Soviet and Post-Soviet Politics and
ISSN 1614-3515

General Editor: Andreas Umland,
Stockholm Centre for Eastern European Studies, andreas.umland@ui.se

EDITORIAL COMMITTEE*

DOMESTIC & COMPARATIVE POLITICS
Prof. **Ellen Bos**, *Andrássy University of Budapest*
Dr. **Gergana Dimova**, *University of Winchester*
Dr. **Andrey Kazantsev**, *MGIMO (U) MID RF, Moscow*
Prof. **Heiko Pleines**, *University of Bremen*
Prof. **Richard Sakwa**, *University of Kent at Canterbury*
Dr. **Sarah Whitmore**, *Oxford Brookes University*
Dr. **Harald Wydra**, *University of Cambridge*
SOCIETY, CLASS & ETHNICITY
Col. **David Glantz**, *"Journal of Slavic Military Studies"*
Dr. **Marlène Laruelle**, *George Washington University*
Dr. **Stephen Shulman**, *Southern Illinois University*
Prof. **Stefan Troebst**, *University of Leipzig*
POLITICAL ECONOMY & PUBLIC POLICY
Dr. **Andreas Goldthau**, *Central European University*
Dr. **Robert Kravchuk**, *University of North Carolina*
Dr. **David Lane**, *University of Cambridge*
Dr. **Carol Leonard**, *Higher School of Economics, Moscow*
Dr. **Maria Popova**, *McGill University, Montreal*

Prof. Gerhard Mangott, *University of Innsbruck*
Dr. **Diana Schmidt-Pfister**, *University of Konstanz*
Dr. **Lisbeth Tarlow**, *Harvard University, Cambridge*
Dr. **Christian Wipperfürth**, *N-Ost Network, Berlin*
Dr. **William Zimmerman**, *University of Michigan*
HISTORY, CULTURE & THOUGHT
Dr. **Catherine Andreyev**, *University of Oxford*
Prof. **Mark Bassin**, *Södertörn University*
Prof. **Karsten Brüggemann**, *Tallinn University*
Dr. **Alexander Etkind**, *University of Cambridge*
Dr. **Gasan Gusejnov**, *Moscow State University*
Prof. **Leonid Luks**, *Catholic University of Eichstaett*
Dr. **Olga Malinova**, *Russian Academy of Sciences*
Dr. **Richard Mole**, *University College London*
Prof. **Andrei Rogatchevski**, *University of Tromsø*
Dr. **Mark Tauger**, *West Virginia University*

ADVISORY BOARD*

Prof. **Dominique Arel**, *University of Ottawa*
Prof. **Jörg Baberowski**, *Humboldt University of Berlin*
Prof. **Margarita Balmaceda**, *Seton Hall University*
Dr. **John Barber**, *University of Cambridge*
Prof. **Timm Beichelt**, *European University Viadrina*
Dr. **Katrin Boeckh**, *University of Munich*
Prof. em. **Archie Brown**, *University of Oxford*
Dr. **Vyacheslav Bryukhovetsky**, *Kyiv-Mohyla Academy*
Prof. **Timothy Colton**, *Harvard University, Cambridge*
Prof. **Paul D'Anieri**, *University of Florida*
Dr. **Heike Dörrenbächer**, *Friedrich Naumann Foundation*
Dr. **John Dunlop**, *Hoover Institution, Stanford, California*
Dr. **Sabine Fischer**, *SWP, Berlin*
Dr. **Geir Flikke**, *NUPI, Oslo*
Prof. **David Galbreath**, *University of Aberdeen*
Prof. **Alexander Galkin**, *Russian Academy of Sciences*
Prof. **Frank Golczewski**, *University of Hamburg*
Dr. **Nikolas Gvosdev**, *Naval War College, Newport, RI*
Prof. **Mark von Hagen**, *Arizona State University*
Dr. **Guido Hausmann**, *University of Munich*
Prof. **Dale Herspring**, *Kansas State University*
Dr. **Stefani Hoffman**, *Hebrew University of Jerusalem*
Prof. **Mikhail Ilyin**, *MGIMO (U) MID RF, Moscow*
Prof. **Vladimir Kantor**, *Higher School of Economics*
Dr. **Ivan Katchanovski**, *University of Ottawa*
Prof. em. **Andrzej Korbonski**, *University of California*
Dr. **Iris Kempe**, *"Caucasus Analytical Digest"*
Prof. **Herbert Küpper**, *Institut für Ostrecht Regensburg*
Dr. **Rainer Lindner**, *CEEER, Berlin*
Dr. **Vladimir Malakhov**, *Russian Academy of Sciences*

Dr. **Luke March**, *University of Edinburgh*
Prof. **Michael McFaul**, *Stanford University, Palo Alto*
Prof. **Birgit Menzel**, *University of Mainz-Germersheim*
Prof. **Valery Mikhailenko**, *The Urals State University*
Prof. **Emil Pain**, *Higher School of Economics, Moscow*
Dr. **Oleg Podvintsev**, *Russian Academy of Sciences*
Prof. **Olga Popova**, *St. Petersburg State University*
Dr. **Alex Pravda**, *University of Oxford*
Dr. **Erik van Ree**, *University of Amsterdam*
Dr. **Joachim Rogall**, *Robert Bosch Foundation Stuttgart*
Prof. **Peter Rutland**, *Wesleyan University, Middletown*
Prof. **Marat Salikov**, *The Urals State Law Academy*
Dr. **Gwendolyn Sasse**, *University of Oxford*
Prof. **Jutta Scherrer**, *EHESS, Paris*
Prof. **Robert Service**, *University of Oxford*
Mr. **James Sherr**, *RIIA Chatham House London*
Dr. **Oxana Shevel**, *Tufts University, Medford*
Prof. **Eberhard Schneider**, *University of Siegen*
Prof. **Olexander Shnyrkov**, *Shevchenko University, Kyiv*
Prof. **Hans-Henning Schröder**, *SWP, Berlin*
Prof. **Yuri Shapoval**, *Ukrainian Academy of Sciences*
Prof. **Viktor Shnirelman**, *Russian Academy of Sciences*
Dr. **Lisa Sundstrom**, *University of British Columbia*
Dr. **Philip Walters**, *"Religion, State and Society", Oxford*
Prof. **Zenon Wasyliw**, *Ithaca College, New York State*
Dr. **Lucan Way**, *University of Toronto*
Dr. **Markus Wehner**, *"Frankfurter Allgemeine Zeitung"*
Dr. **Andrew Wilson**, *University College London*
Prof. **Jan Zielonka**, *University of Oxford*
Prof. **Andrei Zorin**, *University of Oxford*

---

* While the Editorial Committee and Advisory Board support the General Editor in the choice and improvement of manuscripts for publication, responsibility for remaining errors and misinterpretations in the series' volumes lies with the books' authors.

Soviet and Post-Soviet Politics and Society (SPPS)
ISSN 1614-3515

Founded in 2004 and refereed since 2007, SPPS makes available affordable English-, German-, and Russian-language studies on the history of the countries of the former Soviet bloc from the late Tsarist period to today. It publishes between 5 and 20 volumes per year and focuses on issues in transitions to and from democracy such as economic crisis, identity formation, civil society development, and constitutional reform in CEE and the NIS. SPPS also aims to highlight so far understudied themes in East European studies such as right-wing radicalism, religious life, higher education, or human rights protection. The authors and titles of all previously published volumes are listed at the end of this book. For a full description of the series and reviews of its books, see www.ibidem-verlag.de/red/spps.

Editorial correspondence & manuscripts should be sent to: Dr. Andreas Umland, Department of Political Science, Kyiv-Mohyla Academy, vul. Voloska 8/5, UA-04070 Kyiv, UKRAINE; andreas.umland@cantab.net

Business correspondence & review copy requests should be sent to: *ibidem* Press, Leuschnerstr. 40, 30457 Hannover, Germany; tel.: +49 511 2622200; fax: +49 511 2622201; spps@ibidem.eu.

Authors, reviewers, referees, and editors for (as well as all other persons sympathetic to) SPPS are invited to join its networks at www.facebook.com/group.php?gid=52638198614
www.linkedin.com/groups?about=&gid=103012
www.xing.com/net/spps-ibidem-verlag/

Recent Volumes

235 *Eleonora Narvselius, Julie Fedor (Eds.)*
Diversity in the East-Central European Borderlands
Memories, Cityscapes, People
ISBN 978-3-8382-1523-5

236 *Regina Elsner*
The Russian Orthodox Church and Modernity
A Historical and Theological Investigation into Eastern Christianity between Unity and Plurality
With a foreword by Mikhail Suslov
ISBN 978-3-8382-1568-6

237 *Bo Petersson*
The Putin Predicament
Problems of Legitimacy and Succession in Russia
With a foreword by J. Paul Goode
ISBN 978-3-8382-1050-6

238 *Jonathan Otto Pohl*
The Years of Great Silence
The Deportation, Special Settlement, and Mobilization into the Labor Army of Ethnic Germans in the USSR, 1941–1955
ISBN 978-3-8382-1630-0

239 *Mykhailo Minakov (Ed.)*
Inventing Majorities
Ideological Creativity in Post-Soviet Societies
ISBN 978-3-8382-1641-6

240 *Robert M. Cutler*
Soviet and Post-Soviet Foreign Policies I
East-South Relations and the Political Economy of the Communist Bloc, 1971–1991
With a foreword by Roger E. Kanet
ISBN 978-3-8382-1654-6

241 *Izabella Agardi*
On the Verge of History
Life Stories of Rural Women from Serbia, Romania, and Hungary, 1920–2020
With a foreword by Andrea Pető
ISBN 978-3-8382-1602-7

242 *Martin Malek, Sebastian Schäffer (Eds.)*
Ukraine in Central and Eastern Europe
Kyiv's Foreign Affairs and the International Relations of the Post-Communist Region
With a foreword by Pavlo Klimkin
ISBN 978-3-8382-1615-7

243 *Volodymyr Dubrovskyi, Kalman Mizsei, Mychailo Wynnyckyj (Eds.)*
Eight Years after the Revolution of Dignity
What Has Changed in Ukraine during 2013–2021?
With a foreword by Yaroslav Hrytsak
ISBN 978-3-8382-1560-0

Rumena Filipova

CONSTRUCTING THE LIMITS OF EUROPE

Identity and Foreign Policy in Poland, Bulgaria, and Russia since 1989

With forewords by Harald Wydra and Gergana Yankova-Dimova

Bibliografische Information der Deutschen Nationalbibliothek
Die Deutsche Nationalbibliothek verzeichnet diese Publikation in der Deutschen Nationalbibliografie; detaillierte bibliografische Daten sind im Internet über http://dnb.d-nb.de abrufbar.

Bibliographic information published by the Deutsche Nationalbibliothek
Die Deutsche Nationalbibliothek lists this publication in the Deutsche Nationalbibliografie; detailed bibliographic data are available in the Internet at http://dnb.d-nb.de.

Cover picture: Ivan Marc/Shutterstock.com

ISBN-13: 978-3-8382-1649-2
© *ibidem*-Verlag, Stuttgart 2022
Alle Rechte vorbehalten

Das Werk einschließlich aller seiner Teile ist urheberrechtlich geschützt. Jede Verwertung außerhalb der engen Grenzen des Urheberrechtsgesetzes ist ohne Zustimmung des Verlages unzulässig und strafbar. Dies gilt insbesondere für Vervielfältigungen, Übersetzungen, Mikroverfilmungen und elektronische Speicherformen sowie die Einspeicherung und Verarbeitung in elektronischen Systemen.

All rights reserved. No part of this publication may be reproduced, stored in or introduced into a retrieval system, or transmitted, in any form, or by any means (electronical, mechanical, photocopying, recording or otherwise) without the prior written permission of the publisher. Any person who does any unauthorized act in relation to this publication may be liable to criminal prosecution and civil claims for damages.

Printed in the EU

Contents

Acknowledgments 7

Foreword *by Harald Wydra* 13

Foreword *by Gergana Yankova-Dimova* 19

1 Central and Eastern Europe after the 1989 Revolution: Diverging Identities in a Reunifying Era 27

2 Are the Social Sciences Indeed 'Sciences'? Towards a Middle-Ground Methodological Perspective 51

3 Shades of Affinity: An Interactive Constructivist Theory of Self and Other in Bordering Belongingness 67

4 The Interactive Constructivist Theory of Self & Other and IR Debates: Refinement, Dialogue and Challenge 97

5 A European Trailblazer: The Thick Europeanisation of Polish Foreign Policy 135

6 Neither In, Nor Out: The Ambivalent Europeanisation of Bulgarian Foreign Policy 213

7 Europe's Outlier: The Thin Europeanisation of Russian Foreign Policy 283

8 Three Limits of Europe: Poland, Bulgaria and Russia in Comparative Perspective 355

Epilogue: Europe Beyond the 30-year Limit 399

List of Abbreviations 411

Bibliography 415

Acknowledgments

The writing of this book was always motivated by my enduring fascination with the historic social, political, economic and international changes Central and Eastern Europe has been through after the collapse of communism. Growing up in post-1989 Bulgaria imbued me with a burning curiosity about the new phenomena that Bulgarian society was grappling with: How could the country implement 'democratic values', 'privatisation', 'EU and NATO accession talks', which were gaining a foothold in public discourse?

Finding out the answers to these questions took a long intellectual journey, along which I received invaluable guidance from my mentors. The journey started at St. Catharine's College, University of Cambridge, where Harald Wydra lent the decisive intellectual support. It ranged from the most foundational task of learning how to construct and defend a persuasive argument to the thorniest philosophical queries — namely, how should we approach the social sciences? Do they require an 'understanding' or 'explanation', in Max Weber's terms, or both? Was the 'transition' in Central and Eastern Europe only about the fulfilment of formal institutional criteria or was there something more — connected to the 'spirit' of nations?

While at St. Catharine's, I met Gergana Yankova-Dimova, whom I have always looked up to as an academic role model. Our shared concerns about democratisation and Europeanisation and our long-lasting association have since grown into a fruitful professional partnership as part of the Institute for Global Analytics that we founded.

I am grateful to Jean Thomas, Philip Oliver, Miranda Griffin for the stimulating conversations and for bringing forth the example of how academic dedication went hand in hand with care for the community: making sure that St. Catharine's College students grew as professionals as well as individuals. Studying Politics, Psychology and Sociology at the Department of Politics and International Studies at Cambridge was an eye-opening and endlessly absorbing experience based on a multifaceted understanding of the variety of disciplinary approaches within the social sciences. The emphasis on history of ideas and the historical, cultural and national context in the interpretation of politics has become pivotal in my own research orientation.

Continuing my journey to St. Cross College, University of Oxford, opened the gates to the captivating study of the theory and history of international relations. It was there that I embarked on turning the comparison of the Europeanisation process of Poland, Bulgaria and Russia, which had been an idea in gestation, into a fully-fledged DPhil dissertation. As my dissertation supervisor, Neil MacFarlane was an invariable source of intellectual growth and refinement. Our painstaking discussions impressed upon me the outlook that since social and political life is so complex, the explanations that we seek and supply would inevitably involve multiple considerations — rather than singular factors. Hence, as social scientists we should retain a degree of caution and restraint in that we can strive for 'plausibility' but not to once-and-for-all measurable solutions.

I would like to thank Alex Pravda, Jan Zielonka, Roy Allison, Hartmut Mayer, who represented a key influence in framing my understanding of Russian foreign policy and EU-wide policy processes. My research assistance to Yuen Foong Khong widened my perspectives, including through the study of the region of East Asia, and provided an insight into his ever-original analysis of international relations dynamics. I benefited significantly from exchanges with Kalypso Nicolaidis and Kataryna Wolczuk. I owe my maturation as a scholar to the Department of Politics and International Relations at Oxford.

At St. Cross College, Joanna Ashbourn and Glenda Abramson lent moral support and encouraged me along my academic path. The St. Cross community — headed by Mark Jones and Carole Souter, created the most favourable conditions ensuring that graduate experience was full of prolific debates and mutual learning.

During my studies, I also ventured into the think tank world. As an intern at the Russia and Eurasia Programme at Chatham House, I collaborated closely with James Nixey and Lubica

Pollakova, who involved me in every aspect of the think-tank job: from assisting in conferences featuring leading authorities on Russia and the rest of the post-Soviet space to helping out with cutting-edge research reports. It was through this inspiring cooperation that I became convinced that in my future career development I would combine the academic and think-tank track.

Over the course of my research for my DPhil dissertation, I set out to conduct fieldwork in Poland, Bulgaria and Russia. I aimed for a deep immersion in the respective local contexts in order to inquire after what the Poles, Bulgarians and Russians themselves thought about the Europenisation of their countries. Three institutions made this endeavour possible. The Carnegie Moscow Center and its director Dmitri Trenin provided a highly welcoming, expertise- and resource-rich environment that allowed a deep-dive into the intricacies of Russian political and societal developments after the disintegration of the USSR. I deeply appreciate the interviews I carried out in Moscow in 2014 with Nadezhda Arbatova, Vladimir Baranovsky, Irina Busygina, Alexey Fenenko, Alexey Gromyko, Lev Gudkov, Andrey Kortunov, Andrej Krickovic, Maria Lipman, Alexey Malashenko, Olga Malinova, Sergey Medvedev, Andrey Melville, Alexey Miller, Viacheslav Morozov, Yulia Nikitina, Boris Shmelev, Mark Simon, Pavel Smirnov, Alexander Tevdoy-Burmuli, Ivan Timofeev, Dmitri Trenin, Mikhail Troitskiy, Sergey Utkin, Igor Zevelev.

While in Poland, I was hosted by the Polish Institute of International Affairs. The consultation of PISM's expertise and written record of Polish foreign policy was crucial for a detailed understanding of Warsaw's external relations in every step of the post-1989 way. The general ambience in a country that had grown assured of its European-ness, not least through what many Poles judged to be the success of their democratic transformation, made for ardent conversations. I would like to extend my gratitude for the interviews I carried out in Warsaw in 2015 with Łukasz Adamski, Adam Eberhardt, Konstanty Gebert, Leszek Jesień, Piotr Kościński, Jerzy Koźmiński, Marek Krząkała, Roman Kuźniar, Wojciech Lorenz, Anna-Sophie Maass, Marek Madej, Jerzy Nowak, Cornelius Ochmann, Zbigniew Pisarski, Adam Rotfeld,

Patrycja Sasnal, Tobias Schumacher, Stanislav Secrieru, Ryszard Stemplowski, Andrzej Szeptycki, Sergiusz Trzeciak, Witold Waszczykowski, Bartosz Wieliński and three experts, who preferred that their identities be kept confidential.

In Bulgaria, the Centre for Liberal Strategies and its chairman, Ivan Krastev, facilitated a research stay in my homecountry after many years of studying abroad. I benefited immensely from the learned—and frank (i.e. nationally self-critical), conversations with the Centre's experts about the Bulgarian experience of Europeanisation since 1989. I am grateful for the interviews I was able to conduct in Sofia in 2015 with Marchela Abrasheva, Irina Alexieva, Marco Arndt, Iskra Baeva, Tatiana Burudjieva, Dimitar Dimitrov, Boriana Dimitrova, Hristo Georgiev, Zhivko Georgiev, Marin Lessenski, Iliyana Marcheva-Atanasova, Tanya Mihaylova, Ognyan Minchev, Yuliana Nikolova, Krastyo Petkov, Antoaneta Primatarova, Stefan Ralchev, Valeri Ratchev, Ingrid Shikova, Vladimir Shopov, Nikolay Slatinski, Louisa Slavkova, Kristian Vigenin and one expert, who preferred that their identity be kept confidential.

The completion of my doctoral work was followed by the next phase in my professional path based on further building on my academic—an increasingly also policy relevant—study of Central and Eastern Europe. One step of the new journey was established by the Center for the Study of Democracy in Sofia, which provided me with a sense of place and also widened my research vistas.

The other main milestone consisted in turning my DPhil dissertation into a fully-fledged book. I would like to express my special thanks to Andreas Umland, series editor of Soviet and Post-Soviet Politics and Society at ibidem Press, for appreciating this project and enabling its realisation. Valerie Lange has been a source of support ensuring the smooth running of the publication process.

My deepest gratitude goes to my parents. They have been the staunchest pillar of guidance, consolation and forward-looking direction, who made this book possible. I dedicate the book to them.

For my mum, Galina,
and my dad, Valentin

Foreword

I am writing these lines in the week when the Russian Federation closed down its diplomatic mission at NATO and the Polish Constitutional Court ruled that parts of the Polish Constitution are superior to European law. The former is another blow to relations between a key Western alliance and the Russian Federation, whilst the latter undermines one of the EU's fundamental principles and dramatizes an already difficult conflict. The insistence of the Polish government on the sovereignty of the Polish nation against what it claims to be a rising bureaucratic and liberal-secular totalitarianism in the EU reveals that even within Europe, perceptions of common values may be contested. Be it as it may, what matters is such conflicts about sovereignty and national independence have accompanied Europe for a long time. After recent massive drawbacks of the debt crisis, Brexit, and the controversial refugee policies, the recalcitrant attitudes of newer member states such as Poland, Hungary, or Slovenia continue to ask a long-standing question: where does Europe end? How far can enlargement go? Should Europe remain a Europe of homelands and nations or should it become a post-sovereign state?

Rumena Filipova's book does more to illuminate such questions than any other scholarly contribution in the field of International Relations that I know of. Hers is a historically rich, culturally sensitive, and imaginative tour de force through the meanings and layers of Europeanisation after the end of communism. It is a thoroughly researched and lucid book. This work does not design policy agendas or provide recommendations for strategic decision-making. It actually offers something much more valuable. It spells out why Europeanisation has been and will continue to be a moving target. It asks: what do states and societies mean when they invoke their belonging to Europe, to its traditions, values, norms, and horizons? For Filipova, it is identity that defines the limits of Europe. National identities, in particular, are not stable or unequivocal. They are dynamic but also deeply rooted. Unlike many other scholarly treatments of Europeanisation, Filipova acknowledges the reciprocity that underlies ideas, perceptions, and psychological bonds between different cultures and societies. She thus links Europeanisation to deeper long-standing cultural patterns that have dominated public debates in these countries for decades, if not for centuries. Without the ideas that have dominated the self-perception of leaders and followers in the three countries under study, we cannot comprehend the different trajectories that have delineated their current position within Europe.

Long-term trajectories of Europeanisation have indeed gone opposite ways. Few would disagree that the European Community was a project designed, assembled, and deepened by politicians and citizens from the parts of Europe that are usually called 'Western Europe'. As European institutions integrated further within the West, citizens of France, Netherlands, or Germany came to identify Europe with core values such as economic cooperation, capitalist wealth creation, progressive modernization, individualism, and the extension of individual rights and their protection. The ideological traditions of Poland, Russia, and Bulgaria were very different, each of them reflecting each country's historical individuality. Their collective identity has been more fragile, fragmented, and tormented. Poles, for instance, fought to conquer back their sovereignty—from 1956 to 1989—by retrieving traditional republican and spiritual values from its own national heritage. When the streets of Paris in spring 1968 sent shockwaves across Europe, heralding emancipation, anti-traditionalism, and embracing accelerated modernity, Eastern Europe's uprisings in Czechoslovakia and ten years later in Poland pursued projects that were inward-looking and orientated towards their own history. Poles sought to retrieve traditional republican and spiritual values from their own national heritage. The 'spring of the peoples' in 1989 therefore already projected meanings of Europe as culturally tinged by expectations and hope that differed from the acquired status quo in the West. Further South, Bulgaria's self-perception has for a long time oscillated between allegiance to Russia and a tentative openness towards Western institutions, whereas Russia's initial post-1991 liberal-democratic honeymoon with Western values was quickly superseded by a chaotic and painful transition, which turned the leadership towards a centralizing sovereign conception of managed democracy.

This book does not simply deplore the different speeds and depths by which Europeanisation has been sedimented. In a boost to infuse foreign policy analysis with perspectives that are much more fine-grained than traditional premises of conditionalities, national interests, and geo-strategic imperatives, Filipova acknowledges the importance of inter-subjective formation of strategic outlooks and the imitation of foreign models. Western European countries have scrutinized their Eastern neighbours for their 'Europeanness'. The latter were met by trust, fascination, and openness but also, to different degrees, by great caution, diffidence, and stigma. Her thorough analysis leads the author to claim that Poland's encounter with Europeanisation can be considered as 'thick', whereas Bulgaria's has been ambivalent at best. Russia's initial opening to the West was channelled into pragmatic nationalism, before the turn towards restoring Russia's great power identity would create multiple conflicts which have maintained a rather thin form of Westernisation. Filipova's key point is that identity-building in Europe has not been a one-way street. All three countries, to different degrees, learnt political modernity, social progress, and secularism under the iron fist of communism. For them, the question of belonging to Europe is not easily separable from ontological security about one's own borders and self-determination. In the centre are questions of belonging to Europe, which are not primarily understood institutionally, legally, or politically. There is a significant and decisive pre-political element. Integration and proximity to Europe or the West has been a relational, intersubjective process of recognition and acceptance of values, traditions, and self-perceptions that diverged massively between the core of 'Western Europe' and the newcomers in the East.

Different speeds, contradictory conceptions of belonging, and opposed aspirations are the stuff out of which Europe has been made. Multiple crises – many of them considered to be existential – have been and continue to be an inherent part of Europe's construction. The first member state left the alliance, the rifts between the wealthy North and the financially struggling South has gripped

Europeans ever since the financial crisis of 2008. A shrinking population, rising populism, and mounting pressure from strong nations and alliances outside Europe have seriously affected confidence. And yet, in Filipova's panoramic picture there are rays of hope. Europe's *raison d'être* has never been settled around a stable identity. Quite the opposite. The signatories of the treaty of Rome were 'determined to lay the foundations of an ever-closer union among the peoples of Europe'. Such a project with an open horizon requires ideas and leaders. Filipova indicates at some point that any great project requires a genuine elite that is animated by the care of the soul, a project of political morality that precedes institutional engineering. Disaster, crisis, and collapse cannot create a new community without political morality. And yet, with good leadership and a keen eye on essentials there is always hope. The elites that pushed towards European unification post-1945 had grown up far before the beginning of the First World War. Many of the key figures, like Adenauer, de Gasperi, or Robert Schuman came from border regions with high sensitivity for transitional zones, for the undetermined, and the marginal. They had 'learnt'—as many of their contemporaries—that European meant almost always 'somebody else', the 'other', or the former enemy. Europe would become a beacon of hope for the uprooted, an alternative to closed minds and hermetic borders. Although often left undefined and hazy, it was such conflicting aspirations that fuelled the creativity of leaders and followers. The generation of leaders such as Jacques Delors, Helmut Kohl, and François Mitterand pushed European integration to a new level.

Readers should recognize that it cannot be the task of this book to identify potential candidates for such leadership in the third decade of the 21st century. Perhaps the quality of leaders today is indeed not up to the task. Perhaps the tensions between different conceptions of national prestige, collective identity, and democratic legitimacy are too high, and not only in the East of Europe. After all, democratic referenda in France and the Netherlands put the European Constitutional project to rest. Many countries are in the grip of populist projects that are deeply Eurosceptic and inward-looking. Moreover, politicians should be under no illusion that rivalry with Russia will end any time soon. Scepticism towards greater integration will continue in Central and Eastern Europe. But if for Western eyes, they present backward and outdated visions, we must realize that there is no cogent argument to consider them in any way less *European* than narratives based on progressive secularism and liberal individualism that have dominated the 'core of Europe'. As Pope John Paul II once argued, Western Europe has a much richer heritage of Christendom, civilisation, and human freedom. Yet, concomitantly, secularism and rationalistic-technological civilisation have opposed and challenged such traditions. They put in question many of the values and norms that have been so fundamental in the self-extrication of Eastern Europe from communism. Poland's struggle against communism aimed at the recovery of human dignity and personal freedom. It thus pointed to a greater resourcefulness in spiritual values that were invested in the defence of the person and the nation. Whilst such views may be seen as outdated and backward, they should remind us that Europe's legitimacy is not only in European institutions but also in the traditions that are by definition plural, diverse, and often in tension with each other. It may be an irony of history that the old Polish credo of being the *antemurale Christianitatis*, the bulwark of Catholicism against Orthodoxy, is now fuelling deep scepticism against the secular, progressive, and centralized European core values. It may also be seen as irrelevant and outdated what Fyodor Dostoevsky said in 1881, when he argued that in Europe Russians are Tatars, whilst in Asia they are seen as Europeans. And yet, decision-makers in Brussels, Paris, or Berlin should be advised to take such statements as indicative of a very deep sense of how European identity has been and will be shaped by what has been beyond the limits of its core lands. If the limits of Europe are a moving target, as Filipova's important book so lucidly demonstrates, such inter-subjective self-perceptions must not be sidelined by ideological parochialism. As a post-sovereign entity, the European Union will need to accommodate the plurality of national self-perceptions in a political space in which meanings of the people are always—from any vantage point—pointing to 'others'.

Harald Wydra,
University of Cambridge,
United Kingdom

Foreword
Foreign Policy after Regime Change: Articulated Identity vs. Affronted Identity?

Dr Filipova's book "Constructing the Limits of Europe" tells a thought-provoking story, which would be useful to potentially understand the foreign policy choices of various countries, which in the future undergo a transitionary period from one regime type to another. The puzzle that the book seeks to unravel is as follows: for countries, which emerge from one regime type, how do we know which foreign policy orientation they would choose? Would they revert back to the foreign policy orientation they harbored before the transition, or would they choose to belong to the set of institutions and values, which countries of a new regime type espouse? This inquiry is far from a foregone conclusion, especially in the area of foreign policy as a lot of attention has been focused on understanding the domestic choices that transitionary countries make, but not as much scholarly debate has been devoted to comprehending the foreign policies that the same countries make. The puzzle has recently become even more "puzzling" as countries, which had previously been considered as Western-leaning and fully espousing a Central European identity, such as Hungary, have spurned some of the policies of the European Union. The puzzle is also very important because Ukraine's desire to join the European Union sparked the annexation of Crimea and a prolonged international conflict in Donbas.

So, how do transitioning countries make foreign policy choices? The very simplified version of the answer that the book provides is "identity": transitionary countries would pivot to the foreign locus that is closest to the way that they identify themselves as. Thus, Bulgaria's foreign policy, with its perfunctory and formalistic European identity, would take on a course of ambivalent Europeanisation; Russia, based on its fractured and weak cultural-historical basis for European identity, has defied belongingness to the Euro-Atlantic community; and Poland, identifying as through and through European, and most decisively denouncing the Soviet past, has whole-heartedly embraced the foreign policy institutions and policies of the West. The book develops a neat typology of these three outcomes: a thick Europeanization of foreign policy in Poland, an ambivalent Europeanization of foreign policy in Bulgaria, and a thin Europeanization of foreign policy in Russia.

The book offers a constructivist explanation, but with a very important twist: this construction of foreign policy orientation is interactive. The twist comes from the fact that identities are not just "there", automatically prompting states to enter NATO, join the European Union, or revert to the Eurasia Union. The twist is, in my interpretation, in the articulation and implementation of various identities. Dr Filipova calls this an interactive process of mutual recognition of identities. The lesson I took away, especially from the information emerging from the interviews that the author conducted, is that the process through which identity made its way into foreign policy decisions took (at least) two manifestations: the articulated identity and the affronted identity. These two derivations of identity happen at two different levels. The "articulated identity" was the identity, which local political elites verbalized and delivered to the public in the aftermath of the fall of communism. Thus, the articulated identity is domestically embedded. By contrast, the notion of the "affronted identity" I extrapolated from the text is internationally located as it refers to the degree to which the proverbial West has welcomed the transitioning countries, and how these countries have reacted to this reception.

In terms of what I conceive as the problem of "(un)articulated identity", the lesson I learnt from the book is that it is important for the elites to express the principles of identity in public. The Polish case, in my reading, is a case of a well-articulated identity, where the strong anti-communist movements during communism and the vibrant émigré and underground intellectual circles, such as the Kultura intellectuals, had already identified the names for the values and norms that constituted the Western identity. As the German philosopher Martin Heidegger (2015) has suggested, one's language to a large extent defines one's world[1], and the "language of Western identity" was present in the public space right after the fall of communism. It spilled directly out from the underground intellectual discourse. As Sing (1993) would put it, the role of the language was "world-yielding".[2]

By contrast, the Bulgarian case, as described in chapter 6, points to the lack of language describing the key principles of ideational belonging to the West. This is in contrast to the Lech Walesa and the Polish leaders who, as shown in chapter 5, presented to the public a more intricate and fully fledged vision of what it means to feel and be a part of the West. The Bulgarian situation is similar to a case of liking a coat one sees in the shop window versus just dreaming of a new piece of clothing. Actual coats in shop windows people can admire, and occasionally, take a liking of. General ideas about clothes float around, and if they are not anchored by words or images, they can be elusive and evasive. Arguably, the Bulgarian elites from the Union of Democratic Forces, who carried the impetus of the initial post 1989 transition to democracy, failed to draw the coat, they failed to capture in words what it means to belong to the West. Ideas of the transformative power of the free and entrepreneurial individual, of the belief in hard work and meritocratic success, of the American dream, of separation of powers, of respect for minorities, of the power of order and respect for rules, of technological progress and the general feeling of optimism, were never spoken. Because these ideas were never verbalized and explicitly debated in the public space, they failed to offer the opportunity to a large number of people to "try on the coat" of Western identity. Was this simply a failure of words or the presence of an underdeveloped PR strategy? Or was this due to an absence of a sustained preceding intellectual discourse, is a good point for further discussion.

In any case, in the absence of a public discourse, which exemplified, visualized and led on the experiment of testing the

---

1   Rentsch, T., (ed.), 2015, *Martin Heidegger. Sein und Zeit*, Vol. 25, Berlin: de Gruyter.
2   Singh, R.R., 1993, 'Heidegger and the world-yielding role of language', *Journal of Value Inquiry*, Vol. 27, pp.203-214, https://doi.org/10.1007/BF01207378.

limits of belonging to the West (or trying on a new coat), Western identity in Bulgaria came to be interpreted in a variety of ways, and it never acquired a monolithic meaning. Perhaps above all, Western identity was the anti-dote of the lived communist experience. Democracy and capitalism were everything that communist and a command economy were not. Western identity was defined by what it is lacking, not by what it entails. Secondly, Western principles were equalized with economic well-being. Instead of conceiving of the principles of freedom and achievement through hard work, many people in the post-Soviet bloc equated the Western identity with pictures of the clandestine catalogues of goods that somehow made their way into the Soviet bloc from East Germany (the Neckermans) and with the shops selling Westerns goods for dollars. Gradually, their visuals were enriched by observations from their travel to the West and by the communications with the American and Western European tourists who came to visit the Bulgarian resorts. Books containing writings of John Keynes, Thomas Hobbes, Winston Churchill and the Founding Fathers, to name a few, made a very limited presence in elite academic and dissident circles, who- and this is crucial- failed to disseminate them through plain and spoken ideas to the public. In my reading, the elite interviews in the book "Constructing the Limits of Europe" open up the possibility that the political party leaders did not incorporate vivid visions of Western norms and principles in their discourse. The post-communist public sphere, as outlined by Juergen Habermas (1964)[3], lacked the liberal principles that even those people, who did have a predisposition to liberal values, could recognize themselves in.

    The societal members dressed in the Western brands, such as Nike and Puma, but talked about anti-communism, not liberalism. These were people who could have potentially sympathized with liberal political theory, but they were never in a position to make a conscious choice. Consequently, when they were faced with a situation, where they had to make a conscious choice between joining

---

[3]   Habermas, J., 2010, 'The Public Sphere: An Encyclopedia Article (1964)'. In Gripsrud, J., et al., *The Idea of the Public Sphere: A Reader*, pp.114-120.

NATO, the Euro-Atlantic community and the European Union, they were unprepared, and their choices were, as the book argues, situational. In some situations, their ideational proclivities flared up, but this was a sporadic process, that made for a half-hearted choice in favor of Western institutions. As the German philosopher Martin Heidegger has said, my language is my world, and in Bulgaria, it was never in the language, and never in the world. It is easier to understand how an identity, which equalizes principles with products, began to wane, when the economic hardships struck the post-communist economy. When the economy did not deliver, there was very little left to sustain pro-Euro-Atlantic orientation. Such a flimsy and fluid identity orientation was easy to manipulate, undermine and reverse. It was there to change course, when the winds start blowing in another direction.

In addition to the issue of the "(un)articulated identity", Filipova's book, in my reading, also posits the question of the "affronted identity". Filipova lists a number of cases when the West could have integrated Russia into its alliances, but it chose not to integrate it. Russia, for its part, most likely felt affronted. These Western choices, as the book argues, were, among others, the omission to consult Russia about the bombing of Kosovo in 1999, and the non-admission of Russia in NATO. On these occasions, Russia was spurned by its would-be friends, and this affront may have fueled and channeled the anti-Western identity formation. Although there is no counter-factual to show what would have happened if the West had reached out to Russia earlier, if we follow Filipova's logic, we would understand that the West made Russia feel as "the other" and it alienated it in the process. As the text propounds an inherently interactive process of identity recognition, the West's cold-shoulder treatment of Russia may have triggered an equally hostile counter-reaction.

The book offers yet another twist in this constructivist interactive process. It shows that Russia's anti-Western reaction to Clinton's policies were predicated on two internal developments: Yeltsin's proclivity to divide the political elites and the failure of some Western initiatives in Russia. The first factor—the fact that former President Yeltsin kept the ruling classes divided so that they could clamor for his approval and he could centralize his power — in this case had the effect that there were some factions, which were powerful and interested to use the Western foreign policy snub to assert anti-Western tendencies and identities. These "interests" included the armed forces, the military-industrial complex, the gas and oil lobby, the KGB.

The second factor, which according to the book was a part of the interactive process of constructing a more anti-Western identity, and consequently adopting a more anti-Western foreign policy stance on the part of Russia, was that some policies instituted by Western agencies did not produce good results. Some of the IMF's and the World Bank's policies were subject to dissatisfaction in Russia. Particularly, the loans-for-shares and voucher privatisation schemes failed to transform the state-owned companies by issuing vouchers for their shares to the company's workforce. The schemes were largely unsuccessful because most vouchers somehow went into the hands of people in the management or those from the ruling echelons of power. In addition, the book argues, the size of Western aid was perceived to be much smaller than expected. The combination of these factors—the reluctance of the West to incorporate Russia more quickly, the power of anti-Western elites, and the negative economic fallout of Western policies, made for a more solid anti-Western foreign policy orientation. This is partly how Filipova builds up a case for an interactive constructivist explanation for the degree of belongingness to the Euro-Atlantic community.

The book opens up other avenues for discussion. One can argue whether Russia's foreign policy could be explained *only* by the identity-related factors mentioned in the book, in other words whether this ideational explanation is not only necessary but sufficient. A realist perspective would point out that Russia had an alternative, and from the perspective of a rational, interest maximizing country it is easier to turn down an ally on the West, if there is a powerful alternative ally on the East, namely China. Perhaps it is less costly to turn down the European Union, when there is a Eurasian Union in the works. Furthermore, a realist would argue that an affronted identity impacts policy choices mainly when there is a plan B. In this case, an affronted and an unarticulated identity would be a facilitating factor, not the main cause of various degrees of Europeanisation. Thus, while the weighted causality of the interactive constructivist explanation, could be open to scaling, it is still a thought-provoking theorizing, backed by dozens of interviews, about the power of history, culture, and how they interact to define foreign policy choices.

Gergana Yankova-Dimova
Oxford, United Kingdom

1 Central and Eastern Europe after the 1989 Revolution
Diverging Identities in a Reunifying Era

1989 marked a revolutionary time—largely peaceful and non-violent but nonetheless momentously far-reaching in its consequences. The end of the Cold War and the collapse of communism culminated in that year and heralded the beginning of dramatic transformational processes in Central and Eastern Europe (CEE)—i.e., in the countries having formerly constituted the Soviet bloc and the European part of the USSR. These transformational processes encompassed the development of liberal democracy, free market economy as well as integration into and civilizational 'return to Europe'—in contrast to the totalitarian rule, suppressed freedoms and isolation from the West that had previously characterised the predicament of CEE.

Yet, the sweeping changes and reversals that typically accompany the impassioned revolutionary impulse cannot wipe the slate clean and fulfil the ideals for the future in oblivion of historical accretions. So too the promise of 1989 has been unevenly and incompletely realised, remaining just as pertinent nowadays. Indeed, the diversity in the outcomes of the attempted post-communist transformations is striking as CEE states have not managed to join the Euro-Atlantic, liberal democratic community of nations in the same way or at all. In particular, three of those states—Poland, Bulgaria and Russia, have differed among each other in their ability to Europeanise, i.e., to integrate into European (and more generally—Western) institutional structures by enunciating, implementing and sustaining a domestic and foreign policy based on civilizational belongingness to Europe and shared European values. The continuing patterns of differentiation—represented by Poland's assertive determination to become an inseparable part of 'core' Europe, Bulgaria's struggle to find a meaningful and substantive role in the EU and NATO and Russia's repudiation of European values and cooperation with the West, still underline the gap between revolutionary expectations and outcomes in the unfinished journey of European integration.

Hence, a key conundrum of post-1989 transformations is contained in an overarching trend, whereby post-communist states have not transitioned and become Europeanised in a similar way, although their internal, political, economic and social systems as well as external relations had an analogous formal-institutional organisation. The book sets out to account for the diversity in the foreign policy responses of Poland, Bulgaria and Russia to the collapse of formerly similarly established state structures and the international system all three belonged to by considering how these countries' elites have interpreted and reacted to dramatic change on the basis of conceptions of nation-state identity.

In short, identity has shaped patterns of Europeanised transformation of foreign policy after 1989. Since identity is relational and requires both a Self and an Other to become meaningful, the book argues that it has been the interactive process of identification between the Western (European) Other and the CEE Selves that has defined the borders of belongingness to the Euro-Atlantic community. And given that mutual attraction or repulsion in the process of identification depend on degrees of inclusivity and ideational affinity, the following pattern can be observed: the closer the boundaries of similarity and recognition, the more Self and Other will be united in a shared standard of communal belongingness. Accordingly, the extent to which Poland, Bulgaria and Russia have been able to integrate and Europeanise their foreign policy identities has been conditioned by their external acceptance as rightfully 'European' as well as by the normative compatibility of the domestically constructed Polish, Bulgarian and Russian conceptions of 'Europe' with the values and principles benchmarking the Euro-Atlantic community. This ideational benchmark — which CEE states have had to live up to in their bid to rejoin Europe, crystallized after 1989 into a historically and politically informed set of European values, norms and principles emanating from the Western experience (whereby the term 'Western' denotes both West European dominance in defining what Europe stands for as well as the ideational overlaps between Western Europe and America within a values-based Euro-Atlantic community). The different levels of fulfilment of this benchmark constitute what I propose to be 'thick', 'ambivalent' and 'thin' forms of Europeanisation.

The book's argument about differentiated Europeanisation of foreign policy as stemming from differentially domestically constructed and correspondingly externally confirmed culturally-historically shaped visions of Europe, however, stands in contrast to the universalist-rationalist academic and policy-making belief that predominated in the aftermath of 1989. It held that the 'legacies' of the past could be overcome through the implementation of a liberal democratic, market economic blueprint for reform that would eventually lead to sameness and the convergence of East and West.

Most conspicuously embodied in Francis Fukuyama's 'end-of-history' argument, this belief held that the collapse of communism inaugurated the end point of humanity's ideological evolution and the universalisation of Western liberal democracy as the final form of human government (Fukuyama, 1989:1, 1992). Such an assumption proved to be a powerful one, shaping expectations and the conceptual lens through which transformations in CEE began to be perceived.[1] Following Fukuyama, a significant body of the literature on democratic transition treated CEE states as clean slates on

---

[1] In his recent work, Fukuyama takes stock of the trends towards democratic backsliding on a global scale, including in the West, arguing that the rise of identity politics is a key threat to liberal democracy since both left-wing claims to the observance of minority rights and right-wing assertions of nationalist sentiments are said to be particular identifications that undermine civic unity. However, the argument that the demand for recognition of one's identity explains (primarily negative) trends in world politics today is as sweeping as the proclamation of the triumph of democracy three decades ago. Moreover, positing identity as an obstacle to democracy overlooks the inherent interlinkage between the two that is not necessarily pernicious or easily separable. Liberal democracy does not exist for itself as a superior political and civil overlay (which Fukuyama seems to suggest in the claim that 'Liberal democracy has its own culture, which must be held in higher esteem than cultures rejecting democracy's values'). Rather, democratic values are related to national identity, albeit in in a different degree of rootedness. For instance, democracy is an intrinsic part of the development of the American national story as opposed to the 'imported' character of democratic principles in nations having followed a different historical trajectory. Fukuyama also makes little differentiation

which to inscribe a set of institutional-administrative and political-elite behavioural norms that would be conducive to democracy as the end point of political development (Ekiert, 2003; Fish, 2005; Linz, 2000; Linz, Stepan, 1996; Eckstein, 1998; Anderson, Fish, Hanson, Roeder, 2001; Pridham, Lewis, 1996; Higley, Pakulski, Wesołowski, 1998; Dawisha, Parrott, 1997; Kaldor, Vejvoda, 1999). In this view, the past is treated as a 'legacy', which represents a de-historicised abstraction of a set of habits and attitudes inherited from the previous regime and which is a structural variable that either acts as a constraint or permissive force in achieving a predetermined outcome (Wydra, 2007:2-3, 6, 18, 24, 34; Whitehead, 2002:3-4).

However, there are at least two problems with such research premises. First, the underlying assumption of a law-like unfolding of historical development and a structural necessity, according to which political evolution occurs (from one political *system* or *order* to another) and where even if some societies do not manage to become liberal democracies, at least they 'end their ideological pretensions' of representing a higher form of human organisation, often casts CEE countries as *tabula rasa* (Wydra, 2007:41; Fukuyama, 1989:12). This may encourage a sense of 'normative hegemony' and a positivist approach that strictly separates types of domestic and international systems (on the basis of distinctly measurable rational-institutional characteristics), going hand in hand with obliviousness to long-term culturally-historically informed identities and conceptions of 'Europe' that are continuously reproduced

---

between different types of identity (personal, social, national, civilizational) and their distinct content and implications. One consequence of that is that a parallel is drawn between left-wing and right-wing identity groups as equally threatening to democracy, yet the disregard on the part of the latter for democratic values and procedures, particularly evident in the 6th of January 2021 storing of the Capitol, speaks to important differences between identity groups' impact on democracy. Fukuyama, F., 2018, *Identity. The Demand for Dignity and the Politics of Resentment*, Farrar, Straus and Giroux; Fukuyama, F., 2018, 'Against Identity Politics. The New Tribalism and the Crisis of Democracy', *Foreign Affairs*, September/October, https://www.foreignaffairs.com/articles/americas/2018-08-14/against-identity-politics-tribalism-francis-fukuyama

and constitutive of the process of democratisation and Europeanisation. Second, the overwhelming focus on domestic transition has meant that transformations in the issue area of foreign policy (and particularly in Poland, Bulgaria and Russia) have not been adequately, extensively or at all examined by International Relations (IR) or area studies scholars, as is further discussed in Chapter 4.

Hence, in contrast to the predominant, yet empirically unsustainable, universalist-rationalist assumption that exiting one system of international relations (the former Soviet bloc) and integrating into another (the Euro-Atlantic family of nations) was to be primarily a matter of implementing a set of institutional-administrative requirements and demonstrating interest-based behavioural compliance, the book's distinctiveness lies in the argument that it is identity that defines the limits of Europe. Identity shapes the ability to internalise and apply a set of European norms, principles and values posited by the West as embodying European-ness. A number of implications are entailed from this argument.

In particular, the cases of Poland, Bulgaria and Russia exemplify how in their quest to rejoin 'Europe' and become 'Europeanised', post-communist states proceeded in a divergent rather than uniform manner as their understandings of Europe matched and were positively received or were incongruent with European normative standards. That is, the extent of normative affinity, inclusiveness and mutual recognition between Poland, Bulgaria and Russia, on the one hand, and the Euro-Atlantic community, on the other, conditioned the capacity of these countries to converge on the Western European normative framework of international relations. Thus, identity delimits the boundaries of Europe, including the values-based distance between the Western and Eastern parts of the continent as well as among the sub-regions of CEE itself, as expressed in Poland's, Bulgaria's and Russia's respective belongingness to the Central European, Southeast European and former Soviet/imperial Russian region.

Moreover, the post-1989 process of European integration of the CEE states has revealed not only these states' ability to integrate according to a set of European values but has also shone a light on (Western) Europe in general—including its willingness to engage with a variety of constructions of European-ness as well as its own level of espousal of and adherence to these values. Although 'European' values have been (hegemonically) posited as representative of what European-ness stands for, a focus on Polish, Bulgarian and Russian visions demonstrates that a generalised European normative model neither holds sway over the whole continent and nor is it consistently and indisputably followed within the West itself — as the rise of far-right, nationalist ideas and their political empowerment across Europe and the US has evidenced.

Finally, in showing that identity has been a key shaper of the foreign policy transformations of CEE countries, the book makes a reinvigorated case for the significance of ideational factors in the study of International Relations through the development of an interactive Constructivist theory of Self and Other in bordering belongingness. The study also puts forward a middle-ground methodological argument advancing qualified post-positivism. It is grounded in the perspective that context, meaning and flux are crucial to social and political life, while retaining positivist injunctions of scientific enquiry and advocating for a contextual combination of qualitative and quantitative methods.

Why identity matters: A conceptual, theoretical and methodological framework

Identity is a fundamentally constitutive psychological factor both on the personal and group level, as it informs the foundational query about who I am/who we are. The specific answer to this query shapes one's preferences, interests, actions, delineates the boundaries of communal relatedness and situates oneself in the world, which is rendered meaningful on the basis of the guidepost provided by the self's identity map. Indeed, since the inception of the social sciences, scholars have emphasised the centrality of identity. Sigmund Freud, Erik Erikson, George Herbert Mead made it explicit that feelings of contentment are associated with a secure sense of identity, while discomfort and personality breakdown accompany any identity crisis. Ultimately, individuals have a need to defend their identity. For its part, ideology represents a psychological necessity on the social level since it takes on the specific psychological meaning as that generalised identification which is a prerequisite for an adult participation in society (Bloom, 1993:34-38; Stryker, 2008:5; Berger, 1966:9). As further elaborated by Jürgen Habermas (1992), satisfactory group identification is the essential prerequisite for a cohesive social system. And whether in primitive or in industrial societies, humans manifest the same psychological syndrome—social reality must be satisfactorily mediated to them through a myth or ideology which meets the behavioural imperative to identify (Bloom, 1993:50).

Identity thus represents a vital factor in personal and social life, referring to a set of typical characteristics and attributes, which define the outlooks, values, goals and interests of a person or a group. Yet, these typical characteristics and attributes cannot be constructed in a self-standing and isolated manner but require an external reference point to become meaningful. Apart from the internal component, the definition of one's identity further requires an external reference point, a significant Other, comparisons with whom are integral to situating and actualising one's own sense of Self. A core feature of identity is therefore its relationality.

The particular type of (social) identity that the present study focuses on is that of *nation-state* identity, which captures both the interior constructions of those cultural-historical traditions, myths and distinctive traits that mould a *national* entity as well as the latter's projection and concomitant reframing through its organisation in the form of a *state* that operates in the exterior arena of international relations. The book explores the manifestations of nation-state identity in foreign policy, as the domain of external relations epitomises most conspicuously a nation-state's place in the world and civilizational belongingness in interaction with significant Others (Hill, Wallace, 1996:8). Hence, the way that the relevant foreign policy decision-makers within the political elite and the influential international relations experts define and express their nation-state's identity becomes paramount in the examination of Poland's, Bulgaria's and Russia's Europeanisation because external policy is usually the limited preserve of a top professional, policy-making circle. However, this focus does not preclude a comparison as to whether the political elite's articulations of nation-state identity correspond to or diverge from the ideational positions of other societal groups (such as business elites, journalists, the wider populace).

Theoretically, the examination of identity within the discipline of International Relations has been the preserve of Constructivism, which provides the analytical guidelines for exploring how socially constructed rules, norms and ideas shape international politics. The book contributes to the development of Constructivism by putting forward an interactive Constructivist theory of Self and Other in bordering belongingness, which advances a mid-range theoretical exploration of identity construction in an interactive and comparative manner. The theoretical framework is based on the elaboration of the cultural and psychological dynamics that define the mutually constitutive process of identification between Self and Other and that take on an added prominence during times of crisis, destabilising established bounds of mutuality. To investigate whether and how such a destabilisation leads to identity continuity or change, I draw on the discipline of Social Psychology, which supplies an analytical lens for a concrete examination of the operation and effects of identity, which remains a neglected and underdeveloped pathway of analysis in Constructivism, given the latter's predominant meta-theoretical debates. The incorporation of Social Psychological insights points to the persistence as opposed to fundamental change of identities — and hence the re-enactment rather than radical displacement of boundaries of belongingness. It also corroborates the behaviourally consequential effects of identity, which do not remain simply confined to the socio-cognitive realm.

The application of the interactive Constructivist framework to the European context involves the rendering and collective signification of Poland, Bulgaria and Russia as the respective Selves and of Western Europe as the relevant Other, whose interaction determines the extent of belongingness to and limits of the Euro-Atlantic community. Europeanisation thus refers to the dynamic, mutually constitutive process of identification between Self and Other, whereby the scope of mutual acceptance, recognition and ideational affinity conditions Poland's, Bulgaria's and Russia's ability to integrate in the Euro-Atlantic community. The benchmark of that community according to which the ability to integrate is evaluated can be represented in the form of an ideal-typical model of European-ness.

So what is 'European-ness'? The book treats the concept of 'European-ness' as a value-laden notion that denotes the quality of being 'European' in terms of adhering to a set of norms and principles. These norms and principles can be generalised into an ideal-typical model, which generalisation is justified by the Western (European) historical experience and normative projections to CEE as well as CEE's own perceptions. More concretely, a set of norms, values and principles can be extrapolated as being commonly shared by Western Europe: despite the diversity of national traditions, they have emerged as part of the Western political-historical trajectory and have been further projected onto Central and East European states after 1989 in the form of a (hegemonic) normative discourse. Moreover, overall CEE representations have been historically continuous in depicting and perceiving Western Europe through a totalised mythical and utopian image, made up of those norms, values and principles.

As Chapter 3 elaborates, derived from the principled standpoints codified in the strategic documents, treaties, organisational framework, membership criteria of the state and international institutional entities that can be taken to embody the West European experience, the core normative features of the ideal-typical model of European-ness include the rule of law, human rights, tolerance, pluralism, support for civic expressions of nationalism, the free market. The conduct of foreign policy and vision of international relations stem from and are expected to safeguard these values along a number of key (yet overlapping and mutually entailing) dimensions linked to the realisation of a *liberal, rules-based international order and politics, the establishment of regionally cooperative relations and integration within the core European organisations* of the EU, NATO, the OSCE and the Council of Europe.

It should also be noted that the general characteristics of 'European-ness' can be associated with the 'West' more generally, to which the US and Canada also belong. The West can be taken to represent an abstract concept referring to a group of countries sharing a similar civilizational code. Emerging as the most powerful representative of the West particularly after World War II, the US has epitomised Western civilization's progress and modernity, further cementing an institutional link to Europe through NATO, the notion of the 'Euro-Atlantic' community and agreements stipulating the complementarity and interdependence of the transatlantic partners' roles in European affairs (Charter of Paris for a New Europe, 1990:6; Helsinki Document, 1992:2; Study on NATO Enlargement, 1995). So the ideational and institutional closeness between Europe and America (and the predominant conflation of Europe and America into the notion of the West in CEE political imagination) allows studying the impact of the US on the Europeanisation of CEE countries and justifies references to the term 'West' and 'Euro-Atlantic community' instead of just 'Europe'.

The theoretical framework developed in the book refines and addresses some persistent contentious points, gaps and weaknesses in the Constructivist paradigm. A particularly poignant and divisive debate has centred on ontological and epistemological questions. As regards ontology, I weigh in and build on the interactive-holistic strand of Constructivism, which holds that identity construction, continuity and change represent the product of the mutually constitutive interaction of systemic- and unit-level factors. This stands in contrast to those Constructivists, who place an emphasis on either systemic or unit-level factors as respectively taking precedence in affecting ideational outcomes in international relations. The book also makes a case in favour of a middle-ground epistemological position, which mounts a critique both against objectivist expectations of law-like regularities in ideational processes and post-structuralist assumptions of perpetual contingency, malleability and fluidity of identity. Thus, taking an approach that is sensitive to repetitive ideational continuities as well as possibilities for change can accommodate the insights of the different strands of Constructivism—including objectivist, scientifically realist 'conventional' Constructivism and post-structuralist 'critical' and 'linguistic' Constructivism.

Having forged an integrated perspective combining elements of the extremes of Constructivist ontological and epistemological theorising, I further argue for the conduct of mid-range theoretical examinations as a way of moving beyond arguments about the philosophical underpinnings of Constructivism and addressing Constructivists' own self-critique. It consists in identifying the disjuncture that has been created between ontology/epistemology and history/empirics — i.e., between a strong emphasis on ontological and epistemological theorising and an insufficient concrete empirical and mid-range theoretical exploration of how identities are constructed in an interactive and comparative mode and how these identities in turn affect state behaviour. Correspondingly, there is a very limited number of Constructivist studies, which undertake interactive, empirically-informed examinations of identity and its effects on state behaviour as applied empirically to either CEE or other geographical areas. Indeed, there are no systematic comparative investigations of Polish, Bulgarian and Russian foreign policy identities.

Moreover, the book promotes cross-disciplinary dialogue with those areas of study that share common concerns with Constructivism. In this way, mutually beneficial cross-learning can take place, while retaining caution to the limits of disciplinary integration. For instance, although I argue for an ideational definition of European-ness, whose concrete expression and projection is not necessarily institutionally confined to the EU, the Europeanisation literature's findings on how EU member states coordinate their external stances on the Union level, especially by undergoing a process of socialisation, can be usefully taken into account as a facet of foreign policy Europeanisation. Similarly, the overblown academic boundaries between International Relations and Foreign Policy Analysis (FPA) can obscure the avenues for cross-learning, given that both disciplines are ultimately committed to studying the international dimension of politics. Constructivism and FPA's Role Theory (informed by 'roles' as social positions shaping an actor's behaviour) share a general focus on researching the impact of ideas on foreign policy decision-making. Constructivist insights on the interrelation between the socio-cognitive, discursive and behavioural elements of identification can contribute to the resolution of certain weaknesses in Role Theory scholarship (linked to conceptual imprecision and tensions in the treatment of the agent-structure relationship in the formation and effects of roles).

The development of an ideational theoretical perspective by working within Constructivism and simultaneously building bridges to related areas of study additionally goes in hand in hand with defending the persuasiveness of this perspective vis-a-vis materialist approaches. Despite the centrality of identity as a foundational (social) psychological force defining an individual's and a group's self-perception, actualisation and place in the world, the discipline of International Relations has been dominated by interest-based, materialist theoretical explanations, which have downplayed the importance of ideational factors. Yet, the case for reinvigorating the focus on Constructivist studies within the discipline is made by critically interrogating core assumptions of rationalist theories. As against the premium these theories place on power-political, instrumental considerations, I argue that preferences, power-maximisation motives and actors themselves are constituted by norms, intersubjective beliefs and socialisation processes (whereby even instrumentally-motivated actions in pursuit of given means to achieve a specific end are derived from individual/group identity that bestows meaning on those actions). Moreover, the goal pursued by Neoclassical Realism to refine Neo-realism's overly structuralist premises (that privilege the system in determining state behaviour) by introducing unit-level variables leads to conceptual and theoretical inconsistencies and contradictions. Consequently, the attempt to improve upon the systemic Realist bent actually results in undermining the distinctiveness and determinacy of Realism as a research paradigm that can convincingly account for empirical phenomena.

In turn, the book demonstrates Constructivism's conceptual soundness and interpretive power in illuminating the empirical complexity of large-scale transformational processes in CEE. The fact that Constructivism more convincingly accounts for developments as momentous as the restructuring of international relations in Europe since 1989 shows that the explanatory potential of dominant rationalist theories such as Realism is far from comprehensive, while identity-based interpretations represent auspicious avenues for research able to challenge dominant Realist conceptualisations.

Finally, the conceptual and theoretical standpoints of the study are operationalized through the development of a middle-ground methodology based on 'qualified post-positivism'. This perspective defends the robustness and value of the interpretivist-qualitative approach to the social sciences, which privileges in-depth explorations of context, detail and particularity, as against the dominance of statistical-quantitative procedures that aim to model the investigation of social and political life on a set of generalizable and objective laws. At the same time, an integrated view is advanced via the recognition that the positivist striving after the uncovering of regularities in the human world is a worthwhile endeavour. To this end, the methodological procedures of scientific inquiry should continue to be maintained and I argue that these procedures are applicable and relevant not just to positivist-quantitativist research set-ups.

Countries in focus: Poland, Bulgaria and Russia

The book's singling out of Poland, Bulgaria and Russia has been motivated by the goal to understand the driving factors behind the following observations: why was Poland a trailblazer in the EU and NATO accession process on the basis of its advanced domestic and external transformation? Why did Bulgaria achieve accession status at a much slower pace, showing ambivalence about its civilizational orientation? And why is Russia not a member of either the EU or NATO, engaging in normative contestation with the West? The illumination of this patterned Europeanisation through the perspective of national identities shaped by sub-regional belongingness means that regularised similarities and differences among the three states under investigation can be uncovered and that these regularities apply to other countries in the respective, historically bounded parts of CEE. The choice of Poland, Bulgaria and Russia is therefore aimed at ensuring 'representativeness' of countries selected from the three sub-regions of CEE to establish if the culturally-historically shaped sub-regional characteristics (informed and refracted through distinctive national-identity frames) and trends of likeness and differentiation are reproduced in the post-1989 contemporary period.

The overall comparability between Poland, Bulgaria and Russia stems from long-term cultural-historical developments, which have imparted some commonly shared characteristics across the whole of Central and Eastern Europe, while distancing it from the West in political-cultural terms (Dandolov, 2012; Light, 2003; Wydra, 2000). In particular, the consequences of foreign domination and dependence, the historical development of the state and its disconnection from society, the weak democratic tradition, the lagging process of economic modernisation as well as the implications of communist rule, have been invoked as influences upon the political culture of CEE countries (Keane, 1988; Bibo, 2004; Schöpflin, 1990). As Banac (1992) points out, the features of Central-East European societies created by Leninist rules included the perception of the political realm as something dangerous, which strengthened the insular, privatised quality of social life and stifled the development of social trust and civil society.

Moreover, during the Cold War, Poland, Bulgaria and Russia (as part of the then Soviet Union) conducted foreign policies based on three official principles: competition (but also peaceful coexistence) with the West; socialist internationalism (presupposing unity, friendship and close cooperation among the socialist states); and solidarity (with nations in the Third World fighting for national and social liberation) (Zięba, 2011:2). As opposed to the security community (informed by elite ties, economic interdependence and institutional integration) that gradually developed in the West, the Soviet Union's international relations were predicated on the need for allies as buffer zones, which were disciplined by Soviet military preponderance. This logic of international relations led to habits of paternalism in Moscow and passivity in the satellites; the totalitarian mentality was manifested in a vision of the world exclusively in friend-enemy distinctions and fostered zero-sum, bilateral rules of behaviour.

The resemblances inherited from the overarching trends in the historical experience of Central and Eastern Europe have, however, been complemented by distinctions arising from Poland's, Bulgaria's and Russia's respective presence in the Central, Southeastern and the former Russian Empire/post-Soviet European subregions of CEE. Although subject to contested interpretation of boundaries and membership, the concept of Central Europe (encompassing Poland, the Czech Republic, Hungary, Slovakia) generally denotes certain cultural-political differences from Southeastern Europe (the Balkan states of Bulgaria, Romania, the former Yugoslav countries) and the former Russian Empire/post-Soviet area (including the Russian Federation and the rest of the post-Soviet republics other than the Baltic states, whose cultural attributes make them more firmly anchored in Central Europe). Already in mediaeval times, Central Europe forged stronger links to Western civilization through Roman Catholicism, the Latin language and alphabet as well as the emerging practice of self-government and political liberty. All of these formed a political-religious frontier to the Orthodox Christian Slavs, the Cyrillic literary tradition and the despotic Byzantine political habits in the south and Muscovite autocracy in the east (Szücs, 1983; Delanty, 2012).

The three sub-regions were also shaped by the respective animating characteristics of the Austro-Hungarian, Ottoman and Russian Empires that dominated them. Habsburg rule bequeathed to Central Europe a tradition of a hard-working and fairly honest bureaucracy that fostered trust in its inhabitants in the respectability of government. Given the legal and practical limits on their authority, the Habsburgs were often forced to compromise with their subject populations, which led to a degree of political modernisation (Becker, Boeckh, Hainz, Wassmann, 2015:2-3; Subtelny, 1997:88). In contrast, the Ottomans' preoccupation with the supply of revenue and recruits for the army incubated traditions of public ignorance, technological backwardness, local corruption, social injustice and lawlessness, with the subject Christian populations only gaining independence in the late 19th century (Ingrao, 1996). The Russian rulers saw themselves as the sole centres of power and could not envisage the Empire as anything but a unitary entity. While society gradually modernised, the political system remained militantly conservative, focused on the triad of 'Orthodoxy, Autocracy and Nationality' (Subtelny, 1997:89-91). The Soviet Union perpetuated the traditions of a centralised state, unaccountable political power and authoritarian attitudes of the population.

These long-term historical trends further fed into the nature of communist rule. The Polish (like the Hungarian and Czechoslovak) form of governance could be termed 'national-accommodative' in that it permitted modest levels of civil rights and elite contestation, informed by the pre-communist tradition of semi-democratic, modernising-industrialising polities. In contrast, the Balkan form of governance had 'patrimonial' characteristics since it stifled dissent and relied on extensive patronage—built as this was on pre-communist authoritarian habits, weak political modernisation and lagging industrialisation. Finally, the Soviet system came closest to a totalitarian state, whereby an all-powerful bureaucratic regime governed by a disciplined communist party perpetuated tsarist autocratic traditions of crushing societal opposition (Petrescu, 2010:12; Kitschelt, 1999:23-26).

These overall patterns of sub-regional characteristics are still relevant and applicable even in the face of the 'distinctiveness' of the Russian case. That is, although Russia's imperial past, sheer size and prominent role in international relations may be seen as requiring a category of its own that is incomparable to any of the other states in CEE, the book nevertheless argues that the points of Russian distinction are intimately related to, embedded in and informed by nation-state identity and understandings of 'Europe', conditioned by the cultural-historical accretions of sub-regional experience.

Moscow's great power identity does indeed affect receptivity to and contestation of 'standards of European-ness' on the presumption that a great power should receive respect and special status instead of following others' normative prescriptions. Yet, aside from entailing assertiveness, protection of sovereignty and demands for respect, the animating normative basis of great powerhood—that also affects corresponding international recognition or rejection of a state's great power claims, is substantiated by deeply ingrained self-conceptions of civilizational (specifically European) belongingness. A great power may lead by principled exemplariness involving a democratic internal structure and a pursuit of a liberal regional and international order or by projecting and encouraging practices of state capture and the establishment of trans-imperial patrimonial ties (Mäkinen, 2013:4; Conley et al 2016; Wallander, 2007).

Moreover, as elaborated in Chapter 7, the collapse of the multi-national Soviet 'empire' and the ongoing process of nation-building since 1991 marked a deeper identity crisis, whereby the elements of ethnic, civic, nation, state, imperial and civilizational identity were in flux. But this deeper crisis can be argued to be a reflection of the weaker cultural-historical basis for Europeanisation so that the diverse elements of identification were differentially interpreted by the overarching Russian identity groups, whose political-ideational struggles prevented a single-minded commitment to joining the Euro-Atlantic space.

Additionally, the absence of the same extent of institutionalisation as in the Polish and Bulgarian cases (i.e., Russia has never been a prospective or eventually a fully-fledged member of the EU and NATO) stands out as a further distinctive feature of Russian Europeanisation. However, as posited in more detail in Chapter 3, the book's conceptual stance that ideas shape and are reflected in institutional forms means that the weakness of formal institutional ties can itself be understood as conditioned by ideational divergencies between Western Europe and Russia. Hence, if one analyses institutions as ideationally embedded rather than self-standing rationalist-instrumentalist phenomena, then the difference between those within and without institutional confines is not a marker of unique incomparability but can still be examined as part of the identity-based axis of comparison.

Finally, Russia represents an additional significant Other for Poland and Bulgaria. Yet and as concluded in Chapter 8, although the determination with which these two countries pursued their Europeanisation was to some extent informed by the place that the

Russian Other takes in their national-state identity and conceptualisations about the principled compatibility between Russia and Europe, Moscow nevertheless did not pose an ideational and power-based alternative to the Euro-Atlantic framework for — and retreated from, Central and Southeast Europe (Mangott, 1999). Western Europe (and the US, where applicable) remained the most significant, relevant and standard-positing Other for Poland and Bulgaria in the process of establishing affinities to European-ness.

As a result, although some outstanding characteristics of the Russian case contribute to relative distinctiveness, they are also inseparably linked to and informative with the overarching visions, values and norms inherent in nation-state identity and the understandings of Europe rooted in it. The special features do not stand apart from questions of Europeanisation and do not prevent comparisons in ideational terms with Poland and Bulgaria. Russia ultimately shared with these two countries a general commitment to Europeanisation in the 1990s, an overall perception of Europe along the axes of utopia and threat and a common relationship to the West European model as formative of national consciousness.

Elite interviews: obtaining the local perspective

The exploration of the transformations of Polish, Bulgarian and Russian foreign policy since 1989 has necessitated my 'immersion' into the local contexts. It is in this way only that the specificities and nuances of native perspectives can be glimpsed as opposed to a fixation on secondary resources that can obscure the peculiarity of nationally-bounded frames of reference. This consideration led me to conduct fieldwork in Warsaw, Sofia and Moscow with the goal of carrying elite interviews with a designated target group of individuals, who could provide insights into the intricacies, inner workings and overall background of how Poland's, Bulgaria's and Russia's external behaviour was formulated after the 1989 changes.

Who comprised this target group? In general, the subject matter of foreign policy decision-making requires special attention to those political figures in the executive branch of power who are responsible for making and implementing a country's external relations—the Prime Minister, Foreign Minister and President, as well as the deputies in legislative committees tasked with scrutinising the country's international commitments and actions. The foreign policy-making authority among these seats of power may differ depending on the state's constitutional arrangements. In Poland and Bulgaria, which are parliamentary republics, foreign policy decision-making rests principally with the Prime Minister, Foreign Minister and Council of Ministers. In both countries, the President is the supreme representative of the state in external affairs and supreme commander of the Armed Forces. Finally, in Poland—as in Bulgaria, the parliament exercises control over the activities of the Council of Ministers and may appoint investigative committees to examine a particular issue (Constitution of the Republic of Poland, 1997: Articles 95, 111, 126, 133, 134, 146, 148, 149; Constitution of the Republic of Bulgaria, 1991: Articles 62, 79, 85, 92, 98, 100, 105, 106, 115). In contrast, Russia can be classified as a federal, semi-presidential republic, where foreign policy-making is concentrated primarily in the hands of the President, who governs and determines the guidelines of external affairs, holds negotiations, signs international treaties, appoints or recalls diplomatic representatives. The government's duty is to implement the foreign policy line set by the President (Constitution of the Russian Federation, 1993: Articles 80, 83, 86, 114).

But apart from the constitutional stipulations about which members of the executive have the authority to make foreign policy, the debate, formulation and conduct of external relations is influenced by the wider political and social context. This context includes party-political attitudes, political culture, popular opinion as well as the impact of politicians, experts, advisors, intellectuals and public figures, who possess political, moral and intellectual authority without necessarily filling in a particular institutional post. Accordingly, I set out to analyse both the subjective and inter-subjective context of decision-making—aiming to obtain the individual beliefs of particular policy-makers involved in foreign policy decision-making as well as of those politicians and experts, whose influential positions allowed them to shape, communicate and convey to their respective societies the ideational background informing the implementation of foreign policy.

As a result, I conducted a total of 75 interviews (26 in Poland, 24 in Bulgaria and 25 in Russia), the overwhelming majority of which were tape-recorded and on the record. The interviews represented in-depth conversations guided by semi-structured questions that displayed both similarities of formulation among the countries (in order to carry out the cross-case comparison) and differences (to take into account specific national processes, the interviewees' particular experiences and to be able to follow through novel and unexpected information).

The outcomes of the elite interviewing processes in the three countries with regard to the ability to obtain access to political postholders warrants the stipulation of three different levels of openness of the culture of public debate (which is a methodologically inferred differentiation mapping onto levels of Europeanisation). In Russia, I arranged interviews with experts (who nevertheless had some involvement in the political process in an advisory role) rather than politicians. Access to the latter was most likely hindered by the closed character of the political system as well as the concrete situation at the time of the fieldwork in 2014, when increasing tensions between Russia and the West turned foreign policy into a sensitive topic of discussion, especially with scholars from Western institutions (as I was then a DPhil candidate at the University of Oxford). In Bulgaria, I reached an equal balance of interviews with left- and right-leaning politicians, but did not receive responses from representatives of the Movement for Rights and Freedoms (or MRF, whose primary constituency is that of the ethnic Turks) and Citizens for European Development of Bulgaria (or GERB, the center-right party that has dominated the Bulgarian political scene since 2009). This can presumably be explained by the relatively more hierarchical and closed internal structure and political conduct of these parties. In Poland, a wide array of politicians was interviewed without obstacles. Thus, holding constant the effort in gaining access to politicians and my public-political neutrality (i.e., being devoid of political affiliations) regularised non-response from the abovementioned groupings can be explained by levels of political openness and freedom of public debate.

Conclusion

The revolutionary year of 1989 still invokes the image and memory of the striking, avalanche-like and wholesale collapse of the communist political regimes and the bipolar system of international relations. But on a much more fundamental and even subtle level, the events of that year prompted a rethinking of what Europe is. The physical fall of the Berlin Wall may have come to symbolize the reunifying spirit of the times, yet dilemmas about where Europe ends and who belongs to it were to be posed with renewed vigour so that the answers to these dilemmas (or lack thereof) have come to shape European politics to this day. It did not take long after 1989 to see that the transitional process proceeded unevenly and to identify emerging patterns of Europeanisation throughout the former communist space, where some countries (such as Poland) managed to 'return' to the European fold quickly, others (such as Bulgaria) stumbled upon uncertain of their affinities, while still others (such as Russia) repudiated 'European-ness'.

The book's central concern with understanding the differential pace and quality of Europeanisation is motivated by the aim to shed light on the push and pull of European integration. The contradictory impulses to unify and separate, which became highly prominent in the post-1989 period, ultimately represented, as I argue, a re-enactment of culturally-historically bound conceptions of Europe that are not uniformly shared throughout the continent but are rooted in distinct national and sub-regional identities. Such a re-enactment points to the cyclicality in processes of transformation as opposed to a linear, uninterrupted progression towards a predetermined end goal. Hence, Europeanisation is unfinished, continuous and repetitive but is nevertheless marked by distinctive, though not disjointed or completely bounded timeframes, around which the empirical analysis is focused.

As the period immediately following the 'revolutionary' year of 1989, the 1990s were marked by the most strenuous turmoil, flux, uncertainty and crisis, posing the challenge ahead of post-communist states to work out their civilizational response and belonging. In these circumstances, domestic debates were distinguished by their vigour, intensity, symbolic-ideational argumentation, while the West was simultaneously defining the boundaries of Europe and differentiating between potential members and outsiders (Stadtmüller, 2000:29; Szczerbiak, 2001:9; Prozorov, 2009:42-52; Mihaylova, 2015, interview). The civilizational orientation worked out in the 1990s designated the recreation of national conceptions of Europe (of the *longue durée*), which were concretely substantiated in the 2000s and 2010s, when, however, the symbolic dimension was being subdued, the crisis subsided and some previously suppressed ideational strands re-emerged. In turn, the period starting from 2016 inaugurated a weakening of ideal-typical European-ness itself and a resurgence of alternative ideational traditions within the West. Britain's vote to leave the European Union, the populist wave throughout European countries and Donald Trump's election as American President have undermined the liberal international order and the cooperative-multilateral-consensual conception of European-ness as pillars of post-Cold War politics and the Euro-Atlantic community. Therefore, the book focuses its empirical examinations on the period between 1989 and 2015—not because Europeanisation has been 'implemented' or 'finished', but because its salience as a dominant ideational orientation has receded. The ideal-typical model of European-ness that was posited as a benchmark for the transformation of CEE after 1989 has been challenged, while domestic Polish, Bulgarian and Russian political priorities of and societal concern with Europeanisation have simultaneously subsided.

In advancing the argument that historically continuous and recurring ideational traditions define the limits of Europe, the book carves out a distinctive theoretical and empirical space in the discipline of International Relations. The case for a reinvigorated emphasis on and conceptualisation of the significance of ideational factors in politics is made through the development of an interactive Constructivist theory of Self and Other in bordering belongingness (as elaborated in Chapter 3). The theory mounts two main challenges against the Realist paradigm. First, in contrast to Realism's privileging of material over subjective factors, the examination of post-communist transformations substantiates an ideational account of large-scale processes in international relations. The record of Central and Eastern Europe's transformation shows that 'reality' is refracted through the perceptual lenses of political elites, who are part of a given culture constituted by Self-Other affinities and whose foreign policy stances are informed by ideational considerations. Second, as opposed to Realists' positing the autonomy of the international and the domestic level — which has buttressed a general conceptual separation between the different levels of analysis within the discipline of International Relations, and their ultimate theoretical commitment to the system's primacy in determining state behaviour, I argue that it is problematic to isolate the external from the internal as bounded phenomena since they mutually constitute one another (Ripsman, Taliaferro, Lobell, 2016:12, 159; Waltz, 2010:47-58).

The book also fills an empirical gap through a hitherto unexplored juxtaposition of Poland, Bulgaria and Russia on the basis of the distinctive conceptual lens provided by the interactive Constructivist theory of bordering belongingness, in-depth primary interview material and a middle-ground methodological procedure (developed in Chapter 2). Indeed, Constructivist studies have not featured a systematic comparative examination of Polish, Bulgarian and Russian foreign policy transformations since 1989 (Chapters 5, 6 and 7 respectively discuss the Europeanisation of the external behaviour of each of these three country cases). Scholarship that has been much more squarely focused on Central and Eastern Europe has similarly not delivered a comparative investigation of Poland, Bulgaria and Russia. Moreover, the thematic concerns of these scholarly strands have not necessarily been related to foreign policy and a theorisation of the role of ideational factors. For instance, the overwhelming focus of the literature on transition to democracy and a market economy underprivileged the examination of the foreign policy transformations of post-communist states. Additionally, the literature on Europeanisation has presented a more limited focus on the external relations of CEE countries (usually confined within analyses of convergence on the Common Foreign and Security Policy) and has generally drifted away from examinations of European international relations. This is reflected in the move from the study of European integration among states to Europeanisation, whereby the deepening of integration led to the creation of a EU political system that produces decisions and impacts on domestic policies, increasingly explored within the domain of Political Science (Tonra, 2015).

Overall, one of the key conclusions that Chapter 8 sets out points to the fact that there is a significant degree of continuity of culturally-historically shaped patterns of ideas, group self-understandings and sub-regional identifications. Although the historical continuity of identities may be self-evident, its vindication serves to reinvigorate the challenge to rationalist-realist perspectives as well as to revitalise an emphasis on ideational persistence balancing out a prominent social scientific (especially post-modernist) view of the emancipating potential of identities that are constantly fluid, malleable and in flux (Caldas-Coulthard, Iedema, 2010; Howard, 2000:20; McCrone, 1998:47; Dunn, 1998; Powell, 1996:6).

On a more general level, highlighting the importance of continuous ideational attachments, which do not easily yield themselves to rapid and wholesale change, can serve as a reminder of the importance of cultural-historical context when devising theories and policy prescriptions animated by grand narratives of 'convergence', 'democratisation', 'liberalisation' and 'transition from authoritarianism'. Belief persistence still stands out as a poignant factor in the ongoing process of defining the boundaries of Europe, whereby the EU's relations with the Western Balkans, the eastern neighbourhood (Armenia, Azerbaijan Belarus, Georgia, Moldova, Ukraine) and Russia will depend on the reciprocal negotiation of the limits of mutual affinities and ideational compatibilities.

2 Are the Social Sciences Indeed 'Sciences'? Towards a Middle-Ground Methodological Perspective

The mid-range Constructivist theoretical framework that the book puts forward is operationalised through a similarly middle-ground methodological argument advancing 'qualified post-positivism'. The latter defends and justifies the robustness and value of the qualitative approach as against the dominance of quantitativism and proposes an integrated perspective aiming to build bridges in the long-running and hotly contested positivist vs. post-positivist debate on the epistemological and methodological underpinnings of the social sciences.

According to the middle-ground argument, in the epistemological sense the social sciences differ fundamentally from the exact natural sciences. But if social scientists are not to relinquish any claims to objectivity and generalizability and turn the social sciences into an interesting narrative and story-telling, two procedures should be followed. First, the methodological guidelines of scientific inquiry, linked especially to rigorously identifying systematic comparative standards that can yield a degree of generalisation, should be preserved. Second, a contextual, i.e., research-sensitive conjunction of qualitative and quantitative methods should be additionally aimed at.

Before elucidating the concrete choice and combination of methodological techniques that can substantiate qualified post-positivism, a review is in order regarding the respective standpoints of the positivist and post-positivist approaches and their status in the discipline of International Relations, in particular, and the social sciences, in general.

The positivist-quantitative epistemological and methodological orientation has acquired a dominant position in terms of being both a privileged philosophical outlook and a preferred focus in devising research designs. Such a dominance has its long-standing roots in the historical development (and perception of the purpose) of the social sciences. From the latter's very inception and particularly in the writings of August Comte, positivist science was regarded as the highest stage in the development of knowledge. Comte thought that all sciences (including the sciences dealing with society) would eventually be unified methodologically so that the rationale and methods applied to the study of the natural world were also relevant to social phenomena. This view was enormously important in the development of the social sciences throughout the 19th century, fundamentally influencing the classic social theorists, including Karl Marx and Emile Durkheim (Baert, 2005).

Correspondingly, two key propositions have come to characterise the positivist approach to the social sciences. The first proposition holds that there is a distinction between facts and values and that 'facts' are theory-neutral. In philosophical terms, this is an objectivist position that sees objective knowledge of the world as possible, although observations may be subjective. Hence, empirical validation or falsification is the hallmark of 'real' social inquiry, which fitted particularly well, for example, into the trend towards behaviouralist quantification in the 1960s (Smith, 1996:11-47). Second, the positivist approach contains a powerful belief in the existence of regularities in the social—as in the natural—world, licensing both the deductive-nomological and the inductive-statistical forms of law explanation. In International Relations, this assumption lies at the heart of debates about polarity, stability and cycles in world history (Smith, 1996:11-47; Murphy, 1996:157-160).

The historically conditioned propensity to a positivist-quantitative treatment of social scientific subject matter has been continued in a path-dependent manner in contemporary IR studies, where positivism remains the dominant approach (Zarakol, 2017; Eun, 2017). Moreover, the tendency to consider the quantitative-statistical examination of social, political and international phenomena as the ultimate manifestation of 'scientific' procedure (and the complementary accusation of qualitativism as being unprovable by quantifiable standards and therefore unscientific) has yielded itself to preoccupation with methodological procedure as opposed to conceptual-theoretical innovation. The fixation on procedural rigour based on fine-turning particular, primarily formal-quantitative, techniques has led to sidelining the study of research topics that are of substantive importance and interest to both policy-makers and the wider society. The end result of these trends has been the declining policy relevance of the discipline of IR (Desch, 2019:2-4; Shapiro, 2005; Mearsheimer, Walt, 2013).

For their part, strands of social theory sharing a post-positivist orientation (such as interpretivism, critical theory, feminism, postmodernism) have contested the epistemological and methodological implications of equating social phenomena with the natural world and that it is only the utilization of a quantitative-statistical evidence and procedure that can underwrite the rigour, plausibility and usefulness of a study (Shankman, 1984:3). One of the most important elements in the post-positivist, interpretive critique is related to the idea of 'meaning', derived from Max Weber's work. For him, it was not sufficient to simply establish regularities of social life because social explanation demands more. To make sense of the observed regularities, it is necessary to understand why people act in the way they do, while the understanding of motivation has to be further placed in an intelligible and more inclusive social-historical context of meaning (Baert, 2005:5). Moreover, building on Weber's scholarship, subsequent social and political theorists have developed a much more strongly anti-naturalist case. For instance, Wittgensteinians, such as Peter Winch, have insisted that cause and effect relationships do not apply to human action, because instead of causes we talk about reasons for action where reasonableness is a matter of public convention and an action embodies the motive or reason for action (Winch, 1990; Tully, 1988:80; Gadamer, 2013).

Hence, according to post-positivism, social scientific phenomena can be better grasped through in-depth interpretations of meaning and context as opposed to statistical manipulations across aggregated data. Of late it has been the American Statistical Association itself that has pioneered an initiative calling for much greater caution vis-à-vis the overreliance on statistical significance for drawing scientific conclusions, including in the social and political sciences. The predominant 'binarisation', whereby a statistically significant result confirming a hypothesis as true depends on a p-value set at 0.05 calculated as part of a 95% confidence interval, unduly juxtaposes results as significant or not on either side of the 0.05 divide. Although the p-value threshold may designate whether a quantitative effect may exist, it does not measure the size and importance of that effect (Wasserstein, Lazar, 2016; Wasserstein, Schirm, Lazar, 2019).

A preoccupation with reaching quantitative benchmarks thus under-privileges considerations of larger contextual factors that can account for the reasons and substance of an effect. These factors include the complex, co-constitutive variation, contingency and even pervasive uncertainty characteristic of real-world developments—as opposed to the manipulation of 'pure', isolatable variables, whose social and political impact depends on setting a numerical threshold confined within a confidence interval (Filipova, Yalamov, 2021). Moreover, the very quality of the data gathered for carrying out statistical tests shapes the type of effect that is observed. However, the rigour of data collection used for quantitative studies is rarely subject to external verification, given that emphasis is placed on producing equations showing associations between variables rather than scrutinising the input that underwrites the validity of making quantitative estimates in the first place.

A post-positivist case in point: AI and studies of disinformation

The increasing uses of big data operationalised through machine learning and AI further raises ever more urgently the question about the applicability and utility of large-scale algorithmic categorisations to the social sciences, particularly in studies of disinformation. From a qualitative point of view, big data pose even more starkly concerns about the validity of quantitative assessments vis-à-vis considerations of meaning and context. The belief in the impartiality and scientism of automated processes that aggregate and classify large amounts of data comes up against the foundational role of human curation for training machines and inputting information. Hence, the quality of the results produced by machine learning depends on sound expert judgment as incomplete input and in-built bias (for instance towards underrepresented groups) can skew the effectiveness of automatic monitoring of, for instance, harmful online content. Additionally, automated data processing is most suited to identifying repetitive patterns of information that are already fed into the system through key-word/phrase labelling. Yet, machine learning is much less adaptable to classifying new information as well as recognising subtleties of linguistic narration. It is only through a thick description and analysis of the wider narrative context that the meaning of specific statements can be understood, which can be couched through subliminal stylistic and attitudinal means of message transmission rather than be explicitly expressed and conform to a set of pre-defined words and phrases.

Recent experience with the utilisation of machine learning for dealing with disinformation underscores the pitfalls of overreliance on automation. The increase in the application of automated tools during the coronavirus pandemic did not lead to a qualitative change in the detection of harmful material on social media platforms. Rather, dangerous and illegal content was omitted, while legitimate accounts were closed down because of automated processes' difficulty detecting linguistic subtleties (Scott, Kayali, 2020). Such instances have underwritten an emerging academic and policy concern with the ethical implications of artificial intelligence methods. The latter pose a threat to the right to free speech by taking down legitimate content and further raises the issue of the appropriateness of instituting the presumption of prior censorship without adequate oversight and due process (Llansó et al, 2020). European regulations,[2] for example, now stipulate that online platforms shall ensure that content moderation decisions are not solely taken on the basis of automated means and the latter's precise purposes, indicators of accuracy and accompanying safeguards should be clearly detailed.[3]

---

2   According to Article 17, 5.; Article 23 1. (c) of the Digital Services Act.
3   For an exemplification of how to combine qualitative content analysis of disinformation attuned to the meaning, sentiment and style of message transmission and a quantitative-automated identification of the frequency, intensity and vo-

Overall, the middle-ground methodological argument subscribes to the interpretivist epistemological critique of positivist-quantitative injunctions but nevertheless posits the retention and observance of the key guidelines of scientific inquiry so as not to turn interpretive analysis into infinite contextualism without any claim to generalizability. The latter danger can be particularly present in linguistic-discursive, post-structuralist modes of social scientific research that can succumb to the relativism of multiple interpretations whose 'truthfulness' cannot be adjudicated as each interpretation comes from a particular perspective on the world. Therefore, the focus on contextual detail should be coupled with attention to the possibility of larger-scale socio-political regularities in order to capture both the particular and the general. In this way, qualitative analysis becomes no less scientific as it can also provide a comparative and comprehensive perspective by rigorously identifying similar and different conditions across various types of cases—yet through interpretive analysis rather than statistical inquiries.

A middle-ground methodological approach to the social sciences, as charted by classical social theorists and eminent sociologists, needs to be reinvigorated. For instance, Anthony Giddens has pointed out that if we fully commit ourselves to hermeneutics, then the tasks of social science seem limited to ethnography — to the hermeneutic endeavour of the fusion of horizons. Such a paralysis of the critical will is as logically unsatisfactory as the untutored use of the natural scientific method in the social sciences (Giddens, 1984:284, 335). Similarly, Quentin Skinner proposes a middle ground for the social sciences. He argues that there is some hope for the retention of generalizability if we begin our analysis by focusing not on the individual action to be explained, but rather on the conventions surrounding the performance of the given type of social action in the given social situation. The vital importance of

---

lume of disinformation messaging, see Filipova, R., 2021c, 'Russia's Media Capture Power Mix in Southeast Europe', in *Tackling Kremlin's Media Capture in Southeast Europe. Shared Patterns, Specific Vulnerabilities and Responses to Russian Disinformation*, CSD, pp. 34-47, https://globalanalytics-bg.org/wp-content/uploads/2021/08/Tacklin-Kremlins-Media-Capture.pdf

this methodological injunction relates to the fact that understanding what the established, conventional standards are will help us predict or expect to see these standards followed in the case of various types of social action within a given culture. Accordingly, we will not get lost in detail and contextualism that is oblivious to the possibility of generalisation (Skinner, 2002:132-143; Tully, 1988:10, 24, 82). Ultimately, it shall be most instructive to follow Max Weber's advice to social scientists. He disagreed that the task of sociology was to develop an all-embracing deductive science but at the same time Weber did not concur with the view that the study of the social depends on an unfathomable ability to intuition. Sociology as a science, and indeed all of the social sciences, employs interpretative understanding of social action precisely in order to establish an explanation of its itinerary and effects (Baert, 2005:45).

Qualified post-positivism: Research design in practice

A qualified post-positivist perspective retaining the injunctions of scientific inquiry can build the way forward for a middle-ground methodological and epistemological approach to the social sciences and to the contextual combination of qualitative and quantitative methods. Each type of method can contribute its specific analytical insights suited to answering particular kinds of questions and addressing different aspects of the research procedure.

The middle-ground perspective is substantiated by the overall case-study methodological focus as fulfilling the concrete purposes of the present investigation. The selection of three case countries (Poland, Bulgaria and Russia) follows the scientifically-guided preference for going beyond a single-case analysis since only by examining a number of manifestations of a given phenomenon does the impact of factors on the outcomes under examination come into view in a much clearer way that does not show up in single-case explorations (Mahoney, Rueschemeyer, 2003:320-323; Bennett, Elman, 2006:11). The comparative framework allows establishing similar and different conditions shaping particular levels of Europeanisation, thus providing a degree of validity and generalizability as well as attention to context and specificity through the combination of both interpretive and positivist within- and cross-case analytical procedures.

Unpacking the case (1): Discourse analysis and elite interviews

The major methodological challenge, which within-case techniques have to address, is that ideas and identity matter in the process of policy-making. To this end, the adoption of an interpretive framework contributes a 'thick' description of the foreign policy context, revealing in a detailed and in-depth manner the motivations, deliberations and justifications for a given decision and related action.

Two key interconnected methods inform the interpretivist framework. The first is *discourse analysis*, which uncovers meaning from the language that actors use to describe and understand social phenomena (Dunn, Neumann, 2016). To establish intersubjective understandings (rather than contingent, individually idiosyncratic stances), discourse analysis should reconstruct the tacit rules, the shared experience and collective knowledge of social actors by relating texts to context and social practices (Milliken, 1999:10). The appropriate corresponding research strategy includes a thorough review of primary and secondary sources relevant to the topics of Polish, Bulgarian and Russian foreign policy identity, representing a collection of texts constituted as speech, written documents and social practices. These sources encompass the foreign policy-making elites' public statements, speeches, official policy documents, media outlets and commentaries, the academic literature, political observers' expert analyses. The main task would be to analyse Poland's, Bulgaria's and Russia's conceptions of European-ness by examining domestic political debates, influenced as they are by the national and international context.

Second, *elite interviewing* is vitally conducive to discourse analysis. Gathering interview material, which is relevant and directly related to the specific research questions posed can serve to illuminate—i.e., confirm or challenge empirically from a 'hands-on' policy-making and expert lens, key conceptual and theoretical concerns. Although other primary sources (such as public speeches and strategic documents) constitute the backbone of narrative (re)construction, the method of elite interviewing further complements, fills gaps in, resolves ambiguities and enriches such discursive sources by rigorously focusing on the viewpoints of those most engaged with a certain policy decision. Original conversational accounts can thus deliver a deeper discernment and clarification of the nuances of opinion, priorities and accents placed on given issue areas, the motivations behind and relationships of influence in the process of deliberating and choosing a foreign policy course of action.

For the concrete research purposes of the present study, elite interviewing provides more comprehensive insights regarding the conundrum of Europeanisation, given the equivocal and insufficient evidence from the widely available discursive sources and secondary literature. That is, the predominant area studies focus on Poland, Bulgaria and Russia, which speaks to particular issues of their (separately examined) domestic and foreign policies cannot demonstrate the extent to which levels of Europeanisation were established in the context of mutually constitutive interaction between the external and internal dimension of identification as opposed to interest-based single-factor (domestic or international) considerations. Neither can this question be conclusively answered by focusing on publicly accessible speeches and statements only.

Two criticisms of the elite interviewing method—related to sampling procedure and reliability of the material obtained, are usually raised from a positivist perspective. Yet, these criticisms can be addressed in order to fine-tune the method on the basis of qualitative rather than quantitative-statistical techniques, as the latter are not applicable when dealing with human subjects involved in in-depth conversational research.

In terms of sampling strategy, the preferred positivist focus on random sampling cannot be realized not least due to the issue of access—it is impossible to guarantee a fixed positive response rate on the part of designated interviewees so as to fulfil expectations of equal probability of selection providing an unbiased representation of a population. Instead, non-probability sampling procedures should be utilized, given that randomness is not possible and neither is it essential to the goals of the research. More concretely, the aim is not to make quantified statistical inferences based on closed, structured questionnaires (yielding tightly scripted, simplified and easily coded short answers across a randomised population sample) but to obtain qualitative information about specific events and processes, for which one needs interviewees who have had most involvement in or most knowledge about these events and processes, while striving for a degree of representativeness. So the non-probability sampling strategy is 'purposive', guided by the purposes of the study and the researcher's knowledge about the population sample. Also, interviewees are chosen on the basis of reputational criteria — namely, how influential and knowledgeable these people are (Tansey, 2007:3, 18, 21). Therefore, elite interviewing can also be 'scientific' in that its application is based on well-defined and rigorous criteria, yet these are much more responsive and sensitive to the human participants and thorough, though distinctly focused, conversational subject matter of qualitative investigations, where random sampling is not available or necessitated.

Moreover, the elite interviewing method can be subject to criticisms of its reliability. This is emphasized especially strongly from a positivist point of view on the grounds that subjective 'conversational' material is not verifiable enough in contrast to 'hard' quantitative data. Admittedly, problems of reliability can indeed arise due to mendacity, error (as a result of lapses of memory or lack of complete knowledge), self-enhancement (spinning a story to present oneself in the best possible light), concerns with social desirability or simply subjectivity (one's individual or occupational perspective colours unconsciously their recollections). Nevertheless, elite interviewing remains the most direct and relevant source of information for the purposes of studying contemporary decision-making.

Thus, instead of downgrading and sidelining this method, its credibility should be reinforced through the methodological procedure of triangulation. The latter was originally applied to and taken from geographical land surveying on the basis of the laws of trigonometry so that determining the exact position of a point in a landscape depends on conducting three measurements (Yeasmin, Rahman, 2012:4). In social science research triangulation has been adapted as an approach, whereby information about a given phenomenon can be obtained and validated from multiple perspectives in order to confirm reliability (Bryman, Bell, Teevan, 2009). Accordingly, the interview material can be compared with and referenced alongside statements made by the interviewee as well as secondary research about the events in which the interviewee was involved to establish consistency between interviews and documents. As long as the interviewee's credentials are sound, the contours of his/her words and actions provided by other primary and secondary sources are held up and no flagrant discrepancies with the historical record and the inter-subjective views surrounding a given foreign policy development are identifiable, then the reliability of the interviewee's account can be ascertained. Similarly, in the case of generalisations of interviewees' opinions, one should relate a stance enunciated by a set of interviewees (belonging to a given political-intellectual grouping) to that grouping's stated ideas and background politics to control for instrumentalised misrepresentation and spin of party positions when vested interests are concerned.

In this way, a scientific form of inquiry originally pertaining to geographical and navigational calculations can be utilized in social science research—yet by deploying multiple qualitative techniques rather than carrying out quantitative computations.

Unpacking the case (2): Process tracing and the congruence method

The findings produced by within-case discursive-interpretivist methods for the analysis of policy-makers' views and reasons for taking a particular action can be further validated by employing two methodological techniques aimed at establishing causal pathways. First, *process tracing* is a useful method for the identification of correlations because it traces the process, where intervening causal mechanisms link causes and outcomes (with such mechanisms being described in terms of entities that engage in activities) (Beach, 2017). Process tracing can thus be helpful for establishing the intervening steps by which beliefs influence behaviour, in particular how the actors' beliefs affect their assessment of incoming information about a given situation, followed by the identification and evaluation of options that circumscribe the choice of a course of action (Khong, 1992:64; Brady, Collier, 2010:103-104).

Second, the *congruence method* checks for consistency between observed empirical outcomes and the extent to which different theoretical explanations fit with and contribute to those outcomes. Congruence analysis does not subscribe to the strong positivist epistemological position that one can verify, falsify and completely dismiss or discriminate between theories. Rather, there is a supposition that a plurality of approaches may be conducive to understanding the complexity of social and political phenomena, so there is an emphasis on how much or which part of the observed outcome a theory can illuminate (Blatter, Haverland, 2012; Sinkler, 2011:14-15). In the context of the present study, the congruence method can be a complement to process tracing, examining the link between the hypothesised cause and the outcome rather than intervening steps in the process (Khong, 1992:66). In this way, consistency is aimed to be established between the theoretically stipulated importance of identity in decision-making and whether the policies adopted are indeed influenced by ideational factors.

Overall, through the deployment of process tracing and the congruence method, the interpretive framework can draw conclusions about causal pathways. Yet, it should be noted that these methods are not epistemologically suited to fully-fledged causal analysis (where a hypothesised prediction specifies which value of the independent variable causes a particular outcome at the dependent variable along a quantitative data-set that prescribes the empirical values of variables). Process tracing and the congruence method rather remain attuned to detailed and contextual empirical observations and a possibility of a plurality of theoretical explanations for these observations (Blatter, Blume, 2008:4-6).

Collating cases: Structured-focused comparison and the ideal type

In addition to within-case methods, remaining focused on unpacking what goes on 'inside' a case, cross-case comparison contributes to the development of a broader picture that allows to establish trends across multiple instances of a given phenomenon (in the context of the present study this being the Europeanisation of Poland, Bulgaria and Russia). The guidelines of *structured-focused comparison* provide a rigorous methodological procedure for qualitative, small-N studies, which stand in the middle between single-case research (that cannot produce larger-scale generalisations) and large-N studies (oblivious to finer contextual detail), and are thus open to integration of positivist and post-positivist insights. In particular, the method is 'structured' in that the researcher writes general questions reflecting the research objective and that these questions are asked of each case to guide and standardise data collection. This makes systematic comparison and cumulation of the findings of the cases possible. The method is 'focused' in that it deals with specific aspects of the cases examined, guided by a well-defined theoretical goal (George, Bennett, 2005:67).

The comparative benchmark on which the systematic comparisons of the book's investigations are based is informed by an ideal-typical model of European-ness. According to Max Weber's pioneering work on the *ideal type*, no scientific system is ever capable of reproducing all concrete reality, nor can any conceptual apparatus ever do full justice to the infinite diversity of a particular phenomenon. The notion of the ideal type is meant to provide an escape from the dilemma between overgeneralising (leading to obliviousness to the unique features of a given phenomenon) and particularising (rendering even contingent generalisations impossible due to a focus on unique characteristics) (Coser, 1977:223-224; Lindbekk, 1992:7).

The ideal-typical analytical approach to European-ness allows to generalise common normative dispositions in the West (although these may not be consistently espoused and practised, may even be subject to erosion and may have specific connotations depending on distinctive national conceptions of Europe) as well as to gauge Poland's, Bulgaria's and Russia's ideational affinity to that model between 1989 and 2015 (although 'perfect' conformity cannot be expected even in the most Europeanised case).

In the cross-case comparative setup, the study preserves the guidelines for a robust research strategy. The latter's goal is to produce reliable findings, by positing differential outcomes, avoiding the selection bias of choosing similar manifestations of a phenomenon, in order to identify the complexity of conditions that can account for the differences in outcomes (or what positivists would call 'variation') (George, Bennett, 2005:80). The book aims to interpret differential levels of Europeanisation, instead of focusing only on those countries, which were most 'advanced'/ 'successful' in this process.

The investigation consequently steers clear of the selection bias of examining cases clustered at one end of the outcome continuum. The inclusion of contrasting outcomes controls for making implicit and unfounded assumptions about causal (or constitutive) relationships in the whole universe of cases (which are relevant to the argument's domain) through an exploration of only those cases that exhibit a similarity among themselves (Geddes, 2003:91-97). This makes for a non-parsimonious, complex theory claiming cautious generalizability to other CEE states. The aim to understand the differential Europeanisation of Poland, Bulgaria and Russia also aspires to some wider validity by demonstrating these countries' respective belongingness to the three culturally-historically framed sub-regions of CEE (Central, Southeast Europe and former Soviet space). So although the unique distinctiveness of the three states—as indeed of any state, means that the observed similarities and differences in the comparative setup will first and foremost apply to those states, their sub-regional representativeness allows making theoretical conclusions about the larger patterns of sub-regional resemblances and contrasts recreated in the post-communist period, as reflected in the propositions about what 'thick', 'ambivalent' and 'thin' Europeanisation entail.

Indeed, in line with the middle-ground methodological argumentation advancing qualified post-positivism, the focus on constitution (as opposed to clearly separable 'causes') does not preclude positing 'propositions', which is akin to hypothesis-testing. This is so because even though an analysis may be constitutive, qualitative-interpretive (rather than causal, quantitative-statistical), it can also be guided by and incorporate scientific standards of enquiry, including a rigorous-systematic, cross-case comparative, discursive as well as policy-focused empirical investigation of clearly specified suppositions. Such an investigation can provide a degree of validity and generalizability—as opposed to simply narration, directed by intuition, while at the same time being attuned to the vital significance of contextualism and to the possibility that further interpretive evidence may be uncovered (thus avoiding the assertion of confident claims to causality and finality of the data) (Hopf, 2002:29).

Conclusion

The predominant binary division of social scientific research into positivist or post-positivist, mapped respectively on the scientific vs. non-scientific spectrum, can obscure opportunities for methodological bridge-building. In this chapter I propose to relieve the excesses of such binarisation through qualified post-positivism that is concretely informed by interpretive and positivist within-case and cross-case comparative methods encompassing discourse analysis, elite interviews, process tracing, the congruence method, structured-focused comparison and the ideal type. The next chapter turns to elucidating the theoretical standpoints of the book.

3 Shades of Affinity
An Interactive Constructivist Theory of Self and Other in Bordering Belongingness

Emerging in the 1980s through the pioneering work of Alexander Wendt, Constructivism provided a rebalancing of overwhelming focus away from the debate between Realism and Liberalism — both of which share similar rationalist premises, and into the ideational, subjective and normative factors that inform the conduct of international relations. Constructivism turned attention to how the operation of material forces, state interests and systemic constraints is not automatic and predetermined but depends on the eye of the beholder — i.e., on perceptions, shaped by culture and identity, that refract the understanding and consequences of 'materiality'.

In the late 1980s, systemic collapse, which could not be predicted or explained on the basis of Realist premises, and neither could what followed be classified as a 'return to the future' through the reoccurrence of violent crises in Europe (Mearsheimer, 1990), pointed towards the large-scale impact that 'new thinking' can have on international relations.[4] Nevertheless, in the ensuing three decades, Constructivism has far from been firmly secured as a dominant professional practice within the discipline of IR. Constructivist research and teaching have instead been marginalised vis-à-vis Realist, positivist and quantitative approaches.[5]

---

[4] Authoritative analyses of the end of the Cold War illuminate the importance of belief evolution culminating in the rise of a global, Westernising identity among the Soviet elite: English, R., 2000, *Russia and the Idea of the West: Gorbachev, Intellectuals and the End of the Cold War*, Columbia University Press; English, R., 2002, 'Power, Ideas, and New Evidence on the Cold War's End: A Reply to Brooks and Wohlforth', *International Security*, Vol. 26, No 4, pp. 70-92, https://www.jstor.org/stable/3092102?seq=1#metadata_info_tab_contents; Brown, A., 2020, *The Human Factor: Gorbachev, Reagan, and Thatcher, and the End of the Cold War*, Oxford: Oxford University Press. The maturation of popular aspirations for democracy has also been singled out as contributing to the end of the Cold War: Wydra, H., 2007, *Communism and the Emergence of Democracy*, Cambridge University Press.

[5] For a stock-taking on the challenges that Constructivists face in terms of establishing themselves as part of the theoretical and methodological mainstream of

Yet, the disciplinary status accorded to Constructivism does not make the significance of ideas in international politics any less current. It is within the Constructivist theoretical strand that I have sought an answer to a main question underpinning the post-1989 European regional order: Who and how much belongs to the Euro-Atlantic family of nations?

The response that this chapter provides is pivoted on the development of the book's interactive Constructivist theory of the cultural and psychological dynamics between Self and Other—the two inextricably linked participants in any process of identification, which shape the possibility of coexistence as members of a shared group. After unpacking the concept of identity, I show that the conceptualisation of how the characteristic features of the Self-Other relationship play out—particularly in dramatic times of crisis, sheds light on the phenomenon of bordering the extent of belongingness to a joint community. The Self-Other relationship is subsequently contextualised in the case of Europe. The interactive dynamics of identity construction replayed between the Western Other and the CEE Selves since 1989 yield three propositions of 'thick', 'thin' and 'ambivalent' forms of Europeanisation. They denote three different extents of integration in the Euro-Atlantic community benchmarked by an ideal-typical model of European-ness, compatibility with or divergence from which conditioned CEE countries' ability to return to Europe after the collapse of communism.

IR see Bertucci, M., Hayes, J., James, P., (eds.), 2018, *Constructivism Reconsidered. Past, Present and Future*, University of Michigan Press; Steele, B., Gould, H., Kessler, O., (eds.), 2019, *Tactical Constructivism, Method, and International Relations*, Routledge. For a review of Constructivism's place within IR paradigmatic hierarchies particularly regarding faculty composition, graduate training and curriculum development see Subotic, J., 2017, 'Constructivism as Professional Practice in the US Academy', *Political Science & Politics*, Vol. 50, No 1, pp. 84–88 https://doi.org/10.1017/S1049096516002201; Zarakol, A., 2017, 'TRIPping Constructivism', *Political Science & Politics*, Vol. 50, No 1, pp. 75-78 https://doi.org/10.1017/S1049096516002183

Reciprocal bonds: Identity's relationality

Questions and quests of identity arise out of the need to situate oneself among others. The definition of a distinctive 'I' only becomes a meaningful — and possible, pursuit in a world that consists of a significant 'you' and 'they'. Thus, the inherently comparative character of identity underlines its relationality, which requires both a Self and an Other to negotiate mutual boundaries of similarity and difference.

The Self-Other relationship is present in interpersonal as well as group identification processes. In the latter, the collective internal self-definition of a group meets with the external other's categorisation of that group. As Jenkins puts it, each element — the internal/Self and external/Other, is an interrelated part of the collective dialectic of identification, whereby neither comes first or exists without the latter (Jenkins, 2008:109-110). In the interactive constitution of group boundaries, two factors play a definitive role, including level of inclusivity and normative compatibility. It is both the mechanisms of acceptance/positive valuation (or conversely separation/denigration) and the normative standard underlying the substantive meaning of group membership that determine joint belongingness to a community. Hence, assumptions of kinship are inextricably linked to ideational similarity.

In the case of the national collectivity, the Self-Other interactive dialectic is expressed in the domestic impetus to figure out belongingness on the ideological and civilizational map of the world. The book follows a conception of 'nation-state' identity that addresses the ways in which a community identifies as a national entity with distinctive traits, habits, culture and history, while also being politically organized in the form of a state that operates in an international setting populated by other states with which it establishes degrees of commonality or differentiation (Krause, Renwick, 1996:25).

Such a perspective captures both the internal self-understanding of a nation and its positioning within an external framework. The internal and external dimension of identification are therefore inextricably linked although the different theoretical concerns across the fields of Political Science and International Relations may have contributed to separate investigations of 'national' and 'state' identities. Those scholars concerned with domestic politics and nationalism tend to see identity as 'national', while scholars of foreign policy and international relations emphasise the extrinsic dimension of 'state' identity (Alexandrov, 2003:4-5). In particular, national identity is generally approached as the continuous reproduction and reinterpretation of the pattern of values, symbols, memories, myths, traditions that compose the distinctive cultural heritage of a nation and the identification of individuals with that pattern and heritage (Smith, 2009). National identity is thus constituted by religion, language, ethnicity, territory, which circumscribe a community of fate bound by common historical experiences. Moreover, national identity can be further delineated in terms of 'ethnic' or 'civic', depending on whether a greater emphasis is laid on citizenship or ethnic ties as criteria of belongingness to a given nation. In turn, state identity has been associated with an outward orientation referring to a state's characteristic place and conduct within the international community.

However, the analytical distinction between 'national' and 'state' identity can obscure the inseparable link that binds them together. National identity has been a fundamental source of a state's approach to forming allies and enemies in international affairs, while in a reciprocal fashion, the state has itself moulded national identity. Scholars of nationalism such as Ernest Gellner (2006), Benedict Anderson (2006), Eric Hobsbawm (2012), John Breuilly (1993) have stressed the importance of 'invention' and the 'imagining' of community and traditions in the political construction of nation-states within a historical purview. National distinctiveness, language, customs, sensibilities, religion, heritage and shared destiny were not accentuated and insisted upon until internationalisation set in train reciprocal national self-definitions (Krause, Renwick, 1996:41-42).

In the concrete terms of the book's empirical investigations, the continuity and change of the nation-state identities of Poland, Bulgaria and Russia since 1989 are examined as part of the mutually constitutive process of identification between Self and Other. That is, the (Polish/Bulgarian/Russian) nation-state is embodied in the collective signifier of the Self, while the West represents the relevant significant Other. And even as so generalised on the collective level, the Self and the Other need not be treated as abstract notions equivalent to 'individuals' or undifferentiated units with a ready-made outlook. Rather, the various and intricate aspects, processes and developments going on 'within' the Self and the Other need to be scrutinised when aiming to establish the ideational perspective of those collectivities. The Self's perspective can be gleaned on the basis of the leadership positions in the domestic political debate and process that sanction, shape and inform an identity stance, which is associated with the Self and externalised towards the Other, at any given time. Similarly, the Other's image can be discerned through those state-level and international institutional processes, events and policies that most significantly influence and frame its collective representation and power projection in relation to the Self within a particular timeline.

The exploration of the manifestation of the mutually constitutive interactions of Self and Other in the realm of foreign policy entails a focus on the way that the relevant decision-makers within the political elite as well as the influential international relations experts conceptualise and implement their identity stances. Although other societal groups such as business and economic elites, journalists can also express nation-state identity positions, the specific domain of foreign policy is for the most part an elite affair (Hill, Wallace, 1996:8). External relations remain the preserve of a small group of decision-makers and experts, who possess relevant diplomatic information (including intelligence) that is not accessible to the populace, which itself tends to be more concerned with socio-economic issues. Moreover, foreign policy-makers participate in European and international fora and become part of an elite network, which can have a significant effect on their identity stances in contrast to the wider public that is not part of such processes. Thus, while the political elite and the experts belong to the broader national-cultural environment and as a result their identity stances are informed by general popular discourses, it is up to political-intellectual elites themselves to decide when and how to utilise particular identity discourses and to induce innovation in those discourses within the bounds of electoral considerations. Still, the observation that political-intellectual elites matter overwhelmingly in the formulation of foreign policy does not preclude the examination of public opinion in order to compare and contrast the ways in which the politicians and the wider public perceive their country's identity.

The Self-Other relationship in the boundary drawing process of identification

The establishment of the relational underpinnings of identity, in general, and nation-state identity, in particular, poses the need for a concrete and comprehensive answer to a query that immediately follows: What are the distinct attributes of the Self and the Other, which exert an impact on negotiating mutual affinity in the process of identification? As I argue, there are a set of cultural and psychological characteristic features of the Self and the Other that gain prominence in dramatic circumstances and times of crisis and that affect the dynamics of reciprocal identification. They do so by accentuating the urgency of (re)locating borders of similarity and difference, whereby the rethinking of possibilities of shared belongingness to a community generates further questions of identity continuity and change and the specific ways in which identity frames boundary-drawing behavioural practices.

As regards *the Self*, crunch conditions can enhance its specific attributes, which influence the dynamics of the process of identification with a significant Other. In particular, a 'liminal' situation of internal ideational crisis can take the form of status inconsistency and may result in confusion, disorientation, insecurity and enhanced sensitivity to external factors (Greenfeld, 1992:15). Liminality refers to in-between periods distinguished by contingency, uncertainty and flux because of the dissolution of the established social order, triggered by a sudden event such as war, revolution or the collapse of a whole socio-political system. Liminal situations lead to the dislocation of established structures, the reversal of hierarchies and intellectual confusion (Gennep, 1960; Turner, 1995; Thomassen, 2009).

An identity crisis also sharpens the need for external models, guidance and even imitation so that a methodological focus on strategic calculations becomes rather less useful. As against the assumptions that crisis periods require a focus on actors' choices and strategic decision-making, which is present in much of the 'transition' literature, it can be argued that a sharpened awareness and reactions to outside models and actions becomes paramount (Dobry, 2009:75). Individuals trapped in a liminal situation cannot follow their 'rational interests' for two main reasons: first, because the structure on which 'objective rationality' was based has disappeared and second, because the stressful character of a liminal period prevents clear thinking. The search for a solution to the identity crisis therefore involves an escalating process of imitation and hence the greater importance of the example but also behaviour and attitudes of outside actors (Szakolczai, 2009:154). However, the process of comparison with and emulation of these outside actors can give rise to ressentiment – i.e., hostility and defensiveness towards the perceived external source or benchmark of one's inferiority (Greenfeld, 1992:16).

A further feature of the Self, which can become especially prominent in dramatic circumstances, is the need for positive self-identification. Social Identity Theory posits that people have a basic need to see themselves in a positive light in relation to relevant others. This need for prestige and high status means that in times of crisis, usually leading to diminished group esteem, social creativity and social change can take place in order that identity can be enhanced in a positive way. Social Psychological research has pointed that members of a negative group attempt to change their group's status by rating an undesirable attribute more positively or rating the group more favourably on other comparative dimensions (Huddy, 2001:10).

Moreover, the importance accorded to the Other in the Self's consciousness can affect the direction of identity change in periods of crisis that diminish positive esteem. The assumption is that the more important and salient the Other is, the more significant its impact will be in times of identity crisis. But what is the relationship between the Self and the Other?

In the tradition of Hobbes and Machiavelli the foundational political idea is that individual subjects as well as political communities oppose one another in a state of constant competition over interests. For Realists, the logic of security is exclusionist—it proposes to exclude developments deemed threatening to the continued existence of the state and in doing so draws boundaries to discipline the behaviour of those within and to differentiate within from without (Lipschutz, 1995:214). Therefore, the Other is conceived as an enemy. However, this need not be the case and one of the first thinkers to redefine the relations of identity and difference was Friedrich Nietzsche. He argued that the desire for security is manifested as collective resentment of difference—that which is not us, which is not certain and predictable. Complicit with a negative will to power is the fear-driven desire for protection from the unknown. Hence, the attitude to a 'negative' Other is based on competitive animosity, fear and stereotyping exacerbated by cultural incompatibility.

Yet, the positive will to power produces an aesthetic affirmation of difference and the Other need not be an enemy but can also be worthy of admiration and praise (Lipschutz, 1995:33-35). An analysis of identity can thus be situated within the tradition that emphasises not the struggle for self-preservation but the struggle for the establishment of relations of mutual recognition as a precondition for self-realisation. Recognition is worthless if it does not come from someone whom one views as deserving recognition and whose praise can serve as a confirmation of the Self's worth (Honneth, 1995:xi-xix).

In short, critical junctures can augment certain core characteristics of the Self, prompting an impetus to rethink and redefine boundaries of mutuality and affinity with a significant Other. A condition of internal identity crisis can lead to confusion, insecurity and a heightened search for external models. The need for positive self-identification, threatened by the prospect of a loss of status, can easily turn such confusion into resentment of the significant Other and attempts at positive self-inflation. And the more important and valued that Other is in the Self's perception, the more intensely the Self will seek its recognition.

Dramatic times also accentuate qualities of *the Other*, which affect the bounds of commonality with the Self. Consequential actions undertaken by the Other can set in train a process of ideational redefinition. Translated into International Relations terms, the premise is that international institutional events or state policies, which have a regional and even global significance, are very likely to have an impact on other states by leading to the rethinking of self-conceptions or making some identities more salient. This argument has received theoretical substantiation by Social Psychological identity theories, including affect control theory and identity control theory (Berger, 1966:9). Both theories deal with the internal dynamic of selves seeking to restore balance when identities are threatened by external events. In affect control theory, interactions consist of three important elements—self, other, activity—with affective values reflecting meanings resident in existing culture. If an external event disturbs the affective value of an element, adjustment involves altering one or more of the meanings, and therefore the values of elements, including identities, restoring equilibrium. An identity is re-conceptualised, or another identity becomes more salient, when a disturbance is so great that affective values cannot be brought into line with one another without altering the identity somehow (Stryker, 2008:8-9).

The Other's consequential actions can gain additional significance if backed up by outstanding power. That is, the ideational importance of the Other's activities will be amplified by its power capabilities since that Other will be able to influence the Self's perceptions of capacity, efficacy and hierarchical positioning in inter-group relations. For instance, the Other's economic and political power can reinforce its normative and symbolic authority, through which it can confer positive or negative evaluations on the Self. In this vein, the line between international society (defined by certain rules and norms) and the hegemony of the capitalist core can sometimes be difficult to draw. Many states feel threatened by international societal norms (e.g., human rights), as such norms may be incompatible with domestic political and cultural traditions but also define these states' relegation to the periphery of global politics as a result of principled divergence from the powerful core (Lipschutz, 1995:193).

In short, momentous developments unleashed by a powerful Other can initiate a shift in borders of mutuality by inducing a re-conceptualisation of the Self's identity and hierarchical positioning. If in such critical circumstances the Other demonstrates recognition, appreciation and acceptance, it will facilitate positive identification with the Self. But the significant Other can also exclude, insult or sideline the Self, which can accentuate feelings of ressentiment, opposition and attempts at self-enhancement.

On the whole, core characteristics of the Self and the Other manifest themselves with increased prominence and intensity during times of crisis, bringing about a destabilisation of mutual identifications and an impetus to rethink and redefine boundaries of similarity and difference. The sources of conflict that can create upsets in identities are therefore both external and internal. External sources of conflict are related to the Other in the form of critical actions that induce a discrepancy between situationally self-relevant meanings and the meaning contained in the identity standard that the Self measures itself against. Internal sources are linked to the Self and its conditions of identity crisis and liminality. The extent to which the disturbance in conceptions of Self-Other relatedness will result in integration or mutual exclusion depends on two social factors singled out by Social Psychological research: social support (referring to inclusion efforts, positive affirmation and acceptance on the part of the Other) and need satisfaction (referring to the Self's ability to fulfil needs for positive distinctiveness through effort and motivation) (Burke, 2006:4-5; Burlingame, 2008:23-24; Amiot, Terry, Wirawan, Grice, 2010:3).

Yet, is such a disturbance in the boundaries placed between Self and Other capable of engendering identity change or does it in the end only lead to the re-enactment of persistent, deeply ingrained identities? The answer which Psychological investigations provide—and which can advance Constructivism's more limited theorising of the problem of identity continuity and change, is contained in the persistence and only very gradual evolution of identities (Abrams, Hogg, Marques, 2005:21; Huddy, Sears, Levy, 2013:10; Burke, Stets, 2009:177; Jenkins, 2008:123). Habitual thought relieves the burden of effortful information-processing; motivated reasoning urges individuals to preserve their beliefs, oppose challenging views and dismiss the other's side of the argument as far weaker than one's own; while prior beliefs serve as a cognitive anchor that impedes appropriate and efficient updating based on new information not least due to selective attention and aversion to cognitive dissonance (Huddy, Sears, Levy, 2013:10, 13-14; Levy, 2013:311). The operation of these cognitive features in social processes on the international scale can be exemplified by the beliefs and images that people have of other countries becoming assumptions that are so taken for granted that they produce routinised habits that influence perceptions. The existing image operates as a cognitive schema that not only shapes the interpretation of information but also affects the search for new information (Herrmann, 2013:338-343).

Individuals will thus typically use selective perception, tact and sanctions to maintain identifications. For instance, through selective interaction one can choose partners and situations that do not pose a threat to identity, while signalling and displaying cues can let others know what the group is and how it should be treated. If for no other reason, people engage in these strategies because it is generally easier to maintain an identity than to come up with alternative identifications or definitions of a group or situation. Hence, although change and flux in identities are possible, the persistence and stability of identification is likely to be routine (Jenkins, 2008:123; Burke, 2006:14). Moreover, when belief change occurs, it tends to follow the cognitive-consistency tradition of least resistance. As people are faced with repeated inconsistencies between their belief systems and the world they observe, they first change tactical beliefs about the best means to particular ends. Change in fundamental beliefs is often so psychologically difficult that it is likely to occur only in conjunction with a major disruption in circumstances (Levy, 2013:312).

In addition to being paramount for social-cognitive functioning, the maintenance of stable identification entails practical implications in the realm of action by conditioning patterns of behaviour. According to Social Psychological findings — which can further address Constructivism's gap in theorising and specifying the ways in which identity affects behaviour, identities are behaviourally consequential in that they frame relations within the social group and with Others. It is a practical matter to synthesise relationships of similarity and difference — i.e., to identify someone could be enough to decide how to treat them (Jenkins, 2008:6, 18).

As a result, in order to belong to a group, it is not enough to claim an identity: one must also perform and actualise it to be accepted and confirmed as a member (Jenkins, 2008:122-123). Especially if people identify strongly with a group, whose norms prescribe certain actions, then they are more likely to do those things than if they did not identify strongly (Hogg, 2006:124-125). Moreover, identities provide a sense of predictability, anticipation and regularity when dealing with Others. Attribution and stereotyping have a political role in the 'social exorcism' of the Other through the dramatisation of differentiation and boundaries. Ambiguity and uncertainty are characteristics of boundaries, hence the need to map them with imaginary precision and to dramatise them ritually (Jenkins, 2008:150-153).

Ultimately, institutionalisation and allocation are some of the most consequential ways in which individuals participate in collective identifications. Institutionalisation contributes to the reproduction of environments of relatively predictable collective behaviour. The symbolisation of identity is embodied in very material practices: institutionalised collective forms may be imagined, but they are not imaginary since the practices of people and their products constitute these forms as tangible in space and time (through formal or informal organisation) (Jenkins, 2008:154-158; Hogg, Abrams, Marques, 2005:21). Moreover, identification and allocation are mutually entailed in each other since how one is identified influences what and how much one gets. In this way, administrative allocation represents a process of labelling, in which positive and negative stereotypes of particular categories are applied to individuals or groups, influencing the distribution to them of resources and penalties. Indeed, the moral register that resonates with notions of fairness and justice makes stereotyping appropriate to allocatory decision-making (Jenkins, 2008:192-193).

Overall, the features and dynamics characterising the Self-Other relationship, particularly in dramatic times of crisis and uncertainty, take a preeminent role in (re)bordering belongingness and shaping patterns of identity continuity, change and impact on behaviour. However, it must be noted that mutual unintelligibility can be present in Self-Other interactions, as the internal meaning of a group can be different from its meaning to outsiders. Some of the reasons for this include pre-existing stereotypes and cognitive schemas, which affect the intake of new information, as well as group members' attempts to elevate their group's standing by redefining negative identities (Huddy, 2001:18). Consequently, identity as a personal and social psychological phenomenon can be influenced and moulded by cognitive factors such as misperceptions, illusions, negativity bias (the tendency for negative events to have greater effects than positive events in information-processing, decision-making, learning and memory). Affective factors can play a further important role, especially background affective dynamics in the form of subtle intuitions that guide choices, ongoing desires, enduring attitudes and loyalties, deeply held convictions (Johnson, Tierney, 2014; Hall, 2013). So although it takes a mutually constitutive interaction between Self and Other to make identity meaningful, the meaning that Self and Other attribute to each other's attitudes and actions may be rather more subjectively perceived than objectively apprehended.

Conceptualising Europe's limits

Redrawing the borders of Europe became an acutely prominent endeavour after 1989 when the countries of the East of the continent emerged from behind the Iron Curtain and could rejoin the West. As I argue, the post-1989 process of establishing the limits of European-ness—of determining which countries qualified as

'European', can be conceptualised through an application of the interactive Constructivist framework of Self-Other dynamics to the European context. To this end, the book puts forward three propositions of Europeanisation, which specify how the mutually constitutive and reciprocal process of identification shapes three distinct levels of ideational proximity and acceptance into the Euro-Atlantic community that was taking shape following the collapse of communism.

What does it mean to be European?

Before elaborating on why and how differentiated extents of Europeanisation occur, a primary question emerges: How can we define what 'Europe' and 'European-ness' denote? The present study approaches European-ness as a value-laden notion, constituted by a set of rules, norms and principles that designate what it means to be European in an ideational sense. Such an ideational perspective can be juxtaposed to the prevailing trend in the literature on Europeanisation approximating processes of Europeanisation with the EU. Accordingly, a focus on the Union delimits the definition and scope of European developments to an institutional phenomenon emanating from the opportunities and constraints inherent in EU membership.

Instead, the book posits an ideas-based understanding of European-ness that can be discerned and abstracted—despite the presence of diverse specific representations of Europe throughout the continent. The conception of European-ness that has come to dominate has been shaped by the historical experience and cultural traditions of the *Western* European states, whose power-political preponderance has underpinned the ascendancy of their significations of what it takes to be European. The rules, norms and principles that make up this dominant conception can be generalised into a historically and analytically informed ideal-typical model.

The ideal type is not merely an ad hoc construction but is underlined by both longer-term historical developments and post-

1989 trends that point to the genealogical emergence of commonalities in Western understandings and projections of European-ness. The formative historical contributions to these commonalities include Greek science and philosophy, Roman law, Christian thought, the Enlightenment, the industrial and democratic revolutions, which have come to shape the constituent elements of the idea of the West: liberty, democracy, constitutional government, rule of law, private property, individuality (Nemo, 2006; Bavaj, 2011; Kurth, 2004; Daly, 2015).

Moreover, the course of international relations in the 20th century led to the gradual emergence, acceptance and legal-institutional codification of the norms and practices that have come to be associated with the Euro-Atlantic security community. The destructive trends of militarisation, alliance politics, nationalist self-aggrandizement through the use of force and oppression of small states, all of which underpinned the outbreak of two world wars, were renounced and rethought in the direction of the creation of a rules-based, institutionalised liberal international order. Secret treaties and unbridled militarism would give way to the construction of a security community, underpinned by a reduction in armaments and defence planning transparency. Nationalist unilateralism and economic barriers to trade would be replaced by supranational and regional integration, characterised by the pooling of sovereignty and economic interdependence. International legitimacy would be gained not through the exercise of coercive power but commitment to international law and the promotion of human rights and democracy (President Wilson's Fourteen Points, 1918; Jackson, 2011:4, 18-19, 23; Shimazu, 2003:4; Dunbabin, 1993:11-13, 17-19; Webster, 2005:10; Jacobson, 1972:7; Cox, Kennedy-Pipe, 2005:13; Leffler, 1996:15, 20; Bowker, Williams, 1988:62-63, 90-93; Davy, 2014:250-252; Thomas, 2005).

Following the end of communism, the US, Western European states and international institutions posited these norms, which had taken shape and been consolidated in the Western-centric system of international relations during the Cold War, as criteria to be fulfilled by the CEE countries in the latter's quest for cooperation with the Euro-Atlantic community through integration in the EU and

NATO. Such criteria were akin to standards of European-ness forming an integral part of a normative project, underwritten by assumptions of the universalisation of Western liberal democracy and capitalism, which had won over communism. These criteria were also singled out in a normatively selective process that posits certain values and historical experiences as more self-defining than others (such as Marxism, fascism and war, which also represent Western historical traditions and experiences) (Fukuyama, 1989:1; Arfire, 2011; Haukkala, 2008a; Diez, 2013; Medvedev, 2008).

Hence, the commonalities of historical-political experiences in Western Europe (and the US) have conditioned a set of shared understandings of European-ness. Admittedly, there is an undeniable diversity among specific Western national traditions in conceptualising Europe and its values such as different views on the depth and extent of European cooperation as related to national sovereignty, of state intervention in a capitalist economy, of the proper arrangements (presidential, parliamentary, etc.) of distinct visions of democracy. Nevertheless, the common denominator of Western understandings becomes especially generalised and pronounced in interactions with Central-East Europe. This is so because the latter has been historically treated as a constitutive Other, whose economic backwardness, authoritarian traditions and insufficient modernisation demarcate a boundary with the progressive, free and prosperous West of the continent (with a further hierarchy of distance from the West being established between Central Europe, the Balkans and the (former) Russian imperial space) (Neumann, 1999; Kuus, 2004).

In a mirror image, CEE representations of (Western) Europe also reinforce the 'ideal' construction of European-ness. There is a continuous historical perception of Europe as 'utopia', taking the contours of a 'myth' in political imagination. Myth can be understood as a form of ideologised narrative attempting to mediate 'reality', in which the contingent and differentiated manifestations of a given political phenomenon disappear. The result is that the association of modernity, democracy and prosperity with Western Europe has become a commonly accepted and ideologised appraisal in Central-East European thinking (Wydra, 2013:4-5;

Sakwa, 2008:205). As Wydra has clarified, during communism, 'Europe' was a magical point of attraction in the consciousness of Central and East Europeans. After 1989 the image of the liberal and rich Western Europe replaced communism's ideological prescription of totality with a vision of totality of a different kind: an ideal perception of Europe oblivious to finer differences in normative positions within the West of the continent itself (Wydra, 2013:7). This mythical image of the values Western Europe embodies and projects produced an overall commitment to Europeanisation throughout CEE after the fall of the Berlin Wall. Yet, the commitment was differently realised as circumscribed by concrete national traditions of understanding, rootedness and practice of ideal-typical European values within the country-specific context (Wydra, 2013:9).

Finally, apart from the historical reasons for positing European-ness in an 'idealised' and generalised form, the provision of a general standard of European-ness can fulfil the analytical purpose of serving as a comparative benchmark for establishing extent of Europeanisation. As argued in Chapter 2, the ideal type is an analytical-methodological device, which allows carrying out comparative investigations by extrapolating general features without, however, expecting 'perfect' reproduction of the features either on the part of those whom the values emanate from, or on the part of those whose affinity with the values is assessed. Indeed, an insufficient reproduction of the elements of the standard of European-ness does not entail judgements of unfulfilled developmental prerequisites and normative 'lack'. Although the projection of European-ness on the part of the West after 1989 has assumed the contours of normative dominance that aims to socialise the East into the 'correct' norms (given that their previously communist worldview was discredited), the research process is not underwritten by expectations of a normatively necessary linear development towards European-ness. The weak resemblance of ideal-typical values on the part of a national tradition of conceptualising 'Europe' is not a matter of moral opprobrium but of a specific political-historical and cultural process that in itself contains a critical potential. This potential is revealed in the demonstration of the multiplicity of CEE conceptions of Europe, which are formed in relations with the West, limit the possibility of fulfilling the ideal-typical standard of belongingness (for reasons of identification rather than normative insufficiency) and should be taken into account when de-centering Western Europe's own commonly accepted and dominantly projected views (Onar, Nicolaidis, 2013). The recognition of differences can in turn foster greater mutual understanding, reflection and reflexivity instead of an 'overcoming' of those differences.

On the whole, the definition of ideal-typical European-ness as framed by the traditions of the West means that its value-based constitutive elements can be derived from those principles codified as animating the diplomacy, organisational framework and membership criteria of the state- and international institutional actors, who embody, share and project the Western European historical-political experience and normative positions (including individual West European countries, the EU, NATO, the OSCE, the Council of Europe). These normative positions can be gleaned from key documents setting out a state's or institution's goals, policy directions and place in the world, such as national security strategies and landmark institutional treaties.

The major West European states' (and the US's) definition and understanding of themselves as foreign policy actors hinge on the domestic organisation of their societies on the basis of democracy, the rule of law, human rights, tolerance, pluralism, support for civic expressions of nationalism, the free market. The conduct of foreign policy and vision of international relations stem from and are expected to safeguard these values along a number of key (yet overlapping and mutually entailing) dimensions. First, the universality of democracy, human rights and international law should be realised within a *liberal, rules-based international order and politics* oriented on multilateralism, interdependence, the renunciation of spheres of influence and balances of power, democracy- and human rights promotion, good-neighbourliness, institutionalised cooperation on the basis of forging close transatlantic security ties and European partnerships.[6]

Second, the values informing the general conduct of international politics should also be specifically reflected *on the regional level* through the establishment of regionally cooperative, peaceful and friendly relations (in a state's immediate neighbourhood), built on trust, devoid of historical hatreds and embedded in bilateral as well as multilateral arrangements.[7]

Third, adherence to and promotion of European values should be ultimately reflected in *integration within the core European organisations* of the EU, NATO, the OSCE and the Council of Europe. The distinctiveness of debating and conducting foreign policy through institutionalised cooperation is especially centred on the EU (as the most significantly institutionalised cornerstone of European political-economic relations) and is linked to the search for consensus through persuasion, argumentation, cooperation as well as support for the further institutional development of the EU. The reciprocal ability to both 'download' (follow) from and

---

[6] These values-based positions are enunciated and codified in for example: Persuasion and Power in the Modern World, 2014, *Select Committee on Soft Power and the UK's Influence*; Strategic Defence Review White Paper of the UK, 1998, *International Affairs and Defence Section, House of Commons Library*, pp. 12, 17-18; Strategic Defence and Security Review: Securing Britain in an Age of Uncertainty, 2010, *Cabinet Office, National Security and Intelligence*; National Security Strategy and Strategic Defence and Security Review of the UK, 2015, *Prime Minister's Office, Cabinet Office, Department for International Development, Foreign and Commonwealth Office, Home Office, Ministry of Defence*, p.10; Defence Policy Guidelines of the Federal Republic of Germany, 2011, *Ministry of Defence*, pp. 3-4; French White Paper – Defence and National Security, 2013, pp. 25-26; White Paper for International Security and Defence, Italy, 2015, *Ministry of Defence*, pp. 33, 35-38; A Secure Netherlands in a Secure World, 2013, *Ministry of Foreign Affairs*, pp. 3-10; National Security Strategy of the US, 2015, *Barack Obama Administration*, pp. 25-28; National Security Strategy of the US, 2006, *George W. Bush Administration*, pp. 7-12; National Security Strategy for a New Century, USA, 2000, *Bill Clinton Administration*, p. 9.

[7] As gleaned from: European Council Summit in Copenhagen, Presidency Conclusions, 1993; European Convention on Human Rights, amended in 2010, European Court of Human Rights, *Council of Europe*; Framework Convention for the Protection of National Minorities and Explanatory Report, 1995, *Council of Europe*; Partnership for Peace: Framework Document, 1994, *NATO*; Study on NATO Enlargement, 1995, *NATO*; Charter of Paris for a New Europe, 1990, *CSCE*; Helsinki Document: the Challenges of Change, 1992, *CSCE Summit*.

'upload' (create) foreign policy positions onto the Brussels level is also part of the opportunities for diplomatic cooperation and coordination provided by EU membership/accession status (relevant where the latter has been achieved and as linked particularly to the CFSP).[8]

In the realm of European security and defence underwritten by NATO, integration would presuppose a foreign policy, whereby the achievement of peace encompasses conducting democratic reforms (such as civilian and democratic control over the military); increasing transparency in defence planning and military budgets; renouncing the aggressive use of force and spheres of influence and considering soft security issues. This stands in contrast to zero-sum calculations and an overwhelming focus on hard power and hard security linked to balance of power politics and the creation of military alliances. Additionally, cooperation is fostered on the basis of complementary and mutually reinforcing institutions (including NATO, the EU, the OSCE), bilateral and multilateral undertakings and regional cooperation.[9]

---

[8] As gleaned from Davignon Report, 1970, *Bulletin of the European Communities*; Declaration on European Identity, 1973, *Bulletin of the European Communities*; Solemn Declaration on European Union, 1983, *European Council*, Stuttgart 19 June 1983; Treaty on European Union, 1992, *Council of the European Communities, Commission of the European Communities*, p. 7; European Council Summit in Copenhagen, Presidency Conclusions, 1993; European Parliament Resolution of 8 May 2008 on the Annual Report on Human Rights in the World 2007 and the European Union's Policy on the Matter, 2008, *European Parliament*, pp. 5-11; European Parliament Resolution of 22 October 2009 on Democracy Building in the EU's External Relations, 2009, *European Parliament*, pp. 3-7; Chelotti, N., 2014, 'Multiple Practices and Styles: Analysing Variation in EU Foreign Policy Negotiations', *European Foreign Policy Unit LSE, Working Paper 2014/1*, pp. 2-7, https://www.lse.ac.uk/international-relations/assets/documents/efpu/publications/EFPU-Working-paper-2014-1.pdf; Moumoutzis, K., 2011, 'Still Fashionable Yet Useless? Addressing Problems with Research on the Europeanization of Foreign Policy', *Journal of Common Market Studies*, Vol. 49, No 3, pp. 607-629, https://onlinelibrary.wiley.com/doi/abs/10.1111/j.1468-5965.2010.02146.x.

[9] As gleaned from Partnership for Peace: Framework Document, 1994, *NATO*; Study on NATO Enlargement, 1995, *NATO*; Membership Action Plan, 1999, *NATO*; Helsinki Final Act, 1975, *CSCE*; Charter of Paris for a New Europe, 1990, *CSCE*; Helsinki Document: the Challenges of Change, 1992, *CSCE Summit*; Code of Conduct on Politico-Military Aspects of Security, 1994, *CSCE*; Vienna Document on Confidence- and Security-Building Measures, 2011, *OSCE*.

Ideas vs. institutions?

The book takes an ideational approach to European-ness, singling out a set of norms and principles that define what it means to be European according to the politically dominant and historically conditioned understandings of the western half of the continent. Yet, a question can be raised as to how such an ideational approach relates to the issue of 'institutionalisation'. The latter is specifically linked to the present study's inference of value positions from institutional setup and membership as well as the empirical investigation of institutionalised arrangements and practices as part of Europeanisation (such as offer of international organisational membership, attendant conditions and domestic institutional factors).

The answer that I provide is that in contrast to the rational-instrumental approach, which views institutions through a formal means-end, transactional logic, sociological and historical institutionalism underscores the normative-ideational underpinnings that inform the rationale and operation of institutions. Accordingly, the creation, development and sustenance of institutions are shaped by ideational-discursive embeddedness, cultural construction and repeated patterns of interaction that foster normative regularities of behaviour within a cognitively interdependent community (Rosamond, 2000:117-118; Risse, quoted in Rosamond, 2000:121; Acharya, 2001; Ba, 2005).

In short, ideas and identities shape and are reflected in institutional forms. The establishment of relations and boundaries of inclusion or exclusion is crucial to Self-Other, inter-group identification, whereby formally institutionalised membership is a tangible manifestation of inclusivity. Thus, the pace, degree and offer of formalised membership in a given community is vitally determined by views regarding common belongingness and shared values. As previously outlined in this chapter, institutionalisation and administrative allocation do not stand apart from but are entailed in the process of identification as the palpable substantive markers and organisational frameworks of the principles and regularised patterns of behaviour of a collectivity and its distinction from out-groups. Hence, the offer of membership and inclusion in culturally embedded institutional forms and practices would represent the rite of passage from the liminal conditions of status uncertainty to acceptance and positive affirmation of mutuality between Self and Other (Gennep, 1960; Turner, 1995).

Consequently, as opposed to a rationalist view of institutions as intervening variables between actor preferences and policy outputs and an instrumentalist explanation of Europeanisation as rule transfer/institutionalisation (i.e., the transposition of EU legislation in internal institutional forms), determined by the credibility of EU conditionality and domestic costs of rule adoption,[10] the book takes the position that 'institutions are what states make of them'. That is, the offer of membership, conclusion of agreements and attendant conditions and criteria of entry into international organisations would be guided by levels of identification both on the part of the Other (and its ideational-civilizational reasons for extending membership) and on the part of the Self (who conceives of conditionality as a marker of belongingness). Institutionalisation certainly does contribute distinctive practical diplomatic, political, economic effects to Europeanisation. The offer of institutional membership will incorporate a stipulation of formal-objective benchmarks for compliance; conditionality will invoke a calculation of adaptation costs; achieved organisational admission will provide a wider platform for building partnerships and conducting external relations. Nevertheless, these effects will be ultimately conditioned and circumscribed by identity as well as differentially understood and applied in the process of defining and expanding communal boundaries.

Similarly, domestic institutions linked to party politics, the separation and balance between democratic arrangements, can affect the consistency, timing of foreign policy conduct and the relationship between political groupings. But such consequences will be enabled, limited and manifested as part of the general

---

[10] The rationalist-instrumentalist explanation of Europeanisation is exemplified by Schimmelfennig, F., Sedelmeier, U., (eds.), 2005, *Europeanization of Central and Eastern Europe*, Ithaca: Cornell University Press.

political-intellectual frame that informs understandings of a country's place in international relations.

Finally, it should be noted that intra-West European national specificities may lead to the contestation of some institutional practices or to non-participation as in the case of the UK, Switzerland or Norway, for example, with regard to the EU and NATO. Institutional fluidity, however, is not a reason for exclusion from the category of being 'West European'. This is so given the overarching ideational-historical bond of commonality, despite the presence of specific ideas correspondingly reflected in institutional specificities (e.g. about British sovereignty and independence of decision-making).

An ideational approach to European-ness therefore does not exclude or contradict but incorporates an institutional perspective informed by a historical and sociological rather than rationalist-instrumentalist, bureaucratic-administrative understanding. Institutionalisation represents a core manifestation of the dynamic of identification, which justifies the extrapolation of value-based positions from institutional frameworks and treaties as well as the exploration of institutional factors such as formal membership in a group as part of the process of bordering belongingness between Self and Other.

Differential Europeanisation: 'thick', 'thin' and 'ambivalent' Europeans

The chapter has so far laid out an ideal-typical definition of European-ness that represents a dominantly politically posited and historically buttressed yardstick by which to measure a country's European qualities. Yet, it is not equally achievable and applied, particularly across the eastern part of the continent. This unevenness can be understood if one examines the larger context of the interactive dynamics of identification between the Western Other and the CEE Selves. These dynamics construct the boundaries of belongingness to a shared Euro-Atlantic community and the related ability to enunciate and practice the ideal-typical values benchmarking that community.

The main argument of the book holds that by contextualising the interactive model of Self-Other identification, differential Europeanisation can be accounted for on the basis of differentiated levels of inclusion and ideational affinity, which are respectively established between the Polish, Bulgarian and Russian Self and the Western European Other. The greater the Other's acceptance and commitment and the greater the Self's normative similarity and identification with the Other, the more such an interaction defining boundaries of mutuality will (re)produce conceptions and practices on the part of the Self, which match most closely the ideal standard embodying the values and principles of communal belongingness with the Other. In this way, the differential Europeanisation of Poland, Bulgaria and Russia will depend on two interrelated dimensions. The first marks the degree to which these countries' specific, domestically debated and constructed conceptions of Europe normatively match the benchmark of European-ness underwriting the Euro-Atlantic community. The second refers to the extent of receptivity, recognition and commitment that the Western Other grants to the Polish, Bulgarian and Russian Selves.

These interactive dynamics play out especially prominently in dramatic circumstances and times of crisis when characteristic features of the Self and the Other have been theorised to disturb the stability of established identifications and bring about an impetus for a redefinition of mutual boundaries. For instance, and as further elaborated in Chapters 5, 6 and 7, the process of EU and NATO accession, German and American policies of inclusion in/exclusion from the Euro-Atlantic community represent some of those consequential actions taken by a powerful Other that can lead to a re-thinking of the Self's identity. Moreover, the post-1989 changes induced liminal domestic situations of identity crisis and a corresponding search for external models, identity verification and positive distinctiveness in all of the three countries under investigation, whereby heated internal political debates were focused on the urgency of (re)constructing Poland's, Bulgaria's and Russia's place in Europe.

The interactive dynamics between the Western Other and the Polish, Bulgarian and Russian Selves in the process of determining the limits of the Euro-Atlantic community in the critical aftermath of 1989 yield propositions about three distinct levels of Europeanisation. First, the *'thickest' (i.e., deep, extensive, substantial) case of Europeanisation* of foreign policy identity would be characterised by the interaction of sustained, consistent and wide-ranging Western European commitment, recognition and acceptance of a CEE country coupled with a broad-based internal political consensus espousing a strong cultural-historical tradition of identification and normative compatibility with Western Europe. On the other hand, *the 'thinnest' (i.e., shallow, tenuous, insubstantial) case of Europeanisation* would be characterised by the interaction of low and inconsistent Western European commitment and acceptance working in conjunction with serious domestic doubts about the desirability of 'merging' national identity and social-political practices with those of Western Europe. Finally, *an 'ambivalent' (i.e., uncertain, ambiguous) case of Europeanisation* is one in which there is both international and domestic ambivalence about how much a country belongs to Europe. Nonetheless, this ambivalence is not too strong to prevent the gradual albeit difficult movement towards inclusion and (superficial) normative compatibility, pushed along by the provision of European diplomatic and economic support and the achievement of internal consensus about forging a pro-European foreign policy direction.

The three propositions about differentiated forms of Europeanisation underscore that although Europeanisation denotes a dynamic, interactive process between Self and Other, the result of this process is not uniform but can recreate, re-invoke and modify in contemporary circumstances historically-informed national conceptions of 'Europe'. So Europeanisation does not enshrine an assumption of linear progression towards the ideal type of European-ness benchmarking belongingness to the Euro-Atlantic community. It is rather expected to reproduce degrees of distance from it by re-enacting distinct levels of inclusivity and ideational affinity performed between the Western Other and the Polish, Bulgarian and Russian Self.

Measuring Europeanisation

How can a particular extent of Europeanisation—constituted by inclusivity and ideational affinity, be recognised and systematically evaluated? *Inclusivity* can be assessed on the basis of the Other's commitment and acceptance, discerned in such concrete acts as pace and degree of institutional admittance, diplomatic support and economic assistance offered to a given CEE country. This is so because institutionalisation and allocation represent the tangible consequences of a process of collective identification and categorisation. *Ideational affinity* can in turn be gauged in convictional, discursive and behavioural terms by evaluating the genuineness of attachment to ideal-typical values, the consistency, sustenance and (cross-party politically) shared quality of the rhetorical embeddedness of these values and their expression into action.

Comparatively, levels of inclusivity and ideational affinity can be established relationally across the country cases on a continuum from the 'thickest' to the 'thinnest' substantiation and application of European-ness. A 'thickly' Europeanised case would feature a construction of 'Europe' characterised by a desire to belong and integrate with West of the continent based on an ideational internalisation of ideal-typical European values and their corresponding sustained and consistent discursive embeddedness and behavioural manifestation. It would also feature continued and intensive commitment on the part of the Other, expressed in quick and substantial institutional inclusion, diplomatic support and economic assistance, fostering an increased sense of belongingness and status security.

On the other hand, a 'thin' case of Europeanisation would be one in which the construction of 'Europe' only matches the ideal type as a rhetorical overlay. But it is devoid of in-depth consistency, internalised ideational substantiation and behavioural manifestation, which can amount to contestation of the values in the ideal-typical model and of the desirability of integration. This would be consonant with a non-committal Other that fails to provide significant diplomatic, institutional and economic support and hence contributes to disappointment and exclusion.

Finally, an 'ambivalent' case of Europeanisation would combine elements from the aforementioned instances. The construction of 'Europe' would be characterised by discursive enunciation of the values in the ideal type but divergence in substantive understandings. The divergence would be expressed in the prevalence of imitative performativity rather than either the normative internalisation characteristic of 'thicker' conceptions or contestation of these values in 'thinner' ones. The Other would similarly demonstrate slower and less significant diplomatic, institutional and economic support—but without refraining from such support altogether, thus fostering a mix of encouragement and disappointment.

The establishment of conceptions of Europe of differentiated distance from the ideal type and informing thick, thin and ambivalent forms of Europeanisation does not, however, presuppose a black-boxed abstraction of these conceptions, obscuring *alternative strands of thinking*. That is, such conceptions cannot be uncovered in pure and undisputed form. They will, rather, prevail over alternative culturally and historically shaped visions of Europe due to their dominant discursive promotion and foreign policy implementation by the political groupings, who have achieved political ascendancy within a particular timeframe. So in the political process of constructing Europe some ideas become empowered, while others are subdued in influence, although they continue to be enunciated in the public space.

And even when alternative conceptualisations themselves become politically empowered, the book argues that the degrees of distance from the ideal type on the part of the proposed levels of Europeanisation will still be maintained. A thickly Europeanised vision, for instance, will not be contested by alternative traditions to such a fundamental depth and extent that it leads to a comprehensive renunciation of European-ness and belongingness in the Euro-Atlantic community as well as wholesale external marginalisation, similar to thinner Europeanisation. Instead, alternative traditions of thinking Europe can entail a modified understanding and practice of specific value dimensions and limited international criticism, while still preserving a thickly Europeanised character especially in contrast to other countries' level of Europeanisation.

This is so because traditions of conceptualising Europe are co-dependent and coexist within an overall national-intellectual frame, whereby alternative views are not expected to deviate from other traditions in a way that will represent a radical 'break' and leap forward or backward as regards Europeanisation. Such views can introduce uncertainty within a given level of Europeanisation on its own terms but will nevertheless keep the contours of that level — particularly cross-country comparatively. So the return of traditions that are in tension with the overall, dominantly constructed level of Europeanisation should be taken into account as reactions, intimately related to that level of Europeanisation. As the empirical analysis in Chapters 5, 6 and 7 shows, all of the distinct, country-specific, contemporary forms of conceptualising Europe in Poland, Bulgaria and Russia perpetuate historical traditions of identity formation that grapple with the West European model. The model was integral to national consciousness and identity construction, whereby Western values were accepted, assimilated, practiced or criticised, moulded and renounced in nationally specific ways as part of the general CEE representation of Europe along the axis of 'utopia' and 'threat'. Therefore, alternative or contested meanings ascribed to a given level of Europeanisation will not be independently existing of and unrelated to that level but will constitute a reaction, which is borne out of the dualistic, attractive yet repulsive, aspirational and threatening perception of Western Europe and its values.

Conclusion

The interactive Constructivist theory of Self and Other in bordering belongingness developed in this chapter focuses attention on the power of ideational factors in politics. The examination of the dynamics of the Self-Other relationship, which is inherent in processes of identifification especially in times of crisis, is crucial to understanding how and where states in Europe (and beyond) place boundaries among each other. Encircling spaces for joint community and enforcing its limits in turn provide a compass as to the patterns of friendship/cooperation or rivalry/competition in international political life that are not simply an epiphenomenon of relative power position. The degree of European unification since 1989 thus ultimately depended on answering questions about 'who we are' and 'with whom we belong together'.

4 The Interactive Constructivist Theory of Self & Other and IR Debates
Refinement, Dialogue and Challenge

The goal to reinvigorate theorising about the significance of ideas in politics calls for a discussion of the state of related and competing research strands within the discipline of International Relations. The current chapter shows that the book's interactive Constructivist theory of Self and Other positions itself and speaks to IR debates in two main ways. First, it does so by refining, filling in and addressing the persistent gaps and weaknesses of relevant analytical pathways within Constructivism. Additionally, the possibility of inter-disciplinary dialogue with theories related to Constructivism is charted out. Building links particularly to the literature on Europeanisation and Foreign Policy Analysis's Role Theory takes place on the basis of mapping areas of overlap as well as divergence and singling out potential avenues for cross-learning. Second, the book's theoretical framework challenges the conceptual premises and empirical relevance of Realism, questioning its explanatory persuasiveness and dominant status within International Relations.

Constructivism: Improving resilience

Constructivism's pivotal intervention in the discipline of International Relations through the enunciation of the importance of ideational factors in shaping and directing international political events and developments has nonetheless been plagued by persistent intra-theoretical disagreements on questions of ontology and epistemology. The preoccupation with such meta-theoretical issues has in turn given rise to a related self-critique of the insufficiency of concrete empirical and mid-range theoretical exploration of how the key concepts and mechanisms that Constructivists have singled out as central to their theory — including 'identity', the mutual constitution of structures and agents, the inseparable operation of materiality from its socially shared perception — can be examined as part of concrete cases and occurrences in international politics.

Reviewing these points of contention, in what follows I demonstrate how the book's interactive Constructivist theory of Self and Other, informed by a middle-ground methodological perspective, weighs in on and contributes to the resolution of weaknesses in the Constructivist research agenda along three dimensions. The first develops the interactive ontological perspective. The second integrates the positivist and post-positivist strands of the epistemological debates. The third puts forward the mid-range interactive theory of Self and Other as a move away from the Constructivist concentration on philosophical arguments.

Constructivist ontological and epistemological debates

One major axis of difference among Constructivists is based on their *ontological standpoints and commitments*: Constructivists have disagreed over whether international (system-level) or national (unit-level) factors have primacy in the formation of state identities and interests (Wendt, 1992:15-17; Wendt, 1999:11-23). On the one hand, pioneering Constructivists such as Alexander Wendt and Martha Finnemore have elaborated a systemic approach. Wendt claims that identities and their corresponding interests are learned and reinforced in accordance with the way actors are treated by significant Others. So the principles of 'reflected appraisals' or 'mirroring' are crucial because the most important thing in social life is how the Self begins to see itself as a reflection of its appraisal by a significant Other (Wendt, 1999:327-335, 346; Wendt, 1992:16, 17). Similarly, according to Finnemore, the starting point of analysis is the international structure because its rules and values create all actors we might consider relevant in international politics — states, firms, organisations, even individuals. State interests and behaviour are defined in the context of internationally held norms and understandings about what is good and appropriate (Barnett, Finnemore, 2004; Finnemore, Sikkink, 1998; Keck, Sikkink, 1998).

On the other hand, 'unit-level' Constructivists have criticised 'systemic' Constructivists for paying insufficient attention to domestic factors (Katzenstein, 1996; Lapid, Kratochwil, 1996; Hunt, 2009). It is charged that Wendt says next to nothing about actors prior to their interaction and his belief in actors as cultural 'blank slates' prior to contact prevents him from examining the domestic sources of a state's identity and international behaviour. Peter Katzenstein, for instance, takes the position that the structures of meaning are not simply the result of cultural interaction after the first contact. Rather, each culture brings to the interactions images of itself and others that are prefigured by myths, texts and traditions (Katzentstein, 1996:33-72; Inayatullah, Blaney, 1996:73-75).

Moreover, scholars, who propose an agent-centric account of the way identities are formed, stress 'Habermasian' logics of argumentation or the role of communicative action in mediating between agents and inter-subjective values in contrast to 'systemic' Constructivists, who emphasise logics of appropriateness — the constitutive power of structure over interests and behaviour. Kratochwil (1991), Onuf (2013a, b), Reus-Smit (2009), Risse, Ropp, Sikkink (1999) argue that norms do not constitute identity or interests in any straightforward or uncomplicated way. In many situations, actors encounter multiple norms of behaviour, open to varied interpretations. So actors engage in argument: they try to figure out in a collective communicative process whether their assumptions about the world are correct or which norms of appropriate behaviour apply.

Finally, 'holistic' Constructivists have attempted to bridge the divide between the international and the domestic in explaining how state identities and interests are constituted (Schonberg, 2007:15; Rae, 2002; Hall, 1999; Koslowski, Kratochwil, 1995). In this vein, John Ruggie (1998) sets out to integrate the domestically constituted corporate identities of states and their internationally driven social identities into a unified analytical perspective that treats the domestic and the international as two faces of a single social and political order (Behravesh, 2011). The 'practice turn' in IR, which has increasingly been included into Constructivist theorising, also claims to bridge the agency-structure divide by placing ontological primacy on practices (Cornut, 2018:141; Collins, 2019). In this way, as Emanuel Adler explains, the agent-structure dichotomy begins to highlight action and processes rather than separate entities, considering agents and structures as propensities that become actual only in and through practice (Adler, 2019:65).

It is this interactive-holistic strand of Constructivism that the book weighs in and builds upon. Indeed, an interactive perspective upholds most closely and develops the original Constructivist argument that it is impossible for structure to have effects apart from the attributes and interactions of agents (Wendt, 1992:15-17; Wendt, 1999:11-23). Nonetheless, both systemic and unit-level Constructivists have paradoxically sidelined or taken as 'given' this injunction, exclusively focusing their analyses on either the domestic or international level as relevant for identity construction. Caution has to be retained, however, regarding the practice turn's promise of integrating agents and structures due to its behaviouralist bent and overemphasis on action. Adler agrees that cognition does not precede action but represents a phase of action by which action is (re)directed in its situation context. Scientific and social reasoning are therefore not causal forces antecedent to practice but its 'laborious achievement'. In short, 'practice rules' (Adler, 2019:116; 119; 144). Yet, this postulation leads to structuralist implications, whereby practices are unconsciously reproduced by virtue of ingrained, culturally bound habit. Agential perspectives related to subjective and intersubjective cognitive processes that contain the potential for rethinking and changing practices consequently remain underdeveloped—but have to be taken into account, as cognitive factors are not necessarily always visible in and caused by behaviour.

The second main axis of difference among Constructivists is linked to *epistemology*—i.e., whether they adhere to positivist or post-positivist epistemological standpoints (Ish-Shalom, 2019). Positivist Constructivists such as Alexander Wendt, Martha Finnemore, Michael Barnett, Peter Katzenstein, John Ruggie, Emanuel Adler maintain that despite being socially constructed and subject to varied understandings and meanings, the international system contains law-like patterns governing social relations that are amenable to generalisation and falsifiable hypotheses (Hurd, 2008:308). On the other hand, for post-positivist Constructivists, including Friedrich Kratochwil, Nicholas Onuf, Richard Price, Christian Reus-Smit, Thomas Risse, social relations cannot be objectively explained and separated into 'causes' and 'effects' since social and political life is not guided by generalizable laws but exists in contingency and flux. Hence, social inquiry has to be concerned with the social constitution of meaning, the linguistic construction of reality and the historicity of knowledge (Hurd, 2008:308).

Apart from this two-fold overall distinction between positivist and post-positivist Constructivists, the epistemological orientations within Constructivism have also been labelled more specifically as 'conventional' (or also 'modernist' and 'subjectivist'), 'linguistic' and 'critical' (Adler, 1997, 2013; Palan, 2000; Epstein, 2010; Hopf, 1998). The conventional Constructivist approach involves positivist epistemological assumptions (most notably Wendt's Scientific Realism) and draws on phenomenological and sociological perspectives such as Symbolic Interactionism, which is premised on the theory that humans see the world through perspectives that are developed socially and advances a subjectivist, methodologically individualist point of view (Palan, 2000:6-7).

Linguistic Constructivism, exemplified by the works of Friedrich Kratochwil and Nicholas Onuf, subscribes to post-positivist epistemology and follows Ludwig Wittgenstein's philosophy in arguing that social objects are constituted by the description actors give them and therefore have no existence independent of beliefs, utterances and speech acts. So the crude materialist reality (emerging in Wendt's theory as 'brute material forces') is a hypothetical reference point arising out of the properties of language, which warrants a focus on argumentation, speech acts, communicative action and discourse analysis (Palan, 2000:8; Kratochwil, 1991, 2001; Onuf, 2013a, b; Risse, Kleine, 2009).

Finally, critical Constructivism also employs a post-positivist, discursive epistemological perspective but is concerned with a critique of society and power. Drawing on Jacques Lacan's social theory of identity, which does not view the Self as in harmony with its social environment, critical Constructivist research takes issue with 'subjectivism' that does not enquire about the emergence of the subject-as-actor and remains silent on the ways in which identities and 'systems of truths' are constructed through power, repression and exploitation (Palan, 2000:11-12; Epstein, 2010:10). For example, the post-colonial strand of critical Constructivism focuses on embodied experiences, steeped in colonial histories, which are posited as a counterpoint to universalisation as the key historical driver of colonisation (Epstein, 2017:9-11; Adem, 2021). Critical norms Constructivist theorising, for its part, is advanced through an emphasis on the contested-ness of norm generation, validation and legitimacy in contrast to the stability of international normative structures, which represents the analytical preserve of conventional Constructivists (Wiener, 2014).

Conventional, critical and linguistic Constructivist approaches thus each promote a particular perspective on the question of epistemology. However, I propose their integration by retaining as well as critiquing insights from all these three strands of epistemological positioning through the middle-ground methodological argument developed in Chapter 2. This argument forges a qualified post-positivist standpoint that is focused on the central importance of meaning and context in the study of social and political phenomena, while allowing for the establishment of generalizations that contain some wider validity by uncovering regularities across contexts.

By following this argument, the book subscribes to conventional Constructivists' aim to posit regularised conditions under which one can expect to observe a particular identity, being attuned to identity stability and continuity (Hopf, 1998:13). Similar to critical Constructivists' concern with unmasking power relations in identification processes (whereby the Self is assimilated with the Other, if deemed equal, or is oppressed and excluded, if inferior), dynamics of hierarchy and dependence are also recognised in the present study (Hopf, 1998:14-15). This recognition is reflected in the conclusion that Poland, Bulgaria and Russia are not 'clean slates' on which to inscribe a set of normative prescriptions and which need to be 'normalised' because they have their particular historical experiences that shape identity and pose limits to the possibility of ideational alignment with the West. And as with linguistic Constructivists, I examine the discursive representations of identity, which frame public space discussions and in this way structure the possibilities of and constraints on political action.

On the other hand, the middle-ground methodological argument takes issue with those propositions of conventional, critical and linguistic Constructivism—particularly related to a strict adherence to objectivism or, conversely, relativism, which stretch the assumptions of the Constructivist research paradigm too widely on two opposite ends of the epistemological spectrum. Such a concentration on the two extremes prevents fruitful dialogue within the paradigm and is untenable in terms of understanding social processes. Hence, Alexander Wendt's Scientific Realism, in particular, may not be compatible with the Constructivist approach. Contrary to Scientific Realism's contention that the objective world can be apprehended correctly and measured accurately, the problem that Constructivism (and Wendt himself) raises in a big way is not about the essence of existence and 'things in themselves' but what and how things come to be constituted intersubjectively (Wendt, 1999:110-120; 133; Kratochwil, 2000:17, 24; Epstein, 2010:6).

At the same time, critical Constructivism's rejection of the possibility or desirability of even a minimal foundationalism as well as the assumption of the perpetual contingency, malleability and fluidity of identities can be similarly critiqued for their one-sidedness. The empirical chapters of the book demonstrate that an intersubjectively shared meaning and standard of identity conditioning a continuity of ideas can be singled out. Moreover, an insistence on a relativist position that does not leave room for the possibility of generalisation may not be convincingly defended in critical Constructivist theorising itself. For instance, Epstein claims that a discursive-Lacanian approach avoids the problem of essentialising the state as a pre-social Self in the international arena because it does not presume such a Self and accepts that it may remain forever impossible to demonstrate that a state has a Self. To that end, Epstein distinguishes between a subject-position (i.e., a position within a discourse) and subjectivity (i.e., all that has to do with desire and bodily effects) and argues that this distinction allows focusing solely on subject-positions and suspending questions pertaining to subjectivity (Epstein, 2010:18). Yet, falling back on such a distinction shows that the post-modernist approach cannot maintain its argument about the indeterminacy of the Self without itself first stipulating and relying on essentialised understandings, embodied in the idea of subjectivity. Likewise, linguistic Constructivism's privileging of speech acts as constitutive of persons, sociality and action can miss out on those pre-existing subjective and intersubjective socio-cognitive factors that come to shape identity through implicit reflection and behavioural performance — with or without argumentative enunciation.

Therefore, a middle-ground approach unifying different epistemological orientations within Constructivism can offer the opportunity for a more diversified approach to research design and implementation attuned to the consideration of regularised and generalizable as well as contextually-specific, discursive and power-sensitive manifestations of identity in politics. This can be achieved by curbing the excesses of both objectivism and relativism.

From ontology and epistemology to mid-range theory

The heavy emphasis on ontological and epistemological arguments has entailed a lesser focus on the development of mid-range theories operationalising central concepts of Constructivism and substantiating them through rigorous empirical investigations. As much has been admitted by Constructivists themselves. A broadly shared self-critique diagnoses the gap between ontology / epistemology and history / empirics — i.e., between an inordinate fixation on the philosophy of social science and an insufficient concrete empirical and mid-range theoretical exploration of how identities are constructed in an interactive and comparative mode and how these identities in turn affect state behaviour (Palan, 2000; Finnemore, Sikkink, 2001; Moravcsik, 2001; Shannon, Kowert, 2012; Epstein, 2010; Zehfuss, 2001; Checkel, 1998; Wiener, 2009; Bertucci, Hayes, James, 2018:22).

Finnemore and Sikkink argue that the ongoing difficulty in identity research is that there is still no agreed-on definition of what is meant by 'identity'; how researchers can plausibly establish what state identities are; what range of prominent identities may exist in international politics at any particular historical moment; how states with particular types of identities will behave (Finnemore, Sikkink, 2001:9, 21). Richard Ned Lebow takes aim at Constructivist research that examines state identity as stable and unified. Instead, he urges Constructivists to acknowledge that states, like individuals, have many different identifications that vary in appeal and salience. Such a recognition would entail a greater analytical sensitivity to the multiplicity and malleability of identity (Lebow, 2016:183). In a similar vein, Christian Reus-Smit argues against a default conception of culture and norms as coherent, bounded and integrated entities. Culture is, rather, heterogeneous and contradictory, shaping political order not as a deeply constitutive or corrosive force but as a governance imperative (Reus-Smit, 2018:5).

And according to Moravcsik and Checkel, the reason for the above-described gaps and difficulties is linked to Constructivists' preoccupation with ontology. Constructivist scholars have spent excessive time exploring meta-theoretical and ontological distinctions between 'rational' and 'Constructivist' theories and not enough time developing concrete mid-range theories, deriving hypotheses from them and then testing them rigorously. So the challenge is to address how and why social construction occurs, clearly specifying the actors and mechanisms bringing about ideational continuity or change, the scope conditions under which they operate and how they vary across countries (Moravcsik, 2001:2; Checkel, 1998).

Unless such a theoretical and research strategy is taken up, Constructivist studies will continue to result in what Constructivism has itself contended against: accepting identities and the socialisation of actors as 'givens' as well as side-lining the core proposition about the interaction between agents and structures in favour of an exclusive focus on the role of ideas in foreign policy-making and the normative-ideational makeup of the international structure (Moravcsik, 2001:2). As Palan asks, if anarchy is what states make of it, then why have states chosen the particular form of anarchy which they have? The implication of this question is that meta-theoretical, Symbolic Interactionist accounts of international order cannot provide an explanation of the specificity of an order (Palan, 2000:14, 18). Similarly, Epstein argues that for Constructivists researching the impact of norms in international relations, identity tends to be important as the 'given' site that holds the micro-foundations of norm dynamics. In this vein, socialisation features as the activity of adding a new norm onto a stable platform of identity without discussing the process of identification that makes the acceptance of certain new norms as more appropriate and consonant with the Self's character than others (Epstein, 2010:8-9). Likewise, Sjoberg and Barkin argue that 'though the idea of constructivisms in IR is a nice one, the practice of constructivisms in IR is often vague, violent, overstretched, and underspecified'. This is so because understanding social construction means first of all providing an account of how something came to be socially constructed (Sjoberg, Barkin, 2018:238).

The present study aims to address the self-critique shared among Constructivists and fill the gap left by the prioritisation of ontological and epistemological debates through the mid-range interactive theory of identity construction, which is concretely applied to the three cases of Poland, Bulgaria and Russia over a three-decade timeframe. Moreover, the incorporation of Social Psychological insights into the mid-range theory charts a way forward for remedying Constructivism's continuing difficulty in accounting for identity continuity, change and its effect on behaviour.

The mid-range theory in context

In putting forward a mid-range theoretical framework, the book's approach contributes to and improves upon the limited number of Constructivist studies, which undertake interactive, empirically-informed examinations of identity and its effects on state action, while simultaneously carving out a distinctive empirical space in Constructivism by focusing on the region of CEE. The latter does not generally figure in International Relations and, more specifically, Constructivist comparative explorations. Instead, Central and Eastern Europe remains the preserve of area-studies investigations, where ideationally-informed analyses tend to be confined to such issues as the influence of ideology, nationalism and strategic culture rather than presenting elaborate conceptualisations of the mechanisms, constituent norms and effects of identity.

A number of works authored and compiled by Browning (2008), Telhami, Barnett (2002), Hagström, Gustafsson (2015), Banchoff (1998) explore state identity continuity and change, as the book does, as the product of the interaction of international and domestic factors in the concrete cases of Finland, the Middle East, Japan and Germany, respectively. However, in contrast to my middle-ground epistemological stance, Browning analyses Finnish foreign policy identity through a critical, narrative-focused perspective that looks at identities as continuously open to renegotiation and change. In contrast to this, Telhami and Barnett argue that identity can be treated as a variable that can take on different values and can be accurately measured on some scale. None of these studies is simultaneously comparative and examining patterns of identity change and continuity over an extended period of time (Browning does the latter only in the case of Finland, whereas Telhami's and Barnett's volume features separate, stand-alone chapters on Middle Eastern countries).

As far as the region of CEE is concerned, there are no Constructivist studies that analyse comparatively the foreign policy identities of Poland, Bulgaria and Russia, as indeed there is no such comparison in the literature informed by other International Relations theoretical perspectives or by an area studies approach. Also, those works conducting comparative examinations of a different combination of CEE countries through an identity-based analytical lens tend not to present a Constructivist framework. Rather, they operate within the conceptual confines of area studies, which generally eschews theory-based investigations. In the aftermath of the post-1989 changes, these scholarly contributions focused on the ways in which the Soviet ideological legacy in foreign policy was dealt with in the post-communist period as against the background of the resurgence of nationalism and the potential appearance of new foreign policy ideologies (Burant, 1995; Skak, 1992, 1996; Fawn, 2003). As the European integration process accelerated, comparative examinations of CEE states began to be conducted within Europeanisation/EU area studies. They explore how Union accession and membership affected these states' (foreign policy) identities as well as how the candidates' and new entrants' identities have in turn enabled or constrained the ability to contribute to EU foreign policy-making (Šabič and Brglez, 2002; Smith, 2006; Tulmets, 2014; Bossuyt, 2014; Graney, 2019).

Similar to the state of research in comparative CEE studies, works focusing on single country cases in the region (and in particular on Poland, Bulgaria and Russia) are also primarily conducted within an area studies rather than a Constructivist perspective on issues of identity. As regards Poland, a considerable amount of research examines how the historically-informed strategic culture and ideas of nationhood shape Warsaw's foreign policy in the period since 1989: including Sanford (2003), Zaborowski, Longhurst (2003), Longhurst, Zaborowski (2007), Longhurst (2013), Reeves (2010), Osica (2004), Prizel (1998), Chappell (2010), Wawrzyński (2012), Krasnodębska (2021). In addition, many scholarly works deal with the more specific aspects of Poland's relations with the eastern neighbours (Ukraine, Russia, Belarus), whereby a key theme of investigation is the extent to which the 'burdens' of history are being transcended or continue to affect national identity narratives as well as concrete policies: Zarycki (2004), Klatt (2011), Roberts (2014), Copsey (2008), Cianciara (2008), Eberhardt (2006, 2007, 2008), Adamski (2008), Szeptycki (2010). A growing strand of the literature deals with the rise of illiberal populism in Poland (as well as elsewhere in CEE) and its effects on Warsaw's foreign policy and constitutionalism (O'Neal, 2017; Nyyssönen, 2018; Calliess, Schyff, 2019; Sadurski, 2019; Varga, Buzogány, 2020; McManus, 2020; Belavusau, Gliszczyńska-Grabias, 2020).

In the Bulgarian case, a limited number of studies tend to employ a discursive and critical Constructivist approach in analysing processes of Europeanisation. Dimitrova (2002) demonstrates how the Europeanisation discourse became dominant in Bulgaria's domestic and foreign policies. Nancheva (2012) accounts for whether and how Bulgarian national identity narratives with respect to Macedonia[11] have become Europeanised. Kavalski (2003, 2005, 2007 – with Zolkos) shows how historically-informed identity discourses are invoked in foreign policy formulation. He further presents the securitisation of Western norms since the 1999 Kosovo crisis as a process of socialisation based on enforcement and teaching aimed at ensuring rule conformance. Bechev (2004, 2006a) explores the regional identity construction of Southeast Europe by taking into consideration the 'inside' (or national lens of the SEE countries) and the 'outside' (the West European view of the region). However, other works eschew a Constructivist perspective, instead employing an area studies analytical prism on the Europeanisation of foreign policy identity (Katsikas, 2010b, 2012; Ralchev, 2015); a sociological approach to the examination of elite and popular understandings of liberal values (Dawson, 2014); an elite-citizen interactive prism on the rise of identity politics and attitudes to the EU in Bulgaria and Romania (Kolev, 2019; Bankov, Gherghina, 2020); or a historical analysis of the long-term cultural antecedents of Bulgarian foreign policy (Baeva, 1998).

As regards Russia, a few significant studies are informed by Constructivism. Tsygankov (2016) shows how national identity and foreign policy in post-communist Russia are negotiated and constructed as a result of the influence of international and domestic factors. Neumann (1995, 2016) provides a thorough overview of the intellectual and political debate in Russia about its 'European-ness' over the last three decades as well as three centuries by taking into account the impact of major international events and changes in national leadership. Hopf (2002) focuses on the importance of a significant Other for a country's self-understanding and examines the way in which the Russian Self in 1955 and 1999 constituted itself with respect to three kinds of Others – the historical, internal and external Other. Hopf's edited volume (2008) features examinations

---

[11] Following the 2018 referendum, Macedonia was renamed into 'North Macedonia'. Throughout the book, the country is referred to as Macedonia (the short form of Former Yugoslav Republic of Macedonia) in relation to events and developments that took places prior to 2018.

of the normative dynamics between Russia and Europe, where Medvedev argues that through its focus on the importance of shared values for sustainable cooperation Constructivism explains best the difficult relations between Russia and the EU. Morozov (2013) employs a critical Constructivist perspective in presenting Russia as a subaltern empire that engages in the inversion of Western norms. Samokhvalov (2017) places Russia's great power identity in a historical framework that puts an emphasis on Europe's role in shaping this identity. Anno (2018) compares the construction of Russian and Japanese political-elite attitudes to the liberal international order at the end of the 19th and early 20th century.

Yet, the majority of studies focusing on ideational factors in Russian foreign policy making do not operate within a Constructivist (or indeed an international relations) perspective. Such studies can be broadly subdivided into six categories. First, some scholars (Gorodetsky, 2003; Light, 2003; Laruelle, 2012, 2015) examine the influences of the Soviet imperial legacy on Moscow's foreign policy and the re-emergence of a (nationalist) ideology in the conduct of external relations. A second strand of research has provided a detailed treatment of the longer-term cultural-historical foundations of Russia's post-1991 foreign policy, including Trenin (2007), Legvold (2007a), Prizel (1998). Third, other works lay a greater emphasis on Russia's contemporary (i.e., post-Soviet) ideational environment, namely, the country's identity crisis and the political elite's views of Russia's internal and external identity, often classifying them into distinct schools of thought (Baranovsky, 2000b, 2002; Adomeit, 1995; Tsygankov, 2003, 2005; Evans, 2008; Trenin, 2002; Malashenko, 2012; Giles, 2018; Service, 2019). Fourth, many scholars explore Russia-EU relations not least as conditioned by the clash of visions, identities and normative adherences (Webber, 2000; Dragneva, Wolczuk, 2012; Gower, Timmins, 2007; Prozorov, 2006; Allison, Light, White, 2006). A fifth set of works engage in conceptual analysis of the notions of 'nation', 'nationality' and 'civilization' in the context of Russian domestic and foreign policy (Zevelev, 2009; Malinova, 2012; Timofeev, 2008; Miller, 2008; Gudkov, 2010; Bassin, Pozo, 2017; Hale, Laruelle, 2020; Mjør,

Turoma, 2020; Suslov, 2020). Finally, specific emphasis is placed on considerations of 'status' and 'roles' in the international system in Moscow's foreign-policy making (Freire, Heller, 2017; Gunitsky, Tsygankov, 2018; Larson, Shevchenko, 2019; Dal, Erşen, 2020).

Integrating Social Psychology

As I argue in the elaboration of the book's interactive Constructivist theory of Self and Other in Chapter 3, Social Psychology is integral to understanding the cognitive processes that underwrite the phenomena of identity continuity and change as well as identity's impact on behaviour. Hence, the incorporation of Social Psychology's insights can address Constructivism's conceptual deficiencies and help it move towards the mid-range theoretical operationalisation and investigation of ideational persistence, evolution and practical manifestation in concrete IR settings. A feasible cross-disciplinary integration necessitates a clarification as to how distinctive theoretical assumptions and methodological proceedings of Social Psychology, which at first glance sit uneasily within Constructivism, can nevertheless be complemented and refined through a Constructivist lens.

Social Psychology's individualist premises (whereby social behaviour is explained in terms of asocial intrapsychic cognitive and motivational processes) have been subject to a criticism of reductionism, privileging subjectivist standpoints at the expense of an insufficient theorisation of intersubjectivity (Hogg, Vaughan, 2007:23; Shannon, 2012:18). Constructivism's provision of a greater focus on social interaction and cultural context can redress this individualist imbalance and reveal relationality as a constitutive element of cognition. The elaboration of the characteristic features of the Self-Other relationship thus shows how cognitive processes (of identity continuity and change and effect on behaviour) are informed by and situated within social interaction and intersubjectively held ideas, while the empirical investigations in the subsequent chapters present the concrete cultural substantiation of the Self-Other relationship in country-specific contexts.

Moreover, Social Psychology's operation through cognitivist concepts and premises, frequently abstracting from the formative effect of social interaction, also leads to an insufficient unpacking of the content of those concepts and premises. Social Identity Theory, for instance, argues that symbolic concerns related to group standing and perceived inter-group status differences are central to the development of in-group cohesion, identity stability or social mobility among groups since the individual's need for positive distinctiveness is taken as a crucial psychological need (Tajfel, 1974; Tajfel, Turner, 1979; Huddy, 2013:742). So it is enough for two individuals to know that they belong to the same group for them to favour one individual over another. In this way, what the group stands for — its norms and values, is bracketed out given that the overwhelming emphasis is placed on positive valuation (Epstein, 2010:15). Likewise, Social Categorisation theory's cognitivist bent is expressed in the assumption that what matters in the development of social identity is one's perceived similarity to the prototypic group member (Turner, et al., 1987; Huddy, 2013:741). Yet, the book's theoretical framework points out that it is not only dynamics of inclusion and exclusion, belongingness and status that inform the process of identification but also how these are made meaningful by intersubjectively established norms, rules and principles.

Finally, Social Psychology's predominantly positivist reliance on small-scale laboratory experiments means that additional contextual verification of psychological findings has to take place before these findings' cogency can be generalised to less 'pure', 'real-life' conditions. To this end, a mid-range Constructivist theory that applies laboratory-developed results to a wide international political setting can contribute to the establishment of the degree of external validity of Social Psychology's conceptualisations (Hogg, Vaughan, 2007:10-11).

The individualist-cognitivist and positivist underpinnings of Social Psychology do not therefore represent insurmountable obstacles to a fruitful cross-disciplinary integration with Constructivism. Rather, these underpinnings can be built upon through the Constructivist perspective of the socially interactive formation and contextual manifestation of identity, approaching social phenomena as meaningful and normatively constituted.

Literature on Europeanisation: Building bridges (1)

In addition to refining Constructivism 'from within' by addressing intra-theoretical debates, I now turn to elucidating how related disciplines can provide opportunities for dialogue and learning in issue areas of thematic overlap with Constructivism, all the same remaining attuned to the limits of disciplinary cross-fertilisation. Given the application of the book's theoretical framework to the phenomenon of identification and its manifestation in foreign policy in the European context, bridges can be built with the literature on Europeanisation, which can supply specific guidelines to the examination of EU-centred processes. In this regard, I follow the literature's conclusions related to the conduct of foreign policy on the Union level, as shaped and mediated through the mechanism of 'socialisation', while ultimately proposing a distinctive definition of 'European-ness' and hence an approach to analysing Europeanisation that includes but is not confined to developments emanating from the EU.

As outlined in Chapter 3, the present study approaches European-ness in terms of a values-based ideal type, which defines what it means to be European in an ideational sense — as embodied and projected by a variety of state and international institutional actors in the West, given the politically-historically informed commonalities of Western understandings. In contrast, the Europeanisation perspective was originally aimed at the analysis of EU-induced change in the constituent members of the organisation in a variety of policy arenas. The growth of the literature has reflected the institutionalisation of the single market, the advent of the Economic and Monetary Union, market-driven processes such as the regulation of competition as well as enlargement to the East (Bulmer, Radaelli, 2004:1-2). So the deepening and widening of integration in the 1990s consolidated research attention onto the impact of European institutions and processes on member states

(Börzel, 2003:1-2). The research agendas of scholars of Europeanisation have on the whole been underpinned by the goal to stipulate theoretically and examine empirically the extent and scope conditions of the influence of the EU on domestic policies through conditionality that leads to compliant adaptation; through socialisation that leads to normative evolution; or through a combination of both conditionality and socialisation. This 'top-down' perspective has been complemented by 'bottom-up' approaches, which examine member states not simply as responding to Brussels-level initiatives and processes but as actively shaping those initiatives and processes (Börzel, 2003; Bulmer, Radaelli, 2004; Featherstone, Radaelli, 2003; Grabbe, 2001; Sedelmeier, 2011; Epstein, Sedelmeier, 2008; Schimmelfenning, Sedelmeier, 2005; Johnson, 2006; Whitefield, Rohrschneider, 2009; Olsen, 2002; Hughes, Sasse, Gordon, 2004; Cowles, Caporaso, Risse, 2001; Kohler-Koch, 2002; Dimitrova, Rhinard, 2005; Terzi, 2005; Trondal, 2004; Beyers, 1998).

However, when following the ideal-typical justification of European-ness, it is no longer necessary to postulate Europeanisation as inextricably and only linked to the EU. Although the Union may be the key institution providing a framework for the governance of political and economic issues on the European continent, other institutions and states, including NATO, the Council of Europe, the OSCE, individual West European countries, the US, also enunciate and practice the values inherent in European-ness. Hence, this conceptualisation allows the book to examine the projection of European-ness in the process of Europeanisation on the part of a wider array of actors beyond the EU and reflected in the generalised image of the 'Other'. The acceptance and contestation of European-ness can be further examined in acceding and non-acceding states alike, given that the EU is not taken as a proxy for all Europe-level developments and non-accession/member status, such as Russia's, does not preclude examinations of Europeanisation.

Moreover, establishing Europeanisation as extent of ideational affinity with the ideal-typical benchmark means that a Europeanised foreign policy can be discerned in the general approach to international politics, regional relations as well as institutional integration according to a set of norms and rules distinctive of European-ness. That is, institutionalised cooperation centred on the EU — as emphasised by the Europeanisation literature focusing on the normative expectations and diplomatic avenues for cooperation provided by EU membership/accession status, is one aspect to be considered. But it does not exhaust all external political dimensions of European-ness.

Delving deeper into the main premises of the literature on Europeanisation shows that it has placed specific emphasis on the questions of whether and how member and candidate countries experience a convergence of preferences, identities and policies on the strategic and normative provisions contained in the Common Foreign and Security Policy (CFSP) as well as in the Union's other external positions (trade, humanitarian aid, peace-building, conflict prevention) (Manners, Whitman, 2000:1, 7; Allen, 1998; Wong, Hill, 2011; Wong, 2005; Tonra, 2001; Moumoutzis, 2011; Zaborowski, 2002). This perspective expects that convergence with regard to concrete policies and strategic positions will take place since the member state is subject to the constraints, opportunities and influences of the EU, given that being a member of the club means fulfilling the obligations to reason, debate and act in a certain manner (Wong, 2005:146). The CFSP operates at a unique nexus between the constituent countries and European integration and has therefore created a form of symbiosis in which states are increasingly reliant on the efficiency of the collective policy process and this collective policy process itself depends on the political will of the states. This ultimately combines the 'downloading' dimension of adopting policies conceived on the EU level as well as 'uploading' national preferences as common Union strategies (Tonra, 2001:3; Wong, Hill, 2011:12).

And as countries learn to coordinate their positions within a structure consisting of the institutions and the acquis of the CFSP, it is expected that there will be normative convergence since European foreign policy is an inherently normative project enshrining the projection of democratisation and human rights. European Political Cooperation even before the CFSP included as one of its central goals the expression of moral concern about events in non-democratic states, especially in the Third World. After the end of the Cold War, this concern crystallised into a full-blown paradigm that stresses the importance of democratisation and human rights (Hill, 2002:6). Article 11 of the Treaty on European Union stipulates that a major objective of common foreign policy is to 'safeguard common values' and 'to develop and consolidate democracy and the rule of law, and respect for human rights and fundamental freedoms' (Treaty on the European Union, 1992:7).

Concurrence on a principled behavioural style is also expected to take place. The distinctiveness of debating foreign policy positions at the EU level is related to a focus on negotiations, consensus, dense institutional networks and frequent contacts between officials, which puts a premium on cooperative bargaining (Chelotti, 2014:2-7; Moumoutzis, 2011:13).

Cooperation within the CFSP is then a manifestation of Europeanised foreign policy, imparting distinguishing characteristics to EU member and accession states. But as the book argues and empirically demonstrates, European values can be embodied and projected outside of CFSP structures in relation to wider issue areas, where coordination with other European states may not be required or achievable.

Finally, the insights of the literature on Europeanisation regarding the operation of the mechanism of socialisation,[12] particularly in the domain of foreign policy, can illuminate how 'lower-order', non-fundamental ideational change can take place. Reservations should nevertheless be retained about the depth and extent of socialisation's effects when dealing with deeply ingrained views of nation-state identity in large-scale settings involving the national political-intellectual (foreign policy) decision-making elite

---

12 Socialisation can be defined as a process by which social interaction leads novices to endorse and internalise expected ways of thinking and acting characteristic of a group through persuasion, social influence and in the absence of overt coercion: Johnston, A., 2001, 'Treating International Institutions as Social Environments', *International Studies Quarterly*, Vol. 45, No 4, pp. 487-515 https://www.jstor.org/stable/3096058?seq=1#page_scan_tab_contents

as opposed to the national administration and representatives to Brussels institutions.

As scholars working within the literature on Europeanisation make clear, the 'adaptational' model of Europeanisation based on the idea that an institutional misfit between national and European models causes pressures for adaptation typically guided by conditionality is not applicable to the domain of foreign policy. This is so because in policy areas where legally binding instruments are not available at the Brussels level, the misfit between national and EU policy does not produce adaptational pressure and Union policy creates its effects through mechanisms other than conditionality (Moumoutzis, 2011:9). Consequently, in the field of external relations, the mechanism of socialisation takes precedence, whereby through reiterated interactions national foreign policy-makers become convinced of the appropriateness of the EU way of doing things and internalise behavioural rules (Moumoutzis, 2011:9; Bulmer, 2007; Checkel, 2001; Schmidt, 2002). Wong has claimed that the CFSP is hence not just another venue for rational choice but a critical set of social forces that shapes perceptions, structures policy choices and privileges certain courses of national and collective action while constraining others (Wong, Hill, 2011:9).

In support of this, research has shown that the effects of socialisation are most pronounced in situations, where actors find themselves in novel circumstances and are motivated to analyse new information but have few prior, cognitively anchored beliefs (such as deeply rooted societal views of national identity) that are inconsistent with the socialiser's/persuader's message (Checkel, 1999:8; Dimitrova, Rhinard, 2005:6-10). Socialisation is additionally likely to work in smaller, confined (rather than large-scale) settings, featuring more extensive and intensive interactions, which change the views held by bounded, heavily involved groups such as national administrators (dealing with EU accession negotiations) and national representatives to EU fora (including the European Parliament, Commission and Council), and which affect smaller, sector-specific policies (Epstein, 2006; Johnson, 2006; Kaminska, 2007:10; Pomorska, 2011:3; Primatarova 2015, Mihaylova, 2015, Krząkała, 2015, interviews).

However, even among such officials operating under the above conditions, the consequences of socialisation are most significant in relation to altering debating and behavioural style rather than in terms of persuading or socially influencing deep normative change with regard to core national identity beliefs. The key factors implicated in the socialisation processes reviewed in studies of socialisation in European institutions encompass *level of embedded-ness in transnational networks, extent of exposure to EU affairs, frequency, intensity and duration of interactions with European colleagues, length of service in the European Parliament, Commission or working groups of the Council of Ministers, generational change, international educational and professional experiences* and *cultural capital*. Despite nuances as to whether actors socialise for instrumental reasons or are subject to normative suasion, the overall evidence demonstrates that these factors may promote coalition-building habits, mutual trust, a co-ordination reflex and greater focus on the European interest. But they do not supersede national identity considerations by fostering an exponentially more favourable attitude to European integration, the empowerment of supranational institutions such as the Parliament and the Commission or the creation of common foreign policy positions at the expense of core national priorities (Best, Lengyel, Verzichelli, 2012; Bigatto, 2007; Beyers, 1998, 2005; Breuer, 2012; Duke, 2005:29-31; Egeberg, 1999; Hooghe, 2005; Howorth, 2010:17-22; Hube, Verzichelli, 2012; Juncos, Pomorska, 2006; Scully, 2005; Trondal, 2004). Instead, pre-existing national collective experience, political-cultural factors and party ideology retain their key significance in socialising officials into a particular worldview and attitude to European integration (Filipova, Stefanov, 2020:5-6).

Therefore, the empirical investigations in the book are guided by the expectation that even when participating in an interactive European setting, the national decision-makers responsible for formulating Polish, Bulgarian and Russian foreign policy may not have been amenable to comprehensive socialisation with regard to their deeply ingrained beliefs about nation-state identity and conceptions of Europe. Moreover, such participation, especially in the case of Poland and Bulgaria, does not amount to the intensified and frequent socialising experiences as in the more specific and bounded case of national administrators/negotiators and representatives to Brussels. (Experiences even for the latter groups did not commence in a fully-fledged manner before Polish and Bulgarian accession status was agreed in the 1990s and especially after membership was achieved).

However, the process of socialisation is still likely to alter and refine non-fundamental, lower-order, tactical ideas that are implicated in the contemporary circumstances in which the higher-order images of Self and Other are reenacted. Mutually interactive acceptance and desire for integration, fostering positive reinforcement and identification between Self and Other, are expected to encourage and influence the Self to learn and move towards common positions and shared understandings with the Other—as limited, though, by fundamental belief compatibility or contestation.

Overall, the establishment of a dialogue with the literature on Europeanisation can yield a cross-fertilisation with the book's theoretical framework to the extent that the EU is analysed as an institution that embodies European values and through socialisation imparts a normative dimension and specific principles of behaviour to the debate and conduct of foreign policy within the Union framework. Yet, my approach diverges from Europeanisation studies in arguing that European norms can be epitomised and projected by actors other than the EU. These norms can be accepted or challenged by CEE countries, which do not have to be candidates for Union admission and whose deeply ingrained conceptions of Europe may not be changed via socialisation in the European arena. And finally European norms can be manifested in external conduct in fields other than the CFSP and the overlay of (prospective) EU membership.

FPA and Role Theory: Building bridges (2)

The other theoretical strand, which is particularly relevant to International Relations studies focused on the examination of foreign policy, is Foreign Policy Analysis (FPA). The oftentimes tenuous dialogue between IR and FPA can be remedied through charting out avenues for cross-disciplinary learning, whereby each can nevertheless retain its distinctiveness. FPA's Role Theory specifically shares the Constructivist concern with studying the effects of identity in international politics. I argue that the interactive Constructivist theory developed in the book can address the unresolved tensions within Role Theory, linked to the ongoing challenge of achieving conceptual precision with regard to 'identity', 'roles' and the agent-structure relationship, and thus contribute to mutual conceptual fertilisation.

The FPA approach has been oriented on the exploration of the processes, effects, causes and outcomes of foreign policy decision-making in a comparative or case-specific manner (Foreign Policy Analysis Journal). It is distinguished by being agent-oriented and actor-specific in examining the policy process, whereby those with decision-making authority frame problems, assess policy options, prioritise objectives, formally settle on and implement a course of action taken with reference to a particular situation (Hudson, 2005:2-3). This distinctive agentic focus, however, has been taken as reason for the establishment of a firmly sealed disciplinary division between predominantly 'systemically' concerned International Relations and 'sub-systemically' focused FPA. This gap was pioneered by Kenneth Waltz's conception of IR and foreign policy as two separate fields in terms of levels of analysis and was further complemented by Richard Snyder's parallel positioning and development of FPA on the agentic, decision-making level. As a result, a path-dependence disciplinary divide has persisted. Even studies within either discipline, which have moved beyond a single a level of analysis, overall maintain their respective categories and boundaries, without necessarily engaging with and clarifying the relationship to each other (Waltz, 2010; Snyder, Bruck, Sapin, 2002; Houghton, 2006:1-3).

Straddling the overblown disciplinary distinctions of IR and FPA can illuminate the close affinity between international relations and foreign policy, otherwise obscured by stringent academic dividing lines. The general interactions and dynamics between states in the international system have implications for foreign policy decisions, which in turn affect international trends and structures. This inseparable association between international relations and foreign policy means that they are not the exclusive research preserve of IR and FPA, respectively (especially when examinations are attuned to multiple levels of analysis). They can be studied by both IR and FPA, which can borrow from each other's theoretical and conceptual assumptions, while retaining their distinctive contributions, i.e., without there being a complete overlap.

How this disciplinary bridge-building can be effected can be illustrated by the book's interactive Constructivist theory incorporating the structural and agentic dimension in the process of identification and construction of elite conceptions of Europe, which shape external stances. On the one hand, the interactive Constructivist theory generally shares FPA's concern with agency and actor-specificity. The latter rests on clarifying who the relevant decision-makers and 'identity' groups are, examining their views and debates and attending to the effects of the domestic political-institutional environment in mediating the construction and expression of a given identity stance. But, on the other hand, the specific Constructivist value in studying foreign policy behaviour lies in the provision of a wider treatment and understanding of foreign policy as practices of boundary-drawing between political communities. Foreign policy is thus an exercise of situating a state on the international civilizational map — rather than more narrowly defined by FPA as the concrete external actions of a government in bounded cases, casting a distinctive light on a state's external conduct. In particular, a Constructivist perspective of foreign policy behaviour studies how (and whether) subjectively and intersubjectively shared conceptions shaping a given ideational-discursive domestic context inform, direct and circumscribe foreign policy options by serving as a conceptual map, cognitive anchor and guide. This context is expected to frame the overall tenor, character and orientation of external relations as regards the larger questions of identification, integration and belongingness between Self and Other. In contrast, the traditional domain of FPA focuses squarely on the intricacies and steps of decision-making details and mechanisms of implementation of the specific policies that take place as part of the general ideational-behavioural overlay.

Hence, the research priorities of FPA as an applied science, micro-analysing processes and outcomes, should not preclude a more generalised perspective and examination of foreign policy. According to such a perspective, the dominant public-political discursive conceptualisations crucially condition the framework of foreign policy formulation and conduct. That framework is foundational as the diplomatic-bureaucratic apparatus depends on it for direction and it links foreign policy much more closely to the key goals of the state (rather than the procedures and concerns of the concrete execution of those goals) (Chan, 2017).

The ideational dimension of FPA: Role Theory

An ideational focus on foreign-policy making within FPA is developed by Role Theory. But it does not amount to a full-blown consideration of the socially shared, intersubjectively formed context that mediates decision-making. The key concept of 'national role conception' refers to the policy-makers' representations of the kinds of decisions, commitments, rules and actions suitable to their state and of the functions this state should perform in the international system. National role conceptions are concretely expressed through 'national role performance/enactment', and are circumscribed by 'role prescriptions' — the norms and expectations emanating from the external environment about the appropriate role that Ego should play (Barnett, 1993:5; Walker, 1987).

These concepts point to the major theoretical assumptions, as developed by touchstone Role theorists, including Kalevi Holsti, Naomi Wish, James Rosenau. As Holsti explains, in the study of foreign policy, the role performance of governments can be explained primarily by the policy-makers' own conceptions of their nation's role in the international system, domestic needs and demands. Generally, the expectations of other governments, international legal norms and sanctions are ill-defined, too flexible or weak compared to those that exist in an integrated society (Walker, 1987:8-10). Therefore, the perceptions and attitudes of the decision-makers become the crucial independent variables in illuminating foreign policy (Walker, 1987; Holsti, 1970; Chafetz, Abramson, Grillot, 1996).

Guided by this argumentation, Role theorists have constructed typologies of the roles that states can play in the international system. For instance, Holsti (1970) identified 17 major roles expressed by states between 1965 and 1967, connecting role conceptions to different levels of involvement in international politics (Thies, 2009:5). Wish (1980) found out 13 national role conceptions, grouped under the categories of status, motivational orientation and issue area, while Hymans (2006) built his typology on the dimensions of solidarity and status as they key aspects of social comparison (Ifantis, Triantaphyllou, Kotelis, 2015:8-9). Methodologically, Role theorists have predominantly (yet not exclusively) drawn on content analysis, events databases, statistical analysis, with the Comparative Foreign Policy strand being particularly attuned to aggregated, cross-national analyses, correlating national roles to foreign policy along conflict-cooperation dimensions (Thies, 2009:32, Starr, 1988:6; Lantis, Beasley, 2017:14).

The book's interactive Constructivist framework shares a general similarity of approach with Role Theory to the extent that the role (i.e., the primarily behavioural manifestation of identity), its individually subjectivist definition and the interaction of external and internal factors represent common concerns. However, these foundational positions of Role Theory are only partial aspects of identification. I aim to provide a wider and more rounded treatment of the process of identification by pointing out and addressing conceptual and theoretical weaknesses through the interactive Constructivist approach. Indeed, these weaknesses are being increasingly recognised by most recent, contemporary Role Theory scholarship as well.

One of the key problem areas is related to the neglect of conceptual precision in terms of the difference between a 'role' and an 'identity' (Harnisch, Frank, Maull, 2011:9, 13; Lantis, Beasley, 2017:6; Wehner, Thies, 2014:2). Such neglect coupled with the distinct behavioural bent accorded to the definition of a role, the creation of typologies circumscribing the range of roles that can be enacted on the international level and formal-statistical forms of inquiry obscure the context-specific constructions and manifestation of identification, as captured by the concept of identity. The latter contains and unites the socio-cognitive, discursive as well as behavioural element of identification so that it is only when social positions are internalised (as roles refer to behavioural alignment to a social position and purpose) that one can speak of identity. Thus, to say that a state takes the role of and acts like a European power (ally/joiner) or an anti-European power (challenger/competitor), as prescribed by a standard, does not become revelatory enough until one examines the context-specific meanings and various possible expressions imparted to European-ness as part of the Self-Other interactive process of identification. The behavioural aspect of identification should not be disconnected from the internalisation of meaning-formation, which substantiates the performance of an identity and checks against the charge that the role concept can become indistinguishable from instrumentalised conformity (carried out by mask-wearing, image-creating stage actors). Hence, the usage of the overarching term of identity that subsumes the role.

The other key problem area relates to the agent-structure relationship. Role Theory promises an interactive theoretical pathway, particularly by arguing that states and their leaders seek to enact roles consistent with their domestic context and expectations, while international actors may sanction role-inappropriate behaviour and alter-cast states into different roles (Lantis, Beasley, 2017:17). Still, there are a number of tensions in this approach, which limit the potential contribution of an interactive perspective. Despite the fact that Role theorists do not dispute the social origins of individual beliefs, they (predominantly) regard the beliefs held by decision-makers as exerting an independent influence on foreign policy behaviour and, therefore, the individual beliefs of decision-makers are ascribed a great deal of autonomy vis-a-vis their social environment (Houghton, 2006:19; Cantir, Kaarbo, 2016:2). So as it stands, a role-based approach to FPA remains open to the essential thrust of Giddens' criticism that action-oriented approaches of this kind tend to occlude the intimate connection between agents and structures. That is, such approaches are unable to give institutions (and other social structures) their proper theoretical due in social and political analysis (Carlsnaes, 1992:12-13). Instead, Constructivism can point to the social roots of individual beliefs and raise attention to the 'situated-ness' of decision-makers in a wider social setting, characterised by intersubjective beliefs and identities.

The subjectivist treatment of roles at the expense of intersubjectivity in the domestic domain is paralleled by a similar under-emphasis of the international dimension in the formation of role conceptions (notwithstanding the prominence of such concepts as role prescriptions and expectations). The focus of Role theorists on the inner experience and perception of individual leaders in defining national role conceptions may overlook the structure of expectations of the wider international environment (role prescriptions) (Beneš, 2010:12; Barnett, 1993:6-7). It is precisely this structure that an interactive Constructivist framework incorporates theoretically by arguing that states construct their identities through interactions with significant Others.

And, paradoxically, when Role theorists shift their examinations from national role conceptions to their enactment, external factors take on a significant importance in conditioning the range of 'enact-able' national conceptions, whose categorisation into typologies (of ally, bridge, mediator, regional leader, etc.) is much akin to Realist classifications (linked, for instance, to types of status quo and revisionist states) (Thies, 2009:5-6, 2012:9; Schweller, 1994; Lantis, Beasley, 2017:17; Cantir, Kaarbo, 2016:14). External factors tend to be equated with material ones, as the performance of decision-makers' role conceptions hinge on the obstacles conditioned by a state's power position in the international system, which is argued to place roles at the intersection of the agentic-ideational and structural-material aspect of IR (Harnisch, Frank, Maull, 2011:26; Wehner, Thies, 2014:4; Thies, 2010).

All of this may well lead to the pre-imposition of roles distributed among states in the international system—as already generally charted out by Realists. In this way, the exploration of the various manifestations that a given identity makes possible are foreclosed, unduly confining roles to their structural-material determination (despite Role Theory's ideational assumptions) and limiting the conceptualisation of the international structure to its material aspects. In contrast, rather than pre-specifying a role as a parsimonious label with Realist connotations that reflect positional assignment (such as ally/joiner, peripheral state, competitor/challenger), I provide more extensive values-based indicators of behaviour. They are in line with a construction of Europe, which is defined by both an internal and external ideational dimension, along with the Constructivist assumption that structure is not simply material but depends on the distribution of beliefs and ideas and interactions among states to become meaningful.

The most recent wave of Role Theory scholarship has begun to address some of the theory's flaws. Interpretive methods are utilised (Beneš, 2011:8-9; Wehner, Thies, 2014:10-11). Role conflict through domestic political contestation is increasingly explored (Brummer, Thies, 2015; Cantir, Kaarbo, 2016). The importance of the Other's expectations in role conceptions are incorporated (Beneš, 2017; Hermanns, 2013). However, an interactive Constructivist lens can resolve remaining tensions within Role Theory, related to conceptual unclarity and the conceptualisation of the relationship between ideational and material external factors (Malici, Walker, 2016:8). Cross-disciplinary fertilisation can then be established, bridging the gap not only between Constructivist and Role theoretical concerns but also between IR and FPA, which after all share a common primary preoccupation: understanding the international domain of politics.

Realism: Mounting challenges

In parallel to demonstrating how an ideational approach to international relations can be developed by improving the resilience of and building bridges to those theoretical strands that coalesce around a shared focus on the significance of ideas in politics, it remains to be elucidated how rival theories, above all Realism, that hold non-ideational stances can be contended against. In this regard, two challenges are mounted to Realism's critique of Constructivism's core conceptual-theoretical assumptions.

First, I counter the Realist dismissal of the independent effect of ideational factors in international relations. Defending the role of ideas vis-a-vis Realism's materialist approach can also be utilised to argue against Liberalism's more muted criticisms of Constructivism. Although the Liberal perspective allows a greater room for ideas in determining outcomes and for the cooperative, community-building potential of institutions (which are therefore not straightforward epiphenomena of power hierarchies), alongside Realism, it similarly treats ideas and institutions as part of an instrumentalist-rationalist approach.

Second, I show specifically that Realism cannot convincingly account for Poland's, Bulgaria's and Russia's differential Europeanisation and integration in the Euro-Atlantic community on the basis of its own conceptual and theoretical apparatus. This apparatus would posit different levels of integration as the outcome of differential perceptions of threat on the part of three countries distinguished by differential size and power capacities. At first glance, the different weight of a small, medium and large state in the international distribution of power can be argued to be an easy case for a structural, Neorealist explanation, whereby positional placement according to relative power conditions state behavior. A modified, Neoclassical Realist explanation can also be said to fit the empirical record as states react to internally perceived and mediated threats and not only to unproblematically translated systemic constraints alone. However, the plausibility of a Realist explanation is nevertheless far from justified.

The first challenge to Realism is more specifically based on rationalist approaches' positing of the greater explanatory value of a theoretical emphasis on instrumental-rational behaviour that aims at calculating costs and benefits. Neorealism and Neoliberalism relegate norms and identities to a relatively insignificant role as intervening variables explaining residual variance—the unexplained variance which cannot be attributed to specific causes. According to Neorealists, identities matter only at the discretion of or in the service of a power structure. In Neoliberal Institutionalism, norms and institutions matter to the degree that they facilitate cooperation derived from cost-benefit maximisation of pre-existing preferences by reducing transaction costs; identifying focal points for coordinated behavior; and providing frameworks for productive issue-linkage. The origins of norms and identities are thus limited to the pre-existing preferences of agents and their consequences tend to reflect this constraint (Kratochwil, 2001:50-55; Wohlforth, 2008:133-134; Donnelly, 2000:6-12; Keohane, 1984:65-79). Even Liberal theory that focuses on domestic politics and allows for state preferences to be determined by societal values and identities still assumes that once so determined preferences are pursued according to a means-end rational logic. This is argued to distinguish Liberalism from 'non-rational' theories (Moravcsik, 2010:2, 6).

Yet, for Constructivists, preferences and power maximisation are not fixed in time and content but are constituted as meaningful and given substance to on the basis of actors' identities and inter-subjectively held beliefs and interactions between the agent and the social environment (Hurd, 2008:303). Kratochwil has argued that actors in international relations are themselves constituted by norms so the stability, maintenance and effects of international regimes and power relations are crucially related to the identities of actors (Kratochwil, 2001:57-58). As the book demonstrates in the empirical investigations, the conceptual standpoint that 'institutions are what states make of them' (as reflected in a perspective that analyses institutions as culturally and historically embedded) is vindicated since integration with the EU and NATO was not solely focused on the facilitation of cooperation and the provision of economic benefits, as Neoliberal Institutionalism would have it, but was crucially linked to defining the boundaries of 'Europe'. Ultimately, following Max Weber's logic, different types of rationalities—practical, substantive, theoretical, formal, are all socio-cognitive processes, which strive to understand and organise reality and are institutionalised as normative regularities of action within legitimate social and political orders (Kalberg, 1980:16-18).

Moreover, identity does not operate as a causal variable but as a constitutive mechanism that shapes both belief systems and behaviours. Identity has very 'real' practical consequences in that belongingness to a group entails performativity and institutionalisation of distinctive group norms, while the symbolic dramatisation of difference encompasses attribution, stereotyping and discretionary allocation.

In concrete foreign policy terms, identity informs policy-makers' perceptions and understandings of situations; shapes the foreign policy-making context; limits the available and possible range of courses of action; serves as a justificatory and legitimating principle; guides the treatment of significant Others in international relations; and directs internal efforts to confirm and prove belongingness to a community of nations. Ultimately, the Constructivist argument that identity shapes interests is substantiated when action is broadly congruent with both identity and interests (Banchoff, 1998:25-27). That is, for a Constructivist approach to foreign policy to be persuasive, it must demonstrate the existence of a broadly shared collective identity in political discourse and action, which informs the definition, justification and prioritisation of national interests as well as guides the deployment and utilisation of material capabilities. In specific circumstances, the concrete realisation of identity positions (and ideas in general) takes place within a frame of a plethora of instrumental cost-benefit, administrative-organisational, cognitive and emotional factors. These factors may dictate tactical forbearance, pose practical limits to or underwrite the sustainability of an identity vision, affect the consistency and coordination of the implementation of that vision or introduce biases in its perception. But as long as the vicissitudes in the process of the actualisation of ideas leads to a congruence between state identity, interest and actions in overall policy direction, then Constructivism retains its viability.

The second challenge I mount against Realism, contained in questioning the latter's soundness in answering the puzzle of CEE's differential integration in the Euro-Atlantic community, is substantiated by critiquing Neoclassical Realism's conceptual and theoretical assumptions in general terms as well as their specific deficiencies in explaining the empirical record of Poland's, Bulgaria's and Russia's Europeanisation. Theoretical inconsistencies and contradictions arise from Neoclassical Realists' aim to enrich Neorealism by introducing domestic intervening variables as mediating the effects of the system, while maintaining core

Neorealist assumptions. The latter are embodied in positing a rigid separation between 'autonomous' and 'isolatable' levels of analysis, the ultimate primacy of the system in determining outcomes and an objectivist ontological standpoint.

Neoclassical (and Defensive) Realists invoke state preferences, beliefs, strategic culture, state-society relations and international organisations in order to trump the direct effects of material power and structure. In this way, the core underpinnings of Neorealism are stretched to include assumptions and causal mechanisms from alternative paradigms, albeit with little effort to reconcile the resulting contradictions (Legro, Moravcsik, 1999:2-3; Narizny, 2017). Also, to fulfil its claims to determinacy stemming from an objectivist identification of regularities, Neoclassical Realism needs to specify exactly what range of foreign policy options are available to states as a result of the operation of systemic variables and then clarify which options will be more likely to be utilised due to the impact of domestic variables. However, Neoclassical Realists still state rather generally that 'international structures have dominant influence over the range of systemic outcomes that are possible' (Ripsman, Taliaferro, Lobell, 2016:90). And it turns out that domestic-level factors can take precedence over systemic variables. As much is revealed in the statement that 'in the more common circumstances when the international environment does not present a clear and imminent threat, states often have a range of policy options' so that 'the actual choices that states make may have far more to do with the worldviews of leaders, the strategic cultures of the states they lead, the nature of the domestic coalitions they represent...'. Moreover, 'states do not necessarily select the optimal policy response to satisfy systemic constraints, instead, they choose from a range of policy alternatives to navigate between systemic constraints and domestic policy imperatives'. Intervening variables can therefore interact with dependent variables and intervening variables can themselves also be influenced by the independent variables so that ultimately 'in rare times of extreme domestic instability, national leaders might actually conduct foreign policy with greater attention to the domestic audience than to international exigencies' (Ripsman, Taliaferro, Lobell, 2016:30, 35, 94, 168).

Further theoretical difficulties are related to the incomplete treatment of Neoclassical Realism's core conception of perception of threat. The latter are shaped not only by aggregate power, geographic proximity, offensive power and aggressive intentions, as Stephen Walt argues, but also by culture, cognition and affect (Walt, 1987:19-27). Social Psychological research demonstrates that the deeply rooted and routinised images people have of other countries become central building blocks in the identification of the threats and opportunities faced in the international system (Herrmann, 2013:338-343). Moreover, fear conditioning may be more permanent than other kinds of learning so that fear lasts longer than the threat and can become a learned response embedded over time (Stein, 2013:382). In international relations terms, fear can be taken to represent a culturally-bound perception and internalisation of the threat coming from a significant Other. Therefore, the elements of capabilities and intentions, which are at the centre of threat assessment and the modelling of rational deterrence and other strategies in Realist theory, are not borne out by Psychological research. This is so because the drive for consistency, simplicity and fear-motivated patterns of thought and behaviour impair the processes of rational estimation and assessment of threats (Stein, 2013:371-373).

The tenability of Neoclassical Realism's conceptualisations also cannot be sustained in accounting for Poland's, Bulgaria's and Russia's differential Europeanisation. A Neoclassical Realist counter-argument could posit that Poland decided to bandwagon with the West very early on after the collapse of communism because of its strong threat perceptions of Russia. Bulgaria was slower in pursuing a bandwagoning strategy because of less strong fears of Russia. Russia itself perceived the West as an enemy and thus decided to balance against it. However, there are a number of problems with this counter-argument.

Most importantly, Neoclassical Realism, like Neorealism, claims adherence to a structural explanation of international politics, which however is unable to account coherently and adequately for both the effects of identity as well as the interactive dynamic between domestic and international factors. Even if we accept that bandwagoning was Poland's and Bulgaria's motivation, why did the West acquiesce in their demands to be included in NATO and the EU? Arguably, from a realist-rational perspective, it might have been more rational on the part of the West not to antagonise Russia by accepting in its orbit countries from which it gained little in terms of an aggregate enhancement of security, thus re-enacting a great power condominium with Moscow and ignoring the security needs and preferences of smaller states (Kennan, 1997; Mearsheimer, 2014). Additionally, the different timing of the acceptance of CEE countries into the EU and NATO can to an important extent be accounted for by the fact that these organisations have criteria of domestic transformation (successful transition to liberal democracy and market economy), which serve to inform decisions as to whether a country is ready to be accepted or not. This point demonstrates the importance of the degree of domestic political, societal and economic transformation as conditions that are intimately connected with the desire of a particular country to be integrated in the West and the West's own affinity with, support for and acceptance of that country.

The Neoclassical Realist treatment of perceptions of threat also misses crucial elements of the nature of the 'threat' and how exactly it matters in decision-making. For example, judged by Walt's (1987) four criteria of what constitutes a perception of threat, Russia in the 1990s (and indeed until 2014) was not a threatening state to Poland and there was little reason to be concerned that the nationalist trend in Russian politics would produce efforts to restore the Russian sphere of influence in Central Europe (MacFarlane, 1993:18). However, the historical-cultural underpinnings of Polish-Russian relations (namely, the memory of partitioning and subjugation) informed Poland's representations of Russia as an enemy and aggressor, making Warsaw demand quick accession into NATO and further strengthening of the eastern flank of the Alliance.

Ultimately, as will be seen in the empirical chapters, Neoclassical Realism's structuralist, materialist and objectivist assumptions, sitting uneasily alongside the introduction of unit-level variables, fail to account for the foreign policy strategies and choices taken by Poland, Bulgaria and Russia. These strategies and choices were conditioned by the mutual constitution of the international and domestic dimension as well as of ideas and interests.

Conclusion

A reinvigoration of the study of ideational factors rests on charting a way forward for Constructivism that is focused less on foundational intra-subject debates and more on mid-range theoretical, interactive and comparative explorations as well as the promotion of fruitful inter-disciplinary dialogue.

By strengthening Constructivist conceptual and theoretical premises it is then possible to approach the hard and consequential questions of international relations such as the continent-wide re-ordering of Europe after 1989. And this reordering was not just the outcome of power political motivations and the implementation of a set of instrumental-bureaucratic conditions. Rather, it depended first on a much more fundamental (re)establishment of shades of affinity and mutuality between Western Europe and the post-communist CEE states, which would determine practical institutional, diplomatic and financial arrangements. How this happened in the cases of Poland, Bulgaria and Russia forms the main focus of the following three chapters.

5 A European Trailblazer
The Thick Europeanisation of Polish Foreign Policy

Standing on the shoulders of the Solidarity opposition and determinedly renouncing the Soviet-authoritarian past, Poland emerged from the shackles of the defunct communist regime as a trailblazer in the quest to return to Europe. It would subsequently establish itself as a pioneer in democratisation and Europeanisation. Although the more recent heated standoffs with the EU have somewhat shaken the perception of Poland as a committed member of the European family, this has not—as I argue, deprived it of the status of being among the CEE states that share the strongest affinities with the West. How the Polish Self and its Western Other have acquired their distinctive characteristics in the process of mutual identification and how these features concretely played out in forging the thick Europeanisation of Polish foreign policy between 1989 and 2015 thus form the central concerns of this chapter.

So close no matter how far: Constructing Poland and Europe

The ideational backdrop against which the empirical record of Poland's external transformation since 1989 unfolded can be understood in terms of the contextual Polish manifestation of the conceptual-theoretical standpoints of the present study. That is, the operationalisation of these standpoints illuminates the historical framing of Poland's nation-state identity and its contemporary referent groups as well as the distinguishing dynamics of the Self-Other relationship.

Dramatic Polish experiences of loss of statehood and a concomitant struggle for the institutional expression of national identity as part of one political unit have conditioned a simultaneously attractive-aspirational and repulsive dialectic between the 'state' and the 'nation'. Statelessness, foreign domination, oppressive political authority during the Partitions of Poland in the 18th century by Russia, Prussia and Austria, the era of the two World Wars and communism have meant that the Polish concept of the nation and nationality developed in tension to externally imposed state structures. The partitioning powers sought to suppress the expression of Polish nationality and sovereignty. The existence of the Polish state in the course of the World Wars was threatened by foreign aggression, continuing changes in frontiers through partitions and annexations, mass deportations and extinction of the population. All of this brought about alienation from the realm of the political, while during communism such alienation persisted and was coupled with deep-seated disrespect for party-state authority. In the post-communist period, an unprecedented degree of compatibility was achieved between national aspirations, state sovereignty and a democratic political system. Yet, this has not completely superseded the gap between state and society since adversarial politics and factionalism have contributed to the relative delegitimisation of the political elite and state institutions (Davies, 2005:9, 22, 131, 448; Dziubka, 2000:61).

Further constituent elements and processes of modern Polish nation-formation have been related to issues of ethnicity as well as elite and popular beliefs about the nation. The development of Polish nationalism can be analysed as a story about the transfer of national identity from the elite to the popular level and about the transition from a multi-ethnic to a homogenously ethnic nation and hence from a commonwealth to a narrower, ethnic-organic conception of the community (Prizel, 1998; Stauter-Halsted, 2004). The failed 1863 Uprising against the Russian Empire, the demise of the *szlachta* (i.e., gentry), the partitioning of the Commonwealth along ethnic lines contributed to the rise of the belief that only an ethnonational self-conception of the Poles could give them sufficient cohesion against the partitioning powers (Davies, 2005:48, 55, 62; Zielonka, Krok-Paszkowska, 2004:10). During the interwar period, Polish political-military leader Józef Piłsudski tried to recreate the romantic ideal of the Commonwealth as a multi-ethnic great-power, united by history and culture, with a special mission in the eastern borderlands (*kresy*). However, the failure to resolve the minorities question and Poland's declining capabilities ensured that the vision of Piłsudski's chief political and ideological opponent, Roman Dmowski, promoting an ethnic, organic nation, would predominate (Krok-Paszkowska, Zielonka, 2004:10, Davies, 2005:62).

As regards foreign policy, the transformation of the constituent elements of Polish national identity has led to a break with the idea of Poland as a great power, possessing a multinational identity and engaged in a struggle with Germany and Russia. An important conclusion promoted by the intellectually influential Paris-based émigré magazine 'Kultura' was that in order for Poland to become a modern state, it had to overcome ideas of national exclusivity and accept that it is one part of the mighty European culture, which is by definition tolerant and pluralistic (Prizel, 1998:102). This vision was incorporated in the practice of Polish external relations and hinged on the acceptance of Poland as a medium-sized European state; the renunciation of a special mission beyond the frontiers of the country to the east (instead, good relations with Russia and the democratisation of the states between Poland and Russia have been emphasised) and concentration on those international developments that Warsaw can influence (Prizel, 1998:104, 109-110).

In the most recent post-1989 period, historically-informed visions of Polish nation-state identity have been expressed by two main 'identity' groups on the level of the political-intellectual elite clustered around particular political parties — the 'modernists'/ 'integrationists' and 'traditionalists'/ 'isolationists' (Reeves, 2010; Sanford, 2003; Zaborowski, 2002). The 'modernist' view (descended from the historical Polish conception of Europe as 'modernity') is characterised by open/receptive attitudes to the ideal-typical model of European-ness based on liberal democracy, the free market, support for institutionalised European integration, regional cooperation with Germany as well as with the eastern neighbours, a liberal international order, a degree of pooling of sovereignty, multilateralism, consensus and coalition-building in the European arena (Millard, 1996:210; Sanford, 2003:20; Zaborowski, 2002:20). In contrast, the 'traditionalist' view (rooted in the historical Polish defensiveness against perceived 'backwardness' in relation to Europe) expresses more inward-looking nationalist, Catholic values, favouring a degree of conservative isolation and economic protectionism. Traditionalists tend to emphatically associate European-ness with its core Christian identity component, fear the loss of influence of the Catholic Church (as against the background of the spread of secularism and the erosion of conservative morality), see Europe as a club of independent states (and hence the pooling of sovereignty and supra-nationalism are resisted), are wary of German domination and attempt to conduct an independent foreign policy (Sanford, 2003:20-21; Zaborowski, 2002:19-20).

The parties sharing a decidedly pro-integrationist, liberal-modernist stance have included the Democratic Union (UD), the Liberal Democratic Congress (KLD), the Freedom Union (UW), the Civic Platform (PO) (Millard, 1996:210; Zuba, 2009:7). Moreover, parties of social-democratic orientation have espoused a similarly pro-integrationist vision. The Social Democracy of the Republic of Poland (SdRP) renamed into Democratic Left Alliance (SLD) in 1999 and the Labour Union party (UP) have supported vigorously Poland's EU membership and espoused a federal model of the EU. However, they have shared the nationalists' fear of exploitation by the economically stronger West (Millard, 1996:211; Zuba, 2009:7). Some of the 'traditionalist' parties have included the Christian National Union (ZChN), the Polish Peasants' Party (PSL), the Self-Defence party (SRP), the League of Polish Families (LPR), the Law and Justice party (PiS) (Millard, 1996:211; Zuba, 2009:8-10). Since 2005, the PO and PiS have established themselves as the main parties dominating the Polish political landscape, embodying respectively the modernist and conservative perspectives on Polish identity.

However, despite the importance of the general lines of difference between the 'modernists' and the 'traditionalists', some caution is necessary against drawing rigid distinctions between these two identity groups as there are overlaps linked to some commonly shared views across the political spectrum. The shared views include a firm belief in Poland's belongingness to Europe, support for democracy and the liberal international order, wariness of Russia, an active and assertive foreign policy and a strategic orientation on the US. The historical antecedents of these common ideas can be traced to the strategies worked out in response to the country's problematic geopolitical location in Europe between Germany and Russia, which are expressed and reframed in contemporary thinking and practice of foreign policy.

Two main solutions to Poland's geopolitical dilemma emerged over the *longue durée*. The Piast dynasty embodied the 10th-14th century preoccupation with the German threat and a self-contained foreign policy. The Jagiełłonian dynasty maintained the 14th-16th century focus on the Russian threat, Polonisation of the eastern borderlands and romantic messianism. These visions were later reframed respectively by Roman Dmowski and Józef Piłsudski (Sanford, 2003:11-12). Importantly, the foreign policy thinking of contemporary Polish parties tends to correspond closely with either of these two politicians' visions but there are certain commonly shared standpoints, drawing from both traditions (Longhurst, Zaborowski, 2007:3, 18). Piłsudski's legacy has been preserved through the general recognition of the need to conduct an active Eastern policy, the assessment that Russia poses the greatest security threat to Poland and the goal to secure national independence through assertive external behaviour. However, the fact that ideas linked to romantic messianism, Poland as bulwark of West European Christian civilization and as a great power have subsided, while the vision of the ethnically and culturally homogenous nation cooperating on equal terms with other European nations has been fully accepted means that elements of Dmowski's thought are also ubiquitous. Finally, informed by the dramatic experiences of World War II, the belief in the US as a crucial external guarantor of Poland's security is overwhelmingly shared by contemporary Polish political parties.

The Polish Self and the Western Other in the boundary-drawing process of identification

The distinctive features and dynamics of the Self-Other relationship that Chapter 3 has posited as becoming particularly manifest in times of crisis and prompting a rethinking of the bounds of mutuality have been concretely embodied in the post-1989 Polish context. An internal liminal situation of identity crisis, the corresponding need of the Self to emulate a significant Other and to achieve positive self-identification as well as consequential actions on the part of the Other backed up by significant power capacities have all figured prominently in the negotiation of the mutual boundaries between Poland and the West.

At the end of the 1980s and in the 1990s, Poland found itself in a liminal situation, which has been perpetuated at least since the Partitions of Poland, pointing to the presence of elements of 'permanent liminality' (Wydra, 2000). Such permanent liminality grew out of uncertainty, instability and dissatisfaction with socio-political and international arrangements and a corresponding inability to overturn them. That is, starting with the Partitions and continuing with the externally imposed communist system, Polish liminality was manifested in fundamental social discontent, resistance to imperial domination and state authority and utopian visions, whereby the disapproval of the domestic and external order led to taking refuge in collective ideational constructions (Wydra, 2000:31-56).

The liminal situation has persisted in the post-1989 period, albeit assuming less dramatic forms. Although the achievement of independence, the opportunity to become firmly anchored in the West and to overcome economic backwardness represented an attainable societal aspiration (suggesting that liminality may finally be transcended), the need to resolve the challenges of internal reforms and European integration marked a process of transformation that was far from certain or accompanied by the carefully planned objectives, pursued by 'rational' actors. Rather, this process again bore the hallmarks of liminality, characterised by an authority vacuum, reversals and elimination of distinctions of hierarchy, normative void, reliance on cultural guideposts (as practical experience was missing), a gap between reality and desired endpoint (Wydra, 2000:51). For instance, the emerging, Solidarity-based political elite shared pro-Western views. But it lacked political experience and expertise, which coupled with the absence of a fully-fledged institutional framework and firmly established party system, enhanced the role of individuals and their intuitive reactions (Osica, 2004:9-10; Eyal, Szelényi, Townsley, 2000).

In these circumstances of internal crisis, imitation, heightened comparisons and the need for recognition from Poland's significant Other (i.e. the West and its two 'faces' of (Western) Europe and the US) have been further defining features of Polish liminal experiences. As regards Europe, there is on the one hand a strong Polish conviction about Poland being an inseparable part of the cultural-historical developments in the western half of the continent. Indeed, Poland's and the larger Central European region's belongingness to Western Europe is shaped by mental-spiritual links and similarity related to a shared religion (in its Catholic denomination) and a common cultural and scientific development, influenced by the Enlightenment (Baeva, 1998:2). In this regard, Poland's adoption of Christianity from Rome in 966, King Sobieski's victory over the Turks in Vienna in 1683, the 1791 Constitution (which was the first written democratic, European constitution), the traditions of noble democracy, an elected king and the widespread use of Latin among the upper class are some of the landmarks marking Poland's 'European credentials' (Zielonka, Krok-Paszkowska, 2004:9; Rotfeld, 2015, interview). But on the other hand, the economic and political patterns of Poland's development distanced it from the western half of the continent. Lagging industrialisation and modernisation, the dominance of the state administration over economic activities as well as experiences of loss of statehood and imperial domination brought about a disconnection of civil society from the political authorities and a belated nation-building process (Baeva, 1998:2).

Therefore, the combination of Poland's 'mental-spiritual' attachment to Western Europe and political-economic distancing from it have engendered a dual perception of Europe as an entity to which Poland belongs but also as a 'standard of civilization' that contributes to an inferiority complex (stemming from repeated attempts at catching up), ressentiment and the reflex to 'defend' one's indigenous traditions (Baeva, 1998:3). So at least since the 20th century the Polish discourse about Europe has been linked to the notion of 'modernity' and the corresponding recognition of Poland's 'backwardness', associated with belated political, economic and social development (Zielonka, Krok-Paszkowska, 2004:11; Wydra, 2000:83).

In turn, the attitude to the US is closely linked to Polish strategic culture, which has been shaped by a number of crucial historical experiences of geopolitical vulnerability, betrayal and defeat, and which is an important formative aspect of Polish national identity. More specifically, the geopolitical dilemma stemming from Poland's location between Russia and Germany — i.e., between two (formerly) imperial, great powers, has been a core security preoccupation throughout Polish history, as these powers divided, suppressed and deprived Poland of its independent statehood (at least until 1989) (Longhurst, Zaborowski, 2007:6, 8-11).

The experiences of World War II added further dimensions to Poland's strategic culture. The alliance of Nazi Germany and the Soviet Union, Britain's and France's appeasement policies and betrayal of Poland at the hands of German aggression, the defeat of Polish forces in 1939 and the failure of the Warsaw Uprising in 1944 as well as the Yalta agreement, consigning Warsaw to the Soviet sphere of influence, created permanent doubts in Poland about Western Europe's ability and willingness to guarantee Polish national security. These experiences also led to pessimistic assessments about Poland's own capacity to defend itself and engendered firm opposition to Yalta-style divisions of spheres of influence and exclusion from European decision-making (Osica, 2004:5-7; Longhurst, 2013:2; Longhurst, Zaborowski, 2007:11-13). Hence, a crucial conclusion drawn from these dramatic historical experiences was that the US represents the best guarantor of Polish security. American protection is seen as allowing Poland to overcome the status of an 'outsider' in European security matters, i.e., excluded from the top decision-making table and left to fend for itself against overwhelming external aggression. This therefore fosters the Polish conviction that Washington should be an inseparable part of the European security architecture (Longhurst, Zaborowski, 2007:2-3).

Aside from Europe and America representing positive Others, Poland also has a negative Other in the face of Russia. The 'burdens of the past' in Polish-Russian interactions have moulded antagonistic perceptions on both sides, fed by a dissimilarity in values stemming from Polish traditions of democracy, plurality, individual conscience, toleration as against the Russian principles of 'Orthodoxy, Autocracy and Nationality'. Competition for power and influence (in the 17th century) and opposition to subjugation and suppression (on the part of Poland between the 18th and 20th century and continuing until now in a less existential fashion) also reinforced negative perceptions (Davies, 2005:65).

Cultural incompatibility and the acute sense of threat thus interacted to transform Russia into a negative Other in the Polish national psyche. Additionally, the Polish inferiority complex in relation to the West is thought to be compensated by the feeling of cultural superiority over Russia. That is, historical Polish weaknesses such as backwardness, poverty, corruption, frail civil society should pale into insignificance when compared to the scale of Russian social, political and economic problems. These problems position the big eastern neighbour as 'non-Europe' and shape Western perceptions of Poland as the bulwark that defends the continent from the 'eastern threat' (Zarycki, 2004:6, 16).

The impact of Others — both positive and negative, is further accentuated when backed up by power preponderance, which affects the Self's identity definition in liminal periods. For Poland, Western Europe has been a positive as well as a more powerful reference point before and after 1989, whose greater capabilities have also been translated into normative power. This normative power has stemmed both from Poland's cultural identification with Western Europe as well as from the desire to adopt the more advanced and modern forms of European political, economic and social organisation. In the post-1989 period, Poland has retained its role as a norm-taker in the quest to Europeanise itself through the appropriation and implementation of Western models of domestic politics and foreign policy.

And greater normative power and capabilities assume an added importance when manifested in consequential actions, which can lead to the rethinking of the Self's identity by confirming, empowering and making some elements of identity more salient than others. In Poland's case, Western debates and decisions about the EU's and NATO's expansion and integrative processes were crucial at a time of liminality since 1989 when Western Europe's and the US's level of acceptance could affect significantly the re-definition of Polish post-communist self-conceptions.

Poland and Europe in action, 1989-2015: A story of thick Europeanisation

The historically-informed constructions and characteristic features of the Polish Self and its Western Other came to the fore and took on special significance in the dramatic post-1989 circumstances that called for a (re)establishment of mutual boundaries of affinity and kinship. The interactive negotiation of these boundaries promoted Poland's thick Europeanisation, whereby a strong Polish domestic conviction that the country represents an inseparable part of Europe was constitutive with the relatively early and consistent West European (and American) recognition of Poland as rightfully belonging to European civilization and its core structures of the EU and NATO.

The overall direction and substance of the thickly Europeanised character of Polish foreign policy was preserved over time, although the 1990s, 2000s and 2010s left their distinctive mark. The decade of the 1990s posed specific challenges—including the difficulties related to laying the foundations of the domestic liberal democratic and international pro-Western transformation, which were successfully translated into NATO membership and a clear perspective of EU membership by the end of the 1990s. In comparison, in the new millennium, the need to work out and—have confirmed, a civilizational place in Europe subsided in symbolic and political pre-eminence. Instead, the focus shifted onto the more mundane process of learning how to be a fully integrated and trustworthy European power, which represented an adjustment from the achievement of formal membership in the Euro-Atlantic community to the substantiation of the quality of this membership. At the same time, the previously suppressed, 'traditionalist' strand of identification re-emerged in the political arena, as the urgency of having Poland's Europeanised identity accepted by the West was successfully addressed (Cimoszewicz, 2002:29; Kwaśniewski, 2001; State News Service, 2013; Maass, 2015; Szeptycki, 2015; Pisarski, 2015; Krząkała, 2015; Stemplowski, 2015; Gebert, 2015, interviews).

The rest of this chapter first charts out how the Polish Self and its Western Other respectively manifested their particular characteristics in the 1990s and in the 2000s-2010s. It is then shown how the mutually constitutive interaction between Self and Other ultimately shaped Poland's thick Europeanisation since 1989.

The Polish Self, 1989-2000: A determined return to Europe

The Polish political scene in the 1990s was characterised by a consistent, intersubjectively shared overall domestic political consensus about the goal of Euro-Atlantic integration, based on the recognition of cultural-historical affinity with Western Europe. The consensus conditioned the dominance of 'modernist' ideas and policies and shaped a strong positive identification with the West (including Western Europe and the US) as a significant Other, whose praise and acceptance were expected and strived after through a consistent strategy of persuasion. This strategy focused on a reiteration of Poland's ideational belongingness to Western Europe, which had to lead to institutional integration, and on a presentation of the country's success in the post-1989 reform process as further evidence of cultural, political, social and economic compatibility.

This domestic political consensus persisted despite the fragmented institutional setting and acrimonious party-political struggle. Such ideational unity meant that the identity crisis could be located primarily on the institutional and party political level—

in terms of the need to learn and consolidate the habits and institutional practices of democratic political behavior, rather than on the level of ideas and consciousness. That is, a deep-seated disorientation regarding the choice of ideational guideposts for the post-1989 Poland was not present, unlike in Russia and to some extent Bulgaria.

Domestic political consensus

The Polish domestic political consensus, informed by cultural-historical affinity and positive identification with Western Europe, found a twofold foreign policy expression. It was first of utmost importance that the country become integrated in the institutional fora of the Euro-Atlantic community, whose most important elements included EU and NATO membership. This went hand in hand with the establishment of cooperative regional relations with both the Central European states of Hungary, the Czech Republic and Slovakia and with the neighbours to the east—Ukraine Belarus, Lithuania, Russia. The consensually-based goal to join the EU and NATO was also coupled with the determination to fulfil the admission criteria of these organisations because of the recognition that Brussels-disseminated norms resonate with Polish national traditions and with key domestically-defined goals. The latter included overthrowing the heritage of communism through political democratisation, market economy transformation and foreign policy conduct founded on the rejection of spheres of influence and division on the continent, multilateralism, cooperative decision-making and support for a rules-based liberal regional order. Thus, the thick Polish ideational affinity with European-ness was expressed in normative compatibility, whereby there was a concordant, internalised understanding of and convictional adherence to ideal-typical values on Poland's overall political-ideational level as dominated by the 'modernists'.

The interviews I have conducted unanimously confirm the presence of a sustained and internalised identity-informed domestic political and societal consensus in favour of Poland's EU and NATO membership (Kuźniar, 2015; Waszczykowski, 2015;

Kościński, 2015; Jesień, 2015; Lorenz, 2015; Madej, 2015; Gebert, 2015; Szeptycki, 2015; Pisarski 2015; Rotfeld, 2015; Nowak, 2015; Koźmiński, 2015; Stemplowski, 2015; three anonymised participants, interviews). Polish decision-makers and experts portray the strong pro-European course of development after the collapse of communism as a way of 'coming back home'. Prime Minister Mazowiecki had popularised the idea of 'return to Europe', where Poland has always 'naturally' belonged civilizationally and mentally but from where the Poles had been separated and 'kidnapped' by the culturally alien Soviet empire (Kuźniar, 2015; Kościński, 2015; Jesień, 2015; Szeptycki, 2015; Pisarski 2015; Stemplowski, 2015; two anonymised participants, interviews; Kundera, 1984).

Moreover, the deeply held idea of 'return to Europe' informed the strong desire to transform through the fulfilment of the concrete criteria of Europeanisation. Although the Poles' psychological and normative attachment to Europe was shaped by long-term historical memories of Poland's belongingness to European civilization, it was also clear, as Andrzej Szeptycki pointed out, that the country was not returning to the Europe of the 1920s (when Poland was a multi-ethnic republic with great power ambitions) or of the 18th century (i.e., of the end of the aristocratic Polish-Lithuanian Commonwealth) but to the Europe of the late 20th century. That Europe was pivoted on democratic political arrangements, market economy and foreign policy cooperation (Szeptycki, 2015; Nowak, 2015, Koźmiński, 2015, interviews). The general longing to return to Europe thus encompassed both the mental-normative and the institutional aspect of integration through sustained domestic and external transformation (Stemplowski, 2015; anonymised participant, 2015, interviews).

Another important facet of the consensus concerned Poland's Eastern policy. Polish experts concur that both the politicians and the public had been reconciled to the loss of the eastern lands by 1989 and had relinquished territorial and imperial temptations in favour of pursuing friendly and cooperative policies towards Ukraine, Belarus, Lithuania (Secrieru, 2015; Kuźniar, 2015;

Kościński, 2015; Jesień, 2015; Eberhardt, 2015; Adamski, 2015, interviews). This was so for a number of reasons, including the fact that Polish intellectuals were strongly influenced by the communist-era, Paris-based, émigrés-inspired Kultura magazine thinking on this issue. The émigrés argued that in order for Poland to change its position as part of the Soviet bloc, Warsaw had to hope for the dissolution of the Soviet Union and support the independence and the national identities of Ukrainians, Belarusians and Lithuanians, in particular (Kuźniar, 2015; Kościński, 2015, interviews; Szczerbiak, 2012:84). Once these nations had become independent, embarking on a process of democratisation, and the Soviet Union had dissolved, Russia would (supposedly) have no other option but to transform into a European power on the example of its neighbouring states (Eberhardt, 2015, interview).

Therefore, the consensual goal to Europeanise Polish foreign policy also rested on a friendly strategy towards the countries to Poland's east through a cooperative regional policy (rather than revisionism), aiming to bring Ukraine, Belarus and possibly Russia to the European fold on the basis of European standards of democratisation and de-imperialisation (Kuźniar, 2015; Jesień, 2015, interviews). Indeed, an internalised transformation in political thinking followed a mutually constitutive relationship between ideas and reality. The influence of Kultura-magazine views depended on what Poland stood for (liberal democratic values) as well as on changing material conditions from the quasi-imperial, messianic goals pursued by an ethnically heterogeneous commonwealth to the promotion of cooperative regional relations feasible for a 'normal', middle-sized European power (Kuźniar, 2015; Jesień, 2015, interviews).

The genuineness and intersubjective quality of the consensus was further confirmed by the adherence of the 'post-communists' to the ideas comprising that consensus so that the victory of the SLD in the 1993 elections did not lead to a fundamental reorientation of Poland's foreign and domestic policies. As my interviews attest, by 1993 the SLD had become fully supportive of the pursuit of EU and NATO membership, democratisation and market economic reforms (Eberhardt, 2015; Pisarski, 2015; Koźmiński, 2015; Jesień,

2015; Lorenz, 2015; Madej, 2015; Adamski, 2015; Gebert, 2015; interviews). This support was induced by the SLD's strong leadership commitment (in the face of the SdRP's first chairman Aleksander Kwaśniewski) to integration in the Euro-Atlantic community and reframing of the SLD's domestic identity as a social democratic formation on the West European model. Such commitment was reinforced by the realisation that the successors of the communist party could only gain legitimacy in an overwhelmingly pro-European and pro-Atlantic society by taking on a 'European' identity and was underscored by a genuine belief in Europeanisation on the part of the SLD's political figures. As Polish observers have stressed, the majority of these figures were mid-level officials in the Polish communist government, coming from the younger generation that was strongly critical of the 'old guard' and had gained experience in the West, which made them receptive of ideas of democracy, market economy and European integration (Lorenz, 2015; Jesień, 2015; Madej, 2015, interviews; Markowski, 2002:54-58).

So the deeply ingrained ideational convictions related to the overwhelming goal to return to Europe united the Polish political elite. However, the nature and timing of the domestic political consensus was not devoid of instrumental considerations. First, although the consensus was shaped by ideational motives, there was also a clear acknowledgement of Poland's geopolitical and economic interests in becoming part of the Euro-Atlantic community. The Polish desire to integrate in European institutions was to be propped up by the prestige and economic benefits it would acquire as a member of the influential and exclusive Western club consisting of the most developed, democratic countries. Poland's historically-informed threat perception from Russia, the fear of remaining isolated and facing external aggression on its own would be secured by membership in NATO as the most powerful military alliance in the world as well as by the independence and democratisation of Ukraine and Belarus (Kuźniar, 2015; Waszczykowski, 2015; Kościński, 2015; Koźmiński, 2015; Eberhardt, 2015, interviews; Ministry of Foreign Affairs Report, 2012).

Second, as regards timing, there was initial uncertainty about the most appropriate form of Poland's institutional integration in

Europe. Early hopes were placed on the CSCE as a unifying organisation that could include the USSR as a guarantor of Polish security, lest Germany mounted revisionist claims on its border with Poland. This was so due to a delay in the provision of a firm and clear German recognition of the Oder-Neisse border, given Chancellor Helmut Kohl's preoccupation with issues arising out of the collapse of the GDR and the unification of Germany, as well as ongoing negotiations over the withdrawal of Soviet troops from Poland. Yet, once the border question was resolved in the 1990 Treaty on the Final Settlement with Respect to Germany and it was agreed in 1991 that all Soviet troops would leave Poland by the end of 1993, Warsaw was free to pursue EU and NATO membership without potential security threats (Cottey, 1995:33-36; Nowak, 2015; anonymised participant, 2015, interviews).

The domestic institutional and party-political setting

In the aftermath of 1989, Polish politics was characterised by an unstable institutional framework resulting not least from constitutional ambiguities about the delineation of foreign policy-making authority. Party fragmentation, frequent changes of government and the acrimonious struggle for power did not however pose a fundamental alternative to the internal and external course of Poland's development (Groblewski, 1992:12). This was so because of the overall ideational unity among the otherwise diverse political actors, reinforced by a path-dependent foreign policy-making setting and continuity in personnel especially in the realm of international affairs.

The ambiguity of the Small Constitution about the delineation of external decision-making authority and the significant powers it granted the Presidency encouraged an acrimonious struggle for control of foreign policy (Wizimirska, 1996a:191, 193; Sabbat-Swidlicka, 1994b:1). President Lech Wałęsa aimed to assume a leading role in Poland's external relations, which put him at odds with the government on a number of issue areas, especially related to Eastern strategy and NATO enlargement (Spero, 2004:76). While declaring that Warsaw would remain a supporter of united Europe, the President stated that his country would not immediately seek NATO membership. Such a stance pitted Wałęsa against his strongly pro-NATO and anti-Moscow advisors as well as against Foreign Minister Krzysztof Skubiszewski, who strove for closer relations between Poland and the Alliance (Spero, 2004:79). The conflict was exacerbated further when outspokenly pro-NATO politician, Jan Olszewski, became Prime Minister. He accused the President of sacrificing Polish sovereignty in favour of cooperation with Russia particularly in the midst of Wałęsa's proposal of a 'NATO-bis' organisation — a sub-regional security system in CEE, that took both the government and Poland's European partners by surprise (Spero, 2004:81-82).

Still, the pro-Western course of Poland's foreign policy was not revised in any fundamental way, which could be pinned on the general ideational consensus. Wałęsa did not propose significant alternatives to the foreign policy line pursued by the Foreign Ministry because he also focused his activities on the consolidation of Polish independence and argued that Poland's ultimate sovereign decision was to pursue membership in the EU and NATO (Wizimirska, 1996a:193, 194). Thus, Wałęsa shared the Atlanticist orientation of the Olszewski government, but he differed in terms of the analysis of the geopolitical situation and its implications for Poland's NATO membership. Unlike Olszewski's vigorous pursuit of NATO membership as a way of freeing Poland from the Russian sphere of influence, the President was more cautious in pursing Alliance accession. This was because of the fear of the negative repercussions for Poland in the midst of instability in the East, including the disintegration of the Soviet Union and the resurgence of conservative views in Moscow, which could interpret Polish membership in NATO as an open challenge (Millard, 1996:214-215).

The durability and depth of the domestic political consensus was thus underwritten by shared identity perspectives, propped up by the continuity in personnel in the realm of external relations and the path-dependent logic of the foreign and domestic political foundations laid out by the first Solidarity government. In particular, Krzysztof Skubiszewski occupied the Foreign Ministry post between 1989 and 1993, during which period of time he had given

Polish international relations a sound legal foundation through a system of bilateral treaties in the West and East. He involved the country in regional initiatives, secured its acceptance in the international community of democratic nations and succeeded in integrating the interests of the government and the President's office in forging agreement on the strategic direction of foreign policy — even though the opposition on both the left and the right quarrelled over the details of this direction (Sabbat-Swidlicka, 1994a:84). The continuity in foreign policy was further ensured by the PSL-SLD governing coalition's agreement to entrust Poland's Foreign Ministerial post to non-partisan political figures, despite the acrimony between the former communists and the Solidarity-descended anti-communist parties. These figures included Andrzej Olechowski and Władysław Bartoszewski and SdRP member Dariusz Rosati, who were fully dedicated to Poland's Euro-Atlantic course of development (Wizimirska, 1996b:197; Hübner, 1999:220).

On the whole, over the course of the 1990s, Warsaw's broad-based and sustained internal political consensus dominated by 'modernism' promoted a thick ideational affinity with Europeanness on the basis of a firm belief in the cultural-historical similarity between Poland and the West, expressed in the Polish desire for integration in the Euro-Atlantic community and normative resonance with ideal-typical values. The depth and durability of the shared convictions comes into view especially prominently as against the background of the fragmented institutional setting, which did not shake fundamental ideational orientations.

The Polish Self, 2000-2015: A conservative resurgence

By the mid-2000s, Poland had acceded to the EU and domestic priorities shifted onto working out strategies for making Warsaw a respected and substantively — rather than just formally, integrated member state. The internal political scene began to be characterised by a resurgence of the conservative discourse in Polish politics and a 'bipolarisation' of the political scene between PiS and the PO, respectively embodying the traditionalist and modernist vision of Poland's identification with and place in Europe. Despite the intense competition for power between the two parties however, they have shared certain ideational positions linked to the importance of preserving a liberal international order and maintenance of cooperative regional relations. And while PiS' conservative critique of European-ness has challenged particular facets of the ideal-typical model, I argue that this has not resulted in a wholesale repudiation of thick Europeanisation.

A shift to conservatism and 'bipolarisation'

After the 2005 general elections, the domestic political scene in Poland underwent a shift to conservatism through the formation of a right-wing coalition between PiS (as a dominant partner), populist agrarian Self-defence and nationalist League of Polish Families. Fiercely patriotic, socially conservative and drawing on Piłsudski's concept of 'sanacja' (or moral renewal), PiS set its sights on 'cleaning up' public life by purging elements of the consensus governing domestic politics since 1989. According to this consensus, political activities were to be governed only by the rules of the free market, the rule of law minimal state, the independent media and parliamentary democracy, which — in the view of the Law and Justice Party, were devoid of a moral dimension. Such rules also made it possible for the former communists to participate fully in Polish politics and avail themselves of the corruption ridden environment of the 1990s. As a result, the vast majority of the population was deprived of the economic benefits of transformation (Longhurst, Zaborowski, 2007:18; Bobinski, 2007:2; Madej, 2015; Trzeciak, 2015; Gebert, 2015; Pisarski, 2015; interviews).

As regards attitudes to Europe and European integration, PiS' conservative vision has been translated into a wariness of the homogenising and 'corrupting' influence of post-modern European values (such as gay rights) on Polish national identity and morality, which was hence accompanied by a strong attachment to state sovereignty as protecting the moral and political independence of Poland and a sceptical view of deeper European integration (Fotyga, 2008:15; Szczerski, 2005:54-55; Waszczykowski, 2015, interview). Additionally, PiS' sensitivity to the country's geopolitical dilemma of being situated between the two great and aggressive powers of Germany and Russia gave rise to a suspicious, at times confrontational policy towards Berlin and Moscow, and a favourable attitude to Central European cooperation akin to the 'intersea' perspective advanced in the interwar period. That perspective consisted in the creation of a Central European alliance of states between the Baltic, Black and Adriatic seas to act as a bulwark against both Germany and Russia (Szczerski, 2005:49, 62; Waszczykowski, 2016; Wieliński, 2015, Ochmann, 2015, interviews).

It can therefore be concluded that the attitudes of the Law and Justice party dilute the thick Europeanisation of Poland's foreign policy identity on the measures of support for deeper integration and promotion of post-modern liberal values as elements in the ideal-typical conception of European-ness. As my interviews with observers of Polish politics confirm, PiS is indeed perceived as consistently and genuinely holding conservative views on morality and a preference for a Europe of nation-states (Madej, 2015; Trzeciak, 2015; Gebert, 2015; Pisarski, 2015, interviews). But does this dilution amount to a wholesale repudiation of thick Europeanisation? I argue that this is not the case for at least two main reasons, despite a somewhat alarmist domestic and international treatment of the stances adopted by PiS, as is further discussed in Chapter 8. First, there are important limits to the contestation of European-ness stemming from the conservative vision. Such critique is primarily reserved for certain issues of traditional morality (the role of the Church in politics, reproductive practices, national heritage and historical memory) and state sovereignty. At the same time, support for democracy, human rights and a cooperative international liberal order is generally not questioned. In the words of former PiS Minister of Foreign Affairs, Witold Waszczykowski, the conduct of foreign policy through brute force, concerts of powers and divisions into spheres of influence should be firmly rejected. Instead, a European community of interest should be underpinned by the values forming the heritage of European civilization, which encompass Roman law, Greek philosophy, Christian ethics, rationalism, the common good, respect for human rights (Waszczykowski, 2016).

Second, PiS' scepticism of a common EU foreign policy arises out of a much more acute wariness of the potentiality of unified European positions as well as the consequences of the role of Germany in the Union. According to Waszczykowski, the problem with EU foreign policy is that it cannot be developed decisively because the threat perceptions of the European states are different, especially regarding the danger posed by Russia (i.e. as some countries such as Italy are much more lenient towards Moscow) (Waszczykowski, 2015, interview). Moreover, as against the PO's main foreign policy slogan that it is enough for Poland to be part of the European 'mainstream', PiS opposes Warsaw's seemingly unproblematic place in the mainstream because the mainstream to Law and Justice means succumbing to Germany's domination (Waszczykowski, 2015, interview). Krzysztof Szczerski (foreign policy advisor to President Andrzej Duda) has argued that the twin crises around the EU's constitution and budget for 2007-2013 were the result of a misguided and unrealistic attempt at creating a 'Duchy of Europe' (reminiscent of the German duchies after the Reformation) based on an estate division of power with a clearly dominant centre, a guild-like division of interests, an agricultural nature of the economy, market protectionism and defence against outsiders (Szczerski, 2005:54-55).

Hence, given that Law and Justice is not fundamentally conceptually opposed to a common EU foreign policy and indeed deeper integration (other than in the cultural sphere) means that the party is not averse to participating in common positions whenever this is possible — i.e. when threat perceptions converge and when it is in Poland's interest to do so. This flexible attitude has given rise to an inconsistent approach to European integration. On the one hand, the party has called for the strengthening of the intergovernmental nature of the EU. But PiS has nevertheless supported communitarian initiatives through its contribution to the budget debate and insistence on a common agricultural policy; its proposal for a common energy policy; its attempts to forge a more integrated and unified CFSP stance on Russia as well as its calls for the need to develop the eastern dimension of the Union and continue the process of enlargement to the east (Longhurst, Zaborowski, 2007:88).

In turn, the PO, which governed Poland between 2007 and 2015 and has been the main opposition party since 2015, represents a more liberal, Euro-enthusiastic alternative to PiS. After assuming power in 2007, then Prime Minister Donald Tusk declared a shift in Poland's foreign policy approach in the direction of repositioning the country from an unpredictable and obstructionist partner to a core European state through the adoption of a more consensual, persuasive style, support for deeper integration and closer cooperation with Germany on the basis of trust (Cianciara, 2008:10; Świeboda, 2007:3; Trzeciak, 2015, Gebert, 2015, interviews). Former PO Foreign Minister Radosław Sikorski continuously stressed the importance of strengthening the process of European integration and the creation of a stable political union (even in the form of federation). He argued that sharing competences with the EU is consonant with sovereignty, if the latter is understood as voluntary subjection to common rules (Sikorski, 2009, 2012, 2013, 2014; Krząkała, 2015, interview).

Moreover, although the PO continued to pursue an active Eastern policy focused on the democratisation and independence of the eastern neighbours, the party nevertheless began to approach Ukraine, in particular, more cautiously. If earlier relations with Kyiv had been regarded as a value in itself (largely for historical ties and lessons of geopolitics), for the Tusk government the EU became the major reference point for Polish foreign policy. So Ukraine's status as a country outside of the EU, lacking in the required domestic impulse for democratic and market economic reforms, was a constraint on cooperation (Szeptycki, 2010:23). This (relative) shift in Polish foreign policy Sikorski termed to be a modernisation of the Giedroyć doctrine of the Kultura intellectuals through Europeanisation and multilateralisation—i.e., placing Eastern policy in the wider EU framework (Sikorski, 2014; Berdychowska, 2001; Sienkiewicz, 2001). Finally, although the PO continued Poland's pro-Atlanticist orientation, more attention began to be paid to the European framework of security. Sikorski, in particular, became gradually disappointed about the US's lack of reciprocity of Poland's unconditional loyalty, which was especially highlighted by America's unwillingness to help the modernisation of the Polish armed forces in a more committed way (Świeboda, 2007:2).

PO's vision therefore demonstrates normative compatibility with the dimensions of European-ness related to support for the institutional integration of the EU, the conduct of regional relations through a European prism and greater consideration of European security arrangements independent of the US. Yet, the limits to PO's Euro-enthusiastic views have to be taken into account. First, PO has not envisaged a complete 'merger' of national identity with the European model. Although the recognition of common religious ties and political values of liberal democracy, respect for human rights, multilateralism, consensus-building served as the basis for a shared European outlook and even federative political-economic institutions, a complete homogenisation of cultural identities as a possible future development was opposed by the party. Sikorski has argued that 'we will never renounce our Polish identity'. The European identity will not replace but strengthen the Polish one so that the creation of a political union notwithstanding 'identity, culture, religion, way of life, and the principal tax rates should forever remain in the hands of nation-states' (Sikorski, 2012).

Moreover, Polish experts agree that the liberal-internationalist, European integrationist stances that the PO took between 2007 and 2015 were not only ideationally but also pragmatically and instrumentally motivated (Kuźniar, 2015; Madej, 2015; Trzeciak, 2015; Gebert, 2015; Pisarski, 2015, interviews). As Roman Kuźniar explains, at the beginning of the PO's tenure in power there was a more idealistically-informed support for stronger European cooperation, which however evolved in a more pragmatic direction because of the learning process that took place. PO politicians realised that just as Poland was ready to take active part in the debate about EU integration, the majority of the West European states had already been a different, more Eurosceptic mood (Kuźniar, 2015, interview with author). There was also the expectation that making compromises with the EU and being a non-controversial partner could be beneficial for Poland (Kuźniar, 2015; Trzeciak, 2015; Gebert, 2015, interviews).

All in all, the increasing bipolarisation of the Polish political scene since 2015 has meant that a thick Europeanisation of Polish foreign policy has been embodied by the Civic Platform as based on its support for deeper European integration, close cooperation with Germany as Europe's key power and a pragmatic approach to Russia. On the other hand, the conservative outlook of the Law and Justice party has diluted the thickness of Poland's Europeanisation. PiS' stress on morality and sovereignty tends to translate into a preference for a Europe of nation-states, greater assertiveness in external relations (especially with regard to Eastern policy), wariness of Russia and Germany and strong reliance on the bilateral relationship with the US.

Yet, the stipulation of stark substantive differences between the two parties' foreign policies should not be exaggerated. As Polish experts concur, the distinctions between PiS and the PO can be located much more in the realm of style of conducting external relations and in the choice of foreign policy instruments rather than in terms of substantive policy goals (Kościński, 2015; Jesień, 2015; Lorenz, 2015; Eberhardt, 2015; Adamski, 2015, Madej, 2015; Gebert, 2015, interviews with author). There is a shared view on the vital importance of the EU and NATO framework for the security and confirmation of the cultural-historical belongingness of Poland to the West; of the establishment of Poland as an equal and respected partner within Euro-Atlantic institutions; the need to support the democratisation and independence of the eastern neighbours and to prevent the resurgence of a neo-imperial Russia (or limit the consequences thereof). But the attainment of these goals is subject to much more polarised strategies related to PiS' accentuation of historical grievances and the assertion of national sovereignty though confrontational and unilateral behaviour as against PO's focus on a more cooperative outlook readier to transcend historically-loaded problems through coalition-building and consensus.

For instance, with regard to Eastern policy, both parties recognise the same goal of democratising and modernising Ukraine, Belarus, Moldova and Georgia, increasing Polish presence in these countries and winning greater West European support for Ukraine's EU perspective (of association if not membership). The PO pursues this goal on the basis of multilateral cooperation with other EU members, promoting Western standards in the eastern neighbours without actively antagonising Russia. According to a unanimous view emerging from my interviews, it was on the basis of consistent, consensual and cooperative efforts that the PO-led Polish government managed to persuade EU member states, the European Commission and Council to adopt its Eastern Partnership (EP) initiative aimed at the creation of a more intensive bilateral and multilateral framework of relations with the eastern neighbours of Armenia, Azerbaijan, Belarus, Georgia, Moldova and Ukraine (Joint Declaration of the Prague Eastern Partnership Summit, 2009; Secrieru, 2015; Kuźniar, 2015; Kościński, 2015; Lorenz, 2015; Eberhardt, 2015; Admaski, 2015; Schumacher, 2015; Maass, 2015; Nowak, 2015, two anonymised participants, interviews; Kaminska, 2010:11-12; Klatt, 2011:3, 4, 11).

In contrast, PiS being less attached to a consensual form of engagement on the EU level has had greater difficulty of promoting its positions, which may be otherwise shared ideationally by the PO. An example was the veto that the PiS government placed on the European Commission's mandate to negotiate the extension of the Partnership and Cooperation Agreement with Russia in 2006 in response to the Russian embargo on Polish meat products and the failure to reach an agreement with Moscow on common adherence to the EU Energy Charter (Pomorska, 2011:13). As a result of the lack of coordination and communication with European institutions, Poland was pressured to widen the negotiation margin by leaving the issue of the ratification of the Energy Charter Treaty out of the veto negotiations. Warsaw was also subject to European criticisms referring to the Poles' breach of the informal rules of behaviour in the EU based on consensus, institutional coordination and consultation (Kaminska, 2010:11; Pomorska, 2011:13).

The Western Other, 1989-2000: Granting access

The overall external institutional and country-specific attitudes and policies (making up the Other's ideational projection) contributed to the thick Europeanisation of Poland by providing positive reinforcement as well as conferring recognition to the 'modernist' foreign policy identity course taken by Warsaw that was in line with the key dimensions of ideal-typical European-ness. This was achieved through a relatively early rhetorical differentiation and inclusion of Poland in Euro-Atlantic arrangements. Intense bilateral and multilateral institutional links were created, which served to ensure compatibility with standards of European-ness on the basis of membership criteria. Although there were some initial uncertainties as to the pace and depth of the desirable extension of Euro-Atlantic arrangements to Central Europe, these ambivalences were not too strong to turn Poland away from its chosen path.

The European Other's stance towards Poland was critically informed by the key European integration processes related to the pivotal institutions on the continent—the EU, the OSCE, the Council of Europe. The attitudes and policies of Germany were also crucial as this was the West European country most politically and economically invested in Poland's Europeanisation and possessing a decisive weight in European integration developments.

The European Union

The EU provided Poland with relatively early and positive signals, singling it out, along with other Central European countries, as a frontrunner in membership negotiations (in contrast to Bulgaria's later inclusion in membership talks and Russia's exclusion) and assisting Warsaw politically, economically and diplomatically. Favourable Western attitudes stemmed from the perception of the Central European states of Poland, Hungary and the Czech Republic as 'more European' than Southeastern Bulgaria as well as post-Soviet Russia. Central Europe had Western Christian traditions, it could claim deep cultural ties with Western Europe, was more developed economically and overthrew communist regimes very early on (Thatcher, 1988; Prodi, 2001; Sutton, 2007:317-318; UPI archives, 1989; Wedel, 1998:19-20).

However, although the decision to enlarge to Central Europe (and CEE in general) was informed by historical and symbolic reasons based on the West's assumption of 'special responsibility' to overcome the division of Europe (European Council Summit in Strasbourg, 1989:11 and Madrid, 1995:6-7), the pace of the process also depended on negotiating and softening the negative impact from enlargement on Western Europe. For instance, reduced allocations from the common agricultural policy and the costs of liberalising trade in the sensitive areas of coal, steel, textiles and agriculture featured as central concerns (Piedrafita, Torreblanca, 2004:10, 19). This led to some Polish disappointments with the pace of Western European institutional commitment, but the latter nevertheless developed in a manner that confirmed the thick Europeanisation of Polish foreign policy.

More concretely, the Treaty of Association, or Europe Agreement, was signed in 1991 and it was greeted with approval from the majority of the Polish political elite and society, for whom, as Stawarska argues, the prospect of integration with Western Europe appealed to the imagination, evoking a sense of regaining paradise lost (Europe Agreement, 1991; Stawarska, 1999:4; Koźmiński, 2015, interview). In addition, the conclusion of Association Agreements with Poland as well as the other Central European countries of the Visegrad Group (Hungary, the Czech Republic and Slovakia or Czechoslovakia until 1993) represented an important symbolic and strategic gesture. The Central European states were singled out as a distinct group, likely to become integrated with Western European institutions earlier and more quickly than the rest of the post-communist countries (Cottey, 1995:127, 130).

The Association Agreement nonetheless met with some grievances in Warsaw. The disappointment with the lagging inclusion of Poland in the trading arrangements of the EC and the lack of provision of a timetable for accession prompted President Wałęsa to come up with a proposal for a Central European Trade Initiative (or a smaller, EC-like/EC-bis organisation on the regional level) as a way of addressing the uncertain strategic environment Central Europe found itself in (Jesień, 2015, interview; Terry, 2000:10). Moreover, the Polish reaction to West European uncertainties and delays was not only to criticise the lack of clarity but to persuade the West by presenting in a staunch, determined and consistent manner Warsaw's own vision of what a stable and just European order would look like. This vision centred on integration and the enlargement of existing European institutions to include Poland and the rest of the CEE countries as well as on the renunciation of balances of power, concerts of powers and a Yalta-style international order that disregarded the aspirations and interests of smaller states. Thus, Foreign Minister Krzysztof Skubiszewski (1989-1993) argued that Poland should do everything in its power to ensure that bipolarism would not be revived. He firmly rejected the idea of European powers regarding the country as a 'grey', 'buffer' or 'neutral' zone in the centre of the continent, which would inevitably lead to the rivalry of powerful states and the reduction of Poland to a foreground serving foreign interests (Skubiszewski, 1994:21, 26). It was similarly reiterated by Foreign Minister Andrzej Olechowski (1993-1995) that the new Europe had to be formed though integration, whereby the gradual expansion of Western structures to the whole continent would lead to a situation when 'the West becomes Europe and Europe the West'. In particular, an expanding EU had to continue developing and promoting consistently the values of democracy, free markets and human rights, while further intensifying political integration (Olechowski, 1995:21, 22, 24).

Much greater certainty was introduced in Poland's bid for EU membership between 1993 and 1994. At the Copenhagen Summit (1993), the EU endorsed its commitment to the eventual accession of CEE countries and spelled out the general membership criteria (which became known as the 'Copenhagen criteria'). In April 1994, Poland submitted its formal application for admission into the Union. In the same year, the European Council meeting in Essen adopted the pre-accession strategy, which set out to involve the candidate states fully in all areas of the EU, including foreign and security policy. These developments were welcomed with an overall positive reception in Poland. Foreign Minister Olechowski argued that his country's 'energetic efforts' to present to the EU the Polish vision of European integration—according to which eastern enlargement would serve to stabilise and deepen European integration on the basis of shared values—helped the EU recognise that the admission of CEE countries was not only the concern of those nations but of the Union itself, thus securing the decision to establish a pre-accession strategy (Olechowski, 1995:23-24).

By 1993-1994, the EU had also recognised Poland's claim to be included in a more substantive manner in the Union's foreign policy dialogue and decision-making mechanisms. In October 1994, it was agreed that the associate states should participate in EU ministerial meetings on foreign and security policy. This signified that Warsaw could take part in the shaping of the EU's common external policy and express its security concerns, despite not yet being a member of the Union (Cottey, 1995:138; Wizimirska, 1996b:208). Another important step with regard to foreign policy cooperation included greater integration of the associated states with the Western European Union (WEU). 'Enhanced status' within the WEU was first agreed in November 1993, followed by 'associate partnership', agreed in March 1994, stipulating attendance of weekly working meetings and participation in the peacekeeping missions of the WEU (Cottey, 1995:140).

Such moves towards closer political and foreign policy cooperation were greeted positively in Poland as signs that the country was being included in the West European institutional orbit. Foreign Minister Olechowski argued that the offer to become an associate partner of the WEU was 'symbolic but also concrete. We are going to be involved in the decision-making process and the security structure of the European Union' (Weydenthal, 1994b:17). High-profile Polish MPs such as Janusz Onyszkiewicz and Longin Pastusiak, acting as delegates to the Assembly of the WEU, repeated that countries aspiring to EU membership should also participate in the process of shaping the Union's common security policy (Wizimirska, 1996b:208).

A new phase commenced between 1994 and 1998, which was focused on the more practically-oriented work of conducting negotiations and monitoring Poland's progress in meeting the accession criteria. The EU's Agenda 2000, published in 1997, designated Poland as a country qualified to be part of the first group of CEE states ready to begin negotiations for accession. The European Commission also prepared an Accession Partnership, which contained a detailed membership programme (Stawarska, 1999:8). As the Secretary of the Committee for European Integration and Head of the Presidential Chancellery, Danuta Hübner, argued, Poland received the European Commission's opinion (or *avis*) on the country's application for EU membership in July 1997 'with satisfaction'. The *avis* recognised Poland as a democratic country guaranteeing human rights and a functioning market economy, which was therefore ready to begin negotiations for EU accession (Hübner, 1998:230).

However, there was a declining enthusiasm on the part of West European governments for enlargement due to concerns about the pace of domestic reforms and the implementation of EU standards in Poland and calculations of the costs of enlargement. Richer member states were growing reluctant to pay more into the EU budget, whereas the poorer members had to start sharing regional development funds (Terry, 2000:26, 33; Blazyca, Kolkiewicz, 1999:10-11). This declining enthusiasm affected the Polish political elite debate about EU membership in that there was a transition from the proliferation of general, abstract, symbolic-historical arguments for Poland's belongingness to Europe (and hence for its EU membership) to a more specific, realistic appreciation of the costs involved in the accession process (Koźmiński, 2015; Kuźniar, 2015, interviews; Pridham, 2000:13, 18; Stadtmüller, 2000:29). Moreover, the realistic analysis of such costs—related to the difficulties of adjustment to EU standards in agriculture, heavy industry, banking, labour mobility, sales of land to foreigners, enhanced the prominence of European issues in domestic politics in a negative way. The parties began to politicise the question of *how* (and not of *whether*) Polish EU membership was to be achieved. This was especially exploited by the Eurosceptics such as the Christian

National Union in order to present themselves as being 'tough' rather than giving in easily to the EU, as the liberal reformers of the UW ostensibly did (Szczerbiak, 2001:11; Blazyca, Kolkiewicz, 1999:9, 10).

There was a further tendency to turn the debate on the EU into ideological confrontations, for instance between the right-wing representatives of the liberal-conservative coalition of Solidarity Electoral Action (AWS) and the post-communist SLD, about whether Poland wanted to join a 'Christian' or 'secular' Europe (Szczerbiak, 2001:10). Additionally, as regards more staunchly conservative parties, the Christian-National Union was not completely against Poland's EU membership but highlighted the danger posed to Polish sovereignty and national values, rejecting a federal model of the EU and German expansionism (Stadtmüller, 2000:32; Szczerbiak, 2001:11). Also, an overtly anti-EU party — Polish Agreement, was set up in 1999 on a platform of religious and national conservatism (Szczerbiak, 2001:9-10). Ultimately, the most severe criticism of the EU on ideological grounds came from nationalist-traditionalist circles linked to Radio Maria, the Polish Thought daily as well as conservative parties League of Polish Families and Self-Defence. All of them called for the preservation of the Christian identity of Europe and opposed the rise of moral relativism (Krok-Paszkowska, Zielonka, 2004:16-17).

Overall, the beginning of substantive negotiations between Poland and the EU infused the domestic political debate and public opinion with greater realism and some Eurosceptic overtones. But it should be noted that the overwhelming political consensus on EU membership as Poland's key external and domestic political priority was preserved. The ideational setting was influenced to the extent that the differences between the 'modernists' and the 'traditionalists' (and consequently those who were ready to comply with EU procedures and those who represented a 'tougher' attitude) were emphasised more sharply through the politicisation of the EU factor, with the conservative parties being especially vocal. Yet, they commanded a minority of popular votes.

Germany

As the country possessing significant capabilities and decisive weight within the EU, while also having historically loaded relationships with its eastern neighbours, Germany affected notably Polish Europeanisation. Berlin facilitated Warsaw's acceptance by the rest of the West European states and thus anchored Poland firmly within West European institutions.

The guiding principle in Germany's foreign policy towards those states with which it had conflict-ridden relationships in the past is based on 'reconciliation'. It holds that the mistrust and grievances engendered historically need to be addressed in order for sustainable cooperation to take place in the present, which is informed by a dual normative-pragmatic dimension. As Feldman points out, the German rendering of the English term 'reconciliation' refers to both an emotional-philosophical and a practical element, expressed respectively in the words 'Versöhnung' and 'Aussöhnung' (Feldman, 1999:2). So according to the German understanding of 'reconciliation', dramatic historical experiences of victimhood and war, retained in the living memory and consciousness of the former adversary, can be overcome not through forgetting and downplaying but through constant dialogue that finds its material manifestation, reinforcement and future sustenance in bilateral institutionalised cooperation, further embedded into a multilateral framework (Feldman, 1999:2-5).

Polish and German observers have additionally elaborated on the process of reconciliation. As Łukasz Adamski has argued, policy motivations related to historical guilt and the corresponding urge to redress past crimes were interlinked with security considerations and a concomitant intensification of political and economic relations in determining Germany's consistent support for Poland's Europeanisation (Adamski, 2015, interview). And according to Cornelius Ochmann, there was a long-term German strategy based on the assumption of responsibility in CEE, the stabilisation of the eastern border and the transformation of Poland into a strong and predictable neighbour (Ochmann, 2015, interview). Thus, in aiming to address the memory of victimhood and historically-informed lack of trust predominant in Germany's Central European neighbours (especially Poland), while stabilising their politics, Germany created intensive and special relations with Poland, the Czech Republic and Hungary. These countries were singled out as a distinct group likely to be the first ones to join the EU, further prioritising (rhetorically and through the extent and depth of bilateral links) Warsaw's integration in Europe within this group (Ochmann, 2015, interview).

For instance, Helmut Kohl's November 1989 visit to Poland marked a symbolically crucial step towards deepening reconciliation and laying the foundations for post-Cold War Polish-German cooperation within the framework of European integration. Kohl announced that his visit represented 'a task of European dimensions that is comparable with the French-German reconciliation, without which the process leading to the unification of our part of Europe would not exist' (Wieliński, 2015, interview; Spero, 2004:109). In turn, Prime Minister Mazowiecki maintained that 'the separation of Europe can only be eliminated...if a process of growing economic and cultural cooperation occurs' (Spero, 2004:109).

Another decisive step in bilateral relations but also in Poland's Europeanisation was the signing of the 1991 Polish-German Treaty of Good Neighbourliness and Friendly Cooperation, which enshrined the common aspiration to promote Poland's EU membership (Kuźniar, 2015, interview; Traktat, 1991; Feldman, 1999:17). Foreign Minister Skubiszewski's comment on the signing of the Treaty in Bonn was that 'democratic Poland and a united Germany are the expression of the great changes in Europe. From the Polish point of view, this logical consequence in Europeanisation of foreign policy aims to link Poland to the West' (Spero, 2004:127). Also, to the Polish Parliament, he proclaimed that the agreement laid 'the legal and political foundations of a Polish-German community of interests' (Spero, 2004:128). As an anonymised insider to Polish-German relations has clarified, the concept of 'community of interests' reflected the phenomenon that both countries could benefit from developments linked to European integration, which created a common interest and a common responsibility for taking these developments further (anonymised participant, 2015, interview). The 'community of interests' thus reinforced and lent practical commitment to the vision that was agreed to in the Treaty — namely, a united and free Europe based on minority rights, rule of law, border inviolability and regional cooperation (Spero, 2004:127-128).

Moreover, the establishment of the Weimar Triangle in 1991 among Germany, Poland and France served to multilateralise Germany's eastern policy, to include Poland in larger European formats (and hence to promote Warsaw's self-confidence in European international relations) as well as to change France's ambivalent attitudes to eastern enlargement (Górka-Winter, Posel-Częścik, 2002; Hübner, 1999:223; Krząkała, 2015, anonymised participant, 2015, interviews). As Marek Krząkała has confirmed, cooperation within the Weimar Triangle did contribute to the overcoming of the division of Europe and to Poland's gradual inclusion into EU structures by raising Warsaw's reputation in international relations and engendering a greater acceptance of Poland not only in Germany but also in France (Krząkała, 2015, interview).

However, it still needs to be noted that despite Germany's significant normative-practical contribution to Polish Europeanisation through the overcoming of past wrongs, the historically-informed problematic aspects of the bilateral relationship were not completely resolved, with grievances persisting especially among the 'traditionalists'. For instance, at the time, Witold Waszczykowski perceived that the position of the Polish minority in Germany was not satisfactorily solved as part of the reconciliation process. According to a German law introduced in the 1940s (Trzcielińska-Polus, 2011), the Poles lost the status of an official minority, which still continued to be the case in the 1990s and created an imbalance. That is, the small German minority in Poland was granted substantial rights, especially in relation to their language, schooling and culture, whereas the Polish minority in Germany, which is much bigger, does not enjoy such legally enshrined rights (Waszczykowski, 2015, interview). Moreover, as Bartosz Wieliński maintains, the activities of the descendants of the Germans expelled from Poland after World War II served to sour the spirit of reconciliation (Schmemann, 1990; Ther, 2006). Although lacking the support of German politicians, they acted aggressively in trying, among other things, to demand compensations for the property they had lost in their former lands (Wieliński, 2015, interview).

My interviews with Polish representatives of both the 'modernist' and 'traditionalist' identity groups have concurred that once the urgency of reconciliation enabling German support for the thick Europeanisation of Polish identity subsided (especially with the achievement of a firm EU accession perspective), some problematic issue areas, such as the above-mentioned, resurfaced and gained prominence in the late 1990s and the 2000s (Kuźniar, 2015; Waszczykowski, 2015; anonymised participant, 2015, interviews).

The OSCE and the Council of Europe

The OSCE (CSCE until 1995) and the Council of Europe also contributed to the thick Europeanisation of Polish foreign policy in that they disseminated strong norms of liberalisation and democratic accountability to the CEE states and through their organisational authority and reputation could legitimate the actions of Polish governments. These two institutions thus had the symbolic power to confirm (early on) Poland's course of domestic and external development on the basis of consensual democracy, human rights and adherence to the key principles of the European security architecture (Steves, 2001:9-10).

As regards *the OSCE/CSCE*, the Charter of Paris for a New Europe (1990) enshrined the norms of behaviour to be followed by democratic states in the European regional order. The Charter committed the signatories to respect for the rule of law, human and minority rights, market economics as well as to the rejection of the use of force in the resolution of conflicts and border issues, set up an Office for Free Elections in Warsaw and a Secretariat in Prague (Steves, 2001:10; Cottey, 1995:148-149). Poland welcomed these developments as codifying the principles on which the post-1989 European order was to be built—and which Poland itself espoused as part of its vision of European integration. The establishment of a CSCE body in Warsaw reflected especially strongly the recognition of the country's active participation in the Helsinki process (Cottey, 1995:149; Wizimirska, 1996b:209-210). Such positive confirmation was forthcoming throughout Poland's engagement with the OSCE in the 1990s. For instance, at the annual session of the Parliamentary Assembly of the OSCE in 1995, the Economic Committee discussed the report of Senator Kelly who singled out Poland, together with the Czech Republic and Hungary, as a country leading in the economic reforms among former communist states, while the committee dealing with national minorities issues adopted a resolution approving the strengthening of the Warsaw Bureau for Human Rights and Institutions (Wizimirska, 1996b:209-210).

Moreover, the Treaty on Conventional Armed Forces in Europe (CFE Treaty) signed in 1990 together with the CFE 1A agreement, the Vienna Document on confidence and security-building measures and the Treaty on Open Skies (all three signed in 1992) were received by Poland as providing new tools for preventing the re-emergence of aggressive military postures and for laying the foundations of a cooperative security system. This was so because the documents provided for reductions in military equipment, constrained force concentrations and codified predictability and openness (Nowak, 1993:3-6).

As regards *the Council of Europe*, in the very early period after the collapse of bipolarity, membership in this organisation was perceived as a first step towards the institutionalisation as well as symbolic confirmation of Poland's social and cultural ties with Western Europe (Zięba, 2011:4). Early accession, roughly coinciding with the conclusion of the Treaty of Association with the EU, brought greater confidence in Poland that it would be recognised as part of a distinct group of frontrunners, together with Hungary, the Czech Republic and Slovakia, which would gain membership in the more influential Western organisations such as the EU and NATO, contributing to Poland's return to European civilization both normatively and institutionally (Zięba, 2011:4; Cottey, 1995:127).

However, the lesser prominence of formal security guarantees and deeper institutional-legal binding of the OSCE/CSCE and the

Council of Europe reduced their attractiveness to Warsaw, as compared to the EU and NATO. The latter provided both firmer markers of belongingness based on greater selectivity of the membership base and stricter criteria to ensure norm compliance. They also featured much more credible security guarantees through mechanisms enforcing the monitoring and implementation of shared obligations (Cottey, 1995:149-150). As Foreign Minister Skubiszewski maintained, the crucial goals of Polish foreign policy in terms of the European security order included the rejection of domination and deterrence in order to build security on the basis of cooperation among states and international institutions through the highest possible level of coordination and the attainment of collective security. But since the CSCE was a long way off the achievement of such goals, focusing attention on that organisation exclusively could slow down and create setbacks for the Polish policy of joining the Western institutions that could best fulfil these aims (Skubiszewski, 1994:22). And as a participant in the process, Jerzy Nowak has confirmed that since 1991 Polish priorities within the CSCE centred on arms control, confidence-building measures, human rights and conflict prevention to the extent that these could contribute to the stability of the European security order. But the ultimate security goal was attainment of NATO membership (Nowak, 2015, interview; Nowak, 1997:10-11).

The American Other

The European face of the Western Other was complemented by its American counterpart in contributing to Poland's thick Europeanisation. The US's perceptions and policies within the NATO framework and in bilateral relations with Warsaw provided the diplomatic and financial support for firmly anchoring Poland in the Euro-Atlantic community.

NATO accession

American perceptions of Poland in the 1990s were based on an understanding and treatment of the country as a 'protégé' in CEE (Zaborowski, Longhurst, 2003). This was informed both by the fact that Poland was a middle-sized European power (and the largest among the former Soviet satellites), representing an island of stability in contrast to the situation further east, and a 'standard-bearer' of quick and successful internal reforms. The country could thus serve as an example to the rest of the post-communist states and was in line with the American democracy-promotion effort in CEE (Zaborowski, Longhurst, 2003:1-2; Önis, 2004:27). However, despite overall receptive attitudes, a gradual evolution in thinking and policies had to take place before America and its NATO allies could fully sanction Warsaw's accession to the organisation.

The period between 1990 and 1992 was marked by Western uncertainties about the proper security arrangements that could be instituted in a changing European landscape (Koźmiński, 2015, interview; Rotfeld, 1990:9). The North Atlantic Cooperation Council (NACC) was established in December 1991 as a way of promoting dialogue with the former Warsaw Pact adversaries. These developments met with dual reactions in Poland. On the one hand, during a visit to Germany in March 1992, President Wałęsa proposed to create a NATO-bis organisation, which would represent European military forces composed of units of the former Eastern bloc under the aegis of NATO aimed at the joint prevention of conflicts in Central Europe. This conception reflected Polish disappointment with the slow movement towards NATO expansion and called attention to the strategic isolation of the region and the need to extend the protective space of the Alliance over CEE (Wizimirska, 1996a:194-195). But on the other hand, Poland's relations with the NACC subsequently evolved in a way that expanded the range of areas of possible cooperation, deepened Warsaw's political and military ties with America and other NATO members and de facto differentiated Poland together with Hungary and Czechoslovakia (Cottey, 1995:143). As a result, Poland was Europeanising its security policy by modernising its armed forces, establishing civilian control over the military and developing transparent military strategies in consonance with those of NATO members (Cottey, 1995:144).

Starting in 1992 until 1994, NATO took encouraging steps towards moving from dialogue on security issues to action and cooperation in the military field in its relations with the CEE states.

Yet, a concrete timetable, criteria and date of a future NATO entry were not specified (Terry, 2000:11; Reisch, 1994:21). Indeed, partly pushed by Central European pressure and the unstable situation in the Soviet Union/Russia, politicians in the US and other Alliance countries (above all Germany) began to slowly develop a consensus about formalising NATO's ties with Poland, the Czech Republic and Hungary. In November 1992, American Defence Secretary Richard Cheney asserted that 'eventually we will want to expand NATO'. In March 1993, as Ochmann has recalled, German Defence Minister Volker Rühe was one of the first European politicians to claim that there was no reason to deny prospective EU members the opportunity to accede to NATO (Cottey, 1995:145; Ochmann, 2015, interview).

As a key decision-maker in Poland's NATO accession process, Jerzy Koźmiński has emphasised that there were two additional significant developments in 1993 with regard to the possibility of NATO enlargement. The first one was related to the publication of a crucial article by RAND Corporation, which for the first time formulated the concept that the North Atlantic Alliance should expand to the east or else risk becoming irrelevant (Koźmiński, 2015, interview; Asmus, Kugler, Larrabee, 1993). The second development, important from the point of view of the internal American political process, was Senator Richard Lugar's speech at the National Press Club, which made him one of the first American officials embracing the ideas expressed in the RAND article and openly proclaiming himself in favour of including Poland in NATO (Koźmiński, 2015, interview). Therefore, Senator Lugar, Defence Secretary Cheney and Defence Minister Rühe led the way in calling for the expansion of the Alliance specifically to Poland (and also the Czech Republic and Hungary). They cited Warsaw's progress towards domestic political and economic transformation and its ability to project an image of relative stability, which NATO had to further ensure with formal security guarantees (Reisch, 1994:21).

The combined result of the above developments was the Clinton administration's proposal of the Partnership for Peace programme (PfP, 1994), offering CEE states and Russia improvement of the interoperability and compatibility of their armed forced with those of NATO (Cottey, 1995:146). But the PfP, like the NACC, evoked dual reactions. On the one hand, the programme was greeted with disappointment and frustration at Poland's half-hearted inclusion in the system of Euro-Atlantic security (Reisch, 1994:25). As Koźmiński recalls, the PfP was perceived by him and the rest of the Polish decision-makers as a surrogate and not a vehicle for NATO membership (Koźmiński, 2015, interview). On the other hand, the PfP did contribute to the possibility of closer integration and eventual membership. This was so because the PfP for the first time enshrined NATO leaders' expectation that expansion would likely take place in the future, while Russia's claim to a veto over Alliance decisions and CEE security was rejected (PfP, 1994; Cottey, 1995:147; Clinton, 1994; Koźmiński, 2015, interview). Foreign Minister Bartoszewski recognised the 'enormous significance' of the PfP because it allowed Warsaw to build intensive political and diplomatic contacts, which in turn provided an opportunity for Poland to indirectly join the debate about NATO expansion (Bartoszewski, 1996:13).

The period between 1995 and 1999 finally sealed Poland's efforts to join NATO. In September 1995, the Study on NATO Enlargement (1995) was concluded, which enshrined the clear decision that the Alliance would expand and laid down membership criteria, which overlapped with and reinforced the 'standards of European-ness' established by the EU, the OSCE, the Council of Europe and posed further conditions in the area of defence. Indeed, since Poland's motivation to join NATO was so unflinching, Warsaw saw the fulfilment of membership conditions as crucial to its Europeanisation and acceptance in the Western security system. As Koźmiński and Nowak have specified, the overriding goal of NATO accession provided the ideational cohesiveness and commitment on the part of the domestic political forces to push through difficult decisions in compliance with the Alliance criteria — whose substantive implementation was strictly expected by NATO members (Koźmiński, 2015; Nowak, 2015, interviews).

Henceforth, the achievement of NATO membership in 1999 affected Polish policy-makers' security perceptions in a positive way as Poland became part of a broader system of security, which ensured credibly the country's defence and structured intra-Alliance relations on the basis of shared values, cooperation and interdependence. A degree of discrepancy nevertheless remained between Western perceptions, informed by a more benign view of the cooperative potential of Russian foreign policy, as compared to Poland's greater concern with planning for negative contingencies and placing NATO infrastructure in CEE (Koźmiński, 2015; Nowak, 2015; Lorenz, 2015; Madej, 2015, interviews).

America's diplomatic and economic contribution to Poland's Europeanisation

America's contribution to the Polish Europeanisation process was not only limited to the realm of security. The US was also conducive to the diplomatic acceptance of the CEE states in the Euro-Atlantic family and provided direct financial and technical support for Poland's domestic reforms (Koźmiński, 2015; Nowak, 2015; anonymised participant, 2015, interviews).

There were at least two ways in which the US's promotion of the NATO accession process affected the willingness of the West Europeans to accelerate the European integration schemes. First, NATO enlargement gave an added impetus to EU enlargement through the assumption that European security was indivisible and comprehensive and that as a result NATO and EU expansions should go together. The NATO Study on Enlargement (1995) stated that accession to the Alliance extended to new members the benefits of European integration based on shared liberal democratic values and complemented EU enlargement as a mutually supportive and reinforcing process (Clinton, 1994). Moreover, according to Jerzy Nowak's insights into the inner diplomatic workings, a generalisation can be made that the West Europeans were not initially as open to the possibility of NATO enlargement. This was so because they still looked at CEE states in the early 1990s as enemies of the formerly opposing bloc (despite greater receptivity to the Central European countries). In contrast, the Americans showed quicker acceptance because they perceived Europe as a more cohesive unity and were readier to promote integration with the frontrunners of Poland, Hungary and the Czech Republic (arguably also because the US's relationship with CEE did not require the same depth and extent of political-economic enmeshment as was the case of geographically contiguous countries). Thus, 'Once the Americans were convinced that this (i.e., reforms) could be done and that these countries really mattered to NATO, they were instrumental in convincing their European allies that they should change their negative position...' (Nowak, 2015, interview)

Second, Poland's growing association with NATO over the 1990s facilitated building bilateral links with West European countries. For instance, on the heels of the PfP, in March 1994, Polish Defence Minister Piotr Kołodziejczyk met in Paris with his French and German counterparts for talks about expanding cooperation through the exchange of military experts, the organisation of joint military manoeuvres and the possible inclusion of Polish troops in the Franco-German-Belgian Eurocorps fighting force (Weydenthal, 1994a:28).

Furthermore, the Americans provided vital financial and economic assistance for the Polish internal transformation, which affected the success of the country's domestic Europeanisation and hence Western Europe's decisions about how fit Poland was to join European institutions and become part of the Euro-Atlantic community (Wedel, 1998:22, 35-36). American support contributed crucially to the success of the Balcerowicz Plan—Poland's shock therapy programme guiding the transition to a capitalist market economy, especially at the very early stages. The US led an international effort to put in place a one-billion dollar IMF stabilisation plan necessary for the introduction of the convertibility of the Polish złota and subsequently for the restructuring of Polish debt. Jerzy Koźmiński, who was on the Balcerowicz team at that time, has clarified that it was critical to have reserves in dollars in case convertibility led to a run on dollars in Polish banks and hence an economic collapse. Dramatically, three days prior to the introduction of convertibility on 1 January 1990, Poland lacked half a billion, whereby Under Secretary of the American Treasury for International Affairs David Mulford stepped in, ensuring that Poland would obtain the required funds in time (Koźmiński, 2015, interview). Moreover, the US established an Enterprise Fund in

1990 to promote the privatisation of the Polish economy and the development of the private sector in the country, contributing $240 million of capital (Szeptycki, 2015; Koźmiński, 2015, interviews; Hunter, Ryan, 1998:83-85; Polish-American Freedom Foundation, Annual Report, 2000:2).

On the whole, American attitudes and policies reinforced European initiatives in promoting the thick Europeanisation of Poland. The gradual process of conferring recognition and acceptance, concretely manifested in early and intensive rhetorical, diplomatic-political, economic support and institutional inclusion served to confirm Warsaw in its 'modernist' vision of Europeanisation on the basis of a sustained, consistent and intersubjectively shared convictional adherence to the key dimensions of Europeanness. Indeed, in response to EU, German, OSCE, Council of Europe, NATO and US developments, Poland insistently espoused its view of a European order to be informed by institutional integration, overcoming of the burdens of the past in favour of trust, the renunciation of zero-sum balance of power politics and isolation in the direction of shared and comprehensive security.

There were some initial uncertainties as to the pace and depth of the desirable extension of Euro-Atlantic arrangements to CEE, which led to disappointments in Poland and empowered some 'traditionalist' elements on the Polish political scene. Still, these ambivalences were not too strong to turn Poland away from its chosen path or bring about a fully-fledged dominance of the traditionalists with their more nationalist, self-isolating instincts. Instead, external hesitation provided the necessary stimulation for Warsaw to pursue its goal of European integration in an even more determined and persuasively argued manner, which aimed to convince Western Europe and the US of Poland's unquestionable belongingness to European civilization.

The Western Other, 2000-2015: Reconfirming Poland's Europeanness

The very beginning of the new millennium introduced new challenges and dynamics in the Euro-Atlantic community. The terrorist attacks in 2001 represented a critical event in international relations, requiring a delineation between those who joined in the American effort to fight terrorism (and indeed in the US-led international order) and those who stood against the 'civilised' world. The differentiated response to the new security threat and its aftermath among the US and Western European states meant that the complementarity between the European and American face of the Western Other of the 1990s gave way to greater discrepancy. Poland's reactions to 9/11 and to the initiation of the war in Iraq in the form of determined support for the US served to re-confirm the Atlanticist orientation as a key element of the country's strategic culture. But disappointments in America's level of commitment to European and Polish security conditioned an evolution in Warsaw's strategic thinking. This evolution consisted in a greater priority placed on the European as against the North Atlantic dimension of security on the basis of the realisation that Poland's strongly pro-Atlanticist orientation could strain Polish Europeanisation, particularly when European and American security stances diverged.

The new millennium also sealed Poland's accession to the EU. The achievement of formal membership in 2004 accelerated the process of thick Europeanisation by opening up new institutional and ideational opportunities for the continued thick convergence of Poland on the ideal-typical model of European-ness, particularly on the dimension of further institutional integration and socialisation into the behavioural norms of Union policy-making.

The American Other

9/11 brought about important changes to American foreign policy not least by demonstrating the changing order of priority that had to be placed on America's European allies depending on the level of support they provided in the war against terror (Osica, 2004:16). Warsaw's role in transatlantic security was elevated to that of an American protégé with the potential to exercise regional leadership to which some of the US's security-related tasks as the world's sole superpower could be delegated, given Poland's central location in

Europe, loyalty to NATO and strong backing for Washington's foreign policies (Zaborowski, Longhurst, 2003:1-2). Secretary of Defence Donald Rumsfeld praised the Poles — and the other Central and East Europeans who strongly endorsed the war in Iraq, as 'new Europeans', distinguished by their 'love of freedom' and unquestioning support for America (Lansford, 2005:xxi). Such rhetorical recognition of the importance of the CEE allies was also matched by growing financial and military ties. Already in 2002, the US Congress approved of a $3.5 billion loan for Warsaw to purchase 48 F-16 fighter jets, which entailed direct investment in Poland worth $1.5 billion and established a close link between the defence sectors of the two countries (Longhurst, 2013:4).

In turn, Poland's reaction to 9/11 and the initiation of the war in Iraq was to show unstinting solidarity with and determined support for America's war on terror. Warsaw reconfirmed decisively its pro-Atlantic foreign policy identity, presenting itself as a loyal ally, credible member of NATO that stands by the defence of the Alliance's security and fundamental values and making clear its aspirations for regional leadership (Cimoszewicz, 2002:29; Longhurst, 2013:4; Lorenz, 2015; Madej, 2015; Pisarski, 2015; Sasnal, 2015; anonymised participant, 2015, interviews). Recalling Poland's historical experiences, Foreign Minister Włodzimierz Cimoszewicz claimed that 'we understand better than anyone else how priceless and crucial true loyalty and alliance are'. He further declared that 'our principal aim now is to relieve people from fear imposed by the enemies of mankind' through a strategy that leaves no room for relativism when the most fundamental values are attacked (Cimoszewicz, 2002:29-29). Also, President Kwaśniewski argued that the Polish role in the international order emerging after 9/11 was to 'act as a leader to coax Eastern nations into the Western camp and to persuade the West to accept them' (Longhurst, 2013:4). An anti-terrorist conference hosting leaders of CEE states was convened in Warsaw in November 2001, which served to underline Poland's leadership in building regional commitment to Washington's war on terror (Longhurst, 2013:4). In 2003, the Polish Prime Minister signed the Letter of Eight (including the Czech Republic, Poland, Hungary, the UK, Denmark, Italy, Portugal and

Spain), which called for unity and cohesion within the transatlantic community in countering the danger posed by Saddam Hussein's development of weapons of mass destruction. Later on, the Letter of the Vilnius Group (including 10 CEE countries) declared outright support for an international coalition to ensure the disarmament of Iraq (Osica, 2004:18; Europe and America Must Stand United, 2003; Statement of the Vilnius Group Countries, 2003). Warsaw further committed its military assistance to Iraq, which by 2004 had grown to 2500 troops on the ground and involved the command of coalition troops (Osica, 2004:18-19).

The global terrorist challenge of the early 21st century and the American policies that defined the war on terror therefore evoked and reinforced the Atlanticist narrative in Poland's national identity. According to this narrative, compliance with the world's sole superpower and Warsaw's prime security guarantor was a question of the re-confirmation of a key strand of Polish security culture, which places a premium on loyalty and assigns a crucial role to the US in Poland's pursuit of security as a result of Polish experiences of West European exclusionary practices and betrayal. The instrumental benefits of joining the US's war on terror were also not lost on Polish decision-makers as strategic accommodation with Washington would represent proof of Poland's credibility as an ally and an opportunity for the exercise of regional leadership (Lorenz, 2015; Madej, 2015; Pisarski, 2015; Sasnal, 2015; anonymised participant, 2015, interviews with author). And from the Polish point of view, the course Poland had taken in the aftermath of 9/11 had reinforced the country's Europeanisation. Polish decision-makers initially thought that an ever closer partnership with the US based on the American recognition of Warsaw's trustworthiness and international importance would grant Poland prestige and inclusion on an equal footing in European affairs. This view in turn conditioned a Polish reluctance for the development of the ESDP in case it led to the isolation of the US from Europe. The main Polish apprehensions focused on the possibility that an independently developing European defence structure could duplicate the role of NATO and diminish America's presence in European security as well as lead to the exclusion of the non-EU NATO countries from European decision-making (Szeptycki, 2015, interview).

Moreover, although some European countries saw a pro-Atlanticist orientation as conflicting with European objectives, the Poles believed that there was a coincidence between American and European policy priorities. France and Germany (as opposed to the UK, Spain, Portugal and Italy) thought that Poland's strong support for the US undermined European solidarity in the formulation of a common strategic stance and damaged the European credentials of CEE states acceding to the Union. Conversely, it was believed by the Poles that the German and French stance was an attempt to drive a wedge between Europe and America, whose identities could not be defined in opposition to one another (CNN, 2003; Wieliński, 2014:13). Bronisław Geremek (Minister of Foreign Affairs, 1997-2000) argued that the West, including Europe and America, is a construction united by common civilizational values. Dariusz Rosati (Minister of Foreign Affairs, 1995-1997) maintained that the model of foreign policy based on democracy and morality emerged in the 1950s and 1960s in both Europe and the US (Geremek, 2001; Rosati, 2001).

However, the strongly pro-Atlanticist orientation of Polish foreign policy identity nevertheless began to weaken due to a number of disappointments. Warsaw's disenchantment in the aftermath of the Iraq war in late 2003 and 2004 stemmed from moral-ideational reasons, additionally fuelled by pragmatic geopolitical and economic considerations. The tremendous hopes that the Polish political elite and the public placed on the ability of the US to create positive change in the world were being dissipated. There was a growing sentiment that the US had misled its allies (and especially Polish proponents of the war as a humanitarian intervention) into believing that the invasion of Iraq was justified in the name of defending freedom and democracy from dictators who had developed weapons of mass destruction—which turned out not to be the case (Melamed, 2005:10-11). Additionally, Polish officials were beginning to realise that unquestioning loyalty to US policies did not prevent the occurrence of a split in the transatlantic community, grant Poland prestige and inclusion on an equal footing in

European affairs or sustain America's commitment to European security given that the US announced plans for a significant reduction of its military presence on the continent (Longhurst, Zaborowski, 2007:50; Cimoszewicz, 2004:12, 2005:15). The anticipation of economic benefits was similarly disappointed. Polish companies failed to secure reconstruction contracts in Iraq; in 2005 the American House of Representatives did not approve of the provision of military assistance to Poland and other allies; and the Bush administration was unwilling to promise a concrete timetable for progress on waiving visas for Poles travelling to America (Melamed, 2005:12-13).

Polish disenchantment with Atlanticism (especially between 2003 and 2013) was further fuelled by President Barack Obama's review of the missile defence shield agreement, signed in 2008 with President George Bush. The review discontinued the previous plan and entailed a new proposal for stationing smaller SM-3 interceptors (as opposed to Bush's decision to place interceptor missiles and a radar base). This was generally negatively perceived by Polish officials as a sign of declining American commitment to Polish and European security (Baranowski, 2012). Polish concerns as well as those of other CEE states were expressed in an open letter to the Obama administration, which called attention to the negative trends of the diminishing importance of Central and Eastern Europe in American foreign policy, the lack of strong response on the part of the West to Russia's violation of core principles enshrined in the Helsinki Final Act and Charter of Paris during the Russian-Georgian war. Instead, the letter urged greater US vigorousness in defending liberal values rather than succumbing to the 'realism of Yalta' (An Open Letter to the Obama Administration, 2009; Lorenz, 2009:11).

My interviews with Polish experts and decision-makers confirm that disappointments with American policies between 2003 and 2013 led to an evolution—representing a modification rather than a radical departure, in Poland's security thinking towards a less enthusiastic Atlanticism and a stronger focus on Europe as regards security issues. This included a more favourable view of the ESDP (CSDP since 2009) and a relative shift in policy priorities so that the European pillar of national security gradually gained greater prominence, especially as against bilateral relations with the US (Lorenz, 2015; Madej, 2015; Szeptycki, 2015; Pisarski, 2015; Nowak, 2015; anonymised participant, 2015, interviews; Longhurst, Zaborowski, 2007:51).

The change in Polish perceptions took place due to a number of developments. Polish expectations of an enhanced prestige in Europe and the world through determined participation in the Iraq war did not materialise, while Washington did not always reciprocate Warsaw's unconditional support. At the same time, Poland's concerns about its outsider status in the ESDP were alleviated after entry into the EU and Polish confidence in the viability of the ESDP grew with the Union's involvement in missions. In 2003, the security dimension of the EU began to be put into practice with three operations in Bosnia, Macedonia and Congo (Longhurst, Zaborowski, 2007:51). The Polish perceptual evolution was reflected in the difference from the initial scepticism of the ESDP as having little capacity for an independent security role (and hence the overwhelming concern to ensure compatibility between the ESDP and NATO) to the recognition of the increasing potential of the security pillar of the EU to fulfil its functions. The overriding concern with compatibility thus gave way to a more relaxed attitude of supporting the development of the ESDP as long as it did not completely duplicate NATO, challenge its supremacy in hard security issues and undermine Article 5 (Chappell, 2010:17).

The overall tendency that can be observed in Polish security thinking is that in circumstances of increasing contradiction between the European and American faces of the Western Other, the dynamics of commitment or exclusion on the part of the US and Western Europe can shift the priority Poland places on Atlanticism in matters of European security. Up to 2003, when America reconfirmed its acceptance of Poland as a key ally within the Euro-Atlantic community, Warsaw welcomed cooperation with the US as contributing to Europeanisation in terms of enhancing Poland's voice in European security decision-making. Yet, between 2003 and 2013, when American commitment declined, while Poland was being included in the EU's security arrangements, Polish politicians began to think that a greater consideration of the views of the Western European allies was more in line with a pro-European foreign policy. And the Atlanticist ideational strand in Polish thinking has been strengthened once again since the eruption of the Ukrainian crisis. Key factors in this regard relate to Polish interpretation of the vigorousness of US action, the feebleness of the European response to Russian aggression and the stalling development of the CSDP (Waszczykowski, 2015; anonymised participant, 2015, interviews; Woźniak, 2016:10-12).

Hence, external variations in acceptance or exclusion can influence Poland's swing to Europe or America in times of discrepancy between European and American visions and policies, whereby following the US line denotes a deviation from the ideal-typical model of European-ness, particularly on the dimension of diplomatic cooperation with the EU.

The European Other

Entry into the EU altered significantly the institutional and ideational context of Poland's foreign policy-making process. The status of a fully-fledged member and the achievement of the ultimate institutional recognition of European-ness opened up new opportunities for diplomatic cooperation and coordination inside the Union; offered greater possibilities for external activity outside of the EU; attracted attention to Poland; and promoted Poland's further European socialisation, thus accelerating the process of thick Europeanisation (Maass, 2015; Szeptycki, 2015; Pisarski, 2015; Krząkała, 2015, interviews).

As successive Foreign Ministers in the 2000s acknowledged, including Włodzimierz Cimoszewicz, Adam Rotfeld, Stefan Meller, Anna Fotyga, and as it was reflected in Poland's national security strategies, EU membership granted Warsaw more influence and opportunities for foreign policy cooperation within the Union (Cimoszewicz, 2004, 2005; Rotfeld, 2006; Meller, 2007; Fotyga, 2008; National Security Strategy 2003, 2007; Szeptycki, 2015, interview with author). Cimoszewicz argued that the fact that Poland was now a member and not merely an associate partner in an institution, which was a leading international player and a collective superpower, allowed Warsaw to co-create the foreign policy positions of the EU and hence influence the regional and international environment through the reinforcement that the Union imparted to Poland's international message (Cimoszewicz, 2004:10). Similarly, Rotfeld concluded that EU membership shifted the focus of Polish diplomatic activity from the efforts to gain institutional inclusion in the Union to the need to promote Polish interests and win the support of EU partners for Polish goals (Rotfeld, 2006:15).

Moreover, it was recognised that EU membership would initiate Poland into the circle of global issues and relations with non-European states, which would bring economic benefits and an increase in political authority and cultural attractiveness (Cimoszewicz, 2004:19). There was therefore a change from relative disengagement from other regions of the world before 2004 to the need for a serious debate about the profile of Poland's interaction in a global set of relations, introduced by the status of the EU as an important international player (Rotfeld, 2006:15).

For instance, the top-down Europeanisation of Poland's Middle East policy can be traced to 2004 (continuing until 2008 after which year the Poles began to show greater self-initiative) because of the realisation that it became necessary to take stances on a range of developments in the Middle East that the EU was involved in (Sasnal, 2015; Schumacher, 2015, interviews). Up to 2004, Poland's Middle East policy focused on maintaining good relations with Israel: Poland quickly re-established diplomatic relations with Israel in 1990, having repented for its treatment of the Jews during World War II and during communism. Following EU accession, Warsaw had to take a position on such issues as the Israeli-Palestinian conflict, particularly by joining the 'middle' camp in the Union led by France and Germany that maintained a neutral, even-handed attitude to the two sides (Sasnal, 2015, interview; Sasnal, 2015:181, 190). As my interview with Tobias Schumacher confirms, Polish engagement in the Middle East was the result of a learning process within the context of the EU's foreign policy objectives. This engagement however was sustainable as long as it did not fundamentally contradict Poland's key priorities. This could happen if policy towards the southern neighbourhood absorbed more attention and resources than Poland's preferred focus on the eastern neighbourhood (Schumacher, 2015, interview; Schumacher, 2011:9, 11).

EU membership additionally offered Poland the chance to continue working towards thick Europeanisation through deeper socialisation in European structures (Sztompka, 2002:85). European socialisation was particularly necessary for diplomats, who needed to overcome their passivity, instilled by the Soviet domination over Poland, and lack of experience in European ways of behaviour (Stemplowski, 2001:107). According to the testimony of Marek Krząkała, who was himself a participant in these processes, EU membership did contribute to the alleviation of these cultural habits through opportunities for the socialisation of Polish representatives to Brussels, who took part in CFSP and European Council meetings (Krząkała, 2015, interview; Kaminska, 2007:10; Pomorska, 2011:3). Consensus-building and the coordination reflex were some of the most important behavioural norms learnt. They in turn found concrete expression in the fact that Brussels representatives took on the role of 'norm entrepreneurs', translating EU policies onto the national level by legitimating new ideas on the basis of their newly gained expertise (Kaminska, 2007:10-11; Pomorska, 2011:4). Also, a change of approach due to socialisation could be observed with regard to the shifting Polish position on the European Constitutional Treaty. Initially, Warsaw maintained a tough negotiating stance against the extension of qualified majority voting in the EU's Council of Ministers and co-decision-making with the European Parliament. Poland was especially intent on safeguarding the voting system in the Council of Ministers proposed in the Treaty of Nice, giving Warsaw almost the same number of votes as Berlin would have (Longhurst, Zaborowski, 2007:37-38). However, over time, the realisation that consultation, information exchange and consensus-building were crucial to promoting one's position at the EU level led Poland's officials to seek cooperation with Spain and the UK to gain greater support for the Polish stance on Council voting (Kaminska, 2007:11).

EU accession therefore contributed to the continued thick Europeanisation of Polish foreign policy identity. The avenues that membership provided for further institutional integration and socialisation into the behavioural norms of Union policy-making allowed Polish decision-makers and representatives to Brussels to ideationally internalise and behaviourally express the importance of organisational coordination within the EU fora based on the values of consensus-building and persuasive negotiation.

The chapter has so far established those distinctive attributes of the Polish Self and its Western Other which contributed to mapping the boundaries of Poland's belongingness to Europe since 1989. Given the relationality and reciprocity of the process of identification, I now turn to the discussion of how the interactive dynamics between the Polish Self and the Western Other—with their particular features manifested in times of crisis, ultimately shaped the overall character of Poland's thick Europeanisation. In particular, I trace the ways in which this interaction informed the continuity and change of Polish identity both on the level of discourse as well as on the level of concrete policies and behaviour.

The Polish Self and the Western Other, 1989-2000: Requited mutuality

Over the course of the 1990s, the initial internal Polish liminality and uncertainty occasioned by the momentous changes following the collapse of communism was being overcome through a broad-based political consensus. That consensus was shaped by ideational affinity with Europe and was substantiated by the Poles' desire to transform their country domestically and ensure its rightful place in the Euro-Atlantic community of nations. The Polish Self's heightened need for achieving positive self-distinctiveness through approval from and even imitation of its most significant, Western Other was pursued through a determined strategy of persuading the West of Poland's European credentials. For its part, from the position of outstanding diplomatic, normative and economic power, the West's actions with regard to EU and NATO accession were crucial for sanctioning Poland's European self-definition. All in all, sustained West European and American recognition of Poland's cultural-historical belongingness to European civilization as well as the West's (relatively) quick commitment to the acceptance and integration of Poland in the Euro-Atlantic institutions confirmed, complemented and were themselves informed by the broad-based Polish domestic political consensus. The thick Europeanisation of Polish foreign policy identity therefore consisted of the externally sanctioned and internally motivated pursuit of integration. In this process, quick and intensive international inclusion interacting with domestic attachment to ideal-typical values produced a sustained, consistent and intersubjectively shared rhetorical embeddedness of and behavioural alignment with the key dimensions of European-ness.

Poland's key foreign policy-making figures invariably underlined the significance of the mutual relatedness of internal and external factors as well as of identity motivations and security concerns in the process of Europeanisation. Krzysztof Skubiszewski argued that 'the linkage between the state's domestic policy and its foreign policy is unbreakable and decisive for a success of the whole grand design (of returning to Europe)'. The striving for EU membership promoted, harmonised with and at the same time depended on Polish efforts to build political democracy and a market economy, meaning that any major slowdown in internal reforms would undermine the country's European policy and the goal to guarantee Poland a lasting and safe position in Europe (Skubiszewski, 1994:27). Similarly, Skubiszewski maintained that accession to NATO would not only enhance his country's security, but would also provide an important political factor accelerating the Polish domestic reforms. Moreover, the goal of the Eastern policy should be the internationalisation of Poland's democratic transformation for the sake of the stabilisation of the East on the basis of respect for democracy (Skubiszewski, 1994:28-29).

In a further allusion to the importance of the interaction of internal and external factors, Dariusz Rosati clarified that 'to ask what are the conditions for preserving European equilibrium and security is more or less the same thing as to ask what are the conditions for the survival of a democratic and sovereign Poland' (Wizimirska, 1996a:193; Rosati, 1997:11). In Rosati's view, Poland's and Europe's interests and visions were identical because Warsaw's cooperative policies towards the eastern neighbours would make irrelevant the West's historical dilemma as to whether 'there is any point in "boys from Virginia" (or wherever in the West) dying once again for Gdańsk'. In turn, European integration would grant Poland a further guarantee of security and provide proof that unswerving adherence to the path of reform, however great the sacrifices, eventually brings tangible rewards. These rewards consisted in membership in the EU and NATO—i.e., the ultimate confirmation of a country's belongingness to European civilization (Rosati, 1997:12).

Andrzej Olechowski, Dairusz Rosati and Bronisław Geremek underlined the inseparable connections between the symbolic-ideational and self-interested aspects of Poland's pursuit of EU membership. The EU was seen as a symbol of liberal democratic values, which the country was prevented from developing during communism (although Europe had always been the object of Polish dreams of liberty), but it was also an organisation that could grant Poland specific political and economic benefits (Olechowski, 1995:19-20; Rosati, 1997:9; Geremek, 1999:9).

On the whole, the interaction of the external and internal dimension of identification contributed to the sustainability and continuity of the modernist, liberal-internationalist, integrationist Polish foreign policy discourse. The latter focused on the achievement of quick accession to the EU and NATO, the construction of cooperative regional relations (with both Central European countries and the eastern neighbours) and readiness to overcome historically-shaped distrust of and animosity toward Germany and also Russia. Conservative elements of the identity discourse did indeed resurface especially in relation to a supposed cultural and political threat that the EU represented to the traditional values and sovereignty of Poland as well as the alleged contemporary relevance of the geopolitical challenge that Germany and Russia had historically posed to Poland. However, such elements remained on the level of public debate, with the main governing parties and the key decision-makers endorsing the modernist view of Warsaw's external relations.

As regards the EU, my interviews with Polish decision-makers and experts have confirmed the overwhelming importance of the interaction of international and domestic influences in the persistence of the identity discourse in favour of membership (Gebert, 2015; Jesień, 2015; Kościński, 2015; Kuźniar, 2015; Szeptycki, 2015; Pisarski, 2015; two anonymised participants, 2015, interviews). Konstanty Gebert and Andrzej Szeptycki maintained that the early provision of a EU membership perspective—based on Western Europe's recognition of Poland as part of European civilization, legitimised both the difficult domestic reforms and the foreign policy direction of the country in political terms. In technical terms, the EU provided Poland with a roadmap of what should be done to carry out the reforms. So internal modernisation and external integration merged into one single process of EU accession (Gebert, 2015; Szeptycki, 2015, interviews). In this way, the policy of gradual inclusion signalled the acknowledgement of ideational compatibility with Poland's vision of European integration. Warsaw thus received confirmation in its determined pursuit of this vision—based as it was on the rejection of a Yalta-style international order and the extension of the West European security community animated by liberal democracy, rules-based institutional arrangements, sustained cooperation, consensus and coalition-building. As Foreign Minister Dariusz Rosati argued, the expansion of the EU to the countries of its east would create a Europe which would no longer be a Europe 'of divisions, spheres of influence, imperial ambitions, distrust, and balances of terror', making it possible to claim that an integrated continent has brought 'moderation, prudence and stability without sacrificing the cause of liberty, justice, and progress' (Rosati, 1997:13-14).

The foreign policy identity discourse retained the same general contours from the initial period between 1989 and 1993 when Krzysztof Skubiszewski laid the foundations of Poland's European direction. Subsequent Foreign Ministers, including Andrzej Olechowski, Władysław Bartoszewski, Dariusz Rosati and

Bronisław Geremek repeatedly and insistently confirmed the continuity in Polish foreign policy informed by a consensus about the key objective of entering the EU and NATO (Skubiszewski, 1994:22; Olechowski, 1995:19-20, 29; Bartoszewski, 1996:9, 17; Rosati, 1997:9; Geremek, 1998:9, 1999:12-13).

Although some opposition to European integration was identity-based (i.e., linked to the cultural threat that the EU posed to traditional Polish, Christian values), the hard-line, anti-EU 'traditionalists' remained a minority voice, with the majority of the conservative-minded politicians acquiescing in Poland's pursuit of EU membership. The most strongly critical, anti-European integration attitude was exhibited by Catholic Radio Mariya, led by Jan Łopuszański, and newspaper *Nasz Dziennik*. They opposed EU membership on the grounds that the common currency, freedom to purchase land, internationalisation of capital and ownership contributed to the wiping out of national communities, moral relativism and the decline of religion. Yet, the leader of the conservative AWS—Marek Krzaklewski, argued that his party was in favour of EU membership. The latter would help Poland strengthen its national identity based on belongingness to European civilization, albeit the pursuit of accession had to take place on the basis of a tougher Polish attitude in membership negotiations, especially with regard to agriculture (PAP News Wire, 1998; Polish News Bulletin, 1998; Freudenstein, 2002:12). As Gebert clarified, the Catholic Church and the peasantry—the two main opponents of European integration, did not actively challenge Poland's bid for membership. This was especially due to the authority of Pope John Paul II, who strongly endorsed Polish accession to the EU, and due to the realisation on the part of the farmers that EU membership would be beneficial for them (Czaja, 1999:6; Pielacha, 2004:123). So opposition was much weaker than the fundamental internal support for the EU, whose joining was seen as the ultimate confirmation that Poland was 'part of the club' (Gebert, 2015, interview). Therefore, as Kuźniar made clear, the question was not about Europe. It was rather about the hardship of the transformation reforms, which were needed in order to meet the EU criteria (Kuźniar, 2015, interview).

Similarly, with respect to relations with Germany, the formation of a 'community of interests' and 'the substantial concurrence of views' between Bonn and Warsaw about European integration, as Skubiszewski put it, ensured the Europeanisation of Polish foreign policy identity. Accordingly, the majority of Polish policy-makers (and the wider public) could overcome their historically-informed fears of Germany and conduct a policy of intensive cooperation based on mutual trust (Skubiszewski, 1994:23). As my interviewees concurred, the progress of bilateral relations in the 1990s, which contributed significantly to Poland's integration in Euro-Atlantic structures, given Germany's influential voice in the EU and NATO, was conditioned by German feelings of historical guilt and security motivations. A complementary factor was linked to the Polish desire to return to Europe, coupled with the evolving perception of Germany as a country that had relinquished imperial ambitions and through which Poland's road to Europe lay (Kuźniar, 2015; Kościński, 2015; Adamski, 2015; Wieliński, 2015; Ochmann, 2015; Krząkała, 2015; three anonymised participants, 2015; interviews).

Ultimately, upon his receipt of the Charlemagne prize in 1998, Foreign Minister Geremek underscored the key, mutually interactive quality of Polish-German relations, whereby 'in place of geopolitics there appears an even stronger motivation from...the field of geoculture'. This meant that 'the economic tie and the political tie found their foundation in the culture and spiritual life of Europe, and the motivation to unify Europe is not fear but the sense of a common identity' (Geremek, 1999:12). Problems in the bilateral relationship began to appear by the end of the 1990s, including growing German reservations about unconditionally supporting Poland, given the declining confidence in Warsaw's ability to meet the economic criterion for EU membership. There were also Polish grievances about the treatment of the minority of Poles in Germany and the activities of German expellees' descendants. Yet, these problems did not fundamentally change the relationship, with the conservative view of the threat emanating from Germany still remaining in the minority (Cichocki, 2002:172-173).

A further illustration of the continuity of views on Poland's key foreign policy goals as a result of the interaction of the external and internal dimensions of identity construction relates to NATO membership. The evolution of NATO thinking in the direction of greater acceptance of CEE candidates, spearheaded to a significant extent by American perceptions and policies, singled out Poland as part of a distinct group of states being the first ones to join the Alliance. At the same time, this process was itself shaped by Poland's consensually and decisively pursued goal to be included in Euro-Atlantic structures of security. The goal was motivated by both claims to cultural-historical belongingness and security concerns emanating from the possibility of Central Europe's remaining in a grey zone between the West and Russia. As Polish security specialists confirm, Alliance membership criteria reinforced the standards of European-ness set by the EU, the OSCE and the Council of Europe and promoted Poland's Europeanisation, whereas the success with which these standards were implemented domestically further affected Western willingness to admit Poland in the Alliance (Lorenz, 2015; Madej, 2015; Koźmiński, 2015; Pisarski, 2015; Nowak, 2015, interviews).

Overall therefore, there was a significant continuity in Polish foreign policy identity in the 1990s focused on modernist, liberal-internationalist, integrationist principles, with conservative right-wing critique remaining on the level of public debate rather than on the level of the decision-makers' views. Moreover, the interactively conditioned, thick discursive-ideational Europeanisation found expression in concrete action. That is, thick Europeanisation framed the general tenor, context and character of Poland's external relations in such a way as to situate the state on the European civilizational map, guiding the treatment of the Other on the basis of positive identification and pursuit of integration. As a result, a Europeanised identity was actualised by Warsaw—rather than just claimed, on the basis of approaching international politics, regional relations and institutionalised cooperation through the application of ideal-typical principles.

Consistent with the interaction of initial Western European ambivalences about the future shape of the European order after the end of bipolarity and Poland's cautiousness in openly declaring its Euro-Atlantic ambitions due to uncertainties related to the timetable for Soviet troop withdrawal and Germany's confirmation of its western border with Poland, Polish external relations at the end of the 1980s and early 1990s were first directed towards solving these two problematic issues. Despite some disappointments linked to Chancellor Kohl's equivocation on the border question, especially during his November 1989 trip to Poland, Foreign Minister Skubiszewski's cautious approach yielded positive results. Warsaw was included in the penultimate round of the two plus four talks — in stark contrast to the exclusion of Poland from the Potsdam and Yalta summits after World War II in the discussion and resolution of problems crucial to Central European security. The talks culminated in the signing of the Treaty on the Final Settlement with Respect to Germany of 1990 and the German-Polish Border Treaty of 1990 (Spero, 2004:120-121).

Once united, Germany committed itself to the Oder-Neisse border, the Soviet Union ceased being the sole guarantor of Poland's security and Warsaw could pursue with full determination the goal to 'return to Europe'. The agreement on the withdrawal of Soviet forces was signed in October 1991, stipulating that all troops had to leave Poland by the end of 1993 (Cottey, 1995:33-36).

In the still uncertain external circumstances of the late 1980s and very early 1990s, Poland pinned some of its initial hopes on the CSCE/OSCE. However, the absence of formal security guarantees (confirmed at the Paris summit in 1990 by the unwillingness of Western powers to turn the CSCE into a collective security organisation) and the CSCE's ineffectiveness in the Yugoslav conflict in 1991 informed the development of a Polish view of the CSCE as a secondary institution. Henceforth, Warsaw focused its attention on joining the most viable Western institutions — the EU and NATO. Nevertheless, Poland continued to play an active role in developing the CSCE's role in those areas in which it could promote the European security order, including conflict prevention, crisis management, arms control and confidence-building. For instance, when the CSCE Forum on Security Cooperation opened in Vienna in 1992, the Visegrad states established themselves as leading participants. Warsaw showed particular interest in issues related to the military force structures and readiness levels of its eastern neighbours that could be conducive to the possibility of regional arms control measures with these states (Cottey, 1995:152).

So since 1990-1991, Poland made clear its key foreign policy goal of gaining membership in the EC/EU, which met with Western Europe's growing willingness to include Poland (as well as Hungary and the Czech Republic) as a frontrunner in the accession process. Some of the earliest milestones in Polish-EC/EU relations were linked to the signing of the EEC-Poland agreement on trade and commercial and economic cooperation (1989), followed by the Europe Agreement (1991). Polish officials and their Hungarian and Czech counterparts were gradually included in EC decision-making fora. This was exemplified by the opportunity provided to Central European foreign ministers to join for the first time a regular meeting of EC foreign ministers in October 1992 and the 1994 agreement among EU first diplomats stipulating the participation of the associate states in the Union's ministerial meetings on foreign and security policy (Cottey, 1995:137-138). Poland submitted its application for membership in 1994 and established in 1996 the Committee for European Integration, which coordinated the activities of the state administration in anticipation of the country's integration in the EU, shaped government policy and produced a National Strategy for Integration. The Strategy became the first programme paper to be submitted by any associate state outlining the tasks that had to be fulfilled prior to accession (Hübner, 1998:224, 228). At the European Council Summit in Luxembourg (1997), the EU accepted the Commission's opinion to invite six CEE states—among which Poland, to start accession talks, which were formally initiated in the following year.

The Europeanisation of Polish foreign policy through deeper integration with Western Europe was enhanced by the increasingly close cooperation with Germany based on the mutual Polish-German drive for reconciliation, which found concrete expression in the creation of extensive security and economic ties. Chancellor Helmut Kohl and Foreign Ministers Hans-Dietrich Genscher and

Klaus Kinkel consistently lent preeminent support to Poland's EU and NATO membership goals and consolidated Skubiszewski's strategy for ever closer cooperation with Germany based on a 'community of interests' (Cichocki, 2002:169-170; Spero, 2004:129-130).

Bilateral ties were thus focused both on regular high-level political consultations among Prime Ministers, Ministers of Foreign Affairs and Defence (as stipulated in the 1991 Treaty on Good Neighbourliness) as well as on meetings and knowledge exchange among security experts, journalists and scientists. Between 1990 and 2000, Poland and Germany concluded 27 agreements on military and security cooperation. For instance, the 1993 Agreement on Military Cooperation was the first treaty of this kind that Berlin had signed with a former Warsaw Pact member (Górka-Winter, Posel-Częścik, 2002). Moreover, commercial relations between Poland and Germany also developed dynamically. If in 1989 the two German states accounted for 20.6% of imports and 19.2% of exports for Poland, by 1999 these figures had risen to 25.2% and 36.1%, which made Germany Poland's first and most important trade partner. Germany provided significant capital investments, retaining the largest share in the Polish banking sector with respect to equity owned by foreign nationals (ranging between 33% and 26% in the latter half of the 1990s) and playing a major role in the insurance sector (Kleer, 2002).

Furthermore, apart from the gradual steps taken by NATO towards the inclusion of CEE states—such as through the NACC and the PfP, Polish officials worked consistently throughout the 1990s in accelerating the accession process and receiving a firm date for membership on the basis of a strategy of persuasion (Lorenz, 2015; Madej, 2015; Koźmiński, 2015, interviews; Wawrzusiszyn, 2014:4). By 1993, Polish officials were pressing hard for their country's NATO membership. Prime Minister Hanna Suchocka, deputy Defence Minister Jerzy Milewski, deputy Foreign Minister Andrzej Ananicz and Defence Minister Janusz Onyszkiewicz warned that old threats were likely to return in the absence of an Alliance membership perspective. The revival of a bipolar arrangement in Europe and the potential failure of Polish democratic reforms were highlighted (Polish News Bulletin, May 1993, October 1993, December 1993). In the mid-1990s, the push for NATO membership continued. On signing the PfP, Prime Minister Waldemar Pawlak assessed the Partnership as not completely satisfactory but still a promising element of the new European security system, which should culminate in full Polish membership in the Alliance (Polish News Bulletin, February 1994, February 1995). By the end of the 1990s, Poland continued to receive Western support for its bid for NATO membership—as President Kwaśniewski was strongly assured during his 1997 visit to the US. Prime Minister Jerzy Buzek asserted that Polish NATO membership brought 'the true end of World War II' (PAP News Wire, 1997; Associated Press, 1998).

As far as the work of the Polish diplomatic representatives to the US was concerned, the strategy of persuasion was actualised in at least three major tasks, as explained by then Polish Ambassador to the US Jerzy Koźmiński. First, the Polish diplomats set about creating a proper image of Poland as a country with a rich history and a pro-Western attitude, which had embarked upon a path of radical domestic political-economic changes and successfully sustained that course, thus representing a potential asset to NATO. The second task was to exert pressure through active networking with and lobbying those American institutions and policy-makers who were directly or indirectly influencing the decision about NATO expansion. Of crucial importance were the White House, the Department of State, the National Security Council, the CIA, the Pentagon, the US Congress, the media, the opinion-making circles such as think-tanks, academics and influential former politicians, the business and Polish-American interest groups. The third task consisted in contributing to the American discussions about NATO enlargement from a conceptual point of view by clarifying how the process of Alliance expansion would be situated within the broader security context that encompassed relations with Russia, Ukraine and the Baltic states. And it was the Polish diplomats' argument that NATO enlargement was one pillar in a broader security complex that included special relations between NATO and Russia enshrined in the NATO-Russia Founding Act so that Moscow's security concerns about being encircled by the Alliance would be alleviated. A parallel NATO-Ukraine council was also to be created, while the ambitions of the Baltic states to join NATO would have to remain temporarily unfulfilled since a big enlargement to Poland, Hungary and the Czech Republic as well as the Baltics would be both too costly for the Alliance and too offensive to Moscow (strategically, because Estonia, Latvia and Lithuania were neighbours of Russia and, psychologically, because they used to be part of the Soviet Union) (Koźmiński, 2015, interview).

Finally, Warsaw was active in constructing integration initiatives with Hungary, the Czech Republic and Slovakia as a way of proving to Western European and American observers that Poland shared and operated on the key European principle of regional cooperation. The Visegrad summit in 1991 initiated formally the creation of the Visegrad organisation and produced a significant document—the Visegrad Declaration (1991). This document signalled the resolve of the Visegrad states to act together in convincing Western Europe that they were the most Europeanised. That is, the process of Central European regional cooperation was in itself a signal that these countries were willing to put historical disputes behind them, resolve differences peacefully and pursue together EU and NATO membership (Cottey, 1995:132; Spero, 2004:256, 268). In turn, Western Europe's recognition of the special relationship that it was beginning to form with the Visegrad Group was highlighted when the Prime Ministers of Poland, Hungary and Czechoslovakia met together with EC leaders for the first time in 1991. At the 1993 Copenhagen summit, the EU referred to the Visegrad states as a group, whose cooperation it supported (Cottey, 1995:127, 130, 134).

Polish decision-makers further attempted to conduct a friendly and cautious policy towards the eastern neighbours of Ukraine, Belarus and also the Soviet Union/Russia in order to stabilise the security environment in the east through democratisation. As regards Poland's relations with Russia, in particular, the growing recognition of the fundamental differences in Moscow's and Warsaw's visions of how the European security order should be constructed soured interactions (Fedorowicz, 2007:7; Eberhardt, 2015, interview). The Russian ambition to establish dominance over the domestic and external development of the post-Soviet states conflicted with Poland's goal to democratise Ukraine and Belarus and to promote the European integration of these countries. Moscow criticised Ukrainian President Leonid Kravchuk's proposition to establish a security zone from the Baltic to the Black Sea and the formation of a Polish-Ukrainian battalion as attempts on the part of Warsaw to undercut Russia's interests in the post-Soviet area by drawing Ukraine into the West (Longhurst, Zaborowski, 2007:65). Ultimately, as Kuźniar confided, during unofficial meetings, Russian politicians were telling their Polish counterparts that Moscow would not object to Poland's accession to the EU and NATO, especially if Warsaw set aside any dreams of Europeanising Ukraine. This proved to be an unacceptable compromise to the Poles (Kuźniar, 2015, interview).

Regarding Ukraine, on 2 January 1990 Poland became the first country in the world to recognise Ukrainian independence and established full diplomatic relations with Kyiv on 8 January 1990 (Fedorowicz, 2007:4-5). Since the mid-1990s, Poland and Ukraine intensified their cooperation, with Warsaw lobbying in favour of Kyiv's inclusion in Central European institutions such as CEFTA, which was seen as a first step towards EU integration. In the process of Poland's accession to NATO, Warsaw advocated the creation of closer ties between the Alliance and Ukraine, culminating in the Ukraine-NATO Charter (Longhurst, Zaborowski, 2007:65). However, Poland's vision of Ukraine as a Europeanising state became unsustainable over time (Eberhardt, 2015; Adamski, 2015; anonymised participant; Kuźniar, 2015, interviews). By the end of the 1990s, Poland and Ukraine were set on divergent paths of development. Warsaw was completing domestic reforms and becoming integrated in NATO and the EU, while Kyiv pursued a policy of balancing its relations with Russia and Europe, giving more and more precedence to the former and sliding into authoritarianism (Longhurst, Zaborowski, 2007:65).

The Polish Self and the Western Other, 2000-2015: Reaffirmed affinities

The relatively more intense liminality and uncertainty that characterised the Polish Self's internal situation in the 1990s subsided over the course of the 2000s and 2010s. In the latter decades, the question of whether, how and under what conditions Poland would join the EU and NATO had already been resolved. As a fully-fledged member of those institutions Polish concerns shifted onto the ways in which the country could become a substantively as opposed to just formally integrated member state. Warsaw set about achieving this by being an active, self-assertive shaper of the EU's external agenda. On the other hand, the Western Other further alleviated the Polish Self's need for recognition and positive distinctiveness by expanding the range of diplomatic avenues for Poland's continued integration in Euro-Atlantic fora. The thick Europeanisation of Polish foreign policy identity was thus carried on from the 1990s and was similarly ultimately shaped by the interactive identification process between the Polish Self and its Western Other. EU accession in 2004 was a crucial confirmation of Poland's belongingness to European civilization, bestowing on Warsaw greater ideational and strategic opportunities for the further Europeanisation of foreign policy. The country could in turn only avail itself of accession in a fully-fledged manner through a domestically-shaped ambition to play an important role in the Union, necessitating deeper socialisation and operation on the European 'rules of the game'. In this vein, a well-rounded process of Europeanisation comprised the fulfilment of a compliant role of a follower, which was complemented by active contribution to EU policy-making.

As a result, thick Europeanisation was manifested in sustained and intersubjectivley shared rhetorical embeddedness and behavioural alignment with the key dimensions of the ideal-typical model of European-ness linked to support for liberal democracy, cooperative regional relations, rules-based international order and international institutional integration. The conservative Polish identity discourse was indeed resurgent but it introduced nuances of style rather than fundamental ideational change in the expression of Europeanisation, while disappointments with pro-Atlanticist policy oriented Poland towards a focus on the European dimension of security.

Polish decision-makers and experts expressed views that underlined both the international and domestic aspects in Poland's foreign policy-making process within the framework of EU membership (Secrieru, 2015; Kuźniar, 2015; Kościński, 2015; Schumacher, 2015; Eberhardt, 2015; Sasnal, 2015; anonymised participant, 2015, interviews). President Aleksander Kwaśniewski argued that accession to the Union would ensure Polish security, which would be further complemented by the contributions his country would make in terms of stabilising the CEE region, helping draw Ukraine, Russia and Belarus into greater cooperation, enriching 'the palette of cultural impulses for development' and facilitating the search for an appropriate formula for the Atlantic partnership (Kwaśniewski, 2001). Foreign Minister Bartoszewski maintained that the development of Polish external relations illustrated that foreign policy was both correlated with a state's internal political system (whereby building a democratic political system informed successful European integration) and was additionally affected by the penetration of international standards in the field of human rights protection and the *acquis* (Bartoszewski, 2001). Marking the 9th anniversary of Poland's entry into the EU, President Bronisław Komorowski concluded that the Poles had made good use of membership. They pinned their hopes for the resolution of problems on the Union, while also recognising their responsibility for the future of the European project (State News Service, 2013). A case in point was the country's EU Presidency, which Komorowski evaluated as the result of Polish success and hard work. But the Presidency also contributed to the strengthening of Warsaw's international position and image since presiding over European institutions took place on the basis of joint effort, consent, debate and concern for the common good (PAP News Wire, 2011).

As Roman Kuźniar has concluded, Polish EU membership neutralised traditional Realpolitik, dispelled fears of Germany, offered a shield against Russia and provided decision-making comfort through the opportunity to choose whether to join US military operations and how closely to ally with American positions (given that Poland's security situation no longer necessitated unilateral security guarantees). Yet, it was also up to Poland to become part of the core of the European unification project or else risk remaining in the periphery of the EU (Kuźniar, 2005:27; Meeting with Professor Roman Kuźniar, 2013).

Furthermore, politicians and experts noted the mutual relatedness of ideas and interests in the process of Europeanisation. Bronisław Geremek maintained that the reconciliation of realism and idealism, of national interests and national identity had been a prime task for Polish foreign policy since 1989. The realist element referred to offsetting threats, strengthening independence and maximising opportunities for the internal political and economic transformation. The idealistic element included support for democracy and human rights. And both of these elements were best accommodated through the institutional anchoring in the Euro-Atlantic community (Geremek, 2001). Likewise, Radosław Sikorski pointed out that an effective foreign policy was the result of 'the mutual impact of material and immaterial factors'. Indeed, successive Polish Foreign Ministers on the one hand recognised the ideational match that existed between the EU as a normative power and Poland's domestically shaped concern with democracy promotion and the protection of human rights, stemming from its cultural traditions and successful transition experience. On the other hand, they also acknowledged the interest-based motivations for foreign policy cooperation within the EU on the eastern neighbourhood, Russia and energy, given the country's more limited potential in dealing with these issues on its own (Sikorski, 2013, 2014; Cimoszewicz, 2004, 2005; Meller, 2007; Fotyga, 2008).

The recognition of the mutually constitutive relationship between identity and interests in Polish foreign policy was similarly reflected in the country's main strategic documents. The National Security Strategy of 2007 and the Polish Foreign Policy Priorities between 2012 and 2016 state that national interests follow from the fundamental and invariable values that inform Polish national identity, including democracy, the rule of law, respect for human rights, solidarity (National Security Strategy, 2007:4; Polish Foreign Policy Priorities 2012-2016:6). This point is further reinforced in the White Book on National Security of 2013 and the National Security Strategy of 2014, where it is maintained that the lessons of the past speak to the importance of sustaining and cultivating identity for the survival of a nation. In the contemporary period, strengthening identity should be ensured by granting common and equal access to culture, activating social capital, consolidating patriotic attitudes and active citizenship (White Book on the National Security, 2013:9, 30; National Security Strategy, 2014:39).

The views expressed by Polish decision-makers and experts therefore confirmed the importance of the interaction of the internal and external dimension of identification, of ideas and interests in the process of the Europeanisation of Polish foreign policy, which represented an overall continuation of the main tenets of the liberal-internationalist discourse of the 1990s. These tenets put a primacy on the achievement of European integration on the principles of liberal democratic values and the rejection of balances of power, spheres of influence and divisions on the continent in favour of co-operation and multilateralism. However, there gradually appeared at least two shifts in the identity discourse of the 2000s and 2010s.

First, the liberal-internationalist rhetoric predominant until EU accession began to be nuanced by the formation of the first completely right-wing oriented government in 2005 (as opposed to the conservative-liberal coalition between the AWS and the UW in the 1990s) as well as the bipolarisation of the domestic political scene between the Euro-realist/Euro-sceptic PiS and the more enthusiastically integrationist PO. Law and Justice retained the consensually shared positions across the political spectrum that Poland should be a respected member of the EU and NATO as the key institutional anchors of Warsaw's European belongingness; that the eastern neighbours should be democratized; and the rules-based international order should be strengthened. Yet, PiS laid a greater stress on traditional morality and state sovereignty, adopting a much more confrontational style of foreign policy-making.

And this shift was also conditioned by the interaction of international and domestic factors. The conservative identity discourse and policies adopted by the Law and Justice-dominated coalition government between 2005 and 2007 was enabled by the changing external framework. Once Poland achieved EU membership, it had much more leeway to pursue its foreign policy vision in a more assertive manner, given that it had fulfilled the non-negotiable, top-down requirements for EU entry and was now a fully-fledged member. Similarly, the PO's integrationist outlook and policy of greater cooperation with Germany after taking power in 2007 was reinforced by the party's recognition that Poland needed German support for its attempts to become part of the core of the EU's decision-making processes and by Berlin's readiness for a closer partnership with Warsaw as a result of changes in European politics. That is, with the onset of the Eurozone crisis and Germany's emergence as the key European power in solving the financial issues of the continent, Berlin needed a strong ally to make its policies credible (lest it was accused of acting as a hegemon) (Buras, 2013:3).

Second, the strongly enthusiastic Atlanticism of the 1990s also underwent an evolution from the increasing attachment to the transatlantic tie in security matters after 9/11 and in the run-up to the Iraq war to a gradual weakening between 2003 and 2013 and a further strengthening in the midst of the Ukrainian crisis. This evolution was again the result of the interaction of international and domestic factors. For instance, PiS put significant emphasis on Polish-American bilateral cooperation. This emphasis was however diminished due to the combination of the US's (relative) disengagement from Europe and the growing realisation on the part of Law and Justice that the development of the European pillar of security could add an additional layer of protection for Poland. So, as Wojcieh Lorenz pointed out, it was under the PiS government between 2005 and 2007 that Warsaw started to support and contribute to the development of the ESDP, especially by sending troops in 2006 as part of the EU mission to Congo (Lorenz, 2015, interview). Moreover, it was not only the Obama administration's hesitancy in relation to the construction of a missile defence shield in Poland that conditioned Polish disappointments and a greater focus on European coordination as regards security matters. It was also the PO's more nuanced and less enthusiastic approach to privileging Polish-American bilateral cooperation at the expense of relations with the EU partners that played a role. Indeed, when the PO came to power in 2007, talks on the missile defence shield stalled not least because of the new government's caution in pressing for an initiative that might jeopardise ties with the EU and Russia, while it was still unclear whether the new American President would continue the project (Lorenz, 2009:10).

The evolution of Poland's security thinking, whereby greater priority was given to the European dimension of the country's security as against bilateral ties with the US, strengthened Polish Europeanisation. The experts and decision-makers, whom I interviewed, concurred that in general there is complementarity between the Atlantic and the European foreign policy direction, which reinforces Europeanisation. This is so because NATO and the EU complement each other in their security functions. The Union is more effective in non-military areas of security such as energy security, while the Alliance is much more suited to the provision of collective defence against armed aggression. However, a serious contradiction—and a disjunction between the American and European element of Euro-Atlantic security provision, can occur in situations when a stark choice needs to be made between Europe and America akin to George Bush's zero-sum postulate of 'you are either with us or against us', or when the EU attempts to develop exclusive military structures. In such situations, aligning with the (predominant) European position anchors Poland more firmly within the European community (Waszczykowski, 2015; Lorenz, 2015; Madej, 2015; Pisarski, 2015; Gebert, 2015; Nowak, 2015; Stemplowski, 2015, interviews).

On the whole, the examination of the Polish foreign policy identity discourse in the 21st century points to the fact that the achievement of thick Europeanisation remained a key goal and policy trend but Polish attitudes became more attuned to the tasks and challenges emanating from the status of a member state. The strongly enthusiastic pro-European and pro-Atlanticist orientation of the 1990s evolved into a much more critical and nuanced assessment of developments on the EU level, of American attitudes and actions and into a more determined and ambitious strategy to assert one's national objectives and equal standing in European decision-making. These discursively espoused stances were, moreover, translated into concrete actions.

The conjunction of the US's policies during the Iraq war, American disengagement from European security, hesitations about the missile defence shield, which bred disappointments in Warsaw, and Poland's attainment of EU membership led to a weakening of the strongly Atlanticist-oriented Polish security culture and a greater focus on European cooperation as regards issues of security (National Security Strategy, 2007:11). Hence, Poland participated in ESDP military missions in the Congo and Chad, supported the Battlegroup Concept as well as wished to contribute to the Gendarmerie forces and to develop the EU's capabilities through the European Defence Agency (Longhurst, Zaborowski, 2007:53; Chappell, 2010:17).

Although NATO and bilateral ties with the US remained a crucial element of Polish security identity, America began to be treated less as the country's ultimate protector (Michta, 2013; Nowak, 2009:14). This led to a shift in security policy priorities. If the 2003 National Security Strategy placed a premium on NATO and close cooperation with the US for the defence of Poland, by 2007 and especially between 2009 and 2013, the European pillar of security provision together with a greater reliance on national capabilities took a second place after NATO cooperation and ahead of bilateral relations with America (National Security Strategy, 2003, 2007, 2014; Defense Strategy, 2009).

Furthermore, Poland's accession in 2004 opened up new avenues for the expansion of Warsaw's foreign policy vistas. With time Poland became much more confident in asserting its national goals on the EU level, although the degree of effectiveness still depended on acting on the basis of a logic of appropriateness that recognised and followed European norms.

In line with PiS' conservative vision and more aggressive style of promoting Polish national interests, the Europeanisation of the country's foreign policy proceeded more slowly and in a conflict-ridden environment. In addition to applying a veto on the PCA negotiations between the EU and Russia, PiS refused to agree to an EU-wide campaign against the death penalty, signalling a challenge to the liberal consensus on this issue within the Union. The party further alienated European leaders with its antagonistic approach to discussions about the replacement of the failed Constitution with the Lisbon Treaty (Bobiński, 2007:7; Reeves, 2010:8). Law and Justice President Lech Kaczyński refused to accept the proposed double majority voting system at the European Council. His argumentation held that more influence would be given to the big European nations and especially Germany, which having killed so many Poles during World War II had ostensibly deprived Poland of a larger population and hence a larger share of the proposed voting system (Reeves, 2010:8-9). The governing party also reacted sharply to the agreement reached in 2005 between Berlin and Moscow on the construction of the North Stream gas pipeline, branding the project another Ribbentrop-Molotov pact that aimed to bypass and control East European countries (Reeves, 2010:11). In general, Law and Justice did not perceive Germany as a reliable partner for Poland's Eastern policy because of Berlin's alleged submissiveness to Russian interests. The PiS government dismissed the German Presidency of the Council of the EU in 2007 as not attaching enough importance to the eastern dimension of the ENP and further deplored the Union's lack of support for Ukrainian accession (Cianciara, 2008:8-9).

In contrast to this, since PO came to power in 2007, Polish foreign policy underwent a more robust process of Europeanisation that included both conformity to EU norms and policies as well as an active role in shaping the Union's external agenda. Apart from the successful uploading of the EP initiative onto the EU level, another important manifestation of the PO's Euro-enthusiastic stance was the integrationist approach that the government took to Poland's Presidency of the EU in the second half of 2011 (Jesień, 2011; Bajczuk, 2011; Pomorska, Vanhoonacker, 2012). The objectives of the Polish Presidency included the promotion of European cooperation as a source of security on the basis of a strengthened

CSDP and giving the EU Commission the mandate to negotiate the legal framework of the Trans-Caspian Gas Pipeline System. European integration was additionally conceived of as a source of growing international prestige through the conclusion of Association Agreements with the EP states, the creation of a European Endowment for Democracy to support civil society and democratisation in third countries (Bajczuk, 2011:4-5; Pomorska, Vanhoonacker, 2012:4-6; Jesień, 2011:20). Also, the improvement of relations with Germany that Prime Minister Tusk called for on assuming power in 2007 culminated in Foreign Minister Sikorski's dramatic appeal in his 2011 Berlin speech that Germany take more responsibility for further European integration (even in the direction of federation) and the survival of the Eurozone since it was 'Europe's indispensable nation' (Sikorski, 2011). The PO's more conciliatory and pragmatic attitude to Russia was reflected in the withdrawal of the Polish veto on Russia's OECD membership and the PCA; in opening up new channels of communication at the governmental, inter-ministerial, technical levels; and in deciding to set up the Polish-Russian Group for Difficult Matters to discuss unresolved historical issues (Eberhardt, 2008:152-153).

Finally, as confirmed unanimously by Polish decision-makers and experts, the eruption of the Ukrainian crisis at the end of 2013 triggered a Polish response that is strongly critical of Moscow's attempt to revise the European regional order and to create a system based on spheres of influence, the use of force and the subordination of smaller countries to the will of the powerful states (Secrieru, 2015; Kuźniar, 2015; Waszczykowski, 2015; Jesień, 2015; Lorenz, 2015; Eberhardt, 2015; Madej, 2015; Gebert, 2015; Szeptycki, 2015; Koźmiński, 2015; two anonymous participants, 2015, interviews). Hence, Warsaw's strategy has attempted to promote unity within the EU and NATO on the adoption of a robust policy towards Moscow, preferably based on containment, bilateral US-Polish security ties and the strengthening of the Alliance's eastern flank (Radio Poland, 13 August 2015, 4 November 2015).

Ideas all the way through: Constructivism vis-a-vis alternative explanations of Polish foreign policy

Poland's thick Europeanisation since 1989 represents a story of how the Polish Self and its Western Other negotiated the boundaries of their commonality, whereby Poland's ideational affinity and normative compatibility with the West met with the latter's consistent acceptance, inclusion and support. Hence, the process of mutual identification shaped the discursive and behavioural manifestations of Poland as a Central and East European trailblazer in integrating with the Euro-Atlantic community. And to reinforce and reconfirm the robustness of this interactive Constructivist perspective, I argue that alternative explanations of the development of Polish foreign policy do not stand up to scrutiny.

In the 1990s, the absence of other feasible options ahead of Poland's course of action other than joining the West, did not mean that Warsaw simply submitted to strategic necessities and external pressures. For instance, one potential alternative to integration was neutrality, requiring the major powers to respect a neutral country's status, the ability to avoid being drawn into conflicts and the possession of the necessary capabilities to defend one's territory. None of which conditions, however, could be realistically met from Poland's perspective. The highly unstable situation in the Soviet Union, the uncertainties surrounding Germany's recognition of its border with Poland and Central Europe's historical experience (above all the division of spheres of influence on the part of the great powers at Yalta) provided little confidence that external powers (particularly Russia) would refrain from domineering and unjust policies towards Warsaw (Cottey, 1995:16-17).

Another potential alternative was reliance on a pan-European security system focused on the CSCE/OSCE. But both theory and history suggested that defining an act of aggression and determining whether and how to respond would be hard to achieve in a credible way. For example, a reason why the League of Nations collapsed was that its members failed to agree on whether and how to oppose aggression. This was so especially given the fact that formal security guarantees and the commitments of member states attached to them were not enshrined in a legally binding manner in the CSCE/OSCE (Cottey, 1995:22). Also, the creation of a Central European regional security system was hardly feasible both because of the limited military and economic capabilities of Poland, Hungary, the Czech Republic and Slovakia—all inherited inefficient armed forces, which needed significant modernisation, and because of little enthusiasm in these countries for the construction of a regional grouping (Cottey, 1995:18, 24; Kuźniar, 2015; Waszczykowski, 2015, interviews).

Therefore, there were no viable options that could ensure Poland's security in the post-Cold War period other than entry into the Euro-Atlantic institutions. But as Polish experts and decision-makers agree and as the analysis in this chapter has shown, the absence of feasible alternatives did not entail a path of Europeanisation solely determined by geopolitical considerations. Instead, identity informed the interpretation of where the country's security and economic future lay so that Poland's strong positive identification with Europe and the US excluded the range of other conceivable courses of action (Kuźniar, 2015; Waszczykowski, 2015; Kościński, 2015; Nowak, 2015; anonymised participant, 2015, interviews).

Similarly, Realist perspectives that aim to explain Warsaw's ambition to be an important player in the EU in the 2000s and 2010s as the result of relative power and size cannot be wholly sustained. As against an argument which holds that Warsaw's assertive style in the EU is related to the country's relative position as the 6th biggest state by territory, the 7th biggest by population, possessing the 5th largest military (Global Firepower, 2016), I mount two objections. First, it was because of the different ways in which PiS and the PO harnessed the subjective elements of projecting national goals on the EU level (through confrontation or persuasion and consensus-building) that their uploading of initiatives enjoyed different levels of durability, effectiveness and reception by the rest of the European states. And this was so despite the fact that between 2007 and 2009 objective factors such as economic capacity did not change significantly (Copsey, Pomorska, 2010:6; Kaminska, 2010:2-3). Such a perspective corroborates previous research according to which it is not only 'objective' variables such as population and economic weight that contribute to the ability to upload national objectives onto the EU level but also 'subjective' aspects. The latter include the intensity of a state's policy preferences, its capacity to carry out persuasive advocacy of its position and participate in informal bargaining, the domestic political strength of the government, the efficiency and professionalism of the national civil service (Copsey, 2010:6; Kaminska, 2010:2-3).

Second, Poland cannot neatly be categorised as a big power since it straddles a number of European demographic, economic and political boundaries between the EU's major and small players (Longhurst, Zaborowski, 2007:88; Gebert, 2012). Although Poland's GDP expanded by 46% in a decade and income inequality dropped to the EU average, the country's GDP per capita is still lower than that of some of its Central European peers. Real earnings remain less than a third of their German equivalent, with Poland's overall contribution to the EU budget being around 3% in contrast to Germany's 19%, and France's 16% (Pawlak, Goettig, 2015; Statista, 2016). Moreover, although Warsaw's aim is to take a central part in European decision-making, it still lies outside the Eurozone, which means that Poland is not yet fully integrated in the EU's political and economic arrangements (Gebert, 2012). All of these condition the country's awkward position as a state that is large by territory and population but is weak on a range of economic indicators.

So 'size' has become a hindrance to determining the conduct of Polish foreign policy on the basis of big-power ambitions (Longhurst, Zaborowski, 2007:88). Instead, as Jerzy Nowak and Roman Kuźniar pointed out, due to Poland's cultural-historical affinities with the West as well as its interests stemming from its status as a country located at the heart of Europe and sharing political and economic characteristics with both the big and small powers in the EU, the soundest foreign policy strategy is one based on the promotion of closer EU cooperation rather than on the go-it-alone principle (Nowak, 2009:12; Nowak, 2015; Kuźniar, 2015, interviews).

6 Neither In, Nor Out
The Ambivalent Europeanisation of Bulgarian Foreign Policy

Bulgaria's hesitant overthrow of communism and subsequent far from unequivocal enthusiasm to return to Europe prefigured the image of a country that lags behind its Central European counterparts in building a liberal democracy, market economy and integrating in the Euro-Atlantic community. As in the Polish case, it was the dynamic between Self and Other in bordering the limits of mutual belongingness that conditioned Bulgaria's Europeanisation since 1989. Yet, unlike Poland, Bulgarian Europeanisation took on an ambivalent — rather than thick, character.

Loose ties: Constructing Bulgaria and Europe

Bulgaria's ideational scene has historically been defined by the tortuous development of nation-state identity and continuing phenomenon of divided loyalties — between Western Europe as an all too frequent distant paragon of progress and Russia as a culturally and emotionally close 'saviour'.

The concepts of 'state' and 'nation' are frequently juxtaposed by the Bulgarians, being historically loaded with a connotation of opposition. The distrust and disrespect characteristic of the subject Bulgarian population in relation to the Ottoman state-imperial structures — perceived as alien and oppressive, were carried over into the post-1878 independence period. Popular dissatisfaction arose as against the rapacious and self-serving political elite as well as the catastrophically pursued vision of the ideal nation-state, whose boundaries always far exceeded those of the actual Bulgarian state at any given time. That is, this was the ideal enshrined in the 1878 Treaty of San Stefano granting Bulgaria extensive territories from the Black Sea to the Mediterranean and Macedonia, but which were divided by the 1878 Congress of Berlin and whose unification was a key motive for Sofia's involvement in the Balkan and

World Wars of the 20th century. During communism, the state was likewise viewed as a distant, threatening and repressive force, which since 1989 has further found expression in the delegitimation of the political elite and state institutions.

Similar to Russian and Polish, the Bulgarian language distinguishes between the terms *narod* and *natsiya*. The latter denotes the political construction of the nation on the basis of rights, laws and institutions ensuring the freedom and equality of its citizens (Raichev, 2009). The former concept is more akin to 'ethnicity' and a seemingly primordial blood relation among the people, which tends to dominate in the national psyche. The narrative of Bulgarian nationhood emerging in the 19th century was rooted in the historical myth of past glory dating back to medieval times and in a story of national unity constituted by the natural bond of 'brotherhood' that not everybody can share into (Nancheva, 2012:152-153).

This ideal of national unity has both domestic and international consequences. The proverbial Bulgarian 'tolerance' and 'ethnic model' refer to peaceful coexistence as opposed to assimilation, considered impossible, given that the Turkish and Roma minorities do not share the same blood origins as the ethnic Bulgarians. Bulgaria's ethnic model also refers to the presence of a political party claiming to represent the interests of the ethnic Turks, yet encapsulating and isolating rather than emancipating socially and economically its ethnic electorate (Nancheva, 2012:154-155; Zhivko Georgiev, 2015; Dimitrova, 2015, interviews). Moreover, the emphasis on blood links has further implications regarding attitudes to the Macedonian national community, which, although living within the boundaries of its own state, is nonetheless considered connected to the Bulgarian nation by virtue of shared blood. The Macedonians are historically framed as 'brothers', who are members of the primordial ethnos (Nancheva, 2012:155-156).

Another facet forming a key part of Bulgarian nationhood is linked to 'territory', which entails some crucial foreign policy implications. A vital element of Bulgaria's foreign policy identity and geopolitical self-awareness is related to the country's central geographical location on the Balkan peninsula that is also interpreted to be the geostrategic and civilizational crossroads between Europe and Asia. An important consequence of this dimension of territoriality encompasses the narrative of victimisation by the great powers, whose conflicting interests in the Balkans unjustly deprive Sofia of freedom of manoeuvre and subject it to deleterious consequences (i.e., the loss of land). Such discursive victimisation coupled with the memory of betrayal (by Bulgaria's neighbouring allies after the First Balkan War) and defeat (in the Second Balkan and World Wars) serve to shift blame for foreign policy failures to outside culprits and condition passivity in international relations that culminates in a 'satellite syndrome' (Nancheva, 2012:159-160; Kavalski, Zolkos, 2007:12-13). This syndrome is expressed in a reactive conduct of Bulgarian foreign policy, which follows already established agendas rather than contributing to the design and formulation of new ones (Dinkov, 2003; Nikolov, Simeonov, 2009:84; Shopov, 2007).

In the post-1989 period and particularly during the 1990s, the main perspectives of Bulgarian nation-state identity were expressed on the axis of 'post-communism' vs. 'anti-communism', which embodied traditional historical divisions between 'Russophiles' and 'Russophobes' and mapped onto the contemporary party-political opposition between the Bulgarian Socialist Party (BSP) and the Union of Democratic Forces (UDF). Although both parties, dominating the political scene until 2001, were in favour of the European integration of Bulgaria, of good-neighbourliness and institutionalised cooperation, they differed along at least three attitudinal and policy dimensions. The first difference was related to the speed with which the democratic and market economic reforms had to be carried out. The UDF opted for a quick, shock therapy policy, while the BSP preferred a gradualist approach. The second difference was in terms of the parties' willingness to bring the country into NATO, which was pursued in a decisive manner by the UDF unlike the BSP's initial outright opposition and later begrudging acceptance. Third, the parties differed with regard to the overall determination with which the pro-Western course of Sofia's foreign policy was pursued. The UDF favoured a single-minded implementation of the Euro-Atlantic vector, whereas the BSP attempted to balance relations with

Western Europe, the US and Russia. The other influential party in the 1990s (and until today) was the Movement for Rights and Freedoms (MRF), whose liberal and Euro-Atlantic orientation was overshadowed by the commonly perceived 'ethnic' character of the party, aiming to represent the voice of the ethnic Turks and guarantee their inclusion in national politics (Katsikas, 2012:44-52, 54-58, 70-72).

Since 2001, the bipolar model of party competition has been dismantled not least as a result of the emergence of centre-right populist parties, which have amalgamated various identity positions related to leftist and rightist stances (such as the degree of state intervention in the economy, social and tax policy) and mixed a pro-Western course of behaviour with pro-Russian attitudes and initiatives. Such parties have included the NDSV (National Movement Simeon the Second, later called National Movement for Stability and Progress) and GERB (Citizens for the European Development of Bulgaria). Moreover, after 2005, the nationalist party ATAKA appeared, advocating exclusivist, xenophobic, anti-Western, anti-EU and anti-NATO views. VMRO (Bulgarian National Movement) and NFSB (National Front for the Salvation of Bulgaria) also established themselves as nationalist political forces, albeit occupying more critical stances towards Russia than ATAKA. Nationalist parties have nonetheless had a circumscribed impact on Bulgaria's foreign relations.

The Bulgarian Self and the Western Other in the boundary-drawing process of identification

The core characteristics of the Self and Other theorised in Chapter 3 as exerting a significant impact on the process of drawing mutual boundaries particularly in times of crisis could also be identified in the Bulgarian case. The Bulgarian Self's ideational liminality, heightened imitation and need for positive distinctiveness were coupled with the West's power capacities and consequential actions, which defined the degree of Sofia's acceptance within the Euro-Atlantic community.

A liminal ideational crisis has been present in Bulgaria since 1989 and especially in the 1990s. It has taken the form of an ideational predicament that has its roots in the country's history, which points to the persistence of permanently liminal conditions both before and after the collapse of the communist system. The post-communist experience brought about generalised social pessimism, distrust in public institutions and (relative) civic disengagement due to the transformational social-economic challenges. The loss of individual social status began to be contrasted with the idealised socialist past that provided secure income for everyone. Disappointment in democratic and market reforms followed suit and it was thought that the transition benefited the politically connected individuals. Constant—and unflattering to Bulgaria, comparisons with the living standards in Western Europe created further disenchantment (Sardamov, 2007:3-5). On the level of the political elite, political instability, the fluid institutional and party-political environment, the frequently resurfacing discussions about the strength of Bulgaria's Euro-Atlantic commitments and the unresolved question about finding a proper grounding for relations with Russia were exacerbated by the liminal post-1989 conditions. Liminality was characterised by the ongoing accumulation of experience, habits and expertise on the part of the governing class to operate within a democratic political environment and in the Euro-Atlantic geopolitical configuration (Sardamov, 2007:3-5).

Post-communist vicissitudes have to be placed in the context of a much more long-term existential crisis of identity, induced by frequent and wholesale ruptures in the country's social, political, economic and international environment. Three historic ruptures have been notable. 1878 marked the achievement of independence from the Ottoman Empire and subsequent attempts at integration with Europe. In 1944, the communist system was instituted and firm anchoring in the Soviet sphere of influence took place. 1989 inaugurated the democratic transformation and alignment with the West. All of these fundamental changes brought about deep-seated dislocations in the governing political class, ownership of property, societal values and external orientation, which contributed to a sense of status insecurity and a loss of stable normative guideposts (Danov, 2014:9; Avramov, 2007:17-49).

In such conditions of identity crisis, the need for a significant Other that can be emulated and whose recognition can affirm the state in its international role aspirations has been an inseparable element of Bulgaria's permanent liminality. The country's key significant Other is (Western) Europe, which has been perceived both as a utopian, superior form of social, political and economic organisation to be imitated, and as a sometimes hostile, exclusive and distant cultural entity that does not sufficiently appreciate the states in its periphery.

Thus, on the one hand, 'Europe' has been historically synonymous with modernisation, progress and prosperity. This has been so since the national awakening and restoration of Bulgaria's statehood in the 19th century when Western Europe was used as a template for the organisation of social and political life. During communism, the West of the European continent remained an idealised, economically prosperous Other in popular imagination. In the post-1989 period, another wholesale attempt at implementing the European model in the form of democratisation, marketisation and integration in the Euro-Atlantic community has been carried out (Todorov, 1999:6; Katsikas, Siani-Davies, 2010:1-2, 7-8, 11-12; Wydra, 2008:71-72).

On the other hand, the main ideational manifestation of difference and potential exclusion of Bulgaria from European civilization is related to the concept of 'the Balkans'. As Todorova's study pointed out, a negative image of the Balkans crystallised in the West European consciousness in the 18th and 19th century, whereby if Europe set the standard of civilization and progress, the Balkans were characterised by backwardness, perpetual strife, tribal warfare and resistance to modernisation (Todorova, 2009; Bechev, 2006b:7). Such a characterisation of the Balkans has been the result of Western attitudes and stereotypes, which however also mapped onto some 'objective' cultural-historical differences and political self-attributions (Kuus, 2004; Mishkova, 2018). Having been incorporated into the Ottoman Empire, the Bulgarians remained on the periphery of the great social, political and economic transformations taking hold in Western Europe. The Reformation, the Enlightenment, the Industrial Revolution, the French Revolution contributed to the development of liberalism, democracy, the rule of law and free market enterprise as core values of the ideal-typical model of European-ness. Yet, these values became an imported — and superficially understood, rather than an organic part of Bulgarian national identity as the Bulgarians emulated them in the process of catching up with the West rather than experiencing them as part of long-term indigenous historical development (Baeva, 2015; Marcheva, 2015, interviews). Hence, for example, in post-1878 independence Bulgaria, the party-political labels of 'liberals' and 'conservatives' masked a substantive ideational divergence from West European conceptions. The Bulgarian conservatives rejected the ideas of the free market and the non-interventionist state, forming otherwise the core of conservative ideologies in Europe. In turn, the Bulgarian liberals identified with the West on the basis of cultural sympathies but the key liberal idea of support for individual rights and freedoms was transformed into majoritarian populism (Avramov, 2007:326; Crampton, 2007).

Furthermore, apart from Western Europe, Russia is also a significant Other for Bulgaria. The Bulgarians and the Russians share similar languages and the Orthodox Christian religion. Bulgaria owed its liberation from the Ottoman Empire to Russian military and diplomatic activities and therefore Russia was central to the restoration of modern Bulgarian statehood (Rusev, 2005:2-3; Stankova, 2010:45). Nevertheless, Russia has also been perceived as an obstacle to the country's European path of development. Prior to and after the Cold War (when Bulgaria emulated obediently the Soviet social and political model), the majority of the Bulgarian elite and society considered Europe to be the model of modernisation. And the latter was adopted despite the authority of Moscow with its halo of liberator because Russia was perceived as politically and economically backward in comparison with the West (Stankova, 2010:45; Todorov, 1999:7; Katsikas, Siani-Davies, 2010:10-11).

On the whole, (Western) Europe and Russia are key significant Others for Bulgaria. Europe represents an example of social, political and economic development, while Russia plays an important role in the realm of the Bulgarians' cultural sensibilities and emotional attachments linked to religious, ethnic, linguistic similarities and historical gratitude. These overall positive perceptions condition an ambiguity about Bulgaria's Western vs. Eastern civilizational and foreign policy orientation. The ambiguity consists in the recognition of the Bulgarians' points of resemblance and favourable attitudes to both Europe and Russia, while also acknowledging a degree of difference from both of them.

On the one hand, Bulgaria may aspire to liberal democratic, market economic values but, as with other Balkan states, its form of (formerly aggressive) nationalism was born of religious, seemingly primordial ethnic ties and of the memory of past glory rather than of democratic patriotism, attachment to civic rights, liberties, the rule of law and the accountability of public institutions, prevalent in West European societies. On the other hand, the individualistic dispositions of the Bulgarians shaped by the fact that Bulgaria has historically been a country of the small land-owner and mobile entrepreneur is hard to square with the more autocratic and collectivist principles of organisation of the Russian state and society. On the level of the political elite, this civilizational ambiguity runs between the divisions of Russophiles and Russophobes. The Russophiles show greater readiness for foreign policy engagement with Moscow and are warier of Europe's exclusionary practices. The Russophobes prefer the Western internal-organisational model and international leadership, opposing closer political ties with Russia not least due to the latter's imperialistic-authoritarian conduct. But the ambiguity additionally runs within these two groupings: the Russophiles also accept Europe as a model of modernisation and the Russophobes acknowledge the Bulgarians' social sensibilities to the Russians (Atanassov, 2000:55; Abrasheva, 2015, interview).

Finally, the US takes a less historically loaded place as a significant Other in Bulgarian identity, given the weak cultural, social and political ties to America prior to 1989, complemented by Cold War-era ideological opposition. The overall imagery of the US is that of a distant and also admired part of the Western Other, which perception was the subject of one of finest pieces of Bulgarian literary works of the early 20th century. In Aleko Konstantinov's (2013) book, America is regarded for its technological prowess, economic success and freedom, and yet criticised for loss of spirituality, coldness and alienation among the people as contrasted with (alleged) Bulgarian warmth and socially harmonious relationships.

Moreover, the US and NATO were not immediately seen as security guarantors after 1989, given the Bulgarian historical experience. In the country's strategic culture and popular consciousness, Moscow is accorded the role of liberator from the Ottoman Empire and a protector from the superior Turkish army during the Cold War, as Turkey is for Bulgaria a political-cultural negative Other and a security threat (Neuburger, 2004). The Ottoman period is represented as 'enslavement', responsible for destroying the Bulgarian medieval empire, which was at the centre of Orthodox Christian and Slavic religious and literary developments, and it was Russia that restored Bulgarian independence (Danova, 2013; Boneva, 2006).

Furthermore, how the Self-Other relationship played out in the Bulgarian case also depended on core characteristics of the Western Other, especially linked to the latter's capabilities. Western Europe has been immensely more powerful, which, matched by Sofia's striving to catch up economically, politically and culturally with the developed countries on the continent, intensified the Bulgarian receptivity to foreign models and normative guidance (Todorov, 1999:6). The process of Europeanisation has additionally been significantly affected by the degree of Western support and recognition granted to Bulgaria over the course of critical, externally-led actions and developments. These have been linked to the decision of whether and how Bulgaria should accede to the EU and NATO—on an equal footing with the Central European frontrunners, or as part of the category of Balkan laggards.

Bulgaria and Europe in action, 1989-2015: A story of ambivalent Europeanisation

The characteristic features of the Bulgarian Self and its Western Other were prominently manifested in the critical circumstances following the collapse of communism and their mutually constitutive interaction produced Bulgaria's ambivalent Europeanisation. This ambivalent form of Europeanisation can also be described as 'formalistic' and 'superficial'. On the one hand, the West's tenuous commitment and lack of sufficient economic and diplomatic support produced disappointments among the Bulgarian political class at the country's perceived exclusion. On the other hand, the international ambivalence interacted with similarly ambiguous domestic Bulgarian views and actions, defined by a less strong cultural-historical affinity with the West, greater contestation of the pro-Western foreign policy course and a more acrimoniously and slowly reached consensus on the Euro-Atlantic integration of the country. As a result, formalistic Europeanisation was produced by the prevalence of situational behavioural normative adaptation in foreign policy coupled with general (yet not always consistently sustained) discursive compliance with European values but mostly devoid of deeply held convictions and ideational internalisation.[13] This was further complemented by Sofia's uncertainty about how to combine the Western and Eastern dimension of its external relations, in turn creating doubts in the EU and NATO about the sincerity of Bulgaria's pro-Western course. Yet, neither Western Europe's and America's, nor Bulgaria's ambivalences were too extensive and deep-seated as to prevent gradual Europeanisation, which by the end of the decade had become a commonly agreed upon priority of the state (albeit less robustly and successfully pursued than in Poland).

---

13 In this context, 'adaption' and 'compliance' do not simply imply cost-benefit rationalist calculation; rather, civilizational ambivalence conditions the inability to pursue with ideational determination and consistency a given course of behaviour so that imitative performativity proliferates.

The ambivalence of Bulgaria's Europeanisation has persisted over time, although the decades of the 1990s and 2000s-2010s respectively imparted different tasks and challenges. During the 1990s, the challenges ahead of Bulgarian foreign policy were related to the arduous process of achieving a consensus on the country's external orientation and receiving corresponding international recognition of that orientation in the midst of an acute identity crisis and normative disorientation. Both of these internal and external challenges were met by the close of the decade. In the 2000s and 2010s, foreign policy-makers focused on the (more mundane) tasks of fulfilling the EU and NATO accession criteria and attempting to work out Bulgaria's meaningful contribution after gaining membership in the institutions of the Euro-Atlantic community. All the while, however, the vigorous and symbolically-loaded domestic debates of the 1990s lost their intensity, the international uncertainty about Bulgaria's European credentials subsided into relative inattention and the country settled into an augmented ambivalence, as political actors with a doubtful ideational commitment to—but rhetorically aligned with, ideal-typical values took over key positions of authority (Mihaylova, 2015; Alexieva, 2015; Slatinski, 2015; Marcheva, 2015, interviews; Cholova, 2010:3-4; Dainov, 2013; Gocheva, Boncheva, 2012; Dempsey, 2014).

The story of Bulgaria's ambivalent Europeanisation, which follows, is presented through the discussion of how the Bulgarian Self and its Western Other each worked out their specific responses to the tests and trials of Bulgaria's post-communist transformation between 1989 and 2015. In the end, I show that it was ultimately the interactive definition of mutual boundaries between Self and Other that shaped Sofia's European path.

The Bulgarian Self, 1989-2000: A tortuous agreement

The examination of the belief systems and organisational features of the two main parties in the 1990s—the BSP (the former communists) and the UDF (the democratic reformers), as well as the nature and speed with which an internal political consensus about the country's foreign policy priorities was reached reveals long-term historical continuities. The post-1989 period embodied a cultural-historical tradition, where European norms retained an imported rather than indigenously developed character. This affected both the quality of Europeanisation—due to the UDF's somewhat formulaic rather than substantive promotion of European values, and the speed of Europeanisation in terms of Sofia's firm declaration of its EU and NATO membership goals—due to the BSP's lingering pro-Russian ideological and geopolitical sympathies. Thus, it was only in 1997, or seven years after the 1989 changes, that the political class reached a consensus about Bulgaria's Euro-Atlantic foreign policy direction. The consensus henceforth represented a general discursive overlay common to both the 'post-communists' and the 'anti-communists'. But overall normative compatibility with ideal-typical values remained superficial rather than deeply internalised.

The fragmented and unstable Bulgarian institutional landscape was enabled by, and in turn reinforced, the general identity malaise in the country. The ideational crisis could therefore be located both on the level of fundamental value and foreign policy orientation as well as on the level of institutions.

The domestic ideational setting

The UDF was the frontline political force that epitomised the desire to break from the past and forge Bulgaria's European future. The early formative period of the party was marked by an authentic spirit and strong enthusiasm for democratisation as well as for a civilizational and geopolitical 'return to Europe' (Mihaylova, 2015; Slatinski, 2015; Burudjieva, 2015; Dimitrova, 2015, interviews). This spirit was most conspicuously embodied by Dr. Zhelio Zhelev (President of Bulgaria, 1990-1997). His communist-era dissident activities and writings subtly drawing out the similarities between fascist dictatorships and socialist regimes; personal dignity and honesty earned him the status of an emblem of the Bulgarian democratic opposition. Moreover, the early reformist zeal of the UDF was inspired by the conviction that 'time' was on the side of the democrats. That is, even though 'space' belonged to the BSP as the most influential party still holding on to its significant political and economic resources after 1989, 'time' and the 'tide of the future' were believed to inexorably lead to the dominance of the liberal democratic, European vision for Bulgaria (Dimitrova, 2015, interview; National Parliament Proceedings, 1990:4, 6; National Parliament Proceedings, 1991:1).

However, as my interviews with Bulgarian experts of various political leanings concur, despite elements of a genuine democratic-reformist zeal, the overall ideational and organisational character of the UDF could not promote a sufficiently substantive — as opposed to a rhetorical and conformist behavioural, vision and practice of the transformation of the country along the key dimensions of ideal-typical European-ness (Mihaylova, 2015; Slatinski, 2015; Burudjieva, 2015; Dimitrova, 2015; Baeva, 2015; Zhivko Georgiev, 2015, interviews). This was so for a number of reasons.

The UDF was not a consolidated, unitary organisation but comprised a multitude of parties and movements, ranging from monarchist to environmentalist, and some of which were descended from pre-communist times such as the Bulgarian Agrarian National Union and the Bulgarian Social Democratic Party (Baeva, Kalinova, 2011:22; Dimitrov, 2000:3; Zhivko Georgiev, 2015, interview). The presence of the latter had by 1991 led to the marginalisation of the European integrationist discourse in favour of an overwhelming focus on nostalgic memories of an idealised Bulgarian democratic system that had existed between 1878 and 1944, where these parties had been central political players, deprived of such a role by the communists (Dimitrova, 2002:8-9). These memories began to be concretely embodied in revanchist policies (such as the hasty restitution of property) as well as in a fixation on anti-communism as a main form of political identification. This slogan aimed to negate the BSP and the communist legacy but lacked a well-elaborated future-oriented vision of what would happen after communism had been denounced (Abrasheva, 2015; Marcheva, 2015; Baeva, 2015; Alexieva, 2015, interviews).

The centralisation and establishment of a consolidated, unified party political structure initiated by Ivan Kostov's leadership (1994-2001) on the one hand introduced a much needed ideological and organisational coherence (of the UDF as a right-wing party). But on the other hand, political figures, who represented the reformist engines behind the party, were sidelined on account of their ideational incompatibility with and distance from the closed circle at the top of the party (Slatinski, 2015; Mihaylova, 2015; Baeva, 2015, interviews; Gospodinova, 2004). In his interview with me, Krastyo Petkov clarified that from his personal meetings with Kostov he could conclude that the UDF of the early 1990s disappeared (in the sense of its animating spirit), as for Kostov the struggle for power meant that economic assets had to be controlled and for that to happen a unified, like-minded party structure had to be created to execute the process of economic accumulation (Petkov, 2015, interview). So the 'radical' (i.e., categorical, uncompromising but lacking in sound ideational underpinnings) course towards economic reform based on accelerated privatisation resulted in the widespread perception (and reality) of the UDF government's (1997-2001) presiding over corruption on a similar scale to their BSP predecessors (Dawson, 2014:87).

In ideational terms, the UDF's conception of Europe was embodied in an economically neoliberal, politically anti-communist set of ideological views, which fell short of elaborating more fully on a number of other core aspects of liberal democracy (Dawson, 2014:82). The liberalism of the UDF was rooted in economistic visions of the free market that never completely embraced the civic elements of Western liberal philosophy and practice both in terms of encouraging the development of a participatory, politically educated civic society and with regard to the enunciation of an inclusive, multi-ethnic, civic form of nationalism. (The party did not break convincingly from the exclusivist nationalist positions typical of the communist regime, as expressed, for instance, in the declared refusal to form a coalition government with the MRF as an 'ethnic' party in case of victory in the 1997 elections) (Dawson, 2014:82, 87-89). At the same time, as Minchev stresses, the UDF's insistence on transposing the West European experience on Bulgaria was turned into an uncritical admiration for all things foreign. The

Europeanisation effort took on an abstract and moralising character, whereby all things local were flawed and backward. Yet, this approach structured the party political scene in such a way that positions extolling the virtues of national traditions began to be intertwined with anti-European standpoints (as in the rise of nationalist party ATAKA in the 2000s) (Minchev, 2015; Hristo Georgiev, 2015, interviews; Minchev, 2013:1-2).

As regards foreign policy, 'radical' anti-communist change for the UDF meant maximally breaking away from Bulgaria's former Soviet-centred international configuration in favour of integration in the Euro-Atlantic community, which, however, became a pronounced foreign policy trend after 1997. Up to that point, the nostalgic focus on the past and the absence of well-thought out ideational standpoints sidelined a more forward-looking discourse on Europeanisation and led to ambivalent stances on Bulgaria's Euro-Atlantic integration. That is, early on the UDF denounced the principles of 'peaceful coexistence' and 'socialist internationalism' as in practice leading to Bulgaria's complete isolation from the West where borders represented a cordon sanitaire. The party called for the conduct of a moral foreign policy supporting democratisation around the world and stood for integration in Europe. But the UDF nevertheless favoured a more CSCE/OSCE-centred European international system so that both the Warsaw Pact and NATO would be dissolved (UDF electoral platform, 1990). And once the UDF settled on a course towards Bulgaria's membership in both the EU and NATO and the conduct of cooperative regional relations, Europeanisation began to be equated with the imitation of West European behaviour and pursuit of the goal to prove that 'we are good pupils of the West'. Such a focus on behavioural obedience as opposed to forging substantive discussions and understanding of European values hampered the process of internalising these values by virtue of a well thought-out convictional adherence (Slatinski, 2015; Hristo Georgiev, interviews; Avramov, 2007:316-317).

If the substance of Bulgaria's Europeanisation was affected by the nature of the ideational character and corresponding organisational features of the UDF, the speed of the process was further slowed down by the tortuous evolution of the BSP's party-political identity. It was only after 1997 that the socialists began to demonstrate fully-fledged acceptance of some of the key tenets of European-ness in the form of moving away from exclusivist nationalist stances; transforming the BSP from a 'communist' into a social democratic party of the West European type; strategically re-orientating from the East (Russia) towards integration into the EU as well as NATO; and multilateral, consensus-based international relations.

Up to 1997, the BSP supported Bulgaria's EC/EU membership but it was strongly sceptical of the country's possible NATO accession and sought to keep close ties with Russia and the rest of the post-Soviet states (Lukanov, May 1990; National Assembly Proceedings, 1995:1-2; Dimitrov, 2000:2-3; Katsikas, 2012:44-52). So like their Polish counterparts, the Bulgarian socialists were committed to building up links with the EC/EU. But unlike the SdRP/SLD, the BSP did not think that EU membership was intertwined with NATO membership (Lukanov, May 1990; Dimitrov, 2000:2-3; Katsikas, 2012:47). All of these positions amounted to the pursuit of a 'balanced' and even neutral foreign policy, equidistant from West and East (Georgiev, 2011:49). Pro-NATO Bulgarian officials saw through these foreign policy formulations the BSP's lingering Gorbachevian conception of the 'common European home' and affinity with post-Soviet Russia's tendency to promote a pan-European, CSCE/OSCE- rather than NATO-based vision of security on the continent (Ratchev, 2015; Primatarova, 2015, interviews). According to Primatarova's recollections of her involvement in the foreign policy debates at the Ministry of Foreign Affairs, up until 1997, BSP officials endowed the term 'Euro-Atlantic' with a meaning that encompassed the EC/EU and the CSCE/OSCE but excluded NATO as primary providers of security, which was a way of incorporating Russia into trans-Atlantic security arrangements. However, such an understanding of Euro-Atlanticism clashed with the Western conception of EU and NATO expansions as interlinked, parallel and reinforcing processes, with the Alliance representing a cornerstone of European security (Primatarova, 2015, interview).

It should be noted, however, that there existed reformist, liberalising tendencies in the BSP prior to and after 1989. As insiders to socialist circles relate, party reformers such as Andrey Lukanov, Ognyan Doinov, Grisha Filipov favoured the initiation of a social democratic political platform (Decree 56, 1989) along the German or Austrian model and preferred relations with the USSR and then Russia to be kept at a level that would not jeopardise Bulgaria's entry into the EC/EU. They were also ready to accept NATO accession as a forerunner of Sofia's EU membership (Marcheva, 2015; Petkov, 2015, interviews). And this contrasted with the conservative-minded party members such as Alexander Lilov and Zhan Videnov. Their more ideologically rigid views made them sceptical about social democracy and aimed at the preservation of Bulgaria's sovereignty through cooperation with the EC/EU and the USSR/Russia in order to counterbalance US 'imperialism' (Katsikas, 2012:48-51).

So it took two overwhelming shocks to to delegitimise any lingering communist-inherited indoctrination against the free market and cooperation with the West, particularly NATO. The first was related to the socialist government contribution to and failure to manage the 1996-1997 economic and financial crisis, engulfing the country into a spiral of hyperinflation, food shortages, bank bankruptcies. The second was the realisation that the Eastern vector in foreign policy was not a viable option after relations with Russia had sunk to a low following the 1994-1997 BSP government's decline of Moscow's overbearing demand for control over the Bulgarian gas pipeline system (Katsikas, 2012:45-48; Spirova, 2008:10-11; Dimitrova, 2002:10-11).

Bulgarian experts of both left- and right-leaning persuasions confirm that, at least rhetorically, the BSP renounced the communist principles of the dictatorship of the proletariat and the dominance of state ownership, accepting neo-liberal economic trends (Abrasheva, 2015; Baeva, 2015; Zhivko Georgiev, 2015, interviews). Moreover, the party toned down its nationalist stances and focus on state sovereignty in favour of European and SEE regional cooperation processes along standards of democracy and tolerance. This was not least because the socialists could not provide more than verbal opposition—rather than feasible policy proposals, to Western sanctions and military activities against Yugoslavia's regime with which the BSP shared political ties (Vigenin, 2015; Burudjieva, 2015; Minchev, 2015, interviews). Over the course of the 1990s, the BSP gradually (and grudgingly) overcame its resistance to Bulgaria's NATO membership, which process culminated at the 44th Congress in 2000 when party leader Georgi Parvanov fully affirmed and persuaded the socialists to accept Sofia's course towards Alliance accession. This evolution was conditioned primarily for purposes of legitimation. Once all alternative foreign policy directions such as 'equidistance' had proven unviable and the 1997-2001 UDF government had initiated the process of NATO integration so that support for Alliance membership began to be shared by two thirds of the Bulgarians by 2001 (Yordanova, Zhelev, 2002:38-44; Bedrov, 2014), the BSP had no other option but to accept NATO accession. The party had to do so if it wanted to return to power as a forward-looking political force that was not attempting to stop Bulgaria from the achievement of its Euro-Atlantic goals (Dimitrova, 2015; Abrasheva, 2015; Slavkova, 2015, interviews).

Overall, the UDF's performative adherence to West European ideas and the BSP's hesitations about embracing a firm pro-Western direction meant that in the early to mid-1990s Sofia's Euro-Atlanticism lacked a sufficiently deeply-rooted and well-elaborated ideational foundation that could inform a consistent and determined pursuit of Europeanisation. This mirrored the historical trend of 'importing' European principles without the necessary reflexivity and cultural tradition to facilitate ideational internalisation. Hence, my interviews with Bulgarian experts and policy-makers unanimously confirm that it was the catastrophic 1996-1997 economic and financial crisis that served as the overwhelming trigger and motivating factor for Bulgaria's Europeanisation. It led the BSP to reconsider its foreign policy positions and urged the UDF to finally abandon its previously amorphous ideational and organisational structure in favour of a more consistent discourse and policy for Bulgaria's Euro-Atlantic integration (Dimitrova, 2002:13; Slavkova, 2015; Primatarova, 2015; Ralchev, 2015; Burudjieva, 2015; Hristo Georgiev, 2015; Dimitrov, 2015; Nikolova,

2015; Abrasheva, 2015; Minchev, 2015; Ratchev, 2015; Mihaylova, 2015; Lessenski, 2015; Zhivko Georgiev, 2015; Dimitrova, 2015; Marcheva, 2015; Slatinski, 2015; Alexieva, 2015; Vigenin, 2015, interviews).

Ratchev specifically observed that Sofia's consensually-based Euro-Atlantic foreign policy platform did not emerge decisively out of Bulgaria's consistently strongly desired, intentionally pre-planned ideational and strategic choice. Rather, it was stimulated by the fear that there could be another crisis leading to the collapse of banks, hyperinflation and the drastic impoverishment of the population (Znepolski, 2015:51-59). EU and NATO membership began to be perceived as a panacea for domestic problems and the loss of capacity to manage them. And if by 1997 Leszek Balcerowicz had completed the shock therapy in Poland so that the Poles had a growing economy and a resource basis on which to build, Bulgaria was starting more or less from a resource-deficient political and economic scratch (Ratchev, 2015, interview).

The domestic institutional and party-political setting

The Bulgarian institutional, party-political environment in the 1990s was characterised by the acrimonious struggle for power between the BSP and the UDF as well as intra-party conflict and fragmentation. All of these contributed to general political instability, fluid government configurations and decision-making incoherence that further confused Bulgaria's European partners about the country's foreign policy direction (Burudjieva, 2015, interview).

For instance, the pro-Western diplomatic activity of the 1991-1992 UDF government was marked by poor coordination. The Prime Minister, the Foreign Minister and the President struggled for supremacy, often acting independently of each other. A point of divergence was related to Prime Minister Filip Dimitrov's focus of Bulgarian foreign policy on the US (as an ideological counterbalance to the BSP's pro-Russian orientation), which was countered by President Zhelev through his signing of cooperation agreements with France in 1992 and with Russia in the same year

(Dimitrov, 2000:4). Moreover, in an extreme case of political manoeuvring, Prime Minister Lyuben Berov (1992-1994) left the post of Foreign Minister vacant for almost half a year. This was so because Berov had to find a candidate that suited both the BSP and the MRF, on whose support his technocratic-branded government hinged (Engelbrekt, 1994b:21).

This institutional liminality was more fundamental than in Poland. If the Poles' identity crisis was confined to the challenges of constructing a stable liberal democratic political-institutional landscape, whose foreign policy consequences were contained by the ideationally-bound consensus on European integration, in Bulgaria the crisis was reflected on the level of ideas. It enabled and was in turn reinforced by institutional deficiencies in confusing the country's external orientation. Yet, the Bulgarian ideational-institutional predicament was not as deep as in Russia, where the unstable organisational and party-political environment went hand in hand with the delegitimation of the process of Europeanisation, as discussed in the next chapter. So it was only from 1998 onwards when cross-party consensus on joining the Euro-Atlantic community had been achieved that institutional structures were established for an administrative coordination of European integration not exclusively focused on the Foreign Ministry. Rather, coordination councils were created on the level of deputy ministers and ministers, thus uniting the effort at Europeanisation (Dimitrova, Toshkov, 2007:8-19). The achievement of a political consensus on European-ness based on a more consistent discursive embeddedness of regionally and internationally cooperative principles as well as membership in both the EU and NATO therefore alleviated institutional fragmentation and factionalism.

The Bulgarian Self, 2000-2015: Settling into ambiguity

The predominant bipolar political competition between the UDF and the BSP of the 1990s underwent a shift in the 2000s and 2010s towards the emergence of populist parties, particularly in the face of the NDSV and GERB. These parties continued the trend towards ambivalent Europeanisation in that they amalgamated various ideational positions in their attempt to appeal to all sections of society and the intellectual elite, thus aiming to conduct a 'balanced' foreign policy between the West and Russia. Moreover, the character and domestic practices of the populists exposed the Euro-Atlantic value-based rhetoric as more formalistic than substantive. So beneath the overall agreement on the importance of Europeanising foreign policy, East-West ideational and strategic ambivalences persisted both within populist parties and in the remaining broader distinction between centre-right and centre-left forces. Coupled with Sofia's limited capacity and historically informed international passivity, these ambivalences did little to contribute to a deep-seated European integration that included the ability to shape the EU's agenda rather than just follow already established lines of action.

A populist wave

The 21st century inaugurated significant changes in the Bulgarian domestic political scene. They began with the 2001 return to Bulgaria of former king Simeon Sakskoburggotski, crowned in 1943 and exiled by the communist authorities in 1946. His political movement, the NDSV, won by a landslide, putting an end to the UDF's and the BSP's bipolar domination of internal politics. This set a trend towards structuring party formation and competition through the charismatic appeal of a popular figure that stands above the mundane politics of 'left' and 'right', further perpetuating the dualistic quality of Bulgaria's Europeanisation.

On the one hand, the former king represented the symbol and hope for an accelerated process of becoming 'more European'. Simeon was the living legacy of the lost Bulgarian constitutional monarchy, which in the first half of the 20th century was undergoing rapid integration in European international relations and socialisation into Western political and cultural manners. Accordingly, he played heavily on his aristocratic blood connections to all major European royal families (Zankina, Gurov, 2009:18). Moreover, the former king included in his cabinet young

Western-educated and trained Bulgarian experts. This chimed with the population's desire to elect politicians that had already been schooled in European ideational and behavioural styles and would hence represent the country in a way that matched the Europeans' expectations (Burudjieva, 2015, interview; Katsikas, 2012:61-62).

On the other hand, Simeon's political appeal bore populist characteristics based on direct contact with the people to whom drastic social, political and economic transformation was pledged in 800 days. The NDSV also lacked a clear political identity in that it was a broadly liberal movement that advocated new morals in politics and rejected the establishment's partisanship. The public indeed greeted Simeon as a saviour who had come to rescue the long-suffering country from incompetent, corrupt and self-serving politicians (Cholova, 2010:3-4; Zankina, Gurov, 2009:21; Sakskoburggotski, 2001). In the foreign policy realm, the NDSV attempted to incorporate various societal attitudes. Bulgaria's European integration linked to joining the EU and NATO was accompanied by the maintenance of close ties with Russia, which would amount to balanced foreign relations (Ratchev, 2015, interview; Katsikas, 2012:61-62).

The populist trend that gained ground since 2001 was continued by Boiko Borissov (General Secretary of the Ministry of Interior, 2001-2005, Mayor of Sofia, 2005-2009, and Prime Minister, 2009-2013, 2014-2016, 2017-). In 2006, Borissov founded the political party GERB, which has located itself in the right-wing end of the political spectrum and has spoken in favour of European values and loyalty to the West especially in terms of close cooperation with Germany and the US (National Assembly Proceedings, 2009, 2014:2; National Security Strategy, 2011:2-3; Sofia Globe, 2014).

As Bulgarian experts concur, beneath the externally EU- and NATO-compliant rhetoric and behaviour, GERB has acted on a logic that does not necessarily adhere to the values embodied in the ideal-typical model of European-ness. Contrary to rule of law, liberal democratic principles, the party's actions have frequently been informed by authoritarian governance and a hierarchical organisational structure, held together by its leaders' charismatic appeal. Power-seeking motivations have been prominently manifested, all the while media, civic and business freedoms have steadily declined (Abrasheva, 2015; Minchev, 2015; Baeva, 2015; Mihaylova, 2015; Zhivko Georgiev, 2015; Marcheva, 2015, interviews; Dainov, 2013; Filipova, 2021a:63). GERB's external conduct centres on the idea that rhetorical and policy-making conformity to EU and NATO positions would buy European inattention to Bulgaria as a country that does not cause international trouble and sticks to the Euro-Atlantic direction. This European propriety in turn allows a free hand in domestic politics, seemingly making unnecessary serious discussions of Sofia's foreign policy interests and priorities as well as opening up space for manoeuvre in strengthening economic and political relations with Russia in consonance with the preferences of the Russophile sections of GERB's electorate (Katsikas, 2012:63).

Furthermore, despite the fact that populism became a key trend since 2001, the anti-communist vs. former communist opposition of the 1990s still persisted in the general distinctions that could be drawn between centre-right and centre-left parties and additionally contributed to the deepening ambivalence of Bulgaria's Europeanisation. Although experts agree that in the 2000s and 2010s there has been an overall, surface-level consensus on the Euro-Atlantic direction of Bulgaria's foreign policy, this consensus has been nuanced by the differing positions of rightist and leftist political forces, especially with regard to the ideational and strategic stances taken towards Moscow (Slavkova, 2015; Ralchev, 2015; Hristo Georgiev, 2015; Burudjieva, 2015; Abrasheva, 2015; Minchev, 2015; Lessenski, 2015; Dimitrova, 2015; Slatinski, 2015; Arndt, 2015; Vigenin, 2015, interviews).

When in power, centre-left parties such as the BSP and ABV (Alternative for Bulgarian Revival) tend to push for energy projects usually carried out with dominant Russian participation, including the Belene nuclear power plant, South Stream and Turkish Stream. These parties also take cautiously pro-Moscow positions, still conscious of the general EU and NATO strategic framework of Bulgaria's external relations in cases such as Western sanctions on

Russia (Slavkova, 2015; Minchev, 2015; Zhivko Georgiev, 2015, interviews). As Vigenin explained, the BSP does not question Bulgaria's continued belongingness to Euro-Atlantic institutions as a result of the process of Europeanisation within the party and membership in PES (the Party of European Socialists). Yet, the socialists are in favour of a balanced foreign policy that is focused on the development of political and economic ties with Moscow, which is believed to correspond to the majority of the Bulgarians' pro-Russian attitudes (Vigenin, 2015, interview; Borislav Angelov, 2015).

At the other end of the political spectrum, the decidedly pro-Western parties such as the Reformist Bloc (established in 2013 by politicians formerly belonging to the UDF and continuing to exist as a unified formation until 2016/2017) most consistently took anti-Russian stances. Russia's authoritarian political and economic model, attempts to revise the liberal international order and to continue to exercise domination over Bulgaria's politics and economics came in for particular criticism (Minchev, 2015; Zhivko Georgiev, 2015, interviews). For instance, Radan Kanev — former leader of one of the formerly constituent parties of the Bloc, qualified Russian foreign policy as representing a 'threat' to Bulgaria, condemning Moscow's neo-imperial stances as infringing upon Bulgarian sovereignty (Vchas.bg, 2014; Holmes, 2015).

Hence, the lingering opposition between the centre-right and centre-left has perpetuated the duality of Bulgaria's Europeanisation. This duality is informed by an oscillatation between a firmly pro-Western course in favour of deeper European integration and a preference for closer ties to Russia, which dilutes Sofia's Euro-Atlantic orientation and sympathises with the Russian authoritarian model.

Bulgaria's passivity

In additional to ideational ambivalence, Sofia's historically shaped 'satellite syndrome' makes it difficult to upload consistently and successfully domestically-inspired foreign policy initiatives on the Union level and thus to achieve thick Europeanisation as in the

Polish case, informed by both a policy-shaping as well as policy-taking role. This 'satellite syndrome' is complemented by limited resources and institutional capacity to carry out actively and sustainably external goals (Slavkova, 2015; Primatarova, 2015; Minchev, 2015; Shopov, 2015; Vigenin, 2015, interviews). That is, the habit of reactiveness circumscribes the ambition to develop a professionalised civil service and establish clear foreign policy priorities. These are further exacerbated by declining budget allocation to the Ministry of Foreign Affairs and the lack of substantial structural reform that would diminish the dominance of the personnel of the former communist secret services (Ralchev, 2015; Vigenin, 2015, interviews; Georgiev, 2009). As a result, despite Bulgaria's attempt to contribute to the European integration of the Western Balkans, the Black Sea area and the Caucasus, the practical successes of such 'uploading' of policy priorities have been limited and sporadic (Bechev, 2009:13; Shopov, 2015; Minchev, 2015; Lessenski, 2015; Shikova, 2015, interviews).

A cabinet's priorities thus tend to reflect the individual policy interests of Foreign Ministers rather than a continuous pursuit of well-defined state interests, backed up by a professionalised civil service providing constancy and sustained coalition-building with other EU member states within European institutions. For example, former Foreign Minister Nikolay Mladenov's strong focus on the Middle East included early involvement in the Tunisian transition after the Jasmine Revolution by pushing for the establishment of the Tunisian School of Politics and sharing Bulgaria's democratisation experience. The first meeting that gathered all the factions of the Syrian opposition was also organised. However, this policy push was not continued by Mladenov's successor, Kristian Vigenin. The latter laid an emphasis on Bulgaria's relations with the EP countries by engaging politically the Bulgarian minorities in Ukraine and Moldova and making the government in Sofia one of the first signatories of the Association Agreements with these states (Ratchev, 2015; Vigenin, 2015, interviews). And in turn this policy concern was sidelined by Vigenin's successor Daniel Mitov (2014-2016), whose priorities included deepening Bulgaria's Euro-Atlantic partnerships by joining the Eurozone and the Schengen agreement (Gyurova, Georgiev, 2012; Dnevnik, 2013; Vigenin, 2012; Petkova, Popov, 2015).

The alterations in and limited durability of foreign policy priorities also prevented effective coalition-building, persuasion and coordination efforts at the regional and EU level. Sofia's lobbying for an enhanced and less stringent integration process for Serbia may have contributed to the signing of the Stabilisation and Association Agreement between Brussels and Belgrade. But it did not suffice to convince countries such as the Netherlands and Belgium that the implementation of the Agreement should not be blocked on conditions linked to the apprehension and delivery of General Radko Mladic (once heading the Bosnian Serbs' army) to the International Criminal Tribunal for Former Yugoslavia. Instead, the credit for successfully arguing the case for Serbia's European integration went to Slovenia—the European Council President in 2008, and not to Bulgaria (Bechev, 2009:10). Also, as Vigenin shared from his personal experience as an MEP, the governments in Sofia behave too passively to be able to give clear and timely instructions to the Bulgarian representatives in the European Parliament so that the MEPs could weave Bulgaria's positions with the European one in the deliberation of policy issues such as the EP (Vigenin, 2015, interview).

Since becoming a member of the Union, Sofia has also aimed to involve itself more actively in regional cooperation schemes but it has done so primarily on the level of state administration level, contributing much less to intensifying dialogue on the political level (Minchev, 2015; Ralchev, 2015, interviews). Bulgaria's policy towards Macedonia has been generally friendly but passive based on the assumption that as 'brothers' the Macedonians have to be supported in their European aspirations (Minchev, 2013). Yet, such 'positive inertia' devoid of sustained bilateral high-level political dialogue has been mixed with a tacit backing for Greece in its name dispute with Macedonia. More overt suggestions made by Foreign Ministers Kalfin and Mladenov that Skopje's EU integration was not unconditional but depended on Macedonia's toning down of anti-Bulgarian propaganda and falsification of Bulgarian history were hardly conducive to building a solid relationship based on good will and anchored in the EU framework (Bechev, 2009:10; Gyurova, Georgiev, 2012:5).

Overall therefore, Bulgaria's attempts at uploading policy initiatives onto the Union level have been significantly circumscribed by the historically ingrained passive attitudinal and behavioural stance, reinforced by limited institutional capacity. And this passive disposition informed Bulgaria's ambivalent Europeanisation. The readiness to join common European policies (where they exist) has not been matched by sufficient ideational internalisation and the ability to shape rather than simply take policies and hence to avail itself comprehensively of the diplomatic avenues for foreign cooperation provided by EU membership.

The Western Other, 1989-2000: A deferred welcome

Over the course of the 1990s, the Western Other displayed a greater level of uncertainty and hesitation in recognising Sofia's European prospects, as contrasted with the much more eagerly enthusiastic and affirming policies towards Poland. Such uncertainties found a concrete expression in the provision of less extensive, continuous and committed support as measured by the slower pace with which Bulgaria was included in institutionally integrative schemes as well as the more limited diplomatic and economic assistance. All of this created disappointments — among at least the pro-Western part of the Bulgarian political elite, and activated historically-informed perceptions of exclusion from Europe on the basis of the Balkans' peripherality that does not live up to standards of European civilization. The absence of stronger external commitment additionally fell short of establishing an 'external anchor' for Bulgaria's transformation process.

However, the slow steps towards the acceptance of Bulgaria in the Euro-Atlantic family gradually assumed a more determined character so that by the end of the 1990s the EU and NATO granted Sofia a membership perspective. This was positively received in Bulgaria, encouraging, directing and providing a blueprint to the politicians to pursue inclusion in the Euro-Atlantic community on the basis of cooperative international politics, good-neighbourly regional relations and institutionalised integration.

The European Other's stances towards the Bulgarian Self were critically informed by the key EU, Council of Europe and OSCE-related developments that both promoted and delayed Bulgaria's Europeanisation.

The EU

The EU did eventually grant Bulgaria a membership perspective, providing a crucial confirmation of the country's aspirations to be recognised as part of the European family of nations. But it took the Union much more time to do so than in Poland's case. Brussels differentiated Bulgaria and Romania into a class of 'laggards' among the CEE states — motivated not only by the 'objectively' measured progress that Sofia and Bucharest were making towards meeting membership criteria. Admittedly, it was indeed the case that Bulgaria and Romania were lagging behind in their domestic reforms, but the EU member states' own historically-informed perceptions and interests regarding these two countries imparted to the technical task of fulfilling conditions a less than completely objective character.

In the post-1989 period, the unfavourable West European image of the Balkans (and of Bulgaria as part of the peninsula) endured and was further reinforced by the Yugoslav wars, which perpetuated the view of the Balkans as rife with ethnic strife, violence and fragmentation, making the region dangerous for political entanglements as well as economic investment (Baeva, 2015, interview; Bechev, 2006b:7-8; Stankova, 2010:59). The difference between the Western-oriented cultural, religious and economic traditions of Central Europe as opposed to the Byzantine and Ottoman heritage of Southeast Europe was also emphasised (Longworth, 1994; Kaplan, 1994; Schrameyer, 2009:80). And as Shikova has clarified, the lack of sufficient familiarity and more comprehensive knowledge of Bulgaria lent themselves to prejudicial treatment on the basis of the psychological principle that the more unknown something is, the more warily it is approached and the more easily negatively stereotyped it becomes (Shikova, 2015, interview).

Constitutive with these Western attitudes were the weaker historical, political and economic ties that key West European states have with Bulgaria. This conditioned a relatively marginal strategic and economic interest in Sofia on the part of the most influential EU countries (such as France and Germany) that could have otherwise sped up the pace of Bulgaria's European integration (as the final decision on enlargement is taken by the European Council where member states and their national perspectives are of crucial importance). Indeed, Sofia has not had the intense, if conflict-ridden, relations that have existed between Germany and Poland as well as the rest of the Central European countries. Geographically, Bulgaria is further east from the EU's centre of gravity in comparison to all of the other applicant states (Dimitrov, 2000:11-23). So as Bulgarian experts and policy-makers concur, Sofia lacked an external 'patron', whose special attitude, informed by cultural-historical affinity and density of links, would have motivated consistent diplomatic advocacy and in-depth political and economic support (Minchev, 2015; Nikolova, 2015; Ratchev, 2015; Shopov, 2015; Arndt, 2015; Shikova, 2015; Vigenin, 2015, interviews).

For instance, the German interest in Bulgaria was not as special, wide-ranging and intense as it was in Poland (Ratchev, 2015, interview). The relative lack of familiarity with Bulgaria led former German Ambassador to Bulgaria — Walter Lewalter, to confess in hindsight that the West Germans were slow to recognise the significance of the dissident movement that was taking shape in the late 1980s (most prominently embodied by the Public Committee for the Ecological Protection of Ruse). This prevented the early creation of contacts with the oppositional forces that could have aided the subsequent democratic transformation and international visibility of the country (Lewalter, 2009:67; Brahm, 2009:129). Also, former German Ambassador Christel Steffler has argued that Chancellor Kohl's first visit to Sofia in 1994 included many representatives of German business, as Germany was becoming the biggest foreign investor in Bulgaria. Yet, this show of support was modest in comparison to the fact that Kohl's first trip to Poland had already taken place five years before and German investments in the Polish economy were much more significant (Steffler, 2009:107-

108). Over the 1990s, Poland became Germany's top trade partner in CEE. In 1999, total Polish-German bilateral trade amounted to DM 51 billion, with the cumulative value of German FDI since the start of the Polish transformation standing at $40 billion (Małachowski, 2003:19, 21, 24). In stark contrast, in 1999, total German-Bulgarian bilateral trade was DM 2.3 billion, while the accumulated German FDI since 1992 equalled $401 million (Embassy of the Federal Republic of Germany to Bulgaria, 1901-1999). Overall, Southeast Europe received just over $300 per capita of Western FDI, compared with about $1200 per capita in Central Europe and the Baltics, during 1989-2000 (Demekas, Herderschee, McHugh, Mitra, 2002).

Hence, by going beyond the examination of EU integration policy based on objective criteria, one can take into account the variety of historically-informed political and economic motives behind Union (and individual members') policies, which contributed to the partial exclusion and differentiation between the lagging Bulgaria (and Romania) and the more advanced Central European states that would be the first ones to join the Union in 2004 (Mungiu-Pippidi, 2003:4). The 'acts of differentiation' that the EU conducted towards Bulgaria and Romania were linked to the refusal to invite them to negotiate accession in 1990; the attachment of a strong special clause on minority rights to Bulgaria's integration prospects in 1992; the decision to decline Bulgaria's and Romania's participation in the Luxembourg European Council, which itself created the queuing system of enlargement (Arfire, 2011:7-8; Hughes, Gordon, Sasse, 2004:25). Moreover, membership conditionality contained a significant degree of ambiguity since what constituted a stable democracy, functioning market economy or capacity to comply with and implement the acquis was not fully defined or subject to clearly benchmarked assessment. Conditionality was also not fixed in time but depended on the policy area, the country concerned and the political context (Bojkov, 2004:9-10; Hughes, Sasse, Gordon, 2004:26). The ambiguity and unfinished nature of membership conditionality thus increased the EU's power of discretion and selective operationalisation of the Copenhagen criteria. The progress reports prepared by the EU to measure the applicants' compliance were increasingly aimed at justifying the creation of waves of potential entrants by extolling the success of some countries and criticising others (Hughes, Sasse, Gordon, 2004:85-86). So through acts of differentiation, the EU exerted symbolic power not only over the notion of European-ness but also over the political-geographic identity of the Balkans in the 1990s, contributing to the normative (re)construction of the sub-regions of CEE — i.e., of the advanced Central Europeans and the Balkan laggards (Bechev, 2006b:21; Arfire, 2011).

As confirmed by my interviews with Bulgarian experts, the partial exclusion of Bulgaria and Romania was negatively perceived on the part of the Bulgarian policy-making and intellectual elite. Disappointments emerged at the country's sidelining in the European integration process and unequal treatment demonstrated in relation to Sofia, as contrasted with the much more favourable disposition and stronger support that the West provided to the Central European states (Shopov, 2015; Marcheva, 2015; Baeva, 2015; Primatarova, 2015, interviews). BSP Prime Minister Andrey Lukanov had to remind in 1990 that Bulgaria had made its contribution to the development of European civilization, which should not be forgotten by either Western Europe or the Bulgarians themselves. He further stressed the assets (and not just burdens) that Bulgaria would bring to a re-unifying Europe. These included the significant human resources, economic potential and a crossroads geographical location connecting Western Europe, the Soviet Union and the Middle East (Lukanov, May 1990).

Moreover, apart from Bulgaria's irritation over the EC's delay in approving the trade agreement with Sofia in 1993 (resulting in an estimated 200-million-dollar loss in trade revenues), German Chancellor Kohl's statement that priority would be given to the Central European applicants to the EC was negatively received by the Bulgarian foreign policy establishment. Prime Minister Lyuben Berov reiterated Bulgaria's aspirations to accede to all the major European institutions but in the absence of significant Western commitment, the country had to make considerable efforts to revive relations with Russia (Engelbrekt, 1994a:108-109).

UDF Prime Minister Ivan Kostov also made it clear in 1997 that the principle of a 'level playing field' in EU accession negotiations was of fundamental importance to Bulgaria. He acknowledged that better prepared countries would be able to complete the accession process earlier but the predetermined differentiation of applicants into groups would be demoralising (Kostov, 1997). Similarly, Foreign Minister Nadezhda Mihaylova declined to countenance the possibility of even temporarily isolating SEE from the dynamics of integration, deploring the policy vacuum that existed in Western policy-making circles about how to deal with the region. Mihaylova pointed out that Balkan countries' significance was downgraded, no provision for longer-term political and economic investment was made, with the better part of Western efforts focusing on establishing cooperation structures with Central Europe (Mihaylova, 1999:2-3).

Nevertheless, despite Western European ambivalences and partial delay of Bulgaria's entry into the EU, these ambivalences were not so strong as to turn Sofia away from the process of European integration. It was generally believed that Bulgaria did belong to European civilization and that it would eventually join the EU. Official documents of the early 1990s included Bulgaria as part of the CEE countries that would be subject to enlargement policy (Lewalter, 2009:66; European Council Summit in Edinburgh, 1992:105-106, in Copenhagen, 1993:13-18, in Madrid, 1995:6-7). Geopolitical considerations further catalysed the movement towards stronger Western engagement with Sofia.

The gradual incorporation of the country into European institutional schemes was received positively and encouraged the political elite to persevere in their integration efforts. Initially, Prime Minister Lukanov lauded the Agreement on Business and Economic Cooperation and Trade signed in 1990 with the EC as a symbolic confirmation of Bulgaria's political and economic return to Europe (Lukanov, May 1990). Also, although up until mid-1991, it seemed possible that Bulgaria may be left out of the negotiations for an Association/Europe Agreement (unlike Poland, Czechoslovakia and Hungary, which signed their respective agreements in 1991), European hesitation was transformed into more decisive action. Critical in this regard were political-strategic considerations linked to the attempted coup in Moscow in 1991; the dangers of a resurgent Soviet Union under a more conservative leadership; and Yugoslavia's descent into war threatening to destabilise the Balkans. Hence, the EC opened talks with Sofia on the Agreement and the two sides signed it in 1994 (Dimitrov, 2000:8; Papadimitriou, Gateva, 2009:13-14; Katsikas, 2012:92; Europe Agreement between the EC and Bulgaria, 1994).

Moreover, although the European Council Summit in Luxembourg (1997) excluded Bulgaria (together with Romania, Latvia, Lithuania and Slovakia) from the first group of applicants that were going to begin accession negotiations in 1998, the European Council changed its policy at Helsinki (1999) when Bulgaria and Romania were also asked to commence accession talks (Dimitrov, 2000:9; Papadimitriou, Gateva, 2009:15; Katsikas, 2012:94). Indeed, it had taken a war (i.e., the 1999 Kosovo conflict) for the EU to finally appreciate the importance of supporting Sofia in its European aspirations and to overcome the relative Western neglect of the region. The European Council decision in Helsinki came right after NATO's military activities in Kosovo. Over the course of the military operation, Bulgaria had offered its political and logistical assistance primarily by opening its airspace to North Atlantic forces and closing it to the Russian ones. It was in the aftermath of the Kosovo operation that British Prime Minister Tony Blair pledged full-hearted support for Bulgaria's EU membership (Dimitrov, 2000:9; Katsikas, 2012:95-96). The speech that Blair delivered at Sofia University in 1999 — in which he categorically stated his conviction that the European Council in Helsinki would have to invite Bulgaria to begin EU negotiations, is generally commemorated by Bulgarian experts and politicians as the first and only open show of patronage for the country's EU integration goals (Minchev, 2015, interview).

Similarly, the 1999 European Commission progress report for Bulgaria, which recommended that the country begin accession talks, was hailed by the Bulgarian political class as a symbolic milestone recognising Sofia's belongingness to the European cultural, political and economic space (European Commission, 1999). Prime

Minister Kostov and Foreign Minister Mihaylova acknowledged that Western Europe and the US appreciated Sofia's Euro-Atlantic solidarity, its civilised and consistently followed choice in favour of democracy, civic nationalism and the establishment of good-neighbourly regional relations (Kostov, 1999; Mihaylova, 1999). Mihaylova reiterated that Bulgaria considered the EU the cornerstone of the continent's structures of cooperation with the potential to play a main role in building a united Europe based on the principles of a liberal order (Mihaylova, 1999).

The Council of Europe and the OSCE

Apart from Bulgaria's engagement with the European Union, which maintained fundamental leverage in the country's 'return to Europe', the Council of Europe and the OSCE made additional contributions in this regard. Sofia's admission into the Council of Europe was the first occasion upon which the language of human rights, the protection of minorities and liberal democratic values was introduced in a clear and organised way in the Bulgarian domestic and foreign policy discourse (Shopov, 2015, interview). As Mihaylova clarified, due to the fact that Bulgaria was still relatively isolated in the international scene, the Council of Europe became a major reference point for the principled justification of Sofia's external actions, while Catherine Lalumière—the Secretary General of the organisation between 1989 and 1994, was the most frequently cited foreign policy authority among the Bulgarian politicians (Mihaylova, 2015, interview). Former Prime Minister Lukanov turned MP, assured Lalumière that his party (the BSP) had initiated Bulgaria's integration with the Council of Europe led by 'sincere democratic convictions' and the realisation that it was only integration in a united and democratic Europe that would provide the cultural, economic and political anchoring for the Bulgarian internal transformation (Lukanov, August 1992).

As regards the CSCE/OSCE, Bulgaria welcomed the signing of the Charter of Paris and the CFE Treaty in 1990 as codifying the principles on which a united, free, stable and peaceful European security architecture would be built, where Sofia could find its rightful place. Lukanov also argued that the CFE Treaty led to an unrivalled breakthrough in the reduction of weapons through a multilateral effort, dispelling a deeply rooted public fear that international disarmament was impossible (Lukanov, November 1990).

However, despite the fact that Bulgaria took part in the discussions on the Common and Comprehensive Security Model for Europe and the Charter on European Security, it made sure that these documents would not delay or substitute potential cooperation with the EU and NATO. The latter's legally binding arrangements and stricter conditions for membership were considered to provide a firmer security and civilizational anchoring in Europe (Ivanov, Atanassova, 2002:9). Moreover, although the CFE Treaty paved the way for disarmament and a general relaxation of tensions in the Balkans, it also froze strategic regional inequities to Bulgaria's disadvantage. The Treaty only took into account the quantitative dimension of the regional military balance, whereby Bulgaria would indeed maintain parity with Greece and Turkey after reductions. But in terms of the quality of equipment Sofia and Bucharest lagged behind Athens and Ankara. Such inequality was further exacerbated by post-communist economic difficulties and the West's increasing weapons transfers to Greece and Turkey to deter potential antagonists in the Eastern Mediterranean — neither of which issues' consequences for Bulgaria were considered by the West (Engelbrekt, 1994c:47).

So the Council of Europe and the CSCE/OSCE disseminated liberal democratic, human rights norms in Bulgarian political discourse. Yet, the impact of those organisations was diluted in cases of perceived exclusionary practices (from the EU and NATO) or strategic disadvantage and was ultimately confined much more to the early 1990s — before Sofia had received an EU membership perspective.

The American Other

In consonance with the European Other's doubts about how much and how fast Bulgaria could be included in European institutional arrangements, the American Other was similarly ambivalent about Sofia's acceptance into NATO integration schemes. In the absence of strong cultural-historical, political, economic and people-to-people ties between the US and Bulgaria, it was considerations of American national interest and assessments of the strategic relevance of SEE that would push the US's decision to draw Sofia closer into the transatlantic alliance. And for at least the first half of the 1990s, the Balkan region was thought to be of peripheral significance to Washington's European policy. Although the Clinton administration finally decided to get militarily involved in Bosnia through the deployment of NATO forces in 1995 and contributed to the restoration of peace at Dayton (due to the fact that US international leadership and NATO's credibility were at stake as the war raged on), this relatively growing engagement did not lead to a significant reassessment of American attitudes and interests in relation to the Balkans. There, as Secretary of State James Baker declared, 'the US did not have a dog in this fight'. So discussions about the necessity of withdrawal, minimal military presence and of Europe taking over responsibility for the region began to take place immediately after the situation in Bosnia began to improve (Daalder, 2002:7-11; Angelov, 2004:3).

In the context of the US's ambivalence about the importance of SEE in America's European policy, there was little readiness for NATO enlargement to the region (Ratchev, 2015, interview). As Solomon Passy has pointed out, the American attitude was not dissimilar to British Prime Minister Margaret Thatcher's blunt assessment of Bulgaria's chances for gaining membership in NATO. At a meeting in 1994, Thatcher reacted to Passy's eagerness for his country's swift admission to the Alliance by recommending to him to forget about the possibility of Bulgaria entering NATO before Poland because the West had surrendered the Poles to Hitler, which had incurred a moral debt to be repaid through speedier Euro-Atlantic integration (Passy, 2015:6).

In this way, sensing the highly likely prospect of being turned down in their bid for NATO membership, Bulgaria as well as other Balkan countries such as Romania demonstrated restraint in demanding that NATO provide an explicit pledge and a timetable for entry. This stood in contrast to the Visegrad states, which continuously called on the Alliance to make a definite commitment and promise a date for accession, assured as they were by Western perceptions of these states as more advanced in their reform process, more culturally but also geographically closer to the core of Europe, thus meeting the Western, and particularly German, interest in security and stability on the eastern borders (Engelbrekt, 1994c:42).

However, the 1999 Kosovo crisis led to a watershed in Western perceptions of the importance of the Balkans not least because ethnic strife and violence represented a normative threat to the legitimacy of the security community pattern of relations in Europe. Indicative of the growing realisation of this alarming prospect was US Secretary of State Madeleine Albright's statement that Southeast Europe is 'the critical missing piece in the puzzle of a Europe whole and free...That vision of a united and democratic Europe is crucial to our security. It cannot be fulfilled if this part of the continent remains divided and wracked by conflict' (Kavalski, 2005:6-8).

And so from that moment on—and as enshrined in NATO's Strategic Concept (1999), the Balkans became integral to the post-1999 European normative and security order. As Kavalski has observed, the year 1999 was for the Balkans the equivalent of 1989 for Central Europe. The new order required compliance with Euro-Atlantic normative standards, 'securitised' through a process of socialisation and a functional differentiation between the Euro-Atlantic partners in their socialising roles (the EU as a 'civilian power' and NATO as a hard-power organisation) aimed at constraining and modifying the foreign policies of the Balkan states. Then European Commissioner for Enlargement Günther Verheugen argued that the Alliance had to accept Sofia and Bucharest in order to avoid the difficult situation of permanent relegation to peripheral exclusion, renewed ethnic tensions and instabilities, which would result from a double rejection from both the EU and NATO (Kavalski, 2005:6-7; Angelov, 2004:4-7; Pierre, 1999; Ivanov, 2000:15-16; Parvanov, 2000:30-32).

In terms of concrete integration initiatives, prior to 1999 Bulgaria joined the PfP in 1994 and was a founding member of the Euro-Atlantic Partnership Council (EAPC) in 1997. Both the PfP and EAPC laid the foundations for Sofia's security policy and defence structures reform on the basis of the development of interoperability with the forces of the Alliance, the promotion of transparency in national defence planning and the establishment of democratic control over the military. In a speech on Bulgaria's signing of the PfP, President Zhelio Zhelev hailed the scheme as 'a momentous process that will help democracy strike strong roots in Eastern Europe'. Yet, he did not shy away from making it clear that the PfP was an intermediate goal on the way to Bulgaria's full NATO membership (Engelbrekt, 1994c).

Indeed, the PfP and the EAPC still remained vague about Sofia's accession prospects (Ivanov, Atanassova, 2002:17; Cragg, 1995). Bulgaria's further impetus to Europeanise its security policy, changing away from the 'old' mentality—as expressed in the belief that the military should be a black box impenetrable to outsiders, would take a firmer NATO commitment and stricter guidelines for membership (as concrete markers of Sofia's acceptance by the West), which crystallised in 1999 at the Washington Summit announcing the Membership Action Plan (MAP, 1999; Ratchev, 2014:7; Ivanov, Atanassova, 2002:17; Sotirov, 2000). Bulgarian experts concur that the MAP and the reinforced commitment to enlargement it enshrined by putting into place activities and criteria for fully-fledged membership were crucially important in the realm of values, professional military ethos and the evolution of the communist-era mind-set hitherto informed by a lack of transparency, authoritarian attitudes and bilateralism. NATO contributed to the Europeanisation of Bulgarian foreign policy identity by promoting the process of democratisation and transparency of security policies through the required adherence to political and economic liberties, the rule of law, the settlement of ethnic disputes and irredentist claims, peaceful and friendly international relations and the building of consensus (Ratchev, 2015; Dimitrov, 2015, interviews; Ivanov, 2000; Sotirov, 2000).

For instance, in the area of regional relations, security policy had to be based on a more democratic, regionally cooperative plane without historical and ethnic prejudices (Ivanov, 2000:14-18). To that end, the US promoted the establishment of the Southeast

European Cooperative Initiative, fostering political-military cooperation in the Balkans (Ratchev, 2015, interview; Šabič, Freyberg-Inan, 2012:266). Moreover, conforming to NATO standards entailed that the communist-era policy of maintaining a large but insufficiently modernised army had to give way to professionalisation, downsizing and greater efficiency. Defence official Ratchev has explained that at the time he prepared and presented to the politicians a drastic reform plan, whereby out of its 142000-strong army, 1447 tanks, more than 400 ships, hundreds of fighter jets and oversized artillery Bulgaria had to retain only a brigade in order to be in alignment with Alliance criteria (Ratchev, 2015, interview; Military Doctrine of Bulgaria, 1999: Article 93; Agenda 2004).

The increased Western commitment to Bulgaria's integration in NATO following the Kosovo conflict in 1999 therefore provided significant encouragement to Sofia's Euro-Atlantic aspirations and mobilised the political elite's effort to begin to conduct a security policy guided by the values embodied in the ideal-typical model of European-ness. The accelerated process of NATO accession also improved Bulgaria's EU integration prospects, impressing upon the Bulgarian political class that EU and NATO membership were inextricably linked. As Primatarova recalls, at a 1998 conference in Germany organised by the Regional Cooperation Council for the integration of SEE in the Euro-Atlantic space, German politician Gernot Erler said that before Bulgaria had received clear positive signals for its NATO membership and before Sofia had itself declared openly its aspirations towards Alliance accession, the country's EU application did not possess sufficient political weight (Primatarova, 2015, interview).

So once the ambivalences that both the European and American Other harboured in relation to Bulgaria's inclusion in Euro-Atlantic arrangements began to evolve towards a greater diplomatic and institutional commitment, Sofia's Europeanisation was accelerated. Western support promoted a more consistent Bulgarian discursive and policy-oriented adherence to a liberal international order, peaceful regional relations, democratisation of the military and institutionalised cooperation. Nevertheless, the

Bulgarian Self's insufficient internationalisation of these value positions meant that Europeanisation still retained its ambiguous quality.

The Western Other, 2000-2015: Distant togetherness

The push and pull nature of Bulgaria's relations with the West was carried on into the 2000s and 2010s. Developments within the North Atlantic framework of security, catalysed by 9/11 and the Iraq war, as well as the EU accession process confirmed Sofia in its pro-Western ideational and strategic choice and provided opportunities for expanding Bulgarian foreign policy activity not least through socialisation in Brussels fora. Yet, Western ambivalence about Bulgaria persisted. The impetus to integrate the country in the EU and NATO increasingly came from strategic considerations and the path dependence of the accession process rather than a symbolically-inspired commitment to Sofia's return to Europe. This created Bulgarian domestic political disappointments and a backlash in the form of growing nationalist and anti-Western sentiments, which perpetuated the dualistic and ambiguous character of Bulgaria's Europeanisation.

The American Other

9/11 and the war on terror dramatically increased the strategic significance of the Black Sea region, pushing it from the periphery to the centre of Western attention and underscoring NATO's and the EU's lack of a coherent strategy to that area (Linden, 2007:5; Minchev, 2011:2-3). The two countries that represented the most promising and reliable partners of the West by virtue of their (albeit more tenuous) cultural-historical belongingness to Europe and pro-European aspirations and that could add a layer of stability in the otherwise grey zone of insecurity, weak institutions, inter-ethnic strife and terrorist extremism stretching between Vienna and Central Asia/the Middle East, were Bulgaria and Romania. It was therefore beginning to be realised that the admission of these states in NATO would improve the strategic balance in the 'no-man's land' between Central Europe, the post-Soviet space and south-west Asia in favour of the democratic international community. This would take place by fostering the process of democratisation in Bulgaria and Romania and exercising strategic control over the Black Sea area that connects Europe and Asia (Minchev, 2002:25-26).

So post-9/11 security developments provided a stronger impetus to the US (as the dominant power within NATO) to proceed with a 'big bang' second-wave of enlargement to CEE and to include Bulgaria and Romania in it. Although the 1999 Kosovo crisis represented a crucial watershed in Western perceptions about the strategic importance of Sofia to European security, the ensuing standstill in Alliance expansion was linked to a degree of dissatisfaction that arose over the actual preparedness, military contribution and condition of the reform process of the 1999 Central European entrants (Angelov, 2004:8; CRS Report for Congress, 2003:2; Stanev, 2001:2-3). Yet, considerations about the need for a stricter supervision of the fulfilment of NATO accession criteria before membership could be granted were superseded by the strategic necessities of the post-9/11 security environment. As the *New York Times* made it clear, Bulgaria's (and Romania's) previously 'laughable' prospects of joining the Alliance changed dramatically after the terrorist attacks when the southern flank of European security as a connecting link to the Middle East began to matter more than the domestic democratic credentials of acceding countries. So during his visit to Sofia in March 2002, Deputy Secretary of State Richard Armitage praised Bulgaria's quick efforts to help the US and NATO after 9/11. He noted the fact that the Bulgarians had allowed American tanker planes and 200 American soldiers to use an air base at Burgas and concluded that the terrorist attacks had a riveting effect on the process of NATO expansion giving the opportunity for potential candidates to 'step up to the plate' (Erlanger, 2002; Mihalka, 2002:291).

The developments in the post-9/11 North Atlantic framework of security elicited a response on the part of the Bulgarian political elite that represented a blend of moral-civilizational and strategic motivations, confirming and reinforcing Sofia's Euro-Atlantic choice. In the immediate aftermath of the terrorist attacks, Prime

Minister Simeon Sakskoburggotski sent a letter to President George Bush in which he stated that Bulgaria was ready to act in accordance with NATO's Article 5 despite the fact that it was not yet a member state (Bonchev, 2002:21). Bush reciprocated by praising the quick demonstration of support, acknowledging the shared values that bound Bulgaria and the US together in the fight against terrorism (Mediapool, 2001). Moreover, President Stoyanov convened a summit in Sofia in October 2001 that brought together the heads of state of the Vilnius Group countries (an organisation of candidates for NATO membership created to facilitate joint cooperation and lobbying for that cause in May 2000). The Sofia Declaration of Solidarity that came out of the summit enshrined the CEE states' resolve to contribute to Euro-Atlantic security through their determination to stand firmly behind the US in the war on terror on both principled and practical grounds (Bonchev, 2002:20-21). The Iraq intervention provided a further opportunity to the Bulgarian political elite to assert an identity narrative of Bulgaria's democratic values. President Parvanov insisted that the country's military presence in Iraq reiterated one of the most significant elements in Bulgarian history—the fact that the Bulgarian army had taken part only in wars of liberation (Kavalski, 2008:11). Foreign Minister Passy also compared the Bulgarian participation in Iraq to the feats of the 19th century Bulgarian revolutionaries, who sacrificed their lives for the national liberation of other oppressed countries (Kavalski, 2008:13; Dnevnik, 2003).

The accelerated process of NATO enlargement facilitated European integration (Primatarova, 2015; Slatinski, 2015, interviews; Sakskoburggotski, 2002; Kostov, 2004). The clearer American commitment to Sofia's inclusion in the next round of Alliance enlargement necessitated a stricter alignment with international as well as European conventions and agreements in the field of security policy. For instance, Sofia began to implement the EU Action Plan in the Area of Police Cooperation in the SEE and Black Sea region through bilateral and multilateral arrangements with Greece, Turkey, Romania, Macedonia, Georgia, Ukraine, Russia (Ratchev, 2002:45-47). Also, in line with anti-terrorist policy requirements, in 2002 the Bulgarian government adopted the draft amendment to the Law on the Control of Foreign Trade Activities in Arms and in Dual-Use Goods and Technologies, which introduced compulsory lists of states placed under EU and UN embargoes (Ratchev, 2002:49).

The US's deeper strategic focus on the Balkans additionally raised the level of the EU's involvement in the region because of the complementary sharing of roles between the EU and NATO in SEE and Washington's expectations that the West Europeans assume greater responsibilities there. These expectations served to direct European attention to the region and accelerate the integration prospects of Bulgaria and Romania as the two most advanced countries in the domestic reform process and accession negotiations. Thus, despite the post-9/11 trend towards growing disagreements between the US and Europe (especially borne out of the American need for European assets rather than rhetorical initiatives), in the Balkans Washington and Brussels continued to collaborate. This was ensured by the functional differentiation between the EU's civilian mission in the region and NATO's provision of hard security as well as by the 2003 EU-NATO framework for permanent relations, which allowed the Union to draw on the North Atlantic Alliance's military assets in peace-keeping operations (Kavalski, 2005:9, 11; EU-NATO Framework, 2003). Also, the American demand for an increased European commitment to the affairs of SEE began to be realised in the process of transferring Balkan missions from NATO to the EU. Examples included the transition from NATO's Operation Allied Harmony in Macedonia to Operation Concordia and the transfer of the Alliance's Security Force (S-FOR) mission to the Union's Operation Althea in 2004 (Kavalski, 2005:9).

However, the contrasting views of the Central and East Europeans—admired for their 'love of freedom' by American President Bush and reprimanded by French President Chirac as behaving in a 'reckless' and 'infantile' way, made it clear that disagreements between the US and Western Europe could be consequential for the regional definition of CEE. As a country at the periphery of the Euro-Atlantic area, Bulgaria had to balance the goal to keep the US committed to regional security, while maintaining good relations with Germany and France (Kavalski, 2005:3;

CNN, 2003). Nevertheless, despite France's and Germany's initial displeasure with the CEE countries' firm siding with the US, Sofia's increased security cooperation with NATO accelerated the country's EU accession. This was so because of the interlinked nature of the NATO and EU expansion process, the Union's assumption of a more prominent role in the Balkans, as encouraged by the US, and Bulgaria's incorporation of legislation that aligned with EU security regulations.

Yet, such growing cooperation between Bulgaria and the West still took place within the confines of ambivalent Europeanisation. It was events such as 9/11 that served as a catalyst for Sofia's integration with the Euro-Atlantic community rather than a more long-term American strategic and ideational commitment to Bulgaria's NATO membership.

The European Other

The process of EU accession and the subsequent admission of Bulgaria (and Romania) in the Union in 2007 represented a crucial external framework for the Balkan country's Europeanisation. On the one hand, the EU's post-2004 enlargement fatigue, more reluctant and exacting attitude to Sofia and Bucharest as well as the post-2007 imposition of safeguard clauses on the two new entrants fed into and were at the same time a manifestation of the much more ambivalent views that West Europeans harboured about Bulgaria and Romania. All of this led to domestic political disappointments and contributed to the rise of small but vociferously nationalist, anti-Western forces. Yet, on the other hand, the EU was not too ambivalent to prevent the Europeanisation of Bulgaria. The granting of full membership provided wider opportunities for Bulgarian foreign policy-making in terms of intensified diplomatic coordination on the Brussels level and fostered the socialisation of the Bulgarian administrative elite into EU behavioural styles of persuasive consensus-building.

In the run-up to and after the 2004 big-bang expansion to ten states, the EU was already in the grips of enlargement 'fatigue' and 'blues', as stated by two successive Commissioners for Enlargement—Gunther Verheugen (1999-2004) and Olli Rehn (2004-2010) (Phinnemore, 2006:4; Horsley, 2005). The reasons behind such waning enthusiasm abounded: there were concerns about the Union's absorption capacity; fears that decision-making would grind to a halt on the basis of a more diverse membership; complaints about tax competition, social dumping, the financial costs of supporting the integration of poorer CEE states; as well as doubts about the progress of the domestic political and economic reform process in the acceding countries (Phinnemore, 2006:4).

So by the time Bulgaria and Romania had finally received a firm membership perspective, the West European attitudinal tidal wave had turned away from the symbolically-loaded enthusiasm about bringing an end to divisions in Europe through EU enlargement that had accompanied the better part of the 2004 entrants' road to membership (Phinnemore, 2006:15). Moreover, to ensure greater compliance and post-accession cohesion but also to narrow the bigger perceived gap between Bulgaria's and Romania's reform progress and the EU's standards of European-ness, the Union introduced stricter elements of conditionality for the two countries. These were evidenced by the more stringent enforcement of the economic criteria for membership as well as the conditions for democratic governance, minority rights and a peaceful foreign policy (Bechev, 2006b:20-21; Phinnemore, 2006:12-13; Mihaylova, 2015, interview).

The harsher requirements and monitoring that Brussels put in place for Bulgaria (and Romania) shaped a degree of domestic backlash mostly present in party politics and internal debates but limited in its impact on foreign policy. For instance, in a reaction to the perceived greater stringency of Brussels' environmental and safety standards entailing the closure of four reactors of the Kozloduy nuclear power plant, the cabinet of Prime Minister Simeon Saxkoburggotski faced two non-confidence votes in 2002, initiated by both the BSP and the UDF. The votes were motivated by the premature closure of the energy accession negotiation chapter. The government was accused of having failed to take into account national interests and instead conformed obediently to what were perceived as unjust European requirements. These requirements were thought to be based on double standards since some nuclear power plants in certain EU member states (such as Germany and the UK) were argued to be less safe than the Bulgarian one, with the latter's technological construction being moreover different from the technology used to build Chernobyl (Boncheva, Tema archive; Spendzharova, 2003:12; Mandjukov, Gospodinova, 2002). Also, for the first time since 1989, the general elections in 2005 brought to Parliament an openly anti-Western and xenophobic party in the face of ATAKA. Its leader Volen Siderov argued that the party embodied a promise for Bulgaria's revival after 15 years of a 'politics of genocide' carried out on the Bulgarian people under the dictatorship of the 'international oligarchy' (National Assembly Proceedings, 2005:6).

Bulgaria's achievement of formal membership in the EU in 2007 did not alleviate ambivalent Europeanisation and a dualistic impact of European attitudes and policies on the Bulgarian domestic political scene. On the one hand, the EU's differential treatment of the two new Balkan members as well as the Commission's ability to adjust its enlargement strategy on the basis of the particular conditions of member states were continued into the unprecedented safeguard clauses, or also known as the 'Cooperation and Verification Mechanism' (CVM), that Brussels put in place for Bulgaria and Romania after they joined the Union in 2007 (Papadimitriou, Gateva, 2009:22; Commission Decision, 2006). The CVM was aimed at ensuring that Sofia and Bucharest addressed outstanding problems in the fields of judicial reform, tackling corruption and organised crime. As a result, the two countries' performance was monitored every six months with the threat of sanctions (such as withdrawal of funds) in case of non-compliance (Linden, 2009:5; Pop, 2009; Primatarova, 2010:3). Apart from the harsh Commission reports, Bulgaria and Romania came in for more criticism from the European Parliament. MEPs deplored the Balkan countries' premature admission, suggesting that the Commission had itself misled the rest of the Union about these states' ability to fulfil the Copenhagen criteria in areas such as the rule of law (Linden, 2009:5; Pop, 2009; Primatarova, 2010:3).

Although concerns about the rule of law may have been based on an objective assessment of the domestic developments in Bulgaria (and Romania), they were nevertheless perceived as discriminatory and implying a second-class membership status in the EU (Nikolov, Simeonov, 2009:80; Primatarova, 2010:3). Prime Minister Sergei Stanishev reacted to the CVM reports as unjust sanctions on Bulgaria, warning that disparaging European attitudes and policies could boost Euroscepticism in his country (Primatarova, 2010:11; Economist, 2009). Similarly, MEP Kristian Vigenin accused the Commission of adopting double standards in relation to Bulgaria and Romania, surmising about the severity of European reactions had the Bulgarian Prime Minister passed a law that would protect him from prosecution just like Italy's Silvio Berlusconi had done (and in which case such severity was missing) (Sega, 2008).

Yet, on the other hand, as my interviews with Bulgarian experts have confirmed, Bulgaria's entry into the EU provided Sofia with new opportunities for downloading and joining Union-level positions that widened the horizon of the country's external activity and allowed for socialisation into Brussels ways of coalition-building, consensus-seeking and compromise (Mihaylova, 2015; Shopov, 2015; Lessenski, 2015; Vigenin, 2015, interviews). For instance, in 2007, the EU initiated an attempt to develop a coordinated policy approach towards the Black Sea region through the Communication of the Black Sea Synergy document (2007) (Minchev, 2011:6; Linden, 2009:10). As the Union's only member states bordering on the Black Sea, Bulgaria and Romania found themselves at the spearhead of this new initiative. Both of them were expected and encouraged to contribute by taking a pro-active stance in meeting the challenges emanating from the area, including dangers of terrorism, drugs, weapons and human trafficking as well as the need for a better cooperation in border management, energy, transport and economic development (Nikolov, Simeonov, 2009:85; Linden, 2009:10).

EU entry also facilitated the socialisation of the country's administrative elite into European principles and practices (Sakskoburggotski, 2002:3-4; Passy, 2002:2; Vesti, 2003). As participants in this process, Primatarova and Mihaylova attest to the socialising influence of Brussels in terms of the administration's growing acceptance of European values, consideration of Union-level common interests and the acquisition of expertise through learning and observation in the execution of policies such as carrying out Bulgaria's legislative harmonisation with the *acquis* (Primatarova, 2015; Mihaylova, 2015, interviews). Then Prime Minister Sakskoburggotski and Foreign Minister Passy acknowledged that EU conditionality was important not simply with regard to implementing institutional reforms. It was additionally vital in terms of changing the Bulgarians' 'mentality', logic of action and international image in line with European standards by changing the habits inherited from the centralised totalitarian state and economy (Sakskoburggotski, 2002:3-4; Passy, 2002:2; Vesti, 2003).

The distinctive features of the Bulgarian Self and its Western Other presented so far exerted their ultimate impact through the interactive process of mutual identification. This interaction shaped the ambivalent character of Bulgaria's Europeanisation, whose persistent continuity could be observed in both political discourse and action.

The Bulgarian Self and the Western Other, 1989-2000: A cautious embrace

The 1990s pushed Bulgaria into a liminal soul-searching as to its proper place in Europe. The uncertainty was only being slowly overcome through the achievement of domestic political consensus towards the end of the decade. Similarly, the West did not immediately deploy its normative authority and power in order to draw Bulgaria closer into its orbit, given Europe's and America's own ambivalent affinities to Sofia. Hence, the West's more tentative commitment to Bulgaria's integration in the Euro-Atlantic space — as measured by weaker diplomatic and economic support than Poland was given, was complemented and informed by Sofia's own uncertain ideational bonds with the West and difficulties in reaching a domestic political consensus about the country's external orientation. Yet, the West's and Bulgaria's ambivalent identifications with each other were not too deep-seated to prevent an eventual integration. But it took the shock of the 1996-1997 financial and economic crisis and the strategic reconsiderations following the Kosovo conflict for Self and Other to move towards closer cooperation. So as Bulgarian experts and decision-makers agree, Bulgaria underwent ambivalent Europeanisation both because it gained Western European and American acceptance and achieved consensus to integrate in the Euro-Atlantic area more slowly and because once it was set on its pro-Western course, it Europeanised more superficially. That is, it did so on the basis of a general (albeit not always consistent) discursive compatibility and situational behavioural norm compliance, largely lacking, however, a deeply held internalisation of ideal-typical values and a corresponding sustained behavioural manifestation (Slavkova, 2015; Primatarova, 2015; Hristo Georgiev, 2015; Ratchev, 2015; Slatinski, 2015; Nikolova, 2015; Vigenin, 2015, interviews).

Post-1989, serious Western geopolitical and economic interest in Bulgaria was absent. This was shaped by the unwillingness and lack of readiness of Western Europe to offer security guarantees and integration prospects to CEE in general and to get entangled in the affairs of Balkan countries — assumed to be descending into age-old enmities with the disintegration of Yugoslavia (Bechev, 2006b:18-19; Slavkova, 2015; Primatarova, 2015; Hristo Georgiev, 2015; Ratchev, 2015; Slatinski, 2015, interviews). Indeed, the uncertain Western engagement in the Balkans was feeding into Bulgarian disappointments and was not conducive to pushing forward domestic reforms and external reorientation on the basis of both recognition of cultural-historical belongingness and material incentives.

At the same time, however, ambiguous and non-committal Western attitudes and actions were further informed by Bulgaria's own similarly indecisive and shallow embrace of ideal-typical European-ness. The UDF's lack of political experience, opportunism and vociferous fixation on anti-communist rhetoric matched by the initial propensity to expect the simultaneous dissolution of the

Warsaw Pact and NATO as well as the BSP's preference for 'gradualist' economic change and strong attachment to the Eastern vector in foreign policy did not help convince Western Europe and the US of the desirability of including Bulgaria in integration arrangements. Also, as Bulgarian experts concur, the insufficient progress on domestic economic reforms served especially importantly to confirm the EU in its decision not to accept Bulgaria as part of the first wave of CEE entrants (Slavkova, 2015; Primatarova, 2015; Minchev, 2015; Baeva, 2015; Mihaylova, 2015; Slatinski, 2015; Alexieva, 2015; Vigenin, 2015, interviews). Domestic economic reforms proceeded slowly, in a piece-meal and often unthoughtful manner. The 1991-1992 UDF government's first economic reforms focused on the restitution of big city property and agricultural land, which had a negative impact on Bulgarian agriculture. The lack of clarity or availability of pre-1944 records on ownership led to the proliferation of a property mafia, while agricultural land was divided in such small pieces that export competitiveness was obstructed (Alexieva, 2015; Petkov, 2015, interviews; Petar Angelov, 2015; Tsanev, 2010:440). Moreover, privatisation took place slowly. In 1993, the output from the private sector still varied between 18% and 37%, while Parliament had not passed crucial legislation on bankruptcy and the system of taxation (Engelbrekt, 1994b:22). An overview of the European and American press in the mid-1990s shows the growing Western frustration with Bulgaria's domestic political and economic condition. *The Economist, the Independent, the Journal of Commerce (New York)* and *the New York Times* argued that unlike the rest of the CEE states, which were becoming prospering countries, Bulgaria was getting poorer and less economically and politically free. Extensive government intervention in the economy, the slow pace of privatisation, the high levels of corruption and the low quality of the rule of law were all cited as contributing factors (Capital, November 1996).

Hence, in the early 1990s, the emerging rhetorical construction based on ideal-typical European-ness failed to become sufficiently substantiated in both ideational and behavioural (and even discursive) terms due to the interactive operation of the internal and external dimension of identification. On the one hand, Alexander

Lilov (BSP) argued that Bulgaria had to take its rightful place in a uniting Europe as a modern, democratic and dynamically developing, civilised country. Europe's recognition of the freedom and fairness of the first democratic elections in 1990 was one proof of the success of this process (National Parliament Proceedings, 1990:3, 5). Filip Dimitrov (UDF) linked the end of the totalitarian communist regime with the historic opportunity to finally build a 'normal' Bulgarian state, where democracy, individual liberty, domestic and external stability and predictability would boost Bulgaria's image in international relations (National Parliament Proceedings, 1991:1-2). Ahmed Dogan (MRF) argued that Bulgaria's Europeanisation encompassed the democratisation of political life as an irreversible process, the transition to a free market economy and the country's integration in the major European institutions. These institutions' fundamental focus on human rights protection should become a model for the equality of all Bulgarian citizen before the law, which would in turn guarantee social peace (National Parliament Proceedings, 1991:3).

However, this rhetoric was not consistently espoused and practiced. For instance, at the beginning of 1993 Bulgaria tried to demonstrate its commitment to international norms by adhering strictly to UN sanctions against Yugoslavia. Sofia enforced the embargo on Belgrade prohibiting the use of the Danube river for trade or transport as Berov's government was hoping to get in return security guarantees from the EU and NATO (Engelbrekt, 1994a:109). Yet, other than John Shalikashvili's (supreme commander of NATO forces in Europe) praise that Bulgaria had become a well-regarded member of the NACC, Sofia received no further assistance or security guarantees (Engelbrekt, 1994a:109; Tashev, 2005:6). But such Western reluctance had also been informed by the fact that Berov did not take practical steps for increasing Sofia's NATO membership prospects. Instead, he spoke of the formation of a 'Slavic arch' uniting Bulgaria, Russia, Serbia and possibly Greece in a common geopolitical orientation based on pan-Slavism and Orthodox Christianity (Engelbrekt, 1994b:20; Slatinski, 2012; Sofiyanski, 1993; Dimitrov, 2015, interview).

Similarly, the socialists' vision of Bulgaria's Europeanisation was rather more akin to Gorbachev's 'common European home' than to a firm geopolitical anchoring in the West, accompanied by the application of the values embodied in the ideal-typical conception of European-ness. 'Equidistance' and 'neutrality' in Bulgarian foreign policy were aimed at the pursuit of balanced relationships with both East and West. Key BSP figures Alexander Lilov, Andrey Lukanov, Prime Minister Zhan Videnov and Foreign Minister Georgi Pirinski claimed that their government's strategic goals included working towards membership in the EU as well as reviving economic and political relations with the CIS states so that the Bulgarians would be 'finally stepping on our two feet' (National Parliament Proceedings, 1990:5, 1995:1-2; Lukanov, May 1990, March 1992; Capital, 1995, April 1996; Georgieva, 1996:3).

Much greater clarity, decisiveness and cross-party consensus about Bulgaria's Europeanisation were achieved through the mutual reinforcement of the domestic shock experienced from the 1996-1997 financial and economic crisis coupled with the change in Western perceptions about the strategic importance of Bulgaria undergone during the 1999 Kosovo crisis. These two crises served as the complementary internal and external catalysts for Bulgaria's Euro-Atlantic integration. As a result, after 1997 the political elite began to enunciate and uphold the achieved consensus. UDF leader Kostov declared that Bulgaria's salvation lay in the shared national agreement on the country's developmental direction. BSP leader Parvanov affirmed the fundamental consensus that existed on the need for reforms and a Euro-Atlantic geopolitical orientation (National Parliament Proceedings, 1997:3-6, 11; Minchev, Ratchev, Lessenski, 2002:11). Foreign Minister Mihaylova argued that the Bulgarian foreign policy agenda was conditioned on the one hand by the unprecedented changes taking place in the international system since 1989 leading to the erosion of dividing lines on the European continent. But on the other, it was also conditioned by the irreversible domestic political and economic changes in Bulgaria, whose successful completion in turn depended on the country's 'civilised' return to the Euro-Atlantic community of democratic nations. She maintained that Bulgaria was proving its fitness to become an EU and NATO member through a regional policy promoting European patterns of behaviour (such as good-neighbourliness and peaceful cooperation) among the Balkan states. The latter's incorporation into the European organisations could guarantee the avoidance of conflicts and foster democratic reforms (Mihaylova, 1999). President Stoyanov expressed his firm conviction that NATO enlargement should be understood above all as a cause. The West had the historic opportunity to make the whole Euro-Atlantic area stable and democratic, complemented by Bulgaria's adherence to the principles of the Alliance such as regional cooperation (Minchev, Ratchev, Lessenski, 2002:13; Stanev, 1998:1).

Yet, it must be noted that even though after 1997 Bulgaria and the West both settled on the course towards Sofia's Euro-Atlantic integration, the Bulgarian case could nevertheless still be characterised as ambivalently Europeanised. The ambivalence was expressed in the situational behavioural and rhetorical compliance with European norms and principles, which was not accompanied by a deep-seated internalisation that would otherwise entail a consistent and sustained application of these norms and principles externally as well as internally (Slatinski, 2015; Arndt, 2015, interviews).

Bulgarian experts express the concern that the path-dependent logic of the way in which Europeanisation was initiated in the 1990s made it hard to take up the debate about the quality of the application of European principles (Lessenski, 2015; Dimitrova, 2015; Marcheva, 2015; Shopov, 2015; Slatinski, 2015; Alexieva, 2015, interviews). Because of the dominance of the former communist networks, the inexperience of the reformers (who only focused on breaking from the past rather than gaining an in-depth understanding of the various facets of European-ness) and the fact that the EU provided a general institutional blueprint oblivious to domestic habits and traditions, the political elite depoliticised Europeanisation. It was rendered as a process of implementing European sectoral policies and legislation, while politicians' concentration on deriving personal profit and ill-gotten gains was continued. Hence, no significant steps were taken for the practical substantiation of the rhetorically espoused European values, which would have entailed principled discussions about Bulgaria's meaningful contribution to the EU and NATO and about what a long-term strategy of a regionally cooperative policy would look like. And once the European Commission affirmed that the Copenhagen political conditions for joining the Union had been fulfilled (primarily due to the modification of national legislation along Union regulations), all domestic criticism about the substance of the fulfilment of the conditions could be brushed aside (Shopov, 2015; Shikova, 2015, interviews).

The discursive manifestations of the degree of Bulgaria's commitment to ideal-typical European-ness were also reflected in concrete action. Ambivalent Europeanisation framed the tenor of Bulgarian foreign policy in the direction of situational behavioural normative adaptation to European values along the key dimensions of support for a rules-based international order, cooperative regional relations and institutionalised cooperation. Greatest alignment was (imitatively) performed when principles-based action was expected by the West and when an internally enunciated pro-Western ideational position needed to be proven behaviourally. Otherwise, the character of foreign policy lurched between civilizational orientations and value outlooks, given that normative ambiguity prevented a fully-fledged and sustained actualisation of ideal-typical European-ness as well as a more determined pursuit of shared belongingness with the Western Other.

The first government after the 1989 collapse of the communist regime was formed by the BSP with Andrey Lukanov as Prime Minister (1990). The interaction of the absence of a fully-developed EC and NATO vision about the strategies they would adopt towards the Balkans coupled with the BSP's ideological closeness to a Gorbachevian understanding of the 'common European home' meant that Bulgaria's Euro-Atlantic integration remained a distant and less than actively followed possibility. Although the socialists supported Bulgaria's economic integration with the EC (hence signing the Trade and commercial and economic cooperation agreement with the Community in 1990), they were committed to maintaining close ties with the USSR/Russia. The socialists also did not view the dissolution of the Warsaw Pact as a valuable security option and, once this did take place, the government was at a loss about how to produce an alternative security policy. So no serious steps were taken for further integration with the EC and NATO (Tashev, 2005:3-4; Dimitrov, 2000:3; Lukanov, May 1990, March 1992).

The first UDF government (1991-1992) with Filip Dimitrov as Prime Minister engaged in intensive diplomatic activity to compensate for Bulgaria's lag behind the Central European states in the process of European integration by securing Bulgarian entry into the Council of Europe in 1992 and negotiating the Association Agreement with the EC in 1992 (Dimitrov, 2000:4). In turn, the positive signals coming from the EU about Bulgaria's gradual inclusion in the integration process had a crucial impact on the country's external behaviour, which aimed to conform to Brussels norms and expectations — especially in terms of constructing good-neighbourly, peaceful regional relations in SEE and placing an emphasis on a civic form of nationalism. For example, bilateral ties with Turkey began to continually improve after 1989 as a result of the Bulgarian authorities' decision to ensure the political representation of the Turkish minority by granting the MRF the right to participate in elections (Resolution No 4, 1992; Markov, 2015; Hristov, 2014). This step positively advanced Bulgaria's minority policies, which led to a rapprochement with Turkey and the conclusion of the Treaty on Friendship, Good-Neighbourliness, Cooperation and Security between the two states (1992). The Treaty removed impediments to the establishment of contractual relations between the EC and Bulgaria and as a result Sofia signed the Europe Agreement in 1994 (Bechev, 2009:7).

Moreover, the government's strongly US-focused external orientation bore results in that Washington granted Sofia MFN status and chose to engage the country on issues of human rights and the dismantling of Soviet made SS-20 missiles, rather than regard those issues as obstacles to improved relations (Clyatt, 1993:33, 40, 53). Yet, the US stopped short of providing Bulgaria with security guarantees, which was also reciprocated by the UDF government, as it did not seek NATO membership. Many of the constituent parties of the Union opposed the idea of Bulgaria's NATO accession — not least because of the expectation that both the Warsaw Pact and the North Atlantic Alliance had to be dissolved (Passy, 2015; UDF electoral platform, 1990).

After the UDF government failed to win the confidence vote it had itself initiated at the end of 1992, a technocratic (but politically supported by the BSP and the MRF) cabinet with Lyuben Berov as Prime Minister (1992-1994) was appointed by Parliament. Consistent with the interaction of the West's more extensive engagement with Central European states, while the Balkan region was being relegated to conflict-resolution efforts, and the BSP-supported government's unwillingness to complete a firm geopolitical orientation to NATO, few decisive steps were taken with regard to Bulgaria's Euro-Atlantic integration. In 1993, Sofia and Moscow signed an accord on cooperation between their defence ministries (Engelbrekt, 1994c:46). The government did join the PfP in 1994 but did not sanction officially the military doctrine that had been commissioned by former Defence Minister Dimitar Ludzhev (1991-1992) and prepared by officers at the General Staff of the army (Engelbrekt, 1994c:48). As an insider to the process, Ratchev explains that the doctrine aimed at a departure from previous foreign policy and military strategies by prescribing active participation in all European integration processes, deepening of cooperation with NATO and the pursuit of relations of good-neighbourliness with other Balkan states (Ratchev, interview, 2015; Ratchev, 2014:6-7).

During the 1995-1997 BSP government with Zhan Videnov as Prime Minister, serious Western doubts about the reformist, pro-European and pro-American credentials of the socialists matched by the BSP's own ideational predisposition for close cooperation with Russia as well as the EU (rather than NATO) amounted to an uncertain and slowly moving process of Europeanisation. The government attempted to maintain an external course of 'neutrality' and 'equidistance', which in practice led to self-isolation (Ratchev, 2015, interview; Georgiev, 2011:49). Bulgaria's European integration assumed a greater priority in foreign policy so that in 1995 Sofia's official application for EU membership was submitted.

However, despite the symbolic gesture of submitting the application, the socialists were slow in establishing the institutional mechanisms for coordinating work on EU accession and did not advance the process of transposing Union legislation in domestic politics (Dimitrov, 2000:4; Capital, 1995, April 1996).

NATO membership was not a priority. But the Videnov government did not show open opposition to the Alliance, conscious of the discrediting international effects this would have. Instead, there was a focus on the exchange of views through the Intensified Dialogue with NATO without taking practical steps towards deeper cooperation (Bonchev, 2002:9; Tosheva, 1995, 1996; Ratchev, 2015, interview). Sustained military reforms had not been initiated, little progress had been achieved in terms of interoperability with NATO and Sofia had not been active in peace-keeping missions (Simon, 1998:2, 7-8). Indeed, the Bulgarian press acknowledged that then US Secretary of State Warren Christopher did not mention Bulgaria as a prospective NATO candidate country during his 1996 visit to the Czech Republic because Foreign Minister Georgi Pirinski had chosen to maintain 'silence' on Bulgaria's policy line towards the Alliance (Tosheva, 1996:1).

Following the domestic political consensus that was being forged after 1997 and the EU's and NATO's greater commitment to Bulgaria's Euro-Atlantic integration especially after the 1999 Kosovo crisis, the 1997-2001 UDF government with Ivan Kostov as Prime Minister introduced a greater certainty and determination in the pursuit of Bulgaria's Euro-Atlantic orientation. As far as European integration was concerned, in 1998 the government adopted a comprehensive strategy for Bulgaria's accession to the Union, an action programme for the implementation of the strategy and a targeted programme for the transposition of the *acquis* (Dimitrov, 2000:5). In 1999, the Helsinki European Council decided to open accession negotiations with Bulgaria, recognising the government's Europeanisation efforts (Dimitrov, 2000:5).

Significant steps were also taken in relation to Bulgaria's NATO membership. In consonance with President Petar Stoyanov's categorically stated position in favour of Bulgaria's

NATO membership at a January 1997 NACC meeting, Kostov continued this policy through the Declaration on National Accord (1997), which stated that NATO membership was a Bulgarian foreign policy priority (Bonchev, 2002:10-11). The crucial catalyst that sped up Sofia's Euro-Atlantic prospects was the government's policy during the 1999 Kosovo crisis. As tensions intensified, NATO requested unrestricted access to and transit of aircraft through Bulgaria's airspace, which was granted by the government in the April 1999 Agreement between Bulgaria and NATO. Conversely, Sofia turned down Russia's requests for an air corridor to transfer Russian troops as part of Moscow's plans to create its own zone of responsibility in Kosovo (vn.government.bg, Bonchev, 2002:12-16). Henceforth, the government's position on the Kosovo conflict was rewarded with a Membership Action Plan, adopted at the NATO Washington summit in 1999.

Moreover, the overwhelming belief that Macedonia is an inseparable part of the blood-bound national community had to be transcended if Sofia was to conform to European norms of good-neighbourliness. Although Bulgaria became the first country to recognise Macedonia (or FYROM — Former Yugoslav Republic of Macedonia) in 1991, the Bulgarian authorities were quick to clarify that the recognition of a Macedonian state did not imply the recognition of a separate Macedonian nation with its own language and identity. The ensuing diplomatic stalemate was overcome through the intervention of the EU and the US, which led to a common declaration upheld by Bulgaria's Prime Minister Ivan Kostov and FYROM's Prime Minister Ljubco Georgievski in 1999. It stated that the two countries recognised the official language of the other as the language stipulated by the constitutions of the two states. This in effect meant that Bulgaria implicitly recognised the Macedonian language (Katsikas, 2010a:139-140, Bechev, 2009:8).

Nevertheless, beyond behavioural alignment with EU and US expectations, parliamentary debates and statements revealed that the deeply rooted views of Macedonia's place in Bulgarian nationhood that had led to the dispute did not disappear (Nancheva, 2012:235). This was visible both on the right-wing and left-wing end of the political spectrum. Krasimir Karakachanov — leader of nationalist VMRO (Internal Macedonian Revolutionary Organisation), reminded that signing a joint declaration with Macedonia in both languages did not amount to a Bulgarian recognition of a separate Macedonian language. He further argued that the recognition of a 'nation' or 'language' was not up for a political debate and interpretation—they either existed or they did not as a matter of fact, which implied an essentialist denial of a separate Macedonian identity (Nancheva, 2012:235-236). Also, the socialists let it be known that the solution of the language dispute represented a 'grave compromise' with Bulgarian national interests and identity (Nancheva, 2012:237).

Another illustration of situational behavioural normative compliance is provided by the fact that although the 1997-2001 UDF government legitimised itself on the basis of a pro-Western discourse, when there was much less West European and American vigilance, Kostov's government behaved more ambiguously (Ralchev, 2015:5). For example, despite the staunch rhetorical promotion of European standards of transparency and the rule of law coupled with opposition to a geopolitical orientation towards Russia, in substantive matters the UDF sold strategic assets of Bulgaria's economy to Russian companies amid charges of corruption. A case in point was the privatisation of oil refinery Neftochim Burgas to Lukoil in 1999 so that Lukoil-Neftochim still continues to be one of the most profitable businesses in the country and largest contributors to the Bulgarian state budget among privately owned firms (Ralchev, 2015:5; Capital, 2020).

The Bulgarian Self and the Western Other, 2000-2015: Persistent duality

The new millennium continued the trend of Bulgaria's ambivalent place in Europe. The diminishing EU and NATO readiness and desire to enlarge was mutually informative with the emergence of populist parties in the Bulgarian political scene that hollowed out the principled substance and practice of 'European-ness'. The lingering anti-communist vs. former communist opposition of the 1990s additionally perpetuated dualistic, East-West foreign policy leanings. Nevertheless, unlike Russia, Bulgaria proceeded on the path of Euro-Atlantic integration, given the generally undisputed membership perspective, continuing entry negotiations and accompanying opportunities for socialisation, all of which served to prevent an overwhelming internal backlash against Europeanisation. But, as contrasted with the sustained Western embrace of Poland in the process of European reunification backed by sustained Polish domestic reforms, Sofia's return to Europe was pushed by the EU's and NATO's strategic considerations and the Bulgarian political elite's surface-level Euro-Atlantic consensus — based on situational behavioural adaptation to European norms rather than deep internal conviction and aspirations to be an active partner of the West.

As a result of such mutually reinforcing doubts and half-hearted ability and willingness to integrate, Bulgarian political elite commitment to ideal-typical European-ness remained primarily on the level of rhetoric rather than substantive values-based adherence and concomitant principled action. Politicians thus verbally acknowledged the importance of European norms in government affairs and the interaction of international and domestic factors in the process of Europeanisation. Former BSP leader and President Georgi Parvanov insisted that joining the EU and NATO could be successfully achieved on the basis of domestic political consensus, stability and parliamentary scrutiny of and involvement in the accession negotiations. This would in turn inform the European Commission's report on the country's progress and conform to Olli Rehn's expectations about a speedy and effective implementation of the *acquis* (National Assembly Proceedings, 2001:5; 2005:2). MRF leader Ahmed Dogan further warned against the pursuit of European integration as simply a foreign policy priority. Instead, it was both an international and domestic goal, whose attainment hinged on the country's economic, social and political modernisation. Dogan compared EU membership to a hologram, in which the whole reflected its constituent parts in the same way that the parts represented a mirror image of the whole. So Bulgaria's task was to modernise itself in order to become a sufficient segment of the whole — i.e., of the EU (National Assembly Proceedings, 2005:5). Also, NDSV Foreign Minister Solomon Passy (2001-2005) asserted that as the most advanced state in the process of EU negotiations in the Balkans, Bulgaria had a special mission to assist the progress of good-neighbourly regional cooperation. In this way Sofia would make SEE leaders understand that their countries could only change the West Europeans' mistrustful attitudes if the word 'balkanisation' (synonymous with ethnic strife, lack of cooperation and aggression) transformed its meaning to signify 'Balkan Europeanisation and globalisation' (to be associated with peace, integration and multilateral dialogue) (Passy, 2001:2-4). President Rossen Plevneliev also argued against an insular form of nationalism based on a hatred of difference, believing that the Bulgarians had embraced democratic patriotism that was in line with the nature of the EU, created to transcend the boundaries of national egoisms (Plevneliev, 2016).

Yet, such statements affirming the importance of European values frequently diverged from the genuineness with which they were held and their implementation into actual policy both before and after EU accession. This pointed to the fact that Union membership failed to bring about a change in the direction of more substantive as opposed to formalistic Europeanisation. And this was both because of the international and domestic context. The generally technocratic nature of EU conditionality—meant to be universally applied regardless of the cultural and socio-economic circumstances of a given country, was exacerbated by an enlargement fatigue leading to a deficit in symbolic and financial commitment and adding to the already weaker cultural-historical affinity binding the West to Bulgaria. At the same time, Bulgaria's own doubtful commitment to carrying out sustained reforms in order to become a credible and active European partner was manifested in the Bulgarian politicians' and negotiating team's predilection for equating the EU accession process with quick 'harmonisation on paper'. That is, swiftly passing laws in alignment with the *acquis* as well as agreeing with almost everything that Brussels demanded during the negotiations (without conducting internal consultations among the various ministries about the costs of reforms) turned the accession process into a legislative exercise that made Bulgaria qualify formally for membership but not substantively in terms of the actual implementation of the harmonised legislation (National Assembly Proceedings, 2005; Primatarova, 2015; Nikolova, 2015; Slatinski, 2015; Shikova, 2015; Burudjieva, 2015, interviews).

Hence, in the 2000s and 2010s Bulgaria retained (and even deepened) the ambivalent characteristics of its Europeanisation. The result of the formalistic introduction of European norms 'on paper' was to impart an abstract quality to those norms, given that they were imported rather than being born out of the particular domestic social and political reality (Shopov, 2015; Slatinski, 2015, interviews). For instance, the harmonisation of national laws with the *acquis* was not enough in the long-term to sustain a recognisably democratic state and society. As long as illiberal assumptions about the political community—linked to ethnic nationalism and social conservative ideals, remain substantively unchallenged by the elite (with the pro-Western politicians focusing overwhelmingly on economic liberalism at the expense of values of civic participation, tolerance and pluralism), Bulgarian citizens may continue to equate liberal democracy with illiberal majoritarianism (Dawson, 2014:134). As Slatinski clarified, a society that finds itself in a liminal, crisis situation (where emotional reflexes predominate over rational precepts) tends to react to the imposition of an external model—which it does not practice nor understand, on the basis of adaptation through mimicry or deviation expressed in the rejection of the political establishment in favour of populist leaders (Slatinski, 2008:261-262). In foreign policy terms, rhetorical and situational behavioural normative adaptation shaped the country's role in the EU as a formally but not sufficiently substantively integrated member that primarily downloads rather than uploads policies.

Similar to the conclusion that EU membership did not resolve but perpetuated Bulgaria's ambivalent Europeanisation, accession to NATO also failed to bring about a deep-seated change in the majority of the Bulgarian military personnel's security thinking and strategic vision. As Slatinski explains, the piece-meal, ad-hoc adoption of laws and institutional arrangements required to formally fulfil the Alliance's membership criteria met with NATO's own lack of sufficient commitment to the reform of Bulgaria's defence system (reflecting the US's greater interest since 9/11 in the strategic location of the country rather than its defence potential) (Slatinski, 2015, interview). The combination of these international and domestic factors led to Sofia's superficial integration in the Euro-Atlantic security framework. The overwhelming focus on reforming the institutions of governance—primarily establishing civilian control over the military, to live up to NATO's criteria bypassed the reform of the political culture of the military, which Kavalski has found to be unscathed and structurally intact (Kavalski, 2006:14). Indeed, although the old communist-era high-ranking officials were dismissed or retired, pro-Russian sentiments continued to dominate among the military ranks and it was assumed that once the depoliticisation of the army had taken place, a deal had been struck for non-interference in the affairs of the defence sector. So the mindset based on the old Soviet patterns of thinking and behaviour persisted—especially as related to the prevalence of views privileging hard over soft security, the lack of a national security strategy oriented to the risk society and the fixation on military imbalances with the Turkish army (Kavalski, 2006:13-15; Dimitrov, 2015; Slatinski, 2015, interviews).

Overall, Bulgaria's ambivalent Europeanisation in the 2000s and 2010s meant that the Euro-Atlantic rhetoric espoused by most parties (other than the nationalist ones) was expressed in situational behavioural adaptation. But such instrumental adaptation lacked a genuine pro-European and pro-American ideational underpinning, as manifested in illiberal internal policies and continued predisposition for a pro-Russian course of action.

The rise of populist, catch-all parties in the 2000s operating within the confines of EU and NATO accession negotiations and subsequent fully-fledged membership in these organisations, led to Euro-Atlantic compliant international policies. But these policies were mixed with authoritarian domestic tendencies and pro-Moscow rhetoric matched by attempts at conducting a balanced line between East and West. The NDSV's 2001 political platform gave top priority to Bulgaria's accession to the EU and NATO with the reception of an invitation for membership in the Alliance in

2002 and the achievement of membership in 2004 becoming an immediate task for the government (Katsikas, 2012:61). Yet, at the same time that Foreign Minister Solomon Passy was on an official visit to Denmark (known for its active advocacy of the eastern enlargements of the EU and NATO), Vice-Premier and Minister of the Economy Nikolay Vasilev travelled to Moscow to discuss economic ties between Bulgaria and Russia (Capital, 2002:3). Also, in line with Simeon's denial of there being a fundamental choice that Bulgaria had to make between NATO and Russia, he was the only Prime Minister of an Alliance acceding state at the official ceremony in Washington in 2004, who emphasised that the expansion of NATO to the east was not aimed as encircling Russia (Sakskoburggotski, 2002:1-2; Milev, 2004:3).

The divergence between foreign policy rhetoric and compliant actions, on the one hand, and the quality of Bulgaria's Europeanisation, on the other, was further demonstrated by GERB governments. The party acted in line with Borissov's declaration that, unlike many other Prime Ministers, he implemented strictly German Chancellor Merkel's proposals (Kadrinova, 2012). For instance, Borissov enthusiastically supported the Fiscal Compact promoted by Merkel, persuading the Bulgarian public that he had managed to free the Bulgarians from European tax harmonisation, yet having signed a declaration of the European Council calling exactly for tax harmonisation (Kadrinova, 2012). Also, GERB's desire for conformity with US foreign policy positions on the Middle East but without a clear consideration of national priorities was prominently manifested in the fact that Bulgaria organised an unprecedented meeting gathering all the factions of the Syrian opposition in 2012. This move was criticised domestically as embroiling Sofia in a conflict that it had few stakes in and which exposed the country to terrorism (as in the 2012 suicide bombing attack on Israeli tourists in Burgas) (Mediapool, 2012). Additionally, despite the rhetoric about European values, since the beginning of GERB's first term in government in 2009, Bulgaria's ranking in international indices measuring business and media freedom has been declining. Most drastically, as regards media freedom, if in 2009 Bulgaria was ranked 68th (out of 169 countries), in 2016 it was already ranked 113th (out of 180) (World Press Freedom Index, 2016).

The ambivalence of the country's Euro-Atlantic integration was also informed by GERB's attempts to balance the Western and Eastern vector. The Borissov cabinet stopped the project to build the Belene nuclear power plant (with the Russian Atomstroyexport having being contracted as the company to carry out the project) citing lack of financial feasibility and the need to boost energy independence from Moscow (Gocheva, Boncheva, 2012; Sega, March 2012). At the same time, it was the Borissov government that signed the agreement with Russia to build the South Stream gas pipeline (Sega, November 2012; Topnovini, 2015; Dempsey, 2014).

In general, the East-West attitudinal dualism (characteristic of most political parties other than the right-wing, firmly pro-Western Reformist Bloc and nationalist, pro-Russian ATAKA) finds expression in foreign policy inconsistency. Of mainstream parties the BSP demonstrated particular readiness to conduct a Moscow-friendly foreign policy within Bulgaria's overall Euro-Atlantic framework. The 2005-2009 socialist-dominated government signed key agreements with Russia for the construction of the Belene nuclear power plant and the Burgas-Alexandroupoli pipeline (a project for the transportation of Russian and Caspian oil from the Bulgarian city port of Burgas to Greece's Alexandroupoli port) (Borislav Angelov, 2015). At the same time, the government oversaw Bulgaria's accession to the EU and signed an Agreement with the US on defence cooperation (2006). The 2013-2014 BSP-led cabinet similarly tried to pursue a policy based on the rationale that America represented a strategic ally, while Russia was a strategic partner. The idea of the economisation of foreign conduct was promoted in order to search for markets outside of the EU such as in Eurasia (Borislav Angelov, 2015).

The political elite's reactions to the Ukrainian crisis and Russia's annexation of Crimea vividly demonstrated the dualism and ambivalence of Bulgaria observable between the then ruling centre-left and the oppositional centre-right forces. The BSP adopted a party declaration avoiding altogether a discussion and evaluation of Moscow's annexation of Crimea, urging intensified

EU-Russia dialogue and arguing that Western sanctions on Moscow could have a negative economic impact on Bulgaria (Vesti, 2014; Rilska, 2014). The socialists' stance was balanced by GERB's insistence on a more determined condemnation of Russian actions as violating international law. The MRF equivocated, while ATAKA approved of Moscow's policies and stood firmly against the imposition of sanctions (Mediapool, 2014). And in contrast to the lack of consensus in Parliament, the President mounted strong criticism against Russia's annexation of Crimea as a rejection of European values of peace and good-neighbourliness (Novini, 2014; Faktor, 2014; Ralchev, 2015:12). For their part, Western Europe and America worried that any eastward tilt in Bulgaria during the 2013-2014 socialist-led government could undermine efforts by Brussels and Washington to present a united front to Putin (Parkinson, 2014; Komentator.bg, 2014). Once, however, a GERB-dominated coalition government was formed in 2014, the international isolation with which Bulgaria was confronted as a result of its pro-Moscow leanings dissipated. In early 2015, US Secretary of State John Kerry, British Foreign Secretary Philip Hammond and NATO Secretary General Jens Stoltenberg visited Sofia to call for energy independence from Russia. These visits were motivated by the belief that Borissov's rhetorical Euro-Atlanticism entailed pro-Western behaviour, arguably ignoring his illiberal domestic conduct and pro-Russian actions necessary to placate his Russophile electorate (Johnson, 2015; Thorpe, 2015; Staneva, 2015).

On the whole, Bulgaria's generally formalistic situational behavioural normative adherence to European norms as well as continuing East-West hesitations, shaped as all of this has been by the weaker mutual cultural affinity and intensity of political-economic commitment and engagement between Bulgaria and the West, found expression in Sofia's inability to assert a substantively integrated place for itself in the EU and NATO. That is, it has failed to take on the role of an active member state that both downloads but is also capable of uploading its foreign policy positions onto Brussels fora.

Ideas all the way through: Constructivism vis-a-vis alternative explanations of Bulgarian foreign policy

The Constructivist account of the course of Bulgaria's relations with the West since 1989 presented so far can gain additional traction if we further consider competing explanations that Realists can posit for illuminating Sofia's behaviour. Although as a small state Bulgaria would seem to be an easy case for Realist theoretical predictions of inevitable conformity to overwhelming strategic constraints, the record shows a much more complex picture that contradicts an instrumentally-rationally motivated surrender to outside forces.

Bulgarian thinking on the availability of alternative foreign policy options during the 1990s reveals this complexity, warranting the conclusion that foreign policy options are 'what states make of them'. Until 1997, it was believed, especially by BSP politicians and their supporters in society, that there could be alternative courses of action for Sofia. Other than the pro-Western orientation, the transformation of Bulgaria into a neutral bridge between East and West received significant approval among (left-leaning) politicians and intellectuals. This approval was based on the ideational disposition to cooperate closely with Russia and Western Europe (but without participating in Western military structures that could be directed against Moscow) as well as on the mentality of subordination to Russia in terms of perceptions and political-economic dependencies (i.e., many political figures had been bound to the Soviet Union by dependencies originating from the state security apparatus, which after 1989 were transformed into business relations) (Georgiev, 2011:49; Hristo Georgiev, 2015; Ralchev, 2015, interviews).

Yet, the hypothetical model of neutrality proved hardly feasible both for international and domestic reasons. The loss of the Soviet markets, the economic collapse and strategic decline of post-Soviet Russia, Bulgaria's own devastating economic crisis, lack of strong army and external patron or international arrangements to guarantee Sofia's neutrality made expectations about the country's bridge-building role between East and West strategically and economically unviable (Ralchev, 2015; Baeva, 2015, interviews; Metodiev, 2017). As Bulgarian experts concur, there were thought to be alternatives to Euro-Atlantic integration but they were never really materially sustainable (Ralchev, 2015; Hristo Georgiev, 2015; Burudjieva, 2015; Dimitrov, 2015; Abrasheva, 2015; Minchev, 2015; Baeva, 2015, interviews).

Therefore, the fact that it took the Bulgarians an economic shock as well as an extremely unfavourable regional and international environment to come to the realisation that EU and NATO membership were the only possible and viable foreign policy options for the country speaks to the argument that despite the push for Europeanisation after 1997, the determinacy of the evolved identity remained in question, given the underlying civilizational ambivalence of Bulgaria that prevented a single-minded orientation to the West. And this stood in contrast to Poland, where the geopolitical availability of one foreign policy option was reinforced by a genuine, culturally-historically grounded belief in that option.

Bulgaria's passivity within the EU and NATO over the course of the 2000s and 2010s was also not simply a reflection of the country's limited military and economic resource base constraining the exercise of active leverage. Instead, reactiveness is underwritten by the ideationally-shaped lack of willingness to realise the theoretical and empirical possibilities for greater activeness on the part of small states in the framework of international institutions. In the EU setting, there are a number of strategies available to small states to counter the constraints of limited bargaining power and the low number of votes in the European Parliament. Some of those strategies include institutionalised cooperation on a regional basis and building partnerships with bigger states that allow an increase in collective bargaining leverage (Filipova, 2015:7; Panke, 2008:10; Kassimeris, 2009). Moreover, prioritisation of issues and selective engagement allows small states to concentrate their limited capacities on salient matters (Panke, 2008:4-11; Ingebritsen, Neumann, Gstoehl, Beyer, 2006; Bjoerkdahl, 2007).

Accordingly, Bulgaria can choose to be 'smart small' by excelling at coalition-building and focusing on priority areas it has expertise in, for instance in relation to the Western Balkans and the Black Sea region (where it can export its enlargement experience) (Slavkova, 2015; Ralchev, 2015, interviews; Kyuchukov, Benisheva, 2017; Dimitrov, 2017; Borisova, 2017; Petrova, 2017). But the fact that Bulgarian policy-makers have not yet realised their state's strengths in these issue areas speaks to the historically-informed lack of self-confidence in international affairs and the traditional disposition to avoid taking strong stances lest they spell disaster (as in the early 20th century), exacerbated by limited institutional capacity. So Bulgaria's passivity does not have to be a strategically inevitable fate but does remain such due to the continuous ideational impact of culturally-historically ingrained habits of policy-making.

7 Europe's Outlier
The Thin Europeanisation of Russian Foreign Policy

The conundrum about Russia's belongingness to Europe has for centuries preoccupied Russians and foreigners alike. In the early 1990s, it seemed as though this eternal question (*vechnyi vopros*) had finally received a long sought-after answer—Moscow was returning to the common European home. However, gradually the vision of Russia as an integral part of Europe was being replaced by the realisation that the Kremlin was increasingly turning into a normative outlier. Why and how the Russian Self and its Western Other could not sustain the initial hope for a joint future is the subject of this chapter.

Resisting each other: Constructing Russia and Europe

As in the Polish and Bulgarian cases, the cultural-historical framing of Russia's nation-state identity in juxtaposition to Europe (and the West more generally) represents the ideational context that has been reflected into and ultimately shaped the contemporary, post-communist unfoldment of Russian-European and Russian-American relations.

A key distinction that cuts across Russian society is that between *rossiyane* and *russkie*. The former term refers to all Russians as a civic identity that incorporates both ethnic Russian and non-ethnic Russian citizens of the Russian Federation, while the latter only denotes ethnic Russians. Closely linked to this distinction are the concepts of *narod* and *natsiya*. *Narod* can be generally taken to mean a big community, comprised of many nationalities, whereas *natsiya* is akin to the Western concept of the nation-state but has been less than widely applied in the Russian context for at least two reasons. First, historian Alexey Miller explains that problems with *natsiya* in the Russian context began with the French Revolution when the 'nation-state' obtained a distinctly political connotation, relating the nation to certain political arrangements—rights, freedoms, equality guaranteed by the constitution of a sovereign political unit. Since then the concept of *natsiya* has been avoided in Russian politics lest it incited national political emancipation from the oppression of the rulers. Instead, the triad of 'Orthodoxy, Autocracy and Nationality' posited *narodnost* (referring to the national community stripped of its political connotations) as a building block of the empire (Miller, 2008:3-5). Second, *natsiya* has been perceived as entailing correspondence with a given 'ethnos', which would mean the building of a nation-state that encompasses the territories inhabited by ethnic Russians. This, however, has been apprehended as posing a fundamental challenge to the multi-ethnic composition of the Russian state (Zevelev, 2009:6).

The differentiations between *russkie* and *rossiyane* as well as between *narod* and *natsiya* point to the coexistence of two competing elements in Russian identity—the ethnic and the supra-ethnic/supra-national. The ethnic component, although gathering strength especially after the collapse of the Soviet Union, has not had a decisive impact on political arrangements and foreign policy. This trend is partly underwritten by the lack of a consolidated national consciousness (*natsionalnoe samosoznanie*), determined by indistinct boundaries between the empire and the Russian ethnic core that characterised both the Russian Empire and the Soviet Union (Zevelev, 2009:2). The supra-ethnic/supra-national element of identity has moreover been instrumentalised to sustain different imperial visions in Russian history—be it a Slavophile-Orthodox, Eurasian or Soviet empire (Zevelev, 2009:7). These imperial visions differed from the modern Western idea of 'political morality'—understood as universal rights and freedoms, civic societal norms and political accountability of the rulers to the ruled. In Russia's case, the 'common imperial good' was defined in terms of great-powerness, autocracy and military prowess (Gudkov, 2014:4, 6).

Furthermore, the Westerniser-Slavophile opposition has been at the heart of debates about Russian national-civilizational identity. Importantly, the main issue in the differences between 19th century Westernisers and Slavophiles as well as their contemporary counterparts is the proper relationship and cultural compatibility between Russia and Europe, rather than discussions about the internal composition of the Russian Empire, the Soviet Union, or today's Russia (linked to relations and territorial borders between the ethnic-Russians and the non-Russians) (Zevelev, 2009:4).

To categorise political figures and intellectuals according to their views on Russian identity (descended and borrowing as these views are from the Westerniser-Slavophile debate of the 19th and early 20th century), the book follows, but also qualifies, a classification elaborated in broadly similar terms by MacFarlane (1993), Allison, Light, White (2006), Light (2003), Jackson (2003), Prizel (1998), which distinguishes between three groups. The first group is that of the Liberal Westernisers (*zapadniki*), who argue that Russia's identity should be defined as a civic state within the boundaries of the Russian Federation, further informed by the goals of liberal democracy, market reforms and the prioritisation of integration with the West. The Liberal Westernisers are opposed to the nationalist search for a unique Russian 'national idea' that can justify the recreation of an empire in the formerly controlled CIS area. So the Liberal Westernisers relegate relations with the CIS countries to a secondary position vis-à-vis Europe and America (Jackson, 2003:34). Some of the representatives of this group have included politicians Boris Yeltsin, Andrey Kozyrev, Egor Gaidar, Anatoly Chubais, Boris Nemtsov, Alexey Navalny; the Yabloko party, the People's Freedom Party (PARNAS), the Progress Party.

At the other extreme of the identity debate are the Fundamentalist Nationalists (or the conservatives—*pochvenniki*), who understand Russia as a 'Eurasian' power. Eurasianism emphasises Russia's geopolitical and cultural distinctiveness from both the Western and Asian worlds and encompasses authoritarian attitudes of the general population and the leaders, strong state, collectivist values, the Orthodox religion. Correspondingly, the principal foreign policy proposals of the Fundamentalist Nationalists are not centred on cooperative relations with Europe and America. Instead, they want to recreate a Russian empire in Eurasia (i.e., the post-Soviet space), oppose US primacy and the liberal international order as well as cooperate with the East (China and India) (Jackson, 2003:35). Some of the representatives of this identity stance have been Vladimir Zhirinovsky, Gennady Zyuganov, Alexander Prokhanov, Sergey Kurginyan, Alexander Dugin; the Liberal Democratic Party (LDPR), the Communist Party (KPRF). A key distinction that can be singled out within the Fundamentalist Nationalist group is that between the neo-imperialists and the ethno-nationalists. The neo-imperialists (such as Alexander Dugin) assert that Russia is a multi-ethnic great power that has to, if not restore the state within the previous borders of the Soviet Union or the Russian Empire, at least maintain a zone of informal imperial influence. The ethno-nationalists' views (of such figures as Dmitry Rogozin) are based on the writings of Alexander Solzhenitsyn, who defined the nation along ethnic lines and envisaged the unification of all ethnic Russians and most eastern Slavs from Ukraine, Belarus and northern Kazakhstan under one political unit (Zevelev, 2014, interview; Zevelev, 2014).

The third position in the identity debate is espoused by the Pragmatic Nationalists (or the centrists/statists—*gosudarstvenniki/derzhavniki*). They agree with the Fundamentalist Nationalists that the country's former status as a great power should be restored and that Russia possesses elements of a unique, Eurasian identity. The Pragmatic Nationalists also accept the Liberal Westerniser goal of democratisation and cooperation with the West, but wish the transitional process to take Russia's conditions (i.e., collectivist values) into account. The Pragmatic Nationalists hence advocate a unique but non-expansionist foreign policy in the CIS, which would allow Russia to regain its status as a great power without the recreation of empire since cooperation with Europe and America is also considered important (Jackson, 2003:36). Thus, in the Pragmatic Nationalist view, Russia should be a European—but also a great global, power that accepts the importance of democracy, cooperation and integration but nevertheless also places and emphasis on sovereignty, the establishment of a regional sphere of influence and the conduct of vigorously competitive international relations that does not shy away from the aggressive deployment of hard power. Prominent representatives of this group have included Evgeny Primakov and Vladimir Putin (until his third term of office when the President's positions evolved closer to the Fundamentalist Nationalists); the United Russia party, A Just Russia (SR).

In addition to the overall differences among the three identity groups, the identification of within-group nuances speaks to the shared and unifying ideational positions across the political spectrum. For instance, within the category of the Liberal Westernisers, the sub-category of the 'moderate liberals' or 'democratic pragmatists' can be noted, who stand for a democratic but strong state and cooperation with the West based on an equal partnership rather than outright agreement with European and American policies, thus coming close to the stances of the Pragmatic Nationalists. Some of the representatives of this sub-group have included Vladimir Lukin, Grigory Yavlinsky, Alexey Arbatov, Sergey Rogov, Nikolay Smelev (Arbatova, 2005:28, Arbatov, 1993:7). In turn, the centrist orientation of the Pragmatic Nationalists has allowed them to borrow and amalgamate elements from the worldview of both the Liberal Westernisers and the Fundamentalist Nationalists.

The Russian Self and the Western Other in the boundary-drawing process of identification

The core attributes of the Self and its significant Other that are conceptualised in Chapter 3 as gaining particular importance during times of crisis have also been prominently manifested in the Russian case. After the collapse of the Soviet Union, Russia found itself in a liminal identity crisis. This crisis was occasioned both by the challenging post-communist political, economic and social transformation as well by Russia's historically continuous liminal geographical, geopolitical and ideational situation between East and West (MacFarlane, 1993; Jahn, 2009; Puhle, 2009; Sakwa, 2011). The end of the USSR meant an abrupt decline in Russia's great-power status in European and world affairs, reviving the Westerniser-Slavophile debate about Russia's European-ness in the search for a redefined international-civilizational place and introducing a nation-building challenge after the collapse of the multinational Soviet 'empire'. Indeed, Russian intellectuals maintain that identity concerns became crucial during the post-1991 period of extreme flux and that visions of Russian identity were heavily contested — there was no political-elite and societal consensus on what is 'Russia', how it should relate to Europe or to its post-Soviet neighbours (Zevelev, 2014; Trenin, 2014; Medvedev, 2014, interviews).

In this situation of identity crisis, the need for external models as well as comparisons and heightened attention to the behaviour and attitudes of the West — Russia's most significant Other (historically encompassing first Western Europe and then also the US), became even more important. The very beginnings of Russian national consciousness in the 17th and 18th century were linked to the relationship with Western Europe (Greenfeld, 1992:189-275). Peter the Great's sweeping onslaught on pre-modern customs in the direction of adopting European cultural, educational, literary, social and economic styles (while instituting autocratic absolutism) gave birth to the torn Russia of the last three centuries — divided between Slavophiles and Westernisers, the legacy of whose vigorous early 19th century debate lives on (Legvold, 2007b:83). These intellectual currents grappled with the merits and desirability of introducing the Western European model to Russia. The Slavophiles viewed the West as morally corrupt and rejected Western political, economic and societal trends, including materialism, rationalism, constitutional monarchy, the nation-state. Instead, for the Slavophiles, Russia's future lay in a return to nativist principles — of the *sobornost* (organic togetherness) of the peasant commune, bound together by the Orthodox Christian faith and an autocratic government, considered suitable to maintaining social harmony (McDaniel, 1996:17; Pipes, 1995:54-55). The Westernisers, however, rejected autocracy and the claim that Russia was unique, putting strong emphasis on the importance of questions of freedom. They argued that in order for the Russians to prosper, they had to embrace the historical Western path, which served as the model for social, political and economic modernisation, and draw on their own indigenous, democratic traditions. For instance, *zemskie sobory* and *zemstvo* (popular democratic councils) consisted of representatives of the gentry, bourgeoisie and even peasantry to consult the tsar on matters of domestic and foreign policy (Petro, 1995:30-33, 42; McDaniel, 1996:18).

Western Europe is thus viewed both as a utopian model to be emulated and as a threat to national uniqueness. This duality can be seen in all forms of self-representations—both in the assertion that Russia is lagging behind, that it is Asiatic and has to catch up with the US and Europe, which are developed and modern, and in the claim that the Russians are spiritual, warm, emotional in contrast to the cold and pragmatic West. As Gudkov and Utkin have made clear, these polarities form two sides of the same coin and represent a compensatory complex that results either in self-criticism or self-inflation when determining boundaries of mutuality with the significant Western Other (Gudkov, 2014; Utkin, 2014, interviews). Similar dualistic considerations apply to the US as the other face of the West (particularly since its rise to great powerhood and the beginning of the Cold War confrontation), but with a special reference to issues of status and prestige. That is, American pre-eminence in international affairs became a benchmark against which to measure Russia's, or formerly the Soviet Union's, own power and military might, giving rise to admiration but also resentment as Russian status is perceived to be inferior.

Following from the above is an important characteristic of the Other—in terms of economic-technological progress and international political weight the West has been superior to Russia. Both before and during the post-communist period, Russia has been in a weaker power-position (despite its relative economic and international resurgence under Putin), which has put it in the role of norm-taker rather than norm-maker. The Russia-Europe relationship has thus been mostly asymmetrical, with the values of the European powers being projected on Moscow (Haukkala, 2008a:35-36, 2008b; Neumann, 1995). Hence, one can expect Russia's sensitivities to Western normative standpoints to be enhanced, given the West's greater capabilities that can affect both the identity and power positions of the Russian Self, which strives for affirmation by its significant and powerful Other.

Added to this have been external events which were critical for the conceptualisation of Russian identity in the post-Cold War period. In the early 1990s and the immediate aftermath of the collapse of the Soviet Union, the way the 'victorious' side of the West behaved towards Russia could shape both its internal development as well as integration in the Western-centric international system. EU and NATO enlargement were particularly consequential in redefining the civilizational, security and economic borders of the European continent and were therefore of crucial significance to the configuration of Russia's place in Europe.

Russia and Europe in action, 1991-2015: A story of thin Europeanisation

The interactive constitution of the boundaries of shared belongingness between the Russian Self and its Western Other since the collapse of the Soviet Union in 1991 produced Russia's thin Europeanisation. This 'thinness' (i.e., superficiality, insufficiency) was shaped by the lack of a strong cultural-ideational basis for and domestic political consensus about the European direction of the country coupled with a low level of commitment and acceptance by the West.

As in Poland and Bulgaria, the decades of the 1990s, 2000s and 2010s imparted distinctive features to the process of Europeanisation. In the 1990s, the Russian political scene was characterised by specific challenges related to the virulent debates about the country's foreign policy identity and the political-economic chaos, as the West was also trying to work out its stance on Moscow's belongingness to the post-Cold War expansion of the Euro-Atlantic community. Neither of these challenges was resolved by the end of the decade, with Russia and the West becoming increasingly mutually disappointed. In the 2000s and 2010s, Vladimir Putin's first two terms in office as President as well as Dmitry Medvedev's Presidency generally continued the goal of situating Moscow in the European order on the basis of the belief that as an essential element of European civilization Russia had to cooperate with the West, while asserting its cultural and geopolitical distinctiveness. But as

Putin reconstituted state authority, the identity crisis subsided (not least due to the President's grip on the identity discourse) and Europe and America drifted further away from recognising Russia's European credentials, the Fundamentalist Nationalist strand of identification received an added impetus since 2011/2012. Accordingly, the Kremlin put forward its alternative interpretation of European-ness, heavily contesting the ideal-typical model (Busygina, 2014; Melville, 2014; Simon, 2014; Gudkov, 2014; Zevelev, 2014; Trenin, 2014, interviews; Malinova, 2012:77; Morozov, 2008:12, 17, 20; Izvestiya, 2014).

The story of Russia's thin Europeanisation since 1991 is told in the rest of this chapter first through the separate lenses of the Russian Self and its Western Other and then through their interactive conjunction, which ultimately shaped the trend of the gradual mutual divergence rather than joining in a shared community.

The Russian Self, 1991-2000: The road to Europe derailed

Russia's Europeanisation in the 1990s crucially depended on how the pro-Western section of the political elite, which held the reins of power, would steer the course of Moscow's return to Europe. Yet, the Liberal Westernisers fell short of this challenge as their understandings were not only substantively incompatible with the ideal-typical model of European-ness related to support for a liberal international order, regional cooperation and institutionalised integration, but the symbolic and practical institutionalisation of those understandings also failed. Hence, the post-1991 period marked a continuation of the historical tradition of a shallow embeddedness of European values in Russian national consciousness. Moreover, the domestic political consensus on Russia's Europeanisation — even if lacking in sound ideational underpinnings, was confined to the Liberal Westernising governing elite but was not intersubjectively shared across the rest of the political spectrum, being vociferously contested by the conservatively-oriented politicians.

The institutional and party-political setting additionally soured the domestic political atmosphere through heavy partisanship and factionalism. And unlike Poland and (to some extent) Bulgaria, where the unstable political landscape led above all to policy inconsistency but did not fundamentally weaken the resolve to Europeanise given the achievement of ideational consensus, in Russia, political factionalism and institutional deficiencies exacerbated the deep-seated ideational uncertainty. This resulted in the inability to pursue determinedly the discursively enunciated liberal course of integration with the Euro-Atlantic community.

The domestic ideational setting

The Liberal Westerniers' inability to internalise and implement the principled positions informing the ideal-typical model of European-ness took on a number of dimensions. Importantly, Russian liberals' understanding of the EU and NATO was stereotypically- and superficially informed and ultimately differed from the West European animating principles of those organisations. Initially, Moscow was convinced that a new European order would emerge without dividing lines but did not realise the value of institutionalised cooperation for building a rules-bound order placing limits on national sovereignty. Since the EU did not include Russia and was an element of the past (of the bygone era of the Cold War), Russia had no reasons for focusing its foreign policy on such an organisation (Baranovsky, 2002:12-13). Then, as the Union proceeded with its enlargement policies, the whole process of institutionalised integration was dismissed and assessed as driven by economic rather than political considerations.

Yet, following disappointments with NATO-related developments (as clarified later in the chapter), it began to be thought that apart from building a zone of prosperity, the EU could fit into the broader picture of creating a 'greater Europe', in which Russia would play a prominent role—in contrast to a NATO-centred Europe (Baranovsky, 2002:126). Yeltsin's 'Greater Europe' concept posited a Europe without dividing lines, where no single state would impose its will on the rest and where all European states would be equal partners united by common democratic principles (Menkiszak, 2013:9-10). The Russian President also warned against forces in and outside Europe which wanted to isolate Russia and place it on an unequal footing, arguing that Europe could build its security without the US (Menkiszak, 2013:9-10; Gornostaev, 1997; Bangersky, Gornostaev, 1997; Miheev, 1997).

What transpires in this concept of 'Greater Europe' is the blending of power considerations and the desire to belong to European civilization along the Russian elites' perception of European integration as a way of enhancing Russia's prestige, being included in European affairs, recognised as an equal and rightful part of the European family of nations and having influence on European politics, ideally greater than US influence on Europe (Yeltsin, 2001:149). However, the West European understanding of European integration differs as it is focused more on a gradual (albeit difficult and sometimes inconsistent) movement towards interdependence and pooling of sovereignty rather than on a 19th century-like Concert of great European powers seeking to counterbalance US hegemony.

As regards attitudes to NATO, even the Liberal Westernisers harboured significant reservations about the Alliance (Gorskii, 2001:19, 26, 35). In Vladimir Baranovsky's recollections, most liberals argued that NATO expansion would damage Russia's security interests, its relations with the West and its liberal democratic domestic development. The debates about NATO enlargement even led to the 'migration' of liberals from the Liberal Westerniser camp to the Pragmatic Nationalists, as was the case of Sergey Karaganov and Sergey Stankevich (Baranovsky, 2014, interview).

Sharing their close observations of Russian politics in the 1990s, Sergey Utkin and Maria Lipman have clarified that Russian centrists, conservatives as well as liberals were very critical of NATO, not least because of Cold War stereotypes, prejudices and irrational fears. It was a minority view that Russia could benefit from cooperating with the Alliance as for most people NATO represented an unpredictable black box and imaginary monster that stays near Russian borders. Although some realistic security concerns could be derived from NATO's coming closer to Russia's borders with its overwhelming military capabilities as well as lack of clarity and binding agreements regarding the non-deployment of tactical nuclear and conventional weapons and infrastructure beyond the borders of the 16 old member states, Utkin asserts that in rational terms NATO enlargement did not pose an 'objective' threat to Russia (NATO Factsheet, 2016). For example, he cites the argument that without the Alliance's pacifying role, there would be a rise in the defence expenditures and military posturing of European countries, which would worsen stability on the continent and hence Russia's own external environment (Utkin, 2014; Lipman, 2014, interviews).

The Liberal Westernising course towards Moscow's integration in the Euro-Atlantic community was further undermined by the inability to work out a symbolic signification of the enunciated identity of Russia as a European state. That identity also had to be conceptually reconciled with outstanding fissures in the interpretation of the Russian past as well as nagging concerns about the assertion of national interests and the achievement of domestic economic justice.

Olga Malinova has explained that the liberal political elite did not understand the importance of providing symbolic rootedness to the Liberal Westernising identity strand in a fundamentally ideationally divided country. So despite the fact that the official discourse of Yeltsin and his team was dominated by the idea of the 'new, liberal democratic Russia', little was done symbolically to support this idea (Malinova, 2014, interview). For instance, there was a lot of ambiguity surrounding Lenin's Mausoleum in the 1990s. One option was for Lenin to be reburied with his relatives in St. Petersburg, which would have completed the deconsecration of that political figure. But the government's inability to decide how to deal with the mausoleum reflected a wider difficulty of interpreting the past in a way that would have provided a symbolic break with Soviet authoritarianism (exemplified by Lenin) as a precondition for uniting around a new set of liberal democratic national symbols (Morrison, 1993:5, 7).

The difficulty of establishing liberal democratic ideas as part of the political mainstream was also the result of the failure of the Liberal Westernisers to marry their Europeanising rhetoric with a foreign policy agenda that would alleviate political and societal concerns about the assertion of national autonomy. Instead, an overly polarising opposition was drawn, according to which all those who deflected from Ego Gaidar's ideas (including a determined pro-Western orientation and preference for a shock economic therapy), were necessarily Russian nationalist-imperialists (Morozov, 2016). Consequently, as Dmitry Trenin and Alexey Miller have assessed, the liberals became estranged from the pro-European part of the political class and society, who were favourably predisposed to Europeanisation but nevertheless began to see in excessive imitation of and obedience to the West an affront to positive national distinctiveness (Trenin, 2014; Miller, 2014, interviews).

Particularly with regard to economics, the way that the liberals conducted the economic reforms damaged the liberal vision of Russia's internal development and cooperation with the West, as the population associated the painful reforms with the European model, thought to be dictated by the Western powers and carried out by the Russian government. Aside from the 'objective' consequences of the reforms—impoverishment, unemployment, inflation, the problem was not necessarily only in the principle of 'shock liberalisation' itself (as it was also carried out in other CEEs) but in that it was never properly explained to the people. Irina Busygina has stressed that Egor Gaidar and his team did not clarify to the electorate what the economic reforms entailed. Such an attitude was a sign that the Liberal Westernisers did not understand the essence of democracy (importantly constituted by horizontal lines of policy deliberation and accountability of the 'rulers' to the 'ruled') since they wanted to build democracy from above (Busygina, 2014, interview; Nelson, Kuzes, 1995:91-133). Moreover, in their attempt to steer Russia into a course of economic development and 'normality'—i.e., into the 'normal' path of internal modernisation and foreign policy behaviour as a 'normal' European power, the liberals dogmatically ignored the important issue of the negative economic fall-out in the transformation process. As Utkin has explained, by arguing that the social and economic costs of moving towards a capitalist system would simply be resolved as a result of the successful application of the Western model, the Liberal Westernisers 'outsourced' the discussion of those problems to the Fundamentalist Nationalists (especially the communists). The latter employed the rhetoric on social-economic injustice as a way of making their case that Russia should veer away from the European path of development (Utkin, 2014, interview).

In addition to the normative incompatibilities and conceptual deficiencies of the Liberal Westernisers' espousal and practice of European-ness, Russia's thin Europeanisation was further underwritten by the absence of a broader domestic political consensus on the desirability of the country's integration in the Euro-Atlantic community. The Fundamentalist Nationalists (including Gennady Zyuganov's Communist Party and Vladimir Zhirinovsky's Liberal Democratic Party) as well as some moderate Liberal Westerniser politicians and oligarchic economic elites became increasingly vociferous and influential critics of government policy.

The end of 1992 and the whole of 1993 illustrate the oppositional forces that President Yeltsin and his team had to come up against. Yeltsin engaged in fierce confrontation with Ruslan Khasbulatov, speaker of the Russian Parliament, and Alexander Rutskoi, Vice-President, over the Constitution, which culminated in the shelling of Russia's White House of government in October 1993 to forcefully suppress rioting deputies who had occupied the building. And although the President's preferred form of the Constitution (granting the Presidency more powers) was approved, he could still not implement his policies freely (Slater, 1994:22, 25). After the December 1993 Federal Assembly elections, the pro-reformist camp did not fare well enough, taking 35% of the seats in the Duma, and Russia's hard line forces emerged as the winners, together gaining more than 40% of the seats. This ensured a new stalemate in the legislative process (Rahr, 1994:32).

Another brake on the implementation of Yeltsin's pro-European intentions was the reassertion of power of the conservative institutions from the Soviet period: the armed forces, the military-industrial complex, the gas and oil lobby, the KGB, whose mind-set was based on a confrontation rather than integration with the West. Their agitation in 1992 and 1993 and General Alexander Lebed's restoration of the cohesion of the Army could well be understood as a determined attempt at making a political comeback (Duncan, 2007:8). The support that the military provided to Yeltsin during the shelling of the White House additionally strengthened its position. Concessions to the military leadership included more assertive policies in Russia's relations with the 'near abroad' and official opposition to NATO expansion, as opposed to the declared Liberal Westernising goal of peaceful and non-domineering regional relations and institutionalised security cooperation (Foye, 1994:4). The President abandoned reformist premier Egor Gaidar and appointed previous Soviet gas and oil minister Viktor Chernomyrdin as Gaidar's successor in December 1992. The agreements signed by Yeltsin in Beijing and New Delhi on arms trade and joint military production, in late 1992 and early 1993 respectively, were testimony to the impact of the military on directing policies away from a primary focus on a cooperative security European order and towards multipolar assertiveness (Adomeit, 1995:25).

In turn, the moderate liberals also exercised increasing influence on government stances. As regards domestic policies, the proposals of the main moderate Liberal Westernising parties — the Civic Union and the Democratic Party of Russia (DPR), took the middle ground between the radical market economics supported by Russia's Choice and the return to state ownership called for by the Communist Party. In terms of foreign policy, the moderates leaned neither towards seeing Russia as an uncritical ally of the West, nor towards a confrontational and assertive line (Slater, 1994:13). These positions became especially influential as the moderates managed to obtain high posts in the Duma — Valery Bogomolov of the DPR became a deputy chairman of the International Affairs Committee; in the executive, economic portfolios were handed to industrialists close to the Civic Union (Slater, 1994:18). Indeed, in 1993, Deputy Prime Ministers Oleg Lobov and Oleg Soskovets proposed changes to the economic and privatisation programmes, gaining support with Yeltsin to the dismay of the more radical liberals, notably Egor Gaidar (Slater, 1994:18). Organisations such as the Russian Union of Industrialists and Entrepreneurs cooperated with their counterparts in former Soviet republics and lobbied for strong bilateral and multilateral economic links, which were expected to lead to a renewed Russian primacy in the region (Pravda, 1996:185).

Finally, the economic elites, especially in the face of certain oligarchs, played a further role in the hardening of Russian attitudes and policies towards the West. Boris Berezovsky argued that Russia ought to promote the integration of the CIS as a sphere of Moscow's influence at the expense of relations with Europe and America. He worked closely with Foreign Minister Primakov to plan a strategy towards the CIS, strongly opposing NATO expansion (Duncan, 2007:8).

Overall, the developments in Russian politics in the 1990s show that although Yeltsin and his closest circle of liberally-minded politicians held on to the reins of power, various other groups who were not in favour of Russia's Europeanisation managed to assert their ideas and policy-making priorities (MacFarlane, 1993:12; Foye, 1994:2; Talbott, 2003:190; Yeltsin, 2001:52; 54; Arbatov, 1993:16). The communists and nationalist-imperialists exercised an influence on the general atmosphere of intensifying oppositional discourse and parliamentary action against cooperation with the West. The military and oligarchs leveraged policies related to the establishment of a more domineering rather than regionally friendly stance towards the CIS. The centrists took important government positions and called for a less determined effort at integrating with the Euro-Atlantic community and applying domestically the Western liberal democratic, free market economic model.

The domestic institutional and party-political setting

The uncertain ideational path of Russia's Europeanisation was further weakened by the institutional fluidity and instrumentally-motivated concerns that had gripped the Russian policy-making environment. In particular, the President's style of rule made it more difficult for the liberal democratic vision of Russia integrated with the West to take hold in the political and societal mainstream. Yeltsin's team did not lay out a solid political and institutional foundation for democratic reforms. This could have happened by building a political party out of the Democratic Russia movement and cementing a broad coalition of liberal to moderate-centrist parties that would consistently support democratic development and the European integrationist course. Instead, Yeltsin's team relied on the enormous post-August 1991 popularity of the President (i.e., when Yeltsin spearheaded the democratic resistance against the hard line Soviet coup aimed at toppling Gorbachev from power) and counted on the disarray in the communist-nationalist camp (Arbatov, 1993:12-13).

Boris Yeltsin's personalistic bent was also expressed in the creation of a system of competing factions, whereby his 'divide-and-rule' strategy ensured that all the major political figures vied for access to the President as the 'supreme arbiter'. For instance, the lack of a clear line of authority in the foreign policy sphere contributed to increased rivalry between the Defence and Foreign Ministry over a number of issues (such as NATO and Kosovo) but Yeltsin stood at the top of this rivalry in almost all cases (Larrabee, Karasik, 1997:14). The Presidential Apparatus began to show signs of influence with the appointment of Anatoly Chubais as chief of staff who brought a much needed sense of discipline. But by appointing Sergei Shakhrai (a political opponent of Chubais) as a deputy head, Yeltsin created a counter-balancing centre of power, which was an attempt to ensure the President's primacy in foreign policy (Larrabee, Karasik, 1997:38, 46).

The lack of institutionalisation, coupled with a divide-and-rule strategy, only served to encourage authoritarian tendencies, which were incompatible with the professed vision of Russia as a

Europeanised country. The new 1993 Constitution granted extensive powers to the President, raising fears among liberal Russian observers that it would encourage authoritarian government (Slater, 1994:25, 28-29; Hoffman, 2011:325-365). As Alexey Gromyko observed, Yeltsin's inclination to create a tight circle around himself—the so-called 'family', made it possible for the oligarchic politics and economy to emerge despite the professed goal of Europeanisation (Gromyko, 2014, interview). Moreover, painting a psychological portrait of Yeltsin out of her personal experiences at the time, Busygina explained that his authoritarian tendencies were particularly enabled by a prominent attitudinal contradiction. It was expressed in Yeltsin's commitment to democratisation and integration with the West (which was both rhetorical and intuitively aspired to) and his simultaneous insufficient understanding of and desire to learn the conduct of genuine democratic practices of transparency, consensus-seeking and cooperation, which stood in contrast to the President's conflictual assertiveness domestically, regionally and internationally. So Yeltsin called for democracy and European integration but behaved like an authoritarian leader, who was, however, unable to fully assert his power given the strong internal oppositional forces (Busygina, 2014, interview).

And the wider institutional setting could not tame the President's personal idiosyncrasies. The dismantling of the Communist Party apparatus, which had represented the central information-processing, decision-making and monitoring agency for the system of foreign policy before 1991, shook up the distribution of power among the Foreign Ministry, the Security Services and the Ministry of Defence. Yet, efficient coordination was not introduced. The Presidential Security Council was unable to carry out its key role in international affairs, hampered by under-resourcing and political cross-currents. Its broad remit meant that it played only an intermittent part in foreign policy. Hence, in the absence of effective central control, and in the new climate of extreme ideological pluralism, bureaucratic rivalries with roots in the Soviet period acquired a more intense character (Larrabee, Karasik, 1997:38). For instance, as head of the Security Council, General Lebed remarked on a visit to the NATO headquarters in

1996 that Russia was ready to cooperate with NATO and would not object to its expansion. But this statement was at variance with Foreign Minister Evgeny Primakov's tougher line against Moscow's cooperation with the North Atlantic Alliance (Larrabee, Karasik, 1997:8-9).

On the whole, although the liberals' fragile political predominance ensured at least an overall rhetorical attachment to Euro-Atlantic integration, the unstable political-institutional environment of the 1990s prevented the consistent conduct of Russian foreign policy. Ultimately, personalism, institutional incoherence and partisanship went hand in hand with Russian politicians' ideational uncertainties in eroding the possibility for the Europeanised vision of Russia to become consolidated as part of the political mainstream.

The Russian Self, 2000-2015: Europe suspended

The difficulty of sustaining and implementing the Russian Self's declared pro-European path of development in the 1990s was not resolved in the 2000s and 2010s. Despite the fact that in the new millennium the dramatic upheavals of the immediate post-1991 period were replaced by relative stability, Moscow gradually drifted even further away from Europeanisation. The change of the identity discourses in the direction of nationalist conservatism and the evolution of the material basis of Vladimir Putin's regime towards growing authoritarianism led to the contestation of key tenets of the ideal-typical model of European-ness. Accordingly, standards of liberal democratic governance were increasingly substituted with authoritarian leadership justified by the (alleged) collectivist dispositions of Russian society. Principles of good neighbourliness gave way to regional assertiveness, while support for a liberal international order based on cooperation with the West yielded to competition with Europe and America and the attempt to construct multipolar global politics.

The discourses of Russian identity under Vladimir Putin

Over the course of his long reign, Vladimir Putin has presided over a number of shifts in the discourses of Russian identity. Each of these shifts has grappled with and imparted a specific interpretation to ideal-typical European values. Putin's first term in office (2000-2004) provided the contours of the vision of Russia as a partner of Europe and America but also as a great, independent power not entirely at ease with liberal democracy. This was consonant with the views of Pragmatic Nationalists incorporating elements of the Liberal Westernising discourse. The amalgamation of liberal as well as centrist and conservative ideas has been termed a 'deliberate eclecticism/evasiveness' (Putin, 7 May 2000). The eclecticism was deliberate both for ideational and instrumental concerns. The political leadership at once tried to provide an answer to the uncertainties of Russia's post-communist identity by uniting the multi-layered, historically loaded strands of Russian identification. But at the same time this unity was also spurred by the governing elite's strategically-motivated goal to limit divisive public discussions about Russian identity that could challenge the ideological legitimacy of the regime. Building as broad a political-ideational base for regime legitimacy as possible was seen as the way to ensure all-encompassing societal support (Malinova, 2012:77).

Thus, on the one hand, Putin's discourse of legitimation was informed by principles different from Yeltsin's general vision of a liberal democratic Russia cooperating closely with the West. The justificatory pillars of Putin's rule rested on sovereignty, independence and great-powerness. The main idea of this rhetoric was that Russia was returning to its traditional role as a great power, which has always asserted its values and independence from the West. So Russia represents an 'exception' that cannot be just another 'normal' European power—rather, its additional Eurasian orientation presupposes the reintegration of the post-Soviet space. Further specificities included collectivist values and a peculiar understanding of state-ness based on a more centralised view of the state that also fulfils the functions of a great power—as embodied in the concept of *derzhavnost* (Putin, 31 December 1999, 7 May 2000; Busygina, 2014; Melville, 2014; Simon, 2014; Gudkov, 2014, interviews). On the other hand, Putin emphasised the importance of the values of liberal democracy and economic freedom, interpreting the collapse of the USSR as the choice that the Russians made in favour of openness, democracy and cooperation with the West. He also repeatedly argued that there is a unity of European culture, to which Russia has historically belonged and contributed (Putin, 25 September 2001).

Since 2005/2006, Liberal Westernising views were increasingly marginalised within Pragmatic Nationalism so that the identity discourse tilted in the direction of stronger criticism of liberal democracy and building enemy images of the West European countries and the US. The concept of 'sovereign democracy' — put forward by Kremlin ideologue Vladislav Surkov, demonstrated the evolving process of identity construction, whereby Russia was simultaneously trying to distinguish and associate itself with Europe (Surkov, 2006). This duality was — as with deliberate eclecticism, an expression of the ideas that the elite held about Russia as a distinctive European power. But sovereign democracy was also a justification for the growing authoritarianism of the regime: this concept conveyed the message that Russia is a democracy and any attempt at the verification of this claim would be regarded as an infringement on Russian sovereignty (Lipman, 2006).

In particular, sovereign democracy simultaneously accepts a European norm (i.e. democracy), while opposing the view that only the West can impose universal standards on how democracy is to be implemented domestically or promoted internationally. This means that Russia wants to be recognised as a 'normal' country that shares common European values. Yet, Moscow lays strong emphasis on its exceptionalism, thus hoping for special treatment as well as countering the liberal universalist agenda that sovereignty should be limited for the sake of fostering democracy and human rights (Morozov, 2008:12, 17, 20; Makarychev, 2008:4; Surkov, 2006).

During Dmitry Medvedev's Presidency (2008-2012) elements of the pro-Western views once again became influential so that, as

Igor Zevelev has pointed out, an intellectual coalition was formed between the great power and pro-Western thinkers (Zevelev, 2014, interview). On the one hand, Medvedev deplored the fact that Russia's power and position in international relations was still based on oil and gas, nuclear weapons and industrial infrastructure—all a legacy of the Soviet Union, which however could not ensure Russia's success in the 21st century and which could not underwrite the sustainability of the USSR as a superpower (Medvedev, 12 November 2009). Instead, he suggested that pragmatism and the goal of the modernisation of Russia's economy and society should guide Moscow's external relations and determine a cooperative attitude to the West. The President advocated a 'smart' foreign policy, free of stereotypes and confrontational attitudes (Medvedev, 10 September 2009; Medvedev, 12 November 2009; Medvedev, 12 July, 2010).

On the other hand, although the President argued that Russia and Europe as well as the US were united by common democratic values, he still maintained that Russian democracy had its specific characteristics and was conditioned by certain distinctive perspectives. For instance, Medvedev claimed that democratic values had to be endowed with a 'legal framework' in order that it would not be possible for certain (Western) countries to abuse democratic values as a pretext for interventions, which the Russian elite interpreted as catering to geopolitical interests (Medvedev, 10 September 2010; Morozov, 2010). In foreign policy terms, Medvedev still pledged to work towards the creation of a multipolar world order, criticising American unilateralism and the EU's designs for the post-Soviet space (including the EP and the ENP), as they could endanger Russia's primacy in the region (Shkel, 2008; Medvedev, 10 September 2009, 10 September 2010). The President's proposed European Security Treaty (2009) was motivated by the desire to limit American influence on Europe's security matters, while ensuring an equal Russian say. To this end, the treaty stated the aim of indivisible European security and the inadmissibility of seeking to strengthen one's own security at the expense of others, thus implicitly criticising NATO's central role on the continent (Zagorski, 2009:6-7).

When Vladimir Putin returned to the Presidency in 2012, the intellectual coalition between the centrists and the liberals had faded, with Pragmatic Nationalism not only becoming dominant but moving towards the Fundamentalist Nationalist end of the identity spectrum. The general consensus emerging from my interviews with Russian experts is that the 'conservative' discourse promoted since Putin's third Presidency is a politically constructed project that aims to serve elite interests by drawing on pre-existing identities shared by the majority of the political elite figures and the wider population (Simon, 2014; Zevelev, 2014; Miller, 2014; Trenin, 2014; Utkin, 2014; Tevdoy-Burmuli, 2014; Shmelev, 2014; Krickovic, 2014, interviews). The infusion of more 'conservative certainty' into the otherwise dualistic discourses of identity that had been hitherto prevalent was spurred by the protests of 2011/2012 and the Ukrainian crisis, which events presented a grave threat to the internal stability of the regime as well as its regional clout. The response of the leadership was to develop an identity discourse that would cement the power of the governing United Russia party by incorporating the significance of the state as a constitutive part of national identity and by further creating a perception of threat (both internal, coming from the liberals, and external—from the West) (Zevelev, 2014, interview; Rogoża, 2014).

The promotion of conservative values, however, also rests on a pre-existing ideational basis. As my interviews confirmed, both Putin's elite circle—the *siloviki* (strongmen or persons of force) as well as a large part of the populace share a demand for a nationalist-statist, great-power ideology (Krickovic, 2014; Gudkov, 2014; Trenin, 2014, interviews; Kolesnikov, 2015). Andrey Kortunov has explained that the predominant Russian perspective now holds that Western normative decadence (ostensibly following from the loss of traditional family values), economic stagnation, the inability to solve the Constitutional and Eurozone crises, the waves of migrants who change Europe's Christian identity and the emergence of non-Western centres of power in international politics all mean that convergence on the Western model should no longer be Russia's ultimate goal (Kortunov, 2014, interview). According to the Russian point of view, Russia is now the only inheritor of the 'true' European traditions typifying Europe 'at its best', which the Moscow elite judges to be the Europe of the 19th century animated by strong state authority, patriotism, family values, religion, and the conduct of international relations on the basis of the balance of power and spheres of influence (Putin, 19 September 2013; Izvestiya, 2014; Kortunov, 2014; Lipman, 2014, interviews). Moreover, until 2014, the government was very careful about endorsing ethnic nationalism especially by using the term *russkie*. However, the annexation of Crimea led to a major shift in discourse, as this term began to be used much more extensively and Putin laid an emphasis on Russia as a multi-national society but with a Russian (*russkiy*) ethnic core (Putin, 18 March 2014; Zevelev, 2014, interview). The conservative identity politics thus rejects the European concept and practice of multiculturalism because although respect for local cultures has allegedly been a main component in Russian history, such local cultures cannot be allowed to challenge the moral principles of the majority (Putin, 19 September 2013; Izvestiya, 2014).

The conservative view entails a number of foreign policy implications. First, the rejection of the idea that modernisation modelled on the West is the only tool of progress and the consequent proclamation of conservatism as a sounder moral and political ethic represents a normative challenge to individual Western European countries and the EU in general — i.e., an attempt to sway EU politics by influencing the conservative, anti-Union layers of European societies (Filipova, Stefanov, 2021b:29). Second, while conservatism holds that Russia is preserving 'true' European-ness spiritually, in geopolitical terms it is moving towards other centres of power, including the Eurasian and East Asian region. A third foreign-policy manifestation of the conservative discourse is staunch support for international law based on the conservative safeguarding of the original UN principles of non-intervention as opposed to more recent developments related to the responsibility to protect (Paterson, 2014; Tetrault-Farber, 2015; Polyakova, 2016; Troitskiy, 2014; Malinova, 2014, interviews).

Authoritarian consolidation

The key domestic trend that characterised the development of Russian politics in the new millennium has consisted in the consolidation of an autocratic system, which underwrote and was mutually constitutive with the afore-discussed evolution of Russian identity discourses. That is, the growing authoritarianism of the regime incompatible with European expectations of liberal democracy; the building of the country's economic strength, which imparted confidence to policy-makers making them believe that they did not have to cooperate with the West; as well as the gradual creation of a new political class composed of individuals with anti-Western views set Russia on a path away from Europeanisation.

During Vladimir Putin's first term in office (2000-2004), the regime still maintained a semblance of democracy (at least rhetorically) and was concerned with receiving approval from the West. However, a gradual process of increasing authoritarianism already underway between 1999 and 2004 crystallised more fully during Putin's second term in office (2004-2008) with the abandonment of civil liberties, political competition and the principles of self-governance (Mendras, 2012:151-158; Pastukhov, 2012; Shevtsova, 2010). For instance, anti-federalism was the corollary of the policy of 'restoring the state' — i.e., the strengthening of the central executive's powers meant the undermining of the representative and legislative authorities. The decline of the provincial and municipal assemblies went in parallel with the decline of the State Duma and the Federation Council. Following the Beslan hostage crisis in 2004, Putin proposed a reform, whereby regional governors would be nominated by the President rather than elected by direct universal suffrage (Mendras, 2012:158; 175-176). Also, judicial independence was subverted. If until 2004 Supreme Court judges were appointed by the Supreme Qualification Collegium, henceforth members of the Collegium were to be chosen by the Head of State or by the President of the Federation Council (Mendras, 2012: 176).

The consolidation of these illiberal trends was ensured by the creation of a political class bound by networks of loyalty and united by a common worldview. Since 2000, the President began establishing a 'vertical of power', which represents a vertical chain of hierarchical authority with strong government from the top, instilling discipline and responsibility to fulfil tasks in the lower rungs (Monaghan, 2011:8). After the 2011-2012 protests, the regime resorted even further to the 'nationalisation' of the elite, diminishing the possibility that public servants and politicians would have foreign allegiances that could make them less loyal to the Kremlin (by for instance banning government officials from owning financial assets abroad) (Morozov, 2013:1).

So who is this political elite composed of? The majority of the political figures who have been side-lined from Russian politics are the Liberal Westernisers, while the most powerful segments of the political elite have become the *siloviki* — i.e., usually those who work in the power ministries and who were former members of the KGB (Mendras, 2012:248). However, not all of the members of the *siloviki* share this occupational background, such as some powerful business and economic figures. Therefore, the *siloviki* can be most accurately described as being united by a common outlook and common interests (Bremmer, Charap, 2006:3; Kryshtanovskaya, White, 2006:10). As Bremmer and Charap's research has shown, there are a number of ideas that the *siloviki* share. First, they promote the consolidation of political and economic power within a highly centralised state, buttressed by large security and defence structures and economic interventionism. Law and order are thought to take important precedence ahead of the democratic process and the creation of a civil society. Second, the *siloviki* believe that Russia's great power status has to be restored, that the US and NATO still represent important external threats and that the post-Soviet space should be reintegrated with Russia (Bremmer, Charap, 2006:5-6).

The *siloviki's* self-confidence as the ultimate governors of post-communist Russia was further cemented by favourable economic trends. The hike in oil and gas prices since the mid-2000s permitted the Russian political elite to cope with the most pressing social problems in the country, to relieve the burden of foreign debt, to build up military potential and to use the growing energy dependency of other states on Russia to promote its interests (as the utilisation of the energy weapon has shown especially in the case of Ukraine, Belarus, and Georgia) (Medvedev, Jackobson, 2012: 188). However, as Baranovsky has pointed out, the newly acquired sense of self-respect was not used in order to create a more stable course of foreign policy and to build an image of a reliable and predictable partner. Instead, given the animating worldview of the *siloviki*, the opposite happened in that the new feeling of overconfidence, and even self-conceit, led to an imperialistic and forceful foreign policy (Baranovsky, 2014, interview).

The consolidation of the authoritarian political system, propped by a heightened sense of self-assurance, thus meant that a liberal democratic form of political and social organisation could not take hold in Russia. Such sliding back into authoritarian forms of rule, underwritten by a weak cultural-historical tradition of rule of law and free political competition, distanced Moscow from Western Europe in terms of values and laid the foundation for an anti-Western foreign policy.

The Western Other, 1991-2000: Opening the door, restricting entry

In addition to the Russian Self's inability to consistently enunciate, substantiate and implement a vision of shared belongingness with the West, the Western Other also responded in kind. By the mid-1990s, externally-driven attitudes and events making up the overall ideational projection of the Western Other were perceived in the Russian policy-making circle with disappointment due to Moscow's exclusion from or at least tenuous and limited acceptance in NATO and EU integration processes. European and American reluctance to whole-heartedly welcome Russia undermined the latter's attempts to discursively sustain and substantiate its Liberal Westernising identity as a liberal democratic, regionally cooperative, institutionally integrated state and alluded to the Western treatment of the country as a secondary rather than equal partner. Such perceptions had a significant effect on the domestic balance of power leading to the disenchantment and marginalisation of the liberals, some of whom migrated to the Pragmatic Nationalist camp (which was becoming the dominant identity stance), and the empowerment of communist and nationalist groups with their Eurasian vision of Russia.

The American Other

The transatlantic framework of relations, whereby the US is a central and most powerful actor, had important repercussions for Russia's Europeanisation. Some US officials (such as National Security Advisor, 1993-1997, Anthony Lake) believing that post-Soviet Russia was a continued incarnation of the West's archenemy, whereas others (such as then President Bill Clinton) hoped that Moscow could follow a democratic future and become an ally. Yet, the latter group refrained from extending substantive support to the development of democratic institutions in Russia, instead backing individual leaders (Boris Yeltsin) and viewing Russia as too weak to be reckoned with in international affairs (Holmes, Cohen, Weinberger, Woolsey, 1999; Conradi, 2017; Lipman, 2014; Cohen, 2001).

Thus, American exclusion of Russia from the NATO enlargement process, the Alliance-led bombing of Yugoslavia that ignored Russian concerns and the insufficient American financial assistance created a perception of Moscow's marginalisation from European security affairs and treatment as a junior partner. As a result, the Pragmatic and Fundamentalist Nationalists were empowered at the expense of the Liberal Westernisers so that a gradual opposition developed against America's and NATO's role in European security. There was correspondingly a general disappointment with Europeanisation as Russia remained on the sidelines of the core arrangements underpinning the cooperative security community of the West. This side-lining was regarded by the Russians as a denigration of Moscow's special and influential status in European international relations.

NATO expansion

Russia's desire to become America's co-leader and be fully integrated in European security arrangements was disappointed almost immediately. In December 1991, President Boris Yeltsin sent a letter to NATO heads of state, informing them that Russia considered applying for NATO membership. Foreign Minister Andrey Kozyrev further explained that Russia did not deem NATO a threat and was eager to cooperate with it (Adomeit 2007:4). Yet, NATO leaders did not reply. In May 1992, Yeltsin made a plea to George H. W. Bush to conclude a bilateral US-Russia alliance, which was rejected by the American President (Trenin, 2007:71). Moreover, Yeltsin's call to his European and American counterparts not to create new dividing lines on the European continent and plunge it into a 'cold peace' through NATO expansion received a nonchalant reception and it was made clear that it was not up to Russia to set the pace of NATO's expansion (Bovt, December 1994). US officials offered a low-key response to the Russian President's comments. Western European officials also downplayed any harsh implications of Yeltsin's remarks. 'It was very moderate and almost philosophical; it was the minimum that a Russian president would have to say in such a situation', a German diplomat said (Kempster, Murphy, 1994).

Nevertheless, despite pressing ahead with NATO enlargement, President Clinton himself was aware of the adverse consequences that such a policy could have for Russian domestic struggles and hence political-elite identity configurations. As Strobe Talbott recalls, Russian liberals repeatedly warned of the dangers of expanding NATO. Egor Gaidar and Anatoly Chubais regarded NATO enlargement without Moscow's participation as an affront to Russian security interests, a vote of no confidence in Russian reforms and incompatible with the idea of partnership (Talbott, 2003:230). Similarly, Grigory Yavlinsky predicted a hysterical reaction from the Russian political elite and a boost for hard-line communist Gennady Zyuganov and hard-line nationalist-imperialist Vladimir Zhirinovsky. As a result, there would be a damaging fall-out on those in Russian politics, who most wanted Russia to be part of the West (Talbott, 2003:301).

The policy that was thought to soften the impact of NATO enlargement on Russian domestic politics was the acceptance of Russia in other Western institutional schemes. President Clinton believed that the Partnership for Peace would permit the expansion of NATO without giving the impression of recreating dividing lines (Talbott, 2003:111). Other measures that were intended to lessen the effect of NATO expansion included Moscow's entry into the G7 and the OECD. Furthermore, the schedule of enlarging NATO itself (after both Clinton and Yeltsin were re-elected) served a similar purpose – to diminish the impact of expansion on Russian domestic politics by limiting the opportunity for Gennady Zyuganov (the Communist party contender for the Russian Presidency in the 1996 elections) to capitalise on anti-Western grievances (Talbott, 2003:217).

However, despite these measures, the issue of NATO enlargement had serious consequences for Russian identity debates. The Partnership for Peace was not a satisfactory 'compensation' for NATO enlargement as it treated Russia 'like the rest' and established relations with former Soviet republics, which was greeted by Moscow with hostility. The NATO-Russia Founding act was similarly received as unsatisfactory because it fell short of Russian aspirations for a veto on NATO out-of-area deployments or for explicit guarantees that NATO would not forward-deploy nuclear and conventional capabilities in new member states close to Russian borders (MacFarlane, 2001:8-9). As Russian liberally- as well as conservative-minded experts concur in their assessments, the liberals in the administration not only worried that Alliance expansion would strengthen their anti-Western nationalist and communist opponents but were themselves disappointed with the West. Exclusion of Russia from European security arrangements posed questions about the threat to Russian security interests as well as the viability of the liberals' desire for Russia to belong to the Euro-Atlantic community of nations and the West's sincerity about cooperating with Russia through the creation of equal and indivisible security shared by all European states. And as far as the more conservative elites were concerned, NATO expansion gave them additional ammunition in their push for more anti-Western policies, confirming their claims that the West is hostile to the Russians, that the collapse of the Soviet Union was a humiliation inflicted by the US and that NATO was a major military threat to Russia (Baranovsky, 2014; Utkin, 2014; Lipman, 2014; Fenenko, 2014, Shmelev, 2014; Timofeev, 2014; Smirnov, 2014; Kortunov, 2014, interviews).

The bombing of Yugoslavia

The Yugoslav crises of the 1990s, especially the Kosovo crisis, had a very strong impact on the Russian policy-making scene. This was so due to at least two factors, including geopolitical and domestic considerations, whose interpretation was shaped by identity concerns.

First, as regards geopolitical considerations, NATO strikes against Kosovo and the inability of European states to resolve the crisis on their own served to confirm Russian fears of the establishment of a NATO-centred European and international system of security, from which Russia was excluded (Baranovsky, 2000a:4). The Russian reaction against such exclusion was exacerbated by the West's disregard of the UN and the principles of international law (i.e., the more conservative principle of observance of national sovereignty as opposed to the norm of humanitarian intervention to protect human rights). The tendency to sideline the organisation and the preferred Moscow stance in favour of the preservation of sovereignty was thought to seal Russia's isolation from the core states influencing international relations, not least because the Russian seat on the UN Security Council was considered a remaining institutional symbol of the country's great power status.

The feeling that Russia was being isolated and dismissed as weak in European and international decision-making had a significant effect on Russian politicians' evolving view that Russia should distance itself from the West and play a more assertive role (Yeltsin, 2001:256-257). As a closely involved participant at the time, Lipman characterised the approach of Western policy-makers as short-termist, since they were warned by her and others that recognising the independence of Kosovo without regard for Russian sensitivities on the issue would create a precedent, which Russia would use in the future. Lipman further explained how Moscow's inability to effectively oppose Western actions contributed to a sense of national humiliation. An example of this was the dispatch of a unit to Pristina in 1999 to counter NATO but the unit was too small, badly equipped and had to rely on the 'adversary' for food and water (Lipman, 2014, interview).

Second, the bombing of Yugoslavia raised domestic political concerns. The 'internal' aspect of the Kosovo intervention invoked different interpretations in the West and in Russia. If for the West, the bombing of the Serbs was primarily a matter of the protection of the human rights of the ethnic Albanians, in Russia, Kosovo was perceived as the 'Serbian Chechnya', thus being linked to fears about Russia's own territorial integrity should intervention become the norm in international relations (Arbatova, 2005:104-105). Also, the Kosovo crisis provoked anti-NATO sentiments intertwined with moral sympathy for Serbia (as religiously, ethnically and linguistically close to Russia and suffering at the hands of the powerful), utilised by the nationalist forces to argue for an anti-Western foreign policy (Torkunov, 2005:283; Baranovsky, 2000a:3, 6).

Therefore, the NATO bombings of Kosovo discredited democracy and human rights-promotion (as they were associated with derogatory treatment and a threat to national territorial boundaries), further contributing to the identity crisis of the Liberal Westernisers. They began to seriously doubt the feasibility of the pro-Western foreign policy direction of the country (Baranovsky, 2000a:6). Russian experts and participants concur that the Liberal Westernisers' warnings to the West that military strikes would empower the communists and the nationalists (aiming at dealing a blow to Russia's democratic, pro-European orientation), went unheeded (Tevdoy-Burmuli, 2014; Gudkov, 2014; Utkin, 2014; Lipman, 2014, interviews). For instance, Yeltsin argued that the internal political configuration in Russia depended on the situation in the Balkans. The communists and the nationalists played the Balkan card in order to influence the balance of political forces by asserting that the West not only humiliated Russia but also represented a threat to state integrity through its strategies of democratisation and protection of human rights. He asked 'Wasn't it obvious to the West that the NATO bombing was an indirect strike against Russia?' (Yeltsin, 2001:259-260).

Overall, the geopolitical and domestic repercussions of the Kosovo crisis posed serious doubts as to Russia's belongingness to Europe, its place in European and global security matters. The unfoldment of the crisis distanced Moscow from the norm of humanitarian intervention (which was gradually gaining important ground in the foreign policy policies of the European states and the US) and tipped the internal configuration of power towards the conservatives, who contested Russia's European integrationist, liberal democratic vector of development.

The European Other

America's role in Russia's thin Europeanisation over the course of the 1990s was complemented by Europe's stance. The overall West European attitude tended to treat Russia as 'becoming like us', which reflected a historically continuous representation of Moscow as a learner in perpetual transition to Europeanisation (Neumann, 1999:111). Yet, as Neumann has argued, given that Russia also represents a constitutive negative Other in European identity (differing on the basis of a despotic political regime, insufficient 'civility' and posing a military threat), it was not thought that Moscow would become a member of European institutions. The failure of democratic reforms under Yeltsin confirmed particularly strongly the image of 'eternal' Russian otherness (Neumann, 1999:65-112; Malia, 1999:1-15). Hence, the differentiation that was beginning to be made in policy documents between the EU's *enlargement policy* to CEE and *external relations* to the Russian neighbour (European Council Summit in Edinburgh, 1992:105-106, in Copenhagen, 1993:13-18, in Madrid, 1995:6-7). Consequently, although the Union concluded agreements with Russia, which marked prospects for the Europeanisation of Russian foreign policy, these initiatives also contributed to disenchantment in Russia about the degree of the country's acceptance in Europe.

Yet, the EU's impact on Moscow's rhetorically proclaimed goal of Europeanisation was not immediate. In the early 1990s, Russia neglected the Union and put an extensive focus on relations with the US as the most powerful state that could legitimise Russia's belongingness to the Euro-Atlantic community (Arbatova, 2005:129). For instance, as an insider to these processes, Baranovsky recalls that Vladimir Lukin, a member of the Supreme Council of the Soviet Union, summoned experts to discuss Yeltsin's trip to the US in 1991, with the main theme of the discussion revolving around obtaining legitimation for Russia as an actor in international relations (Baranovsky, 2014, interview). Another element of this focus on the US had to do with Yeltsin's reliance on personal relations and diplomacy, which for him were above all centred on President Clinton and to a lesser extent on German Chancellor Kohl and French President Chirac (Arbatova, 2005:129).

However, in the second half of the 1990s, the EU began to play a much bigger role in Russian foreign policy for reasons not directly related to the Union itself — it was Russia's disappointment with NATO expansion, the bombing of Yugoslavia and overall US policy of 'unilateral dominance' in European and global affairs. The change of focus away from an overwhelming reliance on relations with the US became most pronounced when Evgeny Primakov became Foreign Minister in 1996. He perceived the EU as a pole in international relations, which could serve to balance American hegemony (Arbatova, 2005:129). Indeed, heightened attention to the EU was not the result of the deep-seated realisation of the importance of the process of institutionalised cooperation, regional integration or the global advocacy of democracy and human rights, based on soft power and renunciation of the use of force. Rather, the EU was seen as a pole in a multipolar world that could dilute the perceived exclusionary practices of the US. And such an attitude re-enacted the Russian conceptual affinity to 19th century balance of power politics rather than late 20th century politics of interdependence and integration (Arbatova, 2005:129). Along a similar logic, in October 1997, Boris Yeltsin announced his 'Greater

Europe' concept and put forward the initiative to establish a 'troika' dialogue with France and Germany in order to counteract US policies (Menkiszak, 2013:9).

Furthermore, the EU-Russia strategic documents of the 1990s—the Agreement on Partnership and Cooperation (1994) and the Union's Common Strategy (1999), were most important with respect to political dialogue and symbolism, the institutional channels established for communication and socialisation and the declaration of the existence of common values (Baranovsky, 2002:57; Gower, 2000:76-79). The PCA (1994:4) stated that the envisaged political dialogue 'shall foresee that the Parties endeavour to cooperate on matters pertaining to the observance of the principles of democracy and human rights', initiating Russia's interaction with the CFSP (Baranovsky, 2002:57). The Common Strategy (1999:1) also asserted that 'the offer of a reinforced relationship, based on shared democratic values, will help Russia to assert its European identity'.

However, there were different underlying visions regarding the extent to which the two parties should be integrated. As Arbatova makes clear, while carrying out negotiations with the EU over the PCA, Moscow was aiming to draw the document closer to an Association Agreement. Yet, the EU tried to restrict the scope of Russia's integration in Europe, justifying this with the fact that Russia was a great power and not just another ordinary European state, which newspaper *Kommersant* interpreted as an excuse. The then deputy Minister of Foreign Affairs—Sergei Krylov, disappointedly considered the negotiations over the Partnership Agreement between the EU and Russia in June 1994 as a 'failure' due to the limited character of cooperation envisaged between the two sides (Arbatova, 2005:130; Bovt, November 1994). Thus, although Russian leaders made references to Russia's desire for EU membership, by 1994 it was becoming clear that integration with the EU would not even be discussed and the most that Moscow could get was membership in the Council of Europe (Trenin, 2007:70-71). Russian proposals that the CSCE should be developed into a major institution coordinating European security matters were similarly spurned (Ignatenko, 1994). Further disappointments followed from the intransigence on the part of the West to renegotiate the CFE Treaty limits on military presence and equipment on Russia's southern flank (which Russia deemed necessary for the preservation of national unity given Chechnya's desire to secede) (Bovt, Kalashnikova, 1995).

The EU's non-committal attitude to Russia reflected Germany's stance. Despite Chancellor Kohl's close personal ties to Yeltsin (expressed in 'sauna diplomacy') and substantial German government credits (contributing $52 billion in aid), the possibility of Russian membership in European organisations was not considered as Berlin advocated EU and NATO expansion, particularly to the Central European states. The general German view held that as the Cold War memory receded, Russia would eventually — but not in the immediate term, be brought into the Western community of values (Turgunova, 2013:27; Erb, 2003:187; Zaborowski, 2006:112-113; Szabo, 2015:61-62).

Overall, these European developments bred Russian disappointments. Tevdoy-Burmuli argued that unlike in its relations with the CEE states, as regards Russia the EU did not seriously entertain the prospect of offering membership, which would have otherwise provided an anchor to Russia's European belongingness. The EU strategy and the PCA were characterised by a lack of clear vision of what the end result would be (Tevdoy-Burmuli, 2014, interview). Russian experts lament that Brussels proceeded with its enlargement project, which excluded Russia, so that in symbolic terms the notion of 'Europe' and the 'EU' became almost identical and the much cherished idea of the pro-Western liberals of 'Russia in Europe' was supplanted by 'Russia and Europe' (Trenin, 2007:72; Miller, 2014; Timofeev, 2014; Utkin, 2014; Morozov, 2014; Tevdoy-Burmuli, 2014; Arbatova, 2014; Kortunov, 2014; Fenenko, 2014, interviews).

And disappointments with the process of European integration were bound to follow since, as Smirnov and Kortunov argued, the relationship between the EU and Russia in the 1990s was built on illusions. One illusion was that Russia would be able to gradually integrate in the European community. But the very fact that the PCA was signed in the 1990s and there is still no other foundational document to build on it is demonstrative of the absence of a vision of shared belongingness (Smirnov, 2014; Kortunov, 2014, interviews). Arbatova also clarified that in the early 1990s, EU enlargement was viewed favourably in Russia—as the Russian liberals thought that NATO and EU enlargement were two different processes. However, the high-ranking officials in Brussels and Germany insisted that these two processes were complementary, whereby a negative Russian perception was being formed that Union enlargement would be replacing NATO expansion as an overwhelming project creating a new reality in all aspects of social, political and economic development (Baranovsky, 2002:129-130). This led to an intense psychological anxiety about a political-cultural and economic abyss that might develop between the EU member states and Russia (Arbatova, 2014; Fenenko, 2014, interviews).

On the whole, over the course of the 1990s, Western European attitudes and policies exhibited a deep-seated ambivalence towards Russia's European belongingness, providing only limited, non-committal and tenuous diplomatic, institutional and economic support. As a result, the emerging Liberal Westernising rhetoric on the desirability of Euro-Atlantic integration could not be sustained and become infused with discursive references to the key dimensions of European-ness. Exclusion bred disenchantment and activated normatively contested understandings of ideal-typical values, including support for non-infringed upon sovereignty, balance of power politics, multipolarity as opposed to integration, multilateralism and institutionalised cooperation. Russia's great-power self-conception was also invoked in cases of perceived slights to the demand for special status, which further diluted the process of seeking liberal interdependence with the Euro-Atlantic community in the direction of assertiveness against American dominance.

The Western Other, 2000-2015: Better apart

The Western Other's reluctance to admit Russia in the Euro-Atlantic community in a fully-fledged manner further intensified in the new millennium. America's and Western Europe's half-hearted acceptance of Moscow within the post-9/11 North Atlantic framework of security and the EU's deepening enlargement process instilled in Russian experts and policy-makers a perception of Moscow's exclusion from European civilization, politics and security. Hence, the Pragmatic Nationalism closely linked to Liberal Westernising ideas that characterised the beginning of Putin's Presidency was eroded and moved towards Fundamentalist Nationalism.

The American Other

The terrorist attacks on 11 September 2001 reverberated in international relations and forced states to make a choice as to whether they would support the West—i.e., the civilised world, against its war against terrorism. Judging by the immediate response of Russia to the 9/11 events—strong rhetorical, intelligence and logistical support for the US, it can be argued that Moscow perceived itself as being part of the Western-centred coalition of war on terror and an international system dominated geopolitically and ideationally by the US and its West European allies (Pravda, 2003:43-44). Putin's visit to the US on November 12-15 2001 secured a positive turn in bilateral relations. Presidents Bush and Putin signed a joint statement, where the two sides stated the absence of essential difference in ideological, social and economic terms (Melville, 2005:370-371; President of Russia, 13 November 2001; White House Archives, 21 October 2001). Moreover, at a meeting with NATO Secretary General George Robertson, Vladimir Putin was eager to announce the creation of a working body to expand relations between Russia and NATO. This initiative was underwritten by a commitment to common values—as Lord Robertson himself maintained (President of Russia, 03 October 2001). The thaw in US-Russia ties also created a more favourable international context for the EU-Russia relationship. As Richard Wright, then head of the European Commission's delegation to Russia, put it, Moscow's post-9/11 cooperative attitude to the US brought Russia and the EU much closer, while Putin insisted that a significant element in Russian foreign policy is becoming 'truly integrated' into Europe and this was a historical choice that Russia had made (Kuranov, 2002; President of Russia, 18 April 2002, 16 May 2003).

However, the course of close Russia-West cooperation was undermined because of a number of Western policies that were viewed as exclusionary by the Moscow political elite. Already at the end of 2002, relations began to sour and Russia reverted to more assertive rhetoric and actions. On many issues conducive to friction, the US remained reluctant to negotiate and accommodate Russia's concerns. First, the George W. Bush administration was unwilling to go along with Russian demands on missile defence and in particular with Moscow's desire to move beyond the ABM Treaty to a new strategic relationship based on low numbers of offensive weapons stipulated in a formal document (Antonenko, 2001:7). On 13 December 2001, President Bush gave six months' notice that the US intended to abrogate the ABM Treaty. And although he agreed to a bilateral arms reduction treaty, Bush refused to destroy US warheads as part of the agreement (Light, Allison, 2006:11).

Second, the West pressed ahead with NATO expansion to CEE, which gave rise to serious concerns among the Russian political elite about Russia's exclusion from European security matters (Allison, 2006:118-121). The policy move that the West expected would soften the blow of the second eastward NATO enlargement was the creation of the NATO-Russia Council (NRC) in 2002, which replaced the Permanent Joint Council (Light, Allison, 2006:11-12). This development was greeted with some optimism on the part of the Russian political elite, since for Russia the key issue was the capacity of the NRC to act as a genuine mechanism of joint decision-making and the NRC format indeed stipulated joint decision-making through consensus. However, just because a topic is on the NRC agenda does not preclude the Allies from discussing it among themselves; there exists a mechanism of 'retrievability' according to which any NATO member can withdraw an item from the NRC agenda, which displeased Russia (Allison, 2006:105-106).

Third, the view was beginning to be established in Moscow that Putin's support for the US war on terror in terms of providing cooperation in Central Asia was used by the West to isolate Russia from playing a strategic role in the region. Military interaction with Moscow in Uzbekistan and Tajikistan remained limited; the US also provided military assistance to Georgia (through the Georgia Train and Equip Program) in the run-up to the Iraq war and supported Tbilisi diplomatically, economically and militarily in its conflict with South Ossetia and Russia in 2004. The cavalier attitude of the US towards Russia's vulnerabilities in the Trans-Caucasus was interpreted by the majority of the Russian political elite as an attempt on the part of America to exploit the post-9/11 situation in order to promote American dominance in the CIS (Arbatova, 2002:161-162). Also, the US was seen as interfering in Russia's historic zone of influence in the CIS by supporting the 'colour' revolutions in Ukraine and Georgia. Especially important for the deterioration in the relations between Russia and the West was the upheaval in Ukraine during the 2004 Presidential election. What the US and the EU saw as popular outrage over a manipulated vote, Russia perceived as the result of Western design. Coming a year after similar events leading to Georgia's Rose Revolution, the Ukrainian events convinced Putin's conspiracy-minded advisers that influential players in the West used the promotion of democracy to undo Russian influence in the CIS (Legvold, 2007a:9).

Fourth, the Bush administration started the war in Iraq in 2003 despite opposition from Russia and other states in the UN Security Council (Oldberg, 2007:20; Nezavisimaya Gazeta, 2003). Yet, Putin anticipated that, in return for supporting the American antiterrorist campaign, the United States would take Russia's 'right' to be consulted on major international issues into account (Stent, 2008:8). Thus, America's bypassing of the Security Council was thought to be particularly insulting, as Russia's membership of the Council was one of the few markers left of its great-power status in international relations. So Foreign Minister Igor Ivanov clearly conveyed his opposition to American unilateralism, calling the US an 'aggressor' (Golan, 2004:5).

Overall, my interviews with experts and participants in these events convey the sense of disappointment on the level of the political-intellectual elite in the aftermath of 9/11. The US withdrawal from the ABM Treaty, the intention to build an anti-ballistic missile shield in Europe, the Iraq War had a negative effect on Russian politicians' perceptions of the viability of cooperating with the West on matters of European security, as Russia was treated as a junior partner. Especially important from a psychological point of view was NATO enlargement, which created a feeling of encirclement, since Alliance infrastructure came closer to Russian borders and incorporated Moscow's former allies in CEE (Timofeev, 2014; Smirnov, 2014; Nikitina, 2014; Arbatova, 2014; Zevelev, 2014, interviews). Even more dramatically, Alexey Fenenko has conveyed the sense among the conservative Russian political and security elites, who believed that the US wanted to incite a war with Russia, whereby the expansion of NATO and the anti-ballistic missile system were the first steps (Fenenko, 2014, interview). In general, as Shmelev concluded, the Russian path towards Europeanisation based on Putin's Pragmatic Nationalism with strong Liberal Westernising overtones became much harder to sustain among a more disillusioned political elite, the majority of whom found it unacceptable that Russia provided support to the West, which not only failed to provide positive reciprocation but even treated Russia as a junior partner that could be sidelined and displaced from its sphere of strategic interests (Smelev, 2014, interview).

The European Other

Russia initially viewed EU enlargement as a positive force for the development of the CEE region and relied on closer cooperation with the Union in line with Pragmatic Nationalism that employed many Liberal Westernising positions. However, since 2004 a reversal of attitude began to take place, whereby Pragmatic Nationalist stances became more assertive and incorporated some Fundamentalist Nationalist ideas so that the vision of Russia as an inseparable part of the European cultural and geopolitical space evolved into an active contestation of ideal-typical European-ness.

The integration schemes of the EU played an important part in Moscow's ever-thinning Europeanisation as they reinforced Russian anxieties about exclusion, feelings of resentment due to marginalisation in European affairs and doubts about Russia's European credentials. All of this found expression in attempts at positive self-enhancement through the presentation of Russia as a more 'genuine' European power, intent on building an alternative, multipolar international order.

Throughout the 2000s, the EU and Russia concluded agreements that were aimed at bringing the two parties closer together in terms of economics and foreign policy. One such agreement was the Road Map for the Common Spaces agreed in 2003. However, the common space on external security did not manage to contribute significantly to Russia's Europeanisation. The stated goals of 'cooperation' and 'dialogue' were not backed up by a clear vision of practical substantiation—i.e., there was little in the document to suggest how foreign policy coordination would be achieved on a practical level (EU-Russia: Road Map, 2005). Also, the envisaged security cooperation was not informed by the possibility of enhanced cooperation within the European Security and Defence Policy (ESDP). The EU was unwilling to offer Russia regular and institutionalised influence on the ESDP, as decisions related to the ESDP are to be taken by the member states and not by external partners, irrespective of their great power perceptions (Allison, 2006:80-81). Conversely, Russia's vision of the ESDP was related to an expectation that this policy instrument could be turned into a vehicle for creating 'greater Europe', allowing Moscow to have an equal voice in European security affairs (Lynch, 2004:14).

An initiative that was meant to enhance progress on the Common Spaces was the Partnership for Modernisation agreed in 2010. The main goal was to foster the process of modernisation in Russia, including promotion of democratic reforms, economic growth, competitiveness, investment, bilateral trade and science (Joint Statement on the Partnership for Modernisation, 2010). However, overall substantive progress remained limited. The envisaged projects were in the less politically sensitive areas of investment, energy and efficiency. Moreover, neither the EU's proposal to support judicial reform and to strength dialogue with civil society in Russia, nor Moscow's support for visa liberalisation, were transformed into concrete initiatives (Delcour, 2011; Larionova, 2015:8).

Since 2009, the EU attempted to additionally increase its foreign policy and security dialogue with Moscow and define a more active role for itself in the regulation of conflicts in the post-Soviet space. To this end, Germany took the lead, which culminated in the Meseberg memorandum (2010), whereby German Chancellor Merkel and Russian President Medvedev agreed to establish a EU-Russia Committee on foreign and security policy on the ministerial level (Meister, 2011:9). The main aims of the Committee were related to the exchange of views on international politics as well as cooperation with regard to the resolution of the Transnistria conflict. Yet, if Germany and the Union as a whole thought of the Committee as a means to enhance security cooperation with Moscow on the basis of small political steps and dialogue, Russia was much more interested in discussing the big questions of the structure of European security. The Kremlin also suspected that the resolution of the frozen conflicts in the CIS might lead to increased EU influence there and Moscow's normative and strategic marginalisation (Meister, 2011:18).

Furthermore, Union integration schemes excluded Moscow, instilling doubts about Russia's cultural belongingness to a Europe increasingly synonymous with the EU as well as about Russia's status as a European great power. The 'outsider' self-perception was a significant consequence of EU expansion to the majority of the formerly Soviet-allied CEE states, 13 of which had acceded to the Union by 2013 (Casier, 2007:75-76). Moreover, the European Neighbourhood Policy (ENP) outlined in 2003 and the Eastern Partnership (EP) launched in 2009 – embedded within the ENP – placed target countries in Eastern Europe and the South Caucasus in Brussels' orbit of influence through the expectation of strategic and normative convergence (Wider Europe, 2003; Casier, Whitman, Korosteleva, 2013:3). The policy initiative was interpreted from the outset as an anti-Russian move. Foreign Minister Lavrov called the

EP a clear attempt to establish a sphere of influence in an area where Russia claims privileged interests (Casier, Whitman, Korosteleva, 2013:8). Admittedly, it was indeed the case that Russia was originally included along with Ukraine, Belarus and Moldova in the preliminary 'Wider Europe/Neighbourhood' framework published in 2003. Yet, the framework bracketed Russia and the Western CIS countries together with the Mediterranean as states with 'a history of autocratic governance and poor records in protecting human rights and the freedom of the individual'. This was interpreted as an open snub to Moscow's declared commitment to European values. Particularly hard to swallow was the fact that Russia was reduced to one among several Eastern neighbours with little indication of what the Moscow political elite considers to be its special role in European affairs (Commission of the European Communities, 11 March 2003; Arbatova, 2014, interview).

EU integration processes were thus perceived as excluding Russia from European civilization and simultaneously thwarting Moscow's ambitions for regional dominance. Most foreign policy experts expressed anxiety at the Union's refusal to address Moscow's concerns with the argument that enlargement was linked to the EU's bilateral relations with the candidate states and would not be discussed with a third party (Tevdoy-Burmuli, 2014, interview). Moreover, in Arbatova's view, the EU and the US were obsessed with the prospect of the restoration of a new Russian empire but the separation of Russia from the CIS through the ENP was counter-productive in that it agitated the suspicions of Kremlin policy-makers and reinforced the most nationalist sentiments in society (Arbatova, 2014, interview). Also, Brussels' standards of European-ness made the European idea much less attractive to the Russians because of the condescension that accompanies the assumption that certain countries (such as Russia) do not live up to those standards and have to undergo a learning process (Timofeev, 2014; Nikitina, 2014; Baranovsky, 2014; Utkin, 2014; Zevelev, 2014, interviews). Indeed, Russia's current attempt to stipulate what 'genuine' European-ness means—in contradistinction to the ideal-typical model, is fuelled by a reactionary, self-compensatory process, whereby the Kremlin tries to posit its own standards, which it manages to fulfil. But, as Miller has succinctly put it, 'if Europe welcomes Russia, then Russia may forget about Eurasanism' and alternative ideologies (Miller, 2014, interview).

Yet, given that fully-fledged European acceptance was not forthcoming, starting in late 2004 and early 2005, a Pragmatic Nationalist discourse with a strong stress on Fundamentalist Nationalists' Eurasian orientation began to consolidate. Representative of the ever-more Eurasianist bent of Russian elite opinion, Dmitry Rogozin—one of the leaders of the nationalist party 'Rodina', argued that Russia is a 'self-sufficient' civilization and does not need to become part of the EU, which imposes its own standards on Russia, assuming the role of a teacher that draws a dividing line between 'Europeans' and 'non-Europeans' (Rogozin, 2004). Moreover, Liberal-Westernising elites, who were most in favour of Russia's role as a European power, became even more marginalised and/were in a crisis over Russia's engagement with the EU. Liberal politician Anatoly Chubais argued that although Russia had chosen the only possible path—the liberal democratic one, it did not need to become part of the EU and NATO, which have repeatedly tried to exclude Russia. Instead, Russia should become a 'liberal empire' and an equal partner to the US and the EU (Chubais, 2003).

These increasingly anti-European views were sanctioned on the highest level of power. Referring to the EU and the West more generally, Putin talked about the 'dictatorship in international relations, wrapped up in beautiful pseudo-democratic rhetoric' and the danger of 'constructing contemporary civilization on the basis of unipolar designs' (Sysoev, 2004). Dmitry Medvedev also stressed that the EU is not identical with the countries that make up Europe and that decisions about European security should not be based on 'bloc ideas' (President of Russia, 27 June 2008). Ultimately, the establishment of the Eurasian Economic Union (EEU) was Russia's response to EU integration, offering the Kremlin a platform for normative and strategic rivalry with Brussels in the shared neighbourhood (Dragneva, Wolczuk, 2012:9, 15; President of Russia, 18 November 2011, 9 December 2010).

The Russian Self and its Western Other each developed their respective attitudes and stances toward one another since 1991 in an arduous process, whereby Russia had to seek an answer to the question of what it means to be European, while the West had to circumscribe the space within which its affinities extend. I now tie these attitudes and stances together in order to show that it was the mutually constitutive character of the gradual distancing between Self and Other that ultimately sealed Russia's thin Europeanisation, evident in both discourse and policy.

The Russian Self and the Western Other, 1991-2000: A romance that was not to be

The distinctive attributes of Self and Other conceptualised in Chapter 3 as becoming particularly manifest in times of crisis were most dramatically accentuated in the case of Russia-West relations—as contrasted with Poland and Bulgaria. As the 1990s progressed, the liminal uncertainties of Russian identity became the subject of ever-increasing contestation. The inner doubts further gave rise to more aggressive attempts at positive self-inflation through a search of 'uniqueness'. In turn, the West's enhanced power status as the victorious side following the end of the Cold War and consequential policies related to EU and NATO expansion delimiting the bounds of the Euro-Atlantic community exerted a painful effect on the Russians. The latter's diminishment from (almost) equals to the West during the Cold War to followers and imitators after 1991 was all the more negatively experienced, given Moscow's exclusion from the new Europe that was taking shape.

Thus, Russian thin Europeanisation was the outcome of the unwillingness and inability of both Russia and Western Europe and America to forge a vision of shared belongingness. European and American non-committal, half-hearted and tenuous acceptance of Russia's credentials for becoming part of the Euro-Atlantic community was expressed in slow and limited diplomatic, institutional and economic support that did not become more decisive, at least as in the Bulgarian case. This restricted inclusion was simultaneously matched by Moscow's own ideational division over the desirability of integration with the West and substantive normative incompatibility with the ideal-typical values, underpinning the possibility of belongingness to the Euro-Atlantic community. As a result, the Liberal Westernisers, who were politically embattled but still kept the overall reins of power in the 1990s, espoused an identity discourse that was informed by the commitment to Europeanisation, which was not however consistent, intersubjectively shared and substantiated by a deeply internalised adherence to European principles. Instead, the identity discourse gradually incorporated Pragmatic Nationalist views that contested a one-sided orientation to the West. Hence, the initial 'romantic' expectation of Russia building a common home with Europe was only briefly expressed in a decidedly pro-European foreign policy in the early 1990s but could not be sustained and moved towards Pragmatic Nationalist positions of cultural and geopolitical assertiveness against the West.

Telling the story of this evolution in views in further detail shows first that the key tenets of the official identity discourse of the 1990s were based on the goal of Europeanisation. As an observer and participant in these political developments, Andrey Kortunov has argued that the overall rhetorical trend promoted by the Liberal Westernisers over the course of the first post-communist decade remained in favour of Russia's integration in the Euro-Atlantic community. And this commitment to Europeanisation outlived Yeltsin, reflected in the pro-Western statements especially of the first and second administration of President Vladimir Putin (Kortunov, 2014, interview). As further confirmed by Russian experts, the identity politics over the 1990s implied that Russia was a new democratic state, which significantly differed from the Soviet Union in terms of political-social organisation, values and foreign policy. The West was a 'natural' ally as Russia changed itself along a European, liberal democratic, regionally and internationally cooperative path (Timofeev, 2014; Malinova, 2014; Shmelev, 2014; Zevelev, 2014; Busygina, 2014; Simon, 2014, interviews). This identity discourse was conspicuously embodied by Foreign Minister Andrey Kozyrev. His mantra that Russia should become a 'civilised' country and join the democratic West was accepted both by the emerging free market economic elite and most of the liberally-minded foreign policy intellectuals (Stent, 2007:418). In a series of statements in 1991 and 1992, Kozyrev argued that for the first time Russia found itself in a benign security environment, which would allow it to become a truly European power promoting a liberal international order (Kozyrev, 1992a:1-16).

However, although the general official discourse was in favour of Europeanisation, Liberal Westerniser views evolved into a more Pragmatic Nationalist vision of Russia — less hopeful about acceptance by the West and about Russia's ability to undergo a successful transformation on the ideal-typical model; more aware of the country's need for a restored sense of great power-ness; and more assertive in its foreign policy. Russian experts concur that the liberal democratic, pro-European vision of Russia's foreign policy began to lose dominance both because of the lack of external confirmation and support and because of conceptual and practical limitations of liberal ideas as well as the acrimonious political struggle feeding into the unstable institutional setting (Arbatova, 2014; Tevdoy-Burmuli, 2014; Gromyko, 2014; Kortunov, 2014; Melville, 2014; Krickovic, 2014; Shmelev, 2014; Timofeev, 2014; Lipman, 2014, interviews; Trenin, 2007:73).

On the one hand, as summed up by Nadezhda Arbatova, 'Russia's identity in terms of whether it is "Asian" or "European" depends on the balance of force between the liberals and the nationalists' (Arbatova, 2014, interview). And this balance of force can be tipped to one side or another by international developments so that, in the words of Trenin and Miller, the typical Russian psychological reaction to isolation and estrangement when spurned by Europe as 'aliens' is to rediscover Asia (Miller, 2014, interview; Trenin, 2007:73). Such a dynamic led to the gradual sidelining of the most liberally-minded politicians. Zevelev has explained that the demoralisation of the Liberal Westernisers was based on the following line of thinking: 'the Clinton administration started the NATO expansion process, inviting certain countries to join but what about Russia? If the West is honest about its desire to accept Russia as a partner, then it should not create dividing lines' (Zevelev, 2014, interview). Hence, the camp of the liberals gravitated towards the centre, an example of which was Sergey Karaganov—influential intellectual and Presidential adviser to both Boris Yeltsin and Vladimir Putin. Karaganov admitted that after 1999 and the bombing of Yugoslavia he gave up all liberal hopes and moved to the centre (Krickovic, 2014, interview; Karaganov, BBC World Lectures).

Yet, on the other hand, liberal ideas became easily eroded also because they were built on weak cultural-historical and conceptual foundations. The European identity of Russia was to a certain extent 'imagined' and had to be constructed from scratch in some aspects to be truly in line with European values, including democracy, support for a liberal international order, regional integration, institutionalised cooperation. The shared perspective that emerges from my interviews holds that Russia imitated the norms of the West, declared itself to be European and expected the leading European states to give Russia credit for its European-ness. So Russia could only declare that it was a European country but it did not have a deep-seated cultural-historical identification with Europe and was too preoccupied with the conflict between the branches of authority in order to fully implement this European agenda (Busygina, 2014; Smirnov, 2014; Trenin, 2014; Medvedev, 2014; Krickovic, 2014; Gromyko, 2014; Arbatova, 2014, interviews).

Over time, the ever fading possibility of actualising the establishment of a shared community between the Russian Self and its Western Other pushed the Russian identity debate into a Pragmatic Nationalist direction. Even the liberally-minded policy makers and experts had begun to doubt the goal of Russia's Europeanisation. Some academic specialists turned Pragmatic Nationalists, like Georgy Arbatov and Alexey Bogaturov, argued that the 'mindless' following of the West on the part of the Liberal Westernisers only discredited the West in the eyes of the Russian people (Adomeit, 1995:23; Bogaturov, 1994). Vyacheslav Dashichev, Konstantin Pleshakov, Alexey Vasilev made strong statements about Russia's vital interests in the post-Soviet area and warned of the dangers for Moscow's regional primacy following from the equation of Russian policy in the area with that of the US under the banner of friendly regional cooperation (Prizel, 1998:248-

253). Presidential adviser Sergey Stankevich opposed the renunciation of a special Russian 'civilizational mission', imbuing the country with a far more diversified foreign policy orientation than the single-minded European path (Stent, 2007:418; Stankevich, 1992). Vladimir Lukin, the then Russian Ambassador to the US, noted the disillusionment of the elite with the West's policies, which demanded Russia's 'unconditional surrender'. He himself argued that Moscow's security environment was much less benign than Kozyrev thought. Therefore, Russia had to re-orient its foreign policy away from an exclusive focus on building a liberal international order with the West and embrace its identity as a Eurasian country working for multipolararity and defence of regional spheres of influence (Lukin, 1992, 2008).

This evolution in intersubjective views towards Pragmatic Nationalism was paralleled by the transformation in the stances taken by the key decision-makers that set the course of Russian foreign policy. As regards the President, Russian observers, including those who had a direct experience with him, have clarified that Boris Yeltsin was not a foreign policy expert. He was not well-versed in issues of international relations and did not have a firm set of well-elaborated convictions about the conduct of a pro-European external course (and perhaps he did not want to lay out such in-depth convictions, given Kortunov's attestation to Yeltsin's motivation to differentiate himself from his rival Gorbachev's grand visions of international affairs) (Kortunov, 2014, interview). Rather, the President's foreign policy choices were based on instinct, intuitions and generalised predispositions and conceptions. He sensed that the right direction for Russia in international relations was partnership with the West that could legitimise Russia as an international actor and help it both symbolically and economically take its place among the Euro-Atlantic nations (Gromyko, 2014; Baranovsky, 2014; Kortunov, 2014; Arbatova, 2014; Smirnov, 2014; Trenin, 2014; Medvedev, 2014; Krickovic, 2014; Gromyko, 2014, interviews).

These less than well-elaborated views of the President gradually evolved in the 1990s. Yeltsin's hopes for Russia's rapid integration with the West and acceptance as an equal partner were beginning to be replaced by disappointment in Russia's inability to forge for itself and be accepted as a rightful member of the European civilizational space with an equal decision-making in trans-Atlantic affairs. In one of the last messages that he sent in the autumn of 1999 from China, Boris Yeltsin warned Bill Clinton never to forget that Russia was a nuclear power. And this was a very far cry from his early proposals to George H. Bush to accept Moscow as an ally, which could also join NATO. So although Yeltsin did not become an anti-Western politician, he came a long way from his early enthusiastic pro-Western rhetoric, whereby NATO enlargement and the bombing of Yugoslavia proved to be significant disappointments (Trenin, 2014; Smirnov, 2014, interviews; Yeltsin, 2001:164, 250, 257). Thus, Yeltsin urged Russia and the West to find their way 'only by engaging in constant political dialogue, not isolation. Isolation cannot be permitted regardless of the circumstances!' (Yeltsin, 2001:250).

Consistent with the hardening of the President's views, Evgeny Primakov, who took office as Foreign Minister in 1996, inaugurated a period of Russian 'Gaullism' or 'centrism' in foreign policy by trying to reinstate Russian prestige without reverting to anti-Westernism, while shifting the emphasis from the US to Europe (Arbatova, 2014; Baranovsky, 2014, interviews). Russian experts assess Primakov's centrism as based on a definition of Russian identity in the international arena as a great power, moving away from 'romantic' hopes and illusions about rapid integration with the West (as in the case of Andrey Kozyrev) and instead stressing the pursuit of Russia's interests in a multipolar world (Zevelev, 2014; Gromyko, 2014; Busygina, 2014, interviews; Primakov, 2005:208-209; Primakov, 1996). Primakov was therefore in favour of a Pragmatic Nationalist foreign policy that was animated by building a regional sphere of influence in the CIS and a multipolar order with Asia's help, simultaneously still trying to maintain constructive Russia-West relations, exemplified by the conclusion of the NATO Foundation Act (Primakov, 1996; Baranovsky, 2014, interview).

The interaction of growing domestic normative incompatibility with ideal-typical European-ness and external exclusionary practices in shaping the thin character of Moscow's foreign policy Europeanisation can be most vividly demonstrated through the tortuous development of Russian relations with NATO and the EU. NATO expansion contributed to Russia's feeling of exclusion from European political and security arrangements, creating the impression of consolidating the 'gains' of the post-Cold War period in a spirit of triumphalism and in disregard of Russian sentiments and interests. But despite the fact that the Russian reactions to NATO enlargement were indeed predictable and to some degree justified, the extent and intensity of these reactions were determined by a domestic perceptual lens. The disproportionate, emotional and highly charged responses (to what hardly amounted to an 'objective' military threat) can be accounted for by the influence of stereotypes and prejudices, inherited from the Cold War (Black, 2000:240; Tsygankov, 2013).

Moreover, the Russian vision of what NATO integration would entail diverged from that of NATO allies. It is hardly imaginable that Russia would have agreed to wait in the acceding countries' queue, fulfilling criteria and being monitored for its progress on applying principles it had not shown fond adherence to (such as renunciation of zero-sum forceful postures, democratisation and transparency of the military, cooperative rather than sphere-of-influence policies). Trenin has surmised that Moscow would have joined NATO only if there had been an invitation and subsequent entry on the initiative of the West in a quick and unconditional process, granting Russia special status (Trenin, 2006:247). Such a view is in stark contrast to the NATO enlargement process, which includes conditionality and monitoring to ensure both military compatibility and socialisation on the basis of NATO institutional culture and the norms embodied in the ideal type. So there was a clash of visions between Russia and the West, which may not have been overcome by the extension of an invitation to Russia to join NATO.

Similarly, despite Moscow's declared commitment to Europeanisation and disappointment at exclusion from the EU's enlargement schemes, there was once more a clash of visions as to the substance of the process of Europeanisation, which clash may not have been resolved by a more inclusive agenda of the Union with regard to Russia. For instance, the Russian desire to join the EU was not matched by a realistic assessment of what it represented as an organisation. Russian politicians traditionally perceive the EU as one among other international organisations, such as the Council of Europe, the OSCE and NATO, without taking into account the key specificity of the Union—namely, its supranational character. There was also a lack of evidence-based, expert thinking about what Russia's participation in the EU would mean, especially in terms of the large-scale domestic political, economic, social and legal transformation that would have had to take place. Indeed, proponents of accession never even mentioned the *acquis* that any acceding country is obliged to incorporate into its domestic laws (Baranovsky, 2002:32).

Additionally, Primakov's view of the EU as a pole in a multipolar world that could serve as a counterbalance to the US demonstrated that the organisation was perceived along the lines of a 19th century Concert of European powers, rather than a late 20th century union of states gradually pooling their sovereignty to a supranational body. Likewise, Yeltsin's concept of 'Greater Europe' revealed a concern that Russia should not be sidelined in European affairs and should exercise the influence it was due among the ranks of the great European powers.

Moscow thus affirmed its commitment to Europeanisation but the substance of European-ness was differently understood in Western Europe and Russia. Russia saw European integration more as a way of enhancing its prestige, being included in European affairs and having influence on European politics without any diminishment of its sovereignty, whereas in the western half of the continent integration meant the gradual (albeit fitful and difficult) process of pooling sovereignty and domestic policy alignment. It also meant the observance of human rights, democracy and incrementally the norm of humanitarian intervention, which proved to have weak foundations in Russia in light of the war in Chechnya, Yeltsin's authoritarian tendencies and firm stance in support of non-intervention in the Kosovo crisis.

On the whole, the mutually constitutive tenuous affinity between Russia and the West was not only expressed in the evolving anti-Western character of the views and rhetoric espoused by the Russian political elite over the course of the 1990s but also in the concrete policies that they took. In the very early 1990s, it appeared that Russia had no interests which would collide with the interests of the West and this approach became associated with Foreign Minister Andrey Kozyrev (Trenin, 2007:70). He acted along the line that the West was Russia's 'natural' ally in security matters, while the defence of human rights, democratisation and the establishment of a liberal international order were the ultimate goals of Russia's internal and external development (Kozyrev, 1992b:287-293). Yet, changes in these policies (as in views) began to be visible in late 1992 and early 1993 due to the first disappointments with the West, the growing strength of conservative groups and the negative economic and social effects of reforms. From then on there was an increasing assertiveness of Russian foreign policy through the second half of the 1990s in accordance with the Pragmatic Nationalist discourse (Melville, Shakleina, 2005:27-65; Light, 2003:6-7).

As regards relations with Europe and the US, already in December 1992, Kozyrev had stunned his European counterparts at the CSCE summit with his statements that Russia was intent on distancing many of its foreign policy stances — on Serbia and the former Soviet space, from those of the West (Kalashnikova, 1994). Moscow began to adopt more domineering policies contesting the principle of humanitarian intervention, particularly in the conflict in Yugoslavia. This was reflected in Kozyrev's eight-point peace plan of February 1993, which called for a tightening of the arms embargo against the Muslims, Serbs and Croats in Bosnia and for the imposition of UN economic sanctions on Croatia. Moscow subsequently remained adamantly opposed to the adoption of military measures against the Bosnian Serbs on the West's humanitarian grounds (Adomeit, 1995:13). Instead, Russia sent a UN committee overseeing Security Council actions a letter requesting permission to sell natural gas to Serbia and Montenegro for its own 'humanitarian reasons' and engaged in shuttle diplomacy in search of agreements to lift the economic sanctions against Serbia (Lynch, 1994:10-11).

Moreover, Moscow's greater assertiveness in the Yugoslav conflict was part of a larger pattern of growing Russian regional resurgence in CEE, expressed in an opposition to Central East European countries joining the process of NATO institutionalised cooperation (Lynch, 1994:15). Yeltsin sent a letter to Western capitals on 13 September 1993, where he said that NATO expansion would be illegal under the terms of the international deal that led to German unification in 1990 (since a (supposed) pledge was given to Gorbachev that the Alliance would not expand beyond Germany) (Mihalka, 1994:3). Kozyrev attempted to counter Poland, Hungary and the Czech Republic joining NATO, arguing in 1993 that CEE had never ceased to be an area of interest for Russia. However, such a stance was notably absent in 1991 and 1992 (Lynch, 1994:14).

The policy change most indicative of the increasing dominance of Pragmatic Nationalist views was related to the assertion of 'special rights' (as opposed to non-domineering regional cooperation) in the CIS. In February 1993, Yeltsin maintained that 'the moment has come when responsible international organisations, including the United Nations, should grant Russia special powers as a guarantor of peace and stability in the region' (Adomeit, 1995:13-14). This position, however, was in contrast to the prevailing strategy towards the near abroad until 1993 when foreign policy was centred on the West and no explicit and coherent policy towards the near abroad was pursued (Lukin, 1992; Kozyrev, 1994; Primakov, 1996). But more and more figures of the political elite converged on the idea that Russia should have a strategic role in the CIS area, if it was not accepted as a fully-fledged European power (Lukin, 1992; Kozyrev, 1994; Primakov, 1996). The Foreign Policy Concept and Military Doctrines produced in the period were in line with such Pragmatic Nationalist ideas (Jackson, 2003:55-61).

Of crucial importance to Russia was the reestablishment of influence over the Ukrainian-Belarusian triangle—the 'heartland' of the CIS, whose significance was determined not only by geopolitical and economic factors but also by cultural-historical ones, as

Russia considered Ukraine and Belarus 'brotherly nations', rather than independent states. For instance, at the Massandra Summit in 1993 Moscow tried to force Ukraine to relinquish control over its half of the Black Sea Fleet in return for the cancellation of Ukraine's debts to Russia (Teague, 1994:10).

Moscow also forcefully pursued its interests through military involvement in CIS conflicts (Jackson, 2003:76). Russia intervened in the Moldova-Transnistria conflict, Georgia-Abkhazia and Tajik conflict in the early 1990s, with the presumed aim being to provoke instability within a republic that was following an independent path and thereby force it back into Moscow's orbit. In particular, Russia was accused of playing one side against the other in the Nagorno-Karabakh conflict by arming the Karabakh Armenians, while at the same time helping the Azerbaijanis (Teague, 1994:10). Moreover, the ceasefire agreement reached in May 1994 marked the culmination of a single-minded Russian effort to wrest the initiative in the Karabakh mediation process from the CSCE, with General Grachev playing an especially prominent role, which testified to the influence that the Russian military had on the direction of the country's CIS policies (Fuller, 1994:13-14).

All of Russia's interventions in CIS conflicts were consistent with Pragmatic Nationalist views. In the Moldovan case, for example, the consensus over Pragmatic Nationalism suggested that Russia would assert itself cautiously as a great power and precluded Russian military withdrawal from Moldova as well as the disregard of the conflict—courses of action that the Liberal Westernisers suggested. It also made it less likely that Russia would attempt to use military force to impose neo-imperial control over Moldova—an aim of the Fundamentalist Nationalists (Jackson, 2003:175).

Furthermore, as a result of the disappointment with the West and in order to compensate for its weakness in dealing with it, Moscow decided to contest the establishment of a liberal, rules-based international order defined by the West and to turn towards East Asia. The Russian political elite complained that since the end of the Cold War the US had expanded its export of arms, while applying pressure on Moscow to curtail its arms exports to Iran and

India. So Russian actions such as the sale of three submarines to Tehran and of cryogenic rocket engines to Delhi were attempts to pursue a more independent foreign policy and resist the alleged 'hypocrisy' of the West (Prizel, 1998:271; Los Angeles Times, 1992).

The Pragmatic Nationalists favoured closer relations with China and, given the weakened position of the Liberal Westernisers, who preferred improved relations with Japan, there was a marked shift toward a better relationship with Beijing. Although initially Russia had signalled its desire to become a partner of Japan (considered a vital ally of the West) and to reach agreement on the status of the Kurile islands (sovereignty over which is disputed between Moscow and Tokyo), in late 1992 and early 1993 it reversed its position. On 9 September 1992, reflecting the policy change, a well prepared visit by Yeltsin to Japan was abruptly cancelled as opposition in Russia to making any concessions to Japan on the islands issue had hardened (Adomeit, 1995:13). In contrast, relations with China began to improve. In 1994, the two states agreed to refrain from participating in a political or military alliance directed against the other party. Moreover, massive Chinese purchases of Russian military hardware and a boost in the cross-border trade in Russia's Far East further signalled the improvement of relations in the direction of fostering a multipolar order oriented on state sovereignty and balances of power (Ministry of Foreign Affairs, 2002, Prizel, 1998:295-296).

The Russian Self and the Western Other, 2000-2015: Better apart

The inability of Russia and the West to agree on and implement a vision of joint belongingness to a unified community of values continued into the new millennium. The uncertainties of Russian identity were being harnessed and organised through politically-sanctioned discourses, which became ever more uneasy with ideal-typical European-ness as the evolution of the regime was guided by and further solidified a set of domestically autocratic and externally assertive principles, while the search for positive self-distinctiveness perceived as an affront the imitation of the West. At the same time, the Russian incompatibility with liberal democracy and a rules-based conduct of international politics undermined European and American expectations for partnership with Moscow and hardened their policy of defining the limits of Europe through EU and NATO expansion without fully-fledged Russian participation. Thus, the drift toward mutual normative incongruence fed into a cycle of disappointments and unintelligibility so that the hopes for Russia-West cooperation of the early 2000s had thinned into a parting of ways by 2015.

The 'thinning' process of Russia's Europeanisation could be observed on both the subjective and intersubjective political-elite level, expressed in the transformation of the declaratory commitment to Russia's European future into growing criticism of ideal-typical European-ness and the latter's renunciation since 2011. The evolution of Vladimir Putin's views on the relationship between Russia and the West was particularly consequential, as his tight grip on power meant that no discourse of identity could gain ascendancy without his ultimate sanction.

Putin started his Presidency as a 'Europeanist' and reiterated the conviction that Russia was an inseparable part of European civilization (Baev, 2003; Putin, 25 September 2001; Arbatova, 2014, interview). This European outlook had a personal experiential basis in Putin's origins from St. Petersburg (a city historically considered to be Russia's 'door' to Europe), where as Deputy Mayor he was responsible for relations with European countries and was further influenced by Mayor Anatoly Sobchak—a pronounced Anglophile (Baev, 2003:5; Lo, 2003:22). However, this Europeanism was accompanied by latent anti-Westernism—a trend towards 'securitisation' and the defence of sovereignty suggested that cooperation with Western Europe and the US needed to go hand in hand with the recognition of Russia as a great power, which possesses full sovereignty internally and externally (Putin, 7 May 2000, 7 May 2004; Lo, 2002:16-19; Evans, 2008:5-6; Busygina, 2014; Simon, 2014, interviews). Indeed, Putin's conviction in Russia's cultural-historical belongingness to Europe was buttressed by his experience as a KGB officer in the German Democratic Republic, which forged a suspicious attitude to the West as a threat. Putin's admiration for Yury

Andropov (who was instrumental in suppressing the Hungarian revolution, the Prague Spring and the Soviet dissident movement) additionally spoke to his preference for defending order as against democracy (Duncan, 2007:148). Hence, as Bobo Lo has pointed out, the 'securitisation' of Russian foreign policy under Vladimir Putin was informed by an underlying security-based philosophy, which rested on geopolitical assumptions and concepts (including, spheres of influence, balance of power, great-powerness) and found expression in the primacy of hard power, military security over democratisation and liberal interdependence among nations (Lo, 2003:16-19).

My interviews have unanimously confirmed that over time there has been an evolution in elements of Putin's vision of Russian identity as a result of both domestic and international developments. On the one hand, the President believed that West European countries and the US failed to reciprocate his policies aiming at cooperation, showed disrespect, treated Russia as a junior partner and took advantage of Russia's weaknesses. What added even more insult to (perceived) injury was the fact that Putin lived with a personal sense of national humiliation due to the collapse of the Soviet Union, the loss of super-power status and the experience of the 1990s when Russia was in steep decline (Lipman, 2014, interview). Thus, the President's initial expectation that by putting forward a vision of partnership after 9/11 he could negotiate with the US on an equal basis was disappointed when he realised that the America would not recognise parity with Russia (Timofeev, 2014; Smirnov, 2014; Nikitina, 2014; Arbatova, 2014; Zevelev, 2014; Miller, 2014; Shmelev, 2014; Utkin, 2014, interviews). Moreover, the Orange Revolution, the European Neighbourhood Policy and the Eastern Partnership were perceived as an attempt to simultaneously encroach on Moscow's sphere of influence and isolate Russia from European developments (Timofeev, 2014; Nikitina, 2014; Baranovsky, 2014; Zevelev, 2014; Utkin, 2014; Shmelev, 2014, interviews). As Alexey Miller has clarified, the more Europe was seen as siding with America in relation to the CIS, the more European countries were thought of as American 'clients' that wanted to encircle Russia (Miller, 2014, interview).

On the other hand, the President's ever-more authoritarian regime drew on Russian traditions of paternalism and collectivism that were incompatible with ideal-typical European-ness. Indeed, Putin began to realise that simply declaring that Russia wanted to become part of the European family was not enough—as qualitative domestic change was necessary, including democracy, elections and civil society, all the while the country was moving in the opposite direction (Baranovsky, 2014; Medvedev, 2014; Morozov, 2014; Tevdoy-Burmuli, 2014; Malashenko, 2014; Melville, 2014, interviews).

The gradual change of attitudes was reflected in Putin's statements. The President's speech in 2004 after the Beslan crisis emphasised that despite the collapse of the USSR, it was possible to preserve the 'core' of that 'great' country—Russia, which, however, 'external actors' wanted to destroy. Terrorist attacks were singled out as an instrument for attempting to achieve this (Putin, 4 September 2004). Putin's speech at the 2007 Munich Conference on Security Policy further revealed the disappointment that his desire to cooperate with the West was not reciprocated. He noted that 'the Cold War left us with live ammunition…ideological stereotypes, double standards and other typical aspects of Cold War thinking' (Sakwa, 2008:20; Putin, 10 February 2007). Thus, if Putin's Pragmatic Nationalism in his first term tended towards the Liberal Westernising spectrum of identity, his second term was gradually marked by more Fundamentalist Nationalist views about Russia's role in the world.

Since 2011, the above trend intensified. In a 2011 *Izvestiya* article, Putin laid out his plan for the creation of the Eurasian Economic Union that should become one of the 'poles' in a multipolar world order. His vision implied that the EEC and the EU would not try to integrate with one another but would coexist as equal partners in a 'Greater Europe' (Putin, 3 October 2011). Moreover, in his 2014 Crimea speech, Putin denounced Western actions since the collapse of the Cold War, including the bombing of Yugoslavia, the instigation of colour revolutions, NATO expansion, the American missile defence system, the slow progress of visa regime liberalisation with the EU, since they were all considered to aim at

Russia's containment (Putin, 18 March 2014). The President criticised the 'moral degeneration' of Western Europe and defined Russian identity as being constituted by those values that Western Europe had already lost—including patriotism, family and religion (Putin, 19 September 2013, 23 January 2012).

The evolution in the subjective views of Vladimir Putin as the key decision-maker and power-holder was also paralleled by the hardening of intersubjective, Pragmatic Nationalist political elite ideas and their gradual shift towards Fundamentalist Nationalist positions. The political elite's growing dissatisfaction with the US and its perceived insufficient reciprocation of Russia's desire for partnership as well as with the EU enlargement process, which sidelined Moscow from European cultural and strategic developments, led to the disappointment of the liberals. All the while, the conservatives were provided with additional arguments against the Europeanisation of Russia's identity and cooperation with Europe and America. At the same time, continuous domestic movement towards authoritarianism meant that Russia was distancing itself normatively from ideal-typical European-ness, which further tipped the political balance in favour of conservative views and consolidated the dominance of the *siloviki*.

The mutual reinforcement of these international and domestic factors thus contributed to the resurgence of Eurasianist thinking. Igor Ivanov (Foreign Minister between 1998-2004) heavily criticised America's national missile defence system, the situation in the Middle East, Iraq and the bypassing of the UN as unilateral acts aimed at harnessing globalisation in order to defend selfish interests (Ivanov, 2003). Similarly, referring to the US, Sergey Lavrov (Foreign Minister since 2004) denounced unilateralism, the 'inertia of the bloc approach', 'double standards' and stressed the need to 'relinquish the philosophy of the past epoch'. Lavrov endorsed a Pragmatic Nationalist course of foreign policy that could make Russia a civilizational bridge between Europe and Asia (Lavrov, 2005, 2006). And in a vivid expression of the Russian preoccupation with perceived slights, Alexei Bogaturov argued that American policies retained an arrogant view of Russia as a 'beating post', with there being incessant calls 'to demand something from the Kremlin', 'to tell Putin', 'to remind that the US will not tolerate' (Bogaturov, February 2005).

The EU also came in for increased criticism, including from liberal intellectuals. Gleb Pavlovsky lamented that the Union guarded its monopoly on 'European values discourse' and did not recognise other views or contributions to it (Pavlovsky, 2004). Arkadiush Sarna argued that already in 2002, it was clear that the claims of the Central East Europeans to join Europe received a welcoming response, whereas the EU's attitude toward Russia, Belarus and Ukraine remained equivocal (Sarna, 2002). Likewise, Igor Maksimychev maintained that Western European countries promised many times during Perestroika and after the end of the Cold War that a 'Greater Europe' from Reykjavik to Vladivostok would be created with the participation of Russia. However, the EU became synonymous with 'Europe' and EU enlargement, just like NATO expansion, took on an anti-Russian character (Maksimychev, 2003).

Since 2011, the liberal strands within Pragmatic Nationalism were completely marginalised. The governing elite's perception of exclusionary Western attitudes was coupled with the frustration that the 2011-2012 protests in Russia and the Ukrainian crisis were (ostensibly) the ultimate manifestation of how European and American efforts at democratisation and regime change interacting with the local forces that supported such efforts could threaten both the regime's stability as well as Russia's regional and international influence. As a result, the concept of Russia as a distinct civilization, the rejection of Europeanisation, the idea of *russkiy mir* (Russian world) and the protection of compatriots in other countries — standpoints previously supported only by the nationalists, were incorporated in the (former) centrists' thinking, who moved away from centrism to nationalism and conservatism (Zevelev, 2014, interview; Zevelev, 2016). Moreover, the role of the Russian Orthodox Church became more important, with its visions of Russian identity being increasingly included into the political mainstream. In addressing the Duma in 2015, Patriarch Kirill criticised the moral degeneration and rejection of Christian values in Western Europe, defining Russian national and religious identity as consisting of a number of key values—faith, statehood, justice, solidarity, dignity, history and family (Yakovleva, 2015).

All in all, as Andrey Melville has observed, the majority of the foreign policy expert community and the political class converged on the interpretation of Russia's identity since 1991 through the prism of the wounded 'Weimar' Russia. This meant that Gorbachev's opening up to the West inaugurated the country's retreat, betraying its national values and interests. However, it is only since 2014 that Russia has been awakening, beginning to overcome its subjugation to Western hegemony and creating a more equitable international order based on adherence to sovereignty and conservatism (Melville, 2014, interview; Karaganov, 2014; Lukyanov, 2014). In line with this assessment, Presidential adviser Sergey Karaganov has argued that a return to 'New Thinking' in today's Russia would be a disaster because it would mean the collapse of all the achievements of Putin's era and the acceptance of Western hegemony (Karaganov, 2014). Similarly, Fyodor Lukyanov has maintained that Crimea and the Ukrainian crisis marked the end of the period since the collapse of the USSR, during which the West attempted—but failed, to build a new international order based on its own supremacy. Instead, Russia is now acting towards the creation of a more equitable and stable multipolar international order (Lukyanov, 2014).

The ever-thinning Europeanisation of Russia's political-elite and expert discourses was furthermore reflected in concrete policies—namely, in Russia's inability and unwillingness to implement a consistently pro-Western foreign policy based on the practical substantiation of ideal-typical values. The trend towards anti-Westernism that developed over the course of Putin's first two terms as President (2000-2008) was rooted both in the disappointment with the US's and Western Europe's lack of reciprocation of Russia's cooperative stance and the centralisation of Russian state power, which was becoming incompatible with Western standards of liberal democracy. To restore a sense of national pride and shore up regime legitimacy, Putin was thus intent on showing his country's continuing importance in world affairs. Reinforcing the alliance with Iran was one way to do so, which included inviting

Iran to join the Shanghai Cooperation Organisation (SCO) as an observer as well as the planned Caspian Sea security organisation (Freedman, 2007:210). Moscow stepped up its sale of arms to Iran and adopted a more lenient stance in contrast to Western sanctions and suspicions of the purposes of the Iranian nuclear programme (Nezavisimaya gazeta, 2003). Putin further suspended the application of the CFE treaty—a cornerstone of European security and a key post-Cold War arms control treaty. The policy was in response to US plans to base parts of a missile defence system in Poland and the Czech Republic, perceived as yet another example of unilateralist US policy aimed at curbing Russia's influence and security in Europe (BBC, 2007).

The development of Russia-EU relations also stalled as a result of mutual normative incompatibilities. The animating ideas of Putin's identity discourses, including sovereignty, great power status, expansion of Russia's influence in the CIS was coupled with the President's stress on pragmatic relations entailing a vision of Russia-EU relations as a 'grand bargain'. As a result, Putin could only adhere to a declaratory acceptance of European norms, whose substantive implementation was nevertheless expected by Brussels as evidence that Moscow could be included in a more fully-fledged manner within European ranks.

The grand bargain in particular would encompass, from Putin's point of view, the undisputed recognition of Russia's domestic regime; an EU-Russia agreement to respect each other's interests in the shared neighbourhood; and the conduct of business between the two partners on an equal footing (Troitskiy, 2014, interview; Klitsounova, 2005:39). As Utkin and Busygina explain, Putin did not aim to make Russia a member of the EU, as this required domestic transformation in line with European criteria, which he was not able to accept (due to his ambivalence about liberal democratic values and his vision of Russia as a great rather than just a regional European power). Instead, Putin thought that what was feasible to pursue in relations with the EU was visa-free travel and the common economic space, where Russian concerns and interests could be taken into consideration in terms of catching up economically and technologically with the West (Utkin, 2014;

Busygina, 2014, interviews; Lo, 2002:23; Karaganov, 2005). However, the adoption of a narrowly pragmatic approach towards the Union made it impossible for Russia to be accepted as a fully-fledged member of the European community of nations, bound by exactly those values 'set aside' by Moscow as irrelevant to foreign policy (Lo, 2002:25).

And in line with the lack of motivation to pursue the principle of cooperative regional relations coupled with the desire to assert itself against what was seen as the EU's encroachment on the Kremlin's sphere of influence, Russia began to interfere more decisively in the post-Soviet space. Moscow reinforced its connections with the Central Asian states, expanded economic cooperation, backed the ruling elites in their rigged elections and promoted Russian language and culture (Nixey, 2012:2-8). In signing the Kharkiv Accords with Russia in 2010, then Ukrainian President Viktor Yanukovych compromised important elements of Ukraine's independence. The gas subsidy and the accompanying agreement to prolong the lease of the Black Sea fleet in Crimea ensured that Ukraine's relations with Russia would continue to be influenced by economic dependency and limited diplomatic and geopolitical options for Kyiv (Bogomolov, Lytvynenko, 2012:3-4; Sherr, 2010:8). As regards other post-Soviet states, Moscow behaved in a similarly coercive way. It continued its policy of granting citizenship to residents of secessionist regions in Georgia, ignoring Georgia's vehement dissatisfaction with this policy (MacFarlane, 2006:12). And although Russia accepted the establishment of American bases in Central Asia, it reversed this 'intrusion'. For instance, after the Uzbek government's slaughter of protesters in Andijan in May 2005, Russian policy makers exploited the ambivalence of American perspectives on the human rights situation in Uzbekistan to call into question the status of US bases in the region, stressing that what happened in Andijan was Uzbekistan's internal affair (MacFarlane, 2006:12).

During Dmitry Medvedev's tenure as President (2008-2012), the reduction of Western geopolitical pressure on Moscow following its war with Georgia and Medvedev's liberal rhetoric in favour of his country's modernisation determined advances in

Russia's relations with the US within the framework of the 'reset'. Such advances included the signing of the New START treaty (aiming to reduce strategic nuclear weapons), the agreement on sanctions on Iran and joint air defence exercises. However, the general clash of understandings between Russia and the West regarding European values and security led to a dynamic in which a substantive progress in relations was difficult to achieve (Kaczmarski, 2010:2-3). For instance, Medvedev's proposed European Security Treaty failed to elicit much enthusiasm in his European counterparts. It was particularly unclear how the treaty would combine the suggested aims of 'indivisible' security, an equal say for Russia in European security and the implicit goal to limit American influence on European security matters with NATO's pivotal role in the continent's security (Zagorski, 2009:4; Project on a Treaty on European Security, 2009).

Also, one of the major goals of the proposed treaty was to halt EU and NATO expansion in the post-Soviet space and to elicit a recognition of Russia's hegemonic role in the region. This, however, was incompatible with the EU's engagement in the CIS based on European norms of good-neighbourliness and democratisation rather than a zero-sum game that results in the division of spheres of influence. Nevertheless, Moscow pressed ahead with the application of economic, diplomatic and military pressure on the CIS countries, including the recognition of Abkhazia and South Ossetia; a gas war with Ukraine; an agreement with Ukraine on the extension of the deployment of the Russian Black Sea Fleet in Crimea; an extension to Moscow's military presence in Armenia (Lukyanov, 2012). Russia further urged greater cooperation among the BRICs, which would find expression in the striving for a multipolar world order, reform of the major financial institutions (the IMF, the WTO), whose principles were thought to be unfairly skewed in favour of the West (President of Russia, 16 April 2010, 14 April 2011, 29 March 2012).

Since 2011, the centralisation of power and the creation of an enemy image of the West as well as the West's reluctance to integrate Russia in the Euro-Atlantic community led to the intensification of anti-Western trends in Moscow's foreign policy and to a more definitive 'turn to the East' — encompassing both the Eurasian space and East Asia. The Eurasian Economic Union was officially established in January 2015 by Russia, Kazakhstan, and Belarus as founding member states (Armenia and Kyrgyzstan joined later in 2015) (Voloshin, 2012; Dragneva, Wolczuk, 2012). Russia's determination to keep the CIS firmly within its sphere of influence and away from Western interference was most clearly demonstrated in the Ukrainian crisis. The string of events that occurred since late 2013 encompassed Russian pressure on Ukraine not to sign the Association Agreement with the EU, the annexation of Crimea following the Kyiv Maidan protests and a pro-Western interim government (succeeded by a similarly pro-Western elected government) and the destabilisation of eastern Ukraine by 'local' Russian rebels (MacFarlane, Menon, 2014; Arbatova, 2014).

Putin's third term as President also marked increased efforts to forge an alliance with China, which could be instrumental in the creation of a multipolar world order and would signal to the West that Moscow had alternatives to the Euro-Atlantic partnership (Zevelev, 2012:6-7). The Russians stood alongside China at the UN Security Council, the Shanghai Cooperation Organisation and the BRICs as ways of enhancing Russia's international weight. At the UN Security Council China and Russia shared similar positions on the intervention in Libya in 2011, on sanctions against Iran and North Korea and both opposed NATO's use of force against Syria in 2013 (Trenin, 2013:5-6). In the sphere of energy, in May 2014, Russia and China signed a $400 billion gas deal, according to which China would be supplied with Russian gas through a new pipeline over the next 30 years (Mazneva, Kravchenko, Meyer, 2014; Soldatkin, Aizhu, 2014).

Moscow also tried to step up its relations with other non-European actors — including, India, Turkey and Egypt. In 2014, Putin visited India, signing a contract related to the training of Indian soldiers under the Russian Ministry of Defence. Agreements were concluded between the Skolkovo Foundation and the council for companies exporting electronics and software, as well as between the Russian news agency ITAR-TASS and the Press Trust of India (Topychkanov, 2014). Moreover, the difficult relations between the EU and Russia and their negative impact on the South Stream gas pipeline led Putin to cancel the project and sign an alternative gas deal with Turkey. In turn, the Russian President's 2015 visit to Egypt focused on discussions about ending the use of the dollar in bilateral trade and increasing arms sales (BBC, 10 February 2015).

Ideas all the way through: Constructivism vis-a-vis alternative explanations of Russian foreign policy

The development of Russia-West relations since 1991 has demonstrated how deep-seated mutual ambivalences and uncertain affinities undermined the prospect of building a common European home. The thin Europeanisation of Russian foreign policy — that was the ultimate, interactive result of domestic normative divergence from ideal-typical European-ness and external exclusion, conditioned Moscow's place on the outskirts of the Euro-Atlantic community. In the concluding part of this chapter, I further argue that a Constructivist account of the Kremlin's relations with the outside world comes into view even more clearly when juxtaposed to Realist explanations. As opposed to Realism's perspective that Russia's growing assertiveness vis-a-vis the West was determined by a shift in capabilities that warranted a balancing behaviour, it was considerations of identity that circumscribed the 'thinkable' external courses of action and informed the assessment of interests and deployment of available capacities.

As regards trends in the 1990s, Realists have presented Moscow's more domineering foreign policy stances since 1993 as a geopolitical shift, whereby the Russians eventually returned to the Realist tradition of organising their relations with the West on the basis of strategic competition for power and political-military rivalry. An important element in this supposedly timeless, ahistorical geopolitical orientation was the focus on Eurasia (the CIS states) — the space where Russia could advance its great power interests (Morozova, 2011:10, 15-17; Brzezinski, 1997; Skak, 1996; Clover, 1999).

However, such an account faces the challenge that the delineation of a set of 'interests' is inextricably linked to conceptions of national identity — of what Russia is. In the very early 1990s, the leading government politicians thought that Russian interests coincided with those of the West, which flowed from the identity discourse of Russia as a pro-Western, liberal-internationalist, democratic country. Yet, from 1993 onward, Moscow's interests were defined as including the reassertion of power in the CIS and building links with the East in the attempt to establish a multi-polar world order, which was conditioned by the growing political consensus on a Pragmatic Nationalist vision of Russian identity. Hence, 'Eurasianism' was constituted as meaningful by a foreign policy identity paradigm that emerged in reaction to Western practices perceived as exclusionary as well as the increasing influence of anti-Western groups within the polity. These internal and external processes engendered the need for positive self-inflation through a form of identification that asserted Russia's distinctiveness in relation to Europe (Morozova, 2011:34; Tsygankov, 2003:6).

And this reconceptualisation of Russian identity and interests took place despite the fact that a realistic assessment of the country's military and economic capabilities — which declined dramatically over the 1990s, did not warrant a balancing strategy. Russia's GDP dropped by 40% between 1991 and 1999, the population was severely impoverished and state assets were plundered. The 1998 crisis further pushed inflation to 86% and led to the collapse of banks and the stock exchange and to the government's default on debt payments (Bracho, López, 2005:5-6). The military was in a similarly critical condition. Shortcomings in finances for training and exercises and the obsolete status of equipment decreased the combat readiness of the Armed Forces and resulted in a mass exodus of professional servicemen. Between 1991 and 2002, 400 000 officers left, while by 1998 only 17% of potential recruits actually fulfilled their conscription, having to work in circumstances of low morale and poor discipline (Haas, 2011:12-13).

It was therefore the overriding concern with finding Russia's ideational bearings in the post-Soviet world that shaped the

Russian elite's interpretation of interests—in spite of the insufficient capabilities in disposal for the realisation of those interests.

Similarly, the Realist interpretation of Putin's attempt to forge relationships with non-Western states particularly since 2011 as amounting to a balancing act against the West is belied by the actual feasibility of the main vehicles through which the Kremlin has waged this act (i.e., an alliance with China and the creation of the Eurasian Economic Union). A reiteration of the original Russian motivation to seek alternative courses of action despite the viability of the chosen means—namely, the inability of Russia and the West to accommodate each other's visions of the bounds of togetherness, thus speaks once again to the argument that interests and capabilities are what states make of them.

Indeed, despite the development of economic and strategic cooperation between Moscow and Beijing, the track record of bilateral relations up to 2015 did not amount to the ability to comprehensively balance the EU and the US or construct a multipolar world, due to political and strategic limitations to the Russia-China 'axis'. Apart from the common denominator that binds these countries together (opposition to external interference in domestic affairs and US primacy), there was a divergence of positions on various geopolitical issues. For instance, Beijing did not recognise Abkhazia's and South Ossetia's independence, neither did it assume a firm position in the Ukrainian crisis. On the one hand, China abstained when the UN Security Council voted on a resolution condemning Russia's annexation of Crimea as illegal and has not officially recognised that Crimea is part of Russia. On the other hand, China has opposed sanctions against Russia and has implicitly supported the Crimean referendum (Trenin, 2012:41; Tiezzi, 2014; TASS, 2014). Beijing also held ambiguous stances regarding the Russian-Japanese dispute over the Kurile islands, whereas Moscow maintained neutrality regarding the Sino-Japanese standoff over the Senkaku/Diaoyu islands (Trenin, 2012:41-42). Additionally, China's growing military proved to be an unsettling issue for the Russian leadership and military. If in the 1990s and until the mid-2000s, Moscow was an exporter of weaponry to Beijing, this trend had changed because through reverse-engineering China managed to produce its own military hardware and export it to the developing world, thus undercutting Russia's trade positions (Page, 2010). Also, China carried out military exercises that demonstrated the ability of the Chinese ground forces to wage successful war against Russia (Trenin, 2012:59).

China was also unwilling to risk its economic relations with the US and the EU for the sake of forming a balancing Sino-Russian alliance. As a matter of comparison and illustration, the US-China volume of total trade in 2014 amounted to $590.7 billion, with the US becoming China's number one trading partner, while Russia was number 10 (United States Census Bureau, 2014; China Daily, 19 February 2014). In 2013, the total volume of trade in goods between the EU and China reached €428.1 billion (Facts and Figures on EU-China trade, March 2014). In contrast, the Chinese-Russian volume of total trade was at least 5 times less – $88.8 billion in 2013 (Miklushevskiy, 18 April 2014; Xinhua, 14 June 2013; Meyer, Pismennaya, 2014; Wright, 2014). The EU-28 also ranked as one of the top 5 FDI providers to China along with Taiwan, Hong Kong, the USA and Japan (Facts and Figures on EU-China trade, March 2014).

It should be admitted, however, that in recent years China and Russia have moved closer together in strategic as well as ideational terms. Moscow and Beijing have promoted similar anti-Western and anti-democratic narratives that extol the supposed advantages of authoritarian governance over liberal democracy and push for a multipolar world order (Filipova, 2021b:49-53). But Russia's status as a junior partner to Beijing's global ambitions and potential bandwagoner in Realist configurations surrounding a bipolar US-China competition for world leadership would be far from certainly accepted by the Russian elite and little substantive strategic coordination between Moscow and Beijing has taken place (Lo, Lucas, 2021). Russia's place as part of the proclaimed strategic 'turn to East Asia' is also less than clear and assured, given the geopolitical and economic constellation in the region. The most pressing, short- and long-term priority ahead of East Asian leaders is to preserve their autonomy and freedom of manoeuvre through a fine balance between increasing economic interdependence with China and a strategic orientation towards the US (especially in the case of Japan, South Korea, the Philippines, Singapore) (Changsu, 2013;

Watanabe, 2006; Heydarian, 2011; Traywick, 2012; Wallace, 2013; Sukma, 2012; Hiep, 2012).

Furthermore, one can seriously doubt the viability of the Eurasian Economic Union as an alternative to the West. Cohesion within the Union was severely undermined by Russia's annexation of Crimea, as it evoked fears in Moscow's closest allies in the face of Belarus and Kazakhstan, about the possibility of a similar type of intervention in their territories—should Russia decide to 'protect' the status of the Russian language and the Russian ethnic minorities in those countries. Therefore, the Kremlin's actions in Ukraine are fuelling distrust in Moscow's closest partners, which are becoming wary of centralising developments in the EEU that could further compromise their sovereignty as well as preferred multi-vector foreign policy that attempts to navigate between the EU, the US and Russia (Taylor, 2014; Lillis, 2014). Also, there are economic setbacks to the viability of the EEU. For instance, transaction rates between the members of the Union show a very imbalanced pattern of regional trade integration. Belarus is heavily dependent on exports to Russia, with a marginal share of trade with Kazakhstan. On the other hand, Russia and Kazakhstan maintain a relatively low share of exports to other EEU members. These trends combined with a slow movement of capital and labour force impede economic integration and hence prospects for mounting a feasible economic challenge to the EU (Blockmans, Kostanyan, Vorobiov, 2012:14).

The questionable viability of the EEU as well as obstacles and unclarities in Russia's relations with China consequently make it difficult to maintain that 'objective' conditions have dictated a policy of balance of power and the creation of a multi-polar world. Instead, the direction of Russian foreign policy has been informed by the evolution of political elite visions of Russia's identity from the initially favourable outlook on the country's Europeanisation and cooperation with the West to the gradual renunciation of European values and corresponding turn to the 'East'. The stark split in Russia-West relations that has taken place in the stand-off over Ukraine since 2013 represented the catalyst that pushed the Kremlin to search for alternative paths as a form of compensation for Moscow's inability to find and have its place affirmed in the Euro-Atlantic community.

8 Three Limits of Europe
Poland, Bulgaria and Russia in Comparative Perspective

The revolutionary upheaval of 1989 exerted a powerful impact on political imaginations, offering new vistas for a far-reaching change in international politics — more democratic, interdependent and co-operative. The hope for something new was fed by the magnitude of systemic collapse that contained the rarely combined qualities of being both large-scale and (relatively) peaceful. The dissolution of ideological boundaries thus represented a promise of constructing a common European home, where the candidate CEE family members would finally reach the much-coveted goal of becoming like the West.

Yet, the horizon of expectations confronted the totality of experience, since 1989 did not simply inaugurate a radical break from the past and a clean slate on which the 'new' could be inscribed. Instead, in Wydra's terms, the messianic, post-revolutionary time after 1989 represented a period of extraordinary condensation of potentialities — a 'dawn' of a new national constitutive mythology of European-ness, which was, however, conditioned by the continuing hold of the past that could not be swept away as a well-sealed era of bygones (Wydra, 2015; Prozorov, 2009:44, 52).

Indeed, as Poland, Bulgaria and Russia set out on the road to Europe and negotiated with the West their entry into the European home, it once again became clear that the long-standing historical striving for a unified Europe met with the reality of its many manifestations. And as the core argument advanced in this book holds, it was identity that shaped the uneven pattern of Europeanisation that followed in the aftermath of communism's demise. To unify the strands of this story of uneven-ness, I now bring together the empirical record of Poland's, Bulgaria's and Russia's foreign policy transformations told in the previous three chapters and show that a Constructivist perspective provides us with a robust, albeit frequently neglected, lens through which to illuminate the diversity of CEE states' capacity to become integrated in the Euro-Atlantic community. This perspective also underlines the persistence and behavioural consequence of culturally-historically formed conceptions of Europe rooted in nation-state identity and substantiates the significance of ideas in the discipline of International Relations against dominant institutionalist-rationalist, materialist approaches.

Shades of Europeanisation:
The thick, the ambivalent and the thin

The key conundrum that animates the present study asks the following principal question: why did CEE states display such divergent outcomes in the aftermath of 1989? Why did three of those states in particular—Poland, Bulgaria and Russia, differ so starkly among each other in terms of the pace and extent of becoming integrated in the new Europe that was replacing the iron clad divisions of the past? The differences that resurfaced in the post-1989 period pointed to the fact that having formerly shared a similar regime type did not mean that the Central and East European countries had become unified in their social, political and economic characteristics. Moreover, neither could the differential paths these countries took be 'overcome' through the implementation of the same institutional and legislative requirements for building liberal democracy and a free market economy.

Thus, given that suppositions of similar starting and end points in the democratisation and Europeanisation of CEE were not borne out by evidence, I have offered an alternative perspective— based on an interactive Constructivist theory of Self and Other in bordering belongingness, that it was fundamental questions of identity, which shaped the character of post-communist transformations. The exploration of identity construction rests on a threefold theoretical refinement of Constructivism. First, the book builds on the interactive-holistic strand in Constructivist theorising and in this way overcomes a single-minded focus on either systemic or unit-level factors as formative of ideational processes. Second, a middle-ground epistemological position is advanced, which integrates—and simultaneously critiques, objectivist and post-structuralist subjectivist standpoints, attuning the research paradigm to both generalizable regularities and singular, contextual particularities. Third, the interactive Constructivist theory of Self and Other moves past an inordinate emphasis on the philosophical underpinnings and justification of Constructivism to a mid-range theoretical exploration and a firmer empirical understanding of how identities are formed in an interactive and comparative manner. The incorporation of Social Psychological insights further enriches Constructivism's conceptualisation of the patterns of identity continuity, change and impact on behaviour.

According to the interactive Constructivist theory of Self and Other, it was not simply up to Poland, Bulgaria and Russia to decide for themselves where they belonged, as their place on Europe's civilizational map depended on an interactive negotiation with the significant Western Other. In this vein, the ways in which the Polish, Bulgarian and Russian Selves and the Western Other (re)enacted and (re)conceptualised the extent to which they could belong to one community were foundational: the level of external acceptance and internal normative affinity would determine whether a country was in, out or in the hallways of the Euro-Atlantic community. To reiterate and sum up the unfoldment of these mutually constitutive identification processes between 1989 and 2015, I restate and weave together the story of how the Polish, Bulgarian and Russian cases fulfil the book's propositions about thick, ambivalent and thin Europeanisation.

Thick Europeanisation characterises the foreign policy identity transformations of countries, where a resolute, comprehensive and persistent Western (i.e. both Western European and American) recognition meets with a widely shared domestic consensus in favour of integration with the West, informed by a culturally-historically underwritten principled compatibility with ideal-typical European-ness. The course of Poland's relations with the Euro-Atlantic community since 1989 embodied and manifested the conditions of thick Europeanisation. On the one hand, the Polish Self's outlook *shaped a strong positive identification with the*

West; sustained a consistent foreign policy strategy of Euro-Atlantic integration through the determined fulfilment of accession criteria and ambition to become an active and respected member of the EU and NATO; or occasionally *gave rise to Euro-scepticism and empowered the traditionalist strand of identity.* On the other hand, the Western Other *conferred recognition on and lent greater salience to the modernist strand of identity; sped up reforms by providing criteria for transformation and practical support; offered timely and decisive institutional inclusion and socialisation; instilled greater trust and a feeling of belongingness.* Or (only) occasionally and intermittently external influences *failed to give acknowledgement, support and commitment, which bred internal disappointments and empowered the traditionalist strand of identity.*

Poland's thick Europeanisation was ultimately defined by the mutually constituted, internally motivated and externally sanctioned vision of Warsaw's acceptance and integration in the Euro-Atlantic community. In the 1990s, international developments facilitated Poland's inclusion in Western institutions and its domestic transformation. The EU gradually involved Poland in its institutional mechanisms, set conditions for reform and membership. The CSCE/OSCE and the Council of Europe additionally disseminated norms of liberalisation, human rights and democratisation. Germany advocated and accelerated Warsaw's inclusion in the EU, whereas the US further enabled Poland's domestic transformation and NATO membership, with EU and NATO accession developing as parallel and complementary processes. All of these factors strengthened the internal Polish political consensus in favour of Euro-Atlantic integration on the basis of sustained and internalised normative compatibility so that even institutional and party factionalism and fragmentation could not undermine Poland's European direction. In the 2000s and 2010s, EU accession provided Poland with greater opportunities for the Europeanisation of foreign policy, which could only be taken full advantage of on the basis of an internal drive to play an important role in EU decision-making affairs. This trend was further strengthened by the fluctuating level of US commitment to Polish and European security, which weakened the Poles' Atlanticism and fostered a greater focus on the ESDP. So successfully taking and shaping Union policy represented two sides of the same coin. The ability to actively affect the EU's agenda depended on being fully cognizant and integrated into consensual, coalition-building and compromise-oriented European manners that also included acquiescing into and downloading the policy initiatives of fellow member states (but which still varied between consensus-prone PO- and confrontational PiS-dominated governments).

But how could the interactively conditioned thick Europeanisation be evaluated against the ideal-typical standard of European-ness? According to the criteria that Chapter 3 has posited for the systematic establishment of a given level of Europeanisation, the 'thick-ness' of Polish Europeanisation could be discerned in that the conceptions and practices of Europe of the Polish political and intellectual elite *resonated most closely* with ideal-typical values on the basis of consistent, sustained and intersubjectively shared principled internalisation, rhetorical embeddedness and behavioural commitment. This was enabled and maintained by Europe's and America's decisive acceptance, manifested in quick and substantial diplomatic support, institutional admittance and economic assistance. Although such determined adherence to European-ness was particularly prominent in the 1990s, the alternate espousal and pursuit of two conceptions of Europe since 2005 — the modernist-liberal vision of the PO and the traditionalist-conservative vision of the PiS, did introduce an element of contestation. But it did not fundamentally weaken Poland's close affinity to ideal-typical values because of the common ideational bond that modernists and conservatives ultimately share.

Thus, the first post-communist decade was characterised by the dominance and continuity of the Polish modernist, liberal-internationalist discourse. Poland's decision-makers consistently emphasised that the animating principles of their country's foreign policy were those of liberal democracy, respect for human rights, tolerance, a rules-based European and international order focused on institutionalised (especially EU and NATO) cooperation, multi-lateralism, consensual decision-making as well as the rejection of the use of force and a Yalta-style division of the continent, informed by spheres of influence, balances of power, concerts of powers and bipolarism. In addition, the importance of the achievement of mutual trust, reconciliation and the overcoming of historical conflicts was stressed with regard to relations with neighbours, including Germany, the Central European states (the Czech Republic, Hungary, Slovakia) and the countries further to Poland's east (Ukraine, Belarus, Russia). In terms of the latter, special significance was laid on the renunciation of territorial claims, imperial temptations and fixation on past conflicts in favour of friendly and cooperative regional policies coupled with the promotion of democratisation. In the realm of defence, Polish politicians extolled the virtues of a cooperative system of security, whereby states would adhere to civilian control over the military, transparency of their military planning and budgeting and would loyally and in solidarity follow allied commitments.

The dominant liberal-internationalist discourse also shaped the tenor, character and civilizational orientation of the concrete policies that were undertaken in the 1990s. The rhetorical goals aimed at the assertion of Poland's cultural-historical belongingness and normative affinity with Western Europe were enacted through the sustained pursuit of integration in the OSCE, the Council of Europe, the EU and NATO on the basis of the strict fulfilment of accession criteria providing standards of European-ness. Close ties and intense cooperation with Germany were established on the principles of reconciliation and trust. Cooperative regional relations with both the Visegrad states and Warsaw's eastern neighbours were further conducted.

In the new millennium, the PO perpetuated the liberal-internationalist discourse of the 1990s by espousing deeper European integration, trust-based cooperation with Germany and democratisation of the Eastern neighbours by rooting them in a EU-focused framework of relations. In contrast, PiS placed a rhetorical stress on state sovereignty, national traditions and morality (including the Catholic religion, patriotism), statist interventionism in the economy, opposition to a liberalised view on reproductive practices (such as abortion) and uneasiness with homosexuality and gay marriage. The Law and Justice party also made clear its preference for a Europe of nation-states, embraced a suspicious attitude to

Germany and Russia (infused by lingering historical grievances) and promoted Central European cooperation on the basis of the inter-sea concept envisaging greater assertiveness of Central Europe vis-a-vis both the West and Russia. Nevertheless, the limits of PiS' contestation of European-ness, primarily reserved for issues of state sovereignty and traditional morality, meant that key elements of the ideal-typical model have been preserved, which has determined the presence of intersubejctively shared positions with the PO. Both parties have emphasised the goal of establishing Warsaw as a respected member of the EU and NATO, given Poland's cultural-historical belongingness to the West, and promoted the democratisation of Ukraine and Belarus, while guarding against the resurgence of a neo-imperialist Russia through an active Eastern policy.

However, these shared ideas have been enacted through polarised styles comprising the PO's consensus-seeking and PiS' confrontational stances. In line with this, the Civic Platform's policies were based on consistent efforts at making Poland a reliable EU partner that both downloads Union initiatives and is also able to upload Warsaw's own policy objectives through persuasion and negotiation (as manifested in the successful EU uptake of the Eastern Partnership). Conversely, Law and Justice has acted assertively in the EU arena (prominently manifested through the veto on the PCA negotiation between Russia and the Union) and adopting an antagonistic position towards Germany.

In distinction from the Self's convictional tenacity and the Other's keen affirmation that define a case of thick Europeanisation, ambiguity and uncertainty pervade *ambivalent Europeanisers*. In the latter instance, the Self and the Other's ambivalence at once prevents a quick and eager integration with one another, but at the same time does not make impossible the eventual achievement of domestic political consensus in favour of joining the Euro-Atlantic community and the external provision of support. Post-1989 Bulgaria is an exemplar of this form of Europeanisation. On the one hand, the Bulgarian Self's outlook shaped a more uncertain affinity with the West; a weaker attachment to, understanding and cultural rootedness of European norms; a greater contestation of the pro-Western vector of foreign policy; an acrimoniously reached domestic political consensus; a persisting East-West duality of ideational allegiances and strategic orientation. All of these 'hollowed out' and slowed down the quality and speed of Europeanisation, imparting to that process a performative rather than deeply internalised character. On the other hand, the Western Other initially displayed hesitation, uncertainty, reluctance to commit to Bulgarian Europeanisation; partially excluded and delayed Sofia's Euro-Atlantic integration; provided less extensive diplomatic, economic and political support to Bulgaria (than to Poland), which created domestic disappointments and activated historically-informed perceptions of exclusion. Still, international developments also worked in such a way as to gradually and eventually grant Bulgaria a membership perspective; promote and provide a blueprint for internal reforms; introduce the discourse of European values; posit an organising framework that widened Sofia's foreign policy-making opportunities in EU fora, all of which encouraged and motivated Bulgaria's Europeanising efforts.

Ultimately, it was the mutual constitution of the domestic and international dimension of identification that produced Bulgaria's ambivalent Europeanisation. In the 1990s, the EU and NATO took much more time to commit fully to the inclusion of Bulgaria in Euro-Atlantic structures, differentiated Sofia (and Bucharest) into a class of laggards and demonstrated doubts about the country's belongingness as well as preparedness to join. It was a critical event—the war in Kosovo, that catalysed and accelerated the two institutions' readiness to offer membership to Bulgaria. Hence, the Western Other failed to establish an early and substantial external anchor for Bulgaria's domestic and international transformation. In turn, this was complemented and further shaped by Bulgarian political actors' own uncertain identification with the West. The UDF's insufficiently substantive understanding and inconsistent practice of European values; the BSP's gradually evolving ideological adherence away from exclusivist nationalist positions, the Eastern vector of foreign policy and anti-NATO sentiments; the fragmented and unstable institutional and party-political environment reinforced each other towards a slowly attained domestic political consensus.

Similarly, in the 2000s and 2010s, Bulgaria's inability to become a substantively integrated, active and reliable member of the EU and NATO has been the product of the mutually constituted outcome of the internal and external dimension of identification. On the one hand, Western ambivalence about Bulgaria continued as the EU's and NATO's firmer confirmation of Bulgarian membership prospects were significantly informed by strategic concerns and institutional path-dependence rather than a strong symbolic-ideational motivation. And once fully-fledged membership status was granted, Western assessments of Bulgaria's domestic problems (above all deficiencies in the operation of the rule of law) did not lead to a change in ambiguous perceptions. On the other hand, the emergence of catch-all populist parties (some of which only formally paid tribute to European values), the continuing post-communist-anti-communist duality of interpretation and pursuit of external policy and passive mindset determined Sofia's insufficient capacity to move itself from the periphery and contribute to Brussels policy-making. So the formal extensions of the EU and NATO framework to Bulgaria could deepen Europeanisation only given domestic efforts to reform and attempt to both download as well as upload policy initiatives.

Ambivalent Europeanisation was manifest in the political-intellectual elite's conceptions of Europe, which *broadly converged* with the ideal-typical model of European-ness, particularly as a rhetorical overlay, but *frequently diverged* in terms of substantive understandings and sometimes in practice, resulting in superficial normative compatibility and situational behavioural adaptation. Such ambivalent adherence to the ideal type was promoted and sustained by the West's own hesitant commitment to Bulgaria's Europeanisation, expressed in slower and less substantial (than in Poland's case) diplomatic support, institutional admittance and economic assistance.

The interaction of more shallow domestic ideational affinity and international desire for inclusion meant that into the second half of the 1990s the political elite continued to lurch between the post-communist and anti-communist facets of the discourse on Europe before reaching a firmer consensus on Euro-Atlantic integration, with both facets showing a doubtful convictional attachment to the ideal-typical model. The vision of the former communists did acknowledge Bulgaria's cultural-historical belongingness and contribution to European civilization. They stressed that Sofia had to find its rightful place in Europe following the changes in 1989 through adherence to the principles of democracy, human rights, institutionalised cooperation focused on EC/EU membership, multilateralism and cooperative regional relations. Yet, it took a gradual ideational evolution so that the BSP could move away from exclusivist nationalist positions, opposition to economic neoliberalism, preferences for a close strategic cooperation with Moscow, conceptions of European security inspired by Gorbachevian ideas of the 'common European home' and a view of Euro-Atlanticism that included Russia, was sanctioned by the OSCE but excluded NATO. On the other hand, the anti-communist vision of the UDF centred on political anti-communism, economic neo-liberalism, external breakaway from the Russian sphere of influence and the establishment of a strategic partnership with the US. But the either-or, nostalgic-revanchist bent of this anti-communism failed to elaborate sufficiently the principles of civic participation, ethnic tolerance, pluralism, sustainable regional co-operation and was still attached to an OSCE- rather than NATO-based European system of security. It was only after 1997 that the overall Bulgarian discourse began to match more closely the ideal-typical model of European-ness. A more consistent and broad-based espousal emerged of human rights norms, democratic and market economic transformation, EU and NATO institutionalised integration, cooperative security, civilian control over the military, transparency of national defence planning, regional cooperation, good-neighbourliness, peace and stability in European international relations.

In policy terms, there was a congruence between the pre-1997 lack of consensus on Europeanisation, whereby the political dominance of the BSP meant that their ideational dispositions found expression in an ambivalent pursuit of Euro-Atlantic integration and a preference for neutrality, equidistance and balanced relations between East and West. After 1997, the general agreement on Europeanisation was manifested in an external policy of integration in the EU and NATO and regional cooperation. Yet, the UDF's performative-imitative rather than deeply internalised adherence to European norms continued to impart a superficial and situational character to Bulgaria's behavioural commitment to Europeanisation.

In the new century, the predominant bipolar political competition of the 1990s between the UDF and the BSP gave way to the emergence of populist parties (such as the NDSV and GERB). The centre-right populist discourse of Bulgarian foreign policy identity perpetuated the key tenets of the domestic political consensus on the Euro-Atlantic civilizational choice, including an emphasis on liberal democracy, rule of law, multilateralism, good-neighbourliness, institutionalised cooperation and constructive behaviour supportive of deeper European integration. However, beneath the rhetorical surface that matches the ideal-typical model of European-ness, the convictions and political practices of the centre-right populists have revealed ideational and behavioural patterns that deepened the ambivalent incongruence with European norms. These patterns have included forceful, authoritarian governance, illiberal majoritarianism, the conviction that 'might makes right' and that political expedience justifies infringements on fundamental civic and economic freedoms. Moreover, the attempt of the populists to amalgamate various societal preferences (pro-Western and pro-Russian ones) as well as the lingering former communist-anti-communist opposition conditioned a dualistic quality of Bulgaria's external outlooks, still dividing the country's loyalties between East and West.

Accordingly, the rhetorical commitment to ideal-typical values lacking in deep convictional internalisation continued to lend itself to a situational behavioural adaption to European norms and stances forged within the Euro-Atlantic community. Sofia has tried to follow a pro-Western strategic orientation in favour of a liberal regional and international order and act as a loyal EU and

NATO member. But at the same time, Bulgarian politicians have maintained intensive political and economic links with Russia, which together with the historically-informed passivity and propensity to ingratiate with external actors, has limited the ability to develop a longer-term vision of Bulgaria's place in Europe as well as to win respect and trust as a dependable, consistent and committed partner.

The tortuous path and uncertainties of Bulgaria as an ambivalent Europeaniser, however, never amounted to the extent of normative incompatibility and contestation that defines *thin Europeanisation*. Such thin-ness is fed both by an inconsistent support and insufficient recognition on the part of the Western Other as well as by the Self's difficulty reaching a consensus about joining the Euro-Atlantic family of nations, given a tenuous cultural-historical identification with the West. This form of Europeanisation has been vividly embodied by the vicissitudes in Russia's relations with Western Europe and America since 1991. The Russian Self's vision of itself and place in the world *shaped a weak positive identification with the West; made an internal political consensus on the Europeanisation of foreign policy hard to sustain politically and ideationally; laid the foundation for the emergence of normative and regime-institutional developments that contested Europeanisation; and called for a geopolitical reorientation to the East.* All of these *ultimately culminated in a principled and strategic incompatibility with the ideal-typical conception of European-ness.* For its part, the Western Other operated in an exclusionary manner by *side-lining Moscow; displaying nonchalance to Russian ideational and strategic concerns; dismissing Russia at times as weak and irrelevant; and failing to elaborate a vision for cooperation or to provide significant economic aid.* All of these *instilled a perception of the recreation of dividing lines; bred disappointment among the liberals; empowered the anti-Western political forces; confirmed Russian fears of marginalisation from European affairs; and ultimately weakened Moscow' resolve for Europeanisation. Compensatory inclusive schemes and attempts at fostering political dialogue, socialisation and institutionalised cooperation* were viewed as *insufficient and unsatisfactory as a form of acceptance and confirmation of Russia's Europeanisation.*

As in the cases of Poland and Bulgaria, Russia's thin Europeanisation was the product of the interaction of the international and domestic dimension of identification. During the first post-communist decade, the exclusion of Russia from EU and NATO integration processes (i.e., whereby Moscow was not granted membership prospects although alternative schemes for cooperation were devised) as well as the bombing of Yugoslavia empowered and helped tip the Russian domestic political balance in favour of the Pragmatic and Fundamentalist Nationalists. The latter's anti-Western visions and policy preferences together with the institutional factionalism further weakened Russia's course towards joining the Euro-Atlantic family of nations—a goal proclaimed by the Liberal Westernisers, but already hollowed out by the incompatibility of the liberal's conceptions with ideal-typical values and Yeltsin's authoritarian style of rule.

In the 2000s and 2010s, Russia's failure to become part of the Euro-Atlantic community was conditioned by the mutually reinforcing half-hearted Western acceptance and Moscow's growing authoritarianism, whose conservative views, great-power ideology and securitised outlook could not lead to a principles-based integration with the West. Thus, as EU and NATO expansions to CEE were being completed and the Union created new initiatives (such as the ENP and the EP) to cooperate with the post-Soviet states, Russia remained on the side-lines. The US was similarly reluctant to accommodate Moscow's interests. But Russia could not have been included in Western arrangements in a more decisive manner as the Russian identity discourse evolved from the recognition of both normative similarities with and differences from the West (expressed in the 'deliberate eclecticism' and 'sovereign democracy') towards a fully-fledged anti-Western vision (embodied in the 'conservative' rhetoric), whereby the Kremlin sets its own 'standards of European-ness' and pursues a foreign policy that competes with Euro-Atlantic nations.

Overall, Russia's thin Europeanisation has entailed a general conceptual and practice-based *divergence* from European-ness. Even short of the overt repudiation of ideal-typical European-ness (as in the post-2014 stipulation of Russia's own definition of 'genuine' Europe), the declaratory acceptance of the tenets of Europeanisation was never matched by the convictional internalisation of these tenets and their consistent behavioural application.

This divergence has ranged in extent. There was an initial *declaratory acceptance* of the tenets of Europeanisation, particularly by the Liberal Westernisers in the early 1990s and Putin in the early 2000s. This was followed by the *amalgamation* of discursively pro-European positions coupled with normative and behavioural contestation of ideal-typical principles, which was prominent in the Pragmatic Nationalism that gained ascendancy in the 1990s, Putin's discourses of deliberate eclecticism and sovereign democracy as well as Medvedev's rhetoric. The *repudiation* of European-ness was most starkly manifested in the post-2014 stipulation of Russia's own definition of 'genuine' European-ness. This fundamental Russian ambivalence, albeit taking different nuances over time, was maintained by a similarly non-committal Western attitude, manifested in limited diplomatic, institutional and economic support.

The official Russian identity discourse of the 1990s retained its overall Liberal Westernising character, according to which Russia was to become a new democratic state, built on the principles of human rights, economic freedom, political democratisation and aspiring for close cooperation and integration with the EU and NATO. Indivisible European security and the eradication of dividing lines on the continent were called for, given that the Western nations now represented friends and allies rather than enemies. But since 1993, the Liberal Westerniser discourse gradually evolved towards the incorporation of elements of Pragmatic Nationalism with the latter's emphasis on statism, collectivism, great-powerness, sovereignty and independence in international affairs. In this way, the association of Liberal Westernism with Pragmatic Nationalism and the liberals' own conceptual distinctiveness from the ideal type meant that although the principles of liberal democracy and European integration were accepted in official rhetoric, substantive understanding and practice differed from the ideal-typical model. As opposed to the West European interpretation of European integration as being animated by the values of human rights, soft power, democracy promotion, economic interdependence, a degree of pooling of sovereignty, rejection of the use of force and spheres of influence in favour of multilateralism, regional cooperation and a rules-based liberal international order, for Russia European integration — as embodied in Yeltsin's concept of 'Greater Europe', had a different connotation. It represented an opportunity for Moscow's inclusion in European affairs as an influential and equal player, for the creation of a Concert of great European powers to counterbalance US primacy and a NATO-centred European security, for the establishment of the EU as a pole in a multipolar world. All of this was to be informed by a focus on hard security issues, the maintenance of sovereignty, non-interference in domestic affairs and the retention of a sphere of privileged interests in the post-Soviet space. So Russia may have aspired to become a member of the EU and NATO but would not subscribe to the animating principles of those organisations.

In policy terms, there was a congruence between Russian views and actions. The Liberal Westernisers' belief that Russia's interests were identical with those of the West (given Moscow's aspiration to integrate in Europe as a democratic power) was transformed after 1993 in line with the association between Liberal Westernism and Pragmatic Nationalism. The grater rhetorical focus on Russian great-powerness, sovereignty and independence was expressed in the reassertion of Moscow's 'special' Eurasian interests in the post-Soviet space — even through forceful military intervention, and in the attempt to create a multipolar world order opposing US leadership through cooperation with China.

After Vladimir Putin assumed the reins of power, Russia's conceptual and practice-divergence from the ideal-typical model was continued and deepened. By the late 2000s and especially after 2011/2012, the Russian identity discourse had evolved from the Pragmatic Nationalist declaratory acceptance of Europeanisation in the context of 'deliberate eclecticism', to the growing contestation of European norms in the 'sovereign democracy' rhetoric and the fully-fledged normative challenge to ideal-typical tenets and the proposal of alternative European values in the 'conservative' discourse blending Pragmatic and Fundamentalist Nationalist positions. Deliberate eclecticism and sovereign democracy still paid tribute to the values of liberal democracy, economic freedom and cooperation with the West on the basis of Russia's civilizational belongingness to Europe. But at the same time these discourses stressed the importance of sovereignty, great powerness, the primacy of hard power and hard security considerations over soft security and liberal interdependence, regional assertiveness over cooperative good-neighbourliness and the construction of a multipolar world order. The rhetorical reference to ideal-typical European values was completely marginalised in favour of the enunciation of Russia's own standards of European-ness in the conservative vision of Russian identity. This vision prioritises domestically traditional family values, religion, patriotism, a strong state, the reaffirmation of the ethnic dominance of the Russians within the Russian polity and stands for the conduct of international relations in terms of balances of power, spheres of influence, non-interference in the internal affairs of other states and cooperation with the East to oppose the West. Hence, ideal-typical adherence to liberal democracy, multiculturalism, cooperative regional relations and a liberal international order were renounced by the Russians.

Moscow's growing normative incompatibility with Europeanness was congruent with the enactment of concrete foreign policies. The initial goal to maintain close ties with the EU (as in the conclusion of a number of agreements such as the Road Map for the Common Spaces and the Partnership for Modernisation) and to establish a strategic partnership with the US (as in the Kremlin's eager post-9/11 support for America's war on terror) morphed into a full-fledged assertiveness against the West. The creation of the Eurasian Economic Union and forging cooperation with China have been two of the flagship initiatives through which Russia has tried to take on Europe and America.

All in all, the respective form that the process of Europeanisation assumed in Poland, Bulgaria and Russia in the 1989-2015 period denotes the three distinctive, 'thick', 'ambivalent' and 'thin' levels of values-based distance that these countries have maintained with the western half of Europe as well as among themselves. Warsaw's, Sofia's and Moscow's belongingness to the Central, Southeast European and post-Soviet sub-region of CEE also warrants a cautious generalization of these three normative differentiations to the sub-regional level. That is, although the conclusions about a thick, ambivalent and thin Europeanisation apply first and foremost to the country cases examined in the book, the methodological objective to ensure sub-regional representativeness through the selection of Poland, Bulgaria and Russia additionally allows claiming the wider validity of the findings.

In this manner, Central Europe as a whole can be argued to consist of states that proceeded in a quick and determined fashion on the path of re-joining Europe. Southeast European countries have been characterized by the fitfulness and hesitancy of their Europeanisation process. The post-Soviet space has been left on the outskirts of the Euro-Atlantic community. Hence, if one for instance selects the Czech Republic from the sub-region of Central Europe and Romania from the sub-region of South-east Europe, the difference in Europeanisation between them would exhibit similarities to that between Poland and Bulgaria. So despite there being unique processes that characterise Czech and Romanian Europeanisation, there are expected to be regularities due to persistent cultural-historical conditions peculiar to Central and Southeast Europe.

The Western Balkan countries that formerly constituted Yugoslavia have significantly lagged behind in their EU and NATO accession process, thus veering away from the European integration path of Bulgaria and Romania. The experience of being part of a Serb-dominated political unit and its subsequent violent disintegration have left the newly emerging countries preoccupied with state-building, making them focus inwardly on the construction and consolidation of national identities rather than outwardly in terms of joining the Euro-Atlantic family of nations. Yet, despite dramatic experiences of war and uncertainties in drawing the boundaries of national communities, the Western Balkans have similarly exhibited the persistent cultural-historical patterns typical of Southeast Europe. These have included harbouring ambiguous affinities torn between allegiance to Russia and the West and in turn being ambivalently received by Western Europe and the US.

Overall, the identification of cross-country and cross-regional patterns and regularities in the process of Europeanisation might come up against the question of particularity: What if the degrees of distance among Poland, Bulgaria and Russia are themselves diluted by Warsaw's domestic authoritarian tendencies and anti-European rhetoric? And what if sub-regional generalizations cannot be stretched to cover diverse countries, especially in the post-Soviet space?

Poland: Europeanisation gone off track?

Concerns that national distinctiveness may overwhelm cross-country trends can be especially mounted in relation to Poland in the context of the much discussed turn of the country towards the concentration of power and assertive nationalism against the EU (most conspicuously over the rule of law). Yet, I argue that an overly alarmist assessment of Polish developments overlooks the fact that Warsaw has nevertheless retained the qualities of a thick Europeaniser. This is so because PiS attitudes and policies represent a reaction to—rather than a repudiation of, thick Europeanisation, circumscribed by the common ideational bonds unifying Polish national identity strands as well as the socialising effects of the internal opposition and Western normative pressure. The comparison with ongoing developments in Bulgaria and Russia further underscores Warsaw's continuing edge over Sofia and Moscow in the European integration process.

As more specifically discussed in Chapter 5, the conservative critique of European-ness does not by itself lead to a radical break and a 'leap backwards', as it coexists with the liberal modernist strand within an overall national-intellectual frame, which shapes a historically-conditioned conviction of Poland's cultural belongingness to the West. This conviction is concretely expressed in principled positions that PiS and the PO share linked to the aspiration to establish Poland as an equal and respected partner within Euro-Atlantic institutions, to support the democratisation and independence of the eastern neighbours and prevent the resurgence of a neo-imperial Russia. The overarching belief in Warsaw's close affinity with the West also limits PiS' contestation of ideal-typical European-ness. This contestation amounts to a critical-conservative discourse and policy that privilege traditional morality and state sovereignty as well as wariness of Germany's dominant role in Europe rather than a wholesale renunciation of the liberal international order based on cooperation and equality.

The stances adopted by the Law and Justice party do not therefore represent a fundamental repudiation of European values and can instead be viewed through the prism of a reactionary backlash. It stems from what PiS and its supporters perceive to be the elitist and humiliating features of the significant depth of thick Europeanisation, and represents the opposite to the modernist side of the same 'identity coin', rooted in the dualistic, attractive-repulsive, aspirational-threatening conceptualisation of Europe in the Polish national consciousness.

The deep Western political-ideational and economic penetration in Poland as well as the quick pace of Polish European integration have been particularly criticised by PiS as leading to national humiliation, facilitated by the modernists' fervent desire for the receipt of the West's approval and support. The conservative call for asserting sovereignty (as against the liberals' and leftists' ascribed readiness to be '*na kolanach*', i.e., on their knees) conveys the idea that only those who do not overenthusiastically await another's confirmation deserve serious treatment and can defend their positive distinctiveness (Bucholc, 2016:6). Similarly, the PiS ambition to renationalise economic assets has constituted a reaction against the post-1989 economic model, whereby the accelerated integration in the West European markets and especially in the German value chain have contributed to low wages, large shares of foreign capital, dependence on EU subsidies and German economic developments (Buras, 2017:6).

For example, the Law and Justice party's controversial actions on rule of law issues can be interpreted along this line of reasoning that is concerned with asserting positive national distinctiveness, pride and autonomy. Legal changes to the Constitutional Tribunal have been justified by an understanding of the law as an epiphenomenon of the sovereign's will and as subject to the nation's approval (Bucholc, 2016:8-9). Hence, the goal to alleviate the inefficiency and corruption of the judicial system perpetuated by an 'elite and self-serving clique'. Such a position is at once democratic in trying to make the judicial system timely and justly available to everyone, but is admittedly also authoritarian in that 'what the people want' is to be interpreted by the political authorities (Radio Poland, July 2017).

PiS' reactionary stances have in turn been mirrored by Poland's European Other. Apart from addressing rule of law concerns as a matter of principle, the severity of the EU's reaction — threatening to implement Article 7 of the Treaty on European Union that strips a member state of its voting rights, can be attributed to the higher Western expectations of and affinity to Poland that shaped and were themselves informed by the thick Europeanisation of the country (Radio Poland, 5 January 2016, 10 January, 2016, 27 February 2016; Nougayrède, 2017). The eager acceptance of Warsaw as a frontrunner in Europeanisation in the 1990s has entailed higher external demands on the application of ideal-typical values, and consequently a more determined backlash against transgressions. Accordingly, Poland's ambition to be an influential EU member state can continue to be recognised if standards of European exemplariness are maintained.

Moreover, the reassertion of the liberal-modernist political and societal strand of identity and the West's normative effort to bring Poland into line with the frame of an exemplar of Europeanisation have exerted a socialising influence on the Law and Justice party in the direction of softening confrontational conservative stances. Two examples stand out. As Kaminska's study demonstrates with regard to PiS' first tenure in power (2005-2007), the party's application of a veto on the PCA negotiations between the EU and Russia in a unilateral manner — i.e., without a prior warning of European diplomats in the Commission and Council and in disregard for the cooperative and consensual decision-making culture in European fora, had to be eventually reformulated in alignment with European principles on the basis of persuasive

Union normative pressure and domestic criticism (Kaminska, 2014:10, 28, 118-119). The brokerage role that the European Commission played during the Polish-Russian dispute was positively perceived by Law and Justice. Commission President Jose Barroso questioned Russia's motives for continuing the ban on Polish meat, which was viewed by PiS as evidence that Poland was accepted as an equal partner and showed the value of acting in solidarity. So by the end of its tenure in power Law and Justice moved in the direction of adaptation to the European culture of consensus. PiS declared that Polish membership in the EU was beneficial in security and economic terms and that Warsaw could benefit from the communitarisation of the CFSP (Kaminska, 2014:123, 135).

The cabinet reshuffle during PiS' second tenure in power since 2015 represented another example of conservative socialisation (even if just for performative image-making rather than substance). As Roman Kuźniar predicted at the time of my interview with him (in the summer of 2015 and just prior to PiS' election victory), the assumption of confrontation stances on the part of a potential Law and Justice government would have to undergo socialisation towards consensus-seeking and compliance with EU expectations on the basis of critical societal domestic feedback. PiS would particularly need to rebalance its overestimation of Polish society's desire for an assertive policy against European principles and further integration as a counterbalance to the PO's enthusiastic pro-Europeanism (Kuźniar, 2015, interview). Indeed, the new Prime Minister Mateusz Morawiecki stated his position against doctrinal and dogmatic governance, insisting that Poland is part of the West (Davies, Rankin, 2018; Broniatowski, 2017). And in a concrete move towards moderate conservatism, he dismissed Antoni Macierewicz as Minister of Defence (who has close ties to the radical nationalist right) and Witold Waszczykowski as Minister of Foreign Affairs (believed to have complicated Warsaw's relations with the EU) (Dudek, 2018). PiS thus tried to placate the alienated liberal cultural and legal elite and send a positive signal to Brussels about the Polish readiness to cooperate on the rule of law dispute (Szczerbiak, 2018; Radio Poland, 2018).

Finally, the argument that Poland has preserved the qualities of thick Europeanisation becomes especially pronounced in a comparative perspective since the resurgence of the conservative Polish critique of European-ness did not make Warsaw less Europeanised than Sofia or Moscow. Instead, Bulgaria has gradually deepened its ideational ambivalence by sustaining a rhetorical and situational behavioural normative compliance with the ideal type, while substantive value incongruence with European-ness has culminated in illiberal political practices. The latter particularly features the continuous and insidious placement of the judiciary at the service of the government, yet without conspicuous formal-institutional changes, thus trailing at 54.81 percentile Poland's 66.35 percentile rank but ahead of Russia's 25.00 percentile position in rule of law observance (Doichev, 2014; Dainov, 2013; Bregov, 2017; Mediapool, 2017; World Bank, 2020). Correspondingly, the ambivalent Western attitude to Bulgaria has continued to find expression in the relative inattention to the country, occasionally mixed with critique of Bulgarian corruption and poverty typical of delayed Balkan development. Such critique emerges in a circumstantial manner whenever Bulgaria is thrown into the limelight as in its Presidency of the Council of the European Union in 2018 or in the context of the large-scale protest activity in 2020 calling out domestic governance problems (Rankin, 2017; OFFNews, 2018; Barker, 2018).

And in Russia's case, thin Europeanisation has been exacerbated since Putin's third term in office (and catalysed by the Ukrainian crisis) towards the renunciation of Europeanisation, the proposal of alternative, 'genuine' European values, the creation of a fully-fledged authoritarian regime and competition with the West. This has in turn been reciprocated by European and American determination to present a front against Moscow's civilizational and geopolitical challenge, for instance, through sanctions, moral opprobrium and military deterrence (Sokolsky, 2017; Surkov, 2018; Radio Free Europe, 2018).

On the whole, the resurgence of conservatism in Poland, which has received sizeable media attention, as well as the deepening of Bulgaria's ambivalent place in Europe and Russia's fully-fledged normative challenge to European-ness all serve to reconfirm the conceptual point of the book that Europeanisation is a dynamic and interactive process, which does not, however, lead to a progressive, linearly evolutionary outcome towards ever-greater integration and ever-growing normative compatibility on the part of CEE states. Rather, the recreation of historically-informed conceptions of Europe favourably disposed to Euro-Atlantic cooperation throughout the 1990s and into the 2000s in all three countries gave way to the cyclical re-enactment and the achievement of political dominance of (hitherto suppressed as secondary) ideational traditions that criticise and contest European-ness and the integrative aspiration. Nevertheless, even as there is a degree of contestation and disapproval of facets of Europeanisation in Poland, Bulgaria and Russia alike, the three levels of Europeanisation among the countries are preserved. This is so because Europe-critical ideational traditions are part and parcel of—instead of an aberration or a break from—the overarching ideational bonds that unite various strands of conceptualising European-ness in a given country and condition historically continuous degrees of principled compatibility with Western Europe.

A sub-regional escape?

The generalizability of the findings on the three levels of Europeanisation may additionally come up against the 'outlying' qualities of certain post-Soviet states—such as Ukraine and Georgia. At first glance, some would argue, these two states do not fit into a category together with Russia and would most appropriately be distinguished into a league of their own for a number of reasons.

First, the argument goes, Ukraine and Georgia straddle the conflicting and overlapping sub-regional historical, geographical and cultural traditions of Central and Eastern Europe—the Central European and the former Soviet sub-regional heritage in Ukraine's case as well as the former Soviet, South Caucasian, Black Sea, Middle Eastern sub-regional belongingness in Georgia's case. The availability of such diverse traditions contrasts with the more clearly representative countries of the Central, Southeast European and former Soviet areas that Poland, Bulgaria and Russia generally tend to be.

Second, Ukraine and Georgia have demonstrated a strongly determined (although not necessarily consistent) aspiration towards joining the Euro-Atlantic civilizational space, which flourished particularly in the new millennium even in the face of Russian objection leading to a loss of territory and direct military intervention such as the Russia-Georgia War of 2008 and the Ukrainian crisis that began in late 2013 (MacFarlane, 2012:20; Maksak, Mashtaler, 2017:48). This suggests a potential disjuncture between the direction of the domestic and international dimension of identification. Accordingly, the internal push for Europeanisation—reminiscent of a 'thickly' (or at least 'ambivalently') Europeanised desire for a return to Europe, meets with a European and American reluctance to accept fully Ukraine and Georgia in the Euro-Atlantic cultural and organisational mould— as a 'thin' external commitment to the post-Soviet region would presuppose, albeit more engaging politically and institutionally. Conversely, in the cases of Poland, Bulgaria and Russia, the degree of European affinity is matched by a similar national-level enthusiasm for 'returning to Europe'.

Finally, the international context of Ukraine's and Georgia's Europeanisation has been further characterised by Russian great-power assertiveness in the post-Soviet space, where Moscow's regional resurgence has been informed by preferences for 19th-century practices of spheres of influence, use of force and the establishment of organisational alternatives to the EU, especially the Eurasian Economic Union. This may warrant the designation of a distinctive international phenomenon of contested 'Otherness' based on a clash of hegemonic visions and projects of integration between Russia and the West. The phenomenon can be characterised by the involvement of the Russian Other that actively interferes in, contests and blocks the process of identification that concerns the Western European Other who emanates the ideal-typical value standards underlying the (Euro-Atlantic) community to which the Self (Ukraine/Georgia) wants to be included. Yet, for Poland and

Bulgaria, Russia represented an additional—but not crucial and overbearingly defiant, Other.

Overall, the most significant consequence of the availability of multiple identifications and the 'atypical' of the post-Soviet region strong impetus for Europeanisation may be the possibility of greater leeway and social creativity in fashioning a foreign policy identity—such as a Central European one for Ukraine and a Black Sea/Southeast European one for Georgia, both of which apparently draw Kyiv and Tbilisi closer to Europe than the former Soviet markers of identity. This leeway moreover introduces a tension between the reciprocal-mirroring correspondence between Self and Other characteristic of consensually agreed identifications (as in the cases of Poland, Bulgaria and Russia), given the general European hesitation towards Ukrainian and Georgian aspirations for Europeanness. A key question therefore follows: can the potential for a more fundamental change in identity (in contrast to a sub-regionally conditioned continuity) be fulfilled on the basis of a struggle over the renegotiation of identity between Self and Other? Or will this potential be further constrained by the countervailing influence of the rest of the domestically supported sub-regional identifications, European perceptions of difference and Russian imperial-historical claims on Ukraine and Georgia?

Although the answer to this question requires follow-up research that extends the book's findings to the post-Soviet area, a preliminary assessment of the empirical record points that the sustainability and qualitative substantiation of the struggle over renegotiation may indeed be hampered by the constraining counter-influence of domestic and international elements of identification, containing Tbilisi and Kyiv in the realm of thin Europeanisation. For instance, the powerful impact of the Christian Orthodox Church that espouses anti-Western, conservative value positions (e.g., on multiculturalism, sexuality) in Georgia as well as the Eurasian, pro-Russian and post-Soviet strand of identity and the limited ability to carry out domestic reforms on the basis of European standards of democracy and the rule of law in Ukraine hinder substantively the declared aspiration for integration in the Euro-

Atlantic community (Chkhikvadze, 2015:36-37; Jones, 2003; Kakachia, 2014; Wolczuk, 2003, 2004; Lutsevych, 2013; Velychenko, 2007; Lieven, 1999; D'Anieri, 2002; Kuzio, 2002; Prizel, 1998; Proedrou, 2010). Also, the Russian determination to assert its designated sphere of influence in Georgia and Ukraine and the West's weak affinity to these states and corresponding reluctance to provide significant institutional and economic support (despite declared commitments) negatively affect international receptivity to renegotiated change towards thicker Europeanisation (MacFarlane, 2008, 2012:20-23; MacFarlane, Menon, 2014; Allison, 2009; Delcour, Wolczuk, 2015; Dimitrova, Dragneva, 2009; Kasčiūnas et al, 2014; Freire, Kanet, 2012).

Hence, the Georgian and Ukrainian attempts at social creativity come up against the resistance of internal and external ideational continuities limiting the potential for a 'sub-regional' escape. Social Psychologists have similarly expressed caution about the ability of conflict-inducing aspirational identities to finally lead to a dialogical understanding of inter-group relations. This is so because social creativity should be placed in the context of the Other's established beliefs about the Self and the wider cultural values, which limit the content used in the reappraisal of the social identity in question (Weinstein et al, 2017:4; Dashtipour, 2009:2; Swann, Bosson, 2008:461).

Identity continuity and change: On the path of least resistance

The interactive construction of Polish, Bulgarian and Russian identity, in which conceptions of Europe have been shown to be re-enacted in contemporary circumstances, challenges the assumption that identities are necessarily and constantly fluid, malleable and in flux. Instead, the significant degree of continuity of culturally-historically shaped patterns of ideas, beliefs and representations (both on the part of the Self and the Other) points to the prevalence of identity persistence informed by the reproduction of long-term, deeply ingrained views. When internal or external sources of conflict destabilise identities, ideational transformation will therefore follow the path of least resistance. Change is most likely to take place on the level of tactical beliefs and the styles, nuances and accents of belief expression rather than on the level of fundamental beliefs.

Accordingly, ideational redefinition in Poland, Bulgaria and Russia took place through Self-Other socialisation that affected the modalities of understanding and expression of certain non-core identity strands and the varying priorities placed on particular ideas. Moreover, the dynamics of interaction between Self and Other could tilt domestic political balances and frame debates, empowering a particular identity discourse espoused by an ascendant political grouping. Interactive practices also coloured circumstantial attitudinal dispositions (leading to, for example, growing trust or spiralling disappointment).

In *Poland*, historically ingrained conceptions of Europe persisted and were embodied in the alternate discursive dominance of the modernist and traditionalist identity tradition. Modernists have perpetuated a representation of Europe as a utopian ideal to be attained and as the civilization to which the Poles are bound by mental-spiritual affinity based on a shared religion, similar cultural-scientific development and attachment to common values. Conversely, the conservatives have perceived Europe as threatening to Polish traditions, morality and sovereignty, preferring instead a self-contained and defensive safeguarding of national heritage and independence. Self-Other interactive dynamics thus limited a substantive change in the content of the dominant conceptions of Europe so that the evolution in ideas was confined to less fundamental forms and styles.

The support received from powerful, significant Others (Western Europe and the US), the gradual inclusion in EU and NATO arrangements and achievement of 'insider status' to those organisations *dispelled historically-informed fears and mistrust*. A belief began to emerge that for the first time — at least since the partitions, Poland finds itself in a benevolent security environment based on inclusion and allied commitment rather than abandonment, betrayal and occupation. Polish-German bilateral relations underwent an evolution towards greater mutual understanding, trust, cooperation and even forgiveness so that to this day Poles consider Germany to be their state's closest ally in the EU (Radio Poland, 20 June 2016; Łada, 2018). However, it should be noted that the reconciliation process is not yet complete. Polish grievances, particularly pronounced among the traditionalists, have persisted especially as conflicting interests and historical problems remain unaddressed (such as references in German history textbooks and public discourse to Nazi death camps on the then territory of Poland as 'Polish' camps) (Radio Poland, 29 May 2017).

Inclusion in Western organisations also granted Poland greater ideational and institutional opportunities for the *actualisation and practical enactment of the Polish vision of Europe* in concrete domestic and foreign policies. This stood in contrast to a historical pattern of mental-cultural affinity with the West that was in disjuncture with the reality of subordination to outside powers and authoritarian national leaders since the partitions until the end of communism. So the successful liberal democratic, market economic reforms substantiated Poland's belief about its belongingness to West European civilization. The historically-informed, Piłsudskian ambition for Poland to be an influential player in international relations was further strengthened in that the growing recognition and inclusion of Warsaw in EU and NATO decision-making fora allowed a gradual overcoming of historical complexes of inferiority and isolation by the Western powers.

Poland's closer engagement and deeper enmeshment in the EU accession process also *infused attitudes to and views of 'Europe' with more reasoned understanding and less loftiness*. For instance, the fulfilment of the technical conditions for Union accession led to an evolution of the Polish domestic political debate from the symbolically-loaded, enthusiastic and abstract aspiration for a return to the liberal and prosperous Europe of the Polish imagination to a more specific appreciation of the costs and benefits involved in the Europeanisation process.

On the other hand, as opposed to interactive dynamics of inclusion, acceptance and positive identification, (perceived) setbacks in the EU and NATO accession process, relative Western ambivalence and disengagement coupled with domestic-level factionalism and growing conservatism *introduced elements of contestation and shifts in Europeanisation*. For instance, dissatisfaction with the pace of NATO accession, President Wałęsa's struggle for decision-making supremacy and fears of Poland's potential isolation into a grey zone of Central European insecurity *gave rise to short-lived, alternative ideas* for the creation of EU-bis and NATO-bis organisations to foster cooperation among CEE countries as against integration in Euro-Atlantic institutions. Moreover, declining West European enthusiasm for EU enlargement coupled with the growing political, economic and social hardships of domestic transformation along Union criteria *empowered* Eurosceptic politicians; *accentuated* the lines of differentiation among the modernists and the traditionalists; and led to the overall *politicisation* of European issues in domestic politics.

Polish disappointments with developments within the North-Atlantic framework of security and cooperation in the aftermath of the Iraq war and in the wake of America's growing disengagement from Polish and European security led to an *evolution with regard to the priority placed* on US-Polish defence ties. That is, reliance on these ties for ensuring Poland's security was downgraded so that a focus on national capabilities and the European pillar of security took a greater precedence. Still, Poland's Atlanticism has remained a key element of the country's security culture and identity. The evolution has remained on the level of shifting priorities rather than on a fundamental conceptual and ideational change, as seen in Warsaw's quick reorientation to bilateral cooperation with the US, once Washington decided to reengage with Europe following the Ukrainian crisis.

In *Bulgaria*, the dynamics of Self-Other interactions have similarly resulted in the reproduction of the long-term culturally-historically shaped ambivalent conceptions of Europe. The representation of Europe as a positive and significant Other, symbolising modernity, progress and an advanced social, political and economic model to be emulated (not least through normative imitation) persisted in the post-communist period. This representation was embodied in society's and all of the political parties' aspiration to rejoin European civilization. On the other hand, the image of Europe as a distant, exclusive, culturally superior and even 'alien' entity—as contrasted with the backward, peripheral, 'aggressive', authoritarian-prone Balkans, also continued to inform Bulgarian views.

Yet, the Self-Other interactive dynamic was nevertheless conducive to a socialised evolution of Bulgarian perceptions and practices in a number of forms and styles. Inclusive Western attitudes and actions matched by a growing domestic political consensus on Euro-Atlantic integration mobilised the efforts of the political elite, provided reassurance and confirmation of Bulgaria's European identity, which ultimately *encouraged norm compliance and foreign policy alignment with the West through the adoption of the Europeanisation discourse and its behavioural consequences*. Thus, a pro-Western normative and strategic course of action began to be pursued more decisively and consistently based as this was not so much on deeply seated ideational foundations but on the *'import' of values, principles and practices* through a process of 'harmonisation on paper' that imparted to these values, principles and practices an abstract and imitative quality.

Greater external commitment and a more determined internal impetus for Europeanisation shaped evolutionary developments on Bulgaria's domestic and foreign policy scene. Domestically, the UDF's nostalgic revanchism of the early 1990s *gave way to* the espousal of European norms in a more organised and comprehensive manner. This, however, took on an abstract, moralising and performative character since these norms were embraced as part of the post-1989 transformation, lacking in significant substantive pre-1989 ideational antecedents. As regards the BSP, the consensus on Euro-Atlantic integration *delegitimised* doctrinaire principles of the dictatorship of the proletariat and socialist internationalism, while exclusivist nationalist positions and a close strategic focus on Russia were *toned down* and *de-emphasised*.

In the realm of foreign policy, the process of EU accession *promoted the values of regional cooperation and good-neighbourliness*. As a result, there was a *transformation* of Bulgarian-Turkish relations from enmity to relative amity as well as to the *development of friendly relations and greater rapprochement* with Macedonia on the basis of Bulgaria's rhetorical self-enhancement and the gradual evolution of thinking in the direction of conciliation. The achievement of EU membership further *extended the scope and manoeuvrability* of Bulgarian foreign policy options and *facilitated socialisation* (particularly of the administrative elite) in terms of growing acceptance of EU norms, consideration of EU-level interests and acquisition of expertise. NATO accession *fostered the democratisation and reform of the military* and *allowed the development of a conception of security* compatible with European understandings. Finally, the OSCE and the Council of Europe *disseminated* norms of European-ness, which Bulgaria *incorporated* as part of its foreign policy discourse.

On the other hand, European and American (partially) exclusionary, critical or disengaged attitudes and actions coupled with Bulgaria's own lagging internal reforms and ideational ambiguity *enabled the enunciation of alternative foreign policy ideas* (such as neutrality and equidistance as opposed to Euro-Atlantic integration); *created domestic disappointments* at perceived marginalisation and mistreatment; and *generated a greater contestation of European-ness*.

In ***Russia***, Self-Other interactions similarly resulted in the reproduction, continuity and recurring cyclicality of historically ingrained Russian conceptions of Europe. The Liberal Westernising strand of identity gradually incorporating Pragmatic Nationalist positions and the later ascendancy of Fundamentalist Nationalism represented the post-1991 re-enactment of the Westerniser-Slavophile debate about Russia's identity and dual conceptualisation of Europe—i.e., as a utopia to be emulated and as a threat to national culture, giving rise to an inferiority complex, to be compensated through a reversion to conservative Russian traditions.

Against the background of the significant continuity in the content of Russian ideas, ideational evolution took place in more limited ways confined to styles, perceptions and relationship between historically-shaped visions. The interaction of domestic ambivalence about Europeanisation and external exclusionary practices resulted in the *diminishing credibility* and *gradual marginalisation of the liberal vision*; *the resurgence of anti-Western political forces*; as well as the *growing pre-eminence* and *consolidation of Pragmatic Nationalist and Fundamentalist Nationalist views*. During Yeltsin's Presidency, the Liberal-Westerniser discourse was increasingly blended with and gave way to Pragmatic Nationalism. Under Putin, there was a growing nationalist-conservative shift in the conceptualisation of Russian identity so that the 'deliberate eclecticism' and Medvedev's criticisms of Russian democratic shortcomings evolved in the direction of a full-blown swing towards a nationalist, great-power ideology, informed by traditional values.

Russia-EU interactions *transformed* the Russian policy-makers' *initially positive attitude to the Union* and *enthusiasm about prospects for cooperation* into a *psychological anxiety* about Moscow's separation from Europe. Brussels' arrangements for enlargement towards CEE states, excluding Moscow, *enhanced Russia's sense of isolation* from European normative and strategic developments. Russian *doubts increased* about the country's rightful belongingness to the European family of nations; *nationalist sentiments were reinforced*; and *opposition to and contestation of European values were provoked*, matched by a repositioning of Russia towards Eurasia.

Furthermore, Russia-US/NATO interactions in the context of the Kosovo crisis, 9/11, the Iraq war, Alliance expansion *led to a fall in the favourable assessments of America*, seen especially in the early 1990s by Yeltsin as the key state that could legitimate post-Soviet Russia's place in the international system. These developments additionally *spurred a (short-lived) change of foreign policy focus from the US to the EU; fuelled concerns about Moscow's marginalisation from European security developments;* and *sharpened the divide between Russia and the West in terms of conceptions of security* (i.e. between Russian views that privilege a policy of balance of power, spheres of influence, emphasis on hard security, rejection of a NATO-centred European security and Western support for a liberal, rules-based European order, based on multilateralism and collective security ensured by NATO).

On the other hand, cooperative and inclusive interactions between Russia and the West, particularly prominent in the early

1990s and early 2000s, *promoted efforts at building a strategic partnership based on common civilizational roots and economic interdependence.* Some *growing trust was strengthened,* as was *institutional enmeshment* and the *creation of networks and channels of communication.*

On the whole, the post-communist development of Polish, Bulgarian and Russian foreign policy affirms the persistence and cyclical recurrence of foundational ideas about nation-state identity. Contemporary socialisation and change, on the other hand, remain confined to tactical, lower-order beliefs, which do not engender a deep-seated process of learning of new fundamental positions and a qualitative evolution towards ideal-typical values.

However, the conclusion about the continuity of fundamental beliefs should not be taken to entail an overly deterministic – and indeed pessimistic, view about possibilities for ideational change. Rather, it urges caution, as the potential for change is always present but less frequently realised. In each of the three countries under examination, the theoretical and empirical preconditions for a transformation in identities existed in the post-1989 'revolutionary' flux and opening of horizons. Such preconditions particularly related to the potentiality to turn a liminal crisis into an opportunity for renewal and actualise the motivation to achieve positive distinctiveness vis-à-vis a powerful and significant Other. Yet, a crisis in itself does not automatically provide solutions that lead to deep-seated change.[14] Indeed, fundamental aspects of identity refer to the core conceptualisations of the self, establishing meaning, integrity and security, and hence rethinking these aspects is an uphill struggle that meets with the overwhelming urge for identity verification.

---

14 As shown in the analysis of the impact of the coronavirus pandemic on media freedom in Southeast Europe, the unprecedented crisis ushered in by COVID-19 introduced a variety of socio-political, international and technological factors enabling or constraining the exercise of free journalism. Yet, these factors served to reinforce pre-existing trends that have over the years led to the deterioration of freedom of expression in the region: Filipova, R., 2020, *The Shrinking Space for Media Freedom in Southeast Europe in the Midst of COVID-19 Pandemic and State of Emergency*, Sofia: Center for the Study of Democracy/ Konrad-Adenauer-Stiftung Media Programme South East Europe, https://www.kas.de/documents/281902/281951/KAS+CSD+Book+on+Media+Freedom+in+the+Midst+of+Covid-19+Pandemic.pdf/8ab73bd6-a65f-4ccf-5cce-826e61c7b092?version=1.1&t=1600864436285

So the resolution of the problem of change may evoke high standards of political morality. Following Arpad Szakolczai's interpretation of Czech philosopher and dissident Jan Patocka, it can be surmised that the transformation of a collective experience of liminal suffering into a genuine community able to renew itself requires the leadership of a 'genuine' elite.[15] Patocka explained that the 'care of the soul' conducted among a small circle of politically, intellectually and morally enlightened individuals is the effective answer to a situation of crisis. This Platonic focus on the soul thus starts with the unique potentiality of human beings to break away from their habitual, customary, taken for granted ways when they realise that these ways led them astray into vagrancy, error or stagnation (Szakolczai, 2008:56).

Therefore, a crisis can provoke a reckoning and intensive learning if — instead of being accompanied by the glorification of liminal experiences of suffering, the expectation of a just reward and effort-saving attachment to pre-existing ideational guideposts — it becomes the starting point to at once a personal and collective conversion process. This process should rest on honest self-reflexivity that leads to the well-educated evaluation of the past and reading of history, the astute assessment of the present as well as positing clear goals for the future based on the overcoming of trauma and pursuit of sustained international renegotiation (Szakolczai, 2008:56).

The power of ideas in international relations: A Constructivist challenge to Realism

The demonstration that the differential European trajectories of Poland, Bulgaria and Russia since 1989 were shaped by identity brings to bear on the significance of ideas in framing the very character and civilizational situated-ness of state actors in the international arena. The large-scale transformational processes that

---

15 A similar argument was also made by Hungarian intellectual Istvan Bibo: Bibo, I., 2004, 'The Elite and Social Sensitivity', *Review of Sociology*, Vol.10, No 2, pp. 103-114, http://akademiai.com/doi/abs/10.1556/RevSoc.10.2004.2.8

engulfed Europe following the end of communism and bipolarity entailed a reciprocal-interactive definitional reckoning as to who, how much and for what reasons belonged to a newly emerging family of European nations. In contrast, the formulation of grand strategies and a return to the good old European ways of balances of power and forming alliances were not suited to illuminating fundamental questions about bordering belongingness.

Hence, Realist positions related to the privileging of material over subjective factors, the dismissal of the independent impact of ideas and stipulation of the primacy of structural factors in shaping political outcomes lack sufficient explanatory persuasiveness to account for Poland's, Bulgaria's and Russia's foreign policy record between 1989 and 2015. Instead, that record has been consistent with Constructivism as Polish, Bulgarian and Russian discourses and overall policy direction were congruent with a broadly shared nation-state identity as well as state interests. In specific circumstances, the actualisation of ideas took place within a context of a plethora of instrumental cost-benefit, administrative-organisational, cognitive and emotional factors. The latter posed tactical and practical limitations, affected the consistency and introduced biases in identity visions, but did not ultimately undermine the congruence between state identity, interests and actions in overall policy direction.

In the case of *Poland*, ideas about Poland's rightful place in the European regional order were not *ad hoc* constructs worked out in response to the strategic challenges of the post-1989 international environment and the absence of viable alternatives to Euro-Atlantic integration. Rather, these were culturally-historically informed, consistently espoused ideas and identities, whose expression and realisation—suppressed by centuries of foreign domination, dependence and partitions, could finally take place and be enabled by a favourable strategic situation of a retreating Russia and friendly Germany. In this way, in the 1990s, there was a mutually informative conjunction between what was most desirable (the realisation of Poland's identity as part of Western European civilization), possible (joining Western institutions as the only viable foreign policy option) and beneficial (becoming a member of the EU and NATO as conferring strategic and economic gains).

In the new millennium, Poland's ambition to be an important player in the EU was not simply determined and realised on the basis of the country's relative size and power for at least three reasons. First, this ambition was underwritten by a culturally-historically shaped conviction that being active and influential was a reflection of the successful assertion of national objectives, which would in turn be a symbol and proof of the alleviation of Poland's historical inferiority complexes in relation to its significant and powerful Western Other. Second, it was subjective factors related to socialisation in European negotiation and decision-making styles and administrative adaptation that affected Warsaw's ability to upload its policy initiatives on the EU level. In this manner, the vision of Poland as a European normative power, building coalitions and acting efficiently in the European arena, gained recognition within the Union and enabled Polish policies, most conspicuously embodied in the adoption of the Eastern Partnership. Yet, a confrontational demeanour has undermined the country's standing and reputation (in particular as a rule-of-law observant state) and hence hindered the process of uploading policies onto the Brussels level. Third, the case of Poland — a country which is large in terms of population and territory but still lagging behind on economic indicators, illustrates the pitfalls of clear-cut categorisations of size and power and accompanying predictions about the effects of such objective measures on foreign policy behaviour.

Aside from the overall direction of Poland's foreign policy consistent with Constructivist expectations, the specific actualisation of Polish ideational perspectives was worked out in the frame of a variety of countervailing factors. The anticipation of political and economic benefits from taking a particular international stance and lack of sufficient capacities in a bilateral relationship may *dictate tactical caution, temper* ideologies and *pose practical limits to the implementation* of visions and ideas. For instance, in the very early period after 1989, Poland exercised caution and refrained from openly declaring its goal to join the EU, and especially NATO, because of the uncertain international environment. The presence of Soviet troops on Polish territory and the absence of a German confirmation of the border with Poland called for prudence lest Warsaw provoked a Soviet intervention and worsening relations at a time when Poland might need Moscow's protection against irredentist German claims on Polish lands.

Moreover, domestic political-institutional factors—such as factionalism, conflicts over authority, struggles for power, partisanship, political instability, administrative organisation, can affect the *timing, consistency, coordination, determination, sincerity* and *effectiveness* on the basis of which a particular foreign policy identity is pursued. For instance, in the midst of President Wałęsa's struggle for power and the ambiguous constitutional delineation of foreign policy decision-making authority, Wałęsa's hesitant stance on the deepening of Poland's ties with NATO put him at odds with the government, his own advisors and the Sejm. This discrepancy influenced the timing and determination with which Foreign Minister Skubiszewski could pursue his external course focused on Euro-Atlantic integration and impacted the degree of institutional coordination in the realm of foreign policy.

On the other hand, credible, legally-binding and enforceable formal strategic ties, guarantees of security as well as political and economic institutional inclusion can be necessary for making a vision of identity *viable, sustainable* and *irreversible*. Indeed, Poland's enthusiasm about the OSCE and the Council of Europe diminished because other than providing and disseminating strong norms of liberalisation, democracy and human rights through institutional authority and reputation, these organisations could not extend formal security guarantees, legally-binding rules and a firm set of membership criteria ensuring norm compliance both domestically within the state and in member states' interactions.

Finally, cognitive and emotional factors can mould identities and interests by leading to *misperceptions* that can result in *disproportionately strong or weak reactions* on the basis of over- or under-estimating the significance of particular events and developments. For instance, Warsaw's excessively optimistic expectations about the rewards that America would confer on Poland out of gratitude for the Polish participation in the Iraq war were conditioned by the strongly pro-Atlanticist orientation of the country's strategic culture. At the same time, the disappointments following from the US's lack of reciprocation and growing disengagement from Polish and European security were exacerbated by the Poles' negativity bias informed by historical experiences of defeat, abandonment and foreign domination. They seemingly pointed to the conclusion that American disengagement would, as if immediately, encourage the restoration of Russian influence over Central Europe.

In the case of **Bulgaria**, Constructivism similarly illuminates the development of Bulgarian external relations in a more persuasive manner than Realism. Although the pro-Western option was indeed the only viable foreign policy course of action for Sofia, following it was not simply informed by strategic and economic necessity. Rather, it rested on an ideational foundation, embodied by the place that Western Europe takes in national identity as a significant and positive Other. So the swinging of the East-West strategic pendulum in a Western direction had an identity basis in Bulgaria. But given that the country's ambiguous and two-pronged affinities make it broadly ideationally compatible with both a pro-Western and pro-Eastern strategic focus, the Euro-Atlantic choice was arrived at in a less quick and decisive manner. And once this choice began to be pursued, it led to a situationally behavioural Europeanisation rather than to a deeply internalised normative transformation because the identity ambivalence made a thorough belief change difficult to achieve (and not necessarily desired), instead enabling instrumental adaptation.

Likewise, Bulgaria's general foreign policy passivity is not insurmountably determined by external constraints because of the theoretical and empirical possibilities that are available to small states for a more active international stance. Bulgarian passivity is thus ideationally conditioned as historical experiences of victimisation, betrayal and defeat have moulded a submissive and unconfident international behaviour, which conditions the lack of urgency to overcome limitations of institutional capacity, personnel, military and economic capabilities.

As in Poland, in specific circumstances, Bulgarian identity perspectives came up against a variety of countervailing factors. For instance, domestic political and economic considerations hollowed out the substance of ideas in decision-making by *turning norms and values into a convenient veneer* to the pursuit of pragmatic goals. This trend has been particularly evident in GERB's Euro-compliant external behaviour masking unprincipled positions favouring the accumulation of power.

Moreover, *institutional and party-political issues* — related to factionalism, struggles for power, government instability, poor administrative coordination, *exacerbated the confusion and inconsistency* of Bulgaria's foreign policy stances especially with respect to Sofia's already ambiguous ideational commitment to Euro-Atlantic integration in the context of dualistic East-West affinities.

Yet, strategic incentives and domestic interests have also served as *conditions for the sustainability of norms and visions* and as *catalysts for ideational change*. For example, positive incentives linked to expected benefits (primarily of gaining an EU membership perspective) improved the credibility and sustainability of a Bulgarian foreign policy position favouring good-neighbourly relations with Macedonia. Also, the Kosovo crisis was an important trigger that made the West rethink its strategy towards Bulgaria in favour of the country's more decisive inclusion in the EU and NATO.

Finally, cognitive and emotional factors *refracted identities, affecting perceptions, the assessment of events and developments* and *the intensity of reactions*. A stark illustration in this regard is provided by the 1997 economic crisis in Bulgaria, which induced a strong fear in the political class that a similar crisis accompanied by an even deeper delegitimation of the political status quo may happen again. The emotion-driven political considerations thus accelerated the achievement of consensus on the desirability of EU and NATO membership.

The foreign policy course of **Russia** since 1991 is similarly more plausibly accounted for through a Constructivist — as opposed to a Realist, perspective. Russia's cooperative attitudes and policies in the early 1990s were shaped by identity motivations linked to the aspiration to construct the country's Europeanised identity on the basis of integration in the Euro-Atlantic community. This also proved to be the most beneficial choice, given that a bandwagoning strategy with the West could bring both economic profit and international political prestige. However, Moscow's growing focus on balancing the West and opposing American primacy — gaining ground in the mid-1990s, was not necessarily based on an 'objective' assessment of capacities and potential alliances that warranted a balancing strategy. Instead, as Russian policy-makers' desire for integration and cooperation with Europe and America was disappointed, Russian claims to equality with the West were not recognised and Russia's belief in itself as an inseparable part of European civilization was ambivalently received and contested through the West's standards of European-ness (which Moscow could not fulfil), the Russians spurned the Euro-Atlantic community.

Moscow's accelerating shift towards Asia since 2011 was likewise spurred by the inability of Russia and the West to agree on and act as part of a joint, values-bound community rather than by an objectively determined change in Russian capabilities and alliance options that would dictate a policy of competition with Europe and America. The evolving vision of Russia as separate from Europe underlined the redefinition of interests, which now pointed towards the creation of a multipolar world order to oppose the West. Aiming for multipolarity took place even as the means to this end could not be harnessed to fulfil a fully-fledged balancing policy, given the limited political and economic viability of the Eurasian Economic Union and the uncertain underpinning of an alliance with China.

As in the case of Poland and Bulgaria, in specific circumstances, the realisation of Russian identity perspectives took place within the frame of a variety of countervailing factors. Instrumental calculations led to *tactical accommodation that subdued normative visions and ideas* for the sake of *political expediency*. Such was the case with Yeltsin's and his liberal circle's adjustment to some of the foreign policy demands of Pragmatic Nationalist and Fundamentalist Nationalist political forces in return for a continued enunciation of the goal of Europeanisation (MacFarlane, 1993:12). Also, the lack of sufficient strategic, material and interest-focused incentives and foundations *undermined the long-term sustainability of visions and ideas*. For instance, the EU-Russia agreement on the Four Common Spaces was limited in its achievements because it was not underlined by concrete mechanisms of practical substantiation or solutions aimed to alleviate Russian concerns for equal treatment and decision-making.

Moreover, the *sectionalism, partisanship* and *fluidity* of the institutional and party-political environment in Russia contributed to a *disarray* in the Russian foreign policy-making process that exacerbated the ideational divisions through the incoherent espousal of conflicting stances and the creation of an image of unpredictability among Moscow's Western partners. In addition, the institutional exclusion of Russia from deeper integration with the EU (such as visa-free travel for Russians in EU countries) symbolised Moscow's growing civilizational separation from Europe.

On the other hand, ideas can represent and develop into *ideologised conceptions disconnected from an appreciation of material capacities and interests*. In the early 1990s, the liberal view that Russia's interests coincided with those of the West and the proclamation of an 'imagined' Europeanised identity of Russia — expected to be easily achieved and quickly recognised by Europe, overlooked resource constraints that prevented the Russians from transitioning to a market economy and side-lined a consideration of the conflicting external objectives and differences of values and interests between Russia and the West.

Finally, cognitive and emotional biases *reframed identities and interests* and *produced misperceptions*, a *distorted assessment of events and processes* and a *disproportionate intensity of reactions*. Yeltsin's peculiar conduct of foreign policy — informed by his own intuitions and instincts, prevented the development of a well-thought out international direction, which could have otherwise contributed to a more sensitive approach aiming to understand and address (rather than disappointedly deplore) Western anxieties about Moscow. Also, Russia's deeply rooted prejudices and irrational fears of NATO significantly exacerbated Russian policy-makers' negative perceptions of the consequences of NATO expansion for Moscow's security.

Europeanisation: Reclaiming the centre

The recent history of Europe after the end of communism and bipolarity is, crucially, a story about how Western and Central-Eastern European states negotiated the ideational boundaries of the continent. The book's examination of this history leads to three main conclusions. First, identity has shaped patterns of Europeanisation. Second, there is rather more continuity than change in ideas. Third, the prominence of ideational factors in the construction of the Euro-Atlantic community since 1989 challenges the theoretical dominance of Realism.

More generally, the interactive Constructivist theory of Self and Other and the middle-ground, qualified post-positivist methodological argument advanced in this study inform a research direction and simultaneously represent a call to action to reclaim the centre ground — both in Constructivism and the social sciences as a whole. The complexity of social and political life should raise a warning signal against the implementation of totalised political solutions, which usually end in tyranny, and the reduction of social scientific explanation to streamlined, 'elegant' theory that turns its back on real-world intricacies. Recapturing the middle ground can therefore chart a way in between the extremes that tend to haunt social scientific research paradigms. Methodologically, moving towards the centre means forging an integrated perspective that builds bridges between positivists and post-positivists. Ontologically, the centre shines a lights on the interaction between structure and agents, the system and its units. Epistemologically, combining the possibility of law-like generalizations with contextual peculiarity represents the midpoint between objectivism and subjectivism. Theoretically, the promotion of cross-disciplinary dialogue opens up avenues for mutual learning from different perspectives.

In the concrete research ground of European politics, reclaiming the centre first and foremost means recognising Central and

Eastern Europe's own understandings and contributions to the idea of European-ness. The persistent impact of culturally-historically informed visions of Europe in Poland, Bulgaria and Russia shows that Europeanisation is not a linear-evolutionary process in which the 'old legacies' can be easily and quickly overcome through the implementation of a set of new 'rationally engineered' institutions and policies. The diversity of at once nationally specific and sub-regionally conditioned identities of the post-communist states points to the specific historical experiences that lead to thinking and putting 'Europe' into action in CEE in ways that are different from the established Western trajectory.

Reclaiming the European centre also means questioning the West's own, sometimes tenuous hold on a dominant model of European-ness. Indeed, the expected universalisation and 'timelessness' of the liberal democratic, market economic, cooperative-inclusive-multilateral model concealed its temporal political ascendancy, which can subside if disempowered. Britain's decision to leave the EU, Donald Trump's election as President, the multiple crises of Europe (and above all the nationalist-populist trend) have starkly demonstrated that the value dimensions of ideal-typical European-ness are not incontestable but represent one among other Western traditions, including nationalism, total war, politics of spheres of influence and disengagement from Central and Eastern Europe. Such contestation may once again swing the pendulum from the horizon of European unification and solidarity to a retrenchment of the Europeanisation project, whereby coming together as one community is replaced by growing apart and walking alone.

Epilogue
Europe Beyond the 30-year Limit

Where is Europe nowadays—over 30 years after the revolutionary 1989? It finds itself in the realm of diminished self-confidence as regards the ability to uphold its own values and convince others to follow them. The impetus to integrate, unify and define the boundaries of the European community has subsided. The symbolically-loaded times of European unification, the heady *Zeitgeist* of the post-1989 period now seem to be waning into an era of bygones.

The rise of right-wing populism across European countries (as well as the US) has represented a fundamental normative challenge to liberal democracy from within, driven by the resurgence of conservative national traditions, which have been fed and reinforced by economic grievances and disenchantment with political elites. Despite the diversity of populist conceptions rooted in specific national historical experiences, a number of shared overarching features have emerged. Most prominent is the focus on popular sovereignty understood as the exercise of majoritarian power as opposed to the liberal constitutional checks guaranteeing individual rights. The 'people' tends to be represented in narrow confines encompassing a mono-ethnic community and its (ostensibly monolithic) traditions of cultural and national homogeneity, conservative stipulation of gender roles and a sovereign nation-state in contrast to progressive principles of multiculturalism, gender equality and supra-nationalism. For instance, although originating from a French intellectual and cultural background, the Identitarian Movement has attracted a pan-European following. A key ideological postulate centers on 'ethno-pluralism', according to which people of different ethnicities should not live in the same society and should be excluded from democratic participation (Filipova, Stefanov, 2021a:23).

Populist ideas have therefore undermined democratic norms as well as institutional arrangements since populist leaders have been found to curtail freedom of the press, civil liberties and political rights, once elected to political office. It is in particular the liberal aspect of democracy that has come under fire as right-wing populists place a premium on the interests of a self-designated majority against the observance of the individual rights of minorities (Filipova, Stefanov, 2021a:23). In this vein, the ascendancy of illiberal democracy—initially envisaged to be a form of governance that would take root outside of the Western world, has come to characterise developments across European countries. In his seminal article, Fareed Zakaria (1997) argued that 'Democracy is flourishing; constitutionalism liberalism is not', which at the time was an acute observation referring mainly to south-central Europe, Asia, Africa and Latin America. But it is now applicable to social and political trends in the West, too.

The internal values-based contestation and uncertainty has weakened Europe's ability to project normative power both towards European countries seeking closer association and membership in the EU (such as the Western Balkan and eastern neighbourhood states) as well as on the global stage. In stark contrast to the self-assured post-1989 stipulation of a set of 'European' principles as guideposts for the new era of international affairs and as accession conditions for CEE candidates, European institutions have of late engaged in a soul-searching endeavour of re-stating, re-invigorating and re-committing to those very same principles.

The European Democracy Action Plan, for instance, concedes that the EU members' democratic systems, institutions and norms—including the integrity of elections and media freedom, have been subject to increasing attacks from domestic populist challenges and foreign authoritarian state pressure, particularly Russian and Chinese anti-democratic propaganda and disinformation (European Commission, 2020a:2). A conspicuous recognition of the decline of democracy across Europe is manifest in the European Commission's (2019) introduction of an annual rule of law report as part of the European Rule of Law Mechanism aimed at monitoring legal deficiencies in all member states. Thus, if for the better part of the 1990s, 2000s and 2010s the evaluation of the implementation of rule of law criteria was strictly reserved for EU membership candidates or members still falling short of European standards (such as Bulgaria and Romania whose governance was monitored through the Cooperation and Verification Mechanism even after Union accession), there is now an acknowledgement that the observance of the rule of law represents a cross-European concern.

In a similar vein, the NATO Reflection Process, initiated in 2019 with the aim to chart out the priorities and strengthen the resilience of the Alliance for the coming decade, has identified Allied disagreements over values and the erosion of democracy as a key challenge (NATO, 2020:9, 20). An admission that the confidence of the post-Cold War era about the unhindered spread of democracy and free markets has been dented not only by geopolitical threats but also member states' diluted commitment to the animating principles of NATO therefore leads to the conclusion that intra-Allied cohesion will be harder to achieve in the foreseeable future than it ever was in previous decades.

Against this background of wavering internal coherence and consensus on foundational values, the Euro-Atlantic integration of the Western Balkans now represents a far cry from the 2004 and 2007 waves of accession, which were eagerly awaited as the ultimate institutional confirmation of belongingness. Instead, EU enlargement in the early 2020s is more akin to a protracted procedure with no end in sight, hollowed out by a declining enthusiasm and commitment on both sides. On the one hand, paramount questions about the future of the Union in the context of Brexit have placed a stress on self-concentration rather than expansion. The historical task of reuniting Europe has been put on hold and has not proven sufficient to motivate EU member states to offer stronger support to Western Balkan candidates. As much was revealed in the case of France, which blocked the opening of negotiations with North Macedonia and Albania in 2019 and proposed a revised accession methodology as a substitute. For its part, Bulgaria made Skopje's commencement of negotiations conditional on the resolution of bilateral disputes over national identity. On the other hand, the urgent impetus to be accepted in the Euro-Atlantic community and meet the EU and NATO accession criteria that generally defined the social and political landscapes of earlier candidates for membership such as Poland and Bulgaria have faded into a demoralising inertia in the Western Balkans. Resigning to the fact that membership is a distant and uncertain prospect has especially strongly fed into long-running trends of democratic backsliding and societal disenchantment across the region (Filipova, 2021c:24-26).

A key guideline for action in Europe nowadays has thus been informed by a 'community-preserving' rather than 'community-expanding' impulse, which was starkly demonstrated during the coronavirus crisis. At the start of the pandemic, the EU was immersed in questions over the limits of European solidarity in the midst of member states' export bans on medical equipment and border controls threatening a return to nation-state self-containment. The bid to prevent the community from unravelling consisted, among others, in the introduction of an export authorisation scheme that would circumscribe medical exports outside of the bloc, including initially the Western Balkan countries, yet enable intra-EU exchange (Burchard, Gray, 2020; European Commission, 2020b). This move relegated the Western Balkans to a realm that is external to 'Europe' and is comprised of third parties rather than soon-to-be members of the family. Serbia contributed to the process of symbolic distancing calling the Chinese 'brothers' by virtue of the latter's medical donations to the country, contrasting them with the 'fairy tale' of European solidarity (Filipova, 2020:15-16).

In a similar vein, the EU's focus on its own debates and internal accusations about the speed and effectiveness of vaccine procurement once again consigned the provision of assistance to Union candidates to an act that is not fundamentally constitutive of European community relations. The Western Balkans remained excluded from Union-wide mechanisms for vaccination, leaving them to seek assistance from Russia and China (Burchard, Gray, 2020).

And on the global stage, where Moscow and Beijing vie for influence against the West, Europe is trying to find its bearings. Currently, an uncertain balance is being struck between pursuing economic interests and standing up for political values. This tension was evident as the EU rushed to sign an investment deal with China while trying to forge a principled transatlantic response to Beijing's global ambitions. Similarly, the EU's stance in support of Alexey Navalny stands in stark contrast to the continuation of energy projects such as Nord Stream 2 and Turk Stream (Filipova, Stefanov, 2021c).

The difficulties of adjusting Europe's moral and political compass in international affairs is also conspicuously manifest in the challenges encountered by the EU in asserting its role as a norm-setter. Such a role can be pursued in the digital domain, for instance, where Brussels has pioneered a plethora of rule-based policy initiatives, a prominent example of which is the Digital Services Act (European Commission, 2020c). However, nowadays, the barriers to the easy flow of and receptivity to European norms are much higher. What has been termed a 'battle of standards' by the EU's High Representative Josep Borrell (2020) is reflected, for instance, in Russian and Chinese imperviousness to Union-promoted digital principles. The goal shared by Russia and China to create an alternative information ecosystem based on cyber and Internet sovereignty is contained not only in mutual learning with regard to insulating and cracking down on their domestic audiences' access to information but also in relation to forging joint media operations in third countries. These operations are aimed at taking over critical (5G) infrastructure, enabling surveillance, and disseminating disinformation rather than adhering to free speech, data protection, equitable online business practices.

All in all, the weakening of ideal-typical European-ness and the fading of the 'revolutionary' Zeitgeist have meant that the urgent impetus for Europeanisation has subsided. Yet, given that the identification dynamic between Self and Other is constitutive of fundamental psychological and social interactions, it cannot simply be discontinued but is instead accentuated in dramatic circumstances or deflated in more mundane affairs. Hence, the process of Europeanisation, in which the boundaries of European mutuality are drawn, is far from finished or complete. Rather, it continues in a more muted than salient manner.

Developments in Poland, Bulgaria and Russia therefore still exemplify the persistence of historically-shaped attitudes. As a Pew survey has aptly demonstrated, three decades after the end of communism, Warsaw, Sofia and Moscow maintain three levels of difference among each other in terms of their citizens' approval of the shift to a multiparty system and market economy. 85% of Polish respondents approve of these changes; around half of polled Bulgarians do so too, while barely 40% of the polled Russian population expresses satisfaction with the main features of the post-communist transformation (Pew Research Center, 2019:21).

Indeed, zooming in on public dispositions in Poland — much criticized for its anti-democratic turn, shows a significant societal resilience towards authoritarian tendencies. If given a choice, only 26% of Poles would opt for a strong leader, who does not have to comply with a Parliament and multi-party elections, as against 66% who would stick to a liberal democratic system with regular elections. Similarly, in Hungary — another Central European state which has been touted as the ultimate example of democratic backsliding in the region, preferences for a strongman model of leadership and multiparty democracy stand, respectively, at 12% and 81%. In contrast, more of the polled Bulgarians favour governance by a strong leader (45%) over a liberal democratic system (35%) (Filipova, Stefanov, 2020:3). Hence, even though both Bulgaria and Poland (as well as Hungary) have experienced authoritarian political tendencies for more than a decade, this experience does not appear to be primary in forging a predisposition to autocracy, which is more likely the consequence of historically ingrained attitudes. That is, Poland's and Hungary's belongingness to the Central European region, which has been distinguished from the Balkans by the deeper rootedness of the liberal democratic tradition, can account for the greater durability of pro-democracy public tendencies, despite the nature of the political regime (Filipova, Stefanov, 2020:6).

As much is evident from the large-scale civil societal pushback in Poland against infringements on social and political liberties. A stark example is provided by the resistance to the introduction of an almost complete ban on abortion in 2020, resulting in the largest protest movement since 1989 (Armstrong, 2021). Moreover, the increasing crackdown on media freedom in the country—such as through 'Polonising' media ownership by pushing out foreign (primarily German) investors and depriving (mostly private, non-PiS controlled) media outlets of vital funding via an advertising revenue tax, encountered an unprecedented reaction (Ptak, Koper, 2020; Ostruszka, 2021). In a reassertion of press independence, Polish media outlets went on a strike stopping their services for a day. In line with the significant Western attention typically accorded to Poland, EU and US reactions to transgressions on freedoms in the country followed suit closely. The European Parliament (2020a) condemned in a resolution the abortion law as curtailing women's rights, while the European Commission and the Department of State (2021) further criticized the shrinking space for freedom of expression in Poland (Reuters, 2021).

Still, even as Polish political authorities can act contrary to democratic expectations voiced from within and without, they nevertheless acknowledge the fundamental importance of Poland's liberal democratic heritage. On the 40th anniversary of the initiation of the Solidarity movement, Prime Minister Mateusz Morawiecki (2020) declared that the sources of faith for Solidarity in the past as well as for today's Poland are drawn from the centuries-old Polish political tradition based on love of freedom and democracy; on the attachment to Europe and the inspiration provided by Pope John Paul II. Similarly, on the 30th anniversary of the creation of the Visegrad Group, President Andrzej Duda stressed the values-based underpinning of Central Europe as a community of shared fate, success and aspiration whose 'European' credentials are informed by civilizational belongingness to Western Europe for more than a thousand years.

Unlike Poland's certainty of its long-standing rootedness in and contribution to (Western) European civilization, Bulgaria's attachment to Europe has continued to be ambivalent. Although Sofia's Presidency of the Council of the EU in the first half of 2018 marked a symbolic high-point of the country's fully-fledged participation in European institutions gaining the opportunity to set the Union's agenda, deeper internal and external underlying factors conditioned persistent ambiguities.

Even as Bulgaria presided over European affairs, it still looked to the East. The priority placed on the EU integration of the Western Balkans was criticized as a veneer, behind which Prime Minister Borissov developed relations with Russia (including by promoting the Belene nuclear power plant). Such a balancing act was motivated by Borissov's understanding that a choice between Russia and the West did not have to be made since Bulgaria's strategic orientation is underwritten by its membership in the EU and NATO, while historically, culturally and in the realm of business ties, the country is oriented on Russia (Mediapool, 2018a). Yet, this understanding only served to reinforce Western distrust of Bulgarian loyalties and European credentials (Paunova, 2018; Mediapool, 2018b). Indeed, Bulgaria's less than firm commitment to the Euro-Atlantic community was reciprocated by its European partners' critical media fixation on the problems plaguing the country, including corruption, social injustice, inequality (Rankin, 2017; Roser, 2017).

Dissatisfaction with exactly those negative trends erupted into a prolonged civil societal protest activity in 2020 based on the assertion of a set of political-normative standpoints in favor of political transparency, accountability, a meritocratic selection of the governing elite and justice. However, the internal Bulgarian struggle for change and appeals for European solidarity only slowly caught the attention of fellow EU member states (Govedaritsa, 2020). It was the growing normative pressure instigated by the protests and Bulgarian MEPs' active entrepreneurship that ultimately led to a debate at the European Parliament (2020b) on the developments in Bulgaria, later culminating in a resolution condemning the deterioration of the rule of law, democracy and fundamental rights.

For its part, Russia has remained firmly entrenched in its thin form of Europeanisation, whereby it is above all the recognition of common civilizational roots that sustains the narrowing shared bonds between Russia and Europe. Yet, in terms of substantive normative positions—as well as geopolitical stances, Russia and Europe have become accustomed to being opponents.

Indeed, the conservative Russian identity discourse has been externalised through assertive disinformation activities that aim to undermine European societies from within. Forging ideological and interest-based ties to right-wing populists throughout the continent has provided Moscow with a fertile ground on which to disseminate its conservative narratives. Some of the most prominent of those narratives promote a triad of nationalist, anti-migrant and misogynist attitudes. For instance, pro-Kremlin propagandist messaging pushed into the media environments of European countries extols the supposed virtues of Russia's espousal of traditional values as juxtaposed to the West's unbridled liberalism, which is said to lead to moral decadence. The international political implications of the advancement of traditional values are manifested in the presentation of sovereignty as the ultimate safeguard of national identity from external influences and as the major guidepost for maintaining an independent stance in international relations. The European Union model—based on pooling national sovereignty and taking on supranational functions, is derided as dictatorial and offensive to national traditions. Migration is moreover claimed to be a grave challenge to the cultural foundations and very survival of European civilization. The policy of multiculturalism is ostensibly unmasked as a betrayal of nationality and the expression of 'depraved' Western political correctness. Pro-Kremlin messaging also draws a distinction between the West said to be disseminating gender ideology and Russia as a defender of traditional family values (Filipova, Stefanov, 2021b:29-32).

The normative standoff between Russia and Europe is further expressed in the persistent political deadlock. The meeting of the EU's High Representative Josep Borrell with Russian Foreign Minister Sergey Lavrov in February 2021 demonstrated that dialogue cannot facilitate greater mutual understanding when the animating visions of the two sides are diametrically opposed. On the one hand, Borrell (2021) lamented that Russia-EU relations have come full circle since the 1990 Paris Charter, which was informed by the belief in the end of history and envisaged a common European space between Lisbon and Vladivostok. The reason for the inability to realise this vision he pinned on Moscow's refusal to adhere to European values of democracy and human rights, said, however, to be a crucial part of Europe's DNA. On the other hand, Lavrov (2021) followed the well-established Russian line of firmly opposing any (perceived) treatment of Russia as a junior partner. He denounced arrogance and Russophobia in the EU as leading to an aggressive deterrent posture aimed as suppressing Russia's independence in international relations. The normative incompatibility of the Kremlin regime with European values-based expectations made the insistence on uniqueness all the more urgent.

Overall, the Russian viewpoint on the meeting invoked the historically continuous, dualistic representation of Russia and Europe. Former Foreign Minister Igor Ivanov (2021) harked back to Slavophile Nikolay Danilevsky's writings, according to which Europe sees Russia as something alien to it and therefore adopts a hostile stance toward Moscow. While acknowledging the contemporary relevance of this observation, Ivanov also asserted that 'Russia is an inseparable part of Europe, just as Europe cannot be considered "complete" without Russia.' The attractive-repulsive conceptualisation of Russian-European relations and the rhetorical representation of Moscow as seeking cooperation that is not however reciprocated was also vividly advanced in President Putin's (2021) statement: '…love is impossible if it is declared only by one side. It must be mutual'.

Mutuality is crucial indeed for it takes two to tango. But it takes many to form a community. So in a comparative perspective, the differential quality of mutuality—its distinct depths of ideational affinity and readiness for inclusivity, has been critical in the post-1989 bordering of European belongingness. Fast forward 30 years after the fall of the Berlin Wall, which was the most conspicuous landmark of Europe's division, the question of unification and belongingness has given in to concerns about European 'reinvention'.

Re-making and re-imagining Europe nowadays can start by looking back to the experience of the past three decades and the recognition of the many visions of Europe that characterised the process of coming together. These visions serve to remind that Europe is not simply determined by its geographical confines but is circumscribed above all by distinct European ideational spaces, which shape Europe's heart and its limits.

List of Abbreviations

ABM Treaty	Anti-Ballistic Missile Treaty
ABV	Alternative for Bulgarian Revival (initials from name in Bulgarian: *Alternativa za bulgarsko vuzrazhdane*)
AWS	Solidarity Electoral Action (initials from name in Polish: *Akcja Wyborcza Solidarność*; since 1997 renamed into *Akcja Wyborcza Solidarność Prawicy* (AWSP) or Solidarity Electoral Action of the Right)
BCP	Bulgarian Communist Party (English initials commonly used for name in Bulgarian: *Bulgarska komunisticheska partiya*)
BRICs	Brazil, Russia, India, China and South Africa
BSP	Bulgarian Socialist Party (initials in Bulgarian and English coincide—*Bulgarska sotsialisticheska partiya*)
BSS	Black Sea Synergy
CE	Central Europe
CEE	Central and Eastern Europe
CEFTA	Central European Free Trade Agreement
CFE Treaty	Conventional Armed Forces in Europe Treaty
CFSP	Common Foreign and Security Policy
CIS	Commonwealth of Independent States
CSCE	Conference on Security and Cooperation in Europe
CVM	Cooperation and Verification Mechanism
DM	German mark (initials from German—*Deutsche Mark*)
DPR	Democratic Party of Russia
EAPC	Euro-Atlantic Partnership Council
EC	European Communities
EEC	European Economic Community
EEU	Eurasian Economic Union
ENP	European Neighbourhood Policy
EP	Eastern Partnership

ESDP	European Security and Defence Policy, renamed into Common Security and Defence Policy (CSDP) since 2009
EU	European Union
FDI	Foreign Direct Investment
FPA	Foreign Policy Analysis
FSU	Former Soviet Union
FYROM	Former Yugoslav Republic of Macedonia
G7	Group of Seven
GDR	German Democratic Republic
GERB	Citizens for European Development of Bulgaria (acronym from party's name in Bulgarian: *Grazhdani za evropeisko razvitie na Bulgariya*)
IFOR/SFOR	Implementation Force/Stabilisation Force in Bosnia and Herzegovina
IMF	International Monetary Fund
IR	International Relations
KGB	Committee for State Security (initials from name in Russian: *Komitet gosudarstvennoy bezopasnosti*)
KLD	Liberal Democratic Congress (initials from name in Polish: *Kongres Liberalno-Demokratyczny*)
KPRF	Communist Party of the Russian Federation (initials from name in Russian: *Kommunisticheskaya partiya Rossiyskoy Federatsii*)
LDPR	Liberal Democratic Party of Russia (Russian and English initials coincide—*Liberalno-demokraticheskaya partiya Rossii*)
LPR	League of Polish Families (initials from name in Polish: *Liga Polskich Rodzin*)
MEP	Member of the European Parliament
MFN	Most Favoured Nation
MP	Member of Parliament
MRF	Movement for Rights and Freedoms (English initials commonly used; otherwise in Bulgarian

LIST OF ABBREVIATIONS 413

	the initials are rendered as DPS from *Dvizhenie za prava i svobodi*)
NACC	North Atlantic Cooperation Council
NATO	North Atlantic Treaty Organization
NDSV	National Movement Simeon II (initials from name in Bulgarian: *Natsionalno dvizhenie Simeon Vtori*; renamed in 2007 into National Movement for Stability and Progress: *Natsionalno dvizhenie za stabilnost i vuzhod*)
NFSB	National Front for the Salvation of Bulgaria (Initials in English and Bulgarian coincide: *Natsionalen front za spasenie na Bulgariya*)
NRC	NATO-Russia Council
OECD	Organization for Economic Cooperation and Development
OSCE	Organisation for Security and Cooperation in Europe
PARNAS	People's Freedom Party, abbreviation from name in Russian: *Partiya narodnoy svobody*
PCA	Partnership and Cooperation Agreement
PES	Party of European Socialists
PfP	Partnership for Peace
PHARE	Poland and Hungary: Assistance for Restructuring their Economies
PiS	Law and Justice (initials from name in Polish: *Prawo i Sprawiedliwość*)
PO	Civic Platform (initials from name in Polish: *Platforma Obywatelska*)
Progress Party	Partiya progressa
PSL	Polish Peasants' Party (initials from name in Polish: *Polskie Stronnictwo Ludowe*)
RB	Reformist Bloc (Bulgarian and English initials coincide — *Reformatorski blok*)
SCO	Shanghai Cooperation Organisation
SdRP	Social Democracy of the Republic of Poland (initials in Polish and English coincide: *Socjaldemokracja Rzeczypospolitej Polskiej*)
SEE	Southeast Europe

SIT	Social Identity Theory
SLD	Democratic Left Alliance (initials from name in Polish: *Sojusz Lewicy Demokratycznej*)
SR	A Just Russia (initials from name in Russian: *Spravedlivaya Rossiya*)
SRP	Self-Defence of the Republic of Poland (initials from name in Polish: *Samoobrona Rzeczpospolitej Polskiej*)
START	Strategic Arms Reduction Treaty
UD	Democratic Union (initials from name in Polish: *Unia Demokratyczna*)
UDF	Union of Democratic Forces (English initials commonly used; otherwise in Bulgarian the initials are rendered as SDS from *Suyuz na demokratichnite sili*)
UN	United Nations
UP	Labour Union (initials from name in Polish: *Unia Pracy*)
USSR	Union of Soviet Socialist Republics
UW	Freedom Union (initials from name in Polish: *Unia Wolności*)
VMRO	Internal Macedonian Revolutionary Organisation (initials from name in Bulgarian: *Vutreshna makedonska revolyutsionna organizatsiya*). Less frequently, the party's full name is used: VMRO-*Bulgarsko natsionalno dvizhenie* (Bulgarian National Movement)
WEU	Western European Union
WTO	World Trade Organization
ZChN	Christian National Union (initials from name in Polish: *Zjednoczenie Chrześcijańsko-Narodowe*)

Bibliography

A Secure Netherlands in a Secure World, 2013, *Ministry of Foreign Affairs*, pp. 3-10, https://www.bbn.gov.pl/ftp/dok/07/NDL_International_Security_Strategy_2013.pdf

Abrams, D., Hogg, M., Marques, J., 2005, 'A Social Psychological Framework for Understanding Social Inclusion and Exclusion', Ch. 1 in Abrams, D., Hogg, M., Marques, J., (eds.), *Social Psychology of Inclusion and Exclusion*, New York: Psychology Press

Abrasheva, M., 2015, *Interview with Rumena Filipova*, 19 November 2015, Sofia

Acharya, A., 2000, *Quest for Identity: International Relations of Southeast Asia*, Singapore: Oxford University Press

Acharya, A., 2001, *Constructing a Security Community in Southeast Asia: ASEAN and the Problem of Regional Order*, London: Routledge

Acharya, A., 2009, *Whose Ideas Matter? Agency and Power in Asian Regionalism*, Ithaca: Cornell University Press

Adamski, Ł., 2008, 'Poland's Policy Regarding Ukraine', *Yearbook of Polish Foreign Policy*, pp. 214-233

Adamski, Ł., 2015, *Interview with Rumena Filipova*, 19 June 2015, Warsaw

Adem, S., 2021, *Postcolonial Constructivism: Mazrui's Theory of Intercultural Relations*, Palgrave Macmillan

Adler, E., 1997, 'Seizing the Middle Ground: Constructivism in World Politics', *European Journal of International Relations*, Vol. 3, No 3, pp. 319-363, http://journals.sagepub.com/doi/abs/10.1177/1354066197003003003

Adler, E., 2013, 'Constructivism and International Relations', Ch. 5 in Carlsnaes, W., Risse, T., Simmons, B., (eds.), *Handbook of International Relations*, London: SAGE publications

Adler, E., 2019, *World Ordering. A Social Theory of Cognitive Evolution*, Cambridge: Cambridge University Press

Adler, E., Crawford, B., 2002, 'Constructing a Mediterranean Region: A Cultural Approach', *Conference on 'The Convergence of Civilizations? Constructing a Mediterranean Region'*, Arrábida Monastery, Fundação Oriente, Lisboa, Portugal, 6-9 June 2002

Adomeit, H., 1995, 'Russia as a "Great Power" in World Affairs: Images and Reality', *International Affairs*, Vol. 71, No 1, pp. 35-68, https://www.jstor.org/stable/2624009?seq=1#page_scan_tab_contents

Adomeit, H., 2007, 'Inside or Outside? Russia's Policies towards NATO', *Working Paper, German Institute for International and Security Affairs*, https://www.swpberlin.org/fileadmin/contents/products/arbeits papiere/NATO_Oslo_ks.pdf

Agenda 2004, План за организационно изграждане и модернизация на въоръжените сили до 2015 г., (Agenda 2004 for the organisational build-up and modernisation of the armed forces until 2015)

Agreement on Partnership and Cooperation, 1994, http://www.russian mission.eu/userfiles/file/partnership_and_cooperation_agreement _1997_english.pdf

Alexandrov, M., 2003, 'The Concept of State Identity in International Relations: A Theoretical Analysis', *Journal of International Development and Cooperation*, Vol. 10, No 1, p. 33-46, https://ir.lib.hiroshima-u.ac. jp/files/public/1/14409/20141016121246211432/JIDC_10_01_03_A lexandrov.pdf

Alexieva, I., 2015, *Interview with Rumena Filipova*, 14 December 2015, Sofia

Allen, D., 'Who Speaks for Europe? The Search for an Effective and Coherent External Policy', Ch. 3 in Peterson, J., Sjursen, H., (eds.), 1998, *A Common Foreign Policy for Europe? Competing Visions of the CFSP*, London: Routledge

Alliance's Strategic Concept, *NATO*, 1999, http://www.nato.int/cps/on/ natohq/official_texts_27433.htm

Allison, R., 2009, 'The Russian case for military intervention in Georgia: international law, norms and political calculation', *European Security*, Vol. 18, No 2, pp. 173-200, https://www.tandfonline.com/doi/abs/ 10.1080/09662830903468734

Allison, R., Light, M., White, S., 2006, *Putin's Russia and the Enlarged Europe*, London: Royal Institute of International Affairs, Chatham House

Amiot, C., Terry, D., Wirawan, D., Grice, T., 2010, 'Changes in social identities over time: The role of coping and adaptation processes', *British Journal of Social Psychology*, Vol. 49, No 4, pp. 803-826, http:// onlinelibrary.wiley.com/doi/10.1348/014466609X480624/abstract

Anderson, B., 2006, *Imagined Communities: Reflections on the Origin and Spread of Nationalism*, London: Verso Books, Rev. ed.

Anderson, R., Fish, S., Hanson, S., Roeder, P., 2001, *Postcommunism and the Theory of Democracy*, Princeton: Princeton University Press

Angelov, A., 2004, 'The Bulgarian Regional Diplomacy in the Context of the NATO Enlargement toward the Balkans', *Papeles del Este*, No 8, pp. 1-21, http://revistas.ucm.es/index.php/PAPE/article/viewFile /PAPE0404120008A/25847

Angelov, P., 2015, *Разгромът. Откъс от моя несъстоял се диалог с президента д-р Желю Желев*, Български писател, (*Destruction. An excerpt from my conversation with the President, Dr. Zheliu Zhelev, which never took place*, Bulgarian writer)

Anno, T., 2018, *National Identity and Great-Power Status in Russia and Japan: Non-Western Challengers to the Liberal International Order*, Routledge

Arbatov, A., 1993, 'Russia's Foreign Policy Alternatives', *International Security*, Vol. 18, No 2, pp. 5-43, https://www.jstor.org/stable/2539096?seq=1#page_scan_tab_contents

Arbatova, N., 2005, *Национальные интересы и внешняя политика России: европейское направление (1991-1999)*, ИМЭМО Ран, (*National interests and Russia's foreign policy: The European direction (1991-1999)*, IMEMO Ran)

Arbatova, N., 2014, *Interview with Rumena Filipova*, 7 July 2014, Moscow

Arfire, R., 2011, 'The Moral Regulation of the Second Europe: Transition, Europeanization and the Romanians', *Critical Sociology*, Vol. 37, No 6, pp. 853-870, http://journals.sagepub.com/doi/abs/10.1177/0896920510398017

Armstrong, M., 2021, 'Protests against new abortion law continue across Poland', *Euronews*, 30 January 2021, https://www.euronews.com/2021/01/30/protests-against-new-abortion-law-continue-across-pol and

Arndt, M., 2015, *Interview with Rumena Filipova*, 14 December 2015, Sofia

Asmus, R., Kugler, R., Larrabee, S., 1993, 'Building a New NATO', *Foreign Affairs*, Vol. 72, No 4, https://www.foreignaffairs.com/articles/southeastern-europe/1993-09-01/building-new-nato

Associated Press, 1998, 'Polish Prime Minister expresses thanks to US for admission to NATO', 10 July 1998

Atanassov, N., 2000, 'About some national social and economic features and problems in Bulgaria and in the Balkans in the end of the 20th century', *Workshop on Defence Policy Modernisation and Security on the Balkans, University of National and World Economy*, Sofia, 24-25 May 2000

Avramov, R., 2007, *Комуналният капитализъм. Из българското стопанско минало. Том I*, Фондация 'Българска наука и култура', Център за либерални стратегии, (*Communal Capitalism. Though the Bulgarian Economic Past, Vol. 1*, 'Bulgarian science and culture' Foundation, Centre for Liberal Strategies)

Ba, A., 2005, 'On norms, rule breaking, and security communities: a constructivist response', *International Relations of the Asia-Pacific*, Vol. 5, No 2, pp. 255-266, https://academic.oup.com/irap/article-abstract/5/2/255/2357374

Baert, P., 2005, *Philosophy of the Social Sciences: Towards Pragmatism*, Cambridge: Polity

Baeva, I., 1998, 'Когато се спускаше "желязната завеса" (1944-1949): Полша, Чехословакия и Унгария', в Иванова, З., Грозев, К., Мирчева, Х., Баева, И., Драганов, Д., (ред.), *Преди и след "Желязната завеса"*, Тилиа, ('When the Iron Curtain was falling (1944-1949): Poland, Czechoslovakia and Hungary' in Ivanova, Z., Grozev, K., Mircheva, H., Baeva, I., Draganov, D., (eds.), *Before and After the Iron Curtain*, Tilia)

Baeva, I., 2015, *Interview with Rumena Filipova*, 20 November 2015, Sofia

Baeva, I., Kalinova, E., 2011, *Социализмът в огледалото на прехода*, Изток-Запад, (*Socialism in the mirror of the transition*, East-West)

Banac, I., (ed.), 1992, *Eastern Europe in Revolution*, Ithaca: Cornell University Press

Banchoff, T., 1998, 'Germany's European Policy: A Constructivist Perspective', *Program for the Study of Germany and Europe, Harvard University*, Working Paper Series 8.1, http://www.people.fas.harvard.edu/~ces/publications/docs/pdfs/PSGE_WP8_1.pdf

Bangersky, A., Gornostaev, D., 1997, 'Ельцин призвал Европу стать в XXI веке самостоятельным сообществом', *Независимая газета*, 11 октября 1997, ('Yeltsin called on Europe to become an independent community in the 21st century', *Nezavisimaya Gazeta*, 11 October 1997), https://www.uni-potsdam.de/u/slavistik/zarchiv/1097wc/k192-24.htm

Bankov, P., Gherghina, S., 2020, 'Post-accession congruence in Bulgaria and Romania: measuring mass-elite congruence of opinions on European integration through mixed methods', *European Political Science*, Vol. 19, pp. 562-572, https://doi.org/10.1057/s41304-020-00271-0

Baranovsky, V., 2000a, 'The Kosovo factor in Russia's foreign policy', *The International Spectator: Italian Journal of International Affairs*, Vol. 35, No 2, pp. 113-130, http://www.tandfonline.com/doi/abs/10.1080/03932720008458130?journalCode=rspe20

Baranovsky, V., 2000b, 'Russia: A Part of Europe or Apart from Europe?', *International Affairs*, Vol. 76, No 3, pp. 443-458, https://www.jstor.org/stable/2625948?seq=1#page_scan_tab_contents

Baranovsky, V., 2002, *Russia's attitudes towards the EU: Political aspects*, Berlin: Institut für Europäische Politik

Baranovsky, V., 2014, *Interview with Rumena Filipova*, 23 July 2014, Moscow

Barker, A., 2018, 'EU warily welcomes Boyko Borisov's embrace', *Financial Times*, 14 January 2018, https://www.ft.com/content/67bd4b52-f91e-11e7-a492-2c9be7f3120a

Barnett, M., 1993, 'Institutions, Roles, and Disorder: The Case of the Arab States System', *International Studies Quarterly*, Vol. 37, No 3, pp. 271-296, https://www.jstor.org/stable/2600809?seq=1#page_scan_tab_contents

Barnett, M., Finnemore, M., 2004, *Rules for the World: International Organisations in Global Politics*, Ithaca: Cornell University Press

Bartoszewski, W., 1996, '290 days of the Minister for Foreign Affairs', *Yearbook of Polish Foreign Policy*, pp. 9-18

Bassin, M., Pozo, G., 2017, *The Politics of Eurasianism: Identity, Popular Culture and Russia's Foreign Policy*, Rowman & Littlefield Publishers

Bavaj, R., 2011, '"The West": A conceptual exploration', *Europäische Geschichte Online*, https://research-repository.st-andrews.ac.uk/bitstream/handle/10023/2050/Bavaj_The_West_EGO_.pdf?sequence=1&isAllowed=y

Bechev, D., 2004, 'Contested Borders, Contested Identity: The Case of Regionalism in South East Europe', *Journal of Southeast European and Black Sea Studies*, Vol. 4, No 1, pp. 77-96, http://www.tandfonline.com/doi/abs/10.1080/14683850412331321728

Bechev, D., 2006a, 'Carrots, sticks and norms: the EU and regional cooperation in Southeast Europe', *Journal of Southern Europe and the Balkans Online*, Vol. 8, No 1, pp. 27-43, http://www.tandfonline.com/doi/abs/10.1080/14613190600595515?journalCode=cjsb19

Bechev, D., 2006b, 'Constructing South East Europe: The Politics of Regional Identity in the Balkans', *RAMSES Working Paper*, March 2006, http://www.academia.edu/413161/Dimitar_Bechev_Constructing_South_East_Europe_the_Politics_of_Regional_Identity_in_the_Balkans_pdf_

Bechev, D., 2009, 'From Policy-Takers to Policy-Makers? Observations on Bulgarian and Romanian Foreign Policy Before and After EU Accession', *Perspectives on European Politics and Society*, Vol. 10, No 2, pp. 210-224, http://www.tandfonline.com/doi/abs/10.1080/15705850902899248

Becker, S., Boeckh, K., Hainz, C., Wassmann, L., 2015, 'The Empire Is Dead, Long Live the Empire! Long-Run Persistence of Trust and Corruption in the Bureaucracy', *Economic Journal*, Vol. 126, No 590, pp. 40-74, http://onlinelibrary.wiley.com/doi/10.1111/ecoj.12220/abstract

Bedrov, I., 2014, 'Защо днес България нямаше да влезе в ЕС и НАТО', *Дойче Веле България*, 21 март 2014, ('Why today Bulgaria wouldn't join the EU and NATO', *Deutsche Welle Bulgaria*, 21 March 2014), http://m.dnevnik.bg/bulgaria/2014/06/03/2314591_nikolai_malinov_pred_sp_gazprom_ruski_kompanii_smiatat/www.dnevnik.bg/analizi/2014/03/21/2266069_zashto_dnes_bulgariia_niamashe_da_vleze_v_es_i_nato/

Behravesh, M., 2011, 'The Relevance of Constructivism to Foreign Policy Analysis', *e-International Relations*, http://portal.research.lu.se/ws/files/5815015/3053087.pdf

Belavusau, U., Gliszczyńska-Grabias, A., (eds.), 2020, *Constitutionalism under Stress. Essays in Honour of Wojciech Sadurski*, Oxford University Press

Beneš, V., 2010, Role Theory: A conceptual framework for the constructivist foreign policy analysis, *Mezinárodní Vztahy*, Vol. 45, No 4

Beneš, V., 2017, *Temporality, Role Theory and Czech Foreign Policy*, Taylor and Francis Group

Bennett, A., Elman, C., 2006, 'Complex Causal Relations and Case Study Methods: The Example of Path Dependence', *Political Analysis*, Vol. 14, No 3, pp. 250-267, https://www.jstor.org/stable/25791852?seq=1#page_scan_tab_contents

Berdychowska, B., 2001, 'Giedroyć Still Relevant', *Polish Foreign Affairs Digest*, Vol. 1, No 1, pp. 251-257

Berger, P., 1966, 'Identity as a problem in the sociology of knowledge', *European Journal of Sociology*, Vol. 7, No 1, pp. 105-115, https://www.jstor.org/stable/23988309?seq=1#page_scan_tab_contents

Bertucci, M., Hayes, J., James, P., (eds.), 2018, *Constructivism Reconsidered. Past, Present and Future*, University of Michigan Press

Bertucci, M., Hayes, J., James, P., 2018, 'Constructivism in International Relations', Ch. 2 in Bertucci, M., Hayes, J., James, P., (eds.), *Constructivism Reconsidered. Past, Present and Future*, University of Michigan Press

Best, H., Lengyel, G., Verzichelli, L., (eds.), 2012, *The Europe of Elites: A Study into the Europeanness of Europe's Political and Economic Elites*, Oxford: Oxford University Press

Beyers, J., 1998, 'Where does supranationalism come from? Ideas floating through the working groups of the Council of the European Union', *European Integration online Papers* (EIoP), Vol. 2, No 9, http://eiop.or.at/eiop/texte/1998-009.htm

Beyers, J., 2005, 'Multiple Embeddedness and Socialisation in Europe: The Case of Council Officials', *International Organization*, Vol. 59, No 4, pp. 899-936, https://www.jstor.org/stable/3877832?seq=1#page_scan_tab_contents

Bibo, I., 2004, 'The Elite and Social Sensitivity', *Review of Sociology,* Vol.10, No 2, pp. 103-114, http://akademiai.com/doi/abs/10.1556/RevSoc.10.2004.2.8

Bigatto, M., 2007, 'Socialisation of the new Members of the European Parliament: integration in the institutional life', *ECPR Joint Sessions, Helsinki. 7-12 May 2007, Workshop 24 'The European Parliament and the Making of a Supranational Elite'*, https://ecpr.eu/Filestore/PaperProposal/f81bb239-aa62-4f64-bdb0-110e5653b321.pdf

Black, J., 2000, *Russia Faces NATO Expansion: Bearing Gifts or Bearing Arms?*, Lanham: Rowman & Littlefield

Blazyca, G., Kolkiewicz, M., 1999, 'Poland and the EU: Internal disputes, domestic politics and accession', *Journal of Communist Studies and Transition Politics*, Vol. 15, No 4, pp. 131-143, http://www.tandfonline.com/doi/abs/10.1080/13523279908415423

Bobiński, K., 2007, 'Polish Foreign Policy 2005-2007', *Institute of Public Affairs (Warsaw)*, http://www.isp.org.pl/files/20939921610914404001195830246.pdf

Bogaturov, A., 1994, 'Post-election Russia and the West: At a Crossroads?', *The Current Digest of the Post-Soviet Press*, Vol. 45, No 52

Bonchev, P., 2002, 'Bulgaria's way to NATO', in Minchev, O., Ratchev, V., Lessenski, M., (eds.), *Bulgaria for NATO*, Institute for Regional and International Studies, Sofia, http://www.iris-bg.org/fls/intro.pdf

Boneva, T., 2006, 'Власт и идентичност на Балканите', *Анамнеза*, бр. 1, с. 33-51, ('Power and Identity in the Balkans', *Anamnesa*, No 1, pp. 33-51), http://lib.sudigital.org/record/18628/files/SUDGTL-ARTICLE-2011-031.pdf

Borrell, J., 2020, 'The EU in the multilateral system', *Speech by the High Representative/Vice-President Josep Borrell at the United for a New, Fair and Inclusive Multilateralism online International Conference*, https://eeas.europa.eu/headquarters/headquarters-homepage_en/85399/The%20EU%20in%20the%20multilateral%20system:%20Speech%20by%20the%20High%20Representative/Vice-President%20Josep%20Borrell%20at%20the%20UNited%20for%20a%20New,%20Fair%20and%20Inclusive%20Multilateralism%20online%20International%20Conference

Borrell, J., 2021, 'Russia', *Speech by High Representative/Vice-President Josep Borrell at the EP debate on his visit to Moscow*, https://eeas.europa.eu/headquarters/headquarters-Homepage/92876/russia-speech-high-representativevice-president-josep-borrell-ep-debate-his-visit-moscow_en

Börzel, T., 2003, 'Shaping and Taking EU Policies: Member State Responses to Europeanisation', *Queen's Papers on Europeanisation*, No 2

Bossuyt, F., 2014, 'The impact of the Central and Eastern European EU member states on the EU's democracy promotion policy towards Central Asia', *Prospects of EU-Central Asia relations conference*, Almaty, http://iep-berlin.de/wp-content/uploads/2014/10/Paper_Bossuyt.pdf

Bovt, G., 1994, 'Или сверхдержава, или ничто', *Коммерсант*, 26 ноября 1994, ('Either a superpower or nothing', *Kommersant*, 26 November 1994), http://kommersant.ru/doc/96219

Bovt, G., 1994, 'Там, за забором, где любят крепких мужиков', *Коммерсант*, 10 декабря 1994, ('They love strong men abroad', *Kommersant*, 10 December 1994), http://kommersant.ru/doc/97451/print

Bovt, G., Kalashnikova, N., 1995, 'Прогноз на сегодня: "холодный мир" или "холодная война"', *Коммерсант*, 13 января 1995, ('Today's forecast: "a cold peace" or a "cold war"', *Kommersant*, 13 January 1995), http://www.kommersant.ru/doc/99129/print

Bowker, M., Williams, P., 1988, *Superpower Detente: A Reappraisal*, London: Sage

Bracho, G., López, J., 2005, 'The economic collapse of Russia', *PSL Quarterly Review*, Vol. 58, No 232, http://www.networkideas.org/featart/nov2005/Economic_Collapse.pdf

Brady, H., Collier, D., (eds.), 2010, *Rethinking Social Inquiry: Diverse Tools, Shared Standards*, Lanhan: Rowman & Littlefield Publishers, 2nd ed.

Brahm, H., 2009, 'Второто Възраждане на България', в Таслакова, Р., (интервюиращ), *Две десетилетия преход. България през погледа на германски дипломати*, Изток-Запад, ('The second Bulgarian Revival', in Taslakova, R., (intervieweer), *Two decades of transition. Bulgaria through the eyes of German diplomats*, East-West)

Bregov, I., 2017, 'Изборът на нов ВСС се опорочава в зародиш', *Mediapool*, 28 април 2017, ('The election of a new Supreme Court Council is being spoiled from the beginning', *Mediapool*, 28 April 2017), http://www.mediapool.bg/izborat-na-nov-vss-se-oporochava-v-zarodish-news263230.html

Breuer, F., 'Sociological Institutionalism, Socialisation and the Brusselisation of CSDP', Ch. 6 in Kurowska, X., Breuer, F., (eds.), 2012, *Explaining the EU's Common Security and Defence Policy. Theory in Action*, London: Palgrave Macmillan

Breuilly, J., 1993, *Nationalism and the State*, Manchester: Manchester University Press, 2nd ed.

Broniatowski, M., 2017, 'Poland's new PM won't change anything after leadership swap', *Politico*, 12 December 2017, https://www.politico.eu/article/poland-new-prime-minister-mateusz-morawiecki-wont-change-anything-after-leadership-swap/

Brown, A., 2020, *The Human Factor: Gorbachev, Reagan, and Thatcher, and the End of the Cold War*, Oxford: Oxford University Press.

Browning, C., 2008, *Constructivism, Narrative and Foreign Policy Analysis: A Case Study of Finland*, Bern: Peter Lang

Brummer, K., Thies, C., 2015, 'The Contested Selection of National Role Conceptions', *Foreign Policy Analysis*, Vol. 11, No 3, pp. 273-293, https://onlinelibrary.wiley.com/doi/full/10.1111/fpa.12045

Brzezinski, Z., 1997, *Grand Chessboard: American Primacy and Its Geostrategic Imperatives*, New York: BasicBooks

Bucholc, M., 2016, 'The Polish Constitutional Crisis 2015-16: A Figurational Perspective', *Social Character, Historical Processes*, Vol. 5, Issue 2, https://quod.lib.umich.edu/h/humfig/11217607.0005.210/--polish-constitutional-crisis-201516-a-figurational?rgn=main;view=fulltext

Bulmer, S., 'Theorizing Europeanization', Ch. 4 in Graziano, P., Vink, M., (eds.), 2007, *Europeanization: New Research Agendas*, Basingstoke: Palgrave Macmillan

Bulmer, S., Radaelli, C., 2004, 'The Europeanisation of National Policy?', *Queen's Papers on Europeanisation*, No 1

Burant, S., 1995, 'Foreign Policy and National Identity: A Comparison of Ukraine and Belarus', *Europe-Asia Studies*, Vol. 47, No 7, pp. 1125-1144, https://www.jstor.org/stable/152590?seq=1#page_scan_tab_contents

Buras, P., 2017, 'Europe and its discontents: Poland's collision course with the European Union', *European Council on Foreign Relations Policy Brief*, http://www.ecfr.eu/publications/summary/europe_and_its_discontents_polands_collision_course_with_the_eu_7220

Burchard, H., Gray, A., 2020, 'Western Balkans call for exemption from EU medical export restrictions', *Politico*, 9 April 2020, https://www.politico.eu/article/western-balkans-call-for-exemption-from-eu-medical-export-restrictions/

Burke, P., 2006, 'Identity Change', *Social Psychology Quarterly*, Vol. 69, No 1, pp. 81-96, http://journals.sagepub.com/doi/abs/10.1177/019027250606900106

Burke, P., Stets, J., 2009, *Identity Theory*, New York: Oxford University Press

Burlingame, W., 2008, 'Understanding Social Identity Maintenance: An application and extension of the Social Identity Approach', *Department of Organizational Behavior, Weatherhead School of Management, Case Western Reserve University*, https://weatherhead.case.edu/departments/organizational-behavior/workingPapers/WP-10-08.pdf

Burudjieva, T., 2015, *Interview with Rumena Filipova*, 11 November 2015, Sofia

Busygina, I., 2014, *Interview with Rumena Filipova*, 3 July 2014, Moscow

Buzan, B., Waever, O., 2003, *Regions and Powers: The Structure of International Security*, Cambridge: Cambridge University Press

Caldas-Coulthard, C., Iedema, R., (eds.), 2010, *Identity trouble: critical discourse and contested identities*, Basingstoke: Palgrave Macmillan

Calliess, C., Schyff, G., (eds.), 2019, *Constitutional Identity in a Europe of Multilevel Constitutionalism*, Cambridge University Press

Cantir, C., Kaarbo, J., (eds.), 2016, *Domestic Role Contestation, Foreign Policy, and International Relations*, Routledge

Capital, 1995, 'България все по-близко до ЕС', *Капитал*, 11 септември 1995, ('Bulgaria ever closer to the EU', 11 September 1995)

Capital, 1996, 'Пирински зачете европейската интеграция', *Капитал*, 8 април 1996, ('Pirinski paid tribute to European integration', 8 April 1996), http://www.capital.bg/politika_i_ikonomika/1996/04/08/1030506_pirinski_zachete_evropeiskata_integraciia/

Capital, 1996, 'България—срам за Източна Европа', *Капитал*, 4 ноември 1996, ('Bulgaria—Eastern Europe's shame', 4 November 1996), http://www.capital.bg/politika_i_ikonomika/1996/11/04/1006677_bulgariia_-_sram_za_iztochna_evropa/

Capital, 2020, *K100. Най-големите компании в България 2020*, (*K100. The largest companies in Bulgaria 2020*), https://www.capital.bg/k100-2020/#start

Carlsnaes, W., 1992, 'The Agency-Structure Problem in Foreign Policy Analysis', *International Studies Quarterly*, Vol. 36, No 3, pp. 245-270, http://rochelleterman.com/ir/sites/default/files/Carlsnaes%201992.pdf

Chafetz, G., Abramson, H., Grillot, S., 1996, 'Role Theory and Foreign Policy: Belarussian and Ukrainian Compliance with the Nuclear Nonproliferation Regime', *Political Psychology*, Vol. 17, No 4, pp. 727-757, https://www.jstor.org/stable/3792136?seq=1#page_scan_tab_contents

Chan, S., 2017, *Meditations on Diplomacy: Comparative Cases in Diplomatic Practice and Foreign Policy*, Bristol: E-International Relations

Chappell, L., 2010, 'Poland in Transition: Implications for a European Security and Defence Policy', *Contemporary Security Policy*, Vol. 31, No 2, pp. 225-248, http://www.tandfonline.com/doi/abs/10.1080/13523260.2010.491312

Charter of Paris for a New Europe, 1990, *CSCE*, https://www.oscepa.org/documents/all-documents/documents-1/673-1990-charter-of-paris-for-a-new-europe/file

Checkel, J., 1998, 'The constructivist turn in international relations theory', *World Politics*, Vol. 50, No 2, pp. 324-348

Checkel, J., 1999, 'Social Construction and Integration', *Journal of European Public Policy*, Vol. 6, No 4, pp. 545-560, https://www.tandfonline.com/doi/abs/10.1080/135017699343469

Checkel, J., 2001, 'Why Comply: Social Learning and European Identity Change', *International Organization*, Vol. 55, No 3, pp. 553-588, https://www.jstor.org/stable/3078657?seq=1#page_scan_tab_contents

Chelotti, N., 2014, 'Multiple Practices and Styles: Analysing Variation in EU Foreign Policy Negotiations', *European Foreign Policy Unit LSE, Working Paper 2014/1*, pp. 2-7, http://www.lse.ac.uk/internationalRelations/centresandunits/EFPU/EFPUpdfs/EFPU-Working-paper-2014-1.pdf

Chkhikvadze, V., 'A Focus on Georgia', in Gromadzki, G., Sendhardt, B., (eds.), 2015, *Eastern Partnership Revisited*, The Stefan Batory Foundation, Friedrich Ebert Stiftung Representation in Poland, http://library.fes.de/pdf-files/bueros/warschau/12002.pdf

Cholova, B., 2010, 'Populism in Bulgaria: a recent phenomenon?', *9th Belgian-Dutch Political science conference, 27-28 May, 2010, Leuven, Belgium*, https://soc.kuleuven.be/web/files/11/72/W07-04.pdf

Cianciara, A., 2008, 'Eastern Partnership – opening a new chapter of Polish Eastern policy and the European Neighbourhood Policy?', *The Institute of Public Affairs (Warsaw)*, June 2008, No 4, http://www.isp.org.pl/files/8679201040703671001213792577.pdf

Cichocki, M., 2002, 'Polish-German Relations in the Light of Poland's Accession to the European Union', *Polish Foreign Affairs Digest*, Vol. 2, No 1, pp. 169-174

Cimoszewicz, W., 2002, 'New Threats and New Challenges', *Yearbook of Polish Foreign Policy*, pp. 27-31

Clinton, B., 1994, 'Remarks to Multinational Audience of Future Leaders of Europe', *US Diplomatic Mission to Germany*, https://usa.usembassy.de/etexts/ga6-940109.htm

Clover, C., 1999, 'Dreams of the Eurasian Heartland: The Reemergence of Geopolitics', *Foreign Affairs*, Vol. 78, No 2, pp. 9-13, https://www.foreignaffairs.com/articles/asia/1999-03-01/dreams-eurasian-heartland-reemergence-geopolitics

Clyatt, O., 1993, 'Bulgaria's Quest for Security after the Cold War', *McNair Papers*, No 15, The Institute for National Strategic Studies

Code of Conduct on Politico-Military Aspects of Security, 1994, *CSCE*, http://www.osce.org/fsc/41355?download=true

Cohen, S., 2001, *Failed Crusade: America and the Tragedy of Post-Communist Russia*, New York: Norton

Collins, A., 2019, 'W(h)ither the Association of South East Asian Nations (ASEAN)? W(h)ither constructivism? Fixity of norms and the ASEAN Way', *International Relations*, Vol. 33, No 3, pp. 413-432, https://journals.sagepub.com/doi/abs/10.1177/0047117819830469

Common Strategy of the European Union of 4 June 1999 on Russia, http://trade.ec.europa.eu/doclib/docs/2003/november/tradoc_114137.pdf

Conley, H., Mina, J., Stefanov, R., Vladimirov, M., 2016, *The Kremlin Playbook. Understanding Russian Influence in Central and Eastern Europe*, Centre for Strategic and International Studies/Center for the Study of Democracy, http://www.csd.bg/fileadmin/user_upload/160928_Conley_KremlinPlaybook_Web.pdf

Conradi, P., 2017, *Who Lost Russia? How the World Entered a New Cold War*, London: Oneworld

Constitution of the Republic of Bulgaria, 1991, http://www.parliament.bg/en/const

Constitution of the Republic of Poland, 1997, http://www.sejm.gov.pl/prawo/konst/angielski/kon1.htm

Constitution of the Russian Federation, 1993, http://www.constitution.ru/en/10003000-01.htm

Copsey, N., 2008, 'Remembrance of Things Past: the Lingering Impact of History on Contemporary Polish-Ukrainian Relations', *Europe-Asia Studies*, Vol. 60, No 4, pp. 531-560, http://www.tandfonline.com/doi/abs/10.1080/09668130801999847

Cornut, J., 2018, 'New Wine into a (Not So) Old Bottle?', Ch. 9 in Bertucci, M., Hayes, J., James, P., (eds.), *Constructivism Reconsidered. Past, Present and Future*, University of Michigan Press

Coser, L., 1977, *Masters of Sociological Thought: Ideas in Historical and Social Context*, New York: Harcourt Brace Jovanovich, 2nd ed.

Cottey, A., 1995, *East-Central Europe after the Cold War: Poland, the Czech Republic, Slovakia and Hungary in Search of Security*, Basingstoke: Palgrave Macmillan

Cowles, M., Caporaso, J., Risse, T., (eds.), 2001, *Transforming Europe: Europeanization and Domestic Change*, Ithaca: Cornell University Press

Cox, M., Kennedy-Pipe, C., 2005, 'The Tragedy of American Diplomacy? Rethinking the Marshall Plan', *Journal of Cold War Studies*, Vol. 7, No 1, pp. 97-134, http://www.mitpressjournals.org/doi/abs/10.1162/1520397053326202

Cragg, A., 1995, 'The Partnership for Peace planning and review process', *NATO Review*, Vol. 43, pp. 23-25, http://www.nato.int/docu/review/1995/9506-5.htm

Crampton, R., 2007, *Bulgaria*, Oxford: Oxford University Press

Czaja, J., 1999, 'Polish Church and European Integration', *Yearbook of Polish European Studies*, pp. 107-120, http://www.ce.uw.edu.pl/pliki/pw/y3-1999_Czaja.pdf

Daalder, I., 2002, 'The United States, Europe, and the Balkans', *Problems of Post-Communism*, Vol. 49, No 1, pp. 3-11, http://www.tandfonline.com/doi/abs/10.1080/10758216.2002.11655965?journalCode=mppc20

Dainov, E., 2013, *Варварите. Управлението на ГЕРБ (2009-2013)*, Millenium, (*The Barbarians. GERB's Government (2009-2013)*, Millenium)

Dal, E., Erşen, E., (eds.), 2019, *Russia in the Changing International System*, Palgrave Macmillan

Daly, J., 2015, *Historians Debate the Rise of the West*, London: Routledge

Dandolov, P., 2012, 'Bulgarian national identity in an era of European integration', *OpenDemocracy*, https://www.opendemocracy.net/philip-dandolov/bulgarian-national-identity-in-era-of-european-integration

D'Anieri, P., 'Constructivist Theory and Ukrainian Foreign Policy', Ch. 3 in Moroney, J., Kuzio, T., Molchanov, M., (eds.), 2002, *Ukrainian Foreign and Security Policy: Theoretical and Comparative Perspectives*, Praeger

Danov, R., 2014, *Българските освобождения*, Ера, (*The Bulgarian Liberations*, Era)

Danova, N., 2013, 'Османското време в българските текстове през XIX и XX век', *Либерален преглед*, ('The Ottoman times in Bulgarian texts in the 19th and 20th centuries', *Liberal Review*), http://librev.com/index.php/discussion-bulgaria-publisher/1903-2013-01-01-18-41-59

Dashtipour, P., 2009, 'Contested identities: using Lacanian psychoanalysis to explore and develop social identity theory', *Annual Review of Critical Psychology*, Vol. 7, pp. 320-337

Davies, C., Rankin, J., 2018, 'Poland's prime minister sacks ministers in move to mend ties with EU', *Guardian*, 9 January 2018, https://www.theguardian.com/world/2018/jan/09/poland-prime-minister-dismisses-senior-cabinet-members-law-and-justice-relations-eu-mateusz-morawiecki

Davies, N., 2005, *God's Playground: A History of Poland: Volume II: 1795 to the Present*, Oxford: Oxford University Press, Rev. ed.

Davignon Report, 1970, *Bulletin of the European Communities*, https://www.cvce.eu/content/publication/1999/4/22/4176efc3-c734-41e5-bb90-d34c4d17bbb5/publishable_en.pdf

Davy, R., (ed.), 2014, *European Detente: A Reappraisal*, Peterborough: FastPrint Publishing, 2nd ed.

Dawisha, K., Parrott, B., (eds.), 1997, *Consolidation of Democracy in East-Central Europe*, Cambridge: Cambridge University Press

Dawson, J., 2014, *Cultures of Democracy in Serbia and Bulgaria: How Ideas Shape Publics*, Surrey: Ashgate Publishing Limited

Declaration on European Identity, 1973, *Bulletin of the European Communities*, https://www.cvce.eu/content/publication/1999/1/1/02798dc9-9c69-4b7d-b2c9-f03a8db7da32/publishable_en.pdf

Declaration on National Accord, 1997, (Декларация за национално съгласие, 1997), http://www.prehod.omda.bg/page.php?tittle=13_%D0%BC%D0%B0%D0%B9_1997&IDMenu=978&IDArticle=3405

Decree 56 on Economic Activity, 1989, (Указ 56 за стопанската дейност, 1989), http://www.omda.bg/public/arhiv/Realii/Ukaz_%2056_teksta.htm

Defence Policy Guidelines of the Federal Republic of Germany, 2011, *Ministry of Defence*, pp. 3-4, http://www.nato.diplo.de/contentblob/3150944/Daten/1318881/VM_deMaiziere_180511_eng_DLD.pdf

Delanty, G., 2012, 'The historical regions of Europe: civilizational backgrounds and multiple routes to modernity', *Historická Sociologie*, No 1-2, pp. 9-24, http://historicalsociology.cz/cele-texty/1-2-2012/delanty.pdf

Delcour, L., Wolczuk, K., 2015, 'Spoiler or facilitator of democratization?: Russia's role in Georgia and Ukraine', *Democratization*, Vol. 22, No 3, pp. 459-478, https://www.tandfonline.com/doi/abs/10.1080/13510347.2014.996135

Demekas, D., Herderschee, J., McHugh, J., Mitra, S., 2002, 'Southeastern Europe after the Kosovo Crisis', *Finance and Development (IMF)*, Vol. 39, No 1, http://www.imf.org/external/pubs/ft/fandd/2002/03/demekas.htm#author

Dempsey, J., 2014, 'The European Union has an opportunity to increase diversification, transparency, and security across the energy sector. It should seize that chance', *Carnegie Europe*, http://carnegieeurope.eu/strategiceurope/?fa=57386

Department of State, 2021, 'Department Press Briefing—February 11, 2021', https://www.state.gov/briefings/department-press-briefing-february-11-2021/#post-217972-POLAND

Desch, M., 2019, *Cult of the Irrelevant. The Waning Influence of Social Science on National Security*, Princeton University Press

Diez, T., 2013, 'Normative power as hegemony', *Cooperation and Conflict*, Vol. 48, No 2, pp. 194-210, http://journals.sagepub.com/doi/abs/10.1177/0010836713485387

Dimitrov, V., 2000, 'Learning to play the game: Bulgaria's relations with multilateral organisations', *Southeast European politics*, Vol. 1, No 2, pp. 101-114, http://www.seep.ceu.hu/volume12/dimitrov.pdf

Dimitrov, D., 2015, *Interview with Rumena Filipova*, 12 November 2015, Sofia

Dimitrova, A., Dragneva, R., 2009, 'Constraining external governance: interdependence with Russia and the CIS as limits to the EU's rule transfer in the Ukraine', *Journal of European Public Policy*, Vol. 16, No 6, pp. 853-872, https://www.tandfonline.com/doi/abs/10.1080/13501760903087894

Dimitrova, A., Rhinard, M., 2005, 'The Power of Norms in the Transposition of EU Directives', *European Integration online papers* (EoP), Vol. 9, No 16, http://eiop.or.at/eiop/pdf/2005-016.pdf

Dimitrova, A., Toshkov, D., 2007, 'The Dynamics of Domestic Coordination of EU Policy in the New Member States: Impossible to Lock In?', *West European Politics*, Vol. 30, No 5, pp. 961-986, http://www.tandfonline.com/doi/abs/10.1080/01402380701617381

Dimitrova, B., 2015, *Interview with Rumena Filipova*, 1 December 2015, Sofia

Dimitrova, G., 2002, 'The limits of Europeanisation: Hegemony and its misuse in the political field of Bulgaria', *Southeast European and Black Sea Studies*, Vol. 2, No 2, pp. 69-92, http://www.tandfonline.com/doi/abs/10.1080/14683850208454691

Dinkov, D., 2003, 'Сателитният синдром в българската външна политика не е преодолян (българският сателит сменя своята орбита)', *Експерт*, Февруари 2003 ('The satellite syndrome in Bulgarian foreign policy has not been overcome (the Bulgarian satellite changes its orbit)', *Expert*, February 2003), http://www.expertbdd.com/index.php?option=com_content&view=article&id=592:-------------&catid=17:--&Itemid=36

Dirlik, A., 1992, 'The Asia-Pacific Idea: Reality and Representation in the Invention of a Regional Structure', *Journal of World History*, Vol. 3, No 1, pp. 55-79, https://www.jstor.org/stable/20078512?seq=1#page_scan_tab_contents

Dobbs, M., 1996, 'Eastern European Countries Lobby for Seat at the NATO Table', *Washington Post*, 22 October 1996, https://www.washingtonpost.com/archive/politics/1996/10/22/eastern-european-countries-lobby-for-seat-at-the-nato-table/c2397abe-5d0b-4544-909a-76e5da434cd6/?utm_term=.0d1716a0cc09

Dobry, M., 2009, 'Critical Processes and Political Fluidity: A Theoretical Appraisal', *International Political Anthropology*, Vol. 2, No 1, pp.73-89, https://www.researchgate.net/publication/283232605_Critical_processes_and_political_fluidity_A_theoretical_appraisal

Doichev, M., 2014, 'Как да станем правова държава', academia.edu, ('How to become a rule of law state', academia.edu), http://www.svobodata.com/page.php?pid=13165&rid=11104&archive=

Donnelly, J., 2000, *Realism and International Relations*, Cambridge: Cambridge University Press

Dragneva, R., Wolczuk, K., 2012, 'Russia, the Eurasian Customs Union and the EU: Cooperation, Stagnation or Rivalry?', *Chatham House Briefing Paper*, August 2012, https://www.chathamhouse.org/sites/files/chathamhouse/public/Research/Russia%20and%20Eurasia/0812bp_dragnevawolczuk.pdf

Duda, A., 2021, 'Central Europe as a Community of Shared Aspirations', *Website of the Republic of Poland*, https://www.gov.pl/web/usa-en/president-andrzej-duda---central-europe-as-a-community-of-shared-aspirations

Dudek, B., 2018, 'Is Poland's new government a PR stunt or an actual change?', *Deutsche Welle*, 9 January 2018, http://www.dw.com/en/is-polands-new-government-a-pr-stunt-or-an-actual-change/a-42087786

Duke, S., 2005, 'The Linchpin COPS: Assessing the Working and Institutional Relations of the Political and Security Committee', *European Institute of Public Administration*, https://www.eipa.eu/wp-content/uploads/2017/11/20070815142132_FC0505e-1.pdf

Dunbabin, J., 1993, 'The League of Nations' Place in the International System', *History*, Vol. 78, No 254, pp. 421-442, https://www.jstor.org/stable/24422221?seq=1#page_scan_tab_contents

Duncan, P., 2007, '"Oligarchs", Business and Russian Foreign Policy: From Yeltsin to Putin', *Economics Working Papers 83*, Centre for the Study of Economic and Social Change in Europe, SSEES, UCL, http://discovery.ucl.ac.uk/12932/

Dunn, K., Neumann, I., 2016, *Undertaking Discourse Analysis for Social Research*, Ann Arbor: University of Michigan Press

Dunn, R., 1998, *Identity Crises: A Social Critique of Postmodernity*, Minneapolis: University of Minnesota Press

Dziubka, K., 2000, 'Emergent democratic citizenship in Poland: a study of changing value patterns', Ch. 4 in Cordell, K., (ed.), *Poland and the European Union*, London: Routledge

Eberhardt, A., 2006, 'Poland's Relations with Russia', *Yearbook of Polish Foreign Policy*, pp. 115-132

Eberhardt, A., 2007, 'Relations between Poland and Russia', *Yearbook of Polish Foreign Policy*, pp. 128-139

Eberhardt, A., 2008, 'Poland's Policy Regarding Russia', *Yearbook of Polish Foreign Policy*, pp. 139-161

Eberhardt, A., 2015, *Interview with Rumena Filipova*, 19 June 2015, Warsaw

Ecktein, H., 1998, *Can Democracy Take Root in Post-Soviet Russia? Explorations in State-Society Relations*, Oxford: Rowman & Littlefield

EEC-Poland agreement on trade and commercial and economic cooperation, 1989, https://www.cvce.eu/content/publication/2008/1/30/66f3229d-8e28-48a4-a5d5-e2332e168008/publishable_en.pdf

Egeberg, M., 1999, 'Transcending Intergovernmentalism? Identity and Role Perceptions of National Officials in EU Decision-Making', *Journal of European Public Policy*, Vol. 6, No 3, pp. 456-474, https://www.tandfonline.com/doi/abs/10.1080/135017699343621

Ekiert, G., 2003, *Capitalism and Democracy in Central and Eastern Europe: Assessing the Legacy of Communist Rule*, Cambridge: Cambridge University Press

Embassy of the Federal Republic of Germany to Bulgaria, 'Хроника на българо-германските отношения 1901-1999 г.', ('Chronology of Bulgarian-German relations 1901-1999'), http://m.sofia.diplo.de/Vertretung/sofia/bg/03/D__und__BG/Chronik__1900-1999.html

Engelbrekt, K., 1994a, 'Bulgaria: Balkan "Oasis of Stability" Facing Drought?', *RFE/Radio Liberty Research Report*, Vol. 3, No 1, pp. 106-111

Engelbrekt, K., 1994b, 'Bulgaria's Political Stalemate', *RFE/Radio Liberty Research Report*, Vol. 3, No 25, pp. 20-26

Engelbrekt, K., 1994c, 'Bulgaria's Evolving Defence Policy', *RFE/Radio Liberty Research Report*, Vol. 3, No 32, pp. 45-51

English, R., 2000, *Russia and the Idea of the West: Gorbachev, Intellectuals and the End of the Cold War*, Columbia University Press

English, R., 2002, 'Power, Ideas, and New Evidence on the Cold War's End: A Reply to Brooks and Wohlforth', *International Security*, Vol. 26, No 4, pp. 70-92, https://www.jstor.org/stable/3092102?seq=1#metadata_info_tab_contents

Epstein, C., 2010, 'Who speaks? Discourse, the subject and the study of identity in international politics', *European Journal of International Relations*, Vol. 17, No 2, pp. 327-350, http://journals.sagepub.com/doi/abs/10.1177/1354066109350055

Epstein, C., 2017, 'The postcolonial perspective. Why we need to decolonize norms', Ch. 1 in Epstein, C., (ed.), *Against International Relations Norms. Postcolonial Perspectives*, Routledge

Epstein, R., 2006, 'Cultivating Consensus and Creating Conflict: International Institutions and the (De)Politicization of Economic Policy in Postcommunist Europe', *Comparative Political Studies*, Vol. 39, No 8, pp. 1019-1042, http://journals.sagepub.com/doi/10.1177/0010414005279259

Epstein, R., Sedelmeier, U., 2008, 'Beyond conditionality: international institutions in post-communist Europe after enlargement', *Journal of European Public Policy*, Vol. 15, Issue 6, pp. 795-805, http://www.tandfonline.com/doi/abs/10.1080/13501760802196465

Erb, S., 2003, *German Foreign Policy: Navigating a New Era*, London: L. Rienner

Eun, YS., 2016, 'To what extent is post-positivism "practised" in International Relations? Evidence from China and the USA', *International Political Science Review*, Vol. 38, No 5, pp. 593-607, https://journals.sagepub.com/doi/abs/10.1177/0192512116642222

Europe Agreement establishing an association between the European Communities and their Member States, of the one part, and the Republic of Bulgaria, of the other part, 1994, http://ec.europa.eu/world/agreements/prepareCreateTreatiesWorkspace/treatiesGeneralData.do?step=0&redirect=true&treatyId=741

Europe Agreement with Poland, 1991, http://wits.worldbank.org/GPTAD/PDF/archive/EC-Poland.pdf

European Commission, 1999, 1999 Regular Report from the Commission on Bulgaria's Progress towards Accession, https://www.esiweb.org/pdf/bulgaria_EC-Regular%20Report%20Bulgaria_en_1999.pdf

European Commission, 2019, 'Strengthening the rule of law within the Union. A blueprint for action', Communication from the Commission to the European Parliament, the European Council, the Council, the European Economic and Social Committee and the Committee of the Regions, https://eur-lex.europa.eu/legal-content/EN/TXT/PDF/?uri=CELEX:52019DC0343&from=EN

BIBLIOGRAPHY 433

European Commission, 2020a, 'On the European Democracy Action Plan', Communication from the Commission to the European Parliament, the Council, the European Economic and Social Committee and the Committee of the Regions, p.2, https://eur-lex.europa.eu/legal-content/EN/TXT/PDF/?uri=CELEX:52020DC0790&from=EN

European Commission, 2020b, 'Commission Implementing Regulation (EU) 2020/426 of 19 March 2020 amending Implementing Regulation (EU) 2020/402 making the exportation of certain products subject to the production of an export authorisation', *Official Journal of the European Union*, Vol. 63, L 84 I/1, https://eur-lex.europa.eu/eli/reg_impl/2020/426/oj

European Commission, 2020c, Proposal for a Regulation of the European Parliament and of the Council on a Single Market For Digital Services (Digital Services Act) and Amending Directive 2000/31/EC, https://eur-lex.europa.eu/legal-content/EN/TXT/PDF/?uri=CELEX:52020PC0825&from=en

European Convention on Human Rights, amended in 2010, *European Court of Human Rights, Council of Europe*, http://www.echr.coe.int/Documents/Convention_ENG.pdf

European Council Meeting in Essen, Presidency Conclusions, 1994, http://www.europarl.europa.eu/summits/ess1_en.htm

European Council Summit in Copenhagen, Presidency Conclusions, 1993, https://www.consilium.europa.eu/media/21225/72921.pdf

European Council Summit in Edinburgh, Presidency Conclusions, 1992, https://www.consilium.europa.eu/media/20492/1992_december_-_edinburgh__eng_.pdf

European Council Summit in Helsinki, Presidency Conclusions, 1999, http://www.europarl.europa.eu/summits/hel1_en.htm

European Council Summit in Luxembourg, Presidency Conclusions, 1997, http://www.europarl.europa.eu/summits/lux1_en.htm

European Council Summit in Madrid, Presidency Conclusions, 1995, http://www.europarl.europa.eu/summits/mad1_en.htm

European Council Summit in Strasbourg, Presidency Conclusions, 1989, https://www.consilium.europa.eu/media/20580/1989_december_-_strasbourg__eng_.pdf

European Parliament, 2020a, 'Polish de facto ban on abortion puts women's lives at risk, says Parliament', *Press Releases*, 26 November 2020, https://www.europarl.europa.eu/news/en/press-room/20201120IPR92132/polish-de-facto-ban-on-abortion-puts-women-s-lives-at-risk-says-parliament

European Parliament, 2020b, 'European Parliament resolution on the rule of law and fundamental rights in Bulgaria', https://www.europarl.europa.eu/doceo/document/B-9-2020-0309_EN.html

European Parliament Resolution of 8 May 2008 on the Annual Report on Human Rights in the World 2007 and the European Union's Policy on the Matter, 2008, *European Parliament*, pp. 5-11, http://www.europarl.europa.eu/sides/getDoc.do?pubRef=-//EP//TEXT+TA+P6-TA-2008-0193+0+DOC+XML+V0//EN

European Parliament Resolution of 22 October 2009 on Democracy Building in the EU's External Relations, 2009, *European Parliament*, pp. 3-7, http://www.europarl.europa.eu/document/activities/cont/200910/20091030ATT63491/20091030ATT63491EN.pdf

Evans, A., 2008, 'Putin's Legacy and Russia's Identity', *Europe-Asia Studies*, Vol. 60, No 6, pp. 899-912, https://www.jstor.org/stable/20451565?seq=1#page_scan_tab_contents

Eyal, G., Szelényi, I., Townsley, E., 2000, *Making Capitalism without Capitalists: The New Ruling Elites in Eastern Europe*, London: Verso, New ed.

Faktor, 2014, 'Плевнелиев: Русия е агресивна държава, а Путин прави политика от 19-и век', *Фактор*, 3 октомври 2014, ('Plevneliev: Russia is an aggressive state, and Putin conducts a 19th century style politics', 3 October 2014), http://www.faktor.bg/bg/articles/novini/balgariya/plevneliev-rusiya-e-agresivna-darzhava-a-putin-pravi-politika-ot-19-i-vek-29683

Fawcett, L., Hurrell, A., (eds.), 1995, *Regionalism in World Politics*, Oxford: Oxford University Press

Fawn, R., (ed.), 2003, *Ideology and National Identity in Post-Communist Foreign Policies*, London: Frank Cass

Fearon, J., 1999, 'What is identity (as we now use the word)?', *Department of Political Science, Stanford University*, http://www.stanford.edu/~jfearon/papers/iden1v2.pdf accessed 20 February 2013

Featherstone, K., Radaelli, C., (eds.), 2003, *Politics of Europeanization*, Oxford: Oxford University Press

Fedorowicz, K., 2007, 'National Identity and National Interest in Polish Eastern Policy, 1989-2004', *Nationalities Papers: The Journal of Nationalism and Ethnicity*, Vol. 35, No 3, pp. 537-553, http://www.tandfonline.com/doi/abs/10.1080/00905990701368761

Feldman, L., 1999, 'The Principle and Practice of "Reconciliation" in German Foreign Policy: Relations with France, Israel, Poland and the Czech Republic', *International Affairs*, Vol. 75, No 2, pp. 333-356, http://onlinelibrary.wiley.com/doi/10.1111/1468-2346.00075/abstract

Fenenko, A., 2014, *Interview with Rumena Filipova*, 23 June 2014, Moscow

Filipova, R., 2015, 'Bulgaria in the International System: Divided Loyalties?' in Anastasakis, O., et al (eds.), *Critical juncture? Bulgaria after the snap poll in October 2014*, South East European Studies at Oxford

Filipova, R., 2020, *The Shrinking Space for Media Freedom in Southeast Europe in the Midst of COVID-19 Pandemic and State of Emergency*, Sofia: Center for the Study of Democracy/Konrad-Adenauer-Stiftung Media Programme South East Europe, https://www.kas.de/documents/281902/281951/KAS+CSD+Book+on+Media+Freedom+in+the+Midst+of+Covid-19+Pandemic.pdf/8ab73bd6-a65f-4ccf-5cce-826e61c7b092?version=1.1&t=1600864436285

Filipova, R., 2021a, 'Bulgaria' in *Tackling Kremlin's Media Capture in Southeast Europe. Shared Patterns, Specific Vulnerabilities and Responses to Russian Disinformation*, Sofia: Center for the Study of Democracy, p.63, https://globalanalytics-bg.org/wp-content/uploads/2021/08/Tacklin-Kremlins-Media-Capture.pdf

Filipova, R., 2021b, 'Enter China: boosting the authoritarian challenge', in *Tackling Kremlin's Media Capture in Southeast Europe. Shared Patterns, Specific Vulnerabilities and Responses to Russian Disinformation*, Sofia: Center for the Study of Democracy, pp. 49-53, https://globalanalytics-bg.org/wp-content/uploads/2021/08/Tacklin-Kremlins-Media-Capture.pdf

Filipova, R., 2021c, 'Russia's Media Capture Power Mix in Southeast Europe', in *Tackling Kremlin's Media Capture in Southeast Europe. Shared Patterns, Specific Vulnerabilities and Responses to Russian Disinformation*, Sofia: Center for the Study of Democracy, https://globalanalytics-bg.org/wp-content/uploads/2021/08/Tacklin-Kremlins-Media-Capture.pdf

Filipova, R., Stefanov, R., 2020, 'Authoritarian Shadows in the European Union: Bulgarian MEPs' Voting Patterns', *Center for the Study of Democracy*, Working Paper, November 2020, https://www.politicalcapital.hu/pc-admin/source/documents/bulgarian_meps_voting_patterns.pdf

Filipova, R., Stefanov, R., 2021a, 'The Anti-Democratic Turn: Key Trends', *Countering Kremlin's Media Influence in Europe. Patterns of Anti-Democratic Messaging, Disinformation Response, and Resilience Assets*, Sofia: Center for the Study of Democracy, p.21, https://globalanalytics-bg.org/wp-content/uploads/2021/08/Countering-Kremlins-Media-Influence-in-Europe.pdf

Filipova, R., Stefanov, R., 2021b, 'Patterns of Russian Anti-Democratic Disinformation', *Countering Kremlin's Media Influence in Europe. Patterns of Anti-Democratic Messaging, Disinformation Response, and Resilience Assets*, Sofia: Center for the Study of Democracy, p. 29-32, https://globalanalytics-bg.org/wp-content/uploads/2021/08/Countering-Kremlins-Media-Influence-in-Europe.pdf

Filipova, R., Stefanov, R, 2021c, 'The Twin Authoritarian Challenge in the Western Balkans', *Europe's Edge*, Center for European Policy Analysis, https://cepa.org/the-twin-authoritarian-challenge-in-the-western-balkans/

Filipova, R., Yalamov, T., 2021, 'Foreword' in Dimova, G., 2021, *Political Uncertainty — A Comparative Exploration*, Ibidem-Verlag

Finnemore, M., Sikkink, K., 1998, 'International Norm Dynamics and Political Change', *International Organization*, Vol. 54, No 4, pp. 887-917, https://www.jstor.org/stable/2601361?seq=1#page_scan_tab_contents

Finnemore, M., Sikkink, K., 2001, 'Taking Stock: The Constructivist Research Program in International Relations and Comparative Politics', *Annual Review of Political Science*, Vol. 4, pp. 391-416, http://www.annualreviews.org/doi/abs/10.1146/annurev.polisci.4.1.391

Fischer, B., 2007, 'The Vilification and Vindication of Colonel Kuklinski. Entangled in History', *CIA Studies in Intelligence*, https://www.cia.gov/library/center-for-the-study-of-intelligence/csi-publications/csi-studies/studies/summer00/art03.html

Fish, S., 2005, *Democracy Derailed in Russia: The Failure of Open Politics*, Cambridge: Cambridge University Press

Fotyga, A., 2008, 'Government Information on Polish Foreign Policy in 2007', *Yearbook of Polish Foreign Policy*, pp. 11-38

Foye, S., 1994, 'Civilian and Military Leaders in Russia's "New" Political Arena', *RFE/Radio Liberty Report*, Vol. 3, No 15, pp. 1-7

Framework Convention for the Protection of National Minorities and Explanatory Report, 1995, *Council of Europe*, http://www.ecml.at/Portals/1/documents/CoE-documents/FCNM_ExplanReport_en.doc.pdf

Freire, M., Heller, R., 2018, 'Russia's Power Politics in Ukraine and Syria: Status-seeking between Identity, Opportunity and Costs', *Europe-Asia Studies*, Vol. 70, No 8, pp. 1185-1212, https://doi.org/10.1080/09668136.2018.1521914

Freire, M., Kanet, R., (eds.), 2012, *Russia and Its Near Neighbours*, New York: Palgrave Macmillan

French White Paper—Defence and National Security, 2013, pp. 25-26, https://www.defense.gouv.fr/english/dgris/defence-policy/white-paper-2013/white-paper-2013

Freudenstein, R., 2002, 'The Future of Polish-German Relations', *Polish Foreign Affairs Digest*, Vol. 2, No 1, pp. 175-181

Fukuyama, F., 1989, 'End of History?', *National Interest*, Summer, https://ps321.community.uaf.edu/files/2012/10/Fukuyama-End-of-history-article.pdf

Fukuyama, F., 1992, *End of History and the Last Man*, London: Hamish Hamilton

Fukuyama, F., 2018a, *Identity. The Demand for Dignity and the Politics of Resentment*, Farrar, Straus and Giroux

Fukuyama, F., 2018b, 'Against Identity Politics. The New Tribalism and the Crisis of Democracy', *Foreign Affairs*, September/October, https://www.foreignaffairs.com/articles/americas/2018-08-14/against-identity-politics-tribalism-francis-fukuyama

Fuller, E., 1994, 'The Karabakh Mediation Process: Grachev versus the CSCE?', *RFE/Radio Liberty Research Report*, Vol. 3, No 23, pp. 13-18

Gadamer, HG., 2013, *Truth and Method*, London: Bloomsbury Academic

Gebert, K., 2015, *Interview with Rumena Filipova*, 30 June 2015, Warsaw

Geddes, B., 2003, *Paradigms and sand castles: theory building and research design in comparative politics*, Ann Arbor: University of Michigan Press

Gellner, E., 2006, *Nations and Nationalism*, Oxford: Wiley-Blackwell, 2nd ed.

Gennep, A., 1960, *Rites of Passage*, London: Routledge

George, A., Bennett, A., 2005, *Case Studies and Theory Development in the Social Sciences*, Cambridge: MIT Press

Георгиев, Н., 2011, Политика на сигурност на Република България в началото на XXI век, Нов български унивеситет, София, (*Security policy of the Republic of Bulgaria at the beginning of the 21st century*, New Bulgarian University, Sofia)

Georgiev, H., 2015, *Interview with Rumena Filipova*, 10 November 2015, Sofia

Georgiev, Z., 2015, *Interview with Rumena Filipova*, 30 November 2015, Sofia

Георгиева, С., 1996, 'С победата си Елцин прегази и Виденов, и 'левия' му модел', *Капитал*, 8 юли 1996, ('Yeltsin's victory crushed Videnov and his 'leftist' model', *Capital*, 8 July 1996), https://www.capital.bg/politika_i_ikonomika/1996/07/08/1021285_s_pobedata_si_elcin_pregazi_i_videnov_i_leviia_mu_model/

Geremek, B., 1998, 'Continuation and New Dynamism', *Yearbook of Polish Foreign Policy*, pp. 9-13

Geremek, B., 1999, 'Freedom and Solidarity: Polish Message to Europe', *Yearbook of Polish Foreign Policy*, pp. 9-15

Giddens, A., 1984, *Constitution of Society: Outline of the Theory of Structuration*, Cambridge: Polity Press

Giles, K., 2018, *Moscow Rules: What Drives Russia to Confront the West*, Brookings Institution

Gocheva, R., Boncheva, Y., 2012, 'Борисов замени АЕЦ "Белене" с три нови енергийни проекта', *Сега*, 29 март 2012, ('Borissov replaced the Belene nuclear power plant with three new energy projects', *Sega*, 29 March 2012), http://www.segabg.com/article.php?id=595106

Goldberg, C., 1992, 'Lawmakers Force Yeltsin Aide to Defend Russia's Policy toward US', *Los Angeles Times*, 23 October 1992, http://articles.latimes.com/1992-10-23/news/mn-602_1_foreign-policy

Górka-Winter, B., Posel-Częścik, E., 2002, 'New Directions of Polish-German Co-Operation in the Area of Security in the Nineties', *Polish Foreign Affairs Digest*, Vol. 2, No 1, pp. 181-191

Gornostaev, D., 1997, 'Ельцин приехал в Страсбург как европеец', *Независимая газета*, 10 октября 1997, ('Yeltsin arrived in Strasbourg as a European', *Nezavisimaya Gazeta*, 10 October 1997), https://www.uni-potsdam.de/u/slavistik/zarchiv/1097wk/k191-14.htm

Gorodetsky, G., (ed.), 2003, *Russia between East and West: Russian Foreign Policy on the Threshold of the Twenty-First Century*, London: Frank Cass

Gorskii, V., 2001, 'Problems and Prospects of NATO-Russia Relationship: the Russian Debate', *NATO Euro-Atlantic Partnership Council Fellowships Programme*, http://www.nato.int/acad/fellow/99-01/gorskii.pdf

Gospodinova, V., 2004, 'Разцеплението на СДС става неизбежно', *Капитал*, 24 януари 2004, ('The split in the UDF becomes inevitable', *Capital*, 24 January 2004), http://www.capital.bg/politika_i_ikonomika/bulgaria/2004/01/24/224811_razceplenieto_na_sds_stava_neizbejno/

Govedaritsa, S., 2020, 'Протестите срещу Борисов: „ЕС, сляп ли си или го харесваш?"', *Deutsche Welle Bulgaria*, 26 септември 2020, ('Protests against Borissov: EU, are you blind or do you like him?', *Deutsche Welle Bulgaria*, 26 September 2020)

Gower, J., 2000, 'Russia and the European Union', Ch. 4 in Webber, M., *Russia and Europe: Conflict or Cooperation?*, Basingstoke: Palgrave Macmillan

Gower, J., Timmins, G., (eds.), 2007, *Russia and Europe in the Twenty-First Century: An Uneasy Partnership*, London: Anthem

Grabbe, H., 2001, 'How does Europeanisation affect CEE governance? Conditionality, diffusion and diversity', *Journal of European Public Policy*, Vol. 8, No 6, pp. 1013-1031, http://www.tandfonline.com/doi/abs/10.1080/13501760110098323

Graney, K., 2019, *Russia, the Former Soviet Republics, and Europe Since 1989. Transformation and Tragedy*, Oxford University Press

Greenfeld, L., 1992, *Nationalism: Five Roads to Modernity*, Cambridge: Harvard University Press

Greenhouse, S., 1989, '"Shock Therapy" for Poland: Jolt Might Be Too Damaging', *New York Times*, 26 December 1989, http://www.nytimes.com/1989/12/26/business/shock-therapy-for-poland-jolt-might-be-too-damaging.html

Groblewski, K., 1992, 'Fission and Fusion in Polish Politics', *East European Reporter*, Vol. 5, No 4, p. 12

Gromyko, A., 2014, *Interview with Rumena Filipova*, 28 July 2014, Moscow

Gudkov, L., 2010, 'Время и история в сознании россиян (часть II)', *Вестник общественного мнения*, Т. 104, No 2, с. 13-61, ('Time and history in the consciousness of the Russians (part II)', *Public opinion newsletter*, Vol. 104, No 2, pp. 13-61), http://ecsocman.hse.ru/text/33516537/

Gudkov, L., 2014, *Interview with Rumena Filipova*, 25 June 2014, Moscow

Gudkov, L., 2014, 'Имморализм постсоветского общества и европейские ценности', *Лекция*, ('The immorality of post-Soviet society and European values', *Lecture*), http://n-europe.eu/eurocafe/lecture/2014/05/21/immoralizm_postsovetskogo_obshchestva_i_evropeiskie_tsennosti?page=8

Gunitsky, S., Tsygankov, A., 2018, 'The Wilsonian Bias in the Study of Russian Foreign Policy', *Problems of Post-Communism*, Vol. 65, No 6, pp. 385-393, https://doi.org/10.1080/10758216.2018.1468270

Gwiazda, A., 2002, 'Europeanisation in Candidate Countries from Central and Eastern Europe', *paper prepared for the EPIC workshop in Florence, EUI, 19-22 September 2002*, https://pdfs.semanticscholar.org/515d/feee38021026e5559654cccedd41a526fe0c.pdf

Haas, M., 2011, 'Russia's Military Reforms. Victory after Twenty Years of Failure?', *Clingendael Paper No 5*, http://www.clingendael.nl/sites/default/files/20111129_clingendaelpaper_mdehaas.pdf

Habermas, J., translated by Lenhardt, C., and Weber-Nicholsen, S., 1992, *Moral Consciousness and Communicative Action*, Polity

Hagström, L., Gustafsson, K., 2015, 'Japan and identity change: why it matters in International Relations', *Pacific Review*, Vol. 28, No 1, pp. 1-22, http://www.tandfonline.com/doi/abs/10.1080/09512748.201 4.969298

Hale, H., Laruelle, M., 2020, 'Rethinking Civilizational Identity from the Bottom Up: A Case Study of Russia and a Research Agenda', *Nationalities Papers*, Vol. 48, No 3, pp. 585-602, https://doi.org/10.1 017/nps.2019.125

Hall, R., 1999, *National Collective Identity: Social Constructs and International Systems*, New York: Columbia University Press

Hall, T., 2013, 'Affected Actors: Theorizing Affective Politics after 9/11', *Department of Politics and International Relations, International Relations Colloquium, University of Oxford*

Harnisch, S., Frank, C., Maull, H., (eds.), 2011, *Role Theory in International Relations: Approaches and Analyses*, London: Routledge

Haukkala, H., 2008a, 'A Norm-Maker or a Norm-Taker? The Changing Normative Parameters of Russia's Place in Europe', Ch. 2 in Hopf, T., (ed.), *Russia's European Choice*, Basingstoke: Palgrave Macmillan

Haukkala, H., 2008b 'The European Union as a Regional Normative Hegemon: The Case of European Neighbourhood Policy', *Europe-Asia Studies*, Vol. 60, No 9, pp. 1601-1622, http://www.tandfonline.com/doi/abs/10.1080/09668130802362342

Helsinki Document: the Challenges of Change, 1992, *CSCE Summit*, http://www.osce.org/mc/39530?download=true

Helsinki Final Act, 1975, *CSCE*, http://www.osce.org/helsinki-final-act?download=true

Herrmann, R., 2013, 'Perceptions and Image Theory in International Relations', Ch. 11 in Sears, D., Huddy, L., Levy, J., (eds.), *Oxford Handbook of Political Psychology*, New York: Oxford University Press, 2nd ed.

Hermanns, H., 2013, 'National Role Conceptions in the 'Global Korea' Foreign Policy Strategy', *The Korean Journal of International Studies*, Vol. 11, No 1, pp. 55-82, http://www.kaisnet.or.kr/resource/down/11_1_03.pdf

Higley, J., Pakulski, J., Wesołowski, W., (eds.), 1998, *Postcommunist Elites and Democracy in Eastern Europe*, Basingstoke: Macmillan

Hill, C., 2002, 'CFSP: Conventions, constitutions and consequentiality', *The International Spectator. Italian Journal of International Affairs*, Vol. 37, No 4, pp. 75-89, https://www.tandfonline.com/doi/abs/10.1080/03 932720208457003?journalCode=rspe20

Hill, C., Wallace, W., 1996, 'Introduction: actors and actions' in Hill, C., (ed.), *Actors in Europe's Foreign Policy*, London: Routledge

Hobsbawm, E., 2012, *Nations and Nationalism since 1780: Programme, Myth, Reality*, New York: Cambridge University Press, 2nd ed., 18th printing

Hoffman, D., 2011, *The Oligarchs: Wealth and Power in the New Russia*, New York: Public Affairs, Rev. and updated

Hogg, M., 2006, 'Social Identity Theory', Ch. 6 in Burke, P., (ed.), *Contemporary Social Psychological Theories*, Stanford: Stanford Social Sciences

Hogg, M., Terry, D., White, K., 1995, 'A Tale of Two Theories: A Critical Comparison of Identity Theory with Social Identity Theory', *Social Psychology Quarterly*, Vol. 58, No 4, pp. 255-269, https://www.jstor.org/stable/2787127?seq=1#page_scan_tab_contents

Hogg, M., Vaughan, G., 2007, *Social Psychology*, Harlow: Prentice Hall, 5th ed.

Holmes, K., Cohen, A., Weinberger, C., Woolsey, J., 1999, 'Who Lost Russia?', *Heritage Foundation*, 8 January 1999, http://www.heritage.org/europe/report/who-lost-russia

Holsti, K., 1970, 'National Role Conceptions in the Study of Foreign Policy', *International Studies Quarterly*, Vol. 14, No 3, pp. 233-309, https://www.jstor.org/stable/pdf/3013584.pdf?seq=1#page_scan_tab_contents

Honneth, A., 1995, *Struggle for Recognition: The Moral Grammar of Social Conflicts*, Cambridge: Polity

Hooghe, L., 2005, 'Several Roads Lead to International Norms, but Few Via International Socialisation: A Case Study of the European Commission', *International Organization*, Vol. 59, No 4, pp. 861-898, https://www.cambridge.org/core/journals/international-organization/article/several-roads-lead-to-international-norms-but-few-via-international-socialization-a-case-study-of-the-european-commission/6D46B173C967C19F4C26AFB2B84B4A89

Hopf, T., 1998, 'The Promise of Constructivism in International Relations Theory', *International Security*, Vol. 23, No 1, pp. 171-200, https://www.jstor.org/stable/2539267?seq=1#page_scan_tab_contents

Hopf, T., 2002, *Social Construction of International Politics: Identities and Foreign Policies, Moscow, 1955 and 1999*, Ithaca: Cornell University Press

Hopf, T., (ed.), 2008, *Russia's European Choice*, Basingstoke: Palgrave Macmillan

Houghton, D., 2006, 'Reinvigorating the Study of Foreign Policy Decision Making: Toward a Constructivist Approach', *Foreign Policy Analysis*, Vol. 3. No 1, pp. 24-45, https://onlinelibrary.wiley.com/doi/full/10.1111/j.1743-8594.2007.00040.x

Howard, J., 2000, 'Social Psychology of Identities', *Annual Review of Sociology*, Vol. 26, pp. 367-393, https://www.jstor.org/stable/223449?seq=1#page_scan_tab_contents

Howorth, J., 2010, 'The Political and Security Committee: a case study in 'supranational inter-governmentalism'', *Les cahiers Européens*, No 2, https://www.ies.be/files/documents/JMCdepository/Howorth,%20Jolyon,%20The%20Political%20and%20Security%20Committee,%20A%20Case%20Study%20in%20%E2%80%98Supranational%20Intergovernmentalism%E2%80%99.pdf

Hristov, J., 2014, 'Как се опитаха да забранят ДПС през 91-ва и не успяха', *OFFNews.bg*, 18 октомври 2014, ('How they tried to ban the MRF in 1991 but could not do it', *OFFNews.bg*, 18 October 2014), https://offnews.bg/razsledvane/kak-se-opitaha-da-zabraniat-dps-prez-91-va-i-ne-uspiaha-405116.html

Hube, N., Verzichelli, L., 'Ready to run Europe? Perspectives of a supranational career among EU national elites', Ch. 3 in Best, H., Lengyel, G., Verzichelli, L., (eds.), 2012, *The Europe of Elites: A Study into the Europeanness of Europe's Political and Economic Elites*, Oxford: Oxford University Press

Hübner, D., 1998, 'Activities of the Committee for European Integration', *Yearbook of Polish Foreign Policy*, pp. 224-236

Hübner, D., 1999, 'The International Activity of the President of the Republic of Poland', *Yearbook of Polish Foreign Policy*, pp. 219-230

Huddy, L., 2001, 'From Social to Political Identity: A Critical Examination of Social Identity Theory', *Political Psychology*, Vol. 22, No 1, pp. 127-156, https://www.jstor.org/stable/3791909?seq=1#page_scan_tab_contents

Huddy, L., 2013, 'From Group Identity to Political Cohesion and Commitment', Ch. 23 in Sears, D., Huddy, L., Levy, J., (eds.), *Oxford Handbook of Political Psychology*, New York: Oxford University Press, 2nd ed.

Huddy, L., Sears, D., Levy, J., 2013, 'Introduction: Theoretical Foundations of Political Psychology', Ch. 1 in Sears, D., Huddy, L., Levy, J., (eds.), *Oxford Handbook of Political Psychology*, New York: Oxford University Press, 2nd ed.

Hudson, V., 2005, 'Foreign Policy Analysis: Actor-Specific Theory and the Ground of International Relations', *Foreign Policy Analysis*, Vol. 1, No 1, pp. 1-30, https://edisciplinas.usp.br/pluginfile.php/331946/mod_resource/content/1/Hudson-2005-Foreign_Policy_Analysis.pdf

Hughes, J., Sasse, G., Gordon, C., 2004, *Europeanization and Regionalization in the EU's Enlargement to Central and Eastern Europe. The Myth of Conditionality*, Basingstoke: Palgrave Macmillan

Hunt, M., 2009, *Ideology and US Foreign Policy*, New Haven: Yale University Press

Hunter, R., Ryan, L., 1998, *From Autarchy to Market: Polish Economics and Politics, 1945-1995*, London: Praeger

Hurd, I., 2008, 'Constructivism', Ch. 17 in Reus-Smit, C., Snidal, D., (eds.), *Oxford Handbook of International Relations*, Oxford: Oxford University Press

Hymans, J., 2006, *The Psychology of Nuclear Proliferation: Identity, Emotions, and Foreign Policy*, Cambridge: Cambridge University Press

Ifantis, K., Triantaphyllou, D., Kotelis, A., 2015, 'National Role and Foreign Policy: An Exploratory Study of Greek Elites' Perceptions towards Turkey', *GreeSE Paper No 94 Hellenic Observatory Papers on Greece and Southeast Europe*, http://www.lse.ac.uk/europeanInstitute/research/hellenicObservatory/CMS%20pdf/Publications/GreeSE/GreeSE-94.pdf

Ignatenko, A., 1994, 'Геополитический ледоход—не лучшая пора для российской экономики', *Коммерсант*, 17 сентября 1994, ('A geopolitical iceberg—not a good season for the Russian economy', *Kommersant*, 17 September 1994), http://www.kommersant.ru/doc/90004/print

Inayatullah, I., Blaney, D., 1996, 'Knowing Encounters: Beyond Parochialism in IR Theory', Ch. 4 in Lapid, Y., Kratochwil, F., (eds.), *Return of Culture and Identity in IR Theory*, Boulder: Lynne Rienner Publishers Inc.

Ingrao, C., 1996, 'Ten Untaught Lessons about Central Europe: An Historical Perspective', *Center for Austrian Studies Working Paper 96-3*, Minneapolis: University of Minnesota

Ish-Shalom, P., 2019, 'Third generation Constructivism: between tactics and strategy', Ch. 1 in Steele, B., Gould, H., Kessler, O., (eds.), *Tactical Constructivism, Method, and International Relations*, Routledge

Ivanov, I., 2021, 'Why Is Europe Hostile Towards Russia?', *Russian International Affairs Council*, https://russiancouncil.ru/en/analytics-and-comments/analytics/why-is-europe-hostile-towards-russia/

Ivanov, L., Atanassova, M., 2002, 'Bulgaria in the international security organizations', in Minchev, O., Ratchev, V., Lessenski, M., (eds.), *Bulgaria for NATO*, Institute for Regional and International Studies, Sofia, http://www.iris-bg.org/fls/intro.pdf

Ivanov, T., 2000, 'Borderline milestones for Bulgarian defence policy modernisation', *Workshop on Defence Policy Modernisation and Security on the Balkans, University of National and World Economy*, Sofia, 24-25 May 2000

Izvestiya, 2014, 'Минкультуры изложило "Основы государственной культурной политики"', *Известия*, 10 апреля 2014, ('The Ministry of Culture put forward "The bases of state cultural policies"', 10 April 2014), http://izvestia.ru/news/569016

Jackson, N., 2003, *Russian Foreign Policy and the CIS: Theories, Debates and Actions*, New York: Routledge

Jackson, P., 2011, 'French Security and a British "Continental Commitment" after the First World War: a Reassessment', *The English Historical Review*, Vol. 126, No 519, pp. 345-385, https://www.jstor.org/stable/41238643?seq=1#page_scan_tab_contents

Jacobson, J., 1972, *Locarno Diplomacy: Germany and the West, 1925-1929*, Princeton: Princeton University Press

Jahn, E., 2009, 'The state-transformation in the East of Europe. "Second national rebirth". Nationalism, national movements, and the formation of nation-states in late and post-communist Europe since 1985', in Jahn, E., (ed.), *Nationalism in Late and Post-Communist Europe: Volume 1 — The Failed Nationalism of the Multinational and Partial National States*, Baden-Baden: Nomos

Jenkins, R., 2008, *Social Identity*, London: Routledge, 3rd ed.

Jesień, L., 2015, *Interview with Rumena Filipova*, 15 June 2015, Warsaw

Johnson, D., Tierney, D., 2014, 'Bad World: Negativity Bias and the Cycle of War', *Department of Politics and International Relations, International Relations Colloquium, University of Oxford*

Johnson, J., 2006, 'Two-track diffusion and central bank embeddedness: the politics of Euro adoption in Hungary and the Czech Republic', *Review of International Political Economy*, Vol. 13, No 3, pp. 361-386, https://www.jstor.org/stable/25124079?seq=1#page_scan_tab_contents

Johnston, A., 2001, 'Treating International Institutions as Social Environments', *International Studies Quarterly*, Vol. 45, No 4, pp. 487-515, https://www.jstor.org/stable/3096058?seq=1#page_scan_tab_contents

Jones, S., 2003, 'The role of cultural paradigms in Georgian foreign policy', *Journal of Communist Studies and Transition Politics*, Vol. 19, No 3, pp. 83-110, https://www.tandfonline.com/doi/abs/10.1080/13523270300660019

Juncos, A., Pomorska, K., 2006, 'Playing the Brussels game: strategic socialisation in the CFSP Council working groups', *European Integration online Papers (EIoP)*, Vol. 10, No 11, http://eiop.or.at/eiop/pdf/2006-011.pdf

Kakachia, K., 2014, 'Is Georgia's Orthodox Church an Obstacle to European Values?', *Ponars Eurasia*, http://www.ponarseurasia.org/memo/georgia%E2%80%99s-orthodox-church-obstacle-european-values

Kalashnikova, N., 1994, 'Большие маневры', *Коммерсант*, 17 декабря 1994, ('Big moves', *Kommersant*, 17 December 1994), http://kommersant.ru/doc/98069

Kalberg, S., 1980, 'Max Weber's Types of Rationality: Cornerstones for the Analysis of Rationalization Processes in History', *American Journal of Sociology*, Vol. 85, No. 5, pp. 1145-1179, https://www.jstor.org/stable/2778894?seq=1#page_scan_tab_contents

Kaldor, M., Vejvoda, I., (eds.), 1999, *Democratization in Central and Eastern Europe*, New York: Pinter

Kaminska, J., 2007, 'New EU members and the CFSP: Europeanisation of the Polish foreign policy', *Political Perspectives EPRU*, No 2, http://www.politicalperspectives.org.uk/wp-content/uploads/2010/08/EPRU-2007-S1-02.pdf

Kaminska, J., 2014, *Poland and EU Enlargement: Foreign Policy in Transformation*, New York: Palgrave Macmillan

Kaplan, R., 1994, *Balkan Ghosts: A Journey through History*, London: Papermac

Karaganov, S., 'Russia's Uneasy Dance with the West', *BBC World Lectures*, http://www.bbc.co.uk/worldservice/people/features/world_lectures/karag_lect.shtml

Kasčiūnas, L., Ivanauskas, V., Keršanskas, V., Kojala, L., 2014, *Eastern Partnership in a Changed Security Environment: New Incentives for Reform*, Eastern Europe Studies Centre, http://www.eesc.lt/uploads/news/id804/EaP%20In%20A%20Changed%20Security%20Environment%20ENG.pdf

Katsikas, S., 2010a, 'Accession into the Euro-Atlantic Institutions: Effects on Bulgaria's Balkan Policy(ies)', Ch. 8 in Katsikas, S., (ed.), *Bulgaria and Europe: Shifting Identities*, London: Anthem Press

Katsikas, S., (ed.), 2010b, *Bulgaria and Europe: Shifting Identities*, London: Anthem Press

Katsikas, S., 2012, *Negotiating Diplomacy in the New Europe. Foreign Policy in Post-Communist Bulgaria*, London: I. B. Tauris

Katsikas, S., Siani-Davies, P., 2010, 'The Europeanization of Bulgarian Society: A Long-Lasting Political Project', Introduction in Katsikas, S., (ed.), *Bulgaria and Europe: Shifting Identities*, London: Anthem Press

Katzenstein, P., 1996, *Culture of National Security: Norms and Identity in World Politics*, New York: Columbia University Press

Katzenstein, P., 2005, *A World of Regions: Asia and Europe in the American Imperium*, Ithaca: Cornell University Press

Kavalski, E., 2003, 'Theorising Euro-Atlantic Socialisation: Inferences for a Stable Balkan Order', *The Interdisciplinary Journal of International Studies*, Vol. 1, No 1, pp. 17-40, http://journaldatabase.info/articles/theorising_euro-atlantic_socialisation.html

Kavalski, E., 2005, 'The Balkans after Iraq...Iraq after the Balkans. Who's next?', *Perspectives on European Politics and Society*, Vol. 6, No 1, pp. 103-127, http://www.tandfonline.com/doi/abs/10.1080/15705850508438907?journalCode=rpep20

Kavalski, E., Zolkos, M., 2007, 'The Hoax of War: The Foreign Policy Discourses of Poland and Bulgaria on Iraq, 2003-2005', *Journal of Contemporary European Studies*, Vol. 15, No 3, pp. 377-393, http://www.tandfonline.com/doi/abs/10.1080/14782800701683763

Keck, M., Sikkink, K., 1998, *Activists Beyond Borders: Advocacy Networks in International Politics*, Ithaca: Cornell University Press

Kempster, N., Murphy, D., 'Broader NATO May Bring "Cold Peace"', *Los Angeles Times*, 6 December 1994, http://articles.latimes.com/1994-12-06/news/mn-5629_1_cold-war

Kennan, G., 1997, 'A Fateful Error', *New York Times*, 5 February 1997, http://www.netwargamingitalia.net/forum/resources/george-f-kennan-a-fateful-error.35/

Keohane, R., 1984, *After Hegemony: Cooperation and Discord in the World Political Economy*, Princeton: Princeton University Press

Khong, YF., 1992, *Analogies at War: Korea, Munich, Dien Bien Phu, and the Vietnam Decisions of 1965*, Princeton: Princeton University Press

Kitschelt, H., 1999, *Post-Communist Party Systems: Competition, Representation, and Inter-Party Cooperation*, Cambridge: Cambridge University Press

Klatt, M., 2011, 'Poland and its Eastern Neighbours: Foreign Policy Principles', *Journal of Contemporary European Research*, Vol. 7, No 1, pp. 1-16, http://www.jcer.net/index.php/jcer/article/view/259/255

Kleer, J., 2002, 'Implementation of the Polish-German Treaty in the Area of Scientific and Technological Cooperation', *Polish Foreign Affairs Digest*, Vol. 2, No 1, pp. 191-196

Kochanowicz, J., 2001, 'Poland and the West: In or Out?', *Transit online*, Institute for Human Sciences, Vienna, http://www.iwm.at/transit/transit-online/poland-and-the-west-in-or-out/

Kohler-Koch, B., 2002, 'European Networks and Ideas: Changing National Policies?', *European Integration online Papers* (EIoP), Vol. 6, No 6, https://papers.ssrn.com/sol3/papers.cfm?abstract_id=307519

Kolev, K., 2019, 'Weak pluralism and shallow democracy: the rise of identity politics in Bulgaria and Romania', *East European Politics*, Vol. 36, No 2, pp. 188-205, https://doi.org/10.1080/21599165.2019.1700954

Konstantinov, A., 2013, *До Чикаго и назад*, Български писател, (*To Chicago and back*, Bulgarian writer)

Kortunov, A., 1995, 'Russia, the "Near Abroad", and the West', Ch. 5 in Lapidus, G., (ed.), *New Russia: Troubled Transformation*, Oxford: Westview

Kortunov, A., 2014, *Interview with Rumena Filipova*, 9 June 2014, Moscow

Kościński, P., 2015, *Interview with Rumena Filipova*, 15 June 2015, Warsaw

Koslowski, R., Kratochwil, F., 1995, 'Understanding Change in International Politics: The Soviet Empire's Demise and the International System', Ch. 6 in Lebow, N., Risse-Kappen, T., (eds.), *International Relations Theory and the End of the Cold War*, New York: Columbia University Press

Kostov, I., 1997, 'Иван Костов: Получихме уверение за равен старт в преговорите за присъединяване към ЕС', *Демокрация*, 6 юни 1997, ('Ivan Kostov: We received assurance about an equal start in negotiations over accession to the EU', *Democracy*, 6 June 1997), http://www.faktite.bg/person/pm/6852

Kostov, I., 1999, 'Иван Костов: Оценката на ЕК трябва да бъде извор на национално самочувствие', *Демокрация*, 15 октомври 1999, ('Ivan Kostov: The European Commission's evaluation should give rise to national self-confidence', *Democracy*, 15 October 1999), http://www.faktite.bg/person/pm/5149

Koźmiński, J., 2015, *Interview with Rumena Filipova*, 17 July 2015, Warsaw

Kozyrev, A., 1992a, 'Russia: A Chance for Survival', *Foreign Affairs*, Vol. 71, No 2, pp.1-16, https://www.jstor.org/stable/20045121?seq=1#page_scan_tab_contents

Kozyrev, A., 1992b, 'Russia and Human Rights', *Slavic Review*, Vol. 51, No 2, pp. 287-293, https://www.cambridge.org/core/journals/slavic-review/article/russia-and-human-rights/FDE67DFC85E8D0C070AE529FBAA62F49

Kozyrev, A., 1994, 'The Lagging Partnership', *Foreign Affairs*, Vol. 73, No 3, pp. 59-71, https://www.foreignaffairs.com/articles/russian-federation/1994-05-01/lagging-partnership

Krasnodębska, M., 2021, *Politics of Stigmatization. Poland as a 'Latecomer' in the European Union*, Palgrave Macmillan

Krastev, I., 2004, 'We are all Brits today: Timothy Garton Ash's "Free World"', *openDemocracy*, 7 September 2004, https://www.opendemocracy.net/democracy-europe_constitution/article_2078.jsp

Krastev, I., 2005, 'The European Union and the Balkans: enlargement or empire', *openDemocracy*, 8 June 2005, https://www.opendemocracy.net/democracy-europe_constitution/serbia_2585.jsp

Kratochwil, F., 1991, *Rules, Norms, and Decisions: On the Conditions of Practical and Legal Reasoning in International Relations and Domestic Affairs*, Cambridge: Cambridge University Press

Kratochwil, F., 2000, 'Constructing a New Orthodoxy? Wendt's "Social Theory of International Politics" and the Constructivist Challenge', *Millennium*, Vol. 29, No 1, pp. 73-101, http://journals.sagepub.com/doi/abs/10.1177/03058298000290010901?journalCode=mila

Kratochwil, F., 2001, 'How Do Norms Matter', Ch. 3 in Byers, M., (ed.), *Role of Law in International Politics: Essays in International Relations and International Law*, New York: Oxford University Press

Krause, J., Renwick, N., (eds.), 1996, *Identities in International Relations*, Basingstoke: Palgrave Macmillan

Krickovic, A., 2014, *Interview with Rumena Filipova*, 25 July 2014, Moscow

Krząkała, M., 2015, *Interview with Rumena Filipova*, written response to questions submitted on 2 September 2015

Kundera, M., 1984, 'The Tragedy of Central Europe', *New York Review of Books*, Vol. 31, No 7, http://www.bisla.sk/english/wp-content/uploads/2014/03/Kundera_tragedy_of_Central_Europe.pdf

Kurth, J., 2004, 'Western Civilization, Our Tradition', *Intercollegiate Review*, Autumn 2003/Spring 2004

Kuus, M., 2004, 'Europe's eastern expansion and the reinscription of otherness in East-Central Europe', *Progress in Human Geography*, Vol. 28, Issue 4, pp. 472-489, http://journals.sagepub.com/doi/10.1191/0309132504ph498oa

Kuzio, T., 'European, Eastern Slavic, and Eurasian: National Identity, Transformation, and Ukrainian Foreign Policy', Ch. 10 in Moroney, J., Kuzio, T., Molchanov, M., (eds.), 2002, *Ukrainian Foreign and Security Policy: Theoretical and Comparative Perspectives*, Praeger

Kuźniar, R., 2015, *Interview with Rumena Filipova*, 11 and 29 June 2015, Warsaw

Kwaśniewski, A., 2001, 'The President of the Polish Republic in Conversation with the Editor of *The Polish Diplomatic Review*', *Polish Foreign Affairs Digest*, Vol. 1, No 1, pp. 71-94

Łada, A., 2018, 'Germans and Poles A divided past, a common future? Results of the Polish-German barometer 2018', *Institute of Public Affairs/Körber-Stiftung/Konrad-Adenauer-Stiftung*, https://www.isp.org.pl/uploads/drive/oldfiles/A/barometrang.pdf

Lantis, J., Beasley, R., 'Comparative foreign policy analysis', in Thompson, W., (ed.), 2017, *Oxford Research Encyclopedia of Politics* (*Oxford Research Encyclopedias*), Oxford: Oxford University Press

Lapid, Y., Kratochwil, F., (eds.), 1996, *Return of Culture and Identity in IR Theory*, Boulder: Lynne Rienner Publishers Inc.

Larrabee, S., Karasik, T., 1997, *Foreign and Security Policy Decision-making under Yeltsin*, Santa Monica: Rand

Larson, D., Shevchenko, A., 2019, *Quest for Status. Chinese and Russian Foreign Policy*, Yale University Press

Laruelle, M., (ed.), 2012, *Russian Nationalism, Foreign Policy and Identity Debates in Putin's Russia. New Ideological Patterns after the Orange Revolution*, Ibidem Press

Laruelle, M., 2015, 'Russia as a "Divided Nation", from Compatriots to Crimea: A Contribution to the Discussion on Nationalism and Foreign Policy', *Problems of Post-Communism*, Vol. 62, No 2, pp. 88-97, http://www.tandfonline.com/doi/abs/10.1080/10758216.2015.1010902?journalCode=mppc20

Lavrov, S., 2021, 'Foreign Minister Sergey Lavrov's interview with the Solovyov Live YouTube channel, February 12, 2021', *Ministry of Foreign Affairs of the Russian Federation*, https://www.mid.ru/en/foreign_policy/news/-/asset_publisher/cKNonkJE02Bw/content/id/4570813

Lebow, R. N., 2016, *National Identities and International Relations*, Cambridge University Press

Leffler, M., 1996, 'The struggle for Germany and the origins of the Cold War', *German Historical Institute Washington, D.C.*, Occasional Paper No 16, https://www.ghi-dc.org/fileadmin/user_upload/GHI_Washington/PDFs/Occasional_Papers/The_Struggle_for_Germany.pdf

Legro, J., Moravcsik, A., 1999, 'Is Anybody Still a Realist?', *International Security*, Vol. 24, No 2, pp. 5-55, https://www.princeton.edu/~amoravcs/library/anybody.pdf

Legvold, R., (ed.), 2007a, *Russian Foreign Policy in the 21st Century and the Shadow of the Past*, New York: Columbia University Press

Legvold, R., 2007b, 'Russian Foreign Policy during Periods of Great State Transformation', Ch. 2 in Legvold, R., (ed.), *Russian Foreign Policy in the 21st Century and the Shadow of the Past*, New York: Columbia University Press

Lessenski, M., 2015, *Interview with Rumena Filipova*, 30 November 2015, Sofia

Levy, J., 2013, 'Psychology and Foreign Policy Decision-Making', Ch. 10 in Sears, D., Huddy, L., Levy, J., (eds.), *Oxford Handbook of Political Psychology*, New York: Oxford University Press, 2nd ed.

Lewalter, W., 2009, 'Къде са солидните партийни структури', в Таслакова, Р., (интервюиращ), *Две десетилетия преход. България през погледа на германски дипломати*, Изток-Запад, ('Where are the solid party structures', in Taslakova, R., (interviewer), *Two decades of transition. Bulgaria through the eyes of German diplomats*, East-West)

Lieven, A., 1999, *Ukraine and Russia: A Fraternal Rivalry*, Washington, DC: United States Institute of Peace Press

Light, M., 2003, 'In Search of an Identity: Russian Foreign Policy and the End of Ideology', *Journal of Communist Studies and Transition Politics*, Vol. 19, No 3, pp. 42-59, http://www.tandfonline.com/doi/abs/10.1080/1352 3270300660017

Lindbekk, T., 1992, 'The Weberian Ideal-Type: Development and Continuities', *Acta Sociologica*, Vol. 35, No 4, pp. 285-297, https://www.jstor.org/stable/4194790?seq=1#page_scan_tab_contents

Linz, J., 2000, *Totalitarian and Authoritarian Regimes*, London: Lynne Rienner Publishers

Linz, J., Stepan, A., 1996, *Problems of Democratic Transition and Consolidation: Southern Europe, South America, and Post-Communist Europe*, Baltimore: Johns Hopkins University Press

Lipman, M., 2014, *Interview with Rumena Filipova*, 23 June 2014, Moscow

Lipman, M., 2014, 'The origins of Russia's new conflict with the West', *European Council on Foreign Relations*, http://www.ecfr.eu/article/commentary_the_origins_of_russias_new_conflict_with_the_west 330

Lipschutz, R., 1995, *On Security*, New York: Columbia University Press

Llansó, E., Hoboken, J., Leerssen, P., Harambam, J., 2020, 'Artificial Intelligence, Content Moderation, and Freedom of Expression', *Transatlantic Working Group*, https://www.ivir.nl/publicaties/download/AI-Llanso-Van-Hoboken-Feb-2020.pdf

Lo, B., Lucas, E., 2021, *Partnership without Substance. Sino-Russian Relations in Central and Eastern Europe*, Center for European Policy Analysis

Longhurst, K., 2013, 'Where from, where to? New and old configurations in Poland's foreign and security policy priorities', *Communist and Post-Communist Studies*, Vol. 46, No 3, pp. 363-372, http://www.sciencedirect.com/science/article/pii/S0967067X13000299

Longhurst, K., Zaborowski, M., 2007, *New Atlanticist: Poland's Foreign and Security Priorities*, Oxford: Blackwell Publishing

Longworth, R., 1994, 'Bulgaria, Romania Resist Pull of the West', *Chicago Tribune*, 10 October 1994, http://articles.chicagotribune.com/1994-10-10/news/9410120048_1_romania-and-bulgaria-bulgarian-president-zhelyu-zhelev-czech-republic

Lorenz, W., 2015, *Interview with Rumena Filipova*, 16 June 2015, Warsaw

Los Angeles Times, 'Russia Says It Plans to Proceed with the Sale of Submarines to Iran', 3 October 1992, http://articles.latimes.com/1992-10-03/news/mn-272_1_submarines

Lukanov, A., 1990, 'Отиваме към Европа с трудностите си, но и с възможности за сътрудничество', *Дума*, 8 май 1990, ('We are moving towards Europe with our problems but also with opportunities for cooperation', *Duma*, 8 May 1990), http://www.faktite.bg/source/103

Lukanov, A., 1990, 'Създадени са предпоставки за истинско единство в Европа', *Дума*, 22 ноември 1990, ('Preconditions for a genuine European unity have been set', *Duma*, 22 November 1990), http://www.faktite.bg/source/180

Lukanov, A., 1992, 'Съживяването на регионалните източноевропейски връзки е на кръстопът', *Дума*, 19 март 1992, ('The revival of regional East European relations is at a crossroads', *Duma*, 19 March 1992), http://www.faktite.bg/source/352

Lukanov, A., 1992, 'Открито писмо на Андрей Луканов до г-жа Катрин Лалюмиер, генерален секретар на Съвета на Европа', *Дума*, 3 август 1992, ('Open Letter from Andrey Lukanov to Ms. Catherine Lalumière, Secretary General of the Council of Europe', *Duma*, 3 August 1992), http://www.faktite.bg/source/374

Lukin, V., 1992, 'Our Security Predicament', *Foreign Policy*, No 88, pp. 57-75, https://www.jstor.org/stable/1149318?seq=1#page_scan_tab_contents

Lukin, V., 2008, 'From a Post-Soviet to a Russian Foreign Policy', *Russia in Global Affairs*, No 4, http://eng.globalaffairs.ru/number/n_11886

Lutsevych, O., 2013, 'How to Finish a Revolution: Civil Society and Democracy in Georgia, Moldova and Ukraine', *Briefing Paper*, *Chatham House*, https://www.chathamhouse.org/publications/papers/view/188407

Lynch, A., 1994, 'After Empire: Russia and Its Western Neighbors', *RFE/Radio Liberty Research Report*, Vol. 3, No 12, pp. 10-18

Lynch, D., 2000, *Russian Peacekeeping Strategies in the CIS: The Cases of Moldova, Georgia and Tajikistan*, Basingstoke: Macmillan

Maass, AS., 2015, *Interview with Rumena Filipova*, 29 June 2015, Warsaw

MacFarlane, SN., 1993, 'Russia, the West, and European Security', *Survival: Global Politics and Strategy*, Vol. 35, No 3, pp. 3-25, http://www.tandfonline.com/doi/abs/10.1080/00396339308442696?journalCode=tsur20

MacFarlane, SN., 2001, 'NATO in Russia's Relations with the West', *Security Dialogue*, Vol. 32, No 3, pp. 281-296, http://journals.sage pub.com/doi/abs/10.1177/0967010601032003002

MacFarlane, SN., 2002, 'Caucasus and Central Asia: Towards a Non-Strategy', *Geneva Centre for Security Policy Occasional Paper Series*, No 37

MacFarlane, SN., 2008, 'Frozen Conflicts in the Former Soviet Union – The Case of Georgia/South Ossetia', in *OSCE Yearbook*, https://ifsh.de/file-CORE/documents/yearbook/english/08/MacFarlane-en.pdf

MacFarlane, SN., 2012, 'Georgia: National Security Concept versus National Security', *Programme Paper Chatham House*, https://www.chathamhouse.org/publications/papers/view/185193

MacFarlane, SN., Menon, A., 2014, 'The EU and Ukraine', *Survival. Global Politics and Strategy*, Vol. 56, No 3, pp. 95-101, https://www.tandfonline.com/doi/abs/10.1080/00396338.2014.920139

Madej, M., 2015, *Interview with Rumena Filipova*, 25 June 2015, Warsaw

Mahoney, J., Rueschemeyer, D., (eds.), 2003, *Comparative Historical Analysis in the Social Sciences*, Cambridge: Cambridge University Press

Mäkinen, S., 2013, 'European Perceptions of Russia's Image and Identity', *Finnish Centre for Excellence in Russian Studies*, http://ashpi.asu.ru/ic/wp-content/uploads/European-Perceptions-of-Russia%E2%80%99s-Image-and-Identity.pdf

Maksak, H., Mashtaler, O., (eds.), 2017, 'Ukraine in the Coordinates of the Eastern Partnership 2017-2020', *Ukrainian National Platform of the Eastern Partnership Civil Society Forum*, http://eap-csf.org.ua/wp-content/uploads/2017/10/Report_English.pdf

Małachowski, W., 2003, 'Polish-German Economic Relations in the 1990s: The Track Record and Its Implications', Ch. 2 in Stüting, H., Dorow, W., Claassen, F., Blazejewski, S., (eds.), *Change Management in Transition Economies: Integrating Corporate Strategy, Structure and Culture*, Basingstoke: Palgrave Macmillan

Malashenko, A., 2012, Центральная Азия: на что рассчитывает Россия?, *Московский Центр Карнеги*, (Central Asia: What does Russia rely upon?, *Carnegie Moscow Center*)

Malashenko, A., 2014, *Interview with Rumena Filipova*, 16 June 2014, Moscow

Malia, M., 1999, *Russia under Western Eyes: From the Bronze Horseman to the Lenin Mausoleum*, Cambridge: The Belnap Press of Harvard University Press

Malici, A., Walker, S., 2016, *Role Theory and Role Conflict in US-Iran Relations: Enemies of Our Own Making*, London: Routledge

Malinova, O., 2012, 'Российская идентичность между идеями нации и цивилизации' ('Russian identity between the concepts of nation and civilization'), *Kennan Institute Moscow Journal*, No 22, pp. 48-57, https://publications.hse.ru/articles/67718212

Malinova, O., 2014, *Interview with Rumena Filipova*, 31 July 2014, Moscow

Mangott, G., 1999, 'Russian policies on Central and Eastern Europe: An overview', *European Security*, Vol. 8, Issue 3, pp. 44-81, https://www.researchgate.net/publication/232925089_Russian_policies_on_central_and_eastern_Europe_An_overview

Manners, I., Whitman, R., Allen, D., (eds.), 2000, *Foreign Policies of the European Union Member States*, Manchester: Manchester University Press

Marcheva-Atanasova, I., 2015, *Interview with Rumena Filipova*, 3 December 2015, Sofia

Markov, H., 2015, 'Конституционната битка за ДПС—1991-1992 година — как Доган се превърна в проклятие', *Faktor.bg*, 28 януари 2018, ('The constitutional battle over the MRF—1991-1992—how Dogan became a curse', *Faktor.bg*, 28 January 2018), http://www.faktor.bg/bg/articles/petak-13/konstitutsionnata-bitka-za-dps-1991-1992-godina-kak-dogan-se-prevarna-v-proklyatie-37474

Markowski, R., 2002, 'The Polish SLD in the 1990s. From Opposition to Incumbents and Back', Ch. 4 in Bozóki, A., Ishiyama, J., (eds.), *Communist Successor Parties of Central and Eastern Europe*, London: Sharpe

McCourt, D., 2011, 'Role-playing and identity affirmation in international politics: Britain's reinvasion of the Falklands, 1982', *Review of International Studies*, Vol. 37, No 4, pp. 1599-1621, https://www.cambridge.org/core/journals/review-of-international-studies/article/role-playing-and-identity-affirmation-in-international-politics-britains-reinvasion-of-the-falklands-1982/47F2928866C97DAD625FE52CA39065A4

McCourt, D., 2012, 'The roles states play: a Meadian interactionist approach', *Journal of International Relations and Development*, Vol. 15, No 3, pp. 370-392, https://link.springer.com/article/10.1057%2Fjird.2011.26

McCrone, D., 1998, *The sociology of nationalism: tomorrow's ancestors*, New York: Routledge

McDaniel, T., 1996, *The Agony of the Russian Idea*, Princeton: Princeton University Press

McManus, M., 2020, *The Rise of Post-Modern Conservatism. Neoliberalism, Post-Modern Culture, and Reactionary Politics*, Palgrave Macmillan

Mearsheimer, J., 1990, 'Back to the Future: Instability in Europe after the Cold War', *International Security*, Vol. 15, No 1, pp. 5-56, https://www.jstor.org/stable/2538981?seq=1#metadata_info_tab_contents

Mearsheimer, J., 2014, 'Why the Ukraine Crisis Is the West's Fault. The Liberal Delusions That Provoked Putin', *Foreign Affairs*, September/October, https://www.foreignaffairs.com/articles/russia-fsu/2014-08-18/why-ukraine-crisis-west-s-fault

Mearsheimer, J., Walt, S., 2013, 'Leaving theory behind: Why simplistic hypothesis testing is bad for International Relations', *European Journal of International Relations*, Vol. 19, No 3, pp. 427-457, https://journals.sagepub.com/doi/10.1177/1354066113494320

Mediapool, 2017, 'БСП даде своята лепта към паралелната държава', 21 септември 2017, ('The BSP paid tribute to the parallel state', 21 September 2017), http://www.mediapool.bg/bsp-dade-svoyata-lepta-kam-paralelnata-darzhava-news269481.html

Mediapool, 2018a, 'Борисов за избора между Русия и Европа: Едно са историята и бизнесът, друго — западната ориентация', 19 април 2018, ('Borissov on the Choice between Russia and Europe: History and Business Are One Thing; the pro-Western Orientation — Another', 19 April 2018), https://www.mediapool.bg/borisov-za-izbora-mezhdu-rusiya-i-evropa-edno-sa-istoriyata-i-biznesat-drugo-zapadnata-orientatsiya-news278160.html

Mediapool, 2018b, 'Демократична България: Борисов отдалечава страната от европейските ценности', 28 юни 2018, ('Democratic Bulgaria: Borissov Is Distancing Bulgaria from European Vlaues', 28 June 2018), https://www.mediapool.bg/demokratichna-bulgaria-borisov-otdalechava-stranata-ot-evropeiskite-tsennosti-news280852.html

Medvedev, S., 2007, 'The crisis in EU-Russia relations: between "sovereignty" and "Europeanization"', *Political Theory and Political Analysis*, Paper Series WP14, Higher School of Economics, Moscow, https://www.hse.ru/data/2010/05/07/1217274096/WP14_2007_02.pdf

Medvedev, S., 2008, 'Limits of Integration: Identities and Institutions in EU-Russia Relations', *Aleksanteri Papers 2*, https://www.hse.ru/data/617/436/1233/Limits%20of%20Integration%20Medvedev.pdf

Medvedev, S., 2014, *Interview with Rumena Filipova*, 10 July 2014, Moscow

Melville, A., 2014, *Interview with Rumena Filipova*, 30 July 2014, Moscow

Melville, A., Shakleina, T., (eds.), 2005, *Russian Foreign Policy in Transition: Concepts and Realities*, New York: Central European University Press

Membership Action Plan, 1999, *NATO*, http://www.nato.int/cps/en/natohq/official_texts_27444.htm

Menkiszak, M., 2013, *Greater Europe: Putin's Vision of European (Dis)Integration*, Center for Eastern Studies, Warsaw, No 46, https://www.osw.waw.pl/sites/default/files/greater_europe_net.pdf

Metodiev, K., 2017, 'Дебатът за неутралитета на България на границата между XX и XXI век', *Геополитика*, No 1, ('The debate on Bulgaria's neutrality at the threshold of the 21st century, *Geopolitika*, No 1), https://geopolitica.eu/spisanie-geopolitika/58-2017/broy-1-2017/2592-debatat-za-neutraliteta-na-balgariya-na-granitsata-mezhdu-xx-i-xxi-vek

Mihalka, M., 1994, 'Squaring the Circle: NATO's Offer to the East', *Radio Free Europe/Radio Liberty Research Report*, Vol. 3, No 12, pp. 1-10

Mihaylova, N., 1999, 'Priorities in Bulgarian Foreign Policy', *Thesis: A Journal of Foreign Policy Issues*, Autumn 1997, http://www.hri.org/MFA/thesis/autumn97/priorities.html

Mihaylova, T., 2015, *Interview with Rumena Filipova*, 27 November 2015, Sofia

Miheev, V., 1997, 'Европа без России это не Европа', *Известия*, 10 октября 1997, ('Europe without Russia is not Europe', *Izvestiya*, 10 October 1997), http://nostalgie.gershtein.net/1997-dec/ekaterin/news/izvestia/izv97132.htm

Military Doctrine of the Republic of Bulgaria, 1999, https://www.strategy.bg/StrategicDocuments/View.aspx?lang=bg-BG&Id=555

Military Strength Ranking, *Global Firepower*, 2017, http://www.globalfirepower.com/countries-listing.asp

Millard, F., 1996, 'Poland's "return to Europe", 1989-94', Ch. 11 in Bideleux, R., Taylor, R., (eds.), *European Integration and Disintegration: East and West*, London: Routledge

Miller, A., 2008, '"Нация" и "народность" в России XIX века', *Публичные лекции* ('"Nation" and "nationality" in Russia in the 19th century', *Public Lectures*), http://polit.ru/article/2008/12/29/nation/

Miller, A., 2014, *Interview with Rumena Filipova*, 2 July 2014, Moscow

Milliken, J., 1999, 'The Study of Discourse in International Relations: A Critique of Research and Methods', *European Journal of International Relations*, Vol. 5, No 2, pp. 225-254, http://journals.sagepub.com/doi/abs/10.1177/1354066199005002003

Minchev, O., 2013, 'Социален консерватизъм или недовършената архитектура на българския политически живот', *IRIS Strategic Papers Collection*, ('Social conservatism or the unfinished architecture of Bulgarian political life', *IRIS Strategic Papers Collection*), http://www.iris-bg.org/fls/Social_conservative.pdf

Minchev, O., 2015, *Interview with Rumena Filipova*, 20 November 2015, Sofia

Minchev, O., Ratchev, V., Lessenski, M., (eds.), 2002, *Bulgaria for NATO*, Institute for Regional and International Studies, Sofia, http://www.iris-bg.org/fls/intro.pdf

Minesashvili, S., 2016, 'Narrating Identity: Belongingness and Alterity in Georgia's Foreign Policy', in Kakachia, K., Markarov, A., (eds.), *Values and Identity as Sources of Foreign Policy in Armenia and Georgia*, Tbilisi: Universal

Ministry of Foreign Affairs of the Republic of Poland, 2012, *Costs and benefits of Poland's membership in the European Union*, Report, http://www.msz.gov.pl/en/foreign_policy/foreign_economic_policy/costs_and_benefits/

Ministry of Foreign Affairs of the Russian Federation, 2002, 'Перечень действующих российско-китайских межгосударственных и межправительственных договоров', *Министерство иностранных дел Российской Федерации*, ('Overview of active Russian-Chinese interstate and interstate agreements'), http://www.mid.ru/ru/maps/cn/-/asset_publisher/WhKWb5DVBqKA/content/id/538486

Mishkova, D., 2018, *Beyond Balkanism. The Scholarly Politics of Region Making*, Routledge

Mjør, K., Turoma, S., (eds.), 2020, *Russia as Civilization: Ideological Discourses in Politics, Media and Academia*, Routledge

Moravcsik, A., 2001, 'Bringing Constructivist Integration Theory Out of the Clouds: Has it Landed Yet?', *European Union Politics*, Vol. 2, No 2, pp. 226-249, https://www.princeton.edu/~amoravcs/library/clouds.pdf

Moravcsik, A., 2010, 'Liberal Theories of International Relations: A Primer', *Princeton University*

Morawiecki, M., 2020, 'The spirit of Solidarity is necessary for today's Europe', *Website of the Republic of Poland*, https://www.gov.pl/web/southafrica/prime-minister-of-poland-mateusz-morawiecki-the-spirit-of-solidarity-is-necessary-for-todays-europe

Morozov, V., 2008, 'Sovereignty and democracy in contemporary Russia: a modern subject faces the post-modern world', *Journal of International Relations and Development*, Vol. 11, No 2, pp. 152-180, http://www.ingentaconnect.com/content/pal/jird/2008/00000011/00000002/art00004

Morozov, V., 2013, 'Subaltern Empire? Toward a Postcolonial Approach to Russian Foreign Policy', *Problems of Post-Communism*, Vol. 60, No 6, pp. 16-28, http://www.tandfonline.com/doi/abs/10.2753/PPC1075-8216600602

Morozov, V., 2014, *Interview with Rumena Filipova*, 26 August 2014

Morozov, V., 2016, 'What Is the Meaning of "National" in the Russian Debate about the National Interest?', *PONARS Eurasia*, Policy Memo 414, http://www.ponarseurasia.org/memo/russian-debate-about-national-interest

Morozova, N., 2011, *Politics of Russian Post-Soviet Identity: Geopolitics, Eurasianism, and Beyond*, PhD thesis, Central European University, http://stage1.ceu.edu/sites/pds.ceu.hu/files/attachment/basicpage/478/nataliamorozova.pdf

Morrison, J., 1993, *Around the Mausoleum*, unpublished papers

Moumoutzis, K., 2011, 'Still Fashionable Yet Useless? Addressing Problems with Research on the Europeanization of Foreign Policy', *Journal of Common Market Studies*, Vol. 49, No 3, pp. 607-629, http://onlinelibrary.wiley.com/doi/10.1111/j.1468-5965.2010.02146.x/abstract

Mungiu-Pippidi, A., 2003, 'Of Dark Sides and Twilight Zones: Enlarging to the Balkans', *East European Politics and Societies*, Vol. 17, No 1, pp. 83-90, http://journals.sagepub.com/doi/abs/10.1177/0888325402239686?journalCode=eepa

Murphy, J., 1996, 'Rational Choice Theory as Social Physics', in Friedman, J., (ed.), *Rational Choice Controversy: Economic Models of Politics Reconsidered*, New Haven: Yale University Press

Nancheva, N., 2012, *Transforming Identities in Europe: Bulgaria and Macedonia between Nationalism and Europeanization*, PhD thesis, University of Westminster, http://westminsterresearch.wmin.ac.uk/12564/1/Nevena_NANCHEVA.pdf

Narizny, K., 2017, 'On Systemic Paradigms and Domestic Politics: A Critique of the Newest Realism', *International Security*, Vol. 42, No 2, pp. 155-190, https://doi.org/10.1162/ISEC_a_00296

(Grand) National Assembly Proceedings—First solemn proceedings, 10 July 1990, (Първо тържествено заседание на Великото Народно събрание, 10 юли 1990), http://www.parliament.bg/pub/StenD/20130308024827100711990%20_1%20tyrjestveno%20zasedanie.pdf

National Assembly Proceedings, 4 November 1991, (Заседание на Народното събрание, 4 ноември 1991), http://www.parliament.bg/bg/plenaryst/ns/4/ID/1201

National Assembly Proceedings, 15 December 1995, (Заседание на Народното събрание, 15 декември 1995), http://www.parliament.bg/bg/plenaryst/ns/5/ID/2785

National Assembly Proceedings, 7 May 1997, (Заседание на Народното събрание, 7 май 1997), http://www.parliament.bg/bg/plenaryst/ns/6/ID/1056

National Assembly Proceedings, 14 July 2009, (Заседание на Народното събрание, 14 юли 2009), http://www.parliament.bg/bg/plenaryst/ns/7/ID/592

National Assembly Proceedings, 27 October 2014, (Заседание на Народното събрание, 27 октомври 2014), http://www.parliament.bg/bg/plenaryst/ns/51/ID/5305

National Security Strategy and Strategic Defence and Security Review of the UK, 2015, Prime Minister's Office, Cabinet Office, Department for International Development, Foreign and Commonwealth Office, Home Office, Ministry of Defence, p. 10, https://www.gov.uk/government/publications/national-security-strategy-and-strategic-defence-and-security-review-2015

National Security Strategy for a New Century, USA, 2000, *Bill Clinton Administration*, p. 9, http://nssarchive.us/NSSR/2000.pdf

National Security Strategy of the Republic of Bulgaria, 2011, https://www.bbn.gov.pl/ftp/dok/07/BGR_National_Security_Strategy_Republic_Bulgaria_2011.pdf

National Security Strategy of the US, 2006, *George W. Bush Administration*, pp. 7-12, http://nssarchive.us/NSSR/2006.pdf

National Security Strategy of the US, 2015, *Barack Obama Administration*, pp. 25-28, http://nssarchive.us/wp-content/uploads/2015/02/2015.pdf

NATO, 2020, *NATO 2030: Unified for a New Era. Analysis and Recommendations of the Reflection Group Appointed by the NATO Secretary General*, pp. 9, 20, https://www.nato.int/nato_static_fl2014/assets/pdf/2020/12/pdf/201201-Reflection-Group-Final-Report-Uni.pdf

NATO Factsheet, 2016, 'Russia's top five myths about NATO', http://www.nato.int/nato_static_fl2014/assets/pdf/pdf_2016_07/20160627_1607-russia-top5-myths_en.pdf

Nelson, L., Kuzes, I., 1995, *Radical Reform in Yeltsin's Russia: Political, Economic, and Social Dimensions*, London: M.E. Sharpe

Nemo, P., 2006, *What is the West?*, Duquesne University Press, https://muse.jhu.edu/book/14112

Neuburger, M., 2004, *The Orient Within: Muslim Minorities and the Negotiation of Nationhood in Modern Bulgaria*, Cornell University Press

Neumann, I., 1994, 'A Region-Building Approach to Northern Europe', *Review of International Studies*, Vol. 20, No 1, pp. 53-74, https://www.cambridge.org/core/journals/review-of-international-studies/article/regionbuilding-approach-to-northern-europe/6B77683645EBBD2A050227FFF000DA0C

Neumann, I., 1995, *Russia and the Idea of Europe: A Study in Identity and International Relations*, London: Routledge

Neumann, I., 1999, *Uses of the Other: 'The East' in European identity formation*, Minneapolis: University of Minnesota Press

Neumann, I., 2016, 'Russia's Europe, 1991-2016: inferiority to superiority', *International Affairs*, Vol. 92, No 6, pp. 1381-1399, http://onlinelibrary.wiley.com/doi/10.1111/1468-2346.12752/abstract

Nikitina, Y., 2014, *Interview with Rumena Filipova*, 4 July 2014, Moscow

Nikolov, K., Simeonov, K., 2009, 'The Effect of EU Accession on Bulgaria', in Avery, G., Faber, A., Schmidt, A., (eds.), *Enlarging the European Union: Effects on the new member states and the EU*, Trans European Policy Studies Association, https://www.um.edu.mt/__data/assets/pdf_file/0017/71054/Enlarging_the_European_Union.pdf

Nikolova, Y., 2015, *Interview with Rumena Filipova*, 19 November 2015, Sofia

Nougayrède, N., 2017, 'The EU isn't punishing Poland. It's protecting its integrity as a bloc', *Guardian*, 26 December 2017, https://www.theguardian.com/commentisfree/2017/dec/26/brexiters-eu-poland-brussels-warsaw-trade-deals

Novini, 2014, 'Росен Плевнелиев: ЕС трябва да действа срещу Русия', 20 март 2014, ('Rosen Pleveneliev: the EU has to act against Russia', 20 March 2014), http://m.novini.bg/news.php?id=185111

Nowak, J., 1993, *CFE regime and its development as seen from a Polish and Central European perspective*, Vienna

Nowak, J., 1997, 'Poland and the OSCE: In Search of More Effective European Security', *OSCE Yearbook 1995-1996*, https://ifsh.de/file-CORE/documents/yearbook/english/95_96/Novak.pdf

Nowak, J., 2015, *Interview with Rumena Filipova*, 7 July 2015, Warsaw

Nyyssönen, H., 2018, 'The East is different, isn't it? Poland and Hungary in search of prestige', *Journal of Contemporary European Studies*, Vol. 26, No 3, pp. 258-269, https://doi.org/10.1080/14782804.2018.1498772

Ochmann, C., 2015, *Interview with Rumena Filipova*, 14 July 2015, Warsaw

OFFNews.bg., 2018, 'Пак честитка! Журнал дьо Диманш: България е на мафията, една малка Русия', 1 януари 2018, ('Congratulations again! Le Journal du dimanche: Bulgaria belongs to the mafia, a small Russia', 1 January 2018), https://offnews.bg/medii/pak-chestitka-zhurnal-dio-dimansh-balgaria-e-na-mafiata-edna-malka-672143.html

Olechowski, A., 1995, 'Poland's European Foreign Policy Option', *Yearbook of Polish Foreign Policy*, pp. 19-31

Olsen, J., 2002, 'The Many Faces of Europeanization', *Journal of Common Market Studies*, Vol. 40, No 5, pp. 921-952, http://onlinelibrary.wiley.com/doi/10.1111/1468-5965.00403/abstract

Onar, N., Nicolaidis, K., 2013, 'The Decentring Agenda: Europe as a postcolonial power', *Cooperation and Conflict*, Vol. 48, No 2, pp. 283-303, http://journals.sagepub.com/doi/abs/10.1177/0010836713485384

O'Neal, M., 2017, 'The European 'Other' in Poland's Conservative Identity Project', *The International Spectator. Italian Journal of International Affairs*, Vol. 52, No 1, pp. 28-45, https://doi.org/10.1080/03932729.2017.1277645

Önis, Z., 2004, 'Diverse but Converging Paths to European Union Membership: Poland and Turkey in Comparative Perspective', *East European Politics and Societies*, Vol. 18, No 3, pp. 481-512, http://journals.sagepub.com/doi/abs/10.1177/0888325404266936?journalCode=eepa

Onuf, N., 2013a, *Making Sense, Making Worlds: Constructivism in Social Theory and International Relations*, Abingdon: Routledge

Onuf, N., 2013b, *World of Our Making: Rules and Rule in Social Theory and International Relations*, Abingdon: Routledge

Osica, O., 2004, 'Poland: A New European Atlanticist at a Crossroads?', *European Security*, Vol. 13, No 4, pp. 301-322, http://www.tandfonline.com/doi/abs/10.1080/09662830490499984?src=recsys&journalCode=feus20

Ostruszka, L., 2021, 'Seeking new ways to exert pressure on independent media, the Polish government plans to impose a tax on advertising revenue', *Wyborcza*, 3 February 2021, https://wyborcza.pl/7,173236,26752737,seeking-new-ways-to-exert-pressure-on-independent-media-the.html?disableRedirects=true

Paland, R., 2000, 'A world of their making: an evaluation of the constructivist critique in International Relations', *Review of International Studies*, Vol. 26, No 4, pp. 575-598, https://www.cambridge.org/core/journals/review-of-international-studies/article/a-world-of-their-making-an-evaluation-of-the-constructivist-critique-in-international-relations/AEF449AACE997A147DDEA93E3621915

PAP News Wire, 1997, 'Kwaśniewski Assured of US Support for Poland's NATO Bid', 1 April 1997

PAP News Wire, 1998, 'Caucuses approve foreign policy goals', 5 March 1998

Papadimitriou, D., Gateva, E., 2009, 'Between Enlargement-led Europeanisation and Balkan Exceptionalism: An Appraisal of Bulgaria's and Romania's Entry into the European Union', *Perspectives on European Politics and Society*, Vol. 10, No 2, pp. 152-166, http://www.tandfonline.com/doi/abs/10.1080/15705850902899172

Partnership for Peace: Framework Document, 1994, *NATO*, http://www.nato.int/cps/po/natohq/official_texts_24469.htm

Parvanov, A., 2000, 'Aspects and prospects of the regional security in South-east Europe in the 90s', *Workshop on Defence Policy Modernisation and Security on the Balkans, University of National and World Economy, Sofia,* 24-25 May 2000

Passy, S., 2015, *Мемоари на Соломон Паси,* предоставени на Румена Филипова, (*Memoirs of Solomon Passy* shared with Rumena Filipova)

Paterson, T., 2014, 'Putin's far-right ambition: Think-tank reveals how Russian President is wooing — and funding — populist parties across Europe to gain influence in the EU', *Independent,* 25 November 2014, http://www.independent.co.uk/news/world/europe/putin-s-far-right-ambition-think-tank-reveals-how-russian-president-is-wooing-and-funding-populist-9883052.html

Paunova, P., 2018, 'Борисов тежи на България като руска ютия', *Mediapool,* 21 май 2018, ('Borisov Weighs on Bulgaria like a Russian Iron', *Mediapool,* 21 May 2018), https://www.mediapool.bg/borisov-tezhi-na-bulgaria-kato-ruska-yutiya-news279223.html

Persuasion and Power in the Modern World, 2014, *Select Committee on Soft Power and the UK's Influence,* https://publications.parliament.uk/pa/ld201314/ldselect/ldsoftpower/150/150.pdf

Petkov, K., 2015, *Interview with Rumena Filipova,* 16 December 2015, Sofia

Petrescu, D., 2010, *Explaining the Romanian Revolution of 1989: Culture, Structure, and Contingency,* Bucharest: Editura Enciclopedica

Petro, N., 1995, *Rebirth of Russian Democracy: An Interpretation of Political Culture,* Cambridge: Harvard University Press

Pew Research Center, 2019, 'European Public Opinion Three Decades After the Fall of Communism', p. 21, Pew-Research-Center-Value-of-Europe-report-FINAL-UPDATED (1).pdf

Piedrafita, S., Torreblanca, J., 2004, 'The Three Logics of EU Enlargement: Interests, Identities and Arguments', Elcano *Royal Institute,* Working Paper No 51, http://www.realinstitutoelcano.org/wps/wcm/connect/db8f63004f0187e5be18fe3170baead1/051-2004-WP.pdf?MOD=AJPERES&CACHEID=db8f63004f0187e5be18fe3170baead1

Pielacha, S., 2004, *Bargaining for Something Better: The Polish Peasants and the European Union,* Master's thesis, University of Wroclaw/University of British Columbia

Pierre, A., 1999, 'De-Balkanizing the Balkans: Security and Stability in Southeastern Europe', *Special Report, United States Institute of Peace,* https://www.usip.org/publications/1999/09/de-balkanizing-balkans-security-and-stability-southeastern-europe

Pipes, R., 1995, *Russia under the Old Regime,* New York: Penguin Books, 2nd ed.

Pisarski, Z., 2015, *Interview with Rumena Filipova,* 6 July 2015, Warsaw

Pleshakov, C., 2017, *The Crimean Nexus. Putin's War and the Clash of Civilizations*, Yale University Press

Polish-American Freedom Foundation, Annual Report, 2000, http://www.en.pafw.pl/publications/repository/pdf/PAFF_%20Annual_Report_2000.pdf

Polish News Bulletin, 1993, 'Suchocka Visits Council of Europe', 14 May 1993

Polish News Bulletin, 1993, 'NATO Membership: When and How?', 5 October 1993

Polish News Bulletin, 1993, 'Milewski Urges NATO Bid Despite Russian Opposition', 8 December 1993

Polish News Bulletin, 1994, 'Pawlak at NATO', 3 February 1994

Polish News Bulletin, 1995, 'Waldemar Pawlak in US', 3 February 1995

Polish News Bulletin, 1998, 'Poland vs. European Union: Mutual Expectations', 30 July 1998

Polyakova, A., 2016, 'Putinism and the European Far Right', *Institute of Modern Russia*, https://imrussia.org/en/analysis/world/2500-putinism-and-the-european-far-right

Pomorska, K., 2011, 'Are we there yet? From adaptation to Europeanisation of Polish foreign policy', *EUSA Twelfth Biennial International Conference Boston*, 3-5 March 2011, http://www.academia.edu/472461/From_adaptation_to_Europeanization_of_Polish_foreign_policy

Powell, J., 1996, 'The Multiple Self: Exploring between and beyond Modernity and Postmodernity', *Berkeley Law Scholarship Repository*, https://lawcat.berkeley.edu/record/1115675?ln=en

Pravda, A., 'The Public Politics of Foreign Policy', Ch. 3 in Malcolm, N., Pravda, A., Light, M., Allison, R., 1996, *Internal Factors in Russian Foreign Policy*, Oxford: Oxford University Press

President Woodrow Wilson's Fourteen Points, 1918, *The Avalon Project Documents in Law, History and Diplomacy, Yale Law School*, http://avalon.law.yale.edu/20th_century/wilson14.asp

Pridham, G., 2000, 'EU Accession and domestic politics: Policy consensus and interactive dynamics in central and eastern Europe', *Perspectives on European Politics and Society*, Vol. 1, No 1, pp. 49-74, http://www.tandfonline.com/doi/abs/10.1080/1570585008458743

Pridham, G., Lewis, P., (eds.), 1996, *Stabilising Fragile Democracies: Comparing New Party Systems in Southern and Eastern Europe*, London: Routledge

Primakov, Y., 1996, 'Transcript: Primakov Starts with the CIS', *The Current Digest of the Post-Soviet Press*, Vol. 48, No 2

Primakov, Y., 2005, 'International Relations on the Eve of the 21st Century: Problems and Prospects', Ch. 2 in Part 2 in Melville, A., Shakleina, T., (eds.), *Russian Foreign Policy in Transition: Concepts and Realities*, New York: Central European University Press

Primatarova, A., 2015, *Interview with Rumena Filipova*, 3 November 2015, Sofia

Prizel, I., 1998, *National Identity and Foreign Policy: Nationalism and Leadership in Poland, Russia and Ukraine*, Cambridge: Cambridge University Press

Prodi, R., 2001, 'Poland and Europe: building on the past, shaping the future', *Catholic University of Lublin*, http://europa.eu/rapid/press-release_SPEECH-01-115_en.htm

Proedrou, F., 2010, 'Ukraine's foreign policy: accounting for Ukraine's indeterminate stance between Russia and the West', *Southeast European and Black Sea Studies*, Vol. 10, No 4, pp. 443-456, https://www.tandfonline.com/doi/abs/10.1080/14683857.2010.529993?journalCode=fbss20

Prozorov, S., 2006, *Understanding Conflict between Russia and the EU. The limits of integration*, Basingstoke: Palgrave Macmillan

Prozorov, S., 2009, *The ethics of postcommunism: history and social praxis in Russia*, Basingstoke: Palgrave Macmillan

Ptak, A., Koper, A., 2020, 'Poland uses state-owned refiner to buy regional media firm', Reuters, 7 December 2020, https://www.reuters.com/article/us-polskapress-m-a-pknorlen/poland-uses-state-owned-refiner-to-buy-regional-media-firm-idUKKBN28H277

Puhle, HJ., 'New nationalisms in Eastern Europe—a sixth wave', in Jahn, E., (ed.), 2009, *Nationalism in Late and Post-Communist Europe: Volume 1 – The Failed Nationalism of the Multinational and Partial National States*, Baden-Baden: Nomos

Putin, V., 19 September 2013, 'Выступление Владимира Путина на заседании клуба "Валдай"', *Российская газета*, ('Address by Vladimir Putin at the meeting of the Valdai Club', *Rossiyskaya gazeta*), http://www.rg.ru/2013/09/19/stenogramma-site.html

Putin, V., 18 March 2014, 'Обращение Президента Российской Федерации', *Президент России*, ('Address by the President of the Russian Federation', *President of Russia*), http://kremlin.ru/events/president/news/20603

Putin, V., 2021, 'Session of Davos Agenda 2021 online forum', *President of Russia*, http://en.kremlin.ru/events/president/transcripts/64938

Radaelli, C., 2000, 'Wither Europeanisation? Concept Stretching and Substantive Change', *European Integration online Papers (EIoP)*, Vol. 4, No 8, http://eiop.or.at/eiop/pdf/2000-008.pdf

Radio Free Europe, Radio Liberty, 2018, 'Trump Says Putin "May" Bear Responsibility For Syria Deaths, Promises "Major Decisions" Soon', 9 April 2018, https://www.rferl.org/a/syria-israel-blamed-missile-strike-after-douma-chemical-attack/29154339.html

Radio Poland, 2016, 'Poland demands explanation over EU politicians' comments', 5 January 2016, http://www.thenews.pl/1/10/Artykul/235320,Poland-demands-explanation-over-EU-politicians-comments

Radio Poland, 2016, 'EU Parliament chief accuses Poland of "Putin-style" politics', 10 January 2016, http://www.thenews.pl/1/10/Artykul/235922,EU-Parliament-chief-accuses-Poland-of-%E2%80%98Putinstyle%E2%80%99-politics

Radio Poland, 2016, 'Venice Commission warns that democracy in Poland at peril in draft opinion', 27 February 2016, http://thenews.pl/1/10/Artykul/242508,Venice-Commission-warns-that-democracy-in-Poland-at-peril-in-draft-opinion

Radio Poland, 2016, 'Germany is Poland's best EU ally: poll', 20 June 2016, http://www.thenews.pl/1/10/Artykul/257933,Germany-is-Polands-best-EU-ally-poll

Radio Poland, 2017, 'German publishers urged to clean up act over "Polish death camp" references', 29 May 2017, http://www.thenews.pl/1/10/Artykul/309065,German-publishers-urged-to-clean-up-act-over-Polish-death-camp-references

Radio Poland, 2017, 'Poland's ruling conservatives defend court reforms, EU concerned', 14 July 2017, http://thenews.pl/1/9/Artykul/316344,Poland%E2%80%99s-ruling-conservatives-defend-court-reforms-EU-concerned

Radio Poland, 2018, 'Poland close to ending dispute with Brussels: conservative leader', 4 April 2018, http://thenews.pl/1/9/Artykul/357104,Poland-close-to-ending-dispute-with-Brussels-conservative-leader

Rae, H., 2002, *State Identities and the Homogenisation of Peoples*, Cambridge: Cambridge University Press

Rahr, A., 1994, 'The Implications of Russia's Parliamentary Elections', *RFE/Radio Liberty Research Report*, Vol. 3, No 1, pp. 32-38

Raichev, A., 2009, 'Що е то "нация"?', *Дойче Веле България*, 2 март 2009, ('What is a "nation"?', *Deutsche Welle Bulgaria*, 2 March 2009), http://www.dw.com/bg/%D1%89%D0%BE-%D0%B5-%D1%82%D0%BE-%D0%BD%D0%B0%D1%86%D0%B8%D1%8F/a-4066199

Ralchev, S., 2015, *Interview with Rumena Filipova*, 6 November 2015, Sofia

Ralchev, S., 2015, 'Elusive Identity: Duality and Missed Opportunities in Bulgarian Foreign Policy in the Black Sea Region', in Part III of Slavkova, L., Shirinyan, A., (eds.), *Unrewarding Crossroads? The Black Sea Region amidst the European Union and Russia*, Sofia Platform, http://sofiaplatform.org/policy-papers/

Rankin, J., 2017, 'Cloud of corruption hangs over Bulgaria as it takes up EU presidency', *Guardian*, 28 December 2017, https://www.theguardian.com/world/2017/dec/28/bulgaria-corruption-eu-presidency-far-right-minority-parties-concerns

Ratchev, V., 2014, 'Партньорството за мир на НАТО: двадесет години по-късно', *CSDM Views*, Център за мениджмънт на сигурността и отбраната, София, ('NATO's Partnership for Peace: 20 years later', *CSDM Views*, Centre for Security and Defence Management, Sofia), https://procon.bg/system/files/Views_024.pdf

Ratchev, V., 2015, *Interview with Rumena Filipova*, 25 November 2015, Sofia

Reeves, C., 2010, 'Reopening the Wounds of History? The Foreign Policy of the 'Fourth' Polish Republic', *Journal of Communist Studies and Transition Politics*, Vol. 26, No 4, pp. 518-541, http://www.tandfonline.com/doi/abs/10.1080/13523279.2010.519189

Reisch, A., 1994, 'Central Europe's disappointments and hopes', *RFE/Radio Liberty Research Report*, Vol. 3, No 12, pp. 18-37

Resolution No 4 of the Constitutional Court of the Republic of Bulgaria, 1992, (Резолюция No 4 на Конституционния съд на Република България, 1992), http://constcourt.bg/bg/Acts/GetHtmlContent/faa0a5a2-992d-48cf-8e98-820350e42401

Reus-Smit, C., 2009, *Moral Purpose of the State: Culture, Social Identity and Institutional Rationality in International Relations*, Princeton: Princeton University Press

Reus-Smit, C., 2018, *On Cultural Diversity. International Theory in a World of Difference*, Cambridge University Press

Reuters, 2021, 'EU frets over Hungarian radio closure, levy on Polish media', 10 February 2021, https://www.reuters.com/article/eu-media-poland-hungary-idUSL8N2KG4PL

Rilska, B., 2014, 'Пленумът на БСП смекчи декларация за Украйна', *Дневник*, 15 март 2014, ('The BSP's plenum softened the declaration on Ukraine', *Dnevnik*, 15 march 2014), http://m.dnevnik.bg/bulgaria/2014/03/15/2261836_plenumut_na_bsp_smekchi_deklaraciia_za_ukraina/

Ripsman, N., Taliaferro, J., Lobell, S., 2016, *Neoclassical Realist Theory of International Politics*, New York: Oxford University Press

Risse, T., Kleine, M., 2009, 'Deliberation in Negotiations', *UCD Dublin European Institute Working Paper 09-04*, https://www.ucd.ie/t4cms/WP_09-04_Risse_and_Kleine.pdf

Risse, T., Ropp, S., Sikkink, K., (eds.), 1999, *Power of Human Rights: International Norms and Domestic Change*, Cambridge: Cambridge University Press

Roberts, K., 2014, 'Identity, Foreign Policy and the "Other": The Implications of Polish Foreign Policy vis-à-vis Russia', *Affaires publiques et internationals – Mémoires // Public and International Affairs – Research Papers*, University of Ottawa

Rosamond, B., 2000, *Theories of European Integration*, Basingstoke: Macmillan

Rosati, D., 1997, 'Poland's Present and Future in Europe', *Yearbook of Polish Foreign Policy*, pp. 9-15

Roser, T., 2017, 'Korrupt, aber für die EU pflegeleicht', *Zeit Online*, 28 Dezember 2017, ('Corrupt, but easy maintenance for the EU', Zeit Online, 28 December 2017), https://www.zeit.de/politik/ausland/2017-12/bulgarien-eu-praesidentschaft-ratsvorsitz-probleme-korruption?utm_referrer=https%3A%2F%2Fwww.google.com%2F

Rotfeld, A., 1990, 'Changes in the European Security System', *PISM*, Occasional Papers, No 16

Rotfeld, A., 2015, *Interview with Rumena Filipova*, 7 July 2015, Warsaw

Ruggie, J., 1998, *Constructing the World Polity: Essays on International Institutionalisation*, Abingdon: Routledge

Rusev, M., 2005, 'Традиционни и съвременни геополитически предизвикателства пред българската външна политика', *Геополитика*, No 3, ('Traditional and contemporary geopolitical challenges in Bulgarian foreign policy', *Geopolitics*, No 3), https://geopolitica.eu/2007?catid=21:broi6-2007&id=700:sedem-geopoliticheski-stsenariya-koito-mogat-da-raztarsyat-sveta-

Sabbat-Swidlicka, A., 1994a, 'The End of the Solidarity Era', *RFE/Radio Liberty Report*, Vol. 3, No 1, pp. 81-87

Sabbat-Swidlicka, A., 1994b, 'Wałęsa's Conflicts and Ambitions', *RFE/Radio Liberty Report*, Vol. 3, No 14, pp. 1-7

Šabič, Z., Brglez, M., 2002, 'The national identity of post-communist small states in the process of accession to the European Union: the case of Slovenia', *Communist and Post-Communist Studies*, Vol. 35, No 1, pp. 67-84, http://www.sciencedirect.com/science/article/pii/S0967067X01000253

Šabič, Z., Freyberg-Inan, A., 2012, 'Central Europe and the Balkans: So Close and Yet So Far', Ch. 14 in Šabič, Z., Drulák, P., (eds.), *Regional and International Relations of Central Europe*, London: Palgrave Macmillan

Sadurski, W., 2019, *Poland's Constitutional Breakdown*, Oxford University Press

Sakwa, R., 'Myth and democratic identity in Russia', Ch. 10 in Wöll, A., Wydra, H., (eds.), 2008, *Democracy and Myth in Russia and Eastern Europe*, London: Routledge

Sakwa, R., 2011, 'Russia's Identity: Between the "Domestic" and the "International"', *Europe-Asia Studies*, Vol. 63, No 6, pp. 957-975, http://www.tandfonline.com/doi/abs/10.1080/09668136.2011.585749?journalCode=ceas20

Samokhvalov, V., 2017, *Russian-European Relations in the Balkans and Black Sea Region: Great Power Identity and the Idea of Europe*, Palgrave Macmillan

Sanford, G., 2003, 'Overcoming the burden of history in Polish foreign policy', *Journal of Communist Studies and Transition Politics*, Volume 19, No 3, pp. 178-203, http://www.tandfonline.com/doi/abs/10.1080/13523270300660023

Sardamov, I., 2007, 'The Pursuit of Unhappiness: The Puzzle of Bulgaria's Transitional Pessimism', *International Symposium on Post-Communist Social and Political Conflicts: Citizenship and Consolidation in the New Democracies of South East Europe*, New Europe College, Bucharest, 1-3 June, 2007, http://www.academia.edu/318029/The_Pursuit_of_Unhappiness_The_Puzzle_of_Bulgarias_Transitional_Pessimism

Sasnal, P., 2015, *Interview with Rumena Filipova*, 8 July 2015, Warsaw

Sasnal, P., 2015, 'Poland: From Onlooker to Wannabe Agenda-Setter', Ch. 11 in Behr, T., Tiilikainen, T., (eds.), *Northern Europe and the Making of the EU's Mediterranean and Middle East Policies: Normative Leaders or Passive Bystanders?*, Burlington: Ashgate Publishing Limited

Schimmelfennig, F., Sedelmeier, U., (eds.), 2005, *Europeanization of Central and Eastern Europe*, Ithaca: Cornell University Press

Schmemann, S., 1990, 'For the German "Expellees", the Past is a Future Vision', *New York Times*, 4 March 1990, https://www.nytimes.com/1990/03/04/weekinreview/the-world-for-the-german-expellees-the-past-is-a-future-vision.html

Schmidt, V., 2010, 'Taking Ideas and Discourse Seriously: Explaining Change through Discursive Institutionalism as the Fourth 'New Institutionalism'', *European Political Science Review*, Vol. 2, No 1, pp. 1-25, https://www.cambridge.org/core/journals/european-politic al-science-review/article/taking-ideas-and-discourse-seriously-exp laining-change-through-discursive-institutionalism-as-the-fourth-ne w-institutionalism/52E2EB2B9A70D72CEB63CAA0E3B9F516

Schonberg, K., 2007, 'Ideology and Identity in Constructivist Foreign Policy Analysis', *Standing Group on International Relations, European Consortium for Political Research, Sixth Pan-European Conference, Turin, Italy*, http://www.eisa-net.org/be-bruga/eisa/files/events/turin/ Schonberg-Ideology_and_Identity_in_Constructivist_FPA.pdf

Schöpflin, G., 1990, 'The Political Traditions of Eastern Europe', *Daedalus*, Vol.119, No 1, pp. 55-90, https://www.jstor.org/stable/20025284?s eq=1#page_scan_tab_contents

Schrameyer, K., 2009, 'Направете си съдебен борд', в Таслакова, Р., (интервюиращ), *Две десетилетия преход. България през погледа на германски дипломати*, Изток-Запад, ('Create a judicial board', in Taslakova, R., (interviewer), *Two decades of transition. Bulgaria through the eyes of German diplomats*, East-West)

Schumacher, T., 2015, *Interview with Rumena Filipova*, 17 June 2015, Warsaw

Schweller, R., 1994, 'Bandwagoning for Profit: Bringing the Revisionist State Back In', *International Security*, Vol. 19, No 1, pp. 72-107, https:// www.jstor.org/stable/pdf/2539149.pdf?seq=1#page_scan_tab_cont ents

Scott, M., Kayali, L., 2020, 'What happened when humans stopped managing social media content', *Politico*, 21 October 2020, https://www.pol itico.eu/article/facebook-content-moderation-automation/

Scully, R., 2005, *Becoming Europeans? Attitudes, Behaviour, and Socialization in the European Parliament*, Oxford: Oxford University Press

Secrieru, S., 2015, *Interview with Rumena Filipova*, 9 June 2015, Warsaw

Sedelmeier, U., 2011, 'Europeanisation in new member and candidate states', *Living Reviews in European Governance*, Vol. 6, No 1, http:// www.europeangovernance-livingreviews.org/Articles/lreg-2011- 1/download/lreg-2011-1Color.pdf

Sega, 2012, 'Уорлик приветства спирането на АЕЦ "Белене"', 19 март 2012, ('Warlick welcomed the cancellation of the Belene nuclear power plant', 19 March 2012), http://www.segabg.com/article.php? id=593673

Sega, 2012, 'България подписа за "Южен поток"', 15 ноември 2012, ('Bulgaria signed South Stream', 15 November 2012), http://www.se gabg.com/article.php?id=623972

Service, R., 2019, *Kremlin Winter: Russia and the Second Coming of Vladimir Putin*, Picador

Shankman, P., 1984, 'The Thick and the Thin: On the Interpretive Theoretical Program of Clifford Geertz', *Current Anthropology*, Vol. 25, No 3, pp. 261-280, http://www.segabg.com/article.php?id=593 673

Shannon, V., 2012, 'Introduction: Ideational Allies – Psychology, Constructivism, and International Relations', in Shannon, V., Kowert, P., (eds.), *Psychology and Constructivism in International Relations: An Ideational Alliance*, Ann Arbor: University of Michigan Press

Shannon, V., Kowert, P., (eds.), 2012, *Psychology and Constructivism in International Relations: An Ideational Alliance*, Ann Arbor: University of Michigan Press

Shapiro, I., 2005, *The Flight from Reality in the Human Sciences*, Princeton University Press

Shikova, I., 2015, *Interview with Rumena Filipova*, 10 December 2015, Sofia

Shimazu, N., 2003, *Japan, Race, and Equality: The Racial Equality Proposal of 1919*, London: Routledge

Shmelev, B., 2014, *Interview with Rumena Filipova*, 22 July 2014, Moscow

Shopov, V., 2007, 'В ЕС с виртуална външна политика', *Гледна точка*, 20 март 2007, ('In the EU with a virtual foreign policy, *Point of View*, 20 March 2007)

Shopov, V., 2015, *Interview with Rumena Filipova*, 3 December 2015, Sofia

Sienkiewicz, B., 2001, 'Delusions and Dilemmas of Poland's Eastern Policy: In Praise of Minimalism', *Polish Foreign Affairs Digest*, Vol. 1, No 1, pp. 227-237

Sikorski, R., 2009, 'Minister of Foreign Affairs, Mr. Radosław Sikorski, on the goals of Poland's foreign policy for 2009', *Ministry of Foreign Affairs of the Republic of Poland Annual Address*, http://www.mfa.gov.pl/en/news/aktualnosc_25449?printMode=true

Sikorski, R., 2012, 'The Minister of Foreign Affairs on Polish Foreign Policy for 2012', *Ministry of Foreign Affairs of the Republic of Poland Annual Address*, http://www.msz.gov.pl/en/news/the_minister_of_foreig n_affairs_on_polish_foreign_policy_for_2012;jsessionid=21106E0F25 3710F395B542795E70EE0E.cmsap6p

Sikorski, R., 2013, 'Address by the Minister of Foreign Affairs on the goals of Polish foreign policy in 2013', *Ministry of Foreign Affairs of the Republic of Poland Annual Address*, http://www.mfa.gov.pl/en/news /address_by_the_minister_of_foreign_affairs_on_the_goals_of_pol ish_foreign_policy_in2013_

Sikorski, R., 2014, 'Address by the Minister of Foreign Affairs on the goals of Polish foreign policy in 2014', *Ministry of Foreign Affairs of the Republic of Poland Annual Address*, http://www.msz.gov.pl/resource/03ead137-62d8-42d3-9a8a-ed577f19c34a:JCR

Simon, J., 1998, 'Bulgaria and NATO: 7 Lost Years', *Strategic Forum*, No 138-142, https://www.questia.com/library/journal/1G1-130388716/bulgaria-and-nato-7-lost-years

Simon, M., 2014, *Interview with Rumena Filipova*, 23 June 2014, Moscow

Sjoberg, L., Barkin, S., 2018, 'If It Is Everything, It Is Nothing', Ch. 13 in Bertucci, M., Hayes, J., James, P., (eds.), *Constructivism Reconsidered. Past, Present and Future*, University of Michigan Press

Skak, M., 1992, 'Post-Communist Foreign Policies: Initial Observations', *Cooperation and Conflict*, Vol. 27, No 3, pp. 277-300, http://journals.sagepub.com/doi/abs/10.1177/0010836792027003003

Skak, M., 1996, *From Empire to Anarchy: Postcommunist Foreign Policy and International Relations*, London: Hurst & Company

Skinner, Q., 2002, *Visions of Politics. Volume 1: Regarding Method*, Cambridge: Cambridge University Press

Skubiszewski, K., 1994, 'Perspectives of Poland's Foreign Policy in Europe', *Yearbook of Polish Foreign Policy*, pp. 21-31

Slater, W., 1994, 'Russia: The Return of Authoritarian Government?', *RFE/Radio Liberty Research Report*, Vol. 3, No 1, pp. 22-32

Slatinski, N., 2012, 'Ролята и мястото на България в НАТО в условията на променящия се свят', *Ново време*, брой 10, с. 21-100, ('The role and place of Bulgaria in NATO in changing global conditions', *New times*, No 10, pp. 21-100), http://nslatinski.org/?q=bg/node/441

Slatinski, N., 2015, *Interview with Rumena Filipova*, 10 December 2015, Sofia

Slavkova, L., 2015, *Interview with Rumena Filipova*, 28 October 2015, Sofia

Smirnov, P., 2014, *Interview with Rumena Filipova*, 1 July 2014, Moscow

Smith, A., 2009, *Ethno-symbolism and Nationalism: A Cultural Approach*, Abingdon: Routledge

Smith, D., 2003, '"The Devil and the Deep Blue Sea": European Integration, National Identity and Foreign Policy in Post-Communist Estonia', *Journal of Communist Studies and Transition Politics*, Vol. 19, No 3, pp. 156-177, http://www.tandfonline.com/doi/abs/10.1080/13523270300660022

Smith, S., 1996, 'Positivism and beyond', in Smith, S., Booth, K., Zalewski, M., (eds.), *International Theory: Positivism and Beyond*, Cambridge: Cambridge University Press

Snyder, R., Bruck, H., Sapin, B., 2002, *Foreign Policy Decision-Making (Revisited)*, Basingstoke: Palgrave Macmillan

Sofia Globe, 2014, 'Bulgarian Parliament votes Borissov into office as Prime Minister, approves cabinet', http://sofiaglobe.com/2014/11/07/bulgarian-parliament-votes-borissov-into-office-as-prime-minister/

Sofiyanski, S., 1993, 'Национална чест и достойнство', *Демокрация*, 17 май 1993, ('National honour and dignity', *Democracy*, 17 May 1993), http://www.faktite.bg/source/democracia/7053

Sokolsky, R., 2017, 'The New NATO-Russia Military Balance: Implications for European Security', *Task Force White Paper*, http://carnegieendowment.org/2017/03/13/new-nato-russia-military-balance-implications-for-european-security-pub-68222

Solemn Declaration on European Union, 1983, European Council, Stuttgart 19 June 1983, https://www.cvce.eu/en/obj/solemn_declaration_on_european_union_stuttgart_19_june_1983-en-a2e74239-a12b-4efc-b4ce-cd3dee9cf71d.html

Sørensen, G., 2008, 'The Case for Combining Material Forces and Ideas in the Study of IR', *European Journal of International Relations*, Vol. 14, No 1, pp. 5-32, http://journals.sagepub.com/doi/abs/10.1177/1354066107087768

Sotirov, P., 2000, 'Resume of Programme Y2000 of the Bulgarian Membership Action Plan', *Workshop on Defence Policy Modernisation and Security on the Balkans, University of National and World Economy, Sofia*, 24-25 May 2000

Spero, J., 2004, *Bridging the European Divide: Middle Power Politics and Regional Security Dilemmas*, Lanham: Rowman & Littlefield Publishers

Spirova, M., 2008, 'The Bulgarian Socialist Party: The long road to Europe', *Communist and Post-Communist Studies*, Vol. 41, No 4, pp. 481-495, http://www.sciencedirect.com/science/article/pii/S0967067X08000615

Stadtmüller, E., 2000, 'Polish perceptions of the European Union in the 1990s', Ch. 3 in Cordell, K., (ed.), *Poland and the European Union*, London: Routledge

Stanev, I., 1998, 'Хавиер Солана дискретно разузна ситуацията в България', *Капитал*, 4 април 1998, ('Javier Solana discretely inquired into the situation in Bulgaria, *Capital*, 4 April 1998), http://www.capital.bg/politika_i_ikonomika/bulgaria/1998/04/04/243964_havier_solana_diskretno_razuzna_situaciiata_v_bulgariia/

Stankevich, S., 1992, 'Russia in Search of Itself', *The National Interest*, Summer 1992, http://nationalinterest.org/article/russia-in-search-of-itself-1629

Stankova, M., 2010, 'Communism and Cold War in Bulgaria: The Absence of Europe?', Ch. 3 in Katsikas, S., (ed.), *Bulgaria and Europe: Shifting Identities*, London: Anthem Press

Starr, H., 1988, 'Rosenau, pre-theories and the evolution of the comparative study of foreign policy', *International Interactions. Empirical and Theoretical Research in International Relations*, Vol. 14, No 1, pp. 3-15, https://www.tandfonline.com/doi/abs/10.1080/03050628808434686?journalCode=gini20

State News Service, 2013, 'President marks Poland's EU accession anniversary', 1 May 2013

Stauter-Halsted, K., 2004, *The Nation in the Village: The Genesis of Peasant National Identity in Austrian Poland, 1848–1914*, Cornell University Press

Stawarska, R., 1999, 'EU enlargement from the Polish perspective', *Journal of European Public Policy*, Vol. 6, No 5, pp. 822-838, http://www.tandfonline.com/doi/abs/10.1080/135017699343405?journalCode=rjpp20

Steele, B., Gould, H., Kessler, O., (eds.), 2019, *Tactical Constructivism, Method, and International Relations*, Routledge

Steffler, C., 2009, 'На българската политика й липсват млади дипломати', в Таслакова, Р., (интервюиращ), *Две десетилетия преход. България през погледа на германски дипломати*, Изток-Запад, ('Bulgarian politics lacks young diplomats', in Taslakova, R., (interviewer), *Two decades of transition. Bulgaria through the eyes of German diplomats*, East-West)

Stein, J., 2013, 'Threat Perception in International Relations', Ch. 12 in Sears, D., Huddy, L., Levy, J., (eds.), *Oxford Handbook of Political Psychology*, New York: Oxford University Press, 2nd ed.

Stemplowski, R., 2015, *Interview with Rumena Filipova*, 21 July 2015, Warsaw

Stent, A., 2007, 'Reluctant Europeans: Three Centuries of Russian Ambivalence toward the West', Ch. 7 in Legvold, R., (ed.), *Russian Foreign Policy in the 21st Century and the Shadow of the Past*, New York: Columbia University Press

Steves, F., 2001, 'Poland and the international system: external influences on democratic consolidation', *Communist and Post-Communist Studies*, Vol. 34, No 3, pp. 339-352, http://www.sciencedirect.com/science/article/pii/S0967067X01000125

Strategic Defence and Security Review: Securing Britain in an Age of Uncertainty, 2010, *Cabinet Office, National Security and Intelligence*, https://www.gov.uk/government/publications/the-strategic-defence-and-security-review-securing-britain-in-an-age-of-uncertainty

Strategic Defence Review White Paper of the UK, 1998, *International Affairs and Defence Section, House of Commons Library*, pp. 12, 17-18, https://commonslibrary.parliament.uk/research-briefings/rp98-91/

Stryker, S., 2008, 'From Mead to a Structural Symbolic Interactionism and Beyond', *Annual Review of Sociology*, Vol. 34, pp.15-31, http://www.annualreviews.org/doi/abs/10.1146/annurev.soc.34.040507.134649

Study on NATO Enlargement, 1995, *NATO*, http://www.nato.int/cps/po/natohq/official_texts_24733.htm

Subotic, J., 2017, 'Constructivism as Professional Practice in the US Academy', *Political Science & Politics*, Vol. 50, No 1, pp. 84–88, https://doi.org/10.1017/S1049096516002201

Subtelny, O., 1997, 'The Habsburg and Russian Empires: Some Comparisons and Contrasts', in Hara, T., Matsuzato, K., (eds.), *Empire and Society: New Approaches to Russian History*, Sapporo

Surkov, V., 2018, 'Одиночество полукровки', *Russia in Global Affairs*, March/April 2018, ('The loneliness of half-blood'), http://www.globalaffairs.ru/global-processes/Odinochestvo-polukrovki-14-19477

Suslov, M., 2020, *Geopolitical Imagination: Ideology and Utopia in Post-Soviet Russia*, Ibidem Press

Sutton, M., 2007, *France and the Construction of Europe, 1944-2007: The Geopolitical Imperative*, New York: Berghahn Books

Swann, W., Bosson, J., 'Identity negotiation: A theory of self and social interaction', Chapter 17 in John, O., Robins, R., Pervin, L., (eds.), 2008, *Handbook of Personality: Theory and Research*, New York: Guilford Press

Świeboda, P., 2007, 'Poland's Second Return to Europe?', *European Council on Foreign Relations Policy Brief*, http://www.ecfr.eu/page/-/ECFR-03_POLANDS_SECOND_RETURN_TO_EUROPE.pdf

Szabo, S., 2015, *Germany, Russia, and the Rise of Geo-Economics*, London: Bloomsbury

Szakolczai, A., 'The non-being of communism and myths of democratisation', Ch. 2 in Wöll, A., Wydra, H., (eds.), 2008, *Democracy and Myth in Eastern Europe and Russia*, London: Routledge

Szakolczai, A., 2009, 'Liminality and Experience: Structuring transitory situations and transformative events', *International Political Anthropology*, Vol. 2, No 1, pp. 141-173, http://www.politicalanthropology.org/index.php?option=com_content&view=article&id=344:ipa3-liminality-and-experience-structuring-transitory-situations-and-transformative-events&catid=34

Szczerbiak, A., 2001, 'Polish Public Opinion: Explaining Declining Support for EU Membership', *Journal of Common Market Studies*, Vol. 39, No 1, pp. 105-122, http://onlinelibrary.wiley.com/doi/10.1111/1468-5965.00278/abstract

Szczerbiak, A., 2012, *Poland within the European Union: The New Awkward Partner?*, London: Routledge

Szczerbiak, A., 2018, 'The political significance of Poland's government reshuffle', *EUROPP – European Politics and Policy, London School of Economics*, http://blogs.lse.ac.uk/europpblog/2018/02/01/the-political-significance-of-polands-government-reshuffle/

Szczerski, K., 2005, 'The Duchy of Europe or the "Europe" System? Some Observations about the Future of the European Union', *Polish Foreign Affairs Digest*, Vol. 5, No 3, pp. 49-64

Szeptycki, A., 2010, 'Polish-Ukrainian Relations: From the Success of the "Orange Revolution" to Russia-first Policy', *The Polish Quarterly of International Affairs*, Vol. 19, No 3, pp. 5-26

Szeptycki, A., 2015, *Interview with Rumena Filipova*, 3 July 2015, Warsaw

Szűcs, J., 1983, 'The Three Historical Regions of Europe', *Acta Historica Academiae Scientiarum Hungaricae*, Vol. 29, No 2/4, pp. 131-184, https://www.jstor.org/stable/42555425?seq=1#page_scan_tab_contents

Tajfel, H., 1974, 'Social identity and intergroup behaviour', *Social Science Information*, Vol.13, No 2, pp. 65-93, http://journals.sagepub.com/doi/abs/10.1177/053901847401300204?journalCode=ssia

Tajfel, H., Turner, J., 1979, 'An integrative theory of inter-group conflict', Ch. 3 in Austin, W., Worchel, S., (eds.), *Social psychology of inter-group relations*, Monterey: Brooks/Cole

Talbott, S., 2003, *Russia Hand: A Memoir of Presidential Diplomacy*, New York: Random House

Tansey, O., 2007, 'Process Tracing and Elite Interviewing: A Case for Non-Probability Sampling', *PS: Political Science and Politics*, Vol. 40, No 4, pp. 765-772, https://www.cambridge.org/core/journals/ps-political-science-and-politics/article/process-tracing-and-elite-interviewing-a-case-for-non-probability-sampling/8EE25765F4BF94599E7FBD996CBFDE74

Tashev, B., 2005, 'In Search of Security: Bulgaria's Security Policy in Transition', Ch. 7 in Lansford, T., Tashev, B., (eds.), *Old Europe, New Europe and the US: Renegotiating Transatlantic Security in the Post 9/11 Era*, Burlington: Ashgate

Teague, E., 1994, 'The CIS: An Unpredictable Future', *RFE/Radio Liberty Research Report*, Vol. 3, No 1, pp. 9-13

Telhami, S., Barnett, M., (eds.), 2002, *Identity and Foreign Policy in the Middle East*, Ithaca: Cornell University Press

Terry, S., 2000, 'Poland's foreign policy since 1989: the challenges of independence', *Communist and Post-Communist Studies*, Vol. 33, No 1, pp. 7-47, http://www.sciencedirect.com/science/article/pii/S0967067X99000240

Terzi, Ö., 'Europeanisation of foreign policy and candidate countries: a comparative study of Greek and Turkish cases', *Politique Européenne*, Vol. 3, No 17, pp. 113-136, https://www.cairn.info/revue-politique-europeenne-2005-3-page-113.htm

Tetrault-Farber, G., 2015, 'Russian, European Far-Right Parties Converge in St. Petersburg', *Moscow Times*, 22 March 2015, https://themoscowtimes.com/articles/russian-european-far-right-parties-converge-in-st-petersburg-45010

Tevdoy-Burmuli, A., 2014, *Interview with Rumena Filipova*, 9 July 2014, Moscow

Thatcher, M., 1988, 'Speech at dinner given by Polish Government', *Margaret Thatcher Foundation*, http://www.margaretthatcher.org/document/107368

Ther, P., 2006, 'The burden of history and the trap of memory', *Transit*, No 30, https://www.eurozine.com/the-burden-of-history-and-the-trap-of-memory/

Thies, C., 2009, 'Role Theory and Foreign Policy', *International Studies Association Compendium Project, Foreign Policy Analysis section*, http://www.myweb.uiowa.edu/bhlai/workshop/role.pdf

Thies, C., 2010, 'State Socialization and Structural Realism', *Security Studies*, Vol. 19, No 4, pp. 689-717, https://www.tandfonline.com/doi/abs/10.1080/09636412.2010.524084

Thies, C., 2012, 'International Socialization Processes vs. Israeli National Role Conceptions: Can Role Theory Integrate IR Theory and Foreign Policy Analysis?', *Foreign Policy Analysis*, Vol. 8, No 1, pp. 25-46, https://onlinelibrary.wiley.com/doi/abs/10.1111/j.1743-8594.2011.00170.x

Thomas, D., 2005, 'Human Rights Ideas, the Demise of Communism, and the End of the Cold War', *Journal of Cold War Studies*, Vol. 7, No 2, pp. 110-141, https://muse.jhu.edu/article/181904

Thomassen, B., 2009, 'The Uses and Meanings of Liminality', *International Political Anthropology*, Vol. 2, No 1, pp. 5-28

Thompson, M., 2004, *Democratic Revolutions: Asia and Eastern Europe*, London: Routledge

Timofeev, I., 2008, *Политическая идентичность России в постсоветский период: альтернативы и тенденции*, МГИМО (*Russia's political identity in the post-Soviet period: alternatives and tendencies*, MGIMO), http://identityworld.ru/_ld/1/175_pol-id-rus_timo.pdf

Timofeev, I., 2014, *Interview with Rumena Filipova*, 26 June 2014, Moscow

Todorov, A., 1999, *The Role of Political Parties in Bulgaria's Accession to the EU*, Center for the Study of Democracy, Sofia, http://unpan1.un.org/intradoc/groups/public/documents/untc/unpan017021.pdf

Todorova, M., 2009, *Imagining the Balkans*, Oxford: Oxford University Press, Updated ed.

Tonra, B., 2001, *Europeanisation of National Foreign Policy. Dutch, Danish and Irish Foreign Policy in the European Union*, Aldershot: Ashgate

Tonra, B., 'Europeanization', Ch. 12 in Jorgensen, K., et al, (eds.), 2015, *The SAGE Handbook of European Foreign Policy*, London: SAGE Publications Ltd

Torkunov, A., 2005, 'International Relations after the Kosovo crisis', Ch. 1 in Part 3 in Melville, A., Shakleina, T., (eds.), *Russian Foreign Policy in Transition: Concepts and Realities*, New York: Central European University Press

Tosheva, S., 1995, 'Политическата учебна година измести националния дебат за НАТО', *Капитал*, 29 май 1995, ('The new political "school" year displaced the national debate on NATO', *Capital*, 29 May 1995), http://www.capital.bg/politika_i_ikonomika/1995/05/29/1117523_politicheskata_uchebna_godina_izmesti_nacionalniia/

Tosheva, S., 1996, 'БСП изпусна националната идея, дойде часът на псевдонационалистите', *Капитал*, 8 април 1996, ('The BSP let go of the national idea, the time has come for the pseudo-nationalists', *Capital*, 8 April 1996), http://www.capital.bg/politika_i_ikonomika/1996/04/08/1030570_bsp_izpusna_nacionalnata_ideia_doide_chasut_na/

Trade and commercial and economic cooperation agreement between the EEC and Bulgaria, 1990, http://europa.eu/rapid/press-release_MEMO-92-27_en.htm?locale=en

Traktat między Rzecząpospolitą Polską a Republiką Federalną Niemiec o dobrym sąsiedztwie i przyjaznej współpracy, 1991, (Treaty of Good Neighbourliness and Friendly Cooperation between the Republic of Poland and the Federal Republic of Germany)

Treaty on Conventional Armed Forces in Europe, 1990, *CSCE*, http://www.osce.org/library/14087?download=true

Treaty on European Union, 1992, Council of the European Communities, Commission of the European Communities, p. 7, https://europa.eu/european-union/sites/europaeu/files/docs/body/treaty_on_european_union_en.pdf

Treaty on Friendship, Good-Neighbourliness, Cooperation and Security between the Republic of Bulgaria and the Republic of Turkey, 1992, (Договор за приятелство, добросъседство, сътрудничество и сигурност между Република България и Република Турция, 1992)

Trenin, D., 2002, *End of Eurasia. Russia on the Border between Geopolitics and Globalization*, Washington: Carnegie Endowment for International Peace

Trenin, D., 2006, *Интеграция и идентичность: Россия как 'новый Запад'*, Московский Центр Карнеги, (*Integration and identity: Russia as 'the new West'*, Carnegie Moscow Center), http://carnegieendowment.org/files/9819trenin.pdf

Trenin, D., 2007, *Getting Russia Right*, Washington: Carnegie Endowment for International Peace

Trenin, D., 2014, *Interview with Rumena Filipova*, 3 July 2014, Moscow

Troitskiy, M., 2014, *Interview with Rumena Filipova*, 19 June 2014, Moscow

Trondal, J., 2004, 'An Institutional Perspective on EU Committee Governance', in Reinalda, B., Verbeek, B., (eds.), *Decision Making within International Organizations*, London: Routledge

Trzeciak, S., 2015, *Interview with Rumena Filipova*, 30 June 2015, Warsaw

Trzcielińska-Polus, A., 2011, 'Realization of the Rights of Poles in Germany Following the Treaty on Good Neighbourliness', *Przegląd Zachodni*, No 2, http://www.iz.poznan.pl/plik,pobierz,805,b9f6e1b4d487ce8367485900d266a098/9-07.%20Trzcielinska.pdf

Tsanev, S., 2010, *Български хроники. Том 4: История на нашия народ от 1943 до 2007*, Жанет 45, (*Bulgarian chronicles. Vol. 4: History of our nation between 1943 and 2007*, Zhanet 45)

Tsygankov, A., 2003, 'Mastering Space in Eurasia: Russia's Geopolitical Thinking after the Soviet Break-up', *Communist and Post-Communist Studies*, Vol. 36, pp. 101-127, https://is.muni.cz/do/fss/KMVES/40125114/Tsygankov__A._Mastering_Space_Euroasia_Comm.Studes_36_2003.pdf?lang=en

Tsygankov, A., 2005, 'Vladimir Putin's Vision of Russia as a Normal Great Power', *Post-Soviet Affairs*, Vol. 21, No 2, pp. 132-158, http://www.tandfonline.com/doi/abs/10.2747/1060-586X.21.2.132

Tsygankov, A., 2013, 'The Russia-NATO mistrust: Ethnophobia and the double expansion to contain "the Russian Bear"', *Communist and Post-Communist Studies*, Vol. 46, No 1, pp. 179-188, http://www.sciencedirect.com/science/article/pii/S0967067X12000931

Tsygankov, A., 2016, *Russia's Foreign Policy: Change and Continuity in National Identity*, Lanham: Rowman & Littlefield Publishers, 4th ed.

Tully, J., (ed.), 1988, *Meaning and Context: Quentin Skinner and His Critics*, Cambridge: Polity

Tulmets, E., 2014, *East Central European Foreign Policy Identity in Perspective: Back to Europe and the EU's Neighbourhood*, Basingstoke: Palgrave Macmillan

Turgunova, V., 2013, *Nexus of Politics and the Economy: A Case Study of Russian-German Relations*, Master's thesis, University of Tampere, https://tampub.uta.fi/bitstream/handle/10024/85090/gradu07120.pdf?sequence=1

Turner, J., Hogg, M., Oakes, P., Reicher, S., Wetherell, M., 1987, *Rediscovering the Social Group: A Self-Categorization Theory*, Oxford: Basil Blackwell.

Turner, V., 1995, *Ritual Process: Structure and Anti-Structure*, New York: Aldine de Gruyter

UDF electoral platform, 1990, (Предизборна платформа на СДС, 1990), http://www.omda.bg/page.php?IDMenu=209&IDArticle=1631

UPI Archives (United Press International Archives), 1989, 'Mitterrand meets with government, Solidarity leaders', http://www.upi.com/Archives/1989/06/14/Mitterrand-meets-with-government-Solidarity-leaders/4980613800000/

Utkin, S., 2014, *Interview with Rumena Filipova*, 7 July 2014, Moscow

Varga, M., Buzogány, A., 2020, 'The Foreign Policy of Populists in Power: Contesting Liberalism in Poland and Hungary', *Geopolitics*, https://doi.org/10.1080/14650045.2020.1734564

Velychenko, S., (ed.), 2007, *Ukraine, the EU and Russia: History, Culture and International Relations*, Basingstoke: Palgrave Macmillan

Vesti, 2014, 'БСП без "лоша дума" за Русия', 19 март 2014, ('No "bad word" for Russia from the BSP', 19 March 2014), https://www.vesti.bg/analizi-i-komentari/komentari/bsp-bez-losha-duma-za-rusiia-6007863

Vienna Document on Confidence- and Security-Building Measures, 2011, *OSCE*, https://www.osce.org/fsc/86597?download=true

Vigenin, K., 2015, *Interview with Rumena Filipova*, 17 December 2015, Sofia

Visegrad Declaration. Declaration on Cooperation between the Czech and Slovak Federal Republic, the Republic of Poland and the Republic of Hungary in Striving for European Integration, 1991, http://www.visegradgroup.eu/documents/visegrad-declarations/visegrad-declaration-110412-2

Vn.government.bg, 'България и НАТО – дати и събития', ('Bulgaria and NATO – dates and events'), http://www.vn.government.bg/world/stranici/svetat/nato.htm

Walker, S., (ed.), 1987, *Role Theory and Foreign Policy Analysis*, Durham, N.C.: Duke University Press

Wallander, C., 2007, 'Russian Transimperialism and Its Implications', *The Washington Quarterly*, Vol. 30, Issue 2, pp. 107-122, https://www.tandfonline.com/doi/abs/10.1162/wash.2007.30.2.107

Walt, S., 1987, *Origins of Alliances*, Ithaca: Cornell University Press

Waltz, K., 2010, *Theory of International Politics*, Waveland Press

Wasserstein, R., Lazar, N., 2016, 'The ASA Statement on p-Values: Context, Process, and Purpose', *The American Statistician*, Vol. 70, No 2, pp. 129-133, https://doi.org/10.1080/00031305.2016.1154108

Wasserstein, R., Schirm, A., Lazar, N., 2019, 'Moving to a World Beyond "$p < 0.05$"', *The American Statistician*, Vol. 73, pp. 1-19, https://doi.org/10.1080/00031305.2019.1583913

Waszczykowski, W., 2015, *Interview with Rumena Filipova*, 12 June 2015, Warsaw

Waszczykowski, W., 2016, 'Information of the Minister of Foreign Affairs on the Polish Government's Foreign Policy in 2016', *Ministry of Foreign Affairs of the Republic of Poland Annual Report*, http://www.msz.gov.pl/resource/601901dd-1db8-4a64-ba4a-9c80f2d5811b:JCR

Wawrzusiszyn, A., 2014, 'Polish Strategic Thought in Shaping Security Policy', *Security Dimensions. International & National Studies*, No 12, pp. 95-103, http://security-dimensions.pl/wp-content/uploads/2015/07/SD_12_95-103.pdf

Wawrzyński, P., 2012, 'The Usage of Politics of Memory in Polish Foreign Policy: Present State and Perspectives', *Copernicus Journal of Political Studies*, Vol. 1, No 1, pp. 67-91, http://www.academia.edu/7163251/The_Usage_of_Politics_of_Memory_in_Polish_Foreign_Policy_Present_State_and_Perspectives

Webber, M., 2000, *Russia and Europe: Conflict or Cooperation?*, Basingstoke: Palgrave Macmillan

Webster, A., 2005, 'The Transnational Dream: Politicians, Diplomats and Soldiers in the League of Nations' Pursuit of International Disarmament, 1920-1938', *Contemporary European History*, Vol. 14, No 4, pp. 493-518, https://www.jstor.org/stable/20081281?seq=1#page_scan_tab_contents

Wedel, J., 1998, *Collision and Collusion: The Strange Case of Western Aid to Eastern Europe, 1989-1998*, New York: St. Martin's Press

Wehner, L., Thies, C., 2014, 'Role Theory, Narratives, and Interpretation: The Domestic Contestation of Roles', *International Studies Review*, Vol. 16, No 3, pp. 411-436, https://onlinelibrary.wiley.com/doi/abs/10.1111/misr.12149

Weinstein, N., Legate, N., Ryan, W., Sedikides, C., Cozzolino, P., 2017, 'Autonomy support for conflictual and stigmatized identities: Effects on ownership and psychological health', *Journal of Counseling Psychology*, Vol. 64, No 5, pp. 584-599, https://www.ncbi.nlm.nih.gov/pubmed/28493737

Wendt, A., 1992, 'Anarchy is what states make of it: the social construction of power politics', *International Organization*, Vol. 46, No 2, pp. 391-425, https://www.jstor.org/stable/2706858?seq=1#page_scan_tab_contents

Wendt, A., 1998, 'On Constitution and Causation in International Relations', *Review of International Studies*, Vol. 24, pp. 101-117, http://www.jstor.org/stable/20097563?seq=1#page_scan_tab_contents

Wendt, A., 1999, *Social Theory of International Politics*, Cambridge: Cambridge University Press

Weydenthal, J., 1994a, 'Poland Builds Security Ties with the West', *RFE/Radio Liberty Research Report*, Vol. 3, No 14, pp. 28-31

Weydenthal, J., 1994b, 'East Central Europe and the EU: Forging Political Ties', *RFE/Radio Liberty Research Report*, Vol. 3, No 29, pp. 16-19

White Paper for International Security and Defence, Italy, 2015, *Ministry of Defence*, pp. 33, 35-38, https://www.difesa.it/Primo_Piano/Documents/2015/07_Luglio/White%20book.pdf

Whitefield, S., Rohrschneider, R., 2009, 'The Europeanization of Political Parties in Central and Eastern Europe? The Impact of EU Entry on Issue Stances, Salience and Programmatic Coherence', *Journal of Communist Studies and Transition Politics*, Vol. 25, No 4, pp. 564-584, http://www.tandfonline.com/doi/abs/10.1080/13523270903310936

Whitehead, L., 2002, *Democratisation: Theory and Experience*, Oxford: Oxford University Press

Wieliński, B., 2015, *Interview with Rumena Filipova*, 6 July 2015, Warsaw

Wiener, A., 2009, 'Enacting Meaning-in-Use. Qualitative Research on Norms and International Relations', *Review of International Studies*, Vol. 35, No 1, pp. 175-193, https://www.wiso.uni-hamburg.de/fach bereich-sowi/professuren/wiener/dokumente/publikationenaw/ zeitschriftenartikelaw/15-wiener-2009-enacting-meaning-in-use-qu alitative-research-on-norms-and-ir.pdf

Wiener, A., 2014, *A Theory of Contestation*, Springer

Winch, P., 1990, *Idea of a Social Science and its Relation to Philosophy*, London: Routledge, 2nd ed.

Wish, N., 1980, 'Foreign Policy Makers and Their National Role Conceptions', *International Studies Quarterly*, Vol. 24, No 4, pp. 532-554, https://academic.oup.com/isq/article-abstract/24/4/532/18 92386

Wizimirska, B., 1996a, 'Activities of the Sejm in Foreign Affairs', *Yearbook of Polish Foreign Policy*, pp. 187-196

Wizimirska, B., 1996b, 'President Lech Wałęsa's International Activities in 1995. Summing up 1991-1995', *Yearbook of Polish Foreign Policy*, pp. 196-215

Wohlforth, W., 2008, 'Realism', Ch. 7 in Reus-Smit, C., Snidal, D., (eds.), *Oxford Handbook of International Relations*, Oxford: Oxford University Press

Wolczuk, K., 2003, 'Ukraine's Policy towards the European Union: A Case of "Declarative Europeanization"', *The Stefan Batory Foundation*, http://www.batory.org.pl/ftp/program/forum/eu_ukraine/ukra ine_eu_policy.pdf

Wolczuk, K., 2004, 'Integration without Europeanisation: Ukraine and Its Policy Towards the European Union', *Robert Schuman Centre for Advanced Studies, EUI Working Papers, RSCAS No. 2004/15*, pp.1-22, https://papers.ssrn.com/sol3/papers.cfm?abstract_id=2344806

Wong, R., 2005, 'The Europeanisation of Foreign Policy', Ch. 7 in Hill, C., Smith, M., (eds.), *International Relations and the European Union*, Oxford: Oxford University Press, 2nd ed.

Wong, R., Hill, C., (eds.), 2011, *National and European Foreign Policies: Towards Europeanization*, Abingdon: Routledge

World Bank, GDP statistics, 2016, http://databank.worldbank.org/data/ download/GDP.pdf

World Bank, 2020, *World Bank Governance Indicators*, percentile ranks for rule of law chosen for Poland, Bulgaria and Russia in 2019, https:// info.worldbank.org/governance/wgi/Home/Reports

Wydra, H., 2000, *Continuities in Poland's Permanent Transition*, Basingstoke: Macmillan

Wydra, H., 2007, *Communism and the Emergence of Democracy*, Cambridge University Press

Wydra, H., 2008, 'The power of second reality: communist myths and representations of democracy', Ch. 3 in Wöll, A., Wydra, H., (eds.), *Democracy and Myth in Russia and Eastern Europe*, London: Routledge

Wydra, H., 2013, 'Democracy in Crisis? Myth, Ideology, and Reality', *paper presented at conference on The Crisis of Democracy – Evidence from the Post-Communist World, St Catharine's college*, 6 December 2013

Wydra, H., 2015, 'The Dynamics of Memory in East and West: Elements of a Comparative Framework', *Remembrance and Solidarity Studies*, No 1, http://www.enrs.eu/studies/studies1

Yeltsin, B., 2001, *Midnight Diaries*, London: Phoenix

Yordanova, L., Zhelev, I., 2002, 'Public attitudes to NATO membership', in Minchev, O., Ratchev, V., Lessenski, M., (eds.), *Bulgaria for NATO*, Institute for Regional and International Studies, Sofia, http://www.iris-bg.org/fls/intro.pdf

Zaborowski, M., 2002, 'Europeanisation as a consensus building process: the case of Polish-German relations', *European Foreign Policy Unit workshop on 'Europeanisation of national foreign policies'*, June 2002, http://www.lse.ac.uk/internationalRelations/centresandunits/EFPU/EFPUworkshop2002/paper%20-%20Zaborowski.pdf

Zaborowski, M., 2006, 'More than simply expanding markets: Germany and EU enlargement', Ch. 6 in Sjursen, H., (ed.), *Questioning EU Enlargement: Europe in Search of Identity*, London: Routledge

Zaborowski, M., Longhurst, K., 2003, 'America's Protégé in the East? The Emergence of Poland as a Regional Leader', *International Affairs*, Vol. 79, No 5, pp. 1009-1028, http://onlinelibrary.wiley.com/doi/10.1046/j.1468-2346.2003.00351.x/abstract

Zakaria, F., 1997, 'The Rise of Illiberal Democracy', *Foreign Affairs*, Vol. 76, No 6, pp. 22-43, https://doi.org/10.2307/20048274

Zarakol, A., 2017, 'TRIPping Constructivism', *Political Science & Politics*, Vol. 50, No 1, pp. 75-78, https://doi.org/10.1017/S1049096516002183

Zarycki, T., 2004, 'Uses of Russia: The Role of Russia in the Modern Polish National Identity', *East European Politics and Societies*, Vol. 18, No 4, pp. 595-627, http://journals.sagepub.com/doi/abs/10.1177/0888325404269758

Zehfuss, M., 2001, 'Constructivism and Identity: A Dangerous Liaison', *European Journal of International Relations*, Vol. 7, No 3, pp. 315-348, http://journals.sagepub.com/doi/abs/10.1177/1354066101007003002

Zevelev, I., 2009, 'Будущее России: нация или цивилизация?', *Россия в глобальной политике*, No 5, ('The Future of Russia: nation or civilization', *Russia in Global Affairs*, No 5), http://www.globalaffairs.ru/number/n_14037

Zevelev, I., 2014, *Interview with Rumena Filipova*, 27 June 2014, Moscow

Zevelev, I., 2014, 'The Russian World Boundaries', *Russia in Global Affairs*, No 2, http://eng.globalaffairs.ru/number/The-Russian-World-Boundaries-16707

Zięba, R., 2011, 'Twenty Years of Poland's Euro-Atlantic Foreign Policy', *International Studies*, Vol. 13, No 1, pp. 11-21, http://cejsh.icm.edu.pl/cejsh/element/bwmeta1.element.hdl_11089_9956

Zielonka, J., Krok-Paszkowska, A., 2004, 'Poland's Road to the European Union', *Journal of European Integration History*, Vol. 10, No 2, pp. 7-24, http://cadmus.eui.eu//handle/1814/3459

Znepolski, I., 2015, 'Панихида за прехода', в Груев, М., (ред.), *25 Години промени. Граници и периодизация на прехода, институции и качество на демокрацията в България*, Софийска платформа, ('Memorial tribute to the transition', in Gruev, M., (ed.), *25 Years of change. Timeframe and periodisation of the transition, institutions and quality of democracy in Bulgaria*, Sofia Platform, http://sofiaplatform.org/wp-content/uploads/2015/09/25godini-promeni_ebook.pdf

Zuba, K., 2009, 'Through the Looking Glass: The Attitudes of Polish Political Parties towards the EU before and after Accession', *Perspectives on European Politics and Society*, Vol. 10, No 3, pp. 326-349, http://www.tandfonline.com/doi/abs/10.1080/15705850903105744

SOVIET AND POST-SOVIET POLITICS AND SOCIETY
Edited by Dr. Andreas Umland | ISSN 1614-3515

1. *Андреас Умланд (ред.)* | Воплощение Европейской конвенции по правам человека в России. Философские, юридические и эмпирические исследования | ISBN 3-89821-387-0

2. *Christian Wipperfürth* | Russland – ein vertrauenswürdiger Partner? Grundlagen, Hintergründe und Praxis gegenwärtiger russischer Außenpolitik | Mit einem Vorwort von Heinz Timmermann | ISBN 3-89821-401-X

3. *Manja Hussner* | Die Übernahme internationalen Rechts in die russische und deutsche Rechtsordnung. Eine vergleichende Analyse zur Völkerrechtsfreundlichkeit der Verfassungen der Russländischen Föderation und der Bundesrepublik Deutschland | Mit einem Vorwort von Rainer Arnold | ISBN 3-89821-438-9

4. *Matthew Tejada* | Bulgaria's Democratic Consolidation and the Kozloduy Nuclear Power Plant (KNPP). The Unattainability of Closure | With a foreword by Richard J. Crampton | ISBN 3-89821-439-7

5. *Марк Григорьевич Меерович* | Квадратные метры, определяющие сознание. Государственная жилищная политика в СССР. 1921 – 1941 гг | ISBN 3-89821-474-5

6. *Andrei P. Tsygankov, Pavel A.Tsygankov (Eds.)* | New Directions in Russian International Studies | ISBN 3-89821-422-2

7. *Марк Григорьевич Меерович* | Как власть народ к труду приучала. Жилище в СССР – средство управления людьми. 1917 – 1941 гг. | С предисловием Елены Осокиной | ISBN 3-89821-495-8

8. *David J. Galbreath* | Nation-Building and Minority Politics in Post-Socialist States. Interests, Influence and Identities in Estonia and Latvia | With a foreword by David J. Smith | ISBN 3-89821-467-2

9. *Алексей Юрьевич Безугольный* | Народы Кавказа в Вооруженных силах СССР в годы Великой Отечественной войны 1941-1945 гг. | С предисловием Николая Бугая | ISBN 3-89821-475-3

10. *Вячеслав Лихачев и Владимир Прибыловский (ред.)* | Русское Национальное Единство, 1990-2000. В 2-х томах | ISBN 3-89821-523-7

11. *Николай Бугай (ред.)* | Народы стран Балтии в условиях сталинизма (1940-е – 1950-е годы). Документированная история | ISBN 3-89821-525-3

12. *Ingmar Bredies (Hrsg.)* | Zur Anatomie der Orange Revolution in der Ukraine. Wechsel des Elitenregimes oder Triumph des Parlamentarismus? | ISBN 3-89821-524-5

13. *Anastasia V. Mitrofanova* | The Politicization of Russian Orthodoxy. Actors and Ideas | With a foreword by William C. Gay | ISBN 3-89821-481-8

14. *Nathan D. Larson* | Alexander Solzhenitsyn and the Russo-Jewish Question | ISBN 3-89821-483-4

15. *Guido Houben* | Kulturpolitik und Ethnizität. Staatliche Kunstförderung im Russland der neunziger Jahre | Mit einem Vorwort von Gert Weisskirchen | ISBN 3-89821-542-3

16. *Leonid Luks* | Der russische „Sonderweg"? Aufsätze zur neuesten Geschichte Russlands im europäischen Kontext | ISBN 3-89821-496-6

17. *Евгений Мороз* | История «Мёртвой воды» – от страшной сказки к большой политике. Политическое неоязычество в постсоветской России | ISBN 3-89821-551-2

18. *Александр Верховский и Галина Кожевникова (ред.)* | Этническая и религиозная интолерантность в российских СМИ. Результаты мониторинга 2001-2004 гг. | ISBN 3-89821-569-5

19. *Christian Ganzer* | Sowjetisches Erbe und ukrainische Nation. Das Museum der Geschichte des Zaporoger Kosakentums auf der Insel Chortycja | Mit einem Vorwort von Frank Golczewski | ISBN 3-89821-504-0

20. *Эльза-Баир Гучинова* | Помнить нельзя забыть. Антропология депортационной травмы калмыков | С предисловием Кэролайн Хамфри | ISBN 3-89821-506-7

21. *Юлия Лидерман* | Мотивы «проверки» и «испытания» в постсоветской культуре. Советское прошлое в российском кинематографе 1990-х годов | С предисловием Евгения Марголита | ISBN 3-89821-511-3

22. *Tanya Lokshina, Ray Thomas, Mary Mayer (Eds.)* | The Imposition of a Fake Political Settlement in the Northern Caucasus. The 2003 Chechen Presidential Election | ISBN 3-89821-436-2

23. *Timothy McCajor Hall, Rosie Read (Eds.)* | Changes in the Heart of Europe. Recent Ethnographies of Czechs, Slovaks, Roma, and Sorbs | With an afterword by Zdeněk Salzmann | ISBN 3-89821-606-3

24 *Christian Autengruber* | Die politischen Parteien in Bulgarien und Rumänien. Eine vergleichende Analyse seit Beginn der 90er Jahre | Mit einem Vorwort von Dorothée de Nève | ISBN 3-89821-476-1

25 *Annette Freyberg-Inan with Radu Cristescu* | The Ghosts in Our Classrooms, or: John Dewey Meets Ceauşescu. The Promise and the Failures of Civic Education in Romania | ISBN 3-89821-416-8

26 *John B. Dunlop* | The 2002 Dubrovka and 2004 Beslan Hostage Crises. A Critique of Russian Counter-Terrorism | With a foreword by Donald N. Jensen | ISBN 3-89821-608-X

27 *Peter Koller* | Das touristische Potenzial von Kam''janec'-Podil's'kyj. Eine fremdenverkehrsgeographische Untersuchung der Zukunftsperspektiven und Maßnahmenplanung zur Destinationsentwicklung des „ukrainischen Rothenburg" | Mit einem Vorwort von Kristiane Klemm | ISBN 3-89821-640-3

28 *Françoise Daucé, Elisabeth Sieca-Kozlowski (Eds.)* | Dedovshchina in the Post-Soviet Military. Hazing of Russian Army Conscripts in a Comparative Perspective | With a foreword by Dale Herspring | ISBN 3-89821-616-0

29 *Florian Strasser* | Zivilgesellschaftliche Einflüsse auf die Orange Revolution. Die gewaltlose Massenbewegung und die ukrainische Wahlkrise 2004 | Mit einem Vorwort von Egbert Jahn | ISBN 3-89821-648-9

30 *Rebecca S. Katz* | The Georgian Regime Crisis of 2003-2004. A Case Study in Post-Soviet Media Representation of Politics, Crime and Corruption | ISBN 3-89821-413-3

31 *Vladimir Kantor* | Willkür oder Freiheit. Beiträge zur russischen Geschichtsphilosophie | Ediert von Dagmar Herrmann sowie mit einem Vorwort versehen von Leonid Luks | ISBN 3-89821-589-X

32 *Laura A. Victoir* | The Russian Land Estate Today. A Case Study of Cultural Politics in Post-Soviet Russia | With a foreword by Priscilla Roosevelt | ISBN 3-89821-426-5

33 *Ivan Katchanovski* | Cleft Countries. Regional Political Divisions and Cultures in Post-Soviet Ukraine and Moldova | With a foreword by Francis Fukuyama | ISBN 3-89821-558-X

34 *Florian Mühlfried* | Postsowjetische Feiern. Das Georgische Bankett im Wandel | Mit einem Vorwort von Kevin Tuite | ISBN 3-89821-601-2

35 *Roger Griffin, Werner Loh, Andreas Umland (Eds.)* | Fascism Past and Present, West and East. An International Debate on Concepts and Cases in the Comparative Study of the Extreme Right | With an afterword by Walter Laqueur | ISBN 3-89821-674-8

36 *Sebastian Schlegel* | Der „Weiße Archipel". Sowjetische Atomstädte 1945-1991 | Mit einem Geleitwort von Thomas Bohn | ISBN 3-89821-679-9

37 *Vyacheslav Likhachev* | Political Anti-Semitism in Post-Soviet Russia. Actors and Ideas in 1991-2003 | Edited and translated from Russian by Eugene Veklerov | ISBN 3-89821-529-6

38 *Josette Baer (Ed.)* | Preparing Liberty in Central Europe. Political Texts from the Spring of Nations 1848 to the Spring of Prague 1968 | With a foreword by Zdeněk V. David | ISBN 3-89821-546-6

39 *Михаил Лукьянов* | Российский консерватизм и реформа, 1907-1914 | С предисловием Марка Д. Стейнберга | ISBN 3-89821-503-2

40 *Nicola Melloni* | Market Without Economy. The 1998 Russian Financial Crisis | With a foreword by Eiji Furukawa | ISBN 3-89821-407-9

41 *Dmitrij Chmelnizki* | Die Architektur Stalins | Bd. 1: Studien zu Ideologie und Stil | Bd. 2: Bilddokumentation | Mit einem Vorwort von Bruno Flierl | ISBN 3-89821-515-6

42 *Katja Yafimava* | Post-Soviet Russian-Belarussian Relationships. The Role of Gas Transit Pipelines | With a foreword by Jonathan P. Stern | ISBN 3-89821-655-1

43 *Boris Chavkin* | Verflechtungen der deutschen und russischen Zeitgeschichte. Aufsätze und Archivfunde zu den Beziehungen Deutschlands und der Sowjetunion von 1917 bis 1991 | Ediert von Markus Edlinger sowie mit einem Vorwort versehen von Leonid Luks | ISBN 3-89821-756-6

44 *Anastasija Grynenko in Zusammenarbeit mit Claudia Dathe* | Die Terminologie des Gerichtswesens der Ukraine und Deutschlands im Vergleich. Eine übersetzungswissenschaftliche Analyse juristischer Fachbegriffe im Deutschen, Ukrainischen und Russischen | Mit einem Vorwort von Ulrich Hartmann | ISBN 3-89821-691-8

45 *Anton Burkov* | The Impact of the European Convention on Human Rights on Russian Law. Legislation and Application in 1996-2006 | With a foreword by Françoise Hampson | ISBN 978-3-89821-639-5

46 *Stina Torjesen, Indra Overland (Eds.)* | International Election Observers in Post-Soviet Azerbaijan. Geopolitical Pawns or Agents of Change? | ISBN 978-3-89821-743-9

47 *Taras Kuzio* | Ukraine – Crimea – Russia. Triangle of Conflict | ISBN 978-3-89821-761-3

48 *Claudia Šabić* | „Ich erinnere mich nicht, aber L'viv!" Zur Funktion kultureller Faktoren für die Institutionalisierung und Entwicklung einer ukrainischen Region | Mit einem Vorwort von Melanie Tatur | ISBN 978-3-89821-752-1

49 *Marlies Bilz* | Tatarstan in der Transformation. Nationaler Diskurs und Politische Praxis 1988-1994 | Mit einem Vorwort von Frank Golczewski | ISBN 978-3-89821-722-4

50 *Марлен Ларюэль (ред.)* | Современные интерпретации русского национализма | ISBN 978-3-89821-795-8

51 *Sonja Schüler* | Die ethnische Dimension der Armut. Roma im postsozialistischen Rumänien | Mit einem Vorwort von Anton Sterbling | ISBN 978-3-89821-776-1

52 *Галина Кожевникова* | Радикальный национализм в России и противодействие ему. Сборник докладов Центра «Сова» за 2004-2007 гг. | С предисловием Александра Верховского | ISBN 978-3-89821-721-7

53 *Галина Кожевникова и Владимир Прибыловский* | Российская власть в биографиях I. Высшие должностные лица РФ в 2004 г. | ISBN 978-3-89821-796-5

54 *Галина Кожевникова и Владимир Прибыловский* | Российская власть в биографиях II. Члены Правительства РФ в 2004 г. | ISBN 978-3-89821-797-2

55 *Галина Кожевникова и Владимир Прибыловский* | Российская власть в биографиях III. Руководители федеральных служб и агентств РФ в 2004 г.| ISBN 978-3-89821-798-9

56 *Ileana Petroniu* | Privatisierung in Transformationsökonomien. Determinanten der Restrukturierungs-Bereitschaft am Beispiel Polens, Rumäniens und der Ukraine | Mit einem Vorwort von Rainer W. Schäfer | ISBN 978-3-89821-790-3

57 *Christian Wipperfürth* | Russland und seine GUS-Nachbarn. Hintergründe, aktuelle Entwicklungen und Konflikte in einer ressourcenreichen Region| ISBN 978-3-89821-801-6

58 *Togzhan Kassenova* | From Antagonism to Partnership. The Uneasy Path of the U.S.-Russian Cooperative Threat Reduction | With a foreword by Christoph Bluth | ISBN 978-3-89821-707-1

59 *Alexander Höllwerth* | Das sakrale eurasische Imperium des Aleksandr Dugin. Eine Diskursanalyse zum postsowjetischen russischen Rechtsextremismus | Mit einem Vorwort von Dirk Uffelmann | ISBN 978-3-89821-813-9

60 *Олег Рябов* | «Россия-Матушка». Национализм, гендер и война в России XX века | С предисловием Елены Гощило | ISBN 978-3-89821-487-2

61 *Ivan Maistrenko* | Borot'bism. A Chapter in the History of the Ukrainian Revolution | With a new Introduction by Chris Ford | Translated by George S. N. Luckyj with the assistance of Ivan L. Rudnytsky | Second, Revised and Expanded Edition ISBN 978-3-8382-1107-7

62 *Maryna Romanets* | Anamorphosic Texts and Reconfigured Visions. Improvised Traditions in Contemporary Ukrainian and Irish Literature | ISBN 978-3-89821-576-3

63 *Paul D'Anieri and Taras Kuzio (Eds.)* | Aspects of the Orange Revolution I. Democratization and Elections in Post-Communist Ukraine | ISBN 978-3-89821-698-2

64 *Bohdan Harasymiw in collaboration with Oleh S. Ilnytzkyj (Eds.)* | Aspects of the Orange Revolution II. Information and Manipulation Strategies in the 2004 Ukrainian Presidential Elections | ISBN 978-3-89821-699-9

65 *Ingmar Bredies, Andreas Umland and Valentin Yakushik (Eds.)* | Aspects of the Orange Revolution III. The Context and Dynamics of the 2004 Ukrainian Presidential Elections | ISBN 978-3-89821-803-0

66 *Ingmar Bredies, Andreas Umland and Valentin Yakushik (Eds.)* | Aspects of the Orange Revolution IV. Foreign Assistance and Civic Action in the 2004 Ukrainian Presidential Elections | ISBN 978-3-89821-808-5

67 *Ingmar Bredies, Andreas Umland and Valentin Yakushik (Eds.)* | Aspects of the Orange Revolution V. Institutional Observation Reports on the 2004 Ukrainian Presidential Elections | ISBN 978-3-89821-809-2

68 *Taras Kuzio (Ed.)* | Aspects of the Orange Revolution VI. Post-Communist Democratic Revolutions in Comparative Perspective | ISBN 978-3-89821-820-7

69 *Tim Bohse* | Autoritarismus statt Selbstverwaltung. Die Transformation der kommunalen Politik in der Stadt Kaliningrad 1990-2005 | Mit einem Geleitwort von Stefan Troebst | ISBN 978-3-89821-782-8

70 *David Rupp* | Die Rußländische Föderation und die russischsprachige Minderheit in Lettland. Eine Fallstudie zur Anwaltspolitik Moskaus gegenüber den russophonen Minderheiten im „Nahen Ausland" von 1991 bis 2002 | Mit einem Vorwort von Helmut Wagner | ISBN 978-3-89821-778-1

71 *Taras Kuzio* | Theoretical and Comparative Perspectives on Nationalism. New Directions in Cross-Cultural and Post-Communist Studies | With a foreword by Paul Robert Magocsi | ISBN 978-3-89821-815-7

72 *Christine Teichmann* | Die Hochschultransformation im heutigen Osteuropa. Kontinuität und Wandel bei der Entwicklung des postkommunistischen Universitätswesens | Mit einem Vorwort von Oskar Anweiler | ISBN 978-3-89821-842-9

73 *Julia Kusznir* | Der politische Einfluss von Wirtschaftseliten in russischen Regionen. Eine Analyse am Beispiel der Erdöl- und Erdgasindustrie, 1992-2005 | Mit einem Vorwort von Wolfgang Eichwede | ISBN 978-3-89821-821-4

74 Alena Vysotskaya | Russland, Belarus und die EU-Osterweiterung. Zur Minderheitenfrage und zum Problem der Freizügigkeit des Personenverkehrs | Mit einem Vorwort von Katlijn Malfliet | ISBN 978-3-89821-822-1

75 Heiko Pleines (Hrsg.) | Corporate Governance in post-sozialistischen Volkswirtschaften | ISBN 978-3-89821-766-8

76 Stefan Ihrig | Wer sind die Moldawier? Rumänismus versus Moldowanismus in Historiographie und Schulbüchern der Republik Moldova, 1991-2006 | Mit einem Vorwort von Holm Sundhaussen | ISBN 978-3-89821-466-7

77 Galina Kozhevnikova in collaboration with Alexander Verkhovsky and Eugene Veklerov | Ultra-Nationalism and Hate Crimes in Contemporary Russia. The 2004-2006 Annual Reports of Moscow's SOVA Center | With a foreword by Stephen D. Shenfield | ISBN 978-3-89821-868-9

78 Florian Küchler | The Role of the European Union in Moldova's Transnistria Conflict | With a foreword by Christopher Hill | ISBN 978-3-89821-850-4

79 Bernd Rechel | The Long Way Back to Europe. Minority Protection in Bulgaria | With a foreword by Richard Crampton | ISBN 978-3-89821-863-4

80 Peter W. Rodgers | Nation, Region and History in Post-Communist Transitions. Identity Politics in Ukraine, 1991-2006 | With a foreword by Vera Tolz | ISBN 978-3-89821-903-7

81 Stephanie Solywoda | The Life and Work of Semen L. Frank. A Study of Russian Religious Philosophy | With a foreword by Philip Walters | ISBN 978-3-89821-457-5

82 Vera Sokolova | Cultural Politics of Ethnicity. Discourses on Roma in Communist Czechoslovakia | ISBN 978-3-89821-864-1

83 Natalya Shevchik Ketenci | Kazakhstani Enterprises in Transition. The Role of Historical Regional Development in Kazakhstan's Post-Soviet Economic Transformation | ISBN 978-3-89821-831-3

84 Martin Malek, Anna Schor-Tschudnowskaja (Hgg.) | Europa im Tschetschenienkrieg. Zwischen politischer Ohnmacht und Gleichgültigkeit | Mit einem Vorwort von Lipchan Basajewa | ISBN 978-3-89821-676-0

85 Stefan Meister | Das postsowjetische Universitätswesen zwischen nationalem und internationalem Wandel. Die Entwicklung der regionalen Hochschule in Russland als Gradmesser der Systemtransformation | Mit einem Vorwort von Joan DeBardeleben | ISBN 978-3-89821-891-7

86 Konstantin Sheiko in collaboration with Stephen Brown | Nationalist Imaginings of the Russian Past. Anatolii Fomenko and the Rise of Alternative History in Post-Communist Russia | With a foreword by Donald Ostrowski | ISBN 978-3-89821-915-0

87 Sabine Jenni | Wie stark ist das „Einige Russland"? Zur Parteibindung der Eliten und zum Wahlerfolg der Machtpartei im Dezember 2007 | Mit einem Vorwort von Klaus Armingeon | ISBN 978-3-89821-961-7

88 Thomas Borén | Meeting-Places of Transformation. Urban Identity, Spatial Representations and Local Politics in Post-Soviet St Petersburg | ISBN 978-3-89821-739-2

89 Aygul Ashirova | Stalinismus und Stalin-Kult in Zentralasien. Turkmenistan 1924-1953 | Mit einem Vorwort von Leonid Luks | ISBN 978-3-89821-987-7

90 Leonid Luks | Freiheit oder imperiale Größe? Essays zu einem russischen Dilemma | ISBN 978-3-8382-0011-8

91 Christopher Gilley | The 'Change of Signposts' in the Ukrainian Emigration. A Contribution to the History of Sovietophilism in the 1920s | With a foreword by Frank Golczewski | ISBN 978-3-89821-965-5

92 Philipp Casula, Jeronim Perovic (Eds.) | Identities and Politics During the Putin Presidency. The Discursive Foundations of Russia's Stability | With a foreword by Heiko Haumann | ISBN 978-3-8382-0015-6

93 Marcel Viëtor | Europa und die Frage nach seinen Grenzen im Osten. Zur Konstruktion ‚europäischer Identität' in Geschichte und Gegenwart | Mit einem Vorwort von Albrecht Lehmann | ISBN 978-3-8382-0045-3

94 Ben Hellman, Andrei Rogachevskii | Filming the Unfilmable. Casper Wrede's 'One Day in the Life of Ivan Denisovich' | Second, Revised and Expanded Edition | ISBN 978-3-8382-0044-6

95 Eva Fuchslocher | Vaterland, Sprache, Glaube. Orthodoxie und Nationenbildung am Beispiel Georgiens | Mit einem Vorwort von Christina von Braun | ISBN 978-3-89821-884-9

96 Vladimir Kantor | Das Westlertum und der Weg Russlands. Zur Entwicklung der russischen Literatur und Philosophie | Ediert von Dagmar Herrmann | Mit einem Beitrag von Nikolaus Lobkowicz | ISBN 978-3-8382-0102-3

97 Kamran Musayev | Die postsowjetische Transformation im Baltikum und Südkaukasus. Eine vergleichende Untersuchung der politischen Entwicklung Lettlands und Aserbaidschans 1985-2009 | Mit einem Vorwort von Leonid Luks | Ediert von Sandro Henschel | ISBN 978-3-8382-0103-0

98 Tatiana Zhurzhenko | Borderlands into Bordered Lands. Geopolitics of Identity in Post-Soviet Ukraine | With a foreword by Dieter Segert | ISBN 978-3-8382-0042-2

99 Кирилл Галушко, Лидия Смола (ред.) | Пределы падения – варианты украинского будущего. Аналитико-прогностические исследования | ISBN 978-3-8382-0148-1

100 Michael Minkenberg (Ed.) | Historical Legacies and the Radical Right in Post-Cold War Central and Eastern Europe | With an afterword by Sabrina P. Ramet | ISBN 978-3-8382-0124-5

101 David-Emil Wickström | Rocking St. Petersburg. Transcultural Flows and Identity Politics in the St. Petersburg Popular Music Scene | With a foreword by Yngvar B. Steinholt | Second, Revised and Expanded Edition | ISBN 978-3-8382-0100-9

102 Eva Zabka | Eine neue „Zeit der Wirren"? Der spät- und postsowjetische Systemwandel 1985-2000 im Spiegel russischer gesellschaftspolitischer Diskurse | Mit einem Vorwort von Margareta Mommsen | ISBN 978-3-8382-0161-0

103 Ulrike Ziemer | Ethnic Belonging, Gender and Cultural Practices. Youth Identitites in Contemporary Russia | With a foreword by Anoop Nayak | ISBN 978-3-8382-0152-8

104 Ksenia Chepikova | ‚Einiges Russland' - eine zweite KPdSU? Aspekte der Identitätskonstruktion einer postsowjetischen „Partei der Macht" | Mit einem Vorwort von Torsten Oppelland | ISBN 978-3-8382-0311-9

105 Леонид Люкс | Западничество или евразийство? Демократия или идеократия? Сборник статей об исторических дилеммах России | С предисловием Владимира Кантора | ISBN 978-3-8382-0211-2

106 Anna Dost | Das russische Verfassungsrecht auf dem Weg zum Föderalismus und zurück. Zum Konflikt von Rechtsnormen und -wirklichkeit in der Russländischen Föderation von 1991 bis 2009 | Mit einem Vorwort von Alexander Blankenagel | ISBN 978-3-8382-0292-1

107 Philipp Herzog | Sozialistische Völkerfreundschaft, nationaler Widerstand oder harmloser Zeitvertreib? Zur politischen Funktion der Volkskunst im sowjetischen Estland | Mit einem Vorwort von Andreas Kappeler | ISBN 978-3-8382-0216-7

108 Marlène Laruelle (Ed.) | Russian Nationalism, Foreign Policy, and Identity Debates in Putin's Russia. New Ideological Patterns after the Orange Revolution | ISBN 978-3-8382-0325-6

109 Michail Logvinov | Russlands Kampf gegen den internationalen Terrorismus. Eine kritische Bestandsaufnahme des Bekämpfungsansatzes | Mit einem Geleitwort von Hans-Henning Schröder und einem Vorwort von Eckhard Jesse | ISBN 978-3-8382-0329-4

110 John B. Dunlop | The Moscow Bombings of September 1999. Examinations of Russian Terrorist Attacks at the Onset of Vladimir Putin's Rule | Second, Revised and Expanded Edition | ISBN 978-3-8382-0388-1

111 Андрей А. Ковалёв | Свидетельство из-за кулис российской политики I. Можно ли делать добро из зла? (Воспоминания и размышления о последних советских и первых послесоветских годах) | With a foreword by Peter Reddaway | ISBN 978-3-8382-0302-7

112 Андрей А. Ковалёв | Свидетельство из-за кулис российской политики II. Угроза для себя и окружающих (Наблюдения и предостережения относительно происходящего после 2000 г.) | ISBN 978-3-8382-0303-4

113 Bernd Kappenberg | Zeichen setzen für Europa. Der Gebrauch europäischer lateinischer Sonderzeichen in der deutschen Öffentlichkeit | Mit einem Vorwort von Peter Schlobinski | ISBN 978-3-89821-749-1

114 Ivo Mijnssen | The Quest for an Ideal Youth in Putin's Russia I. Back to Our Future! History, Modernity, and Patriotism according to Nashi, 2005-2013 | With a foreword by Jeronim Perović | Second, Revised and Expanded Edition | ISBN 978-3-8382-0368-3

115 Jussi Lassila | The Quest for an Ideal Youth in Putin's Russia II. The Search for Distinctive Conformism in the Political Communication of Nashi, 2005-2009 | With a foreword by Kirill Postoutenko | Second, Revised and Expanded Edition | ISBN 978-3-8382-0415-4

116 Valerio Trabandt | Neue Nachbarn, gute Nachbarschaft? Die EU als internationaler Akteur am Beispiel ihrer Demokratieförderung in Belarus und der Ukraine 2004-2009 | Mit einem Vorwort von Jutta Joachim | ISBN 978-3-8382-0437-6

117 Fabian Pfeiffer | Estlands Außen- und Sicherheitspolitik I. Der estnische Atlantizismus nach der wiedererlangten Unabhängigkeit 1991-2004 | Mit einem Vorwort von Helmut Hubel | ISBN 978-3-8382-0127-6

118 Jana Podßuweit | Estlands Außen- und Sicherheitspolitik II. Handlungsoptionen eines Kleinstaates im Rahmen seiner EU-Mitgliedschaft (2004-2008) | Mit einem Vorwort von Helmut Hubel | ISBN 978-3-8382-0440-6

119 Karin Pointner | Estlands Außen- und Sicherheitspolitik III. Eine gedächtnispolitische Analyse estnischer Entwicklungskooperation 2006-2010 | Mit einem Vorwort von Karin Liebhart | ISBN 978-3-8382-0435-2

120 Ruslana Vovk | Die Offenheit der ukrainischen Verfassung für das Völkerrecht und die europäische Integration | Mit einem Vorwort von Alexander Blankenagel | ISBN 978-3-8382-0481-9

121 *Mykhaylo Banakh* | Die Relevanz der Zivilgesellschaft bei den postkommunistischen Transformationsprozessen in mittel- und osteuropäischen Ländern. Das Beispiel der spät- und postsowjetischen Ukraine 1986-2009 | Mit einem Vorwort von Gerhard Simon | ISBN 978-3-8382-0499-4

122 *Michael Moser* | Language Policy and the Discourse on Languages in Ukraine under President Viktor Yanukovych (25 February 2010–28 October 2012) | ISBN 978-3-8382-0497-0 (Paperback edition) | ISBN 978-3-8382-0507-6 (Hardcover edition)

123 *Nicole Krome* | Russischer Netzwerkkapitalismus Restrukturierungsprozesse in der Russischen Föderation am Beispiel des Luftfahrtunternehmens „Aviastar" | Mit einem Vorwort von Petra Stykow | ISBN 978-3-8382-0534-2

124 *David R. Marples* | 'Our Glorious Past'. Lukashenka's Belarus and the Great Patriotic War | ISBN 978-3-8382-0574-8 (Paperback edition) | ISBN 978-3-8382-0675-2 (Hardcover edition)

125 *Ulf Walther* | Russlands „neuer Adel". Die Macht des Geheimdienstes von Gorbatschow bis Putin | Mit einem Vorwort von Hans-Georg Wieck | ISBN 978-3-8382-0584-7

126 *Simon Geissbühler (Hrsg.)* | Kiew – Revolution 3.0. Der Euromaidan 2013/14 und die Zukunftsperspektiven der Ukraine | ISBN 978-3-8382-0581-6 (Paperback edition) | ISBN 978-3-8382-0681-3 (Hardcover edition)

127 *Andrey Makarychev* | Russia and the EU in a Multipolar World. Discourses, Identities, Norms | With a foreword by Klaus Segbers | ISBN 978-3-8382-0629-5

128 *Roland Scharff* | Kasachstan als postsowjetischer Wohlfahrtsstaat. Die Transformation des sozialen Schutzsystems | Mit einem Vorwort von Joachim Ahrens | ISBN 978-3-8382-0622-6

129 *Katja Grupp* | Bild Lücke Deutschland. Kaliningrader Studierende sprechen über Deutschland | Mit einem Vorwort von Martin Schulz | ISBN 978-3-8382-0552-6

130 *Konstantin Sheiko, Stephen Brown* | History as Therapy. Alternative History and Nationalist Imaginings in Russia, 1991-2014 | ISBN 978-3-8382-0665-3

131 *Elisa Kriza* | Alexander Solzhenitsyn: Cold War Icon, Gulag Author, Russian Nationalist? A Study of the Western Reception of his Literary Writings, Historical Interpretations, and Political Ideas | With a foreword by Andrei Rogatchevski | ISBN 978-3-8382-0589-2 (Paperback edition) | ISBN 978-3-8382-0690-5 (Hardcover edition)

132 *Serghei Golunov* | The Elephant in the Room. Corruption and Cheating in Russian Universities | ISBN 978-3-8382-0570-0

133 *Manja Hussner, Rainer Arnold (Hgg.)* | Verfassungsgerichtsbarkeit in Zentralasien I. Sammlung von Verfassungstexten | ISBN 978-3-8382-0595-3

134 *Nikolay Mitrokhin* | Die „Russische Partei". Die Bewegung der russischen Nationalisten in der UdSSR 1953-1985 | Aus dem Russischen übertragen von einem Übersetzerteam unter der Leitung von Larisa Schippel | ISBN 978-3-8382-0024-8

135 *Manja Hussner, Rainer Arnold (Hgg.)* | Verfassungsgerichtsbarkeit in Zentralasien II. Sammlung von Verfassungstexten | ISBN 978-3-8382-0597-7

136 *Manfred Zeller* | Das sowjetische Fieber. Fußballfans im poststalinistischen Vielvölkerreich | Mit einem Vorwort von Nikolaus Katzer | ISBN 978-3-8382-0757-5

137 *Kristin Schreiter* | Stellung und Entwicklungspotential zivilgesellschaftlicher Gruppen in Russland. Menschenrechtsorganisationen im Vergleich | ISBN 978-3-8382-0673-8

138 *David R. Marples, Frederick V. Mills (Eds.)* | Ukraine's Euromaidan. Analyses of a Civil Revolution | ISBN 978-3-8382-0660-8

139 *Bernd Kappenberg* | Setting Signs for Europe. Why Diacritics Matter for European Integration | With a foreword by Peter Schlobinski | ISBN 978-3-8382-0663-9

140 *René Lenz* | Internationalisierung, Kooperation und Transfer. Externe bildungspolitische Akteure in der Russischen Föderation | Mit einem Vorwort von Frank Ettrich | ISBN 978-3-8382-0751-3

141 *Juri Plusnin, Yana Zausaeva, Natalia Zhidkevich, Artemy Pozanenko* | Wandering Workers. Mores, Behavior, Way of Life, and Political Status of Domestic Russian Labor Migrants | Translated by Julia Kazantseva | ISBN 978-3-8382-0653-0

142 *David J. Smith (Eds.)* | Latvia – A Work in Progress? 100 Years of State- and Nation-Building | ISBN 978-3-8382-0648-6

143 *Инна Чувычкина (ред.)* | Экспортные нефте- и газопроводы на постсоветском пространстве. Анализ трубопроводной политики в свете теории международных отношений | ISBN 978-3-8382-0822-0

144 *Johann Zajaczkowski* | Russland – eine pragmatische Großmacht? Eine rollentheoretische Untersuchung russischer Außenpolitik am Beispiel der Zusammenarbeit mit den USA nach 9/11 und des Georgienkrieges von 2008 | Mit einem Vorwort von Siegfried Schieder | ISBN 978-3-8382-0837-4

145 *Boris Popivanov* | Changing Images of the Left in Bulgaria. The Challenge of Post-Communism in the Early 21st Century | ISBN 978-3-8382-0667-7

146 *Lenka Krátká* | A History of the Czechoslovak Ocean Shipping Company 1948-1989. How a Small, Landlocked Country Ran Maritime Business During the Cold War | ISBN 978-3-8382-0666-0

147 *Alexander Sergunin* | Explaining Russian Foreign Policy Behavior. Theory and Practice | ISBN 978-3-8382-0752-0

148 *Darya Malyutina* | Migrant Friendships in a Super-Diverse City. Russian-Speakers and their Social Relationships in London in the 21st Century | With a foreword by Claire Dwyer | ISBN 978-3-8382-0652-3

149 *Alexander Sergunin, Valery Konyshev* | Russia in the Arctic. Hard or Soft Power? | ISBN 978-3-8382-0753-7

150 *John J. Maresca* | Helsinki Revisited. A Key U.S. Negotiator's Memoirs on the Development of the CSCE into the OSCE | With a foreword by Hafiz Pashayev | ISBN 978-3-8382-0852-7

151 *Jardar Østbø* | The New Third Rome. Readings of a Russian Nationalist Myth | With a foreword by Pål Kolstø | ISBN 978-3-8382-0870-1

152 *Simon Kordonsky* | Socio-Economic Foundations of the Russian Post-Soviet Regime. The Resource-Based Economy and Estate-Based Social Structure of Contemporary Russia | With a foreword by Svetlana Barsukova | ISBN 978-3-8382-0775-9

153 *Duncan Leitch* | Assisting Reform in Post-Communist Ukraine 2000–2012. The Illusions of Donors and the Disillusion of Beneficiaries | With a foreword by Kataryna Wolczuk | ISBN 978-3-8382-0844-2

154 *Abel Polese* | Limits of a Post-Soviet State. How Informality Replaces, Renegotiates, and Reshapes Governance in Contemporary Ukraine | With a foreword by Colin Williams | ISBN 978-3-8382-0845-9

155 *Mikhail Suslov (Ed.)* | Digital Orthodoxy in the Post-Soviet World. The Russian Orthodox Church and Web 2.0 | With a foreword by Father Cyril Hovorun | ISBN 978-3-8382-0871-8

156 *Leonid Luks* | Zwei „Sonderwege"? Russisch-deutsche Parallelen und Kontraste (1917-2014). Vergleichende Essays | ISBN 978-3-8382-0823-7

157 *Vladimir V. Karacharovskiy, Ovsey I. Shkaratan, Gordey A. Yastrebov* | Towards a New Russian Work Culture. Can Western Companies and Expatriates Change Russian Society? | With a foreword by Elena N. Danilova | Translated by Julia Kazantseva | ISBN 978-3-8382-0902-9

158 *Edmund Griffiths* | Aleksandr Prokhanov and Post-Soviet Esotericism | ISBN 978-3-8382-0903-6

159 *Timm Beichelt, Susann Worschech (Eds.)* | Transnational Ukraine? Networks and Ties that Influence(d) Contemporary Ukraine | ISBN 978-3-8382-0944-9

160 *Mieste Hotopp-Riecke* | Die Tataren der Krim zwischen Assimilation und Selbstbehauptung. Der Aufbau des krimtatarischen Bildungswesens nach Deportation und Heimkehr (1990-2005) | Mit einem Vorwort von Swetlana Czerwonnaja | ISBN 978-3-89821-940-2

161 *Olga Bertelsen (Ed.)* | Revolution and War in Contemporary Ukraine. The Challenge of Change | ISBN 978-3-8382-1016-2

162 *Natalya Ryabinska* | Ukraine's Post-Communist Mass Media. Between Capture and Commercialization | With a foreword by Marta Dyczok | ISBN 978-3-8382-1011-7

163 *Alexandra Cotofana, James M. Nyce (Eds.)* | Religion and Magic in Socialist and Post-Socialist Contexts. Historic and Ethnographic Case Studies of Orthodoxy, Heterodoxy, and Alternative Spirituality | With a foreword by Patrick L. Michelson | ISBN 978-3-8382-0989-0

164 *Nozima Akhrarkhodjaeva* | The Instrumentalisation of Mass Media in Electoral Authoritarian Regimes. Evidence from Russia's Presidential Election Campaigns of 2000 and 2008 | ISBN 978-3-8382-1013-1

165 *Yulia Krasheninnikova* | Informal Healthcare in Contemporary Russia. Sociographic Essays on the Post-Soviet Infrastructure for Alternative Healing Practices | ISBN 978-3-8382-0970-8

166 *Peter Kaiser* | Das Schachbrett der Macht. Die Handlungsspielräume eines sowjetischen Funktionärs unter Stalin am Beispiel des Generalsekretärs des Komsomol Aleksandr Kosarev (1929-1938) | Mit einem Vorwort von Dietmar Neutatz | ISBN 978-3-8382-1052-0

167 *Oksana Kim* | The Effects and Implications of Kazakhstan's Adoption of International Financial Reporting Standards. A Resource Dependence Perspective | With a foreword by Svetlana Vlady | ISBN 978-3-8382-0987-6

168 *Anna Sanina* | Patriotic Education in Contemporary Russia. Sociological Studies in the Making of the Post-Soviet Citizen | With a foreword by Anna Oldfield | ISBN 978-3-8382-0993-7

169 *Rudolf Wolters* | Spezialist in Sibirien Faksimile der 1933 erschienenen ersten Ausgabe | Mit einem Vorwort von Dmitrij Chmelnizki | ISBN 978-3-8382-0515-1

170 *Michal Vít, Magdalena M. Baran (Eds.)* | Transregional versus National Perspectives on Contemporary Central European History. Studies on the Building of Nation-States and Their Cooperation in the 20th and 21st Century | With a foreword by Petr Vágner | ISBN 978-3-8382-1015-5

171 *Philip Gamaghelyan* | Conflict Resolution Beyond the International Relations Paradigm. Evolving Designs as a Transformative Practice in Nagorno-Karabakh and Syria | With a foreword by Susan Allen | ISBN 978-3-8382-1057-5

172 *Maria Shagina* | Joining a Prestigious Club. Cooperation with Europarties and Its Impact on Party Development in Georgia, Moldova, and Ukraine 2004–2015 | With a foreword by Kataryna Wolczuk | ISBN 978-3-8382-1084-1

173 *Alexandra Cotofana, James M. Nyce (Eds.)* | Religion and Magic in Socialist and Post-Socialist Contexts II. Baltic, Eastern European, and Post-USSR Case Studies | With a foreword by Anita Stasulane | ISBN 978-3-8382-0990-6

174 *Barbara Kunz* | Kind Words, Cruise Missiles, and Everything in Between. The Use of Power Resources in U.S. Policies towards Poland, Ukraine, and Belarus 1989–2008 | With a foreword by William Hill | ISBN 978-3-8382-1065-0

175 *Eduard Klein* | Bildungskorruption in Russland und der Ukraine. Eine komparative Analyse der Performanz staatlicher Antikorruptionsmaßnahmen im Hochschulsektor am Beispiel universitärer Aufnahmeprüfungen | Mit einem Vorwort von Heiko Pleines | ISBN 978-3-8382-0995-1

176 *Markus Soldner* | Politischer Kapitalismus im postsowjetischen Russland. Die politische, wirtschaftliche und mediale Transformation in den 1990er Jahren | Mit einem Vorwort von Wolfgang Ismayr | ISBN 978-3-8382-1222-7

177 *Anton Oleinik* | Building Ukraine from Within. A Sociological, Institutional, and Economic Analysis of a Nation-State in the Making | ISBN 978-3-8382-1150-3

178 *Peter Rollberg, Marlene Laruelle (Eds.)* | Mass Media in the Post-Soviet World. Market Forces, State Actors, and Political Manipulation in the Informational Environment after Communism | ISBN 978-3-8382-1116-9

179 *Mikhail Minakov* | Development and Dystopia. Studies in Post-Soviet Ukraine and Eastern Europe | With a foreword by Alexander Etkind | ISBN 978-3-8382-1112-1

180 *Aijan Sharshenova* | The European Union's Democracy Promotion in Central Asia. A Study of Political Interests, Influence, and Development in Kazakhstan and Kyrgyzstan in 2007–2013 | With a foreword by Gordon Crawford | ISBN 978-3-8382-1151-0

181 *Andrey Makarychev, Alexandra Yatsyk (Eds.)* | Boris Nemtsov and Russian Politics. Power and Resistance | With a foreword by Zhanna Nemtsova | ISBN 978-3-8382-1122-0

182 *Sophie Falsini* | The Euromaidan's Effect on Civil Society. Why and How Ukrainian Social Capital Increased after the Revolution of Dignity | With a foreword by Susann Worschech | ISBN 978-3-8382-1131-2

183 *Valentyna Romanova, Andreas Umland (Eds.)* | Ukraine's Decentralization. Challenges and Implications of the Local Governance Reform after the Euromaidan Revolution | ISBN 978-3-8382-1162-6

184 *Leonid Luks* | A Fateful Triangle. Essays on Contemporary Russian, German and Polish History | ISBN 978-3-8382-1143-5

185 *John B. Dunlop* | The February 2015 Assassination of Boris Nemtsov and the Flawed Trial of his Alleged Killers. An Exploration of Russia's "Crime of the 21st Century" | ISBN 978-3-8382-1188-6

186 *Vasile Rotaru* | Russia, the EU, and the Eastern Partnership. Building Bridges or Digging Trenches? | ISBN 978-3-8382-1134-3

187 *Marina Lebedeva* | Russian Studies of International Relations. From the Soviet Past to the Post-Cold-War Present | With a foreword by Andrei P. Tsygankov | ISBN 978-3-8382-0851-0

188 *Tomasz Stępniewski, George Soroka (Eds.)* | Ukraine after Maidan. Revisiting Domestic and Regional Security | ISBN 978-3-8382-1075-9

189 *Petar Cholakov* | Ethnic Entrepreneurs Unmasked. Political Institutions and Ethnic Conflicts in Contemporary Bulgaria | ISBN 978-3-8382-1189-3

190 *A. Salem, G. Hazeldine, D. Morgan (Eds.)* | Higher Education in Post-Communist States. Comparative and Sociological Perspectives | ISBN 978-3-8382-1183-1

191 *Igor Torbakov* | After Empire. Nationalist Imagination and Symbolic Politics in Russia and Eurasia in the Twentieth and Twenty-First Century | With a foreword by Serhii Plokhy | ISBN 978-3-8382-1217-3

192 *Aleksandr Burakovskiy* | Jewish-Ukrainian Relations in Late and Post-Soviet Ukraine. Articles, Lectures and Essays from 1986 to 2016 | ISBN 978-3-8382-1210-4

193 *Natalia Shapovalova, Olga Burlyuk (Eds.)* | Civil Society in Post-Euromaidan Ukraine. From Revolution to Consolidation | With a foreword by Richard Youngs | ISBN 978-3-8382-1216-6

194 *Franz Preissler* | Positionsverteidigung, Imperialismus oder Irredentismus? Russland und die „Russischsprachigen", 1991–2015 | ISBN 978-3-8382-1262-3

195 *Marian Madeła* | Der Reformprozess in der Ukraine 2014-2017. Eine Fallstudie zur Reform der öffentlichen Verwaltung | Mit einem Vorwort von Martin Malek | ISBN 978-3-8382-1266-1

196 *Anke Giesen* | „Wie kann denn der Sieger ein Verbrecher sein?" Eine diskursanalytische Untersuchung der russlandweiten Debatte über Konzept und Verstaatlichungsprozess der Lagergedenkstätte „Perm'-36" im Ural | ISBN 978-3-8382-1284-5

197 *Alla Leukavets* | The Integration Policies of Belarus and Ukraine vis-à-vis the EU and Russia. A Comparative Case Study Through the Prism of a Two-Level Game Approach | ISBN 978-3-8382-1247-0

198 *Oksana Kim* | The Development and Challenges of Russian Corporate Governance I. The Roles and Functions of Boards of Directors | With a foreword by Sheila M. Puffer | ISBN 978-3-8382-1287-6

199 *Thomas D. Grant* | International Law and the Post-Soviet Space I. Essays on Chechnya and the Baltic States | With a foreword by Stephen M. Schwebel | ISBN 978-3-8382-1279-1

200 *Thomas D. Grant* | International Law and the Post-Soviet Space II. Essays on Ukraine, Intervention, and Non-Proliferation | ISBN 978-3-8382-1280-7

201 *Slavomír Michálek, Michal Štefansky* | The Age of Fear. The Cold War and Its Influence on Czechoslovakia 1945–1968 | ISBN 978-3-8382-1285-2

202 *Iulia-Sabina Joja* | Romania's Strategic Culture 1990–2014. Continuity and Change in a Post-Communist Country's Evolution of National Interests and Security Policies | With a foreword by Heiko Biehl | ISBN 978-3-8382-1286-9

203 *Andrei Rogatchevski, Yngvar B. Steinholt, Arve Hansen, David-Emil Wickström* | War of Songs. Popular Music and Recent Russia-Ukraine Relations | With a foreword by Artemy Troitsky | ISBN 978-3-8382-1173-2

204 *Maria Lipman (Ed.)* | Russian Voices on Post-Crimea Russia. An Almanac of Counterpoint Essays from 2015–2018 | ISBN 978-3-8382-1251-7

205 *Ksenia Maksimovtsova* | Language Conflicts in Contemporary Estonia, Latvia, and Ukraine. A Comparative Exploration of Discourses in Post-Soviet Russian-Language Digital Media | With a foreword by Ammon Cheskin | ISBN 978-3-8382-1282-1

206 *Michal Vít* | The EU's Impact on Identity Formation in East-Central Europe between 2004 and 2013. Perceptions of the Nation and Europe in Political Parties of the Czech Republic, Poland, and Slovakia | With a foreword by Andrea Pető | ISBN 978-3-8382-1275-3

207 *Per A. Rudling* | Tarnished Heroes. The Organization of Ukrainian Nationalists in the Memory Politics of Post-Soviet Ukraine | ISBN 978-3-8382-0999-9

208 *Kaja Gadowska, Peter Solomon (Eds.)* | Legal Change in Post-Communist States. Progress, Reversions, Explanations | ISBN 978-3-8382-1312-5

209 *Paweł Kowal, Georges Mink, Iwona Reichardt (Eds.)* | Three Revolutions: Mobilization and Change in Contemporary Ukraine I. Theoretical Aspects and Analyses on Religion, Memory, and Identity | ISBN 978-3-8382-1321-7

210 *Paweł Kowal, Georges Mink, Adam Reichardt, Iwona Reichardt (Eds.)* | Three Revolutions: Mobilization and Change in Contemporary Ukraine II. An Oral History of the Revolution on Granite, Orange Revolution, and Revolution of Dignity | ISBN 978-3-8382-1323-1

211 *Li Bennich-Björkman, Sergiy Kurbatov (Eds.)* | When the Future Came. The Collapse of the USSR and the Emergence of National Memory in Post-Soviet History Textbooks | ISBN 978-3-8382-1335-4

212 *Olga R. Gulina* | Migration as a (Geo-)Political Challenge in the Post-Soviet Space. Border Regimes, Policy Choices, Visa Agendas | With a foreword by Nils Muižnieks | ISBN 978-3-8382-1338-5

213 *Sanna Turoma, Kaarina Aitamurto, Slobodanka Vladiv-Glover (Eds.)* | Religion, Expression, and Patriotism in Russia. Essays on Post-Soviet Society and the State. ISBN 978-3-8382-1346-0

214 *Vasif Huseynov* | Geopolitical Rivalries in the "Common Neighborhood". Russia's Conflict with the West, Soft Power, and Neoclassical Realism | With a foreword by Nicholas Ross Smith | ISBN 978-3-8382-1277-7

215 *Mikhail Suslov* | Geopolitical Imagination. Ideology and Utopia in Post-Soviet Russia | With a foreword by Mark Bassin | ISBN 978-3-8382-1361-3

216 *Alexander Etkind, Mikhail Minakov (Eds.)* | Ideology after Union. Political Doctrines, Discourses, and Debates in Post-Soviet Societies | ISBN 978-3-8382-1388-0

217 *Jakob Mischke, Oleksandr Zabirko (Hgg.)* | Protestbewegungen im langen Schatten des Kreml. Aufbruch und Resignation in Russland und der Ukraine | ISBN 978-3-8382-0926-5

218 *Oksana Huss* | How Corruption and Anti-Corruption Policies Sustain Hybrid Regimes. Strategies of Political Domination under Ukraine's Presidents in 1994-2014 | With a foreword by Tobias Debiel and Andrea Gawrich | ISBN 978-3-8382-1430-6

219 *Dmitry Travin, Vladimir Gel'man, Otar Marganiya* | The Russian Path. Ideas, Interests, Institutions, Illusions | With a foreword by Vladimir Ryzhkov | ISBN 978-3-8382-1421-4

220 *Gergana Dimova* | Political Uncertainty. A Comparative Exploration | With a foreword by Todor Yalamov and Rumena Filipova | ISBN 978-3-8382-1385-9

221 *Torben Waschke* | Russland in Transition. Geopolitik zwischen Raum, Identität und Machtinteressen | Mit einem Vorwort von Andreas Dittmann | ISBN 978-3-8382-1480-1

222 *Steven Jobbitt, Zsolt Bottlik, Marton Berki (Eds.)* | Power and Identity in the Post-Soviet Realm. Geographies of Ethnicity and Nationality after 1991 | ISBN 978-3-8382-1399-6

223 *Daria Buteiko* | Erinnerungsort. Ort des Gedenkens, der Erholung oder der Einkehr? Kommunismus-Erinnerung am Beispiel der Gedenkstätte Berliner Mauer sowie des Soloveckij-Klosters und -Museumsparks | ISBN 978-3-8382-1367-5

224 *Olga Bertelsen (Ed.)* | Russian Active Measures. Yesterday, Today, Tomorrow | With a foreword by Jan Goldman | ISBN 978-3-8382-1529-7

225 *David Mandel* | "Optimizing" Higher Education in Russia. University Teachers and their Union "Universitetskaya solidarnost'" | ISBN 978-3-8382-1519-8

226 *Mikhail Minakov, Gwendolyn Sasse, Daria Isachenko (Eds.)* | Post-Soviet Secessionism. Nation-Building and State-Failure after Communism | ISBN 978-3-8382-1538-9

227 *Jakob Hauter (Ed.)* | Civil War? Interstate War? Hybrid War? Dimensions and Interpretations of the Donbas Conflict in 2014–2020 | With a foreword by Andrew Wilson | ISBN 978-3-8382-1383-5

228 *Tima T. Moldogaziev, Gene A. Brewer, J. Edward Kellough (Eds.)* | Public Policy and Politics in Georgia. Lessons from Post-Soviet Transition | With a foreword by Dan Durning | ISBN 978-3-8382-1535-8

229 *Oxana Schmies (Ed.)* | NATO's Enlargement and Russia. A Strategic Challenge in the Past and Future | With a foreword by Vladimir Kara-Murza | ISBN 978-3-8382-1478-8

230 *Christopher Ford* | Ukapisme – Une Gauche perdue. Le marxisme anti-colonial dans la révolution ukrainienne 1917-1925 | Avec une préface de Vincent Présumey | ISBN 978-3-8382-0899-2

231 *Anna Kutkina* | Between Lenin and Bandera. Decommunization and Multivocality in Post-Euromaidan Ukraine | With a foreword by Juri Mykkänen | ISBN 978-3-8382-1506-8

232 *Lincoln E. Flake* | Defending the Faith. The Russian Orthodox Church and the Demise of Religious Pluralism | With a foreword by Peter Martland | ISBN 978-3-8382-1378-1

233 *Nikoloz Samkharadze* | Russia's Recognition of the Independence of Abkhazia and South Ossetia. Analysis of a Deviant Case in Moscow's Foreign Policy | With a foreword by Neil MacFarlane | ISBN 978-3-8382-1414-6

234 *Arve Hansen* | Urban Protest. A Spatial Perspective on Kyiv, Minsk, and Moscow | With a foreword by Julie Wilhelmsen | ISBN 978-3-8382-1495-5

235 *Eleonora Narvselius, Julie Fedor (Eds.)* | Diversity in the East-Central European Borderlands. Memories, Cityscapes, People | ISBN 978-3-8382-1523-5

236 *Regina Elsner* | The Russian Orthodox Church and Modernity. A Historical and Theological Investigation into Eastern Christianity between Unity and Plurality | With a foreword by Mikhail Suslov | ISBN 978-3-8382-1568-6

237 *Bo Petersson* | The Putin Predicament. Problems of Legitimacy and Succession in Russia | With a foreword by J. Paul Goode | ISBN 978-3-8382-1050-6

238 *Jonathan Otto Pohl* | The Years of Great Silence. The Deportation, Special Settlement, and Mobilization into the Labor Army of Ethnic Germans in the USSR, 1941–1955 | ISBN 978-3-8382-1630-0

239 *Mikhail Minakov (Ed.)* | Inventing Majorities. Ideological Creativity in Post-Soviet Societies | ISBN 978-3-8382-1641-6

240 *Robert M. Cutler* | Soviet and Post-Soviet Foreign Policies I. East-South Relations and the Political Economy of the Communist Bloc, 1971–1991 | With a foreword by Roger E. Kanet | ISBN 978-3-8382-1654-6

241 *Izabella Agardi* | On the Verge of History. Life Stories of Rural Women from Serbia, Romania, and Hungary, 1920–2020 | With a foreword by Andrea Pető | ISBN 978-3-8382-1602-7

242 *Martin Malek, Sebastian Schäffer (Eds.)* | Ukraine in Central and Eastern Europe. Kyiv's Foreign Affairs and the International Relations of the Post-Communist Region | With a foreword by Pavlo Klimkin | ISBN 978-3-8382-1615-7

243 *Volodymyr Dubrovskyi, Kalman Mizsei, Mychailo Wynnyckyj (Eds.)* | Eight Years after the Revolution of Dignity. What Has Changed in Ukraine during 2013–2021? | With a foreword by Yaroslav Hrytsak | ISBN 978-3-8382-1560-0

244 *Rumena Filipova* | Constructing the Limits of Europe. Identity and Foreign Policy in Poland, Bulgaria, and Russia since 1989 | With forewords by Harald Wydra and Gergana Yankova-Dimova | ISBN 978-3-8382-1649-2

245 *Oleksandra Keudel* | How Patronal Networks Shape Opportunities for Local Citizen Participation in a Hybrid Regime. A Comparative Analysis of Five Cities in Ukraine | With a foreword by Sabine Kropp | ISBN 978-3-8382-1671-3

246 *Jan Claas Behrends, Thomas Lindenberger, Pavel Kolar (Eds.)* | Violence after Stalin. Institutions, Practices, and Everyday Life in the Soviet Bloc 1953–1989 | ISBN 978-3-8382-1637-9

247 *Leonid Luks* | Macht und Ohnmacht der Utopien Essays zur Geschichte Russlands im 20. und 21. Jahrhundert | ISBN 978-3-8382-1677-5

ibidem.*eu*